THE CAMBRIDGE COMPANION TO
GENESIS

The Cambridge Companion to Genesis explores the first book of the Bible, the book that serves as the foundation for the rest of the Hebrew Scriptures. Recognizing its unique position in world history, the history of religions, as well as biblical and theological studies, the volume summarizes key developments in biblical scholarship since the Enlightenment, while offering an overview of the diverse methods and reading strategies that are currently applied to the reading of Genesis. It also explores questions that, in some cases, have been explored for centuries. Written by an international team of scholars whose essays were specially commissioned, the Companion provides a multi-disciplinary update of all relevant issues related to the interpretation of Genesis. Whether the reader is taking the first step on the path or continuing a research journey, this volume will illuminate the role of Genesis in world religions, theology, philosophy, and critical biblical scholarship.

Bill T. Arnold is the Paul S. Amos Professor of Old Testament Interpretation at Asbury Theological Seminary. Previous publications include biblical commentaries (*Genesis*, Cambridge, 2009; and *1–2 Samuel*, HarperCollins-Zondervan, 2003), *A Guide to Biblical Hebrew Syntax* (coauthored with John H. Choi, Cambridge, 2003 and 2018), and *Introduction to the Old Testament* (Cambridge, 2014). He was awarded a Lilly Faculty Fellowship for his proposal to study the oneness or singularity of God in the Old Testament.

CAMBRIDGE COMPANIONS TO RELIGION

This is a series of companions to major topics and key figures in theology and religious studies. Each volume contains specially commissioned chapters by international scholars, which provide an accessible and stimulating introduction to the subject for new readers and non-specialists.

Other Titles in the Series

THE COUNCIL OF NICAECA Edited by Young Richard Kim

APOSTOLIC FATHERS Edited by Michael F. Bird and Scott Harrower

AMERICAN CATHOLICISM Edited by Margaret M. McGuinness and Thomas F. Rzeznick

AMERICAN ISLAM Edited by Juliane Hammer and Omid Safi

AMERICAN JUDAISM Edited by Dana Evan Kaplan

AMERICAN METHODISM Edited by Jason E. Vickers

ANCIENT MEDITERRANEAN RELIGIONS Edited by Barbette Stanley Spaeth

APOCALYPTIC LITERATURE Edited by Colin McAllister

AUGUSTINE'S CITY OF GOD Edited by David Vincent Meconi

AUGUSTINE'S "CONFESSIONS" Edited by Tarmo Toom

KARL BARTH Edited by John Webster

THE BIBLE, 2ND EDITION Edited by Bruce Chilton

THE BIBLE AND LITERATURE Edited by Calum Carmichael

BIBLICAL INTERPRETATION Edited by John Barton

BLACK THEOLOGY Edited by Dwight N. Hopkins and Edward P. Antonio

DIETRICH BONHOEFFER Edited by John de Gruchy

JOHN CALVIN Edited by Donald K. McKim

CHRISTIAN DOCTRINE Edited by Colin Gunton

CHRISTIAN ETHICS Edited by Robin Gill

CHRISTIAN MYSTICISM Edited by Amy Hollywood and Patricia Z. Beckman

CHRISTIAN PHILOSOPHICAL THEOLOGY Edited by Charles Taliaferro and Chad V. Meister

CHRISTIAN POLITICAL THEOLOGY Edited by Craig Hovey and Elizabeth Phillips

THE CISTERIAN ORDER Edited by Mette Birkedal Bruun

CLASSICAL ISLAMIC THEOLOGY Edited by Tim Winter

JONATHAN EDWARDS Edited by Stephen J. Stein

EVANGELICAL THEOLOGY Edited by Timothy Larsen and Daniel J. Treier

FEMINIST THEOLOGY Edited by Susan Frank Parsons

(Continued after the Index)

THE CAMBRIDGE COMPANION TO

GENESIS

Edited by

Bill T. Arnold
With the assistance of Brian T. Shockey

CAMBRIDGE
UNIVERSITY PRESS

CAMBRIDGE
UNIVERSITY PRESS

University Printing House, Cambridge CB2 8BS, United Kingdom

One Liberty Plaza, 20th Floor, New York, NY 10006, USA

477 Williamstown Road, Port Melbourne, VIC 3207, Australia

314–321, 3rd Floor, Plot 3, Splendor Forum, Jasola District Centre,
New Delhi – 110025, India

103 Penang Road, #05–06/07, Visioncrest Commercial, Singapore 238467

Cambridge University Press is part of the University of Cambridge.

It furthers the University's mission by disseminating knowledge in the pursuit of
education, learning, and research at the highest international levels of excellence.

www.cambridge.org
Information on this title: www.cambridge.org/9781108423755
DOI: 10.1017/9781108529303

First published 2022

A catalogue record for this publication is available from the British Library.

ISBN 978-1-108-42375-5 Hardback
ISBN 978-1-107-63602-6 Paperback

Contents

List of Abbreviations   *page* ix

List of Contributors   xiv

1   Introduction: Genesis and the *status quaestionis*   1
     BILL T. ARNOLD

Part I: ***Composition and Structure of Genesis***   9

2   Genesis in the History of Critical Scholarship   11
     JEAN-LOUIS SKA

3   Genesis in Source and Redaction Criticism Today   53
     JAN CHRISTIAN GERTZ

4   Genesis in Form and Tradition Criticism Today   74
     CHRISTOPH LEVIN

5   Rhetorical Features and Characteristics: The Literary
     Function of Genealogies, Itineraries, and Other
     Etiologies in the Book of Genesis   99
     MICHAELA BAUKS

Part II: ***Social World of Genesis***   119

6   Genesis and Its Ancient Literary Analogues   121
     ALICE MANDELL

7   Genesis and the Conceptual World of the Ancient
     Near East   148
     JOHN H. WALTON

8   Family, Clan, and Tribe in the Book of Genesis   168
     NAOMI A. STEINBERG

9   Women's Status and Feminist Readings of Genesis   188
     SARAH SHECTMAN

Part III: *Themes and Literary Motifs of Genesis*   209

10   From *Imago* to *Imagines*: The Image(s) of God in
     Genesis   211
     BRENT A. STRAWN

11   Genesis, Science, and Theories of Origins   236
     JITSE M. VAN DER MEER

12   Genesis and Ethics   262
     ECKART OTTO

13   Genesis and the Problem of Evil: Philosophical
     Musings on the Bible's First Book   281
     PAUL M. GOULD

Part IV: *Reception History of Genesis*   301

14   Modern Philosophical Receptions of Genesis   303
     FREDERICK D. AQUINO

15   Jewish Reflections on Universalism and Particularism
     in Genesis   322
     JOEL S. KAMINSKY

16   Before Moses: Genesis among the Christians   341
     IAIN PROVAN

     Scripture Index   361
     Subject Index   371

Abbreviations

AB	Anchor Bible
ABD	*Anchor Bible Dictionary*
ABRL	Anchor Bible Reference Library
ACCS	Ancient Christian Commentary on Scripture
ADAIK	Abhandlungen des Deutschen Archäologischen Instituts Kairo
AEL	*Ancient Egyptian Literature*
AJBI	*Annual of the Japanese Biblical Institute*
AJSR	*Association for Jewish Studies Review*
ANF	*Ante-Nicene Fathers*
ANET	*Ancient Near Eastern Texts Relating to the Old Testament*
AOAT	Alter Orient und Altes Testament
ARM	Archives royales de Mari
ATANT	Abhandlungen zur Theologie des Alten und Neuen Testaments
ATD	Das Alte Testament Deutsch
AWEAT	*Archiv für die wissenschaftliche Erforschung des Alten Testaments*
AYBRL	Anchor Yale Bible Reference Library
BA	*Biblical Archaeologist*
BAR	*Biblical Archaeology Review*
BASOR	*Bulletin of the American Schools of Oriental Research*
BBB	Bonner biblische Beiträge
BEATAJ	Beiträge zur Erforschung des Alten Testaments und des antiken Judentums

BETL	Bibliotheca Ephemeridum Theologicarum Lovaniensium
BEvT	Beiträge zur evangelischen Theologie
BHTh	Beiträge zur historischen Theologie
BHQ	Biblia Hebraica Quinta
BIAS	Bible in Africa Studies
Bib	*Biblica*
BibS(N)	Biblische Studien (Neukirchen, 1951–)
BJRL	*Bulletin of the John Rylands University Library of Manchester*
BJS	Brown Judaic Studies
BKAT	Biblischer Kommentar, Altes Testament
BWANT	Beiträge zur Wissenschaft vom Alten und Neuen Testament
BZABR	Beihefte zur Zeitschrift für altorientalische und biblische Rechtsgeschichte
BZAW	Beihefte zur Zeitschrift für die alttestamentliche Wissenschaft
CAD	*The Assyrian Dictionary of the Oriental Institute of the University of Chicago*
CBQ	*Catholic Biblical Quarterly*
CHANE	Culture and History of the Ancient Near East
CML	*Canaanite Myths and Legends*, ed. G. R. Driver (Edinburgh, 1956; 2nd ed. J. C. L. Gibson 1978)
ConBOT	Coniectanea Biblica: Old Testament Series
COS	*The Context of Scripture* (Brill, 1997–2002)
CTA	*Corpus de tablettes en cunéiformes alphabétiques découvertes à Ras-Shamra-Ugarit de 1929 à 1939*, ed. A. Herdner, Mission de Ras Shamra 10 (Paris 1963)
CTJ	*Calvin Theological Journal*
CUSAS	Cornell University Studies in Assyriology and Sumerology
CV	*Communio Viatorum*
DBW	Dietrich Bonhoeffer Works
EBR	*Encyclopedia of the Bible and Its Reception*
EncJud	*Encyclopedia Judaica*
EvT	*Evangelische Theologie*

FAT	Forschungen zum Alten Testament
FC	Fathers of the Church Patristic Series
FCB	Feminist Companion to the Bible
FOTL	Forms of the Old Testament Literature
FRLANT	Forschungen zur Religion und Literatur des Alten und Neuen Testaments
FzB	Forschung zur Bibel
HBM	Hebrew Bible Monographs
HBOT	*Hebrew Bible/Old Testament: The History of Its Interpretations* (Göttingen, 2000)
HBS	Herders Biblische Studien
HBT	*Horizons in Biblical Theology*
HCOT	Historical Commentary on the Old Testament
HKAT	Handkommentar zum Alten Testament
HThKAT	Herders theologischer Kommentar zum Alten Testament
HTR	*Harvard Theological Review*
HUCA	*Hebrew Union College Annual*
IEJ	*Israel Exploration Journal*
Int	*Interpretation*
JAAR	*Journal of the American Academy of Religion*
JAJSup	Journal of Ancient Judaism, Supplements
JANER	*Journal of Ancient Near Eastern Religions*
JANES	*Journal of the Ancient Near Eastern Society of Columbia University*
JAOS	*Journal of the American Oriental Society*
JBL	*Journal of Biblical Literature*
JCS	*Journal of Cuneiform Studies*
JHS	*Journal of Hebrew Scriptures*
JITC	*Journal of the Interdenominational Theological Center*
JNES	*Journal of Near Eastern Studies*
JSOT	*Journal for the Study of the Old Testament*
JSOTSup	Journal for the Study of the Old Testament, Supplements
JTI	*Journal for Theological Interpretation*
JTISup	Journal for Theological Interpretation, Supplements

JTS	*Journal of Theological Studies*
KTU	*Die keilalphabetischen Texte aus Ugarit*, ed. M. Dietrich, O. Loretz, and J. Sanmartín, AOAT 24/1 (Neukirchen-Vluyn, 1976)
LHBOTS	The Library of Hebrew Bible/Old Testament Studies
MThSt	Marburger theologische Studien
NCBC	New Cambridge Bible Commentary
NCHB	*New Cambridge History of the Bible*
NIV	New International Version
NOAB	*New Oxford Annotated Bible*
NPNF¹	*Nicene and Post-Nicene Fathers*, Series 1
NRSV	New Revised Standard Version
OBO	Orbis Biblicus et Orientalis
OBO.SA	Orbis Biblicus et Orientalis, Series Archaeologica
OBT	Overtures to Biblical Theology
Or	*Orientalia* (NS)
OTL	Old Testament Library
OTS	Old Testament Studies
PEQ	*Palestine Exploration Quarterly*
PTMS	Pittsburgh Theological Monograph Series
RA	*Revue d'assyriologie et d'archéologie orientale*
RAI	Rencontre assyriologique internationale
RB	*Revue biblique*
SAAS	State Archives of Assyria Studies
SBL	Society of Biblical Literature
SBLRBS	SBL Resources for Biblical Study
SBLSymS	SBL Symposium Series
SBLWAW	SBL Writings from the Ancient World
SemSt	Semeia Studies
SNT	Studien zum Neuen Testament
SSN	Studia Semitica Neerlandica
TB	Theologische Bücherei: Neudrucke und Berichte aus dem 20. Jahrhundert
ThPh	*Theologie und Philosophie*
ThSt	Theologische Studiën

TLZ	*Theologische Literaturzeitung*
TynBul	*Tyndale Bulletin*
UBL	Ugaritisch-biblische Literatur
UF	*Ugarit-Forschungen*
VT	*Vetus Testamentum*
VTSup	*Vetus Testamentum*, Supplements
VWGTh	Veröffentlichungen der Wissenschaftlichen Gesellschaft für Theologie
WBC	Word Biblical Commentary
WMANT	Wissenschaftliche Monographien zum Alten und Neuen Testament
WUNT	Wissenschaftliche Untersuchungen zum Neuen Testament
ZAW	*Zeitschrift für die alttestamentliche Wissenschaft*
ZTK	*Zeitschrift für Theologie und Kirche*

Contributors

Frederick D. Aquino is Professor of Theology and Philosophy at the Graduate School of Theology, Abilene Christian University.

Bill T. Arnold is the Paul S. Amos Professor of Old Testament Interpretation, Asbury Theological Seminary.

Michaela Bauks is Professor of Old Testament and the History of Religion, Universität Koblenz-Landau.

Jan Christian Gertz is Professor of Hebrew Bible, Ruprechts-Karls-Universität Heidelberg.

Paul M. Gould is Associate Professor of Philosophy of Religion, Palm Beach Atlantic University.

Joel S. Kaminsky is the Morningstar Professor of Jewish Studies and a Professor of Religion, Smith College.

Christoph Levin is Professor (Emeritus) of Old Testament, Ludwig-Maximilians-Universität München.

Alice Mandell is the William Foxwell Albright Chair of Biblical and Ancient Near Eastern Studies, Johns Hopkins University.

Jitse M. van der Meer is Professor (Emeritus) of Biology and the History and Philosophy of Science, Redeemer University College.

Eckart Otto is Professor (Emeritus) of Old Testament, Ludwig-Maximilians-Universität München, and Honorary Professor, University of Pretoria.

Iain Provan is the Marshall Sheppard Professor of Biblical Studies, Regent College.

Sarah Shectman is an editor and independent academic living in San Francisco, California.

Jean-Louis Ska is Professor of Old Testament Exegesis (Emeritus), the Pontifical Biblical Institute.

Naomi A. Steinberg is Professor of Religious Studies, DePaul University.

Brent A. Strawn is Professor of Old Testament and Professor of Law at Duke University.

John H. Walton is Professor of Old Testament, Wheaton College and Graduate School.

1 Introduction: Genesis and the *status quaestionis*

BILL T. ARNOLD

The book of Genesis never seems to go away. Whether we roam the corridors of human philosophies and theological speculations, or walk among the literary giants of past generations, we always seem to find Genesis. It is, in fact, inescapable, given a name like "Genesis" or "Beginnings." Its position as the first book of the Bible, and the one that establishes so many of the themes to follow, gives Genesis a unique position in world literature and in the history of religions. Indeed, Genesis addresses the most profound questions of life. Who are we? Where are we? Why are we here? And it has answers. Whether we are believers or skeptics, Genesis answers questions about who God is, what God's nature is like, and how God relates to humankind. Since the beginning of civilization, most societies have speculated about these or similar philosophical questions, but none has left such an impact on world history and thought as Genesis. Besides addressing the beginnings of the cosmos, of humanity, and of human civilization, the book is also about the origins of God's chosen people, the Israelites, who produced the traditions that came to be preserved in the Hebrew Bible, traditionally known as the Old Testament. As such, the book of Genesis is one of the first steps one must take along the path to understanding the world religions we now know as Judaism, Christianity, and Islam, and the variety of theologies and philosophical principles related to them.

For the history of biblical studies more precisely, the role of the book of Genesis cannot be overstated. During the Enlightenment, when traditional understandings of the Bible were thoroughly reevaluated, long-held assumptions about the composition of the Pentateuch became a topic of intense interest. Indeed, the first eleven chapters of Genesis became the focal point of the first investigations of modernity's historical-critical research of the Bible. Building upon the philosophical foundations of Spinoza, Hobbes, and Richard Simon, among others from a previous era, two notable researchers of the eighteenth century theorized that different names for God in the opening chapters of Genesis reflected original sources behind the text. The first was a German pastor, Henning Bernhard Witter in 1711, who was followed independently by a French physician, Jean Astruc in 1753 (see Chapter 2 below for discussion of both). The pastor and the physician were largely forgotten at first until their work was disseminated more widely at the close of the eighteenth century in what became the beginnings of biblical historical criticism. Since those early days, engaging the book of Genesis has been one the first steps one must take along the path to understanding the world of critical biblical scholarship.

Because of its importance in so many areas of research, the secondary literature on Genesis is immense, and continues to grow every year. Indeed, this is an interesting moment in the history of biblical studies, especially as it relates to the study of the book of Genesis. Several large-scale and important commentary projects are under way on the book just now, including volumes in Hermeneia, the International Exegetical Commentary on the Old Testament, the International Critical Commentary, the New International Commentary on the Old Testament, the Old Testament Library, the Yale Anchor Bible Commentary, and others. We can expect to see several interesting and innovative approaches to the book in coming decades. This volume attempts to provide an overview of a wide variety of approaches and interpretations of Genesis at this pivotal moment in the field, as well as to provide original insights and proposals that will be useful to all interpreters of the book for the foreseeable future.

Certain questions about the Bible have been front and center since the beginning of critical investigation, and without doubt, the composition of Genesis is one of those. Part I addresses the structure and message of Genesis, tracing the history of research through to the leading critical approaches, including the more recent investigation of its rhetorical features. In Chapter 2, Jean-Louis Ska traces the history of critical interpretation of Genesis back to debates between the rabbinical schools of Rabbi Ishmael (90–135 CE) and Rabbi Aqiba (40–137 CE), showing that the impulses at work in those early approaches remain at the foundation of the origins of critical biblical interpretation. The rabbinical school that admits and explores the human dimension of Scripture gave rise eventually, after a long and drawn-out process, to the Renaissance and Enlightenment. Ska's chapter reveals (1) the degree to which some things have remained the same, and (2) the way in which Genesis especially has been at the center of questions about biblical authority from the early rabbinic period all the way to the present critical investigation of the Bible.

The book of Genesis has, of course, played a central role in the early history of biblical scholarship. Jan Christian Gertz shows in Chapter 3 how critical research on the Pentateuch began with Genesis and considers the implications of its ongoing significance in such research. Some questions will simply never cease to fascinate us, compelling us to revisit the answers offered in the past. The nature of the underlying sources and of the redactional processes that led to the composition of the book of Genesis is certainly one of those questions. Gertz surveys developments as they occurred especially related to Genesis, and concludes with a summary of his own reconstruction of the composition of the book. In Chapter 4, Christoph Levin takes up the contributions of form and tradition criticism since their emergence at the beginning of the twentieth century. After a critique of those early contributions, Levin offers a helpful refinement of the circumstances of the earliest literary traditions from ancient Israel, placing special attention on their royal focus, even as they were developed further by the administrative and cult aristocracy after the collapse of the monarchy. Michaela Bauks in Chapter 5 provides an overview of the literary mechanisms that drive Genesis forward as a unified whole. As a representative of more recent approaches to the book, Bauks demonstrates how earlier critical methods evolved by giving special attention to its most relevant rhetorical features, first its formal elements, such as reports, etiologies, genealogies, travel reports, cult notices, etymological notices, etc., and then its motifs and semantic structuring elements (keywords, wordplays, etc.).

Having considered the world *in* the text, Part II turns to consider the world *behind* the text. In Chapters 6 and 7, Alice Mandell and John H. Walton place the book of Genesis squarely in its ancient Near Eastern context by exploring both its literary analogues from the surrounding cultures and its conceptual worldview as compared to Israel's neighbors in the ancient world. The history of comparative work is itself a lesson in caution, as Mandell has helpfully shown in a history of the scholarship. Her chapter returns to the relevant comparanda in order to contextualize Genesis in the first millennium BCE. The result of her work is an understanding of the book as unifying the disparate peoples of Israel and Judah into a cohesive family unit in the context of Mesopotamian imperial oppression. John H. Walton explores intercultural commonalities between Genesis and the ancient Near Eastern world, giving focused attention to creation and humanity, perceptions of the divine, and the uses of ancestral narratives. His study helpfully shows how a fixation or preoccupation among scholars to compare individual passages of the Hebrew Bible to individual texts from the ancient world needs to be balanced by comparative analysis that takes into full account the cognitive environment shared by the cultures producing those texts. His work is especially helpful when we consider that the distance between our contemporary setting and the world of the Hebrew Bible is much greater than that between the Bible itself and its environment in the ancient world (culturally, socially, linguistically, etc.).

In Chapter 8, Naomi A. Steinberg offers a fresh analysis of the Israelite conceptions of kinship units in order better to understand the Israelite family as something more than blood relationship. Steinberg shows how errant Western assumptions from a contemporary perspective can be avoided by focusing on such kinship studies in order to understand traditional roles of family, clan, and tribe. Her study illuminates institutions such as marriage, adoption, bartering, children, and the roles of women in society. On this last point, few other books in the Hebrew Bible have as many women characters as Genesis, making it a fruitful object of study for feminist analysis. Thus in Chapter 9, Sarah Shectman shows how feminism is not itself a distinct method but a perspective on the text that chooses to focus on women, which therefore also engages all the traditional methodological approaches and serves a complementary role to those methods. In the process, Shectman illustrates how feminist analysis enhances our understanding both of the text itself and of related issues of power, status, and autonomy.

Of the many notable themes of the book of Genesis, Part III offers representative discussions of a few of the most important. In Chapter 10, Brent A. Strawn courageously turns to the question of the "image of God" (*imago Dei*), which is famously an important statement of the book's anthropology (Gen 1:26, 27; 5:1–3; 9:6). Strawn considers the theological, historical, and comparative approaches to the question, but then asserts that the book contains not a singular image of God but many images. Whatever else we make of the significance of this phrase, its use must be analyzed in the canonical book as a whole rather than only these few occurrences. By giving attention to the book's holistic message, Strawn emphasizes the functional (as opposed to essential) category of the divine image, suggesting that humans *become* the image of God only as they *actually image* God (reflecting thus an action more than a state of being).

This is followed by another complex issue arising from the book of Genesis. Indeed, the most frequently asked question among lay readers of the book is the relationship of Genesis to science, which is all too often assumed to be adversarial. In Chapter 11, Jitse M. van der Meer offers a compelling investigation of the material realities in the experimental and historical natural sciences that intersect with our reading of Genesis. His chapter is a helpful survey of developments in recent decades as a guide for the non-specialist in both cosmic and human evolution showing the reliability of science and suggesting methodological principles in its interaction with Genesis. He argues that the supposed conflict between Genesis and science is an occasion for reevaluation of both, accepting the presuppositions and limitations of science while also reassessing independently the hermeneutical principles at work in the interpretation of Genesis.

Eckart Otto has made significant contributions to the study of the Hebrew Bible as it relates to the field of ethics, both regarding the Bible's internal system of moral versus immoral behaviors, and regarding the contribution of the Hebrew Bible to contemporary ethics. In Chapter 12, he gives special attention to Genesis by distinguishing between two basic types of narratives in the book. On the one hand, "didactic-sapiential narratives" are accounts in which authors of the text invite the readers to imitate the story's moral "heroes" as representatives of an implicit moral behavior. An example of a didactic-sapiential narrative is the Joseph Novel (Gen 37; 39–50). On the other hand, however, much more common in the book of Genesis are narrative tractates, or treatises, on "meta-ethics." In these accounts, human behaviors were valued negatively or positively based on criteria and implicit values arising from "an inner-biblical meta-ethics." Readers of texts such as Gen 2–3, Gen 22, and Gen 38 are invited to evaluate the behavior of the characters based on implicit values taught across a metanarrative, and thus to receive ethical guidance for their own lives. Otto's adroit use of this distinction is helpful in showing the reader how to avoid simplistic, moralistic readings of the multidimensional narratives of Genesis.

In Chapter 13, Paul M. Gould takes up explorations of the origin, nature, and explanation of evil among analytic philosophers, who often have not given enough attention to individual narratives of Genesis in the larger framework of the biblical metanarrative. He offers a fresh investigation based on more than Genesis 1–3, which is as far as many similar investigations go, while Gould considers the narrative arc of the book as a whole.

The final collection of essays, Part IV of the volume, pulls together many of the themes and reading strategies in the history of interpretation to explore the role of Genesis in diverse venues. In Chapter 14, Frederick D. Aquino explores the reception of Genesis among philosophers by considering the relationship between divine commands, what those commands imply about the concept of divine nature, and ultimately the principle of ethical evaluation. After surveying recent philosophical engagements with Genesis, Aquino turns to the account of the Aqedah (also known as the binding of Isaac; Gen 22:1–19), where many philosophical issues converge, as an investigation of contemporary philosophical readings of the story.

Joel S. Kaminsky in Chapter 15 observes that classical Jewish interpreters sought to explain why the Torah, the majority of which contains divinely issued laws, does not begin with the Passover legislation of Exodus 12 containing the first instructions God gives to all Israel, or with the giving of the Ten Commandments, but rather with an extended prologue – the book of Genesis. He acknowledges a productive tension between the wider universalistic scope of Genesis 1–11 and much of the rest of the Hebrew Bible that is generally more particularistic and focused on Israel. Yet Kaminsky adroitly shows that the more universalistic Primeval History found in Genesis 1–11 contains substantial elements of particularism, while on the other hand, the particularizing ancestral narratives of Genesis 12–50 are more universalistic than often noted. Thus, Genesis anticipates the inseparability of the Bible's particularism (God's election and love of Israel) from the universal ideals it also projects (God's relationship to and concern with non-Israelite peoples and the larger natural world). Such universal ideals grow out of and make sense only in relation to the specificity of the Bible's theological claims. The Bible's universalistic and particularistic impulses are not trapped in a zero-sum game where one must wane if the other waxes. Rather, as Israel's understanding of its unique identity before God deepens so does their awareness of God's relationship to the rest of humanity and of Israel's role in God's larger universal vision for the world.

Finally, in Chapter 16, Iain Provan considers the diverse ways in which Christians have read Genesis from the beginning of the Christian movement. Some early Christians promoted a reading that sought the meaning of the original author, as a literal or historical interpretation, such as Augustine and others. Provan traces the influences of this approach through history to the Renaissance preparing the way for the Protestant Reformation. At times, however, because the early Christians embraced Scripture as a unified and self-consistent text, they also moved beyond the literal sense to other levels of meaning, as Augustine himself even allowed wherever he believed it was warranted. Many others in the post-apostolic Church explored figural and allegorical readings, Origen being the best example. Thus these interpretive strategies could and often did exist side by side until the middle of the seventeenth century, when modernism's emphasis on the historical sense predominated. Provan's chapter helpfully illustrates the ways in which Christians have read each canonical portion of the book of Genesis.

In sum, the authors of this volume approach Genesis from diverse methods and reading strategies, and they address questions that have in some cases been explored for centuries. In other cases, they raise questions that we have only begun to ask in recent decades. By bringing together leading voices on each of these topics, the cumulative effect is, we hope, a dependable guide to understanding the book of Genesis both now and in the future. Whether the reader is taking the first step on the path or continuing a journey with many miles behind them, this volume will illuminate the role of Genesis in the history of world religions and critical biblical scholarship.

Part I
Composition and Structure of Genesis

2 Genesis in the History of Critical Scholarship*
JEAN-LOUIS SKA

INTRODUCTION: INSPIRED WORD OR HUMAN LANGUAGE?

"The Torah speaks a human language" – the saying, accredited to Rabbi Ishmael (90–135 CE) and found in the Midrashic treatise *Sifre to Numbers* 112, is at the root of a critical reading of the Scriptures. It underscores that Scriptures, considered divine revelation, are formulated in a language that follows the rules of any language and the conventions of human communication. R. Ishmael had his opponents, obviously, who belonged to the school of Rabbi Aqiba (40–137 CE) and affirmed that every detail in the Scripture is divinely inspired and therefore meaningful, a tendency for which recent scholarship coined the term "omnisignificance."[1] On the one hand, the school of R. Ishmael thinks of the Bible as having divine origin, but also as being a book like many other books and, on the other hand, R. Aqiba affirms the uniqueness of the Bible and detects a deeper, theological, meaning in every peculiarity of the biblical text.[2] For R. Ishmael's disciples, we may perceive errors, inconsistencies, differences, and imperfections in Holy Scriptures as in other human work.[3] For R. Aqiba's school, Holy

---

* I would like to thank Ronald Hendel and Marc Brettler for precious pieces of advice. All shortcomings are mine, however.

[1] See James L. Kugel, *The Idea of Biblical Poetry: Parallelism and Its History* (New Haven, CT: Yale University Press, 1981), 104–5. Cf. Yaakov Elman, "Omnisignificance," in *Hebrew Bible/Old Testament: The History of Its Interpretations, I.2: The Middles Ages*, ed. Magne Sæbø (Göttingen: Vandenhoeck & Ruprecht, 2000) (abbreviated henceforth as *HBOT* I.2), 419–20. This tendency is present in several modern studies using the method of "close reading." On this method, see Tom Gibbons, *Literature and Awareness: An Introduction to the Close Reading of Prose and Poetry* (London: Edward Arnold, 1979).

[2] On this problem, see Richard Kalmin, "Patterns of Developments in Rabbinic Midrash of Late Antiquity," in *Hebrew Bible/Old Testament: The History of Its Interpretations. I,1: Antiquity*, ed. Magne Sæbø (Göttingen: Vandenhoeck & Ruprecht, 1996) (abbreviated henceforth as *HBOT* I.1), 295–99. There are similarities between the two schools besides some clear differences.

[3] This is the opinion, among others, of Rashbam, Rashi's grandson (Samuel ben Meir; Troyes, c. 1085–c. 1158) in his commentaries on the Pentateuch. For him, there are real

12 JEAN-LOUIS SKA

Scriptures are "cryptic, relevant, perfect, and divine."[4] For the first school, Genesis will reflect the opinions of human beings in their historical contexts. For the other school, Genesis will contain absolute, eternal, and immutable truths, revealed by God, about our human destiny. Or as Hans Frei would have it, Genesis was for a long time supposed to tell a history of the universe and humankind; this history is the real history of the world, and this is a history that determines everyone's destiny.[5]

An important pillar of this construction is the Mosaic authorship of the whole Pentateuch and, in particular, of Genesis. Great works required great authors, and inspired works required inspired authors. Based on some biblical texts (Exod 24:4; Deut 31:9), the belief that Moses, the greatest among all prophets (Deut 34:10–12), had written the Pentateuch is present in the New Testament (cf. Luke 24:27, 44), in Philo and Josephus, and in the Talmud, where there is a discussion about the account of Moses's death in the last verses of Deuteronomy (34:1–12). Some rabbis attribute these verses to Joshua and others say that God dictated these verses to Moses who was "in tears."[6] This is certainly one of the first critical questions about Moses's authorship of the Pentateuch.

Over time, the critical reading of Genesis will change, as the views of R. Ishmael gradually undermined R. Aqiba's presuppositions. Genesis will become less cryptic, less relevant, less perfect and less divine. It will grow plainer, more qualified, more limited, and more human. Origen, Ibn Ezra, Galileo Galilei, Spinoza, Richard Simon, de Wette, and some others are the main architects of this evolution.

ANTIQUITY

Biblical exegesis never developed in an ivory tower. In the first centuries, it was influenced by Platonic philosophy on the one side and, on the other, by the philological study of Homer.

Especially problematic in Homer were two items, namely the coarse descriptions of the gods and goddesses, and the not always edifying behavior of some heroes. In those cases, Hellenistic commentaries

contradictions in the Pentateuch. See *Rabbi Samuel Ben Meir's Commentary on Genesis: An Annotated Translation by Martin I. Lockshin* (Lewiston, NY: Edwin Mellen Press, 1989).

[4] See Ronald Hendel, *The Book of Genesis: A Biography*, Lives of Great Religious Books (Princeton, NJ and Oxford: Princeton University Press, 2013), 50–60.

[5] Hans W. Frei, *The Eclipse of Biblical Narrative: A Study in Eighteenth and Nineteenth Century Hermeneutics* (New Haven, CT: Yale University Press, 1978).

[6] See Philo of Alexandria, *De Vita Mosis*, I.1, II.45–48; Josephus, *Against Apion*, I.7–8; Babylonian Talmud, *Baba Bathra* 14b–15a.

recommended abandoning the literal reading and favoring an "allegorical" interpretation. The Jewish scholar Philo of Alexandria (c. 20 BCE–c. 45 CE) applied this method to his reading of biblical texts, among others to the book of Genesis.[7]

Christians such as Origen followed suit in their interpretation of Scriptures, but Origen was the first to lay down a theoretical treatise about this procedure and inquire about *principles* of reading the biblical text in *De principiis*, as he was the first Christian to apply to the biblical text the rules of the Alexandrian grammarians. For this reason, he can be called the founder of Christian biblical exegesis as of biblical text criticism.

Among his predecessors, we may count the Jewish interpreter Aristobulus of Alexandria, whose *Fragments* Origen was one of the last writers to have accessed. The *Fragments* were written around 180–145 BCE and defend the idea that most Greek poets and thinkers drew their ideas from Jewish sages. In these *Fragments*, Aristobulus treats some problems about Gen 1:3 and 2:2, saying that "light" may have a metaphorical meaning and that God's rest must not be interpreted literally.[8]

Origen of Alexandria (c. 184–c. 253 CE) belonged to a learned generation of Christians imbued with Greek culture. Alexandria was a major center in the Hellenistic world and possessed one of the most famous libraries of that time. In a reflection on Genesis 1–3, Origen notices that several texts cannot be interpreted literally. For instance, light is created on the first day, before the sky, the sun, the moon, and the stars, which are created on the fourth day (Gen 1:2 and 1:16). In the same way, it is difficult to believe that, in Genesis 2–3, God is a gardener who plants trees, that eating a fruit can give life, that the knowledge of good and evil can be obtained in chewing another fruit, or that God goes every evening for a stroll somewhere on earth. Concerning Genesis 4, Origen wonders what the literal meaning of Cain's condemnation could be, that is, to be hidden from God's face or presence (Gen 4:14). What is the literal meaning of "God's presence"? In all these cases, treated in *De principiis* IV:17, Origen tries to determine whether a text conforms the rules of reason or not.

Among Origen's heirs, we should mention first Jerome (347–420), famous for his *hebraica veritas* and for his new translation of the Bible

---

[7] On Philo's exegesis, see, among others, Peder Johan Borgen, *Philo of Alexandria: An Exegete for His Time*, SNT 86 (Leiden: Brill, 1997); Folker Siegert, "Philo of Alexandria," in *HBOT* I.1, 163–89.

[8] On Aristobulus, see Folker Siegert, "Aristobulus," in *HBOT* I.1, 154–62. See also Carl R. Holladay, *Fragments from Hellenistic Jewish authors*. III: *Aristobulus*, SBL Texts and Translations 39 (Atlanta, GA: Scholars Press, 1995).

from the original Hebrew into Latin. Jerome, however, did not write any
treatise on exegesis, but a letter entitled *On the Best Method of
Translating*, where he affirms that he translates not word for word but
sense for sense.[9]

Another heir is Augustine of Hippo (354–430), who wrote his *De
Genesis ad litteram*, completed in 415.[10] Like Origen, Augustine
defends the view that texts that contradict either science or reason,
which is God's gift, should be interpreted metaphorically. Every text
has a "literal sense," but this sense is not always "history." It can be
a "metaphor" and must be understood accordingly, that is, figuratively. This theory is exposed at length in his treatise *De doctrina
christiana*, written between 397 and 426, especially in Book 3.10.14–
15: "Whatever appears in the divine Word that does not literally
pertain to virtuous behaviour or to the truth of faith you must take
as to be figurative."[11] Moreover, Augustine also invites the use of
classical literature for a better understanding of history, geography,
and rhetoric (*De doctrina christiana* 2.42.63). He can be considered
one of the precursors of comparative literature. Eventually, he insists
on the need to know the original languages of the Bible (*De doctrina
christiana* 2.11.16–13.19) although he himself read the Scriptures
mainly in a Latin translation.[12]

MIDDLE AGES

The Cultural Background of the Middle Ages

The Middle Ages are often considered a time of obscurantism, especially
because medieval exegesis was mostly theological, mystical, and
devotional.[13] Scholastic exegesis was also based almost exclusively on
the Latin text of the Vulgate. Moreover, the authority of the Church or
the Synagogue mattered more than a critical reading of the text. This was
not always true, however, and we must mention several important
exceptions, namely Isaac ibn Yashush (d. 1056), the renowned Ibn Ezra

---

9   On Jerome, see Adam Kamesar, "Jerome," in *NCHB* 1, 653–75, esp. 669–70; see also
    René Kiefer, "Jerome: His Exegesis and Hermeneutics," in *HBOT* I.1, 663–81; on his
    principles of interpretation and translation, see 670–75.
10 See David F. Wright, "Augustine: His Exegesis and Hermeneutics," in *HBOT* I.1, 701–
    30; Carol Harrison, "Augustine," in *NCHB* 1, 676–96.
11 Quoted by Harrison, "Augustine," 690.
12 For a translation, see *De doctrina christiana*, ed. and trans. R. P. H. Green (Oxford:
    Clarendon, 1995).
13 For the first part of the Middle Ages, see Aryeh Grabois, "Political and Cultural
    Changes from the Fifth to the Eleventh Century," in *HBOT* I.2, 28–55.

(1092–1167) and some other Jewish exegetes in Spain or France, and the Victorines (1096–1141) and Nicolaus of Lyra (1270–1349) in Paris.

To be sure, important social, economic, and cultural changes were observed around year 1000: first, an increase in the European population; second, the rise of the first cities and their upper middle classes challenging the country aristocracy living in its castles; third, the upsurge of an economy based more on craftsmanship (especially textiles), financial exchanges, and commerce (e.g., a market economy) than on husbandry and cattle breeding; fourth, a shift from a Platonic and hierarchical thinking to a more pragmatic and "down-to-earth" Aristotelian viewpoint where "biblical writings were no longer seen as repositories of divine mysteries only but could also be appreciated as works of an (inspired) human mind to be analyzed like other literature."[14] These phenomena explain, at least partly, the advent of new questions and perspectives on the book of Genesis.

At this time, Spain was a very important cultural melting pot to which Muslims, Jews and Christians contributed in different ways.[15] The knowledge of Arabic and Hebrew in Jewish circles and the influence of Aristotelian philosophy (Ibn Rushd – Averroes; 1126–98) impinged upon the reading of the Bible in a more literal and rigorous way, paying attention to the context (*peshat*), although the usual midrashic reading (*derash*) was surely not abandoned.[16]

Saadiah ben Joseph – Gaon of Susa (882–942)

One of the leading figures in Jewish commentaries on Genesis in the early Middle Ages was Saadiah Gaon.[17] He was born in Egypt and spent some years in Palestine with the Jewish scholars at Tiberias, but was active most of his life in medieval Babylonia (Iraq) under the Abbasside Caliphate. He was Gaon, the leading academic, of the community of Sura. He is also known for his many controversies, and his surly and touchy character. Jewish communities faced a complicated situation at that time in history. On the one hand, the rapid Arabo-Muslim conquests had led several Jews to convert to Islam.[18] On the other hand, the

---

[14] See Karlfeld Froehlich, "The Impact of the Reception of Aristotle," in *HBOT* I.2, 519–22, here 522.
[15] See the articles on "The Flourishing Era of Jewish Exegesis in Spain," in *HBOT* I,2, 261–320; "Jewish Exegesis in Spain and Provence, and in the East, in the Twelfth and Thirteenth Century," ibid., 372–466.
[16] See Stephen Garfinkel, "Clearing *Peshat* and *Derash*," in *HBOT* I.2, 129–34.
[17] See Robert Brody, "The Geonim of Babylonia as Biblical Exegetes," in *HBOT* I.2, 74–88.
[18] See Aryeh Grabois, "The Rise of Muslim Civilization," in *HBOT* I.2, 39–43.

movement of the Karaites, with its rejection of the rabbinic traditions in favor of a literal, and often fundamentalist, reading of the Scriptures, divided many communities.[19] This Karaite attention to the "letter" had significant, either direct or indirect, influence on Jewish exegesis.

In his commentary on the Pentateuch, written in Judeo-Arabic, Saadiah states that there are three sources of knowledge of the Torah:[20]

> The first precedes this Book and the other succeeds it. The one that precedes it is intuitive knowledge, which is created in one whose mind is devoid of [all] impediments and pure of [any] defect. The one succeeding it is the knowledge transmitted by God's messengers that His righteous prophets passed over by informing [us of] the authentic reports. These three sources [of knowledge] – I mean intuitive, written and received – when they meet, give people perfection.

Another passage insists on the literal reading of the Scriptures according to our human capacities, our senses and our intellect:[21]

> One who has sound mind should take the Book of the Torah at all times to be [understood] in the manner apparent from its words, I mean one that is known and frequently used among the people of its language, for every book is composed so that its ideas reach the mind of the listener entirely unless the knowledge of the senses, or of the intellect opposes the popular explanation of the statement, or that this popular explanation would contradict another verse [whose meaning is] clear, or one of the traditions. If he sees that, were he to leave this statement according to the literal meaning of its words, that this would lead him to believe one of the four things that I have expounded [just now], then he should know that this statement is not to be [understood] according to its popular meaning but that it has a word or words that are metaphorical and that he should deliberate which type of metaphor it is until he brings it to its definite meaning. This verse will [then] return to agreement with the senses, the intellect, the other verse, and with tradition.

---

[19] See Daniel Franck, "Karaite Exegesis," in *HBOT* I.2, 110–28. For the Karaites, "The task of the honest interpreter is to discover the *one* correct of every biblical verse through the exercise of reason" (114). For this motive, one of its main representatives, Al-Qirqisâni, quotes the rabbinic dictum mentioned at the beginning of this article: "The Torah speaks a human language" (b. Ber. 31 b).

[20] *Rabbi Saadiah Gaon's Commentary on the Book of Creation*, ed. Michael Linetsky (Northvale, NJ and Jerusalem: Jason Aronson, 2002), 4.

[21] *Rabbi Saadiah Gaon*, 30.

This principle of metaphorical reading of difficult texts that we already met in Origen and Augustine was therefore quite common in this period among both Jews and Christians. This way of interpreting difficult texts has its origin, as we saw, in the Hellenistic interpretation of Homer. Let us also note that Saadiah tries, by all means, to keep to the traditions of his ancestors, against the Karaites, although there are many similarities between their modes of doing exegesis.[22]

Just to name one example of this "reasonable" exegesis, Saadiah believes that neither the snake in Genesis 3 nor Balaam's donkey in Numbers 24 spoke since language is a unique property of human beings. Therefore, an angel spoke for them.

Saadiah can be credited for making popular in the Jewish world philological and grammatical methods common in the Arabic world in the study of the Quran, called *tafsīr* ("explanation").[23] His influence was important, especially in Spain. Abraham ibn Ezra often quotes Saadiah, even though he likes disagreeing with him on concrete points.

Rabbi Isaac ibn Yashush (d. 1056)

Rabbi Isaac ibn Yashush, also known under his Arabic name Isaac Abu Ibrahim (Toledo, 986–1056, Denia, Costa Brava, Spain), is one of the first known rabbis who applied new insights to the book of Genesis.[24] For instance, he pinpointed a historical problem in Gen 36:31–39 that speaks of Edomite kings who ruled "before any king ruled over Israel" (Gen 36:31). Moses, according to our author, cannot have written this text because he could not have known that Israel would have kings one day. The text was written under King Josaphat instead. Isaac ibn Yashush also identifies Hadad of Gen 36:39 with Hadad the Edomite of 1 Kgs 11:14 and Mehetabel of Gen 36:39 with the sister of Tahpenes of 1 Kgs 11:19. Abraham ibn Ezra, however, seems to have disagreed with his

---

[22] See Frank, "Karaite Exegesis," 114–16. Both Saadiah and the Karaites exploited the resources of Arabic and even Christian models. "This enterprise gave birth to the first true Jewish commentaries on the Bible. Unlike Midrashim, these works project clear authorial voices and offer systematic interpretation" (116).

[23] This method is to be distinguished from that of *kalam* ("word"), a more speculative and theological exegesis. This is similar to the distinction between *peshat* and *derash* in Rabbinic exegesis and between *sensus literalis* and *sensus allegoricus* in Christian exegesis. See Stephen Garfinkel, "Clearing *Peshat* and *Derash*," in *HBOT* I.2, 129–34. On patristic medieval exegesis, see Henri de Lubac, *Medieval Exegesis: The Four Senses of Scripture*, trans. E. M. Macierowski. 4 vols. (Grand Rapids, MI: Eerdmans; Edinburgh: T&T Clark, 1998–2009).

[24] Cf. José Martínez Delgado, "Ibn Yashūsh, Isaac (Abū Ibrāhīm) Ibn Qaṣṭār," in *Encyclopedia of Jews in the Islamic World*, vol. 2 (Leiden: Brill, 2010), 556.

predecessor on several points. Moreover, Rabbi Isaac had little influence on subsequent developments in the field.

France and Spain: Rashi de Troyes (Rabbi Shlomo ben Isaac; 1040–1105), Maimonides (Rambam; 1135–1204), the Qimhi Family, and Nachmanides (1194–1270)

Rashi, who studied in Germany and lived in France, is the most popular and influential commentator of the Bible in general and of Genesis in Jewish circles.[25] He is more accessible, less technical and closer to Midrashic exegesis than most of his contemporaries. From the point of view of critical exegesis, his contribution is perhaps more important in the field of grammar and philology than in critical matters. His attention to the plain, literal, meaning of the text and its context (*peshûtô shel miqra*) and to realia is conspicuous, besides his frequent use of *midrashim*. As he himself asserts in a comment on Gen 3:8, "As for me, I am only concerned with the plain meaning of Scriptures and with such *aggadah* as explains the biblical passages in a fitting manner."[26]

Maimonides, certainly the greatest Jewish philosopher and jurist, did not write any biblical commentary, but he exposes a theory of exegesis in the introduction to his major work, *The Guide of the Perplexed* (see Exod 14:3).[27] He distinguishes two types of problems that require explanation, namely individual words and textual units called 'parables.' 'Parables' are single verses or passages with two levels of meaning, a revealed and a hidden level.[28] He also tried to reconcile philosophy and religion, as Muslim thinkers such as Ibn Rushd and Avicenna. In several instances, he proposes a psychological exegesis similar to Philo of Alexandria. For instance, he identifies the serpent of Genesis 3 with human appetite and

[25] For his commentary on Genesis, see *The Torah with Rashi's Commentary Translated, Annotated, and Elucidated. 1. Bereishis – Genesis*, ed. Rabbi Yisrael Isser Zvi Herczeg in collaboration with Rabbi Yaakov Petroff et al. (Brooklyn, NY: Mesorah Publications, 1995). On Rashi himself, see Avraham Grossman, "Solomon Yishaqi/Rashi (1040–1105)," in *HBOT* I,2, 332–46. On the rabbinic exegesis in northern France, see Avraham Grossman, "The School of Literal Jewish Exegesis in Northern France," in *HBOT* I,2, 321–71. On a discussion on the book of Genesis by a Muslim scholar, see Joshua Berman, "The Biblical Criticism of Ibn Hazm the Andalusian: A Medieval Control for Modern Diachronic Method," *JBL* 138 (2019), 377–90.

[26] Grossman, "Rashi," 335. See also Edward Greenstein, "Medieval Bible Commentaries," in *Back to the Sources*, ed. Barry Holtz (New York: Summit Books, 1984), 213–59.

[27] On Maimonides, see Sara Klein-Braslavy, "Moses ben Maimon/Maimonides (Rambam)," in *HBOT* I,2, 311–20.

[28] Ibid., 313.

the sin with following these "irrational appetites" (*Guide*, chap. 13).[29] Maimonides often uses R. Ishmael's dictum to justify his exegesis, "the Torah speaks in language of human beings."[30]

The Qimhi family emigrated from Andalusia (Muslim Spain) and settled in Narbonne, in France's southeastern region of Provence.[31] The father, Joseph (c. 1105–70), and his two sons, Moses (d. c. 1190) and David, also called Radak (c. 1160–1235) are those who brought to Provence the mature Andalusian exegesis and its scientific *peshat* tradition. Reacting against the midrashic perspective of the patriarchs, Radak offers a portrait of Abraham that is more attentive to human, psychological, and historical aspects.[32]

Moses ben Nahman or Nachmanides (1194–1270) must be mentioned here because he is considered the heir of three main schools of thought, the more literal and linguistic school of Ibn Ezra (see below), the more midrashic school of Rashi, and the more philosophical school of Maimonides. He is also more on the side of R. Aqiba than on that of R. Ishmael, and often a representative of "omnisignificant" exegesis.[33]

Christian exegesis benefited from the contributions of rabbinic exegesis through the school of Saint Victor and Nicolas of Lyra (see below).

Abraham ibn Ezra (1092–1167)

Ibn Ezra is known for his enigmatic way of challenging the Mosaic authorship of the Pentateuch in his exegesis of Gen 12:7, 22:14 and some other passages.[34] The Mosaic authorship of the Pentateuch is a traditional belief of both Jews and Christians and is attested in the New Testament, Philo of Alexandria, and Flavius Josephus. As for Genesis, Ibn Ezra doubted that Moses could have written "*Then* the Canaanites were in the land" (Gen 12:7) and "On the mount of YHWH there is vision" (Gen 22:14) since the verse alludes to the Jerusalem

---

[29] Ibid., 317–18. This kind of exegesis is again popular today in some circles. See, for instance, André Wénin, *Abraham ou l'apprentissage du dépouillement. Lecture de Genèse 11,27–25,18*, Lire la Bible 190 (Paris: Le Cerf, 2016), influenced by the works of Marie Balmary.

[30] Klein-Braslavy, "Maimonides," 314.

[31] On this family, see Mordecai Cohen, "The Qimhi Family," in *HBOT* I.2, 388–415.

[32] Ibid., 409.

[33] Yaakov Elman, "Moses ben Nahman/Maimonides," in *HBOT* I.2, 416–32, esp. 419–20.

[34] See Uriel Simon, "Abraham ibn Ezra," in *HBOT* I,2, 377–87 (bibliography: 377–8); Irene Lancaster, *Deconstructing the Bible: Abraham ibn Ezra's Introduction to the Torah*, Routledge-Curzon Jewish Philosophy Series (London: Routledge-Curzon, 2003); Shlomo Sela, *Abraham Ibn Ezra and the Rise of Medieval Hebrew Science*, Brill's Series in Jewish Studies 32 (Leiden: Brill, 2003).

temple. Ibn Ezra's reading of the text is guided by a series of principles which look beyond theological or devotional meanings to identify the human author of the text.

In a short poem prefacing his commentary on the book of Genesis, Abraham Ibn Ezra rejects most allegorical readings and prefers an exegesis "bound by cords of true grammar." His interest in the literal meaning of the text and his attention to Hebrew grammar are some of his main contributions to biblical exegesis.[35] There is a very clear statement about his method in the introduction to his commentary on Genesis. Like many others, for instance Saadia Gaon before him and Nicolas of Lyra after him, Ibn Ezra shows much respect for what he calls "the tradition":

> The fifth method is the one upon which I will base my commentary. [...] I will, to the utmost of my ability, try to understand grammatically every word and then do my best to explain it. [...] However, with regard to verses which deal with laws, statutes and regulations, if we find two possible interpretations for a verse and one of them is in keeping with the interpretation of the transmitters of the tradition, all of whom were righteous men, then without reservation and with all our might we will rely on the truth of their words. Heaven forbid that we should join the Sadducees who claim that the traditions of the Rabbinic sages contradict the literal meaning of the Scriptures and the rules of grammar. The fact of the matter is that our ancient sages are true, and all their words are true. May the Lord God of truth lead his servant in the way of truth.

According to his principles, Ibn Ezra studies the chronology of Genesis and discovers that Terach was still alive when Abraham left Harran for the promised land, that Abraham was still alive when Esau and Jacob were born, and that Isaac was still alive when Joseph was sold by his brothers. He also considers that Genesis 38, the story of Judah and Tamar, cannot be easily reconciled with Gen 46:12, since, according to this latter text, Perez, Judah's and Tamar's son, has already two sons himself and only twenty-two years of narrative time separate Genesis 37 from Genesis 46. R. Joseph ben Eliezer (Tuv Elem) Bonfils (late 14th cent.), in his commentary on ibn Ezra, *Tzafnat Pa'aneach*, clearly

---

[35] For Ibn Ezra's commentary on Genesis, see *Abraham Ibn Esras Kommentar zur Urgeschichte. Mit Einem Anhang: Raschbams Kommentar zum ersten Kapitel der Urgeschichte*. trans. Dirk U. Rottzoll, Studia Judaica 15 (Berlin: de Gruyter, 1996); *Ibn Ezra's Commentary on the Pentateuch*, vol. 1: *Genesis (Berešit)*, trans. H. Norman Strickman and Arthur M. Silver (New York: Menorah Publishing Company, 1988).

explains his predecessor's reasoning, as Baruch Spinoza (1632–77) will do some centuries afterwards.[36]

The School of Saint Victor in Paris

Some medieval authors deserve a special mention for their attention both to the Hebrew language and to the literal meaning of the Scriptures, whereas a majority of commentaries favored a figurative and mystical exegesis. This special attention to the Hebrew language was the origin of a more literal reading of Genesis.

In the Christian world, a very important figure is that of the canon regular Hughes of Saint-Victor (1096–1141), who used his knowledge of Hebrew, philosophy, and science to correct many mystical interpretations of the Bible.[37] He is the founder of a school in the monastery of Saint-Victor (Paris) to which Abelard, Andrew of Saint-Victor, Richard of Saint-Victor and Godfrey belonged. His works were well-known and widespread in medieval Europe.[38]

His exegesis developed along the line of Augustine's *De doctrina christiana*, endeavoring to integrate a rational dimension into the theological reading of the Scriptures.[39] In this, he is an heir of Origen, Augustine, Jerome, and Gregory the Great, authors whom he often quotes.[40] Andrew of St. Victor is another important figure of this school.[41] He was active both in the abbey of Wigmore (Wales) and in Paris. His work is exclusively exegetical and dedicated solely to the Old Testament. Jerome was his guide and he tried, following his example, to

---

[36] See Jon Douglas Levenson, *The Hebrew Bible, the Old Testament, and Historical Criticism: Jews and Christians in Biblical Studies* (Louisville, KY: Westminster John Knox Press, 1993), 67; *Encyclopedia Judaica*, vol. 4 (Detroit, MI: Macmillan, 2007), 62.

[37] On the knowledge of Hebrew in this time, see Gillian R. Evans, "The Impact of Christian Contact with Jewish Exegesis: Knowledge of Hebrew," in *HBOT* I.2, 254–57, and "The Victorines in Paris," ibid., 257–60; Rainer Berndt, "The School of St. Victor in Paris," ibid., 467–95, here 486–89.

[38] See Berndt, "The School of St. Victor"; for a selection of texts, see Franklin T. Harkins and Frans van Liere (eds.), *Interpretation of Scripture: Theory: A Selection of Works of Hugh, Andrew, Richard and Godfrey of St Victor, and of Robert of Melun*, Victorine Texts in Translation 3 (Turnhout: Brepols, 2012).

[39] See Grover A. Zinn, Jr., "The Influence of Augustine's *De doctrina christiana* upon the Writings of Hugh of St. Victor," in *Reading and Wisdom: The* De doctrina christiana *of Augustine in the Middle Ages*, ed. Edward D. English, Notre Dame Conferences in Medieval Studies (Notre Dame, IN: University of Notre Dame Press, 1995), 48–60.

[40] See Berndt, "The School of St. Victor," 474.

[41] See William McKane, "Andrew of St. Victor," in McKane, *Selected Christian Hebraists* (Cambridge: Cambridge University Press, 1989), 42–75; Rainer Berndt, "Andrew of St. Victor," in *HBOT* I.2, 479–84.

enable the readers of his translation to have access to the *hebraica veritas*. His translation is also an attempt to explain the original text, in a similar manner to that of his Jewish colleagues with whom he was constantly in dialogue.

Nicholas of Lyra (1270–1349)

Nicholas of Lyra, a Franciscan, is another important medieval scholar.[42] His commentary on the whole Bible, *Postillae perpetuae in universam S. Scripturam* ("Commentary notes on the whole of the Holy Scriptures"), was the first printed commentary on the Bible (Rome, 1471). Three elements are important in his exegesis. First, he can be considered a forerunner of biblical text criticism since he rejected several allegorical readings of the Bible after examining the original, Hebrew, text. Second, he favored the literal and historical interpretation of the text. Third, he knew several Jewish commentaries, especially Rashi, and drew copiously from these Jewish authorities in his exegesis. Nicholas of Lyra was one of the most influential commentators of the Bible in his time until the sixteenth century and the Renaissance. Even Martin Luther depends on Nicholas of Lyra in his exegesis as seen in his *Lectures on Genesis*.[43] Despite his emphasis on the text, Church tradition remained the highest authority for Nicholas of Lyra. This changed with the spirit of the Renaissance and the Reformation.

RENAISSANCE AND MODERN TIMES

Some Important Cultural Innovations

Two important elements mark this new period of biblical exegesis. First, the Renaissance favored a return to the original languages, Hebrew, Greek, and Aramaic, which had a strong impact on the interpretation of the biblical text. From this point of view, the Reformation can be considered a daughter of the Renaissance especially for its insistence on going back to the sources of revelation instead of relying on later traditions, and on reading the texts in their original language and not in

---

[42] For a general view on this period, see Gilbert Dahan, "Genres, Forms and Various Methods in Christian Exegesis of the Middle Ages," in *HBOT* I.2, 196–236; on Nicholas of Lyra, see Lesley Smith, "Nicholas of Lyra and Old Testament Interpretation," in *HBOT II: From the Renaissance to the Enlightenment*, ed. Magne Saebø (Neukirchen-Vluyn: Neukirchener Verlag, 2008) (henceforth abbreviated as *HBOT II*), 49–63.

[43] Hence the Latin saying: *Si Lyra non lyrasset Luther non saltasset* – "If Lyra had not played the lyre, Martin Luther would not have danced."

GENESIS IN THE HISTORY OF CRITICAL SCHOLARSHIP 23

a Latin translation (Vulgate). Second, the invention of the printing press by Johannes Gutenberg (1455) made the Bible available to many more people and scholars than before. The *sola scriptura* of the Reformation would have sounded differently if Martin Luther had been born before Johannes Gutenberg. He may not have spoken with the same insistence on *Heilige Schrift*.[44]

We may identify two phases in this period. In the first, the attention is focused on text criticism, philology and translation. In the second phase we observe an important development in new modes of interpretation, especially with Baruch Spinoza (1632–77) and Richard Simon (1638–1712).

The first phase is marked by the publication of a printed edition of the Bible with critical apparatus (Robert Estienne, Paris, 1550), the first of this kind;[45] the publication of several polyglot editions of the Bible, namely the *Complutensis* of Alcalá (Spain, 1514–17), the *Biblia Polyglota* of Antwerp (1569–72), the Polyglot of Paris (1645), the Polyglot of London or of Robert Walton (1657);[46] and some very important translations of the whole Bible in modern languages, among others the Old Belarussian translation by Francysk Skaryna (Prague, 1517–19), the German translation by Martin Luther (Wittenberg, 1522), the Dutch translation by Jacob van Liesvelt (Antwerp, 1526), the first complete translation in French by Lefèvre d'Étaples (Antwerp, 1530), the Polish Brest Bible (Brest – Brześć, now in Belarus, 1563), the Spanish *Biblia del Oso* ("Bible of the Bear," Basilea, Swiss, 1569), named *Biblia de Reina Valera* after its revision in 1602, the Czech Melantrich Bible (Prague, 1549) or the Bible of Kralice (Kralice nad Oslavou, 1579–93), and, in English, after several other attempts, the *King James Version* (London, 1611).[47]

---

44 On this point, see Trond Berg Eriksen, "From Manuscripts to Books: The Significance of the Printing Invention of Johann Gutenberg," in *HBOT* II, 103–5: "The Reformation was throughout a movement that exploited the potential created by the new technique and printed books hastened the development of reading skills in general" (104).

45 See Eldon J. Epp, "Early Critical Edition and Emerging Criteria for the Priority of Reading," in *The New Cambridge History of the Bible*, vol. 3: *From 1450 to 1750*, ed. Euan Cameron (Cambridge: Cambridge University Press, 2016) (abbreviated henceforth as *NCHB* 3), 116–27, esp. 116–19.

46 See, on this point, Alastari Hamilton, "In search of the most perfect text: The early modern printed Polyglot Bibles from Alcalá (1510–1520) to Brian Walton (1654–1658)," in *NCHB* 3, 138–56; cf. Adrian Schenker, "From the First Printed Hebrew, Greek and Latin Bibles to the First Polyglot Bible, the Complutensian Polyglot: 1477–1517," in *HBOT* II, 276–91; Adrian Schenker, "The Polyglot Bibles of Antwerp, Paris and London: 1568–1658," in *HBOT* II, 774–84.

47 See, on this point, the articles on "Producing and Disseminating the Bible in Translations," in *NCHB* 3, 159–383.

The study and diffusion of the biblical text, in its original languages and in modern translations, explains the flourishing of commentaries in this period, and prepares for the work of Baruch Spinoza and, in a special way, of Richard Simon, who extensively discussed the different versions and editions of the Bible, as well as the works of his predecessors, either translators or commentators.

Elijah Levita (1469–1549), Louis Cappel (1585–1658), and Jean Morin (1591–1659): A Better Knowledge of the Masoretic Text

Some of the most influential works of this period were the studies on the Masoretic text. Scholars, such as Elijah Levita, Louis Cappel, and Jean Morin, questioned the originality of the Masoretic vowels.[48] The Jewish scholar and grammarian Levita had already expressed doubts about this since neither the Talmud nor Jerome seem to be acquainted with them. The French Huguenot scholar Cappel went further and affirmed that the vowels and accents were inserted by the Masorete Jews of Tiberias not before the fifth century CE. He also asserted that the primitive Hebrew alphabet was that used by the newly discovered Samaritan Pentateuch and that the square characters of Aramaic origin were introduced during the exile and gradually substituted for the more ancient alphabet. The Dead Sea scrolls confirmed Cappel's view over against the criticisms of his numerous adversaries. Moreover, Cappel compared the Hebrew Masoretic text with the Samaritan Pentateuch and ancient versions. His controversial conclusions were that the Hebrew text had been subject to changes, errors, and human interventions. This amounted to an attack on the sacredness of the authoritative text and, specifically, on the doctrine of verbal inspiration. Another French scholar, from a Calvinist family but a convert to Catholicism, Jean Morin, supported Cappel after studying closely the Samaritan Pentateuch and comparing it to the Greek version of the Septuagint (LXX). Morin is the editor of the Samaritan Pentateuch and of the Targum in the Paris Polyglot. He went perhaps too far when he depreciated the Hebrew Masoretic text in his polemics against the Protestant *hebraica veritas*. But today, several scholars admit that, in a certain number of cases, the Samaritan Pentateuch and the Septuagint preserve more original readings than the Masoretic text as, for instance, in the LXX version of Gen 47:1–6.[49]

---

[48] See, on Eliyahu Levita, Sophie Kessler Mesguich, "Eliyahu (Elias) Levita/Ashkenazi," in *HBOT* II, 272–75; on Louis Cappel, see Johann Anselm Steiger, "*Critica Sacra*," in *HBOT* II, 747–49; on Jean Morin, see Pierre Gibert, "Jean Morin," in *HBOT* II, 767–73.

[49] See, for example, Julius Wellhausen, *Die Composition des Hexateuchs und der historischen Bücher des Alten Testaments* (Berlin: Georg Reimer, 1885; Berlin: de

From the point of view of the critical reading of the book of Genesis, these researchers opened new perspectives on the Hebrew text, a text that had undergone changes and evolution. Henceforth, it became possible to inquire about a human aspect of the Scriptures, namely the history of its composition. This is what happens in the next phase of this period.

The Anthropocentric World of Renaissance Humanism

The change of mentality from the Middle Ages to the Renaissance with the rise of a humanist spirit can be encapsulated in Descartes' famous saying, "Cogito, ergo sum" – "I am thinking, and therefore I am."[50] The center of attention is no longer the universe, the cosmos, or the mystery of God. The point of departure of every investigation is henceforward human mind. This is the result of a slow evolution rather than of a revolution. A major interest in humanity is felt already in the Middle Ages, for instance in Francis of Assisi (1181/82–1226), in Franciscan spirituality, and in the paintings of Giotto (1267–1337). But the clear formulation of this new way of thinking is typical of the Renaissance and of modern times, with its passage from a more theocentric way of thinking to a more humanist and anthropocentric one. In this context, it is understandable that biblical studies will also focus the attention on the human origin of biblical literature.

In this new phase of research, the object of biblical studies also changes. In the first phase, the study was mainly philological and focused on the language of the biblical books in its different forms. Now, the study becomes more historical, in the sense that scholars study the gradual development of the text itself.

Baruch Spinoza (1632–1677)

Baruch Spinoza was of Jewish Sephardi Portuguese origin.[51] His family emigrated from Portugal to the Netherlands in the wake of the Portuguese Inquisition, under king John III (1536), to avoid forced

---

Gruyter, 1963), 51–52; Marie-Joseph Lagrange, "Les sources du Pentateuque," *RB* 7 (1898): 10–32, here 15–16.

[50] See, for instance, Jeremy Catto, "The Philosophical Context of the Renaissance Interpretation of the Bible," in *HBOT* II, 106–22.

[51] See, among many others, Steven Nadler, "The Bible Hermeneutics of Baruch de Spinoza," in *HBOT* II, 827–36; Travis L. Frampton, *Spinoza and the Rise of Historical Criticism of the Bible* (London: T&T Clark, 2006); Jeffrey L. Morrow, *Three Skeptics and the Bible: La Peyrère, Hobbes, Spinoza, and the Reception of Modern Biblical Criticism* (Eugene, OR: Pickwick, 2016); Rudolf Smend, *Kritiker und Exegeten: Porträtskizzen zu vier Jahrhunderten alttestamentlicher Wissenschaft* (Göttingen: Vandenhoeck & Ruprecht, 2017), 50–66, who begins his portrait with a fitting quotation from Heinrich Heine: "All our contemporary Old Testament

conversion. Baruch Spinoza is perhaps more a philosopher than a real
exegete, and his reflections on the Bible from his rational – some would
say rationalistic – viewpoint are part of a vast project of rethinking
religion and politics. His first aim was to justify a new
Weltanschauung at a time when Europe was the scene of gruesome
wars of religion. His ideal was a republic where reason would be the
foundation of religious tolerance and human benevolence. "Religion
divides, reason unites" could be a good summary of Spinoza's philosophy. Because of his views on the Bible and religion, Spinoza was ostra-
cized from the Jewish community in 1653. The exact reason is not
stated in the verdict of the Synagogue authorities, but Spinoza denied,
for instance, the immortality of the soul, the existence of a providential
God, and the Mosaic authorship of the Pentateuch.

   As for the Pentateuch, Spinoza applied to the biblical texts a method
typical of ancient and modern historians. He quotes Abraham ibn Ezra's
doubts and declares, in plain language, that Moses could not have written
the Pentateuch. He goes much further, however, and provides evidence
to support the assertion. According to Spinoza, Ezra the scribe (cf. Neh
8:1) is the author of the Pentateuch as well as of the so-called historical
books of the Old Testament. This idea was already present in Andreas
Masius's commentary on the book of Joshua.[52]

   What enables Spinoza to ask these critical questions is his conviction that reason and not authority is the final judge in the interpretation of literary texts. Moreover, he is persuaded that biblical
literature should be read and interpreted the same way as other
historical documents. Like Cappel, he also claims that the Bible
contains in some parts errors, imperfections, and inconsistences,
and that we possess only fragments of it. This roused harsh opposition and led to his condemnation by both Jewish and Christian
authorities, and even by the civil authorities of Amsterdam. In the
long run, however, several of his views proved to be right, helping to
distinguish true religion, inscribed in the heart and mind of human
beings, from the letter of ancient texts. The foundations for a critical
reading of the texts are laid because the "truth" of the Bible in general
and of the book of Genesis, in particular, is no longer fully identified
with its human expression.

---

scholars, perhaps often unwittingly, look through the lens that Baruch Spinoza pol-
ished" (my translation).
[52]   Andreas Masius, *Iosuae imperatoris historia illustrata atque explicata* (Antwerp:
Plantin, 1574), 2.

Richard Simon (1638–1712)

Richard Simon, an Oratorian priest, is at the same time an heir, a colleague, and a staunch adversary of Spinoza.[53] All in all, however, the similarities between both men are more important than their differences, despite the polemics of Simon against Spinoza. Simon is often a bitter and sarcastic polemist. On the other hand, he is sometimes hailed as the real founder of modern biblical criticism. This is true in the sense that he is the first well-known exegete who proposed a systematic view of the development of the biblical text. He goes one step further than Spinoza who, after all, simply substituted the traditional Moses with Ezra as the author of the Pentateuch. For Simon, the text of the Pentateuch can be explained only by resorting to a long chain of public scribes and writers. The biblical text, therefore, was not written at once by one unique author, but is the result of a long and complex process of composition.

Simon's research is guided by four principles he exposes at length in the first part of his *Histoire critique du Vieux Testament*. (1) The first task, according to Simon, is to establish the text, comparing for instance the Masoretic text with the other versions. In this chapter he discusses, among others, the value of the different polyglots available in his time (see above). This part of Simon's work is still valuable today since he does not privilege the Masoretic text in biblical exegesis, although this was almost a dogma for many of his contemporaries. (2) Simon's second principle is probably one of his most original contributions. There existed in ancient Israel, in "the Republic of the Hebrews," a guild of public writers the function of which was on writing the "acts" of the most important events of public life and to convey the old traditions to the next generations. These public writers constitute a continuous chain linking Moses to Ezra. It means that the text was modified and completed several times after Moses, and that some parts of the Pentateuch cannot have been written by Moses in person. We have here the starting point of many inquiries about the sources and the redactions of the Pentateuch in general and the book of Genesis in particular. (3) Another principle that was reinstated recently is that of the concision of ancient biblical texts. We do not have complete versions of the ancient traditions of Israel, but sometimes short and even abridged versions of them were preserved in the archives of the Republic of the Hebrews. This

---

[53] See Richard Simon, *Histoire critique du Vieux Testament (1678)* suivi de *Lettre sur l'inspiration*. Nouvelle édition annotée et introduite par Pierre Gibert (Paris: Bayard, 2008); John W. Rogerson, "Richard Simon," in *HBOT* II, 838–43; Smend, *Kritiker*, 67–96.

solves many problems, Simon asserts, especially with respect to chron-ologies and genealogies. (4) Simon affirms the value of a tradition, both oral and written, behind the actual text of the Bible. We do not have the originals and the text we have now is the fruit of a long process of transmission. Many changes occurred during this oral transmission and many changes were also introduced by the copyists.

As we can see, most of the work done on the book of Genesis in the next centuries finds its source in Simon's *Histoire critique du Vieux Testament*. First, he affirms the existence of different "hands" and opens thus the way to research into the sources of the Pentateuch. Second, we find some foreshadowing of Hermann Gunkel's theory of the existence of an oral tradition preceding the redaction of the actual text of Genesis. Third, Simon insists on the importance of the versions for establishing the text. Today's textual criticism still lives on this principle.

Like Spinoza, Simon was condemned at the instigation of Bossuet, and the 1,300 copies of his *Histoire critique* were sequestered and burnt in public in Paris because it questioned Moses's authorship of the Pentateuch. By chance, a few copies were saved by the executioners themselves and sold in England and in the Netherlands. Otherwise we would not know anything about his research.

THE SOURCES OF THE BOOK OF GENESIS

Historical and Cultural Context

"We are not to renounce our Senses, and Experience; nor (that which is undoubted Word of God) our natural Reason".[54] This sentence by Thomas Hobbes (1588–1679) condensed the new spirit of the time, the spirit that would lead biblical research from this point forward in a systematic way.[55] Hobbes is among the first intellectuals of this time to deny the Mosaic authorship of the Pentateuch because of the many repetitions, inconsistencies, contradictions, and anachronisms present in it.[56]

---

[54] Thomas Hobbes, *Leviathan*. Edited by Richard Tuck Cambridge: University Press, 2005), III.xxxii.2.

[55] See Charlotte Methuen, "On the Threshold of a New Age: Expanding Horizons as the Broader Context of Scriptural Interpretation," in *HBOT* II, 665–90; Peter Harrison, "The Bible and the Emerging 'Scientific' World-View," in *NCHB* 3, 620–40; Henning Graf Reventlow, "Between Humanism and Enlightenment: Morality, Reason and History as Factors in Biblical Interpretation," in *NCHB* 3, 641–56.

[56] Jean Bernier, *La critique du Pentateuque de Hobbes à Calmet*, Libre pensée et littérature clandestine 42 (Paris: Honoré Champion, 2010).

Empirical observation, and exegesis based on philology and a careful analysis of the text, had become the rule. This can be summarized by a famous sentence by Galileo Galilei: "Ciò che l'esperienza, e il senso ci dimostra, si deve anteporre ad ogni discorso, ancorché ne paresse assai ben fondato" – "What experience and senses show us must precede any kind of discourse, even if the latter seems very well founded."[57] This means that the Bible will be studied as any other book and with methods used in other disciplines. Other important names to be mentioned as leading spirits of the time are those of Francis Bacon (1561–1626), John Locke (1632–1704), and David Hume (1711–76) in Britain or Immanuel Kant (1724–1804) in Germany.

Historical research is another essential element of this time.[58] Edward Gibbon (1737–94) published *The History of the Decline and Fall of the Roman Empire* between 1777 and 1788. He is often considered one of the first modern historians because of his insistence on relying on primary sources. Searching for "sources" in the book of Genesis participates in the same spirit, although there is no direct influence by Gibbon on biblical exegesis of that time. In Germany, other historians became famous later. Leopold von Ranke (1795–1886), the father of *Weltgeschichte* (*World History*), is famous for his scientific method, free from ideology, captured in his famous saying that history must show the facts exactly as they happened – "wie es eigentlich gewesen ist."[59] This principle is problematic according to some more recent historians, but Ranke's first purpose was to liberate history from philosophy (against Hegel) and moral judgment. The works of de Wette and Wellhausen should be understood in this light. Their views of the development of Israel's literature, especially with respect of the book of Genesis, are an example of historical research which distinguishes the facts from the religious ideas informing them. We find also here the roots of the distinction between "biblical Israel" and "ancient Israel."

Interest in history increased in Europe after the French revolution (1789) and the Napoleonic wars (1792–1815) with their social and political upheavals.[60] "Happy peoples do not have history," according to an old

---

[57] Galileo Galilei, *Dialogo* (Florence: Giorgio Batista Landini, 1632), VII, 80.

[58] See Euan Cameron, "The Bible and the Early Sense of History," in *NCHB* 3, 657–85.

[59] Leopold von Ranke, *Geschichten der romanischen und germanischen Völker von 1494 bis 1535*, Band I (Leipzig: G. Reimer, 1824), v–vi; see Fritz Stern, *The Varieties of History: From Voltaire to the Present* (New York: Vintage, 1973), 54–62, here 57.

[60] See Henning Graf Reventlow, "The French Revolution of 1789: A Symptom of a New Political and Cultural Situation," in *HBOT* II, 1024–34.

French saying. Wars and revolutions brought about the awareness of a "before" and an "afterwards." A world had gone, and a new world had arrived; with this, the difference between past and present became evident. The romantic movement and its characteristic longing for a "golden age" also encouraged exegetes to inquire about the remote past of Israel in the book of Genesis.[61]

Eventually, biblical studies on the book of Genesis developed in a way strikingly similar to Homeric studies.[62] François Hédelin d'Aubignac (1604–76), in his *Conjectures académiques ou dissertations sur l'Iliade* (written in 1679, published in 1715 by François Fournier), affirms that a careful reading of the Iliad enables one to distinguish in it different dialects and therefore different authors who wrote in different places and in different times. This theory was taken over and developed in a systematic way by Friedrich August Wolf (1753–1824).[63] For him, we have at the beginning separate poems, transmitted orally because there was no literacy at that time, and these poems were therefore modified and amplified in the course of their transmission. They were put in writing later, in the sixth century BCE. The name of Peisistratos (d. 528/7 BCE), ruler in Athens between 561 and 528/527 BCE, is often quoted in this context.

Anyone will notice the strong resemblance of this theory with that of Hermann Gunkel, because for him too the origin of the book of Genesis can be found in single tales transmitted orally. The combination of philology and history, another mark of Wolf's research, would become characteristic of studies on Genesis as well. Moreover, specialists of Homer proposed theories about the formation of the Iliad and the Odyssey which are very close to the theories elaborated later by biblical exegetes. They distinguished different sources and authors, each one with a distinctive style and vocabulary (a theory of sources); or there was a first, original, poem, supplemented subsequently (a theory of supplements); or different fragments were

---

[61]   Asko Nivala, *The Romantic Idea of the Golden Age in Friedrich Schlegel's Philosophy of History* (London: Routledge, 2017).

[62]   See, on this point, Margalit Finkelberg and Guy G. Stroumsa, eds., *Homer, the Bible, and Beyond: Literary and Religious Canons in the Ancient World*, Jerusalem Studies in Religion and Culture 2 (Leiden and Boston, MA: Brill, 2003); Maren R. Niehoff, ed., *Homer and the Bible in the Eyes of Ancient Interpreters*, Jerusalem Studies in Religion and Culture 16 (Leiden: Brill, 2012).

[63]   Friedrich August Wolf, *Prolegomena ad Homerum* (Halle: Waisenhaus, 1795); English edition: *Prolegomena to Homer (1795)*, trans. with an introduction and notes by A. Grafton, G. W. Most, and J. E. Z. Zetzel (Princeton, NJ: Princeton University Press, 1985).

eventually put together by one compiler at a later stage of composition (a theory of fragments). Several specialists combined these theories.[64]

One more point could be of some interest, namely the concept of "diaskeuastai" copyists or editors of Homeric epics who, first of all, "cleaned" the Homeric manuscripts, eliminating spurious glosses. Some scholars also suggest that they revised, elucidated, reelaborated, and completed the copies in their possession. Biblical scholars such as Abraham Kuenen used the same term when speaking of "redactors" or "editors" who had an active role in the composition of biblical texts, compiling, arranging, changing, completing, and sometimes rewriting entire sections of older texts.[65]

Henning Bernhard Witter (1683–1715)

In this new phase of biblical research, the book of Genesis became the center of attention. Simon's intuitions had borne fruit, but now exegetes went one step further and tried to identify the different hands at work in the Pentateuch, beginning with Genesis. The first author to be mentioned is Henning Bernhard Witter, who wrote and published his work in 1711 when he was only 28, and just four years before his death. The starting point of Witter's research, limited to Genesis 1–3, is the observation that the chapters use different appellations for God. In Gen 1:1–2:4a, the deity is simply called "God" (Hebrew: 'ĕlōhîm), whereas, from Gen 2:4b, the appellation is most of the time double: "Lord God" (Hebrew: YHWH 'ĕlōhîm). The use of different appellations for the deity led Witter to the hypothesis that these chapters were written by two different authors. Unfortunately, this work was completely ignored, but his insights reappeared in other publications not much later. It seems that the discovery was "in the air of the time."[66]

---

[64] See Umberto Cassuto, *The Documentary Hypothesis and the Composition of the Pentateuch* (Jerusalem: Magnes Press, 1961), 10–11.

[65] Konrad Schmid, "Von der Diaskeuase zur nachendredaktionellen Fortschreibung. Die Geschichte der Erforschung der nachpriesterschriftlichen Redaktionsgeschichte des Pentateuch," in *The Post-Priestly Pentateuch: New Perspectives on Its Redactional Development and Theological Profiles*, ed. Federico Giuntoli and Konrad Schmid, FAT 101 (Tübingen: Mohr Siebeck, 2015), 1–18. The very existence of "redactors" or "editors" in Antiquity is fiercely opposed by John Van Seters, *The Edited Bible: The Curious History of the "Editor" in Biblical Criticism* (Winona Lake, IN: Eisenbrauns, 2006).

[66] See Adolphe Lods, "Un précurseur allemand de Jean Astruc: Henning Bernhard Witter," *ZAW* 43 (1925): 134–5; Smend, *Kritiker*, 108–23.

Jean Astruc (1684–1766)

Jean Astruc was a member of an old family of Jewish origin.[67] His father was a Protestant pastor who had converted to Catholicism. Astruc was a physician who had studied in Montpellier, a city which possessed a renowned school of medicine. He practiced medicine first at the university of Montpellier and afterwards in Paris where he even became the personal surgeon of Louis XV. His major work, however, was not in medicine, but in biblical exegesis, a work published cautiously in Brussels and not in Paris, *Conjectures sur les mémoires originaux dont il paroit que Moyse s'est servi pour composer le livre de la Genèse. Avec des remarques qui appuient ou qui éclaircissent ces conjectures* (*Conjectures on the original documents that Moses appears to have used in composing the Book of Genesis. With remarks that support or throw light upon these conjectures*) (Brussels: Fricx, 1753).[68]

Ironically, Astruc's first purpose was to defend Moses's authorship against the attacks of Hobbes, Spinoza, and other "enlightened" spirits. His main thesis is that Moses must have used "original memoirs," previous documents, to compose the Pentateuch. Applying to the biblical texts methods solidly established in classical, especially in Homeric, studies, he identified two major and ten minor documents in the first part of the Pentateuch. His main criterion was that of Witter, namely the divine appellations. A first major document used the divine appellation "God" (Hebrew: '*ĕlōhîm*), and the second, the divine name YHWH (Hebrew, without vowels, *yhwh*). Astruc, went further than Genesis 3 and stopped with the analysis of Exodus 2 for one simple reason, namely that God reveals his sacred name YHWH to Moses in Exod 3:14. After this, Astruc felt the use of the criterion of the divine appellations was no longer possible. The other "documents" are fragments which cannot be attributed to the two main sources, A and B.

Astruc's methodology used the criterion of repetitions more thoroughly than others. He noticed that the same incident was sometimes told more than once. For instance, there are two creation accounts in Genesis 1 and 2. After Astruc, the presence of "doublets" will be one of the main criteria used by scholars such as Eichhorn and Ilgen to distinguish different sources within the book of Genesis. Some of the clearest examples, after the two creation accounts, are the threefold narrative of

---

[67] On Astruc, see, among others, Rudolf Smend, *From Astruc to Zimmerli: Old Testament Scholarship in Three Centuries*, trans. Margaret Kohl (Tübingen: Mohr Siebeck, 2007), 1–14.

[68] Newly edited under the title *Conjectures sur la Genèse: Introduction et notes de Pierre Gibert* (Paris: Noêsis, 1999).

the patriarch and his wife-sister (Gen 12:10–20; 20:1–18; 26:6–11); the two covenants of God with Abraham (Genesis 15 and 17); and the two appearances of God to Jacob at Bethel (Gen 28:10–22; 35:9–15). In other cases, as in the flood narrative (Genesis 6–9) or in the first chapter of the Joseph Story (Genesis 37), two parallel threads are interwoven in the same literary composition. Later, Astruc admitted the existence of numerous "fragments" besides his two main "sources" or "memoirs." In this sense, he is one of the fathers not only of the documentary hypothesis, but also of the fragmentary hypothesis.

Johann David Michaelis (1717–1791)

Before turning to Eichhorn and Ilgen as is frequently the case following a study of Astruc, we turn our attention to Johann David Michaelis, who is often bypassed.[69] He deserves special mention for several reasons. He was a layperson, a theologian, and an orientalist who lectured in Halle (1739–45) and Göttingen (1746–91). His contribution to the critical study of Genesis is twofold. First, although he had first defended the Hebrew vowels' antiquity and divine authority, after a journey through England and the Netherlands he changed his mind. Following Levita, Cappel, and Morin, he affirmed that Hebrew was a language like all the other languages and that it must be studied according to the philological methods used for other languages. He was in some respect a pioneer of comparative Semitic linguistics since he knew Syriac and some Arabic. Second, he approached the Bible from a cultural point of view and encouraged a study of all aspects of the Bible as, in other faculties, scholars had studied classical culture. Nobody did as much as Michaelis to make the study of Hebrew antiquity an academic discipline equal to other academic disciplines and to integrate it into the study of ancient Near Eastern civilizations. This is a major contribution, although Michaelis did not express much sympathy for Astruc's intuitions.

Johann Gottlieb Eichhorn (1752–1827)

This was not the case with Johann Gottlieb Eichhorn, who taught in Jena (1775–88) and Göttingen (1788–1827).[70] He picked up explicitly

---

[69] On Michaelis, see John Sandys-Wunsch, "Johann David Michaelis," in *HBOT* II, 980–4; Michael C. Legaspi, *The Death of Scripture and the Rise of Biblical Studies*, Oxford Studies in Historical Theology (Oxford: Oxford University Press, 2011); Smend, *Kritiker*, 140–53 = *From Astruc to Zimmerli*, 30–42.

[70] See Henning Graf Reventlow, "Johann Gottfried Eichhorn: His *Einleitung in das alte Testament* as a 'Summa' of the New 'Higher Criticism'," in *HBOT* II, 1051–57;

Spinoza's, Simon's, and especially Astruc's legacy, and carried on the search for sources through the whole of the Pentateuch. He is sometimes acclaimed as the "the founder of modern Old Testament criticism," but, as we have seen, there are other candidates for the same title. As in other cases, his main merit is to have developed systematically some original insights of his predecessors, especially those of Astruc even though he did not always recognize his debts very willingly. Following Michaelis, he also compared biblical literature with other Semitic writings.

As for Genesis, he distinguished two main sources, with the help of three main criteria. (1) Repetitions, namely the double or triple version of the same event. The example chosen is that of the flood narrative (Genesis 6–9). (2) Style, for instance the use of different divine appellations or of favorite expressions. (3) Content, for instance geographic or cosmographic genealogies on the one side and chronological genealogies on the other side. The main work, at this stage, consists in separating different sources within Genesis. Scholars have not yet asked questions about dating and relative chronology.

Besides the two main sources – the one using the divine appellation "God" (*'ĕlōhîm*), therefore called the Elohim document, and the other Yhwh (*yhwh*), called the Jehovah document – he identified several other pieces. Among them, we should notice the presence of Genesis 2:4–3:19, the second creation account, the Eden narrative.[71] For Eichhorn, the childish tone of these two chapters and the unusual presence of both divine appellation, Yhwh and Elohim, oblige to set this narrative apart. Other texts are Genesis 14; 33:18–34:31; 36:1–43; 49:1–27, texts that are still today the object of many debates.

As for the history of the text, Eichhorn develops a theory that owes something to Richard Simon. At the beginning of the process, we find single, oral, units that were put into writing in a second phase. In a third phase, the single units were put together into larger documents. And the larger documents were united at the time of Moses or later. Eichhorn does not believe in Mosaic authorship, although he thinks that many

---

Rudolf Smend, *Deutsche Alttestamentler in drei Jahrhunderten* (Göttingen: Vandenhoeck & Ruprecht, 1989), 25–37; Smend, *Kritiker*, 176–91.

[71] See, for instance, Joseph Blenkinsopp, *Creation, Un-creation, Re-creation: A Discursive Commentary on Genesis 1–11* (London: T&T Clark International, 2011), who considers Genesis 2–3 as a late, post-exilic and post-priestly text; for the opposite view, see now Walter Bührer, *Am Anfang ... : Untersuchungen zur Textgenese und zur relativ-chronologischen Einordnung von Gen 1–3*, FRLANT 256 (Göttingen: Vandenhoeck & Ruprecht, 2014); Walter Bührer, "The Relative Dating of the Eden Narrative Gen *2–3," *VT* 65 (2015): 365–76.

parts of Genesis predate Moses. The latter is never mentioned as the author of Genesis before Philo, Josephus, and the Talmud.

Another point of Eichhorn's investigation deserves a short mention. For him, the simpler the style, the older the text. This principle was be often used by later generations of scholars but was very often questioned as well. It is because of the simplicity of its style that the Priestly Writer – the source Elohim or the Elohist for the first generations – was considered the oldest source of Genesis.

Eichhorn also deserves attention for introducing the concept of "myth" into the academic landscape, a concept that had much influence on the exegesis of Genesis. Once again, the idea comes from classical studies, more concretely from Christian Gottlob Heyne's (1729–1812) studies on Homer. Eichhorn attended a seminar by Heyne, who often compared Homer and Moses and interpreted old myths as expressions of a still childish humankind. Myth has many meanings, but here is the definition given by Johannes Philipp Gabler: "Myths are in general popular narratives of the ancient world in the sensory way of thinking and speaking of that time."[72] Two elements are essential in this sentence, namely the conviction that our way of thinking and speaking is different from that of the ancient world, and that the ancient world preferred a "sensory" experience to a more rational or Cartesian way of thinking and speaking. Owing to this distinction, Eichhorn thought that he could overcome the gap separating supernaturalistic and naturalistic ways of reading biblical texts in general and Genesis in particular. Like R. Ishmael, Eichhorn looks for a solution in the conventions of human language. For instance, Eichhorn considered that Genesis 1–3 used this "mythical" language to describe the origins of the world and of humankind, and that these texts did not contain a precise account of actual events.

Karl David Ilgen (1763–1834)

The name of Karl David Ilgen is much too often attached to the "invention" of a second Elohist.[73] He would have separated the future Priestly

---

[72] Text quoted by Smend, *Kritiker*, 187, and stemming from Johannes Philipp Gabler, in his new edition of Eichhorn's *Die Urgeschichte* II/1 (Altdorf: Monath & Kussler, 1792), 482. Heyne can be considered as the founder of the *mythische Schule* in Göttingen. He would have many followers, Rudolf Bultmann not being the least of them.

[73] See Bodo Seidel, *Karl David Ilgen und die Pentateuchforschung im Umkreis der sogenannten Älteren Urkundenhypothese: Studien zur Geschichte der exegetischen Hermeneutik in der späten Aufklärung*, BZAW 213 (Berlin: de Gruyter, 1993).

Writer from what was to become the Elohist of the classical
Documentary Hypothesis. But this is not exactly the case since Ilgen
speaks of two Elohists only with respect to the Joseph Story. He explains
in this way the presence of doublets in a text where the divine name
YHWH appears very rarely, apart from Genesis 39.

Karl David Ilgen was also a classical philologist who taught Homer
in the university of Jena. He is credited for having coined the term
epyllion in Homeric studies when speaking of Homer's Hymn to
Hermes. There are some striking similarities between his theory of the
composition of Genesis and the ideas of Lachmann, although we do not
know whether the two men knew each other.[74] Lachmann argued that
the *Iliad* is made of sixteen originally independent units that were
successively augmented and interpolated. This theory had much success
in the nineteenth century. Ilgen, for his part, distinguishes seventeen
"pieces" (*Stücke*) in the book of Genesis, that is, seventeen narrative
units. In Ilgen's theory, however, these "units" belong to three main
sources, a Jehovist, who will become the Yahwist of the classical documentary hypothesis, and two Elohists. These "pieces" were separated
and organized in a chronological order to form the actual book of
Genesis.

The results of Ilgen's research were contested by Eichhorn, among
others, because he often corrected the Hebrew text, following, for
instance, the Greek version of the Septuagint or other versions. His
main contribution, however, is in the field of methodology and on one
of the important exegetes of the next generation, Hupfeld, who praised
his work.[75]

Ilgen's criteria were: (1) titles, namely the *toledot*-formulae (Gen 2:4;
5:1; 6:9; 10:1; 11:10, 27; 25:12, 19; 36:1, 9; 37:2); (2) repetitions or doublets
(cf. Astruc); (3) differences in style, for instance the use of different divine
appellations; (4) differences in content and theology, what Ilgen calls
"character."[76] These criteria, very similar to those of Eichhorn, are still

[74] Karl Konrad F. W. Lachmann, *Betrachtungen über Homers Ilias* (Berlin: G. Reimer,
1837, 1841). Lachmann is also known for his work on New Testament textual criticism. See Elon Epp, "The rise of an eclectic text and the departure from the *textus
receptus* – Dominance of external evidence," in *The New Cambridge History of the
Bible*, vol. 4: *From 1750 to the Present*, ed. John Riches (Cambridge: Cambridge
University Press, 2015), 14–17.

[75] Hermann Hupfeld, *Die Quellen der Genesis und die Art ihrer Zusammensetzung von
neuem untersucht* (Berlin: von Wiegandt & Grieken, 1853), viii-ix.

[76] See Karl-David Ilgen, *Die Urkunden des ersten Buchs von Moses in ihrer Urgestalt
zum bessern Verständniß und richtigern Gebrauch derselben in ihrer gegenwärtigen
Form aus dem hebräischen mit kritischen Anmerkungen und Nachweisungen auch*

valid today. Exegetes refined their mode of applying them, but they did not introduce completely new elements into the field.

The critical study of Genesis owes much to Ilgen for another reason. He worked to reconcile his church and his fellow believers with the results of his research. For him, critical study is not a lack of respect toward sacred and inspired books, nor should reverence toward the Holy Scriptures prevent critical study of its errors, tensions, contradictions, and anachronisms. Ilgen noticed that many elements in Genesis do not reflect the time they describe, but the time of those who put the texts into writing, something that Wellhausen would repeat almost one century later. "One does not yet know", as he said, "how to detect the point where popular legend [German: "Sage"] finishes and history begins."[77]

Wilhelm Martin Leberecht de Wette (1780–1849)

With Wilhelm Martin Leberecht de Wette, we come to a turning point in the critical reading of Genesis.[78] Apart from his "discovery," which is more a rediscovery of the connection between Deuteronomy and Josiah's reform described in 2 Kings 22–23, de Wette is responsible for several innovations in biblical studies.

First, de Wette is a disciple of the *Aufklärung*, the Enlightenment, but there are also elements of romanticism and pietism in his writings and the influence of the great romantic Herder is undeniable, especially in his sensitivity for poetry.[79] De Wette's main interest is similar to that

---

einer Abhandlung über die Trennung der Urkunden (Halle: Hemmerde und Schwetschke, 1798), 351–62, 362–76, 376–400, 400–9.

[77] See Ilgen, Urkunden, xii–xiii.

[78] On W. M. L. de Wette, see, first of all, John W. Rogerson, *W. M. L. de Wette, Founder of Modern Biblical Criticism: An Intellectual Biography*, JSOTSS 126 (Sheffield: Academic Press,1992); Henning Graf Reventlow, "Vernunft, Ästhetik, Glaube und historische Kritik: Wilhelm Martin Leberecht de Wette," in Reventlow, *Epochen der Bibelauslegung. IV. Von der Aufklärung bis zum 20. Jahrhundert* (Munich: Beck, 2001), 227–40. See also Thomas Albert Howard, *Religion and the Rise of Historicism: W. M. L. de Wette, Jacob Burckhardt, and the Theological Origins of Nineteenth-Century Historical Consciousness* (Cambridge: Cambridge University Press, 2000); Smend, *Kritiker*, 192–206, who quotes at the beginning of his biographical sketch Wellhausen's opinion about de Wette: "An intelligent guy! All that I did in Old Testament [field] is already in his work!" (192) (my translation); English translation: *From Astruc to Zimmerli*, 43–56.

[79] See, above all, Johann Gottfried von Herder, *Vom Geist der Ebräischen Poesie: Eine Anleitung für die Liebhaber derselben und der ältesten Geschichte des menschlichen Geistes* (Dessau: Buchhandlung der Gelehrten, 1782; Leipzig: Barth, 3rd ed., 1825). On Herder, ee, among others, Henning Graf Reventlow, "Johann Gottfried Herder – Theologian, Promotor of Humanity, Historian," in *HBOT* II, 1041–50; Smend, *Kritiker*, 154–75.

of Spinoza, he is interested in "truth": "Truth is the first important law
of history, love for truth is the historian's first duty."[80] In this sense, de
Wette applied to historical research Spinoza's rational principles. De
Wette reads Genesis as a historian and tries to define the kind of
"truth" the book contains according to criteria common in historical
research. He lists five criteria: (1) History is based on documents. There is
no history if there are no documents. (2) These documents must be
credible and reliable. They are such if they do not contradict the laws
of nature and reason (cf. Origen's *Principles* and Spinoza) and come from
reliable persons. (3) Not every narrative is a historical document. There
are legends, myths, and fables in the Bible – and in this, de Wette anticipates Gunkel's literary genres. Moreover, the more distant the documents are from the events recounted, the less reliable they are. The
most reliable documents are those going back to eyewitnesses. De
Wette distinguishes what historians will call primary and secondary
sources, firsthand and secondhand documents. For de Wette, the distance between the redaction of Genesis and the events recounted
makes it impossible to treat Genesis as a historical document. This is
an important step in research about Genesis since we know, by now, that
it was not written by Moses in person, that it is a human work, and,
finally, that the world described in it is not historical reality. De Wette
calls it "myth," that is, popular and picturesque narratives intended to
create the identity of Israel's nation. As for Herder, he thinks than these
narratives belong more to poetry than to history. In this, he is also
a disciple and a companion of Heyne, Eichhorn, and Gabler, a member
of the *mythische Schule* (see above).[81] (4) Likelihood and impartiality are
necessary characteristics of historical documents. When narratives
describe events that we consider as impossible or unthinkable, these
cannot be considered as historical documents. We can trace back the
origin of this way of thinking to Origen and Greek historians. (5)
"Tradition" as such is suspect for the historian. Popular traditions tend
to be poetic and patriotic; they are not interested in informing with rigor
and precision about the past. Imagination and fantasy come into play
when the information about the past is too fragmentary. The more
marvelous, the better is one of the principles of popular traditions. As

---

[80] "Wahrheit ist das erste große Gesetz der Geschichte, Wahrheitsliebe die erste Pflicht
      des Geschichtsforschers." Wilhelm Martin Leberecht de Wette, *Beiträge zur
      Einleitung in das Alte Testament*, vol. 2: *Kritik der Israelitischen Geschichte*, pt. 1:
      Kritik der mosaischen Geschichte (Halle: Schimmelpfennig, 1807; Hildesheim and
      New York: Georg Olms, 1971), 1.
[81] See ibid., 81, 93, 353 and *passim*.

we will see, all these elements will reappear in the next generation of scholars, especially in Wellhausen's and, perhaps even more, in Gunkel's research.[82]

The exegesis of Genesis during this period became more and more aware of two gaps: first, a gap between our modern way of thinking and the ancient world's way of thinking, and second a gap between the real world and the biblical narratives, especially in Genesis.

Wilhelm Martin Leberecht de Wette's Posterity: Supernaturalism Versus Humanism

Handbooks and introductions usually summarize the developments of the study of the book of Genesis in a discussion about three models: a supplementary hypothesis attached to the name of Heinrich Ewald, a fragmentary hypothesis attached to the name of Friedrich Tuch, and finally a documentary hypothesis that gained the upper hand thanks to Hupfeld first, and then triumphed with Reuss, Graf, Kuenen, and Wellhausen. The latter is the name most often quoted by the manuals in the field, and for good reasons. This is, however, a simplified view on the matter.

First, most of the theories combined different models, although one of them prevailed in many cases. Distinctions are not clear cut. Some exegetes, for instance de Wette, changed their minds. It is possible to find elements of both fragmentary and supplementary hypotheses even in Wellhausen.

Second, handbooks usually ignore a fierce battle that took place around the critical reading of the book of Genesis, especially about the dating of the so-called *Grundschrift*, today's Priestly Writer. The idea that Genesis 1, the first creation account, could have been written after the exile was appalling to most specialists in the middle of the nineteenth century. The battle took place not only in academic circles, but also in political circles and church institutions. Several well-known exegetes were condemned both in Germany and in Great Britain. We may at least mention William Robertson Smith in Aberdeen (Scotland), condemned for having translated Wellhausen into English, or Marie-Joseph Lagrange, from the École Biblique in Jerusalem, who could never publish his commentary on Genesis.[83]

---

[82] See ibid., 1–29.

[83] For more details, see John W. Rogerson, *Old Testament Criticism in the Nineteenth Century: England and Germany* (Philadelphia: Fortress, 1985); John W. Rogerson, *The Bible and Criticism in Victorian Britain: Profiles of F. D. Maurice & William*

Two points were objects of contention. First, a certain conviction that the truth of the "history of salvation" depends on the historicity of the biblical narratives about it. Second, the problem of interpretation raised by the opinion that many important texts about Israel's legislation, and especially Israel's cult, are late.

Hermann Hupfeld (1796–1866)

Hermann Hupfeld was the successor of the famous Hebraist, Wilhelm Gesenius, at the university of Halle.[84] One year before his death, in 1865, he was accused of heretical doctrines by some followers of the orthodox exegete Hengstenberg.[85] All his colleagues sided with him, however, and he was cleared of this accusation. As for the book of Genesis, his main contribution is a strong plea in favor of a documentary hypothesis, namely the idea that we find in the book of Genesis, as in the rest of the Pentateuch, independent and complete sources, running parallel to each other. The book of Genesis combines two or three versions of the origins of the world and of the origins of Israel. Hupfeld is also the first scholar who clearly distinguished two strands in the so-called Elohist. One will become the (northern) Elohist and the other the Priestly Writer. To be

---

Robertson Smith, Journal for the Study of the Old Testament. Supplement Series 201 (Sheffield: Academic Press, 1997). On William Robertson Smith, see William Johnstone, ed., *William Robertson Smith: Essays in Reassessment*, JSOTSS 189 (Sheffield: Academic Press, 1995); Gillian M. Bediako, *Primal Religion and the Bible: William Robertson Smith and His Heritage*, JSOTSS 246 (Sheffield: Academic Press, 1997); Bernhard Maier, *William Robertson Smith: His Life, His Work and His Times*, FAT 67 (Tübingen: Mohr Siebeck, 2009). On Lagrange, see, among others, Bernard Montagnes, *The Story of Father Marie-Joseph Lagrange: Founder of Modern Catholic Bible Study*, trans. Benedict Viviano (Mahwah, NJ: Paulist Press, 2006).

[84] See Otto Kaiser, "An Heir of Astruc in a Remote German University: Hermann Hupfeld and the 'New Documentary Hypothesis'," in *Sacred Conjectures: The Context and Legacy of Robert Lowth and Jean Astruc*, ed. John Jarick, LHBOTS 457 (London: T&T Clark, 2007), 220–48.

[85] On Hengstenberg, see, among others, Smend, *Kritiker*, 240–57. Smend quotes one of the most famous sentences of this exegete, in his thesis defended in Bonn in 1823: "Falsa est de Wettii de Pentateucho sententia" – "De Wette's opinion on the Pentateuch is wrong" (240). See also Rudolf Smend, "A Conservative Approach in Opposition to a Historical-critical Interpretation: E. W. Hengstenberg and Franz Delitzsch," in *Hebrew Bible/Old Testament. The History of Its Interpretation. III: From Modernism to Post-Modernism (The Nineteenth and Twentieth Centuries). Part 1. The Nineteenth Century, a Century of Modernism and Historicism*, ed. Magne Sæbø (Göttingen: Vandenhoeck & Ruprecht, 2013), 495–520; Matthias A. Deuschle, *Ernst Wilhelm Hengstenberg: Ein Beitrag zur Erforschung des kirchlichen Konservatismus im Preußen des 19. Jahrhunderts*, BHTh (Tübingen: Mohr Siebeck, 2013).

sure, Genesis contains two main sources, an Elohist and an Yhwh-ist, an abbreviation coined by Hupfeld. The second Elohist is often fragmentary.

More important, perhaps, is Hupfeld's reflection about the human aspect of Genesis, in a spirit that reminds one of R. Ishmael: "[We must recognize] the full humanity of the Scripture, in order to recognize at the same time its true divinity, its full divine-humanity."[86]

Julius Wellhausen (1844–1918), and Congenators

Wellhausen deserves special mention for several reasons.[87] First of all, more than any other, he succeeded in putting together the insights of several colleagues and elaborating a clear, understandable, and convincing theory about the origins of the Pentateuch. Second, as for Genesis, his contribution in the field of patriarchal narratives is decisive. But there would not have been any Wellhausen without several other eminent scholars before and around him, including de Wette. Wellhausen himself said once of de Wette: "A clever guy! You can already find in his work all that I did in the Old Testament."[88]

Three of de Wette's intuitions produced fruit in the following years. First, there is the thesis that the original core of Deuteronomy relates to Josiah's reform (622 BCE) and therefore is much later that Moses. Second, there is a considerable distance between the world described in biblical texts, for instance in Genesis, and the time these biblical texts were put in writing. Third, the narratives in Genesis are "myths", that is, popular ways of explaining the world's or a nation's origins.

A further step toward a new understanding of Genesis is related to the name of Abraham Kuenen (1828–91).[89] Building on Hupfeld's work,

---

[86] Hupfeld, *Die Quellen*, xiv: "[Wir müssen die] volle Menschlichkeit der Schrift [erkennen], um darin zugleich ihre wahre Göttlichkeit, ihre volle Gottmenschlichkeit zu erkennen."

[87] On Wellhausen, see, among many others, Rudolf Smend, *Julius Wellhausen: Ein Bahnbrecher in drei Disziplinen* (Munich: Carl von Friedrich Siemens Stiftung, 2006); Walter Brueggemann and Davis Hankins, "The Invention and Persistence of Wellhausen's World," *CBQ* 75 (2013): 15–31; Aly Elrefaei, *Wellhausen and Kaufmann: Ancient Israel and Its Religious History in the Works of Julius Wellhausen and Yehezkel Kaufmann*, BZAW 490 (Berlin: de Gruyter, 2016); Smend, *Kritiker*, 343–56; id., *From Astruc to Zimmerli*, 91–102.

[88] Rudolf Otto, *Kantisch-Fries'sche Religionsphilosophie und ihre Anwendung auf die Theologie*, 2nd ed. (Tübingen: Mohr Siebeck, 1921), 250, quoted by Smend, *Kritiker*, 192 (my translation).

[89] On Kuenen, see Piet B. Dirksen and Arie van der Kooij, eds., *Abraham Kuenen (1828–1891): His Major Contributions to the Study of the Old Testament*, OTS 29 (Leiden: Brill, 1993); Smend, *Kritiker*, 300–16; English translation: Smend, *From Astruc to Zimmerli*, 76–90.

he came to a "four-document-hypothesis," the so-called newer documentary hypothesis, as early as 1861.[90] He also coined in a definitive
way the abbreviations of these sources, P for the Priestly Writer, J for the
Yahwist ("Jahwist" in German), E for the Elohist, and D for
Deuteronomy. The oldest source was the Priestly Writer. But Kuenen
came also to the conclusion that the Priestly, cultic, legislation was very
late, later than Deuteronomy. He stopped there and did not draw the next
and apparently obvious conclusion that the Priestly narratives, including
Genesis 1, were also late. Three personalities helped him wade across
this ford. The first was the Anglican bishop of Natal, South Africa, John
Colenso (1814–83).[91] This learned man had problems with Church
authorities and had therefore to leave Great Britain for South Africa.
His "exile" did not prevent him from studying critically Genesis and
other biblical books. As a good "enlightened" spirit, he observed that the
narratives, genealogies, and lists attributed to the Priestly Writer (the so-
called *Grundschrift*, "basic document") could not be historical because
they contradicted the laws of likelihood more than other parts of
Genesis.

The second personality is Julius Popper, a Jewish scholar (1822–84),
who published in 1862 a detailed study on the tabernacle in the desert
(Exod 25–31 and 35–40).[92] His conclusion was that these texts were much
later than the Babylonian exile and were added by "diaskeuasts" (on
which, see above).

The third person was an Alsatian, Karl Heinrich Graf (1815–69).[93] After
a thorough study of the Priestly laws, he concluded they were all later than
the Deuteronomic laws. Kuenen noticed that it was not possible to separate
Priestly narratives from priestly laws and that they must be both late. Graf
was convinced and published these conclusions just before he died.[94]

---

[90]   Abraham Kuenen, *Historisch-critisch Onderzoek naar het Ontstaan en de
       Verzameling van de Boeken des Ouden Verbonds* (Leiden: Engels en Zoon, 1861).
[91]   On Colenso, see Jonathan A. Draper, ed., *The Eye of the Storm: Bishop John William
       Colenso and the Crisis of Biblical Inspiration*, JSOTSS 386 (London: T&T Clark,
       2003); Hans Ausloos, "John William Colenso (1814–1883) and the Deuteronomist,"
       RB 113 (2006), 372–97.
[92]   Julius Propper, *Der biblische Bericht über die Stiftshütte: Ein Beitrag zur Geschichte
       der Komposition und Diaskeue des Pentateuchs* (Leipzig: Heinrich Hunger, 1862;
       Florence: Nabu Press, 2010).
[93]   See Karl Heinrich Graf, *Die geschichtlichen Bücher des Alten Testaments: Zwei
       historisch-kritische Untersuchungen* (Leipzig: T. O. Weigel, 1866). On this exegete,
       see Joachim Conrad, *Karl Heinrich Grafs Arbeit am Alten Testament: Studien zu
       einer wissenschaftlichen Biographie*, BZAW 425 (Berlin: de Gruyter, 2011).
[94]   Karl Heinrich Graf, "Die sogenannte Grundschrift des Pentateuchs," *AWEAT* 1
       (1869), 466–77.

Actually, the idea had already been proposed by Eduard Reuss (1804–91), his mentor and friend in Strasbourg, himself a disciple of Eichhorn. But Reuss had hesitated to publish the results of his critical research.

Kuenen and Graf convinced Wellhausen and this is the reason why the latter did not hesitate to place all the Priestly texts after Deuteronomy. Genesis 1 was no longer the oldest cornerstone of biblical revelation. Wellhausen created even more turmoil when he said:

> The materials here [in the patriarchal narratives] are not mythical but national and therefore more transparent, and in a certain sense more historical. It is true, we attain to no historical knowledge of the patriarchs, but only of the time when the stories about them arose in the Israelite people; this later age is here unconsciously projected, in its inner and its outward features, into hoar antiquity, and is reflected there like a glorified mirage.[95]

Wellhausen distinguishes very clearly Genesis 1–11 ("myths") from the patriarchal narratives which belong to a different type. The consequences of this statement, nonetheless, are clear. "The God of Abraham, Isaac, and Jacob" is a God of legendary figures, at least of personalities lost in a foggy past and almost impossible to trace back historically. Wellhausen avoids the word "myth" used by Eichhorn and de Wette in this context, but the difference is minimal. We have history, but it is the history and the ideas of those who put it in writing. In other words, the God of Abraham, Isaac and Jacob is first the God of the Yahwist and the Elohist, and sometimes of the Jehovist, the redactor who combined these two early documents.

One more point deserves attention. Wellhausen is much too often considered as the father or the main herald of the documentary hypothesis. In its classical form, and according to summaries and handbooks, this theory supposes that the Pentateuch is the result of a combination of four independent and complete documents about the origins of Israel.

---

[95] Julius Wellhausen, *Prolegomena zur Geschichte Israels* (Berlin: Georg Reimer, 1878, 2nd ed.,1883; 5th ed.,1899); reprinted in de Gruyter Studienbuch (Berlin: de Gruyter, 2001); English translation: *Prolegomena to the History of Israel*. With a Reprint of the article *Israel* from the *Encyclopaedia Britannica*. Preface by W. Robertson Smith (Edinburgh: A. & C. Black, 1885) now in: Reprints and Translations Series (Atlanta, GA: Scholars Press, 1994), quotation on pp. 318–19. German text: "Der Stoff ist hier nicht mythisch, sondern national; darum durchsichtiger und in gewissem Sinne historischer. Freilich über die Patriarchen ist hier kein historisches Wissen zu gewinnen, sondern nur über die Zeit, in welcher die Erzählungen über sie im israelitischen Volke entstanden; diese spätere Zeit wird hier, nach ihren inneren und äusseren Grundzügen, absichtslos ins graue Altertum projicirt und spiegelt sich darin wie ein verklärtes Luftbild ab" (*Prolegomena*, 316).

The Yahwist (J), written in a fresh and spontaneous style and using the divine name YHWH from the start, was composed at the beginning of the united monarchy, probably under Solomon, in Jerusalem. Genesis 2–3 and the appearance of the Lord to Abraham in Gen 18:1–15 are good examples of J's style. The Elohist (E) was written one century later in the Northern Kingdom. The style is dryer, the theology more elaborated – E often speaks of the "fear of God" – and the name Elohim is used until the name YHWH is revealed to Moses in Exod 3:14. Some scholars try to find E in Genesis 15, but the most characteristic texts are rather in Genesis 20–22, especially in Abraham's test, Gen 22:1–19. Deuteronomy (D) is, as we saw, related to Josiah's reform in Jerusalem and Judah in 622 BCE, and insists on the centralization of the cult. D is hardly present in Genesis, but its typical language is often identified in Gen 26:2–5, a divine discourse to Isaac. The Priestly Writer is postexilic and mostly interested in cultic matters. P is often connected with the return from the exile and the reconstruction of Jerusalem and its temple under Ezra and Nehemiah. Genesis 1 and 17 are typical of its style, which is fond of repetitions, formulae, and the use of cultic or juridical language.

This presentation corresponds only to a certain extent to Wellhausen's theory, which is somewhat more complex. On two points Wellhausen prepares for later developments. First, he affirms that the later documents were most probably redacted with an eye on former written sources. This entails a certain continuity between the documents, the latter extending, correcting, and completing the former.[96] Second, Wellhausen also affirms very clearly that, in Genesis, we find at the beginning of the process of composition, in general, individual narratives which were put together and integrated into larger documents in a second step. We find in these insights some seeds which will grow later in Hermann Gunkel's, Martin Noth's, and, eventually, Rolf Rendtorff's fields.[97] In this respect, Wellhausen is surely a faithful disciple of his master, Heinrich Ewald. Franz Delitzsch aptly coined the term "hypothesis of crystallization" to characterize this way of explaining the composition of Genesis.[98]

---

[96] Cf. *Prolegomena*, 293.

[97] Cf. ibid., 324–25, 334.

[98] Franz Delitzsch, *Die Genesis: Einleitung und Kommentar*, 2nd ed. (Leipzig: Dörffling und Franke, 1852), 29. Quoted by Smend, *Kritiker*, 269, n. 48. On Ewald, see Smend, *Kritiker*, 258–77; on Franz Delitzsch, see Smend, *Kritiker*, 278–99. Wellhausen exposed his ideas on the same topic also in *Der Text der Bücher Samuelis* (Göttingen: Vandenhoeck & Ruprecht, 1871), xi–xii, quoted by Smend, *Kritiker*, 269.

Hermann Gunkel (1862–1932)[99]

Among all commentaries on the book of Genesis, that by Hermann Gunkel is undoubtedly the most famous and the most influential. Gunkel is often considered the founder of the form-critical and the history of religion schools. He was interested in literary genres and in *Sitz im Leben* ("setting in life"), as in comparisons with other religions. As for the critical reading of Genesis, his contribution is twofold.[100]

(1) Like de Wette, he saw an insurmountable gap between the Genesis narratives and history.[101] Genesis narratives are about private, not public events; history is founded on witnesses and documents, the narratives in Genesis are not. These narratives do not intend to inform about the past, they want to move, to delight, and to edify. History supposes a developed and literate culture, whereas the legends of Genesis belong to an undeveloped culture and its oral traditions. Popular stories such as those in Genesis do not shrink from telling extraordinary and "incredible" events, such as divine oracles and miracles, something a historian would carefully avoid. Eventually, history is prosaic whereas oral, popular traditions found in Genesis are poetic (cf. de Wette, again). There is also an important gap of several centuries between the events recounted and the time these "events" are put in writing. Oral tradition is not able to preserve exact records of the past for so long a time. For instance, there is no trace of Babylonian religion or culture in the Abraham cycle (Genesis 12–25), although the narrative mentions that Abraham came from "Ur of the Chaldeans" (Gen 11:28, 31; 15:7; cf. Neh 9:7). Hugo Gressmann, Gunkel's friend and colleague, adds one more argument to Gunkel's demonstration, namely that the patriarchs lived mostly in the wilderness and "there is no history in the wilderness."[102] It is useless to look for documents or monuments

---

[99]   On H. Gunkel, see Werner Klatt, *H. Gunkel . Zu seiner Theologie der Religionsgeschichte und zur Entstehung der formgeschichtlichen Methode,* FRLANT 100 (Göttingen: Vandenhoeck & Ruprecht, 1969); Konrad Hammann, *Hermann Gunkel: Eine Biographie* (Tübingen: Mohr Siebeck, 2014); Smend, *Kritiker,* 501–14 = *From Astruc to Zimmerli,* 118–31.

[100] See Martin J. Buss, *Biblical Form Criticism in Its Context,* JSOTSS 274 (Sheffield: Academic Press, 1999); Martin J. Buss, *The Changing Shape of Form Criticism: A Relational Approach,* ed. Nickie M. Stipe, HBM 18 (Sheffield: Sheffield Phoenix Press, 2010).

[101] Hermann Gunkel, *Genesis,* trans. M. E. Biddle (Macon, GA: Mercer University Press, 1997), vii–xi. German original: *Genesis* (Göttingen: Vandenhoeck & Ruprecht, 3rd ed., 1910, 1969), vi–xiii.

[102] Hugo Gressmann, "Sage und Geschichte in den Patriarchenerzählungen," *ZAW* 30 (1910): 1–34, esp. 34.

in the desert. This is perhaps exaggerated, some modern historians would object, but it remains true that it is very difficult to identify and date with certainty the few artifacts and items found in the wilderness.

(2) On the other side, Gunkel contributed in a unique way to a literary and stylistic reading of Genesis, going much further than de Wette, for instance. This is perhaps his main contribution to the field. His analysis anticipates modern approaches to biblical narratives, such as those by Robert Alter, Meir Sternberg, and their followers.[103] Gunkel noticed most of the typical features of biblical narratives in a chapter entitled "Kunstform der Sagen in Genesis" – "The Artistry of the Legends in Genesis."[104] Gunkel develops for the first time a method to explain and interpret the Genesis narratives, paying attention to form and content. The whole chapter deserves close attention, but I will mention here only the most important features. Among these are the fact that the legends of Genesis avoid physical and psychological descriptions; that characters are less important than dramatic action; that dialogues play an essential role; that only two characters can be active at same time in a scene; and that characters often appear in pairs with opposite features, as Cain and Abel, Abraham and Loth, Sarah and Agar, Ismael and Isaac, Esau and Jacob, Lea and Rachel, etc.

Gunkel is also known for the first line of his introduction: "Genesis ist eine Sammlung von Sagen" – "Genesis is a collection of popular tales."[105] This sentence is applauded by some or contested and even rejected by others. For Gunkel, however, it was crystal clear that we have at the beginning of the composition of Genesis small and independent narrative units, or short cycles of stories, such as the Abraham–Lot cycle, the Esau–Jacob cycle, or the Jacob–Laban cycle. These units were put together or compiled in larger collections rather than literary composition to form the actual book of Genesis. This idea was already present in Wellhausen, as we saw earlier. Gunkel summarizes his view pertinently by saying that we do not have a biblical Homer.[106] Nobody unified the older tradition in form, style and content, as in the *Iliad* or the

[103] Robert Alter, *The Art of Biblical Narrative* (New York: Basic Books, 1981); Meir Sternberg, *The Poetics of Biblical Narrative: Ideological Literature and the Drama of Reading*, Indiana Literary Biblical Series (Bloomington, IN: Indiana University Press, 1985).

[104] Gunkel, *Genesis*, xxvii–lvi; English translation: xxiii–xlviii.

[105] Gunkel, *Genesis*, vii; English translation, vii (Biddle translates: "Genesis Is a Collection of Legends"). The translation of the German word "Sage" is not easy.

[106] Gunkel, *Genesis*, xcix; English translation, lxxxvi. Gunkel also uses the term "diaskeuès" ("editing," "reworking") for the last phases of the composition of Genesis; *Genesis*, xcix; English translation, lxxxv.

Odyssey. It is legitimate, therefore, to start the analysis with the single narratives or the small cycles or stories. This is what Rolf Rendtorff recommended and was achieved by his disciple and follower, Erhard Blum.[107] The latter starts his research with the small units in the Jacob cycle and follows the developments of the text of Genesis until the last, Deuteronomistic and Priestly, redactions.

Among Gunkel's followers, we should mention Gerhard von Rad (1901–71), whose commentary on Genesis became a bestseller. It was revised and reprinted more than ten times and translated into several languages.[108] Another follower is Martin Noth (1902–68) who, tried to save the historicity of the patriarchs despite Gunkel's skepticism in this respect. His solution, however, was a kind of Pyrrhic victory since he identified the patriarchs' migration with the peaceful and progressive settlement of half-nomadic tribes in Canaan, his explanation of the conquest of the Promised Land.[109]

The Aftermath of Wellhausen's and Gunkel's Research in the Twentieth Century

We can summarize the developments in the critical study of the book of Genesis during the twentieth and the beginning of the twenty-first centuries in a few words. The nineteenth century, as we have seen, is dominated by two main tendencies, first a certain rationalism – in the line of de Wette, followed by a strong interest in history and in historical documents ("the sources of Genesis" and the "documentary hypothesis"), a school where the figure of Wellhausen looms large. The twentieth century adds a new attention to style and literary features, the famous "literary genres" often connected with the name of Gunkel. For a long time the two methods, source criticism (*Literarkritik*) and form criticism (*Formgeschichte*), contracted a kind of marriage of convenience. A study started with the determination of the source of the text, then of its literary genre. This lasted until Rendtorff contested the legitimacy of this

---

[107] Rolf Rendtorff, *Das überlieferungsgeschichtliche Problem des Pentateuch*, BZAW 147 (Berlin: de Gruyter, 1977); English translation: *The Problem of the Process of Transmission in the Pentateuch*, JSOTSS 89 (Sheffield: Academic Press, 1990); Erhard Blum, *Die Komposition der Vätergeschichte*, BWANT 57 (Neukirchen-Vluyn, Neukirchener Verlag, 1984).

[108] Gerhard von Rad, *Das erste Buch Mose. Genesis*, ATD 2–4 (Göttingen: Vandenhoeck & Ruprecht, 1961, 1987)= *Genesis*, OTL (London: SCM, 1972, 1985). On von Rad, see, among many others, Smend, *Kritiker*, 794–824 = *From Astruc to Zimmerli*, 170–97.

[109] Martin Noth, *Geschichte Israels* (Göttingen: Vandenhoeck & Ruprecht, 1950; 2nd ed., 1954) = *History of Israel* (London: Adam & Charles Black, 1958; 2nd ed., 1960). On Martin Noth, see Smend, *Kritiker*, 825–46 = *From Astruc to Zimmerli*, 198–211.

marriage and proclaimed the divorce of source criticism and form criticism.[110] He advocated a study that starts, not with the long documents, but with the "small literary unit." In this way, form criticism precedes and sometimes substitutes for source criticism. For Rendtorff, there are two main phases in the composition of the book of Genesis. First, we have small literary units or short series of narratives around the same character. Second, we have a redactional work or a series of redactional works, the purpose of which is to compile these narratives or cycles of narratives in some major units, for instance the history of the origins of the universe (Genesis 1–11) and the Patriarchal Narratives (Genesis 12–50), the latter made of three main secondary units, the Abraham cycle (Genesis 12–25), the Jacob Cycle (Genesis 25–36), and the Joseph story (Genesis 37–50).[111] This induced some scholars to bid farewell to continuous "sources," more concretely to the Yahwist.[112] The existence of an ever shadowy Elohist had already been questioned much earlier.[113] Of course, as usual, a theory, a method or a trend does not replace previous ones. Many scholars kept on following the old and beaten paths of exegesis.

Around the same time, a group of scholars picked up one of Wellhausen's and Gunkel's main ideas, namely the gap between the Genesis narratives and historiography. Using the results of archaeology, ancient Near Eastern documents, and a close comparison with other biblical texts, these scholars demonstrated that the patriarchal narratives have little to do with history. Thomas L. Thompson is probably the most prominent in this respect.[114] John Van Seters reached similar conclusions, but using literary rather than historical tools.[115] Even Roland Guérin de Vaux, who is often quoted as an unbending defender of the historicity of the patriarchs, came, at the end of his life, to similar

[110] Rendtorff, *Das überlieferungsgeschichtliche Problem des Pentateuch*.
[111] Ibid.
[112] See especially Jan Christian Gertz, Konrad Schmid, and Markus Witte, eds., *Abschied vom Jahwisten: Die Komposition des Hexateuch in der jüngsten Diskussion*, BZAW 315 (Berlin: de Gruyter, 2002); Thomas B. Dozeman and Konrad Schmid, eds., *A Farewell to the Yahwist? The Composition of the Pentateuch in Recent European Interpretation*, SBLSymS 34 (Atlanta, GA: Society of Biblical Literature, 2006).
[113] Paul Volz und Wilhelm Rudolph, *Der Elohist als Erzähler: Ein Irrweg der Pentateuchkritik. An der Genesis erläutert*, BZAW 63 (Giessen: Töpelmann, 1933).
[114] See the explicit title of Thomas L. Thompson's monograph, *The Historicity of the Patriarchal Narratives: The Quest for the Historical Abraham*, BZAW 133 (Berlin: de Gruyter, 1974; reprint: Harrisburg, PA: Trinity Press International, 2002).
[115] John Van Seters, *Abraham in History and Tradition* (New Haven, CT: Yale University Press, 1975; Brattleboro, VT: Echo Point Books & Media, 2014).

conclusions.[116] These results were contested, sometimes in polemical tones, by other specialists.[117]

Genesis was more frequently considered as a collection of ancient folktales about the origins of the world and the origins of the people of Israel. These narratives were composed and compiled gradually to create a common tradition and unite different groups (clans, tribes, social, political, and religious groups). These narratives reflect more popular interests and should be distinguished from historical and theological documents. In other words, these narratives are expressions of beliefs common among the (extended) families in ancient Israel. Only in a later phase do they become part of the official "creed" of a nation called Israel. In this phase of critical reading, Genesis is read more as a "monument" of Israel (popular) literature than a "document" of Israel's history.

If Thompson – and his companions and followers – broach the problem from a historical and archaeological point of view, others part company with historical questions to study the text of Genesis in its canonical form, in a purely synchronic way. Most of these scholars are disciples of the so-called New Criticism of I. A. Richards and J. C. Ransom. They study literature in a positive or even positivistic way, as a scientific object, independently of its author, its historical setting, and its original audience. Literary study is something different from historical, psychological, and sociological study, and uses its own methods. The study is mostly linguistic, stylistic, and structural. Jan Peter Fokkelman is a pioneer in the field and Robert Alter is another innovator who had many followers, especially in the field of narratives (narratology).[118] Unintentionally however, they follow a path trodden earlier by de Wette and especially Gunkel.

Rendtorff, to come back to the problem of composition, was contested in his turn by the so-called neo-documentarians.[119] But, strangely

---

[116]   Roland de Vaux, *Histoire ancienne d'Israël. 1: Des origines à l'installation en Canaan*, Études Bibliques (Paris: J. Gabalda, 1971).

[117]   See, among many others, on this problem, Lester L. Grabbe, *Ancient Israel: What Do We Know and How Do We Know It?* (London: T&T Clark, 2007). See also Marc Brettler, "The Copenhagen School: The Historiographical Issues," *AJSR* 27 (2003): 1–22.

[118]   Jan Peter Fokkelman, *Narrative Art in Genesis: Specimens of Stylistic and Structural Analysis*, SSN 17 (Assen: Van Gorcum, 1975); reprinted in the series The Biblical Seminar 12 (Sheffield: Academic Press, 1991); Jan Peter Fokkelman, *Reading Biblical Narrative: An Introductory Guide* (Louisville, KY: Westminster John Knox Press, 1999). For Robert Alter, see n. 106.

[119]   See especially Joel S. Baden, *J, E, and the Redaction of the Pentateuch*, FAT 68 (Tübingen: Mohr Siebeck, 2009); Joel S. Baden, *The Composition of the Pentateuch: Renewing the Documentary Hypothesis*, Anchor Yale Bible Reference Library (New

enough, the neo-documentarians follow Gunkel more than Wellhausen in one aspect at least. For them, the real problem of Genesis is literary, not historical. They go back to the usual four documents (J, E, D, P), three of them present in Genesis (J, E, P), but they do not inquire about the historical setting of these documents. They depart from history in a way like Gunkel or Thompson, to study Genesis as mere literature. In this respect, they are also close to New Criticism in that they give history the slip.

A third field of research was triggered by the discovery of the Dead Sea Scrolls. Only fragments of the book of Genesis were discovered, but they confirmed the opinion that the Proto-Masoretic Text was not the only authoritative version of the Hebrew text circulating in the last centuries of the first millennium BCE and the first century CE. There were at least four different forms of the text: (1) the Proto-Masoretic text, the *Vorlage* (or the *Vorlagen*) of the Septuagint; (2) the Alexandrian translation of Genesis into Greek;[120] (3) the copies of Genesis present in the Qumran caves; (4) and the Genesis of the Samaritan Pentateuch. The differences are perhaps not as relevant as in other books of the Old Testament.[121]

CONCLUSION

Among the many theories proposed about the origin of the book of Genesis, we may simply distinguish in Israel's ancient traditions two main "foundation myths" or "foundation traditions."[122] On the one

Haven, CT: Yale University Press, 2012); Joel S. Baden, *The Promise to the Patriarchs* (Oxford: Oxford University Press, 2013). On this discussion, see the many articles in Jan Christian Gertz, Bernard M. Levinson, Dalit Rom-Shiloni, and Konrad Schmid, eds., *The Formation of the Pentateuch: Bridging the Academic Cultures of Europe, Israel, and North America*, FAT 111 (Tübingen: Mohr Siebeck, 2016).

[120]   For a critical edition, see John William Wevers, *Genesis*, Septuaginta. Vetus Testamentum Graecum 1 (Göttingen: Vandenhoeck & Ruprecht, 1974). For a translation, see Marguerite Harl et al., *La Genèse: Traduction du texte grec de la Septante, introduction et notes*, La Bible d'Alexandrie 1 (Paris: Le Cerf, 1986); Susan Ann Brayford, *Genesis*, Septuagint Commentary Series (Leiden: Brill, 2007); Albert Pietersma and Benjamin G. Wright, eds., *A New English Translation of the Septuagint and the Other Greek Translations Traditionally Included under that Title* (Oxford: Oxford University Press, 2007); Martin Karrer and Wolfgang Kraus, *Septuaginta Deutsch – Erläuterungen und Kommentare*, vol. 1: *Genesis bis 4. Makkabäer* (Stuttgart: Deutsche Bibelgesellschaft, 2011).

[121]   Let use note, however, three examples: Gen 4:6, Gen 18:3, and Gen 47:5.

[122]   For more details on the book of Genesis, see Craig A. Evans, Joel N. Lohr, and David L. Petersen, eds., *The Book of Genesis: Composition, Reception, and Interpretation*, VTS 152 (Leiden: Brill, 2012); see also Hendel, *The Book of Genesis*.

side, a popular, familiar, and genealogical tradition present in Genesis and on the other side a more official and juridical tradition present especially in Exodus and related to the figure of Moses. According to Genesis, a member of Israel is a descendant of Abraham, Isaac, and Jacob. According to Exodus, a member of Israel is a member of a nation that YHWH brought out of Egypt to conclude with her a covenant at Sinai/ Horeb, a nation that promised in return to observe God's law.[123]

These ancestral narratives are a common heritage for Jews, Muslims, and Christians, who, each in their own way, find in them basic elements of their identity – and not only of their identity, but also of their faith and their culture. In the course of history, Genesis may have lost some of its "supranatural" qualities and we read it now more and more "as book like all other books." But this reading enhanced one of its fundamental features. These stories lie at the root of our collective memory or, as Ronald Hendel has it, they are "our stories, and we are their children."[124]

SELECT BIBLIOGRAPHY

Berndt, Rainer. "The School of St. Victor in Paris." Pages 467–95 in *Hebrew Bible/Old Testament: The History of Its Interpretation*. Vol. I.2: *The Middles Ages* Edited by Magne Sæbø. Göttingen: Vandenhoeck & Ruprecht, 2000.

Borgen, Peder Johan. *Philo of Alexandria: An Exegete for His Time*, SNT 86. Leiden: Brill, 1997.

Cameron, Euan. "The Bible and the Early Sense of History." Pages 657–85 in *The New Cambridge History of the Bible*. Vol. 3: *From 1450 to 1750*. Edited by Euan Cameron. Cambridge: Cambridge University Press, 2016.

Evans, Craig A., Joel N. Lohr, and David L. Petersen, eds. *The Book of Genesis: Composition, Reception, and Interpretation*, VTS 152 (Leiden: Brill, 2012).

Finkelberg, Margalit and Guy G. Stroumsa, eds. *Homer, the Bible, and Beyond: Literary and Religious Canons in the Ancient World*, Jerusalem Studies in Religion and Culture 2. Leiden and Boston, MA: Brill, 2003.

Frampton, Travis L. *Spinoza and the Rise of Historical Criticism of the Bible*. London: T&T Clark, 2006.

---

[123] The fullest presentation of this idea is that by Konrad Schmid, *Erzväter und Exodus: Untersuchungen zur doppelten Begründung der Ursprünge Israels innerhalb der Geschichtsbücher des Alten Testaments*, WMANT 81 (Neukirchen-Vluyn: Neukirchener Verlag, 1999) = *Genesis and the Moses Story: Israel's Dual Origins in the Hebrew Bible*, trans. James D. Nogalski, Siphrut 3 (Winona Lake, IN: Eisenbrauns, 2010).

[124] Hendel, *The Book of Genesis*, 245.

Gunkel, Hermann. *Genesis* (Göttingen: Vandenhoeck & Ruprecht, 3rd ed.,1910, 1969); English translation: *Genesis*. Translated by M. E. Biddle. Macon, GA: Mercer University Press, 1997.

Hendel, Ronald. *The Book of Genesis: A Biography*, Lives of Great Religious Books (Princeton, NJ and Oxford: Princeton University Press, 2013).

Maman, Aharon, Mordechai Cohen, and Sarah Klein-Braslavy, "The Flourishing Era of Jewish Exegesis in Spain." Pages 261–320 in *Hebrew Bible/Old Testament: The History of Its Interpretation.* Vol. I.2: *The Middles Ages* Edited by Magne Sæbø. Göttingen: Vandenhoeck & Ruprecht, 2000).

McKane, William. *Selected Christian Hebraists*. Cambridge: Cambridge: University Press, 1989.

Morrow, Jeffrey L. *Three Skeptics and the Bible: La Peyrère, Hobbes, Spinoza, and the Reception of Modern Biblical Criticism* (Eugene, OR: Pickwick, 2016).

Reventlow, Henning Graf. "Between Humanism and Enlightenment: Morality, Reason and History as Factors in Biblical Interpretation." Pages 641–56 in *The New Cambridge History of the Bible*. Vol. 3: *From 1450 to 1750*. Edited by Euan Cameron. Cambridge: Cambridge University Press, 2016.

Riches, John, ed. *The New Cambridge History of the Bible*. Vol. 4: *From 1750 to the Present*. Cambridge: Cambridge University Press, 2015.

Smend, Rudolf. *From Astruc to Zimmerli: Old Testament Scholarship in Three Centuries*. Translated by Margaret Kohl. Tübingen: Mohr Siebeck, 2007.

Smend, Rudolf. *Kritiker und Exegeten: Porträtskizzen zur vier Jahrhunderten alttestamentlicher Wissenschaft*. Göttingen: Vandenhoeck & Ruprecht, 2017.

3 Genesis in Source and Redaction Criticism Today

JAN CHRISTIAN GERTZ

THE LONGUE DURÉE OF PENTATEUCHAL RESEARCH

Research on the Pentateuch began in the eighteenth century with the book of Genesis. This has had noticeable consequences for the current literary-historical analysis of both the Pentateuch as a whole and Genesis in particular. It is clear that the question of the sources and redactions in Genesis cannot be answered without the whole Pentateuch in view. However, the exact impact of the earliest questions of Pentateuchal research upon the research approaches of later generations, even in areas in which the directions of inquiry have clearly shifted, is rarely considered. In its beginnings, Pentateuchal research was defined entirely by the question of Mosaic authorship of the Pentateuch. It focused particularly on Genesis and its depiction of the "pre-Mosaic period." With the advent of historical thought in theology and the detachment from the dogma of verbal inspiration, an answer appeared almost automatically: Moses could have relied on reports from contemporary witnesses from earlier time periods. Thus, "Moses, the inspired author" became "Moses, the informed historian," who collected, edited, and compiled documents handed down to him from ancient times. With this paradigm shift, the influential search for "documents" or "sources" had begun. Jean Astruc, the "grandfather of all documentary hypotheses," explained the formation of Genesis through the secondary combination of two continuous documents and ten others preserved only in fragments. Moses, trying to maintain their integrity, neatly placed them side by side in four columns.[1] Only through a later redaction were these columns pushed together,

---

[1] Jean Astruc, *Conjectures sur les mémoires originaux dont il paroit que Moyse s'est servi pour composer le Livre de la Genèse* (Brussels: Fricx, 1753; repr., Paris: Noêsis, 1999; ed. Pierre Gibert). On Astruc, see Jan C. Gertz, "Jean Astruc and the Quellenscheidung in the Book of Genesis," in *Sacred Conjectures: The Context and Legacy of Robert Lowth and Jean Astruc*, ed. John Jarick (Sheffield: T&T Clark, 2007), 188–201.

53

resulting in chronological discrepancies, perturbing repetitions, and the shift between "Elohim" (God) and the Tetragrammaton "Yʜwʜ" as the names for God. In this way, Astruc could (1) make Mosaic authorship of the Pentateuch historically plausible, (2) explain the contradictions and doublets, and (3) exonerate Moses of accusations of sloppy or flawed work.

Well over 250 years later, the field has long since abandoned the picture of Moses as an author or compiler of sources. Nevertheless, in contrast to the scholarship on the other writings of the Hebrew Bible, documentary hypotheses continue to dominate in Pentateuchal research and seem to be part of the field's DNA. This focus may at times restrain scholars from considering other explanations for phenomena in the text. Thus, a field that has been searching for "documents" from its beginnings questions only secondarily (if at all) whether repetitions like the three narratives of a matriarch's endangerment by sexual assault from a foreign ruler (Gen 12:10–20; 20:1–18; 26:1–11) could have been the result of commentating additions or a deliberate literary configuration rather than simply the transmission of parallel traditions. The attempt – for the sake of the biblical witness's reliability – to exonerate Moses from accusations of negligence has also left its mark on recent research. This can be found in the often-uncritical assumption that the earliest biblical authors composed "good" and "sound" texts, unlike later redactors or the compilers of the source documents. This is the only way to explain why an appreciation of the text's final form entered Pentateuchal research only indirectly, through avenues of literary approaches.[2] This process has not yet been completed, as seen from the field's occasional, genuine discussions concerning whether and in what respect the present form of the Pentateuch is "unreadable."[3]

Jean Astruc had confined his search for source documents to the "pre-Mosaic period," spanning the texts from the creation of the world in Genesis 1 to the birth of Moses in Exodus 2. This documentary model developed from Genesis was later extended to the other books of the Pentateuch, tying the term "document" to the idea of continuous

---

[2] E.g., Jan P. Fokkelman, *Narrative Art in Genesis: Specimens of Stylistic and Structural Analysis*, SSN 17 (Assen: van Gorcum, 1975); Robert Alter, *The Art of Biblical Narrative* (New York: Basic Books, 1981).

[3] On this debate, see the contributions in *The Formation of the Pentateuch: Bridging the Academic Cultures of Europe, Israel, and North America*, ed. Jan C. Gertz et al., FAT 111 (Tübingen: Mohr Siebeck, 2016), 197–292 ("Part Two: Can the Pentateuch Be Read in Its Present Form? Narrative Continuity in the Pentateuch in Comparative Perspective").

historical or source writings spanning the entire Pentateuch. Thus, the eighteenth-century beginnings of Pentateuchal research have deeply shaped broader research concerns. To the present day, Genesis (especially the Primeval History in Genesis 1–11) is often regarded as paradigmatic for the entire Pentateuch, even when the textual evidence speaks clearly against the extension of literary-historical assumptions into the other books.[4] The conclusion, already burgeoning with Astruc and Johann Gottfried Eichhorn,[5] that a single hypothesis could not adequately explain the complicated situation in the Pentateuch as a whole has been and can still easily be overlooked. This also applies to counterproposals that criticize the scholarly concentration on Genesis and then, in turn, hastily transfer their rejection of a documentary hypothesis for the following books of the Pentateuch to the book of Genesis itself. In both cases, the danger arises of a model of formation proven in one specific text prefiguring the results of analysis on other texts and excluding more appropriate explanations from the outset. Generally, advocates of documentary, supplementary, or fragmentary hypotheses counter this danger by respectively incorporating elements of the other, competing models. From early on Julius Wellhausen, the "Nestor" of the ("Newer") Documentary Hypothesis, recognized throughout the course of source differentiation numerous redactional transformations and elaborations of the source documents, more or less confirming the "supplementary hypothesis."[6] He also credited some pivotal texts to the source documents' compilers, regarding them as the actual authors.[7] Ultimately, Wellhausen reckoned with later and latest additions that were "the final sediment settled at the surface of the whole debris."[8] This "literary process"[9] was far more

---

[4] See Martin Noth's infamous verdict on the book of Numbers: "If we were to take the book of Numbers on its own, then we would think not so much of 'continuing sources' as of an unsystematic collection of innumerable pieces of very varied content, age and character ('Fragment Hypothesis'). [...] It is, therefore, justifiable to approach the book of Numbers with the results of Pentateuchal analysis elsewhere and to expect the continuing Pentateuchal 'sources' here, too, even if, as we have said, the situation in Numbers, of itself does not exactly lead us to these results" (Martin Noth, *Numbers: A Commentary*, trans. James D. Martin, OTL [London: SCM Press, 1968], 4–5).

[5] Johann G. Eichhorn, *Einleitung in das Alte Testament*, 5 vols., 4th ed. (Göttingen: Rosenbusch, 1823–24), 2: 59.

[6] Julius Wellhausen, *Die Composition des Hexateuchs und der historischen Bücher des Alten Testaments*, 4th ed. (1885; repr. Berlin: de Gruyter, 1963), 314–15.

[7] E.g., ibid., 94–95.

[8] Ibid., 315.

[9] Ibid., 207.

complicated than the "mechanical mosaic hypothesis (*Mosaikhypothese*)" that he rejected and dismissed as "crazy".[10] This should be emphasized because in the current debate, the individual formation models differ primarily in how they weight the ratio of sources to redactions. This has led to a very wide spectrum of conceptions. Here is one example of a current "mosaic hypothesis": according to the "Neo-Documentarians," the four sources of the Pentateuch were combined by a compiler who essentially limited himself to "mechanically" weaving together previously independent sources that had been written and transmitted without knowledge of one another.[11] On the other side of the spectrum stand models for the formation of the Pentateuch (and thus Genesis) that attribute the largest body of text to a gradual process of continuous updating and only reckon with a very narrow corpus of sources, or have bidden farewell to the classical assumption of source texts altogether.[12] Insofar as both sides like to invoke Julius Wellhausen, the current debate is invariably also a disagreement over his legacy.

---

[10]   The two previous citations come from a letter from Wellhausen to Adolf Jülicher of November 18, 1880, in which he argues against a kind of document hypothesis that does not reckon with editorial adjustments and extensions by later redactions. See Julius Wellhausen, *Briefe*, ed. by Rudolf Smend (Tübingen: Mohr Siebeck, 2013), no. 94.

[11]   This primarily concerns a group of exegetes around Baruch Schwartz and his students. On the research approach and "self-designation" as "Neo Documentarians," see, for example, Jeffery Stackert, *A Prophet Like Moses: Prophecy, Law, and Israelite Religion* (Oxford: Oxford University Press, 2014), 1–35. On the description of the operating principle as "mechanical" see ibid., 91 fn. 50. For the exemplaric analysis of a text from Genesis see Baruch J. Schwartz, "How the Compiler of the Pentateuch Worked: The Composition of Genesis 37," in *The Book of Genesis: Composition, Reception, and Interpretation*, ed. Craig A. Evans, Joel N. Lohr and David L. Petersen, VTSup 152 (Leiden: Brill, 2012), 263–78. For a detailed discussion of the basic assumptions of the "Neo-Documentarians" cf. Konrad Schmid, "The Neo-Documentarian Manifesto: A Critical Reading," *JBL* 140 (2021): 461–79.

[12]   See with all their radical differences the positions of Christoph Levin, *Der Jahwist*, FRLANT 157 (Göttingen: Vandenhoeck & Ruprecht, 1993); Reinhard G. Kratz, *Die Komposition der erzählenden Bücher des Alten Testaments* (Göttingen: Vandenhoeck & Ruprecht, 2000); trans. *The Composition of the Narrative Books of the Old Testament*, trans. John Bowden (London: A&C Black, 2005); Christoph Berner, *Die Exoduserzählung: Das literarische Werden einer Ursprungserzählung Israels*, FAT 73 (Tübingen: Mohr Siebeck, 2010). Berner characterizes the formation of the exodus narrative – a range of text in which the Documentary Hypothesis for a long time went almost as unchallenged, as in Genesis – as a "process of 'midrashic' self-interpretation" (ibid., 7) and promotes the "complete farewell to the Documentary Hypothesis, which as a paradigm rooted in nineteenth-century thought is simply outdated" (ibid., 449).

FROM CONSENSUS TO CRISIS

In the last third of the nineteenth century, the ("Newer") Documentary Hypothesis as established by Karl Heinrich Graf, Abraham Kuenen, and Julius Wellhausen among others began its triumphant march, with its validity virtually unquestioned until the 1970s.[13] For the Hexateuch (the Pentateuch plus Joshua), the Documentary Hypothesis works from four formerly independent literary works: the Yahwist ("J," from the German *Jahwist*), from the Southern Kingdom of Judah in the ninth century BCE; the slightly younger Elohist ("E"), from the Northern Kingdom of Israel in the eighth century BCE; Deuteronomy ("D"), originally connected to King Josiah's reforms in the seventh century BCE; and the exilic/early-postexilic Priestly Writing ("P"), from the sixth century BCE. The Yahwist owes its name to its consistent use of the personal name for God "Yhwh," while the Elohist uses the general term "Elohim" until the revelation of the name of God in Exod 3:14. These four sources were then compiled by redactors through a multi-staged process and subjected to further independent expansions. The hypothesis was particularly persuasive because of Wellhausen's connection of the literary analysis to the religio-historical thesis that, so far as he could demonstrate, the identified sources represented specific stages in the history of ancient Israel.[14] It also represents a case of a relatively simple hypothesis being able to explain the basic features of such a complicated work of literature with little conjecture. As mentioned, Wellhausen knew (unlike some of his self-proclaimed heirs) that the focus upon four primary sources and their gradual combination heavily oversimplified the process of literary growth.[15]

In the years that followed, literary-critical means were used in the attempt to understand this process more precisely. However, these

---

[13]   Karl H. Graf, "Die s.g. Grundschrift des Pentateuchs," in *Archiv für wissenschaftliche Erforschung des Alten Testaments* 1/4 (1869): 466–77; Abraham Kuenen, *An Historico-critical Inquiry into the Origin and Composition of the Hexateuch*, trans. Philip H. Wicksteed (London: Macmillan, 1886); Wellhausen, *Composition*.

[14]   Julius Wellhausen, *Prolegomena zur Geschichte Israels* (Berlin: Reimer, 1883; 6th ed. 1927; repr. Berlin: de Gruyter, 2001); trans. as *Prolegomena to the History of Israel*, trans. J. Sutherland Black and Allan Menzies (Edinburgh: A&C Black, 1885; repr., Atlanta: Scholars Press, 1994). Wellhausen described a literary division of sources without historical inquiry as a boring "game of ninepins." See Wellhausen, *Briefe*, no. 94.

[15]   See Wellhausen, *Composition*, 207: "J and E likely experienced several editions themselves ($J^1\ J^2\ J^3$, $E^1\ E^2\ E^3$) and were combined together not as J^1 and E^1, but rather as J^3 and E^3. This similarly applies to JE [i.e., the combination of J und E], Dt and Q [i.e., P], before they were incorporated into their respective larger wholes."

attempts did not lead to a satisfactory and generally recognized conclusion, so that in 1938 Gerhard von Rad noticed a certain exhaustion:

> No one will ever be able to say that in our time there has been any
> crisis in the theological study of the Hexateuch. On the contrary, it
> might be held that we have reached a position of stalemate ... So
> far as the analysis of source documents is concerned, there are
> signs that the road has come to a dead end ... On the other hand,
> in the examination of isolated passages ... we must frankly admit
> that we have by no means done all that might have been done. But
> in this field, too, controversy has ceased, and it may be said with-
> out exaggeration that scholars, especially the younger ones, are
> weary of research in hexateuchal studies.[16]

Yet three decades later, von Rad concluded the last edition of his
Genesis commentary with the oft-cited challenge for "a comprehensive new analysis of the Pentateuchal narrative material, which we
urgently need."[17] What had happened? An immediate occasion for this
challenge was his analysis of the Joseph story in Genesis 37–50, which
had long been one of the classic examples for the "J" and "E" source
divisions. In contrast, von Rad had observed that the Joseph story,
which had been designated by him as a "novella," clearly stands out
from the patriarchal narratives and that "it is from the beginning to
end an organically constructed narrative, no single segment of which
can have existed independently as a separate element of tradition."[18]
In spite of this assessment, von Rad adhered to the source differentiation in the Joseph story (and beyond). Yet, he also had to admit that
the small discrepancies in Gen 37–50 could easily be explained
through glosses and later interpolations, and that this led to an
increased rejection of the division of Gen 37–50 into separate sources.
Only the demanded "new analysis of the Pentateuchal narrative
material" could bring about a decision. After all, von Rad's characterization of the Joseph story as a literary masterpiece could hardly be

---

[16] Gerhard von Rad, "The Form Critical Problem of the Hexateuch," in *The Problem of
the Hexateuch and Other Essays*, ed. von Rad, trans. E. W. Trueman Dickens
(Edinburgh: Oliver & Boyd, 1966; repr., London: SCM Press, 1984), 1–78, here 1;
trans. of "Das formgeschichtliche Problem des Hexateuchs [1938]," in von Rad,
Gesammelte Studien zum Alten Testament, TB 8 (Munich: Kaiser, 1958), 9–86,
here 9.

[17] Gerhard von Rad, *Genesis: A Commentary*, trans. John H. Marks, rev. 3rd ed. (London:
SCM Press, 1972), 440.

[18] Ibid., 347. This passage is also in earlier editions of the commentary, but without the
aforementioned postscript.

reconciled with its distribution between the Yahwist and the Elohist.[19] Yet if the Yahwistic and Elohistic sources could not be verified in this section, both Pentateuchal sources would lose their necessary ties between Genesis and Exodus. The Documentary Hypothesis could only be saved though complicated contrivances – such as the supposition that the redactor had substituted the Yahwistic and Elohistic accounts of the tribes of Jacob's descent into Egypt with a previously independent Joseph story.[20]

The evidence from the Joseph story is by no means the only reason why the Documentary Hypothesis has been heavily criticized since the 1970s, however. Between von Rad's two positions concerning the state of Pentateuchal research lies a pervasive reformulation of the Documentary Hypothesis by von Rad himself and by Martin Noth.[21] Although it is difficult to reconcile their positions with one another, clearly it is less the original shape of the Documentary Hypothesis than its modification and connection with form-critical inquiry through Noth and von Rad that has reopened old questions and, through further discussion, led to a broad differentiation of research positions.

QUESTIONS NEW AND OLD

When we ask about additional reasons for the serious challenge to the previous consensus, the following points become of particular interest in view of the formation history of Genesis: (1) the connection of the individual traditions to a larger narrative work; (2) the rejection of an Elohistic source; (3) the original character of the Priestly texts; and (4) the theological and literary profile of the Yahwistic texts.

---

[19]   See R. Norman Whybray, "The Joseph Story and Pentateuchal Criticism," *VT* 18 (1968): 522–28; Herbert Donner, "Die literarische Gestalt der alttestamentlichen Josephsgeschichte [1976]," in Donner, *Aufsätze zum Alten Testament aus vier Jahrzehnten*, BZAW 224 (Berlin: de Gruyter, 1994), 84: "One cannot have it both ways, with the Joseph story as a novella and as part of the Pentateuchal sources J and E."

[20]   Donner, "Gestalt."

[21]   von Rad, "Problem"; Martin Noth, *The Deuteronomistic History*, trans. Jane Doull, JSOTSup 15 (Sheffield: JSOT Press, 1981); trans. of *Überlieferungsgeschichtliche Studien I: Die sammelnden und bearbeitenden Geschichtswerke im Alten Testament* (Halle: Niemeyer, 1943); Noth, *A History of Pentateuchal Traditions*, trans. Bernard W. Anderson (Englewood Cliffs, NJ: Prentice-Hall, 1972); trans. of *Überlieferungsgeschichte des Pentateuch* (Stuttgart: Kohlhammer, 1948).

"Genesis is a Collection of Legends"

The famous introductory sentence to Herman Gunkel's Genesis commentary[22] not only initiated the form-critical studies of Genesis,[23] but also had consequences for the field in source and redaction criticism. Two questions with far-reaching consequences emerged from the identification of the individual narratives in Genesis as "legends." Legends are the oral form of historical tradition. The characterization as legends, thus, raised the question of the texts' oral precursors and initial compositions. Legends are likewise individual traditions, standing by themselves and being passed down accordingly. Thus, the arrangement of the legends in a particular narrative sequence is not predefined by the legends themselves but relies upon the creative will of their compiler. Here arises the second question, of how the Pentateuchal narrative's individual legends were linked together and then elaborated through the addition of further characters and narrative content. Gunkel had characterized "J" and "E" as narrative schools through which the oral traditions were collected and written down. According to von Rad, however, this line of inquiry could not explain "the co-ordinating power of the writer's overall theological purpose, and the gathering of the separate materials around a very small nucleus of basic concepts" in the historical narrative of the Yahwist.[24] Instead, the Yahwistic narrative was an elaboration of the so-called small historical credo (e.g., Deut 26:5b–9). With that, pre-monarchic Israel brought to life the fundamental themes of its sacred history (the patriarchal period, the oppression in Egypt, and the exodus from Egypt together with the entrance into the land of Canaan) at the Festival of Weeks in Gilgal (e.g., Josh 3–4). In the Solomonic period, the Yahwist expanded the credo with the Sinai tradition, originally from a covenant festival at Shechem (e.g., Deut 31; Josh 24), elaborated on the patriarchal narratives, and prefixed the Primeval History. His theological interest concerned the verification that the Solomonic Empire was the fulfillment of all of Yhwh's promises. All

---

[22] Herman Gunkel, *Genesis*, trans. Mark E. Biddle (Macon, GA: Mercer University Press, 1997), vii; trans. of *Genesis übersetzt und erklärt*, HKAT 1.1; 3rd ed. (Göttingen: Vandenhoeck & Ruprecht, 1910).

[23] See Chapter 4 of this volume.

[24] von Rad, "Problem," 51; see also what follows. In von Rad's argumentation, the Elohist merely plays a subordinate role: "The process by which E and P are superimposed on J ... is a purely literary question ... The form of the Hexateuch had already been finally determined by the Yahwist. The Elohist and the priestly writer do not diverge from the pattern in this respect: their writings are no more than variations upon the massive theme of the Yahwist's conception, despite their admittedly great theological originality" (ibid., 74).

promises concerning nationhood, blessing, and land possession given to Abraham according to Gen 12:1–3, as the core, programmatic text for the Yahwist, had been made a visible reality under Solomon, while the promised "great name" had been awarded to David (Gen 12:2; 2 Sam 7:9). Noth modified this thesis by ascribing the formation of the Pentateuchal narratives to the process of coalescence of the traditions as well as their tradent groups. Thus, he concluded that the general outline of the Yahwist and Elohist should be traced back to an older, shared *Grundlage* ("G") from the cultic context of the twelve-tribe confederation in pre-monarchic times.[25]

The strongest point of this reformulation of the Documentary Hypothesis is how it locates the literary development of old material in the institutions of ancient Israel. Yet, this is exactly where the fundamental assumptions could not be maintained. Neither the theory of a sacred twelve-tribe confederation ("amphictyony") nor the reconstruction of a Festival of Weeks at Gilgal and a covenant festival at Shechem hold up to scrutiny. The hypothetical construction of an ancient Israelite amphictyony was already being opposed early on, since the biblical depiction of the pre-monarchic period shows no knowledge of a central sanctuary for the twelve tribes, the Ark is described not as a cult place but as a cult object, and the number of tribes at "twelve" finds inconsistent attestation across Old Testament texts.[26] The texts cited for the anchoring of the particular Pentateuchal themes in Gilgal and Shechem (Josh 3–4; Deut 31; Josh 24), like the idea of a covenant and the credo formulations, belong to the context of Deuteronomy in the late monarchic or early exilic periods.[27] Thus, the assertion that the fabric of the Pentateuchal narratives had been interwoven already in the pre-monarchic period within the context of cultic celebration was thoroughly refuted.

There was also a methodological objection raised in an influential study from Rolf Rendtorff:[28] the Documentary Hypothesis takes the composite nature of the Pentateuch as its point of departure and seeks to explain its genesis through the literary-critical identification of source

---

[25]   Noth, *Pentateuchal Traditions*, 38–41.

[26]   Christoph Levin, "Amphictyony," *EBR* 1: 1044–47.

[27]   Lothar Perlitt, *Bundestheologie im Alten Testament*, WMANT 36 (Neukirchen-Vluyn: Neukirchener, 1969); for an overview, see Christoph Koch, "Covenant II. Hebrew Bible/Old Testament," *EBR* 5: 900–8.

[28]   Rolf Rendtorff, *The Problem of the Process of the Transmission in the Pentateuch*, trans. John J. Scullion, JSOTSup 89 (Sheffield: JSOT Press, 1990); trans. of *Das überlieferungsgeschichtliche Problem des Pentateuch*, BZAW 147 (Berlin: de Gruyter, 1976).

documents. In contrast, questions of transmission history initiated by Gunkel and continued by von Rad and Noth had begun with the individual narratives and then worked outwards through their further developments. According to Rendtorff, a methodologically consistent history of transmission must set the source theory aside and instead inquire about how the smallest units had developed into the larger composition. He saw this consistent transmission history leading to the conclusion that the Pentateuch consists of larger, relatively self-contained literary units, with only a few, very late lines of connection in between: the Primeval History (Gen 1–11), the patriarchs (Gen 12–50), the exodus from Egypt (Exod 1–15), Sinai (Exod 19–24; Exod 32–34), the wilderness sojourn (Exod 16–18; Num 11–20), and the conquest of the land (Numbers and Joshua). These were, according to Rendtorff, first connected through texts of Deuteronomic character.[29]

"The Elohist as Narrator: A Misguided Path of Pentateuchal Criticism?"

From early on, the theory of the Elohistic source was considered a weak spot in the Documentary Hypothesis. The Elohist contained neither a proper beginning nor a proper end. The texts designated as "Elohistic" provided no continuous narrative thread, and no unified theology could be identified. Wellhausen had already understood a precise division between "J" and "E" to be impossible.[30] Nevertheless, he reconstructed an Elohistic thread by looking for connections between distinct, supposedly Elohistic text blocks like Gen 20–22, 28:10–22, and 37:3–11. Paul Volz and Wilhelm Rudolph labeled this treatment as a "misguided path of Pentateuchal criticism" and supported the counterhypothesis that the Elohistic portions belonged partly to the Yahwist and partly to later additions to the Yahwist.[31] This proposal did not initially take hold, largely due to an intense objection from Noth. As Volz and Rudolph pointed to the fragmentary state of the supposed "E" source, Noth countered with evidence of a redactional

[29] Already by 1972, Rainer Kessler – in his Heidelberg dissertation, published only in 2015 – had found evidence that the cross-references in the non-P material were later additions and could not be taken as evidence for an "early" Yahwist or Elohist (Rainer Kessler, *Die Querverweise im Pentateuch: Überlieferungsgeschichtliche Untersuchung der expliziten Querverbindungen innerhalb des vorpriesterlichen Pentateuchs*, BEATAJ 59 [Frankfurt: Lang, 2015]).

[30] Wellhausen, *Composition*, 32–35, 207 et passim.

[31] Paul Volz and Wilhelm Rudolph, *Der Elohist als Erzähler: Ein Irrweg der Pentateuchkritik? An der Genesis erläutert*, BZAW 63 (Giessen: Toepelmann, 1933).

procedure that only incorporated parts of the Elohistic source into the Yahwistic work and led to a significant loss of text.[32] This caused subsequent discussion to refer to "fragments" of the Elohistic writing.[33]

In the long term, these fragments were hardly able to escape the wake of the supplementary hypothesis. This becomes apparent through the fate of both classical arguments for differentiating between Yahwist and Elohist, the alternating use of the generic term for a deity "Elohim/El" and the personal name "YHWH" and the repetitions of particular stories. Critics of the Elohist hypothesis reject the shift in names for God as an unpersuasive criterion for source division, and even most supporters have heavily relativized or outright rejected its significance.[34] For example, the story of Jacob's Ladder in Gen 28:10–22 – a text of fundamental importance for the emergence of the Elohist hypothesis[35] – very clearly shows an intentional shift between "Elohim" and "YHWH."[36] The reader knows from the outset that it is about an appearance of YHWH (v. 13a), while Jacob first recognizes this during his dream. He begins with seeing heavenly beings ("messengers of God/*Elohim*;" v. 12). Only when YHWH introduces himself by name (v. 13b) does Jacob know which deity is present (v. 16) at the previously unknown sanctuary (v. 11, 17). Since the narrative is the founding legend for the sanctuary in Beth-*El*, he speaks of the "House of God" (*bêt ĕlōhîm*) after he wakes up. The actual highlight of the narrative is in the fact that YHWH is the God (*ĕlōhîm*) of Jacob (vv. 20–21).

The fact that repetitions of whole narratives need not necessarily be ascribed to parallel narrative threads as per the Documentary Hypothesis can be shown in the narratives of the threat to the matriarch. The episode is told three times, with the threats to Rebekah and Sarah by Abimelech (Gen 20:1–18 "E"; 26:1–11 "J") considered to be doublets. Within the text generally ascribed to the Yahwist, the episode also appears with the threat to Sarah by Pharaoh (Gen 12:10–20). Obviously, a narrative plot

---

[32]   Noth, *Pentateuchal Traditions*, 20–37.

[33]   Hans Walter Wolff, "Zur Thematik der elohistischen Fragmente im Pentateuch," *EvT* 29 (1969): 59–72; trans. as " The Elohistic Fragments in the Pentateuch," *Int* 26 (1972): 158–73.

[34]   Erhard Blum, "Der vermeintliche Gottesname 'Elohim'," in *Gott Nennen. Gottes Namen und Gott als Name*, ed. Ingo Dalferth and Philipp Stoellger (Tübingen: Mohr Siebeck, 2008), 97–119.

[35]   See Hermann Hupfeld, *Die Quellen der Genesis und die Art ihrer Zusammensetzung* (Berlin: Wiegandt & Grieben, 1853), 38–40. Gen 28:10–20 is one of the few texts in which the separation of the supposedly interwoven J and E threads is carried out in almost complete agreement by different source critics.

[36]   See the recent analysis of Gen 28:10–20 in Erhard Blum, "The Jacob Tradition," in Evans et al., *The Book of Genesis*, 181–211, esp. 197–203.

may be taken up multiple times within a literary work without one needing
to speak of doublets. The supposedly Elohistic Abimelech episode in Gen
20:1–18 is a late reflection on whether there is also a "fear of God" in foreign
lands (v. 11). This question was essential for the diaspora and is debated by
taking up the thread of the endangered matriarch from Gen 12 and 26. Thus,
the episode draws upon the "doublets" in Gen 12 and 26 and presupposes its
readers' familiarity with both texts.[37] Similarly, a plethora of new analyses
reach the conclusion that the core Elohistic texts are either an integral
component of the texts ascribed to the Yahwist, or that they supplement
these texts and, in some cases, the priestly texts.[38] However, these findings
can be explained much more plausibly through a supplementary hypothesis
than with the assumption of a secondary connection of source documents
formerly transmitted independently from one another.

"Neither Source nor Edition": The Janus-Faced Priestly Writings
The identification of the Priestly Source is regarded as one of the few
anchors of Pentateuchal research, with the definition of the P texts
practically undisputed since Theodor Nöldeke 150 years ago.[39] Yet,
conceptions of the Priestly Source diverge significantly in their details,
such as the literary differentiation within the priestly texts, the scope of
the core priestly texts, the source's datings and literary character (as
a formerly independent work or redactional layer), as well as its relationship to the non-P texts. These questions are interlocked with one
another, and the debate is correspondingly complex.[40] The prevailing

---

[37]   Matthias Köckert, "Abraham: Ahnvater, Fremdling, Weiser: Lesarten der Bibel in Gen
       12, Gen 20 und Qumran," in *Das Buch der Bücher – gelesen: Lesarten der Bibel in den
       Wissenschaften und Künsten*, ed. Steffen Martus and Andrea Polaschegg,
       Publikationen zur Zeitschrift für Germanistik 13 (New York: Lang, 2006), 139–69.

[38]   John Van Seters, *Abraham in History and Tradition* (New Haven, CT: Yale University
       Press, 1975); Claus Westermann, *Genesis 12–36: A Commentary*, trans. John J. Scullion
       (Minneapolis: Fortress, 1985); Westermann, *Genesis 37–50: A Commentary*, trans. John
       J. Scullion (Minneapolis: Fortress, 1986); Erhard Blum, *Die Komposition der
       Vätergeschichte*, WMANT 57 (Neukirchen-Vluyn: Neukirchener, 1984); Timo Veijola,
       "Das Opfer des Abraham – Paradigma des Glaubens aus dem nachexilischen Zeitalter,"
       ZTK 85 (1988): 129–64; Levin, *Jahwist*; David M. Carr, *Reading the Fractures of Genesis*
       (Louisville: Westminster John Knox, 1996).

[39]   Theodor Nöldeke, "Die s.g. Grundschrift des Pentateuchs," in Nöldeke,
       Untersuchungen zur Kritik des Alten Testaments (Kiel: Schwers, 1869), 1–144. The
       characterization of the Priestly Source as "neither source nor redaction" comes from
       Erhard Blum, *Studien zur Komposition des Pentateuch*, BZAW 189 (Berlin: de
       Gruyter, 1990), 221–85.

[40]   See Friedhelm Hartenstein and Konrad Schmid, eds., *Abschied von der
       Priesterschrift? Zum Stand der Pentateuchdebatte*, VWGTh 40 (Leipzig:
       Evangelische Verlagsanstalt, 2015); Sarah Shectman and Joel Baden, eds., *The Strata*

consensus until the 1970s, with P being a formerly independent source document that has been almost completely preserved, was first challenged by Frank Moore Cross and Rolf Rendtorff.[41] Both vigorously argued for P as a redactional layer that integrated older writings into its work. Scholars such as John Van Seters and Erhard Blum have taken up this position,[42] while the majority in the field maintain the "classical" position of a formerly independent Priestly Source. Yet, the evidence in the priestly texts is actually ambiguous, as can best be seen from Genesis: in the Primeval History in Gen 1–11, P provides a coherent and independent text with a clear theological and compositional profile. Likewise, the continuous intertwining of the non-priestly and priestly passages in the Flood Story (Gen 6–9) is best explained through a source model. No editor would have unnecessarily caused the present factual tensions that show no concern for clean editing.[43] On the other hand, the P texts in the ancestral narratives in Gen 12–36 and in the Joseph story in Gen 37–50 do not provide a coherent narrative by themselves and appear incomplete without knowledge of the non-P tradition. This changes once again with the exodus narrative in Exod 1–14, in which the theological profile of the priestly depiction of the call of Moses, plagues, and departure can only be identified when disregarding the non-P texts. Thus, it might be adequate to describe P as a compositional layer that had first formulated its own tradition – for instance, in the Primeval History or in the exodus narrative – and then connected it with the older non-P texts.[44] Given the extreme sparsity of priestly texts in Gen 12–50, it should also be considered that the P account in Gen 12–50 was based on the non-priestly corpus. P would then be seen in this section as a redaction that, following an independently formulated Primeval History, furthered a redacted history of the patriarchs and Joseph with its own depiction of the formation of the Israelites in Egypt and the ensuing Mosaic period.[45]

---

of the Priestly Writings. Contemporary Debate and Future Directions, ATANT 95 (Zurich: Theologischer Verlag, 2009).

[41]   Frank M. Cross, "The Priestly Work," in Cross, Canaanite Myth and Hebrew Epic (Cambridge, MA: Harvard University Press, 1973), 293–325; Rendtorff, Problem.

[42]   John Van Seters, Prologue to History: The Yahwist as Historian in Genesis (Zurich: Theologischer Verlag, 1992); Blum, Komposition; Blum, Studien.

[43]   On the Priestly Source in Gen 1–11, see Jan C. Gertz, Das erste Buch Mose (Genesis): Die Urgeschichte Gen 1–11, ATD 1, 2nd. ed. (Göttingen: Vandenhoeck & Ruprecht, 2021) (English translation forthcoming in HCOT, Leuven: Peeters).

[44]   Blum, Studien, 221–85, esp. 278–85 on P in Gen 1–11.

[45]   Jakob Wöhrle, Fremdlinge im eigenen Land: Zur Entstehung und Intention der priesterlichen Passagen der Vätergeschichte, FRLANT 246 (Göttingen: Vandenhoeck & Ruprecht, 2012). Cf. already Jan C. Gertz, Tradition und Redaktion in der

Another approach to the priestly texts in Genesis ultimately emerged from study of the so-called Holiness Code in Lev 17–26. Conceptually and linguistically, it is equally close to P and Deuteronomy, and can be seen as a redactional harmonization of both conceptions in order to complete the formation of the Torah. Since traces of this redaction can also be found scattered across the Pentateuch (e.g., Gen 17:9, 13–14*; Exod 12:14–20; Exod 31:12–17; Lev 11:41–45) and since it is centered on the Holiness Code, it has been referred to as the "Holiness School."[46] Recently, the hypothesis has been raised for Genesis that the first creation account in Gen 1:1–2:3, the arrangement through the *Toledot* formula ("These are the generations of N.N."; Gen 2:4a; 5:1; 6:9; 10:1; 11:10, 27; 25:12, 19; 36:1, 9; 37:2), the covenant with Abraham in Gen 17, and a number of other redactional verses all stem from the Holiness School. Its authors largely relied on material from the Priestly Source and connected it with Israel's older epic traditions (JE).[47] However, the feasibility of this hypothesis's presupposition of a literary-critical division of the texts commonly assigned to P into (scarce and insubstantial) P and (extensive) Holiness School should be questioned, as should whether the food laws in Lev 17 (H) and the allowance of meat consumption for humans in Gen 9:4–6 come from the same source. Rather, Lev 17:3–7 seems to be a revision of the P text in Gen 9.[48]

Finally, what remains to be investigated are P's absolute and relative chronologies. According to the Documentary Hypothesis, P is the latest

Exoduserzählung. Untersuchungen zur Endredaktion des Pentateuch, FRLANT 186 (Göttingen: Vandenhoeck & Ruprecht, 2000), 391.

[46] Israel Knohl, *The Sanctuary of Silence: The Priestly Torah and the Holiness School* (Minneapolis: Fortress, 1995); Christophe Nihan, *From Priestly Torah to Pentateuch. A Study in the Composition of the Book of Leviticus*, FAT II/25 (Tübingen: Mohr Siebeck, 2007).

[47] Jacob Milgrom, "H$_R$ in Leviticus and Elsewhere in the Torah," in *The Book of Leviticus: Composition and Reception*, ed. Rolf Rendtorff and Robert A. Kugler, VTSup 93 (Leiden: Brill, 2003), 24–40; Bill T. Arnold, *Genesis*, New Cambridge Bible Commentary (Cambridge: Cambridge University Press, 2009), 12–18; Arnold, "The Holiness Redaction of the Primeval History," *ZAW* 129 (2017): 483–500; Arnold, "The Holiness Redaction of the Abrahamic Covenant (Genesis 17)," in *Partners with God: Theological and Critical Readings of the Bible in Honor of Marvin A. Sweeney*, ed. Shelly L. Birdsong and Serge Frolov, Claremont Studies in Hebrew Bible and Septuagint 2 (Claremont: Claremont Press, 2017), 51–61; Megan Warner, "The Holiness School in Genesis?" in *Current Issues in Priestly and Related Literature: The Legacy of Jacob Milgrom and Beyond*, ed. Roy E. Gane and Ada Taggar-Cohen (Atlanta, GA: SBL Press, 2015), 155–74 (focusing on the ancestral narratives).

[48] For the (substantial) uniformity of the P part of Gen 1–11 and the conceptual coherence of this section, foundational for the overall breakdown of P, see Gertz, *Das erste Buch Mose*, 9–11 et passim; for the relationship between Gen 9,1–4 and Lev 17 see Nihan, *Torah*, 412–13.

source and dates back to the time of the consecration of the Second Temple in the late sixth century BCE. Nevertheless, some scholars date P to the monarchic period due to its archaic language.[49] It has correctly been observed that the rituals depicted in P and its conceptual ideas stem in part from the cultic practices of the First Temple. Yet, P's exhibition of several linguistic and factual contacts with Deuteronomism, Deutero-Isaianic texts, and Ezekiel should not be ignored. P presupposes the cult centralization stipulated by Deuteronomy in the late pre-exilic period. The monotheism represented by P in Gen 1 is first found in the Hebrew Bible in Deutero-Isaiah. The universalism of the priestly creation account and Table of Nations in Gen 10 reflect the intellectual and political circumstances of the Achaemenid empire. In this respect, P represents a priestly knowledge base that grew over the centuries and was codified in the early postexilic period. Regarding relative chronology, the old preconception that considered most non-P texts as unquestionably pre-priestly has largely been abandoned. Indeed, the narrative substance of the non-P texts is considered older, but their arrangements are often more recent than P and Deuteronomy. As one example, Gen 15 was long considered one of the bedrocks of Genesis (if only because of its supposedly archaic rite requiring Abraham to walk through a row of halved animals). Yet now, the text is frequently dated to many centuries later. The "archaic" rite has become a controversial theological text that presupposes P in Gen 17 and belongs to the context of a dispute based on the example of Abraham regarding the distinctive identity of Judah in the late Persian period.[50]

"The Elusive Yahwist"

In the mansion of the Documentary Hypothesis, the Yahwist has invariably occupied the *bel étage*.[51] According to von Rad, the Yahwist created

---

[49] See Erhard Blum, "Issues and Problems in the Contemporary Debate Regarding the Priestly Writings," in Shectman and Baden, *Strata of the Priestly Writing*, 31–44, here 31–33 (with further literature). Regarding the problems of "linguistic dating" see Blum, "The Linguistic Dating of Biblical Texts," in Gertz et al., *Formation of the Pentateuch*, 303–25.

[50] See Matthias Köckert, "Gen 15: Vom 'Urgestein' der Väterüberlieferung zum 'theologischen Programmtext' der späten Perserzeit," *ZAW* 125 (2013): 25–48; Jean-Louis Ska, "Some Groundworks on Genesis 15," in Ska, *The Exegesis of the Pentateuch: Exegetical Studies and Basic Questions*, FAT 66 (Tübingen: Mohr Siebeck, 2009), 67–81.

[51] On the history of research and the state of the debate, cf. Thomas C. Römer, "The Elusive Yahwist: A Short History of Research," in *A Farewell to the Yahwist? The Composition of the Pentateuch in Recent European Interpretation*, ed. Thomas B. Dozeman and Konrad Schmid, SBLSymS 34 (Atlanta, GA: SBL Press, 2006), 9–27.

a work that may be considered "one of the greatest accomplishments of all times in the history of thought."[52] Together with the History of David's Rise and the Succession Narrative, the Yahwist's work was an expression of a historical process of thought that ancient Israel developed long before the Greeks, and into a completely distinct form. In all of this, the Yahwist was a product of the "freethinking era of Solomon."[53] In the current discussion, however, nearly everything concerning the texts traditionally ascribed to the Yahwist has been available for renegotiation: age and scope, internal coherence and theological conception. Thus, the amounts of text characterized in the field as Yahwistic vary substantially. At best, the common thread has been the supposition that it was the first overall draft of the Pentateuchal narrative. The alteration in dating has been particularly incisive. John Van Seters considers the majority of the Abraham traditions in Gen 12–25 to have stemmed from the exilic period, with Abraham, first mentioned outside of the Pentateuch in Ezekiel (Ezek 33:23–29) and Deutero-Isaiah (Isa 41:8–9; 51:2), as a role model for exilic Israel.[54] Against Albrecht Alt or Gerhard von Rad, the promises to the patriarchs were not the precipitation of experiences from the early, nomadic days of Israel written down in the monarchic period. Rather, they came about from historical-theological reflections that were responding to the experiences of exile and giving new confidence to a dejected people. The Yahwist was thus a historian akin to Greek historiographers like Herodotus and Hellanicus, who in the exilic period compiled Israel's various foundation legends and whose work was later subject to a priestly revision. Christoph Levin sees the Yahwist similarly, but in some respects also very differently.[55] For him, the Yahwist was a diasporic redactor working with various older sources. In the ancestral narratives, he polemicized against the Deuteronomic stipulation that YHWH only be worshiped at the one legitimate sanctuary (e.g., Deut 12 vs. Gen 12:7–8; 13:8). Also differing from Van Seters, Levin's P was a formerly independent work combined with the Yahwistic narrative by a redactor. According to Levin, with this connection the formation of the text was – even in Genesis – far from complete.

---

[52]   von Rad, *Genesis*, 25.
[53]   Ibid., 29. The memorable phrase "Solomonic Enlightenment" first appears in Gerhard von Rad, "Der Anfang der Geschichtsschreibung im Alten Israel [1944]," in von Rad, *Gesammelte Studien*, 187; trans. as "The Beginnings of Historical Writing in Ancient Israel," in von Rad, *Problem*, 203.
[54]   Van Seters, *Abraham*.
[55]   Levin, *Jahwist*.

While Van Seters and Levin both agree with previous research that the overall design of the Pentateuchal narrative can be traced back to the Yahwist, this has otherwise been heavily questioned in recent years. For Genesis, this primarily concerns the Primeval History in Gen 1–11 and the book's connection with the exodus narrative.[56] The broad thematic and compositional coherence of the traditionally Yahwistic texts in Gen 1–11 on the one hand and their rather loose connection to the Yahwistic patriarchal history on the other has led to the theory of an originally independent non-P Primeval History.[57] Others, however, attribute the traditionally Yahwistic texts to a post-priestly redaction that used older material to revise the priestly Primeval History.[58] Further on, there has been intense discussion on whether there was a "Yahwistic" transition from the Joseph story to the exodus narrative or if P, coming later, first connected the patriarchal and exodus narratives.[59] In the latter case, the non-P ancestral and Moses/Exodus narratives would be considered competing conceptions of Israel's origins.[60] Yet one can assume the non-P

[56] Already by 1961, Samuel Sandmel presented the theory that J "never was a long, connected document" and emphasized the differing character of the four primary sections of Genesis, the Primeval History and the narratives of the three patriarchs (Samuel Sandmel, " The Haggada within Scripture," JBL 80 [1961]: 105–22, here 115).

[57] See already Robert H. Pfeiffer, Introduction to the Old Testament (New York: Harper & Brothers, 1941), 159–67. The seminal study on this topic: Frank Crüsemann, "Die Eigenständigkeit der Urgeschichte: Ein Beitrag zur Diskussion um den 'Jahwisten'," in Die Botschaft und die Boten: FS Hans Walter Wolff, ed. Jörg Jeremias and Lothar Perlitt (Neukirchen-Yluyn: Neukirchener, 1981), 11–29. See also Blum, Komposition, 349–61; Carr, Reading, 234–48; Markus Witte, Die Biblische Urgeschichte: Redaktions- und theologiegeschichtliche Beobachtungen zu Genesis 1,1–11,26, BZAW 265 (Berlin: de Gruyter, 1998), 192–205; Jan C. Gertz, "The Formation of the Primeval History," in Evans et al., The Book of Genesis, 107–36.

[58] Joseph Blenkinsopp, "A Post-Exilic Lay Source in Genesis 1–11," in Abschied vom Jahwisten: Die Komposition des Hexateuch in der jüngsten Diskussion, ed. Jan C. Gertz, Konrad Schmid, and Markus Witte, BZAW 315 (Berlin: de Gruyter, 2002), 49–61; Andreas Schüle, Der Prolog der hebräischen Bibel, ATANT 86 (Zurich: Theologischer Verlag, 2006); Albert de Pury, "Pᵍ as the absolute Beginning," in Les dernières Rédactions du Pentateuque, de l'Hexateuque et de l'Ennéateuque, ed. Thomas Römer and Konrad Schmid, BETL 203 (Leuven: Peeters, 2007), 99–128, here 113–18; Martin Arneth, Durch Adams Fall ist ganz verderbt … Studien zur Entstehung der alttestamentlichen Urgeschichte, FRLANT 217 (Göttingen: Vandenhoeck & Ruprecht, 2007).

[59] See Jan C. Gertz, "The Relative Independence of the Books of Genesis and Exodus," in Book-Seams in the Hexateuch I: The Literary Transitions between the Books of Genesis/Exodus and Joshua/Judges, ed. Christoph Berner and Harald Samuel, FAT 120 (Tübingen: Mohr Siebeck, 2018), 55–72 and cited literature. Already Frederick V. Winnett, "Re-examining the Foundation," JBL 84 (1965): 1–19, proposed that the combination of the non-P ancestral narrative and the non-P exodus narrative postdated P.

[60] Konrad Schmid, Erzväter und Exodus: Untersuchungen zur doppelten Begründung der Ursprünge Israels innerhalb der Geschichtsbücher des Alten Testaments,

authors' familiarity with both traditions, though P would have been the first to connect the ancestors with Moses for a continuous historical scheme.

WAYS OUT OF THE CRISIS?

The field is currently far removed from a consensus, whether it pertains to the formation of the Pentateuch or of Genesis. In English-speaking scholarship, and especially North American research, the Documentary Hypothesis still finds broad representation in its modified form by Noth. Additionally, the circle of Neo-Documentarians in Israel and the United States has returned to the mechanical source separation that had already been forcefully rejected by Wellhausen.[61] Meanwhile especially in continental European research, in addition to variants of a modified version of the Documentary Hypothesis, models are increasingly supported that reckon with compositions of varying sizes that developed independently and at different times and were joined through redactional brackets into even larger units. Lastly, synchronic approaches must also be mentioned, which differ wildly in their specifics and are all generally subsumed under the term "Literary Criticism."[62] These approaches, initially predominant in English departments, share a view of the biblical texts as unitary works of literature. They generally lack a historical dimension, instead understanding the texts' end-forms as works of art and focusing on their internal structural features and literary strategies. For diachronic research, these contributions are nevertheless of great

WMANT 81 (Neukirchen-Vluyn: Neukirchener Verlag, 1999); trans. as *Genesis and the Moses Story: Israel's Dual Origins in the Hebrew Bible*, trans. James D. Nogalski, Siphrut 3 (Winona Lake: Eisenbrauns, 2010); Jan C. Gertz, *Tradition und Redaktion in der Exoduserzählung: Untersuchungen zur Endredaktion des Pentateuch*, FRLANT 186 (Göttingen: Vandenhoeck & Ruprecht, 2000).

[61] See above, p. 56 and fn. 11. Cf. furthermore Joel S. Baden, *The Composition of the Pentateuch: Renewing the Documentary Hypothesis*, AYBRL (New Haven, CT: Yale University Press, 2012).

[62] Here a terminological ambiguity must be acknowledged. The expression "literary criticism" and the corresponding German term "Literarkritik" originally referred to the historical-diachronic question of the text's formation history and the reconstructed sources and redactions. Since the 1970s, the meaning of the English expression has shifted. The historical-diachronic approach is commonly designated "literary-historical criticism," while synchronic or text-immanent approaches fall under "new literary criticism." For an overview, see David J. A. Clines, "Contemporary Methods in Hebrew Bible Criticism," in *Hebrew Bible/Old Testament: The History of Its Interpretation. Vol. III/2: The Twentieth Century – From Modernism to Post-Modernism*, ed. Magne Sæbø (Göttingen: Vandenhoeck & Ruprecht, 2015), 148–69.

interest, since they broaden the view for the idiosyncrasies of biblical narratives and show that not every repetition and supposed linguistic imperfection indicates a literary seam. A particularly apt example is the analysis of the Jacob's Ladder story in Gen 28 by Jan P. Fokkelman.[63] It has been significantly influential for subsequent diachronic analyses that reject the classical division between Elohistic and Yahwistic versions of the text and instead postulate a basic text with several additions.[64]

Given the variety of differing approaches, it may appear daring to conclude with an overview of possible sources and redactions in Genesis. Nevertheless, the course of the discussion may allow for some insights to be gained and the contours of a picture to be revealed that may at least help differentiate between certainties and uncertainties and identify open questions regarding the formation of the book.[65] Very important is the early insight that neither Genesis nor the Pentateuch as a whole can be measured by a single stick. Supporters of documentary, supplementary, and fragmentary models each integrate components of their competing models, as they should. Moreover, regarding formation history, a distinction must be made between the larger units of the Primeval History, the ancestral narratives – and here between the Abraham, Isaac, and Jacob narratives – and the Joseph story. In the Primeval History the two-source theory (P and non-P) has basically been proven, although some texts may be attributed to later redactions. The P texts in Gen 1–11 unmistakably exhibit a larger priestly conception of Israel's history that stretches at least until God's revelation on Sinai, yet there is much reason to suppose that the non-P Primeval History was a formerly independent composition. Moving further, the oldest corpus of ancestral narratives is found in the Jacob/Esau/Laban story in Gen 25–33* and stems from the Northern Kingdom of Israel. It was presumably combined with the Southern Kingdom narratives of Isaac and Abraham after the fall of the Northern Kingdom in 722 BCE. The Isaac story is conspicuously concentrated within Gen 26 and largely consists of variants to the Abraham and Sarah narratives, with the threats to the matriarch (Gen

---

[63] Fokkelman, *Narrative Art*, 46–81.
[64] See above, p. 63 on Gen 28.
[65] The following outline is kept so short that I refrain from using references. Relevant arguments may be found in the aforementioned works by Blum, Gertz, Kratz, Levin and Schmid, which can differ greatly in their details and approaches. For a summary, see Gertz, "Tora und Vordere Propheten," in *Grundinformation Altes Testament*, ed. Jan C. Gertz et al., 6th ed. (Göttingen: Vandenhoeck & Ruprecht, 2019), 193–312; trans. from 3rd ed. (2008) as *T&T Clark Handbook of the Old Testament*, ed. Jan C. Gertz et al. (London: T&T Clark, 2012), 235–382.

12; 20; 26) and the covenant with Abimelech over well rights (Gen 21; 26) probably having originated with Isaac. It seems that these stories were assumed by Abraham as the later, more popular, and more important figure. The core of the Abraham narratives is found in the Abraham/Lot Cycle (Gen 13:1–13*, 18; Gen 18–19*; 21:1–7*). Geographically, it comes from the area of Hebron and thus from Judahite territory. The main stock of the Abraham narratives, however, was filled out later and presupposes the connection to the Jacob narratives. The great attractiveness of Abraham as a role model in post-exilic times becomes apparent with the diversity of late additions such as the courting of Rebekah (Gen 24), Abraham's intercession for Sodom (Gen 18) and Abimelech (Gen 20), as well as the Binding of Isaac (Gen 22). Written in quintessential novelistic style, the story of Joseph and his brothers in Gen 37; 39–50* is a formerly independent narrative vis-à-vis the ancestral history and the exodus narrative. The literary ties are all secondary, but the party responsible for the connection of the larger portions is currently a topic of intense debate. Was it the work of a "late" Yahwist before the connection with the Priestly Source? Did P integrate the non-P blocks into its work? Or does the connection trace back to a redactor who combined P with the non-P literary works? The findings regarding the Priestly Source in Gen 12–50 are also difficult to assess. It is possible that a formerly independent Priestly Source offered only a reduced version of the ancestral narratives and the Joseph novella, presupposing its readers' familiarity with the non-P texts. Yet it is also possible that the Priestly Source in Gen 12–50 is better spoken of as an editorial or compositional layer.

SELECT BIBLIOGRAPHY

Blum, Erhard. "The Jacob Tradition." Pages 181–211 in *The Book of Genesis: Composition, Reception, and Interpretation*. Edited by Craig A. Evans, Joel N. Lohr, and David L. Petersen. VTSup 152. Leiden: Brill, 2012.

Blum, Erhard. *Die Komposition der Vätergeschichte*. WMANT 57. Neukirchen-Vluyn: Neukirchener, 1984.

Carr, David M. *Reading the Fractures of Genesis*. Louisville: Westminster John Knox, 1996.

Gertz, Jan C. "The Formation of the Primeval History." Pages 107–36 in *The Book of Genesis: Composition, Reception, and Interpretation*, Edited by Craig A. Evans, Joel N. Lohr, and David L. Petersen. VTSup 152. Leiden: Brill, 2012.

Gunkel, Hermann. *Genesis*. Translated by Mark E. Biddle. Foreword by Ernest W. Nicholson. Macon, GA: Mercer University Press, 1997. Translation of the 9th printing (1977) of *Genesis: übersetzt und erklärt: Mit einem Geleitwort von Walter Baumgartner*. 3rd ed. HKAT 1.1. Göttingen: Vandenhoeck & Ruprecht, 1910.

Hartenstein, Friedhelm, and Konrad Schmid, eds. *Abschied von der Priesterschrift? Zum Stand der Pentateuchdebatte*. VWGTh 40. Leipzig: Evangelische Verlagsanstalt, 2015 (English translation forthcoming in SBL Ancient Israel and its Literature Series, Atlanta: SBL Press).

Levin, Christoph. *Der Jahwist*. FRLANT 157. Göttingen: Vandenhoeck & Ruprecht, 1993.

Rendtorff, Rolf. *The Problem of the Process of the Transmission in the Pentateuch*. Translated by John J. Scullion. JSOTSup 89. Sheffield: JSOT Press, 1990. Translation of *Das überlieferungsgeschichtliche Problem des Pentateuch*. BZAW 147. Berlin: de Gruyter, 1976.

Römer, Thomas C. "The Elusive Yahwist: A Short History of Research." Pages 9–27 in *A Farewell to the Yahwist? The Composition of the Pentateuch in Recent European Interpretation*. Edited by Thomas B. Dozeman and Konrad Schmid. SBLSymS 34. Atlanta: SBL Press, 2006.

Schmid, Konrad. *Genesis and the Moses Story: Israel's Dual Origins in the Hebrew Bible*. Translated by James D. Nogalski. Siphrut 3. Winona Lake, IN: Eisenbrauns, 2010. Translation of *Erzväter und Exodus: Untersuchungen zur doppelten Begründung der Ursprünge Israels innerhalb der Geschichtsbücher des Alten Testaments*. WMANT 81. Neukirchen-Vluyn: Neukirchner, 1999.

Van Seters, John. *Prologue to History: The Yahwist as Historian in Genesis*. Zurich: Theologischer Verlag, 1992.

Ska, Jean-Louis. "Some Groundwork on Genesis 15." Pages 67–81 in *The Exegesis of the Pentateuch: Exegetical Studies and Basic Questions*. By Jean-Louis Ska. FAT 66. Tübingen: Mohr Siebeck, 2009.

4 Genesis in Form and Tradition Criticism Today

CHRISTOPH LEVIN

Since the beginning of the twentieth century, the book of Genesis has increasingly come to be studied in terms of form and genre as well as of the history of tradition. One of the reasons was Hermann Gunkel's epochal commentary on Genesis, published in 1901, which was soon to become authoritative.[1] Gunkel's often-quoted statement that "Genesis is a collection of legends"[2] ("Die Genesis ist eine Sammlung von Sagen") determined the path future research would take, though he had not meant to say that Genesis was only that.

More recently, scholars have emphasized the multiplicity of processes that shaped the history of tradition, as well as the wide range of genres involved. "The tradition, the crystallization of which has formed the Old Testament, is multiplex in character."[3] One has also generally become more conscious of the fact that the written form was essential to preserving this tradition.

THE SITUATION SINCE HERMANN GUNKEL

Recent research has shown that some of the premises that have so far determined scholarly judgment on early forms of tradition are not sufficiently well-founded.[4]

---

[1] Hermann Gunkel, *Genesis: Translated and Interpreted*, trans. Mark E. Biddle, Mercer Library of Biblical Studies (Macon, GA: Mercer University Press, 1997); trans. of *Genesis übersetzt und erklärt*, HKAT 1,1 3rd rev. ed. (Göttingen: Vandenhoeck & Ruprecht, 1910).

[2] Gunkel, *Genesis*, vii.

[3] James Barr, *Old and New in Interpretation: A Study of the Two Testaments* (London: SCM Press, 1966), 15.

[4] On criticism of Gunkel see John W. Rogerson, *Myth in Old Testament Interpretation*, BZAW 134 (Berlin: de Gruyter, 1974), 57–65; John Van Seters, *Abraham in History and Tradition* (New Haven, CT: Yale University Press, 1975), 131–34; Alois Wolf, "H. Gunkels Auffassung von der Verschriftlichung der Genesis im Licht mittelalterlicher Literarisierungsprobleme," *UF* 12 (1980): 361–74.

(1) Gunkel's conception of the genre of saga does not stand up to comparison with documented sagas and their modes of transmission. He presupposes that sagas are orally transmitted by definition, but this is by no means necessary. He was further misguided by the prejudice that tradition in an unwritten form presented a naive view of the world that differs markedly from the modern state of mind. It is easy to see that this reasoning is circular.[5]

(2) Gunkel was of the opinion that only short units that "hardly extend beyond ten verses" could derive from oral tradition.[6] "The tales all stem from the oral tradition, in which each story was told in turn."[7] This is contradicted by how heavily the narratives in Genesis are woven together.[8]

(3) For the third edition of his commentary Gunkel referred to Axel Olrik's "Epische Gesetze der Volksdichtung."[9] The rules of storytelling discerned by Olrik are not, however, as universal as Olrik thought and, moreover, they are not well suited to marking out a fundamental difference between "folk poetry" and "art poetry." As such, observing these rules being used does not unequivocally say that such texts derive from oral tradition.[10]

(4) Our reservations against the view that Genesis is a collection of sagas are also valid if one applies the definition put forward by André Jolles.[11] In his view, the genre of saga derived from the fact that the oral memory of historical events could only be handed down by being transposed into the family as its frame of reference. Claus Westermann in particular adopted this definition to explain the

---

[5]   See esp. Sean M. Warner, "Primitive Saga Men," *VT* 29 (1979): 325–35.

[6]   Gunkel, *Genesis*, xxix.

[7]   Hermann Gunkel, "Die israelitische Literatur," in *Die orientalischen Literaturen*, Die Kultur der Gegenwart I.7 (Leipzig: Teubner, 1906), 51–102: 72 (my translation).

[8]   See also Wolf, "H. Gunkels Auffassung," 366: "In the period immediately before the narrative tradition was recorded in writing, the poets' and their audiences' capacity for memorizing was presumably high" (my translation).

[9]   Axel Olrik, "Epische Gesetz der Volksdichtung," *Zeitschrift für deutsches Altertum und deutsche Literatur* 51 (1909): 1–12; English trans. (by J. P. Steager) "Epic Laws of Folk Narrative," in *The Study of Folklore*, ed. Alan Dundes (Englewood Cliffs, NJ: Prentice-Hall, 1965), 129–41.

[10] See, for example, Robert C. Culley, *Studies in the Structure of Hebrew Narrative* (Philadelphia, PA: Fortress, 1976), 29–30.

[11] André Jolles, *Simple Forms: Legend, Saga, Myth, Riddle, Saying, Case, Memorabile, Fairytale, Joke*, trans. Peter J. Schwartz (New York: Verso Books, 2017); trans. of *Einfache Formen: Legende, Sage, Mythe, Rätsel, Spruch, Kasus, Memorabile, Märchen, Witz* (Halle: Niemeyer, 1930), 62–90.

process by which the patriarchal narratives came into being.[12]
Jolles developed his definition largely on the basis of an
interpretation of the *Icelandic Sagas* by Andreas Heusler
(1913).[13] Many of the latter's views later turned out to be
untenable.[14] "Many authorities on Icelandic sagas regard them
as primarily literary works with only a limited amount of oral
tradition behind them."[15] "At any rate the whole discussion of
Sage since the time of Gunkel has done little to clarify the form
of the tradition in the Abraham stories."[16]

(5) Gunkel determined the purpose of many sagas as "etiological."[17]
That means that the narratives seek to explain facts of the present by
unfolding their (supposed) historical origin. "In contemporary Bible
scholarship, 'etiology' stands for a narrative that appears to offer
a tradition on the past, but aims solely to explain, justify or
confirm something in present reality."[18] It is obvious that this
does indeed apply to the tradition of the book of Genesis,
especially to the primeval history. It is every bit as obvious,
however, that the etiological aspect has often been supplemented
and hence does not reflect the story's original impetus.[19]

(6) Albrecht Alt attempted to approach the era of the patriarchs as the
Bible presents it by means of the history of religion.[20] He assumed

[12] Claus Westermann, "Arten der Erzählung in der Genesis," in *Forschung am Alten
     Testament: Gesammelte Studien*, TB 24 (Munich: Kaiser, 1964), 9–91, here 36–39.
[13] Andreas Heusler, "Die Anfänge der isländischen Saga" (1913), in *Kleine Schriften*,
     vol. 2 (Berlin: de Gruyter, 1969), 388–460.
[14] See Theodore M. Andersson, *The Problem of Icelandic Saga Origins: A Historical
     Survey*, Yale Germanic Studies 1 (New Haven, CT: Yale University Press, 1964).
[15] Van Seters, *Abraham*, 136.
[16] Ibid., 138.
[17] Gunkel, *Genesis*, xviii–xxi.
[18] Isaac Leo Seeligmann, "Ätiologische Elemente in der biblischen Geschichtsschreibung,"
     in *Gesammelte Studien zur Hebräischen Bibel*, FAT 41 (Tübingen: Mohr Siebeck, 2004),
     77–118: 78 (my translation); Hebrew original: "יסודות איטיולוגיים בהיסטוריוגראפיה המקראית," *Zion*
     26 (1961): 141–69. See also Sigmund Mowinckel, "Das ätiologische Denken," in
     *Tetrateuch – Pentateuch – Hexateuch: Die Berichte über die Landnahme in den drei
     altisraelitischen Geschichtswerken*, BZAW 90 (Berlin: Töpelmann, 1964), 78–86;
     Rudolf Smend, "Elements of Historical Thinking in the Old Testament," in *"The
     Unconquered Land" and Other Old Testament Essays: Selected Studies*, trans.
     Margaret Kohl (Farnham: Ashgate, 2013), 73–98, esp. 79–84; trans. of *Elemente alttesta-
     mentlichen Geschichtsdenkens*, ThSt 95 (Zurich: EVZ-Verlag, 1968).
[19] See Seeligmann, "Ätiologische Elemente," 92; see also Brevard S. Childs, "A Study of
     the Formula 'Until this day'," *JBL* 82 (1963): 279–92; Westermann, "Arten der
     Erzählung," 39–47.
[20] Albrecht Alt, "The God of the Fathers," in *Essays on Old Testament History and
     Religion*, trans. R. A. Wilson (Oxford: Blackwell, 1966), 1–77; trans. of *Der Gott der*

that the frequent references to "the God of the father"[21] represent a form of religion that preceded the commitment of the later Israelites to worship the god YHWH. In his view, this allowed him to identify at least the rough outline of the patriarchal era and its form of life. It has since been shown that the occurrences of "the God of the father" are all part of later revisions of the narratives and not of their basic form.[22] They do not represent a pre-Yahwist stage, but reflect the later development, especially in the Jewish diaspora, when, roughly speaking, the practice of the YHWH religion had moved from the people and the kingship to the family.[23]

(7) What is to be said about the references to "the God of the father" applies equally to the promises to the patriarchs. They too have consistently proved to be the work of later editors[24] and are hence unsuited to providing access to the origins of the tradition. The commonly held view that the promises are intended to link the patriarchal era with the exodus narrative and are hence essential to the structure of the Pentateuch[25] cannot be maintained.[26]

(8) Regarding the narrative structure of the Pentateuch as a whole, Gerhard von Rad assumed that "the basic concepts which bind together the whole structure are not, of course, the products of the personal theological genius of the Yahwist, nor do they represent one of many possible formative lines which might have been chosen. They are themselves an extremely ancient traditional

---

Väter: Ein Beitrag zur Vorgeschichte der israelitischen Religion, BWANT 48 (Stuttgart: Kohlhammer, 1929).

[21] Esp. Gen 26:24; 28:13; 31:5, 29, 42, 53; 32:10; 43:23; 46:1, 3; 48:15; 49:25; 50:17.

[22] See esp. Matthias Köckert, *Vätergott und Väterverheißungen: Eine Auseinandersetzung mit Albrecht Alt und seinen Erben*, FRLANT 142 (Göttingen: Vandenhoeck & Ruprecht, 1988).

[23] See Christoph Levin, *Der Jahwist*, FRLANT 157 (Göttingen: Vandenhoeck & Ruprecht, 1993), 420–22.

[24] See, for example, Jean Hoftijzer, *Die Verheissungen an die drei Erzväter* (Leiden: Brill, 1956); Köckert, *Vätergott und Väterverheißungen*.

[25] Influentially put forward by Martin Noth, *A History of Pentateuchal Traditions*, trans. Bernhard W. Anderson (Englewood Cliffs, NJ: Prentice-Hall, 1972), 54–58; trans. of *Überlieferungsgeschichte des Pentateuch* (Stuttgart: Kohlhammer, 1948). But see Rainer Kessler, *Die Querverweise im Pentateuch: Überlieferungsgeschichtliche Untersuchung der expliziten Querverbindungen innerhalb des vorpriesterlichen Pentateuchs*, BEATAJ 59 (Frankfurt am Main: Lang, 2015).

[26] See Christoph Levin, "Die Väterverheißungen: Eine Bestandsaufnahme," in *The Post-Priestly Pentateuch: New Perspectives on Its Redactional Development and Theological Profiles*, ed. Federico Giuntoli and Konrad Schmid, FAT 101 (Tübingen: Mohr Siebeck, 2015), 125–43.

deposit, and there was no alternative to using them."[27] In support of
this judgment, von Rad pointed to the "short historical creed," three
instances of which he identified in Deut 6:20–24; 26:5b–9, and Josh
24:2b–13. He assumed that examples of this creed had been
regularly recited in the cult at the large annual festivals.[28] This
hypothesis soon turned out to lack support. The passages in
question are no old tradition, but late summaries that largely
presuppose the existing text of the Pentateuch.[29] "This raises the
very serious question of whether any of the thematic structures in
the Pentateuch can be traced back to an oral tradition basis, or
whether they are not all the result of literary composition by
a redactor/collector."[30]

(9) On the basis of von Rad's hypothesis, Martin Noth searched for "the
historical presuppositions of the formation of the tradition."[31] He
too held the distinction between saga and historiography to be the
key to the history of tradition. Historiography, he argued, emerged
only under the monarchy, because the extant written testimonies all
date from this period. Saga, by contrast, and with it the narrative
matter of Genesis, belonged to an earlier time, in which the tribes
determined the people's lives. "The Pentateuchal tradition is on the
whole a *saga*-tradition, in the sense that it had no particular 'author'
or even 'authors' but rather emerged, developed, and was
transmitted through the mouth of 'narrators' within the
anonymous totality of the tribes [...]. A saga-tradition in this sense
is usually found in a situation where the history of a people is borne
by the community of its tribes [...] before a state government in the
proper sense takes over with its own organs of leadership and
responsibility."[32] In offering this interpretation, Noth explicitly

[27] Gerhard von Rad, "The Form-Critical Problem of the Hexateuch," in *The Problem of the Hexateuch and Other Essays*, trans. E. W. Trueman Dicken (Edinburgh: Oliver & Boyd, 1966), 1–78, here 51; trans. of *Das formgeschichtliche Problem des Hexateuchs*, BWANT 78 (Stuttgart: Kohlhammer, 1938).

[28] von Rad, "The Form-Critical Problem," 3–8.

[29] See esp. Wolfgang Richter, "Beobachtungen zur theologischen Systembildung in der alttestamentlichen Literatur anhand des 'Kleinen geschichtlichen Credo'," in *Wahrheit und Verkündigung*, vol. 1, ed. Leo Scheffczyk et al. (Paderborn: Schöningh, 1967), 175–212; Brevard S. Childs, "Deuteronomic Formulae of the Exodus Traditions," in *Hebräische Wortforschung*, ed. Benedikt Hartmann et al., VTSup 16 (Leiden: Brill, 1967), 30–39: 39. N. Lohfink, "Zum 'kleinen geschichtlichen Credo' Dtn 26, 5–9," ThPh 46 (1971): 19–39, has traced the textual connections in detail.

[30] Van Seters, *Abraham*, 143.

[31] Martin Noth, *Pentateuchal Traditions*, 42–45.

[32] Ibid., 44.

referred to Gunkel and Jolles, and as such, he also exposes himself to the criticism levelled at them.

(10) In addition, even Noth's historical presuppositions proved to be untenable. He insisted that "the orientation of the Pentateuchal tradition in terms of all Israel [...] belongs to the fundamental substance of the Pentateuch."[33] In a period before the state formation, "all Israel" can refer only to the tribal league, the constituents and structure of which Noth undertook to determine in his well-known monograph published in 1930.[34] Noth's hypothesis has not stood the test of time.[35] All references to the system of the twelve tribes have proven to be late in terms of literary history.[36] There is much to suggest that it was the kingship and not the tribal league that molded the tribes and regions into "all Israel" (2 Sam 2:9) as an integrated unit.

THE CIRCUMSTANCES OF EARLY TRANSMISSION

More recent research has become cautious regarding the possibility that the pre-redactional material was transmitted orally. The reasons are as follows:

(1) The Israelite, Judean and Jewish tradition is accessible to us only through the preserved texts. All considerations regarding oral transmission are limited by the fact that the potential oral narratives must have been written down at some point in order to be available to us at all.[37] Under what circumstances did this occur? To what extent was the tradition reshaped or even reframed when it happened? How much was lost? And in any case, writing down

---

[33] Ibid., 42.

[34] Martin Noth, *Das System der zwölf Stämme Israels*, BWANT 52 (Stuttgart: Kohlhammer, 1930). For the history of research see Cornelis H. J. de Geus, *The Tribes of Israel: An Investigation into Some of the Presuppositions of Martin Noth's Amphictyony Hypothesis*, SSN 18 (Assen: Van Gorcum, 1976); Otto Bächli, *Amphiktyonie im Alten Testament: Forschungsgeschichtliche Studie zur Hypothese von Martin Noth* (Basel: Reinhardt, 1977).

[35] See A. Graeme Auld, "Amphictyony, Question of," in *Dictionary of the Old Testament: Historical Books*, ed. Bill T. Arnold and Hugh G. M. Williamson (Downers Grove, IL: InterVarsity Press, 2005), 26–32; Christoph Levin, "Amphictyony," *EBR*, vol. 1 (Berlin: De Gruyter, 2009), 1045–47.

[36] See Christoph Levin, "Das System der zwölf Stämme Israels," in *Congress Volume Paris 1992*, ed. John A. Emerton, VTSup 61 (Leiden: Brill, 1995), 163–78.

[37] See the debate documented in *The Interface of Orality and Writing: Speaking, Seeing, Writing in the Shaping of New Genres*, ed. Annette Weissenrieder and Robert B. Coote, WUNT 260 (Tübingen: Mohr Siebeck, 2010).

originally oral traditions must have been prompted by some kind of occasion and carried out in a specific institutional framework.

(2) Human memory has limits. This is true also of the collective memory of families, groups and peoples. Wherever we can observe oral transmission, it goes along with some modification of what is transmitted. Stable traditions require a regularly recurring occasion as well as institutional support. Oral tradition that is to survive in a fairly fixed form requires what is called a *Sitz im Leben*, that is, a firm place in public life, especially in the regular cult.

(3) Written tradition and oral transmission are not mutually exclusive. This applies particularly to largely illiterate societies, in which only a small elite possesses the skill to read and write. Texts were generally written to be read out and have therefore always been subject also to oral transmission and explication. David Carr has even plausibly suggested that for the narrative transmission of the Bible writing and memorizing went hand in hand: the texts were an indispensable aid in preserving oral memory and shaping a collective identity.[38] As a result, the written form automatically takes precedence over the oral tradition.

(4) Those texts that go back to the era of the monarchy before the Babylonian conquest of Jerusalem and were included in the Tanakh can only have been taken from official records. One can with good reason assume that the royal courts in Samaria and Jerusalem, as well as the associated temples had professional scribes and a scriptorium where traditional material was collected and recorded and the scrolls stored. This applies not only to legal documents and wisdom literature (which can be plausibly associated with kingship), and not only to cult-related texts (such as psalms), but also to the collected words of the prophets and the narrative tradition. What the royal archives had not preserved, no longer existed in the Second Temple period. The entire further text of the Bible was hence newly written under the circumstances of that time, which for the most part differed markedly.

A ROYAL FOCUS

The consequence of this last circumstance is that the truly old texts have a more or less pronounced royal focus. When they represent events or

---

[38] See David M. Carr, *Writing on the Tablet of the Heart: Origins of Scripture and Literature* (New York: Oxford University Press, 2005).

conditions of life, they are automatically guided by the worldview and interests of kingship. Even after the fall of the monarchy, further engagement with them was at least initially determined by the administrative and cult aristocracy.

Such a focus is to be assumed also for the book of Genesis. It has always been taken for granted for the primeval history, albeit generally tacitly rather than explicitly. After all, the ancient Near Eastern parallel texts, which have heavily influenced the interpretation of biblical accounts, usually have a royal focus: *Enuma elish* for the creation,[39] and the *Atraḫasīs Epic*[40] as well as the epic of *Gilgamesh*[41] for the flood story.

But it applies equally to the patriarchal narratives. To see this, one need not even point to the related promises such as: "Kings shall spring from you" (Gen 17:6; 35:11). Even in the late form of the present text, the patriarchal narratives echo the circumstances and values of kingship. Their focus is on the succession of the generations. The birth of sons, mostly with the aid of the deity, is the most important motif. This is reminiscent of the *Kirtu Epic* and the *'Aqhatu Legend* from Ugarit, both of which are set in a royal milieu and circle around the lack of offspring or of an heir to the throne.[42] A concern with genealogy is conspicuous throughout Genesis. This interest does not echo the self-image of tribes and families, as was long thought, but reflects the dynastic principle on which the kingship was founded.[43] In the Second Temple period this principle was gradually transferred to the Jewish community.

Even the chronology, which is extraneous to the narrative interest, imitates the royal succession. It is striking that all of the patriarchs are said to have been buried. This otherwise does not happen for ordinary

---

[39] Wilfred G. Lambert, *Babylonian Creation Myths* (Winona Lake, IN: Eisenbrauns, 2013); "Epic of Creation," trans. Benjamin R. Foster (*COS* 1.111).

[40] Wilfred G. Lambert and Alan R. Millard, *Atra-Ḥasīs: The Babylonian Story of the Flood* (Oxford: Clarendon Press, 1969); "Atra-Ḥasis," trans. Benjamin R. Foster (*COS* 1.130).

[41] Andrew R. George, *The Babylonian Gilgamesh Epic: Introduction, Critical Edition and Cuneiform Texts*, 2 vols. (Oxford: University Press, 2003); Stephanie Dalley, *Myths from Mesopotamia: Creation, the Flood, Gilgamesh, and Others*, rev. ed. (Oxford: University Press, 2000); "Gilgamesh," trans. Benjamin R. Foster (*COS* 1.132).

[42] CTA 14–16 = KTU 1.14–1.16 and CTA 17–19 = KTU 1.17–19; English translation: "The Legend of King Keret," trans. H. L Ginsberg (*ANET* 142–55); "Keret," trans. J. C. L. Gibson (*CML* 82–122); "The Kirta Epic," trans. Dennis Pardee (*COS* 1.102); "The 'Aqhatu Legend," trans. Dennis Pardee (*COS* 1.103).

[43] Tomoo Ishida, *The Royal Dynasties in Ancient Israel: A Study on the Formation and Development of Royal-Dynastic Ideology*, BZAW 142 (Berlin: de Gruyter, 1977), esp. 6–25: "The Dynastic Principle in the Monarchies in the Ancient Near East."

people, but does for kings. Abraham and Jacob found temples (see esp.
Gen 28) in the way as kings used to do. Isaac concludes a contract with
a king (Gen 26). The Joseph story takes place at Pharaoh's court. It is not
surprising that what is clearly the youngest text of Genesis, the narrative
of the war of the kings (Gen 14), has Abraham acting as a military
commander.[44]

PRE-EDITORIAL SOURCES WITHIN THE PRIMEVAL HISTORY

The creation account, with which the primeval history begins, derives
from a written source that the author of the Priestly Writing (P) used for
his account and commented on extensively. Here is a hypothetical version from before his additions:

> 1:1 In the beginning God created the heavens and the earth. 2 The
> earth was without form and void. ... 4b Then God separated the
> light from the darkness, 5 and God called the light Day, and the
> darkness he called Night. ... 7 And God made the firmament and
> separated the waters which were under the firmament from the
> waters which were above the firmament. ... 8 And God called the
> firmament Heaven. ... 9b (LXX) And the waters under the heavens
> were gathered together into their places, and the dry land appeared.
> 10 And God called the dry land Earth, and the waters that were
> gathered together he called Seas. ... 12 The earth brought forth
> vegetation, plants yielding seed according to their own kinds, and
> trees bearing fruit in which is their seed, each according to its
> kind. ... 16 And God made the two great lights, the greater light
> to rule the day, and the lesser light to rule the night; he made the
> stars also. 17 And God set them in the firmament of the heavens to
> give light upon the earth. ... 21 And God created the great sea
> monsters and every living creature that moves, with which the
> waters swarm, according to their kinds, and every winged bird
> according to its kind. ... 25 And God made the beasts of the earth
> according to their kinds and the cattle according to their kinds, and
> everything that creeps upon the ground according to its kind. ...
> 27 And God created man in his image. ... 2:1 Thus the heavens and
> the earth were finished, and all their host.

---

[44] On the late origin of Gen 14 see already Theodor Nöldeke, "Die Ungeschichtlichkeit
der Erzählung Gen. XIV," in *Untersuchungen zur Kritik des Alten Testaments* (Kiel:
Schwers, 1869), 154–72.

This document, which can be extracted from the extant text with ease, is an example of a speculative explanation of nature, one could say: an early form of natural science.[45] The original state is imagined as chaos and from it, everything existing is developed in only a few steps. Chaos is separated into its components and these are assigned temporal and spatial boundaries. They are defined (in the basic sense of the word) and hence given distinctive names. As soon as the change from day to night has been established, as soon as the heavenly ocean has been shielded by the firmament and the dry land has been separated from the seas, the plants emerge. Then the sky, the seas and the land are provided with living beings. This is done not by way of example, but by category, "according to their kinds." And finally humankind comes into being, whose sovereign task it will be to preserve the world order.

This account belongs more to the Persian than the Neo-Babylonian period. In its analytical style, it is close to early Greek philosophy of nature, which also emerges around this time. A single, unchallenged God brings forth the existing world. This is also why the frequent attempts to compare this account with Near Eastern myths produce only uneven results. The worldview put forward is so radically different from that of myth that it would be wrong even to identify here an attitude critical of myth, which has so often been sought in Gen 1.[46]

The situation is different for the second creation account, which is faintly reminiscent of the Babylonian epic of creation (and other myths) at least in its beginning, where the primordial world is characterized, among others, by the absence of plants:

> 2:5 When no plant of the field was yet in the earth and no herb of the field had yet sprung up ... 7 then ... God formed man ... and breathed into his nostrils the breath of life. ... 8 And ... God planted a garden in Eden, in the east; and there he put the man whom he had formed. ... 19 Then ... God formed ... every beast of the field and every bird of the air and brought them to the man. ...

---

[45] See Christoph Levin, "Tatbericht und Wortbericht in der priesterschriftlichen Schöpfungserzählung," *ZTK* 91 (1994): 115–33. See also Werner H. Schmidt, *Die Schöpfungsgeschichte der Priesterschrift*, WMANT 17, 3rd ed. (Neukirchen-Vluyn: Neukirchener Verlag, 1973), 160–63.

[46] See Jan Christian Gertz, "Antibabylonische Polemik im priesterlichen Schöpfungsbericht?" *ZTK* 106 (2009): 137–55, against Hermann Gunkel, *Creation and Chaos in the Primeval Era and the Eschaton: A Religio-Historical Study of Genesis 1 and Revelation 12*, trans. K. William Whitney Jr. (Grand Rapids, MI: Eerdmans, 2006); trans. of *Schöpfung und Chaos in Urzeit und Endzeit: Eine religionsgeschichtliche Untersuchung über Gen 1 und Ap Joh 12* (Göttingen: Vandenhoeck & Ruprecht, 1895).

20 And the man gave names to all the birds of the air and to every beast of the field. ... 21 Then ... God caused a deep sleep to fall upon the man, and while he slept took one of his ribs and closed up its place with flesh. 22 And ... God made the rib ... into a woman and brought her to the man, ... 3:20 and the man called his wife's name Eve, because she was the mother of all living. 21 And ... God made for the man and his wife garments of skins, and clothed them. ... 4:1 Now the man knew Eve his wife, and she conceived and bore Cain.

Compare *Enuma elish* I 6–7, 9: "(When) no cane brake was intertwined nor thicket matted close, when no gods at all had been brought forth, ... then were the gods formed ... " In contrast, in Gen 2 it is not the gods that are created first, but the one God creates man. In doing so, he works like a potter. After blowing breath into the nose of his creation, he plants a garden in the East, in Eden, for him to live in. Then God creates the animals and finally woman from a rib taken from man. Soon, the first humans have a son, Cain. The sequence of generations that begins with him leads to Noah and his three sons Shem, Ham and Japheth. This sequence, to which notes on the development of cultural techniques were later added (4:2, 17, 20–22: sheep farming, agriculture, building of towns, music, blacksmithing), leads onto the table of nations 10:2–7, 20, 22–23, 31, which registers the peoples of the contemporary world by location and language, and inscribes them in a genealogy. The table of nations was originally an independent document of ancient geographical history. It was probably created in the seventh century, since Babylonia and Persia are not mentioned, but Assyria is. It is remarkable that the Mediterranean West (Javan = Greece, Elishah = Cyprus, Tarshish = Spain) is included in detail.

At a later, already editorial stage, the anthropogony, which is the foundation of the primeval history, saw a number of significant additions.

(1) A first addition is that of Abel (= Hebr. "vanity") as the brother of Cain, the first human son, who was soon to be murdered by his elder brother in the first occurrence of human death (Gen 4).

(2) To the creation of man was added the motif that man and his wife lost their state of childlike innocence by an (involuntary) transgression of divine commandment and suddenly came to know good and evil, meaning that they acquired adult judgment.

(3) Even later, the figure of the tempter was added in order to relieve the humans once again of the burden of this sin.[47] The role of the snake has triggered many associations with mythical traditions, but no clear parallels are evident. The cherubs, who guard the way to the tree of life, have many iconographical parallels, however.[48]

(4) The story of the flood was also inserted. With it, chaos makes a return before mankind spreads across the earth. A similar sequence of events is also known from the Akkadian *Atraḫasīs Epic*. Thanks to the care of the god YHWH, the flood hero Noah survives and becomes the second father of mankind.

In the extensive flood story Gen 6–9, only a brief kernel of the Yahwist's version can be identified as pre-editorial text:

> 7:10 After seven days ... 12 rain fell upon the earth forty days and forty nights. ... 17 And the waters increased, and bore up the ark, and it rose high above the earth. ... 22 Everything on the dry land in whose nostrils was the breath of life died ... 23 and were blotted out from the earth. ... 8:6a At the end of forty days ... 2 the rain from the heavens was restrained, 3 and the waters receded from the earth continually. ... 6b Then Noah opened the window of the ark which he had made, 7 and sent forth a raven; and it went to and fro until the waters were dried up from the earth.

The editor has rendered the religiously significant scenes at the beginning and end in his own words. Where the Akkadian epics speak of the conflict among the gods, the Bible has the monologue of the god YHWH. The later elaboration of the flood account clearly also incorporates additional knowledge of the narrative tradition. This is evident especially in the birds scene 8:8–12, which has a parallel in Gilgamesh XI 145–54.[49] External influence is also apparent in the version in the Priestly Writing, which has further details, such as the building of the ark.

The primeval history ends with the account of the building of the tower of Babel, which results in the diversity of languages and the scattering of mankind across the earth. Contrary to earlier attempts to

---

[47] See Christoph Levin, "Genesis 2–3: A Case of Innerbiblical Interpretation," in *Genesis and Christian Theology*, ed. Nathan MacDonald et al. (Grand Rapids, MI: Eerdmans, 2012), 85–100.

[48] In its broad strokes, this addition was identified by Hartmut Gese, "Der bewachte Lebensbaum und die Heroen: Zwei mythologische Ergänzungen zur Urgeschichte der Quelle J," in *Vom Sinai zum Zion*, BEvT 64 (Munich: Kaiser, 1974), 99–112.

[49] See Othmar Keel, *Vögel als Boten*, OBO 14 (Freiburg [Schweiz]: Universitätsverlag, 1977), 79–91.

identify a pre-existing tradition in this account,[50] more recently the view that this text is editorial in origin has been gaining momentum.[51]

PRE-EDITORIAL SOURCES IN THE PATRIARCHAL NARRATIVES

The story of Abraham, Isaac and Jacob is based on three great, elegant narratives: (1) the courtship on Isaac's behalf in Gen 24, (2) the stealing of the blessing by Jacob in Gen 27, and (3) Jacob's marriage with the daughters of Laban and the birth of his sons in Gen 29–30. These three narrative units have been sewn together with only a few stitches to create a sequence of generations. The courtship leads directly into Rebekah's pregnancy, which in turn produces the two rivals of Gen 27:

> 24:67aβ And he (Isaac) took Rebekah, and she became his wife; and he loved her, ... 25:21bβ and Rebekah his wife conceived. ... 24 When her days to be delivered were fulfilled, behold, there were twins in her womb. 25 The first came forth ..., and they called his name Esau. 26 Afterward his brother came forth, and his hand had taken hold of Esau's heel, so his name was called Jacob. ... 27 When the boys grew up, Esau was a skillful hunter, a man of the field, while Jacob was a quiet man, dwelling in tents.

Once Jacob has cheated his brother Esau of his father's blessing with his mother's aid, he flees to Rebekah's brother Laban (28:10). At this point, the story of how he acquired his wives and children begins. Then he returns and reconciles with Esau (Gen 31–33).

These three narratives, which contain numerous extensions in their present form, are preceded by the birth of Abraham's two sons. Since Sarah did not give birth to a child at first, she supplies Abraham with her maid Hagar as a wife, who bears him Ishmael (16:1, 3aα, b, 4a, 15). Later, Sarah too becomes pregnant and gives birth to Isaac (21:2–3, 8), whose marriage is related in Gen 24.

---

[50] See recently esp. Christoph Uehlinger, *Weltreich und "eine Rede": Eine neue Deutung der sogenannten Turmbauerzählung (Gen 11,1–9)*, OBO 101 (Freiburg [Switzerland]: Universitätsverlag, 1990).

[51] Levin, *Der Jahwist*, 127–29; Reinhard G. Kratz, *The Composition of the Narrative Books of the Old Testament*, trans. John Bowden (London: T & T Clark, 2005), 255–56; trans. of *Die Komposition der erzählenden Bücher des Alten Testaments* (Göttingen: Vandenhoeck & Ruprecht, 2000); Jan Christian Gertz, *Das erste Buch Mose (Genesis): Die Urgeschichte Gen 1–11*, ATD 1 (Göttingen: Vandenhoeck & Ruprecht, 2018), 330–31.

These stories also have been determined by the interests and experiences at court. This is evident from the fact that they correspond to numerous such motifs found within and outside the Old Testament.[52] The family constellations that serve as the stories' basis reflect processes which have been decisive for the survival of a dynasty. All events play out within the family and what is more, the continuity of the family is their main subject. The stories relate how the protagonists acquire their wives, how the wives could become pregnant, and how the sons are born. The order of succession is always particularly important and indeed seems important to such an extent that one might think that dynastic succession rules applied to Abraham, Isaac, and Jacob.

With every change in generation, a struggle breaks out.[53] The first case of rivalry is that of Isaac and Ishmael. Since Sarah has no children, she offers Abraham her maid Hagar, an Egyptian woman. Since Hagar is Sarah's property, Hagar's son is, at least legally speaking, also Sarah's son. When this threatens to challenge Sarah's status as mistress ($g^e bir\bar{a}h$), she appeals to Abraham, who allows her to exile Hagar and Ishmael (16:1–3aα, b–6). When Sarah does finally become pregnant herself, this then allows her to make her natural child Isaac the sole heir (21:1b–2a, 3).

The role-play is even more transparent during the conflict between Jacob and Esau.[54] Already the sentence framing the scene is reminiscent of the transition from David to Solomon: "Now King David was old and advanced in years" (1 Kgs 1:1), – "When Isaac was old" (Gen 27:1). The driving force behind the plan to invert the brothers' ranks is the mother.[55] When the plot is revealed, Rebekah bids her son flee abroad to her brother Laban (27:43–45) – a pattern commonly found with usurpers, who bide their time abroad, waiting for an opportunity: David fled to king Achish of Gath (1 Sam 27:2), Absalom to king Talmai of Geshur (2 Sam 13:37), Jeroboam to Pharaoh Shoshenq of Egypt (1 Kgs 11:40). This role-play thus has Jacob embody the stock

---

[52] See Urmas Nõmmik, *Die Vätererzählungen im Licht höfischer Erzählkunst: Motivkritische Studien zu den Überlieferungen von Lot, Isaak, Rebekka und Jakob,* FAT (Tübingen: Mohr Siebeck, 2022).

[53] See also Benedikt Hensel, *Die Vertauschung des Erstgeburtssegens in der Genesis,* BZAW 423 (Berlin: de Gruyter, 2011), who moreover sees the basic structure of the book's narrative revealed in this motif. This is not borne out by the evidence.

[54] See the analysis of the history of this motif in Nõmmik, *Die Vätererzählungen,* 38–57.

[55] See Christoph Levin, "Das Amt der Königinmutter in Israel und Juda," in *Natur – Geschlecht – Politik,* ed. Andreas Höfele and Beate Kellner (Paderborn: Fink, 2020), 37–67, here 50–51.

character type of the "king of Israel," as well as potentially being their ancestor.

Only the two stories about Isaac in Gen 26 that interrupt the continuity from Gen 25 to 27 have a different subject matter. They are probably a fragment of another set of narratives that is otherwise lost. Here, Isaac too has a royal counterpart: King Abimelech of Gerar. The depiction adheres to the narrative formula of "conflict resolution," which is amply attested.[56]

A number of scenes were later added to this family story in order to turn it into a history of the origins of the people of Israel. Jacob especially, the third one in this sequence of generations, was given the role of a representative. On his flight to Laban, he founds the shrine at Bethel as though he were one of the early kings of Israel (28:11–19). The dream of Jacob also has a parallel in Solomon's dream at the beginning of his reign (1 Kgs 3:4–15).[57] Upon his return, Jacob names the hill country of Gilead (31:48), founds Mahanaim in Transjordan (32:2–3), plants the Deborah tree at Luz (35:8) and builds the tomb of Rachel near Ephrath (35:20). Particularly spectacular is his wrestling match with a demon while crossing the Jabbok (32:23–33). The event is comparable to the fight between Enkidu and Gilgamesh, the legendary king of Uruk, on the second tablet of the epic of Gilgamesh.[58]

The story of Abraham was expanded by adding the tradition of Lot, a local etiology that claims that the city of Sodom once stood where the Dead Sea is now. It perished because of the blasphemy of its inhabitants (Gen 19). Having escaped the inferno, Lot sired Moab and Ammon with his two daughters, and these two sons in turn became the progenitors of the kingdoms of Transjordan (19:30–38).

The setting of this ex-post nationalization is the Northern Kingdom of Israel as well as its sphere of influence. It is hence remarkable that the monarchy is not mentioned in the stories. Instead, Jacob especially assumes the role of the king. With due caution, one might therefore suggest that this transformation of the text took place after the end of the monarchy, which was defeated by the Assyrians in 722. It may have been carried out by members of the elite, who fled to Judah during the conquest of Samaria. This may be supported by the (superficial) impression that the stories reflect the situation of an itinerant minority. One is struck, for instance,

[56] See Nõmmik, *Die Vätererzählungen*, 157–81.
[57] Ibid., 67–78, who also gives numerous examples of kings' prophetic dreams.
[58] Old Babylonian version according to the Pennsylvania Tablet, lines 196–240, and Standard version, column II, lines 100–15. See Esther J. Hamori, "Echoes of Gilgamesh in the Jacob Story," *JBL* 130 (2011): 625–42.

by the wide geographical horizon of the tales: Abraham settles in the steppe near Egypt (20:1). Isaak lives in Beer-sheba on the south-western border of Judah (28:10). Their clan of origin, however, lives in northern Syria (24:4, 10; 27:43).

THE PRE-EDITORIAL JOSEPH STORY

The oldest form of the story of Joseph and his brothers is a folktale (German *Märchen*). Its setting is, as in many such tales, the family and it begins with a conflict among brothers. The father prefers his youngest son and thus makes him the object of his brothers' jealousy. They rid themselves of him by selling Joseph to travelling merchants (Gen 37). These take him to Egypt, where he ends up a slave in a wealthy man's house (Gen 39). The man's wife attempts to seduce him, but when he rejects her, she wrongfully accuses him to her husband. Innocent, he is thrown in jail. Fate has now struck him twice. In prison, he proves a successful interpreter of dreams, who can reveal the futures of the other captives (Gen 40). Sometime later, the pharaoh is troubled by worrying dreams, yet no one can make sense of their portents. This prompts the cupbearer to remember the slave who predicted his fortune in prison. Joseph is brought and can immediately reveal the meaning of the pharaoh's dreams (Gen 41). The pharaoh makes Joseph second only to himself and Egypt is spared a terrible famine thanks to his help.

This sequence of events fits a folktale perfectly. As such, no religious justification of the events was originally given. The injustice Joseph experiences corrects itself, as is usually the case in such kinds of narrative. Behind the seduction by "Potiphar's wife" (39:6–20) one can detect the Egyptian *Tale of the Two Brothers* documented in the papyrus D'Orbiney, dating to the late nineteenth dynasty.[59] Yhwh's intervention was added only later (39:2, 3, 5, 21, 23). In this way, the story of Joseph was fleshed out and transformed into a novella that portrays the eventful life of its protagonist as an example of Yhwh's guidance.

THE EDITORIAL SHAPE OF THE BOOK

Form and tradition criticism of the book of Genesis encompasses all phases of its literary process of transformation, beginning with oral

---

[59] English translation: "The Two Brothers" (*AEL* 2:203–11); "The Two Brothers," trans. Miriam Lichtheim (*COS* 1.40).

tradition and ending with the current state of the extant book. Or, if one
were being more methodologically precise: it begins with the extant
book and challenges it step by step, all the way back to the oral prehistory
some of its different elements may have had.

The narrative outline of the book is based on a historiographical
work that largely consists in the part of the text that was traditionally
assigned to the Yahwist (J) under the documentary hypothesis. Since the
1960s, however, redaction-critical study has ultimately shown that the
older view of the Yahwist as a storyteller who, much like the Greek
historian Herodotus, compiled traditional stories and rendered them in
his own words, cannot explain the state of the matter.[60] As such, this
view is now held only by few.[61] The literary structure of the text shows
that the Yahwist compiled his work from existing literary sources,
choosing and taking out of context those parts he wished to use, and
then arranged them and added his comments. The Yahwist worked the
way an editor does.[62]

Similar things can be said of the younger Pentateuch source, the
Priestly Writing (P). In its case, its literary origin is evident and scholars
broadly agree on this.

Another, later redaction created the basis of the extant book of
Genesis (including the subsequent historical accounts extant in the
books Exodus to Deuteronomy) by combining the two continuous historiographical works J and P into a single narrative.[63] In the primeval
history Gen 1–11 the compiler used the Priestly Writing as the main
source. Beginning with Gen 12, this changes and the Yahwist's history
becomes the literary basis due to the predominance of its narrative
substance. The thin thread of the Priestly Writing was woven into the

---

[60] See Hans Walter Wolff, "Das Kerygma des Jahwisten," in *Gesammelte Studien zum
       Alten Testament*, 2nd ed., TB 22 (Munich: Kaiser, 1973), 345–73; Rudolf Kilian, *Die
       vorpriesterlichen Abrahamsüberlieferungen literarkritisch und traditionsgeschichtlich
       untersucht*, BBB 24 (Bonn: Hanstein, 1966); Volkmar Fritz, *Israel in der Wüste:
       Traditionsgeschichtliche Untersuchung der Wüstenüberlieferung des Jahwisten*,
       MThSt 7 (Marburg: Elwert, 1970); Erich Zenger, *Die Sinaitheophanie: Untersuchungen
       zum jahwistischen und elohistischen Geschichtswerk*, FzB 3 (Würzburg: Echter, 1971).

[61] An important exception is John Van Seters, *Abraham in History and Tradition* (New
       Haven, CT: Yale University Press, 1975); John Van Seters, *Prologue to History: The
       Yahwist as Historian in Genesis* (Zurich: Theologischer Verlag, 1992); John Van
       Seters, *The Edited Bible: The Curious History of the "Editor" in Biblical Criticism*
       (Winona Lake, IN: Eisenbrauns, 2006).

[62] Levin, *Der Jahwist*; Christoph Levin, "The Yahwist: The Earliest Editor in the
       Pentateuch," *JBL* 126 (2007): 209–30.

[63] See Christoph Levin, "Die Redaktion R^{JP} in der Urgeschichte," in *Auf dem Weg zur
       Endgestalt von Genesis bis II Regum: Festschrift Hans-Christoph Schmitt*, ed.
       Martin Beck and Ulrike Schorn, BZAW 370 (Berlin: de Gruyter, 2006), 15–34.

tapestry of stories. This has raised the question, whether in the extent of the patriarchal history the Priestly Writing was really an independent work or rather a literary supplement.[64] As it stands, this question remains difficult to answer.[65]

After the literary framework of the book had been created in this way, a history of literary addition and adaptation began.

THE GENRE OF THE PRESENT BOOK

The final version of Genesis is firmly attested in the second century BCE through the Greek translation of the Septuagint. It is an integral part of the Torah. "*Torah*" is also an appropriate term for the *literary genre* that this book represents as a whole: "Teaching", or normative religious writing. It is crucial to understand that Genesis was not declared Torah by an external act at some later point in time, but that the literary process that gave the book its current shape was from very early on affected by the fact that the texts it contains have religious significance or even a normative quality. As such, the book of Genesis could also be categorized as *religious tradition literature*. One must add, however, that ancient Judaism also drew its ethnic identity from religious tradition. Genesis is therefore, together with the following books of the Torah, akin to a *Jewish national epic*, with a significance comparable to that of Homer for the Greeks and of Virgil's *Aeneid* for Rome.

As both ethnic origin story and religious norm, the book of Genesis continued – like the entire Torah – to be added to and updated into the late period. The process of exegesis so characteristic of its impact on Judaism and the Christian churches begins already in the biblical text itself. The extent of these additions is substantial. At least half its current text was added to the "completed" book in this manner. Almost no passage is without trace of this process of self-exegesis. This too informs an aspect of the book's genre, making it *religious exegetical literature*. These additions are the literary result of an extensive debate about the text that may be plausibly imagined to have taken place in a temple school, library and scriptorium, most likely in Jerusalem.

---

[64] Frank M. Cross, *Canaanite Myth and Hebrew Epic: Essays in the History of the Religion of Israel* (Cambridge, MA: Harvard University Press, 1973), 324–25; Erhard Blum, *Die Komposition der Vätergeschichte*, WMANT 57 (Neukirchen-Vluyn: Neukirchener Verlag, 1984), 426–27.

[65] See Erhard Blum, "Once Again: The Literary Historical Profile of the P-Tradition," in *A Farewell to the Priestly Document?*, ed. Friedhelm Hartenstein and Konrad Schmid (Atlanta, GA: SBL-Press, 2022), forthcoming.

The parts of the present book produced in that way can best be designated and organized by subject. They deal with questions relating, for
instance, to the ethnic identity of Judaism in the ancient world. They
establish religious customs of the Jewish community and prescribe the
behavior of its members. They contemplate fundamental anthropological
questions regarding man's role and station in the world. They discuss
theological problems, especially the question of God's justice, which grew
particularly acute in Hellenistic Judaism due to the emergence of
monotheism.

There are three reasons why such questions have left their traces
predominantly on the book of Genesis:

(1) Important developments, decisions or rules are often placed at the
beginning of history. This makes them truly fundamentally valid.
The book of Genesis provided the means of making some of them
prior even to the creation of God's people, thus rendering them
anthropological universals.

(2) The patriarchal narratives being framed as family history resonated
with the reality of Jewish life in the Hellenistic world, which for the
most part no longer lived in a homogenous, contiguously resident
population, but in family structures, which were now the social
context in which the religious and ethnic specificity of Judaism
were experienced and passed on. This naturally included the
discourse about rites, customs, and law.

(3) The story of Jacob and his sons provided a framework in which the
development of the exceptional identity of Judaism and its relation
to God could be presented and justified.

These three reasons have in common that they all derive and justify
a current situation, real or ideal, from an alleged origin in a protological time.

At a literary level, these additions have in common that they are
presented not as the descriptions and discussions they de facto are, but
have been dressed up as storytelling. They integrate into the narrative
flow of the book rather than interrupting it with elaboration. This makes
them part of the narrated world.

In many cases, the questions arose from the extant text. They antici-
pate that form of exegesis for which later Judaism coined the term
midrash.[66] The difference is merely that the later midrash, transmitted

---

[66]   See Isaac Leo Seeligmann, "Voraussetzungen der Midraschexegese," in *Congress
Volume, Copenhagen 1953*, ed. G. W. Anderson et al., VTSup 1 (Leiden: Brill, 1953),
150–81.

primarily in Genesis Rabba,[67] keeps interpretation and its biblical basis separate. Inner-biblical midrash, by contrast, introduces its interpretation into the handed-down text. Since Genesis consists mainly of narrative, inner-biblical midrash too is mainly *haggadah*, as narrative midrash was later called. This does not exclude the possibility that the *haggadah* is combined with pedagogical and instructive intent; that is, with what was later called *halachah*. The boundaries between the two forms have been fluid in any case.

EXAMPLES OF LATE ADDITIONS

Ancient Judaism is characterized by a close relation between ethnic and religious identity. The ethnic identity is determined by genealogy, the religious mainly by custom and law.

The *idea of the tribes of Israel* emerged to serve as the foundation of this ethnic identity and eventually led to the system of the twelve tribes. In 29:31–30:24 and 35:16–18 political and topographical units of Israel and Judah were gradually added onto the birth of Jacob's sons Reuben, Simeon, Joseph, and Ben-Oni in a series of steps. Judah, Dan, Naphthali, etc. were declared sons of Jacob by personalizing them in ancestral fathers. Gen 35:22b–26 later summed up the matter: "The sons of Jacob were twelve."

In 46:8–27 a tribal list of seventy descendants of Jacob was derived from the twelve eponyms. These seventy were thought to have come to Egypt with Jacob. In 49:1b–28 the dying Jacob was made to grant his sons a blessing. To create it, an older sequence of tribal sayings was used, as is evident especially from the animal similes in vv. 9, 14, 17, 21, 27. Other information was extrapolated from the narratives of Genesis (vv. 3–7). Older than the blessing given the twelve sons is Jacob's blessing of Ephraim and Manasseh in Gen 48. They are sons not of Jacob but of Joseph (41:50–52). In order to correct this incongruence, Jacob adopts them and grants them the same status as Reuben and Simeon (48:5). This shows that the tribal system could not be implemented without contradictions and upheaval. In the Joseph story, Reuben (37:21–22, 29–30; 42:22, 37) and Judah (37:26–27; 43:3–5, 8–10; 44:14–34) take turns acting as spokesman of the brothers. In 49:3–4 Reuben finally loses this privilege with reference to 35:22a. In the basic version of the Tamar

---

[67] *Midrash Bereshit rabah*, vols. 1–3, ed. J. Theodor and H. Albek, 2nd ed. (Yerushalayim: Sifre Yahrman, 1965); English translation: J. Neusner, *Genesis rabbah: The Judaic Commentary to the Book of Genesis: a new American Translation*, vols. 1–3, BJS 104–6 (Atlanta, GA: Scholars Press, 1985).

story, extant in 38:1, 6*, 18b, 27–30, the birth of Jacob and Esau (25:24–
26) is re-enacted through the birth of the twins Perez and Zerah in such
a way that Judah is put into Isaac's position as if he were the father of
Jacob/Israel.[68]

The special relationship between Israel and God is also prefigured in
Genesis. This is done through the motif of the covenant that the Priestly
Writing understood as a promise of the relation with God. The promise is
first expressed in the covenant with Noah after the primordial catastrophe of the flood (9:1, 11). It is repeated in the covenant with Abraham
(17:4–8), is reaffirmed for Jacob (35:10–12) and finally leads into the
promise of the Shekinah at Sinai (Exod 25:1–2, 8; 29:43, 45).

Two important *boundary markers of Judaism* seem likewise to have
been given their origin stories in the book of Genesis. The Sabbath was
linked to the creation of the world and added into the creation account of
the Priestly Writing. It is considered so fundamental that even God
himself is said to have submitted to the rhythm of six working days
and a day of rest when he created the world (Gen 1:5b, 8b, 13, 19, 23,
31b; 2:2–3). Circumcision was connected to Abraham, who circumcised
his sons and male household slaves at God's command (17:10–14; 21:4)
and was also circumcised himself (17:23–27).

Questions of family law were also dealt with. The story of Jacob's
daughter Dinah treats the circumstances under which a Jewish woman
could be married to a non-Jew:

> 34:1 Dinah the daughter of Leah, whom she had borne to Jacob,
> went out to visit the daughters of the land; 2 and when Shechem
> the son of Hamor ..., the prince of the land, saw her, ... 3 his soul
> was drawn to Dinah the daughter of Jacob, and he loved the
> maiden. ... 4 So Shechem spoke to his father Hamor, saying, Get
> me this child for my wife. ... 7 The sons of Jacob came in from the
> field, ... 8 and Hamor spoke with them, saying, The soul of my son
> Shechem longs for your daughter; I pray you, give her to him in
> marriage. ... 13 The sons of Jacob answered Shechem and his father
> Hamor ... 14 and said to them, We cannot do this thing, to give our
> sister to one who is uncircumcised. ... 15 However, on this condi-
> tion will we consent to you: that you will become as we are and
> every male of you be circumcised. ... 19 And the young man did

---

[68] Christoph Levin, "Tamar erhält ihr Recht (Genesis 38)," in *Diasynchron: Walter
Dietrich zum 65. Geburtstag*, ed. Thomas Naumann and Regine Hunziker-Rodewald
(Stuttgart: Kohlhammer, 2009), 279–98.

not delay to do the thing, because he had delight in Jacob's daughter. He was the most honored of all his family.

The sons of Jacob tell Hamor that circumcision is imperative, quoting the commandment of Gen 17:10 in support, and Shechem submits to it without hesitation. The further development of this intricate story is then determined by the prohibition of the connubium in Deut 7:3 coming into play.[69]

Another paradigm case for family law is the later version of the Tamar story in Gen 38. It relates how Tamar craftily enforces the right to offspring Deut 25:5–10 accords her.[70]

In addition to providing justification for specific modern practices, some later editions can also be categorized based on specific theological concerns which they add to the text, such as humility or justice. The primeval history, for example, saw an anthropologically significant expansion that one might call the *humility edition*.[71] This edition added the tree of life to Gen 2–3 and had God bar access to it, rendering immortality a missed opportunity (2:9bα; 3:19b, 22, 24). In Gen 6:3 God limits the lifespan of humans to 120 years and in the story about the Tower of Babel, he confuses the language of humankind to limit their power (11:1, 3a, 6b–7, 8b–9).[72]

Old Testament wisdom is made evident especially in the story of Joseph. The figure of Joseph transformed from the blessed child of the original folktale into a pious sage, who abides by the Torah (Gen 39:9). His knowledge of the future comes from God (40:8; 41:16, 25, 39). Joseph is presented as the righteous prophet.[73] It was not long before he became the model for the apocalyptic prophet Daniel.

The most fundamental problem of Jewish religion is that of *the justice of God*. The premise that God acts justly under any circumstances is in evidence throughout the additions to the narrative texts of the Tanakh. In the book of Genesis there are numerous additions that

---

69   See Christoph Levin, "Dina: Wenn die Schrift wider sich selbst lautet," in *Schriftauslegung in der Schrift: Festschrift für Odil Hannes Steck*, ed. Reinhard G. Kratz et al., BZAW 300 (Berlin: De Gruyter, 2000), 61–72.

70   See Levin, "Tamar erhält ihr Recht."

71   Following Markus Witte, *Vom Leiden zur Lehre: Der dritte Redegang (Hiob 21–27) und die Redaktionsgeschichte des Hiobbuches*, BZAW 230 (Berlin: de Gruyter, 1994), esp. 175–79. Note the quotation of Job 42:2 in Gen 11:6.

72   The essential features of this edition were identified by Hartmut Gese, "Der bewachte Lebensbaum und die Heroen" (see above n. 48).

73   See Christoph Levin, "Josefsgeschichte und späte Chokma," in *Fromme und Frevler: Studien zu Psalmen und Weisheit: Festschrift für Hermann Spieckermann*, ed. Corinna Körting and Reinhard G. Kratz (Tübingen: Mohr Siebeck, 2020), 353–70.

can be summarized under the heading of *justice edition*.[74] Especially the great catastrophes invariably raise the question of God's justice. The question is made explicit in the conversation between Abraham and YHWH that has obviously been inserted between Gen 18:22a and 33b.[75] The base version identifies the problem at stake:

> 22b Abraham remained standing before YHWH. 23 Then Abraham came near and said, Will you indeed sweep away the righteous with the wicked? 24 Suppose there are fifty righteous within the city. . . . 25 Far be it from you to do such a thing, to slay the righteous with the wicked, so that the righteous fare as the wicked! . . . 26 And YHWH said, If I find at Sodom fifty righteous in the city, I will forgive the whole place for their sake.

This dialogue with God is in fact a theological debate. As far as its literary form is concerned, what Gerhard von Rad observed for Gen 15 applies: "The dialogue between Yahweh and Abraham is supplied with the bare minimum of background, and certainly owes much more to rigidly theological cogitation than to popular narrative tradition."[76] It is typical of the problem being discussed that the dialogue was further extended in two additional steps until God finally grants that he will spare the entire town if ten just people are to be found within it. The Sodom story in Gen 19 was extended at the same time to make clear that the inhabitants of the town had all sinned, ensuring that the punishment was indeed just.

The other great catastrophe was the great flood, which no one but Noah and his family survived. It is theologically imperative that God acted righteously even in this unsurpassable summary judgment. To ensure this, a claim was added to both prologue and epilogue: "YHWH saw . . . that every inclination of the thoughts of their hearts was only evil continually" (Gen 6:5). All who perished in the flood were sinners at heart.

As regards action and suffering, justice mainly has an impact on the individual. The motif is at its most dramatic in the Aqedah narrative in Gen 22:1–19, in which God commands Abraham to sacrifice his son Isaac

---

[74] On this see also Christoph Levin, "Gerechtigkeit Gottes in der Genesis," in *Studies in the Book of Genesis: Literature, Redaction and History*, ed. André Wénin, BETL 155 (Leuven: Peeters, 2001), 347–57.

[75] See Julius Wellhausen, *Die Composition des Hexateuchs*, 4th ed. (Berlin: de Gruyter, 1963), 25: "I think at any rate that 18:22a and 18:33b originally joined" (my translation).

[76] Gerhard von Rad, "Faith Reckoned as Righteousness," in *The Problem of the Hexateuch and Other Essays*, trans. E. W. Trueman Dicken (Edinburgh: Oliver & Boyd, 1966), 125–30, here 125.

and thus controverts the promise given. The story is not traditional, but uses the older patriarchal narratives as building blocks to illustrate a theological problem.[77] Abraham obeys without hesitation. He is rewarded with a replacement sacrifice and God vigorously renews the promise made.

The story of Abraham and Sarah encountering king Abimelech in Gerar (Gen 20) was likewise constructed for theological reasons. It makes use of the example of adultery, which is prohibited in Deut 22:22, to discuss the problem of subjective innocence in the face of objective guilt. To do so, the story uses a traditional case, that of Isaac and Rebekah narrated in Gen 26:1–11.

Another example is that of Joseph in Gen 39, who resists being tempted by another man's wife in Egypt and thus provides a model of obedience to the Torah. References to the prohibition of adultery in Deut 22:22 were later added into the story in verses 8–11, 13–15, 18–19.[78]

The justice edition deals extensively with the behavior of Joseph's brothers. Since the brothers are the fathers of the people of God, they too must have been righteous, strictly speaking. Judah and Reuben are hence retroactively said to have wanted to save Joseph from death in Gen 37. In Egypt, the brothers are badly frightened and thus punished for the injustice they inflicted on Joseph. Ultimately, however, through God's guidance, everything turns out well: "Joseph said to them, Do not be afraid! As for you, you meant evil against me; but God meant it for good" (Gen 50:20). God can bring his good intention to fruition even through the evil will of men. And with this reassuring conclusion, the book of Genesis ends in its current form.

SELECT BIBLIOGRAPHY

Blum, Erhard. *Die Komposition der Vätergeschichte*. WMANT 57. Neukirchen-Vluyn: Neukirchener Verlag, 1984.

Carr, David M. *Writing on the Tablet of the Heart: Origins of Scripture and Literature*. New York: Oxford University Press, 2005.

Gertz, Jan Christian. "Antibabylonische Polemik im priesterlichen Schöpfungsbericht?" *ZTK* 106 (2009): 137–55.

---

[77] See Christoph Levin, "Die Prüfung Abrahams (Genesis 22) und ihre innerbiblischen Bezüge," *ZTK* 118 (2021): 397–421.

[78] See Christoph Levin, "Righteousness in the Joseph Story: Joseph Resists Seduction (Genesis 39)," in *The Pentateuch: International Perspectives on Current Research*, ed. Thomas A. Dozeman et al., FAT 78 (Tübingen: Mohr Siebeck, 2011), 223–40.

Gunkel, Hermann. *Genesis: Translated and Interpreted*. Translated by Mark
    E. Biddle. Mercer Library of Biblical Studies. Macon, GA: Mercer
    University Press, 1997. Translation of *Genesis übersetzt und erklärt*.
    HKAT 1.1. 3rd revised edition. Göttingen: Vandenhoeck & Ruprecht, 1910.

Köckert, Matthias. *Vätergott und Väterverheißungen: Eine Auseinandersetzung
    mit Albrecht Alt und seinen Erben*. FRLANT 142. Göttingen: Vandenhoeck
    & Ruprecht, 1988.

Levin, Christoph. "Gerechtigkeit Gottes in der Genesis." Pages 347–57 in *Studies
    in the Book of Genesis: Literature, Redaction and History*. Edited by
    André Wénin. BETL 155. Leuven: Peeters, 2001.

Levin, Christoph. *Der Jahwist*. FRLANT 157. Göttingen: Vandenhoeck &
    Ruprecht, 1993.

Levin, Christoph. "Das System der zwölf Stämme Israels." Pages 163–78 in
    Congress Volume: Paris, 1992. Edited by John A. Emerton. VTSup 61.
    Leiden: Brill, 1995.

Levin, Christoph. "Tatbericht und Wortbericht in der priesterschriftlichen
    Schöpfungserzählung." *ZTK* 91 (1994): 115–33.

Mowinckel, Sigmund. "Das ätiologische Denken." Pages 78–86 in *Tetrateuch –
    Pentateuch – Hexateuch: Die Berichte über die Landnahme in den drei
    altisraelitischen Geschichtswerken*. BZAW 90. Berlin: Töpelmann, 1964.

Nõmmik, Urmas. *Die Vätererzählungen im Lichte höfischer Erzählkunst:
    Motivkritische Studien zu den Überlieferungen von Lot, Isaak, Rebekka
    und Jakob*. FAT. Tübingen: Mohr Siebeck, 2022 (forthcoming).

Seeligmann, Isaac Leo. "Ätiologische Elemente in der biblischen
    Geschichtsschreibung." Pages 77–118 in *Gesammelte Studien zur
    Hebräischen Bibel*. Edited by Erhard Blum. FAT 41. Tübingen: Mohr
    Siebeck, 2004.

Smend, Rudolf. "Elements of Historical Thinking in the Old Testament." Pages
    73–98 in *"The Unconquered Land" and Other Old Testament Essays:
    Selected Studies*. Translated by Margaret Kohl. Farnham: Ashgate, 2013.

Van Seters, John. *Abraham in History and Tradition*. New Haven, CT: Yale
    University Press, 1975.

Westermann, Claus. "Arten der Erzählung in der Genesis." Pages 9–91 in
    Forschung am Alten Testament: Gesammelte Studien. TB 24. Munich:
    Kaiser, 1964.

5 Rhetorical Features and Characteristics: The Literary Function of Genealogies, Itineraries, and Other Etiologies in the Book of Genesis

MICHAELA BAUKS

The study of the rhetorical features and characteristics in Genesis was started by Hermann Gunkel at the beginning of the twentieth century.[1] He demonstrated how the narratives originated in the folklore of Israelite and pre-Israelite cultures, and how they were transformed into larger collections and finally into the literary documents which formed the book of Genesis. Although today few believe we can illuminate the history of pre-literary traditions and identify any orally based subunits of minor literature (*Kleinliteratur*) according to their initial setting of genre (*Sitz im Leben*), we can focus on the setting of the primary readership of the final written form.[2] In addition, Gunkel's observations on formal criteria and comparisons with other ancient Near Eastern literature are still a valuable foundation for contemporary exegesis. He distinguished clearly between (modern) historiography as prose and the legends of Genesis in their poetic and novelistic character, *which does not proclaim historicity or factuality*. His introduction to the commentary on Genesis dedicates itself to several kinds of legends (§ 2) such as

[1] Hermann Gunkel, *Genesis: Translated and Interpreted*, trans. Mark E. Biddle (Macon, GA: Mercer University Press, 1997) preceded by a foreword by Ernest W. Nicholson emphasizing his pioneer status. Gunkel considered himself as an executor of the testament of Johann Gottfried Herder, *Vom Geist der Ebräischen Poesie: Eine Anleitung für die Liebhaber derselben und der ältesten Geschichte des menschlichen Geistes* (1782/83); see Gunkel, *Genesis*, v.

[2] Hyun Chul Paul Kim, "Form Criticism in Dialogue with Other Criticisms: Building the Multidimensional Structures of Texts and Concepts," in *The Changing Face of Form Criticism for the Twenty-First Century*, ed. Marvin A. Sweeney and Ehud Ben Zvi (Grand Rapids, MI: Eerdmans, 2003), 85–104, esp. 92–97. He emphasizes the important distinction between *setting in life* as an extratextual reality and *setting in text/book/reader/literature*, and claims to study the plurality with regard to the stages of settings we can identify in the texts. See also Erhard Blum, "Formgeschichte – a Misleading Category: Some Critical Remarks," in Sweeney and Zvi, *The Changing Face*, 32–45, summarizing the research history.

cosmogonic and ancestral legends (*Sagen*), myths, etiologies with ethnological, etymological, cultic, or topographical concerns; and also to the
artistic form of legends (§ 3). His study includes issues such as the
"poetical" Hebrew prose style of the legends besides the other genres,
and the literary structure, composition, character and number of figures,
description, speech, the arrangement of motifs, keywords or wordplays,
and reflections about the role of the narrator.

Since Gunkel, the research has evolved significantly. The commentary series "Forms of Old Testament Literature" with the first volume on
Genesis by George W. Coats manifests an upcoming interest in rhetorical
and literary features of the Hebrew Bible.[3] Scholars such as Robert Alter[4]
and others are especially interested in the multiformity of the texts in
Genesis. Alongside the mix of genres in the book, the texts may switch
from the narrative flow to poetic units, which can consist of one single
verse in triadic lines.[5] Occasionally, the switch is explicitly marked.[6]
Small poetic units create moments of reflection within the narrative
flow or summarize relevant topics.[7] Otherwise, we do not always have
a well-balanced narrative, where report/description and speech together
carry the plot.[8] Likewise the length of texts differs between short and
dramatic narratives such as the Aqedah in Gen 22 or Jacob's night-time
encounter in Gen 32:22–32, and the epic breadth as in Gen 26.

My survey is less oriented toward the classic composition schemes
such as primeval history (Gen 1–11) – ancestral narratives (Gen 12–36) – and
the Joseph story (Gen 37–50) than to present the material according to the
most relevant rhetorical features. In a first step, I deal with formal elements
in the sense of literary units and genres, and in a second step with motifs
and semantic structuring elements (keywords, wordplays, etc.).

Already the opening portion of Genesis, the primeval history (Gen 1:1–
11:32), is surprising:[9] the text assumes the function of a large exposition or

[3] George W. Coats, *Genesis with an Introduction to Narrative Literature*, FOTL 1
(Grand Rapids, MI: Eerdmans, 1983).
[4] Robert Alter, "Literature," in *Reading Genesis.: Ten Methods*, ed. Ron Hendel
(New York: Cambridge University Press, 2010), 13–27; Robert Alter, *The Art of
Biblical Narrative* (New York: Basic Books, 1981).
[5] E.g., Gen 1:17; 2:23; 4:23–24 (cf. 27:39b–40); 8:22; 14:19–20a; 25:23 (cf. 4:6–7); see Jan P.
Fokkelman, "Genesis," in *The Literary Guide to the Bible*, ed. Robert Alter and
Frank Kermode (Cambridge, MA: Harvard University Press, 1987), 36–55, 36f. with
further examples.
[6] Cf. Gen 4:23a and 49:1b.
[7] Cf. Fokkelman, "Genesis," 44.
[8] Cf. Gen 24; 27; 38.
[9] The end of the primeval history is the object of discussion, see Jan Christian Gertz,
"The Formation of the Primeval History," in *The Book of Genesis: Composition,*

a prologue to the upcoming story of Israel, which starts only in Gen 12 with the patriarchs. Although the narratives[10] about creation, *hybris* and different forms of "fall" presented in Gen 1:1–4:16, 6:1–9:17, or 11:1–9 dominate the text, these narratives are periodically interrupted by extended genealogies (4:17–26; 5:1–32; 9:17–29; 10:1–32; 11:10–23) which overlap the rest of the book of Genesis. Furthermore, the whole corpus is composed of etiological formulas (e.g., Gen 2:24; 3:20; 4:20–22, 25, 26; 6:4b; 9:25), sayings (Gen 4:1; 8:22; 9:25), songs (4:23f.), date formulas (7:11; 8:4, 5, 13, 14)[11], age formulas (Gen 7:6; 9:28 f), conclusion formulas (Gen 1:1, 4a), and several *tôlədôt* formulas (2:4a; 5:1–2a; 6:9; 10:1, 32; 11:10, 27); the latter generally precede a list of personal names (6:10; 9:18; 10:3–18, 21–29).[12] In Gen 1–11, genealogies set an overarching structure that finally organizes the entire book of Genesis,[13] combining primeval, patriarchal, and Israelite "history."[14] Genealogies assume together with other genres an etiological concern within a chronological, ethnological, topographical, etymological, or cultic perspective.

FORMALIZED NARRATIVES: "REPORT"

The Hebrew Bible opens with a prototype of a well-structured text which integrates numerous formulas (Gen 1:1–2:4a). Eight stages in creation are designed in parallel to the seven-day enumeration scheme, framed by an introduction (1:1–2) and a conclusion (2:1–3[.4a]). The ensemble in between is shaped by repetitive formulas concerning God's implicit or explicit commands (v. 3a, 6, 9a, 11, 14–15a, 20, 24, 26), execution (v. 3b,

---

     Reception, and Interpretation, ed. Craig A. Evans, Joel N. Lohr, and David L. Petersen, VTSup 152 (Leiden: Brill, 2012), 107–35, esp. 109–10.

[10]   Coats suggests that "narrative is the art form, symbolic and imaginative in its representation, that combines description and dialogue in order to depict principals in a particular span of time" (*Genesis*, 4 [quotation]); see also pp. 38 and 47. He qualifies the genre of Gen 1–11 as a primeval saga, a term I do not want to reiterate because the texts seem to be more mythical than older positions would suggest; however, Coats sees only "fragments of myth" in Gen 6:1–4.

[11]   Especially the flood narrative has a second and more precise dating system starting in 7:4, which does not correspond to the Priestly concept (see 7:6, 11, 24; 8:3–5, 13–14; 9:28) according to Noah's age.

[12]   Gen 2:4b and 10:32 form an exception (see infra).

[13]   In Gen 2:4a (secondary) the scheme is firstly introduced. The LXX promotes them when it adds the term ספר still in 2:4a for labeling the whole as Βίβλος γενέσεως.

[14]   The last *tôlədôt* in Ex 6:16–25 and Num 3:1–4 are part of a post-priestly redaction for anchoring the Aaronide and Zadokide priesthood in the Tora; see Thomas Hieke, *Die Genealogien der Genesis*, HBS 39 (Freiburg im Breisgau: Herder, 2003), 214–33, 263–65; cf. David M. Carr, "Βίβλος γενέσεως Revisited: A Synchronic Analysis of Patterns in Genesis as Part of the Torah (Part 1)," *ZAW* 110 (1998) 159–72, esp. 171–72.

7b, 9b, 11b, 15b, 24b, 30b), valuation (v. 4a, 10b, 12b, 18b, 21b, 25b, 31a), naming (v. 5a, 8a, 10a), and blessing (1:22, 28; 2:3). Several formulas are used regularly, others infrequently. The binary pair structure in Gen 1 (heaven – earth; wind – water; darkness – light) reminds one of Near Eastern theogonies given that their primordial gods were transformed into natural objects.[15] Already the formal character of the text is note-worthy, which is why O. H. Steck and others[16] characterized Gen 1 as a creation "report." The succeeding paradise narrative (Gen 2:4b–4:16) is differently shaped as a sapiential reflection transformed from a mythical tale.[17] Coats defines the intention of a report as "to record without developing the points of tension characteristic for a plot."[18] Short and focused on a single event, a report stands out with its accuracy and repetition in linguistic terms and provides key events in the past such as a birth report,[19] death report (with burial notice),[20] or marriage report.[21] These minor forms of report unfold the genealogical frame in the ancestral stories up to the Joseph story.

GENRES WITH ETIOLOGICAL CONCERNS

Genealogies (*tôlᵊdôt*) and other Genealogical Lists

Gen 5 as the genealogy of Adam and his ten succeeding generations opens a series of genealogical lists which structure the Torah texts up to Num

---

[15] Cf. Enuma Elish I:1–10 introducing a theomachy succeeded by the cosmogony; Arnold wants to oppose both genres, which is not yet the case in Enuma Elish I. Bill T. Arnold, *Genesis*, NCBC (Cambridge: Cambridge University Press, 2009), 46; cf. Michaela Bauks, *Die Welt am Anfang: Zum Verhältnis von Vorwelt und Weltentstehung in Gen 1 und in der altorientalischen Literatur*, WMANT 74 (Neukirchen-Vluyn: Neukirchener Verlag, 1997), 212–13, 246–48.

[16] Odil H. Steck, *Der Schöpfungsbericht der Priesterschrift: Studien zur literarkri-tischen und überlieferungsgeschichtlichen Problematik von Gen 1,1–2,4a* (Göttingen: Vandenhoeck & Ruprecht, 1981). Gerhard von Rad characterizes the narrative as "Priestly doctrine" with a "concentrated doctrinal content" ("Priesterlehre" mit "konzentriertem Lehrgehalt"); see von Rad, *Genesis*, trans. John H. Marks, OTL (London: SMC Press, 1972), 47–48.

[17] See, for example, Konrad Schmid, "The Ambivalence of Human Wisdom: Genesis 2–3 as a Sapiential Text," in *When the Morning Stars Sang: Essays in Honor of Choon Leong Seow on the Occasion of His Sixty-Fifth Birthday*, ed. S. C. Jones and C. R. Yoder, BZAW 500 (Berlin: de Gruyter, 2017), 275–86 (with bibliography).

[18] Coats, *Genesis*, 10 (cf. pp. 41–43) qualifies the text as an "enumeration report."

[19] Gen 4:25–26 (Seth and Enosh); 21:1–7 (Isaac); 26:19–26 (Jacob and Esau).

[20] Gen 23:1–2.19 (Sarah); 25:7–11 (Abraham); 25:17–18 (Ishmael); 35:8 (Deborah), 19 (Rachel), 28f. (Isaac); 47:28–31 (Jacob without burial notice); 49:29–33 (Jacob); 50:22–26 (Joseph). The notice of Esau's death is omitted.

[21] Gen 19:35–38 (Lot); 25:1–6 (Rebekah); 26:34 (Esau); the marriages of Jacob with Leah and Rachel are communicated in a tale (Gen 31). See below.

3.[22] Generally these *tôlədôt* are patrilineal lists including material about patriarchs and their succeeding firstborns. In just a few passages these vertical lists are enlarged with segmented information about other descendants in a horizontal perspective (Gen 4:19–24; 5:21–24; 10:1, 32; 11:11; cf. Gen 25:12; Ex 6:16, 19). Gen 6:9 forms an exception as the formula is not succeeded by a genealogy (in v. 10 only Noah's sons are listed; cf. 2:4b and 10:32), but by the narrative of the flood. Usually the patrilineal lists follow a more or less regular pattern comprising three parts: a birth report of the ancestor accompanied by the age of the father, a notice of the years of life for the father after the birth, and the death report.[23] Within the primeval history, the narrative expansions to the list concern three figures in particular: Adam is the God-like being who fathered a child in his own image and according to *his* likeness (5:2–3); Enoch is presented as the rightful man elected by God, who walked with God (Hitpael of *hlk*[24]; 5:22, 24; cf. Noah at 6:9 and Abraham at 17,1; 24:40) and was "taken by him" (5:24) instead of living and dying like the other forefathers (cf. Gen 5:5, 8, 11, 14, 17, 20, 27, 31); Noah, Lamech's son, is highlighted by a name etiology (*nōaḥ/nḥm*) explaining that he will be able to invert the curse which effected human labor in a negative way (5:29; cf. 3:17). Gen 5 points out the life-giving aspect within the primeval history and demonstrates implicitly that the blessing of Gen 1:28 has been fulfilled.[25] *Tôlədôt* formulas in the ancestral stories sometimes have extensions too (e.g., Gen 37:2 concerning Joseph).[26]

---

[22]   Gen 5:1, 32 (from Adam to Noah + his sons); 6:9–10 (Noah + his sons); 9:28–29 (Noah's death); 10:1, 32 (Noah's sons; segmented list); 11:10–26 (Shem to Terach; lineal list), 27–32 (Terach); 25:12, 19; 36:1, 9; 37:2, and the last entries in Ex 6, 16, 19 and Num 3:1–4 (post-P?). Carr describes the P-version of the ancestral traditions like "a covenant-focused expanded genealogy" which reconceptualizes non-P-traditions (David M. Carr, *Reading the Fractures of Genesis: Historical and Literary Approaches* [Louisville, KY: Westminster John Knox Press, 1996], 127).

[23]   The same formulas are used in Gen 11:10–26 (genealogy of Seth), but the summing up of the patriarch's life is omitted.

[24]   In Gen 3:8 the term refers to God himself and in 2 Sam 11:2 to King David in a profane context; in the texts cited above, the term characterizes the strong relationship to God.

[25]   The life-giving function of Gen 5 is inverted to annihilation in the genealogical list from Cain to Lamech (cf. Gen 4:17–24). The secondary v. 25 is a nearly verbatim reprise of v. 17 but the focus changes from Cain to the third son of Adam, Seth. Thus, Seth becomes the representative descendant of the Adamic line (cf. 5:4).

[26]   The list of the Jacob sons in Gen 35:32 is introduced by an addition about Reuben's incestuous relationship with Bilhah, arranged in parallel to the negative evaluation of Simeon and Levi because of the Shechem massacre in Gen 34, which prepares their judgment within the Judah blessing at 49:4–7 (see below, on tribal sayings).

Segmented genealogies have varying uses. The Noah genealogy in Gen 10 aims to present three tables of genealogy, each more or less synchronically according to the sons of Japhet (10:2-5), Ham (v. 6-20), and Shem (v. 21-31), while the list in Gen 35:22-29 seeks to enumerate the twelve sons of Jacob according to his wives, which form the twelve tribes of Israel. In Gen 10 the regular patterns of a linear list (cf. Gen 5) are lacking. In a segmented form, distinct groups belonging to each son within a name list[27] are encountered. These include either the first and the second generation or the first up to the fifth generation in the case of Shem (10:24b-30) – who is the most important ancestor for Israel. A list of the sons introduces each section (vv. 2, 6, 31) and a conclusion resumes their territorial extension (vv. 5, 30, 31, and v. 32 for the whole list). Exceptionally Nimrod, son of Ham, is presented with more details, which places him in a more prominent position (10:8-10).

At least, the function of segmented lists is different from the linear type. They do not focus on time and continuity, but on space and geographic expansion, because each descendant is presented as an independent tribe or people with its own territory and language. These notices are resumed by conclusions in 10:5, 20, 31-32 or by descriptions of kingdoms and cities in 10:10-12, 22, of peoples in v. 13-14, 16-18 and of territorial limits in v. 18b-19, 30. Each table concludes with a statement on the diffusion of the postdiluvian nations, a topic which is also reflected in the tale of Gen 11.

The overarching genealogical structure, which starts in Gen 5:1, links the founder of humanity, Adam, with the re-founder Noah, son of Enosh, after the flood. Another tôlədôt formula in Gen 6:9 focuses on Noah, who is used as a bridge from the antediluvian to the postdiluvian age. This verse is a priestly extension of the originally pre-P genealogical scroll beginning in Gen 5, and aims at a "*gradual* stretching of the *toledot* system as it was extended to encompass ever larger amounts of non-genealogical material."[28] The tôlədôt notice of Noah ends in 9:28-29 according to the regular pattern of Gen 5 which remembers the span of life and his death (cf. 5:1, 32).

In fact, Gen 5:1 affiliates a tôlədôt of heaven and earth in Gen 2:4a and another genealogical list in Gen 4:16-25 ("Kenite list"). While Gen 2:4a is a redactional verse linking together the two creation texts, referring back to Gen 1 (bəhibbārə'ām) and working like a colophon to the priestly account of cosmogony, Gen 5:1 marks a starting point of

---

[27] Concerning *bn* in nominal clauses, cf. Hieke, *Die Genealogien der Genesis*, 101-7.
[28] Carr, "Βίβλος γενέσεως Revisited 1," 170.

humankind's life evolution up to the formation of Israel by Jacob and his sons (cf. Gen 35:22–26; cf. Ex 1:1–11). From a literary perspective, the lists in Gen 4:1, 17–26 and Gen 5 are doublets and form a good example for source criticism. Both lists belong to a common topic of the ancient Near East[29] introducing the distinction between a pre-flood and post-flood humanity. The antediluvian age starts in Gen 4 with Cain, son of "the man" and Eve, the second list in Gen 5 begins with Adam, the father of Seth.

Bill T. Arnold[30] states that the book of Genesis includes 10 explicit *tôlǝdôt* formulas that not only embrace a simple name list but narrative portions as well. They introduce temporal clauses (2:4b and 5:1 – creation topic), descriptive nominal clauses in 6:9; 11:10; 37:2 or narrative verbal clauses (11:27 birth announcement). The formulas structure the entire book in a twofold way: the first five formulas stand within the primeval history and are devoted to the origins of the universe and humanity (2:4a, bridging Gen 1 and Gen 2–4; 5:1 Adam; 6:9 Noah; 10:1 sons of Noah; 11:10 Shem), the other five formulas provide a genealogical structure for the ancestral history forming the genesis of the Israelite history (11:27 Terah; 25:12 Ishmael; 25:19 Isaac; 36:1, 9 Esau; 37:2 Jacob; cf. tribal list Gen 49). The narrative portions which interrupt the genealogical scheme are very disparate. Although, surprisingly, a *tôlǝdôt* formula for Abraham is omitted,[31] the *tôlǝdôt* scheme forms the overarching structure of the whole book (see below).

Travel Reports, Settlement Reports, and Other Topographical Notices

While genealogies are primarily interested in explaining time spans (chronography) and the growth of life as a consequence of divine benediction, travel reports (itineraries) and other topographical notices focus

---

[29] Cf. Robert Wilson, *Genealogy and History in the Biblical World* (New Haven and London: Yale University Press, 1977), 56–136 for Sumerian and Akkadian genealogies found in royal inscriptions, Mesopotamian king lists containing compiled genealogical fragments, sometimes within an ante- et postdiluvian section and non-royal, scribal and priestly genealogies. Most ancient Near Eastern genealogies are linear in form and do not extend ten generations; often they are related to narratives (ibid., 134–35). The preference for segmented data in the biblical literature reflects other sociological conditions, including a tribal instead of monarchic concept (196).

[30] Arnold, *Genesis*, 5.

[31] See, however, the death and burial notice and the list of his sons with Keturah in Gen 25:1–11 succeeded by the list of Ishmael's sons (25:13–18) and the *tôlǝdôt* of Isaac's sons (25:19), which in fact introduces an extended narrative starting with the birth story of the twins and ending with the death notice of Isaac in 35:29 (cf. the *tôlǝdôt* formula in 2:4a; 6:9a; 11:27a).

on space. In the case of the lists of people, chronological and spatial aspects are combined (Gen 10 [cf. 1 Chr 1]; Gen 15:19–21; cf. Act 2:9–11; Jub 8–9). Topographic notices in the primeval history are vague: the east of Eden (2:8; 3:24; 4:16) has a mythical background.[32] Mount Ararat in Gen 8:4 is an isolated folkloric notice.[33] The topographical information in Gen 10 provides a social identification locating the addressee of the list, Israel, in relation to other people or tribal groups by highlighting the ancestor Eber ('br in 10:21, 24–25; cf. the short linear notice in 11:14, 16), whose name is etymologically related to the demonym 'bry ("Hebrew"). "[B]y means of this process of genealogical differentiation ('divergence') Genesis gives an explanation to other populations in a kind of *ethnic map of the world* and explains further the way Israel related to those populations."[34]

After Gen 11:26, the branching of the world's population is contrasted by Israel's narrowed lineage from Adam to Jacob, who embodies Israel. The unexpected beginning with a divine speech in 12:1 is a telescoping of attention from a broader segmented genealogy to Abram, the first patriarch. While the narratives about him are concentrated in the south of the Levant and Egypt (cf. Gen 12:10–20)[35] after having moved from Ur to Haran (11:31), the Jacob cycle is situated in the northern part of Israel (Gilead: Mizpah, Penuel, or Bethel/Luz and Shechem[36]) and at Padan-Aram and Haran in the north, or in Egypt or Edom/Seir in the south (for the Esau-traditions[37]). The latter cycle presents several ancient traditions.[38] The itineraries correspond to the

---

[32] Cf. Gunkel, *Genesis*, 25–27; Claus Westermann, *Genesis 1–11*, BKAT I/1 (Neukirchen-Vluyn: Neukirchener Verlag, 1974), 292–94; differently Philip S. Alexander, "Early Jewish Geography and the Bible," *ABD* 2: 977–88, esp. 978–79, who speaks about exercises in cognitive mapping which aim to present real geographical space (*qdm* concerns the cardinal point "east").

[33] Cf. the land Ararat in 2K 19:37 par. Is 37:38; Jer 51:27.

[34] Arnold, *Genesis*, 115 (emphasis added by author).

[35] Exceptions are formed (e.g.) by the secondary additions of Bethel in Gen 12:3; 13:3 (inspired by Gen 28:19; 31:13) and Shechem in Gen 12:6 (cf. 33:20); see Konrad Schmid, *Erzväter und Exodus: Untersuchungen zur doppelten Begründung der Ursprünge Israels innerhalb der Geschichtsbücher des Alten Testaments*, WMANT 81 (Neukirchen-Vluyn: Neukirchener Verlag, 1999), 287–89.

[36] Jacob's burial place was transferred from Shechem (Gen 33:18–20; 50:5) to Hebron (Gen 49:30; 50:13; cf. 35:27) for tradition-historical reasons.

[37] See the extended birth report (Gen 36:1–5) and genealogy of Esau (vv. 9–14) or Seir (vv. 20–30), name lists about the sons of Esau organizing the tradition contained in the list (vv. 15–19), an Edomite king list interested in political structures (vv. 31–39), and the Esau name list (vv. 40–43); cf. Coats, *Genesis*, 246–57.

[38] See Isaac Finkelstein and Thomas Römer, "Comments on the Historical Background of the Jacob Narrative in Genesis," *ZAW* 126/3 (2014), 317–38, esp. 324–25.

nomadic and – in the case of Jacob for conflictual matter – itinerant lifestyle of the patriarch which is concentrated on the process of movement from place to place. In general, an itinerary comprises stereotyped formulas informing about the route, the place of departure, the place of arrival, and (brief) notes about events on the journey (cf. Gen 11:31; 12:4–9, 10–11, 20 to 13:1; 20:1; 22:19; 26:1f., 6, 17, 23).[39] Especially the itineraries of the Jacob cycle are extended by important episodes on the way in between: first, when he flees from his brother to Haran (28:2–29:13) and second, when he comes back (cf. 31:17–33:18). As in Gen 11:31, when the forefather Terah is described gathering his family and travelling from Ur to Haran, the same is true of Esau when he departs from Canaan to Seir (36:6).[40] Abraham's purchase of the cave of Machpelah, near Hebron (Kiriath-Arba), from the Hittites (Gen 23) is a request for permanent ownership in the promised land (v. 4). The conclusion in v. 17–20 reminds one of a legal text which emphasizes the formal transaction and the intention to possess an ancestral burial ground for the patriarchs and their families (see Gen 25:9; 49:29–30; 50:13). Several settlement notices appear to be paired when they describe the settlement of the patriarchs in the land and of the descendants excluded from the promise outside the land (Gen 16:6 Abram, cf. 16:21 Lot; Gen 21:11, 20 Ismael, cf. 25:11 Isaac; 36:6–8 Esau, cf. 37:1 Jacob).

Cult Notices (*hieros logos*) and Other Religious Customs

In an etiological perspective these formulas set out to explain the origin of the sacredness of a place together with several customs which are observed at it. The tale of the celestial stairway at Luz (28:10–20) is considered to be a cult legend. Just after his flight, Jacob gets a nocturnal theophany followed by a blessing (vv. 12–15). Discovering the awesome character of the place he erects a stone to mark the holy place (vv. 17–18), which is renamed in Beth-El ("House of God"). Furthermore, he vows that the pillar will become a temple and that he will introduce the custom of returning a tenth of his gain to God, on condition that God protects him and supports his return (vv. 20–23). In

---

[39] Claus Westermann, *Genesis 12–36*, BKAT I/2; (Neukirchen-Vluyn: Neukirchener Verlag, 1981), 49–51.

[40] Cf. Carr, *Reading*, 103–13, esp. 104 for the particular terminological similarities in Gen 12:5; 13:6, 11–12; 31:17–18; 36:6–7; 46:5–7 (*lqḥ/qwm* + *nś'*; list of family, livestock, possessions; *bw'*; [*šebet yaḥdāw*]). Exemplary is the Priestly system of travel, burial, marriage and settlement notices, which concludes in Gen 50:22–23, 26a (110). The non-P-texts combine travel commands and (land) promise (cf. Gen 12:1; 26:2–3; 31:3, 13b; 46:3b–4); Carr, *Reading*, 178–80.

fact, the cult notice is succeeded by a religious custom in order to attribute a temple tax to God. Considering the cultic significance of Bethel in 1 Kgs 12, Gen 28 has the proleptic function of underscoring the great antiquity of the Northern Kingdom's cult place.

A second cult notice in the Jacob cycle is encountered at Gen 32 when Jacob comes back to the promised land and meets a supernatural person fighting with him. At the end of the struggle Jacob is blessed by his opponent and names the place close to the Jabboq by the theophoric name Peni-El "[in] the face of God" (v. 30; cf. below). A further etiological note in verse 32 concerns a dietary restriction: when Jacob is limping because he is struck on the hip, the "thigh muscle that is on the hip socket" is hereafter exempted from alimentation. The explanation introduced by "therefore" (*'al-kēn*) marks the etiological character of the passage explicitly.

Further cult notices (see below) are encountered in Gen 12:6–7 (oak of Moreh; cf. 31:33 tamarisk at Beersheba); 26:25 (altar at Beersheba); 33:18–20 (altar called El-Elohe-Israel in Shechem), 35:1–7 (altar in Bethel) and possibly in Gen 22:14[41] (Moriah). Another explicit etiology, again introduced with "therefore" (*'al-kēn*), for marriage as a custom is introduced in Gen 2:24. In an implicit way Gen 1:1–2:3 forms a cult etiology in the form of an explanation for the institution of Sabbath representing a "temple in time", a chronotope (cf. Ex 20:10–11; Deut 5:14–15).

Etymological Notices and Wordplays

Etymology and wordplay also serve a rhetorical function with etiological importance in the book of Genesis. A human being (*'dm*) taken from the dust of the ground (*'dmh*; Gen 2:7) combines an account of the close etymology of the human function as a gardener *and* his destination to finitude and mortality (3:19). The traditional (not technical) sound-alike etymology *'îš* – *'iššâ* (2:23) underlines the particular relationship between man and woman. The term *'rwm* describes either the nakedness of the human couple or the smart character of the serpent (Gen 2:25; 3:1, 7). Noah shall bring us relief of our work (*nḥm*; see below) and Abram receives from God the new name Abraham explaining that he made him "the ancestor of a multitude of nations" (*'b hmwn*; 17:5). Also Jacob is renamed in "Isra-El" at the end of the nighttime struggle at the Jabbok

[41] Siegfried Mittmann, "ha-Morijja-Präfigurationen der Gottesstadt Jerusalem (Gen 22,1–14.19)," in *La Cité de Dieu: Die Stadt Gottes*, ed. Martin Hengel, Siegfried Mittmann, and Anne-Marie Schwemer (Tübingen: Mohr Siebeck, 2000), 67–97.

(32:28) because he has striven (yśr) with God and represents the eponym of the people.[42] With regard to proper names several wordplays are encountered: the first son of Abraham and Sarah is named Isaac because "God has laughter (ṣḥq) for me; everyone who hears will laugh (yṣḥq) with me" (Gen 21:6; cf. 18:12–15). The name of Jacob remembers that during the birth of his twin brother, he was gripping the heel ('qb) resonant in his name (y'qb). A second etymology of his name is offered by Esau: "Is he not rightly named Jacob? For he has supplanted ('qb) me these two times. He took away my birthright; and look, now he has taken away my blessing" (27:36; NRSV). The right of primogeniture (bkwrh) presents a pun with the similar sound of "blessing" (brkh) in Gen 27:36a. Tamar's twins are named Perez and Zerah by two sayings of the midwife (Gen 38:28f.). Perez is named alluding to the birth process ("What a breach [prṣ] you have made [prṣ] for yourself!") and proves the reversal of the right of primogeniture in Ruth 4:18–22, when Perez is considered as ancestor of King David in the line of Boaz, Obed, and Jesse (NRSV). Another pun is formed in Gen 22 by yḥd "one" – yḥyd "only one" – yḥdw "together" in the context of speech (v. 2, 12, 16) and report (v. 6, 8, 19): "This ingenious wordplay creates a paradox at the heart of the message: by showing his willingness to give up his only son, Abraham gets him back, and a much deepened togetherness begins, both between father and son and between the Lord and his obedient follower."[43]

Etymologically operating etiologies are especially propagated in topographical or ethnical contexts such as Gen 10:21, 24–25 (Eber – 'ēber, "Hebrew"). In Gen 19:22 the town where Lot fled from is named Zoar, because it is a little one (myṣr, v. 20). In Gen 21:31 the explicit etiology (lkn, "therefore") about the seven lambs which Abraham offers to Abimelch for bearing witness that he dug a well (Beer-Sheba = oath-well). We know almost nothing about the "land of Moriah" in Gen 22:14,[44] but the paronomasia with the verb r'h ("to see"; hiphil "to provide") announces a possible resort for Abraham's dramatic situation to sacrifice his son. Another topographic wordplay is encountered in 31:48 when the heap of stones which seals the covenant between Jacob and Laban is called in Hebrew gl'd by Jacob and in Aramaic ygr hdwt'ś by Laban, which means "head of witness" (vv. 47, 52) and implies an

---

[42]   "You shall no longer be called Jacob, but Israel, for you have striven with God and with humans, and have prevailed" (NRSV).

[43]   Fokkelman, "Genesis," 46–50, here 50.

[44]   Arnold, Genesis, 204, 207–8; cf. Fokkelman, "Genesis," 50; in 1 Chr 3:1, Moriah is connected to Jerusalem's place for the first temple (see for an identification of the places Mittmann, "ha-Morijja-Präfigurationen").

etiology of border stones (*kudurru*).[45] The following verses identify the Galeed with "the pillar Mizpah" (*hmṣph* = watchpost) which is explained by the pun: "The LORD watch (*yṣp*) between you and me, when we are absent one from another" (NRSV). In the next chapters we have etiologies for three locations close to the Jabbok: at 32:2–3 Jacob met messengers of God and considers the place as God's temporary encampment and calls it Mahanaim (dual: "two camps") reminding one of a place where "heaven and earth melted into one"[46] (cf. 28:17, 19). At 32:30, the place is called Peniel "for I have seen God face to face." Literally, the name means: "[in] the face of God" and denotes the place where Jacob fought against a divine being. In 33:17 it is related to how he constructed the place Succoth, the "booths" for his livestock, before he came to Shechem, where he erected the altar El-Elohe-Israel (v. 20; see above). In the Joseph story, a wordplay is introduced to emphasize the lack of recognition from the brothers when they met Joseph for the first time and Joseph's dissimulation of his identity (42:7–8: he recognized them [*wykrm*] but he treated them like strangers [*wytnkr*]). This tension is only resolved when Joseph reveals himself to them (45:3 – see below).[47]

Paronomastic plays are also frequent in the tribal sayings, as at Gen 49:8, *yəhûdâ ... yôdûkā*, "Judah, they praise you", at v. 16, *dān yādîn*, "Dan shall judge," or the expression at v. 19, *gād gədûd yəgûdennû*, "Gad, who will be raided by raiders but will raid (*ygd*) at their heels."

Short Poems and Sayings

Short poems and sayings have a special literary function by crystallizing and summarizing what is most important. When the first poetic elements occur in Gen 1:27 (*imago Dei*), the aspect of a human being's entering into a close relationship with God is emphasized as a theological *leitmotiv*. The relationship is enlarged in Gen 5:3 from the God–human connection to two men (Adam–Seth), and its validity is reconfirmed after the flood in a chiastic wordplay (Gen 9:6: "Whoever sheds the blood of a human, by a human shall that person's blood be shed; for in his own image God made humankind"; NRSV). A short poem is encountered in

---

45 Cf. Finkelstein and Römer, "Comments," 324.

46 Cf. Cornelis Houtman, "Jacob at Mahanaim: Some remarks on Genesis xxxii 2–3," *VT* 28 (1978) 37–44, here 37. He rates the verses among the examples of a *hieros logos* (40). Other etymological etiologies are allusive and philologically incorrect – e.g., Gen 35:18, 30:23–24 or 50:10–11; see Isaac L. Seeligman, "Ätiologische Elemente in der biblischen Geschichtsschreibung," in Seeligman, *Gesammelte Studien zur Hebräischen Bibel*, FAT 41 (Tübingen: Mohr Siebeck, 2004), 77–110, here 100–1.

47 Cf. Coats, *Genesis*, 352.

Gen 2:23 to explain the strong relationship of man and woman, which is succeeded by an etiological notice of marriage (v. 24). In Gen 3:14–19 the spells of punishment have the etiological task to explain the resultant state of life according to the serpent and to the first couple in a functional and relational way. These conditions persist in the human experience and characterize the *conditio humana* forever. In 4:6–7 we have a three-line poem including a divine exhortation to Cain which is theologically important because Cain's wrongdoing manifests humanity's aim to get knowledge of good and evil as failed.

The name of Noah is etymologically of interest (5:29). The saying "Out of the ground that the LORD has cursed this one shall bring us relief from our work and from the toil of our hands" (NRSV) is a wordplay of Noah (*nwḥ*, "to rest" [cf. Judg 3:1, and 1 Chr 8:2 for the name]) relating to *nḥm*, "bring relief." The relief refers back to the curse of the ground in 3:17 (cf. 4:11), but the notice does not exhibit how the relief is brought about. The song of Lamech in 4:23–24[48] highlights the patriarch by his seventh position within the Kenite list (4:17–24)[49], which is in contrast to the seventh position attributed to Enoch in Gen 5:22. The genealogical extension emphasizes that he "walked with God" and broke the cycle of death because he did not die as the other patriarchs, but rather "God took him" (v. 24). Instead, Lamech is pointed out for excessive vengeance and escalating violence within a – lastly – failed lineage with no other descendants. However, this negative lineage has also positive effects: the segmented part of the list (Gen 4:20–22) dealing with the sons of Lamech gives an account of three cultural innovations that they present, such as pastoral nomadism (Jabal), musicians (Jubal), and metallurgy (Tubal-Cain = *qyn* "forger" or "spear" cf. 2 Sam 21,16). The paronomasia between the three names is evident, but we have no plausible etymological origin for the names.[50] The surname of the last son, Cain, is not only thematically fitting, but also forms at least an introduction to the beginning of the list: the lineage starts and ends with Cain. The non-priestly flood story

---

[48] "Adah and Zillah, hear my voice; you wives of Lamech, listen to what I say: I have killed a man for wounding me, a young man for striking me. If Cain is avenged sevenfold, truly Lamech seventy-sevenfold" (NRSV).

[49] See Jack M. Sasson, "A Genealogical 'Convention' in Biblical Chronography?" *ZAW* 90/2 (1978), 171–85, esp. 172 for the role of the seventh position in genealogies.

[50] The commentaries give no explanation for the paronomasia, only the name of Tubal is encountered in other contexts. Gunkel, *Genesis*, 51 qualifies Lamech (and his sons) as the patriarchs of the desert and the Bedouin (or nomads): Georg Fischer, *Genesis 1–11*, HThKAT (Freiburg: Herder, 2018), 312–15; critically Jan Christian Gertz, *Das erste Buch Mose (Genesis 1–11)*, ATD 1/1 (Göttingen: Vandenhoeck & Ruprecht, 2018), 179; Hieke, *Genealogien*, 55 underlines the inclusion of the surname with the beginning of the list.

"culminates in an explanatory limerick":[51] "As long as the earth endures, seedtime and harvest, cold and heat, summer and winter, day and night, shall not cease" (Gen 8:22; NRSV). Gen 10:9 attests explicitly the aphorism "Like Nimrud a mighty hunter before the LORD," reminding one of a Mesopotamian tradition. Another saying in the form of a blessing is encountered twice in Gen 14:19–20, 22. Beyond that we have a birth oracle according to the eponymous founders of two rival people in Gen 25:23 and a paternal blessing pronounced to Esau (27:39b–40) which confirms finally the validity of Jacob's stolen blessing (vv. 28–30.).

At the end of the book a collection of tribal sayings (Gen 49:2–27) is encountered that are later organized in the context of a speech of death-bed blessings[52] pronounced by Jacob (49:1, 28; cf. Gen 27:28–29, Isaac). This collection is defined by the order of twelve sons of Jacob according to their mothers Leah, Bilhah, Zilpah and Rachel, and concludes the Jacob cycle interrupted by the Joseph story in Gen 36, 39–48.[53] However, we have only eleven sayings about the sons because those of Simeon and Levi have been combined. "It must be interpreted as a numerical saying which is the result of human reflection on the course of history, discovering and defining a certain order or structure in the events of history: There were twelve tribes who once united to form Israel."[54] Another blessing of Jacob according to Ephraim and Manasseh is transmitted in Gen 48:20. While we have generally only one saying for each tribe, several sayings appear for Judah, Dan, and Joseph.

RHETORICAL FEATURES IN THE FORM OF KEYWORDS

The main topic of the book of Genesis is life. Life becomes reality in the act of creation by God with the introduction of time by the creation of light, the separation of spaces, and the accommodation and cultivation of both. At the end of the creation report it is stated that God ordered humankind to be "fruitful and to multiply, and to fill the earth [and to subdue it]" (Gen 1:28) which becomes a formula and reappears continually in the book of Genesis.[55] The ancestral stories tell about the

---

51   Arnold, *Genesis*, 108.

52   Concerning his first sons he pronounces curses (vv. 3–7; referring to Gen 34:25–30; 35:22).

53   See the distinctly composed lists in Gen 29:31–30:24; 35:22b–26 or 48:8–27.

54   The number *twelve* is the most elaborated numerical saying within the genealogical lists (cf. Gen 35:22b–26 for a narrative setting), see Wolfgang M. W. Roth, *Numerical Sayings in the Old Testament: A Form-Critical Study*, VTSup 13 (Leiden: Brill, 1965), 13.

55   See *prw wrbw* [wml'w] + place at Gen 1:[22,] 28; 8:17; 9:1, 7; [26:22]; 35:11; 47:27; [Ex 1:7].

fulfillment of divine benediction, especially with regard to increasing fertility of the offspring and to landholding. The genealogies and itineraries bear witness to them in a greatly reduced form.

While Gen 1:28 suggests that life-bearing is a natural process (the woman in Gen 3:20 is herself named Ḥawwâ "life"), the ancestral stories emphasize at least the high engagement of God in this process. In fact, the birth notices of Isaac, Jacob, Esau, Joseph, and Benjamin are not formulated in terms of begetting by the father (yld, Hiphil; 5:1–32 Adam etc.) or of bearing by the mother (cf. Gen 4:1,17–26, Kain's wife, etc.;[56] Gen 36,4f., 12 Esau; 46:18–25), but since Gen 11:30 children are born from barren women (cf. 11:30; 16:1 Sarah; 25:21 Rebekah; 29:31; 30:1 Rachel) whose wombs were opened by God in order that they can give birth.[57] According to these birth notices, only God can enable continuity of life. This perception is counterbalanced within the tôlədôt lists, which are patrilinear and emphasize the significance of the patriarchs for life giving.[58]

In the Joseph story, life becomes again reality by divine providence, but in a more abstract way. The formula against fear in Joseph's reconciliation speech (50:19–21) manifests his trust in God. In Gen 39:2–3, the introduction of Joseph's encounter with his master's wife uses wordplay to characterize Joseph, who was a successful man (ʾîš maṣlîaḥ) whom God let succeed in all things (maṣlîaḥ). Because God is with Joseph, he has success in all circumstances (see 39:23) and finally embodies God's blessing.[59] Prospection constitutes here the leitmotiv which aims to show how God makes sense of the past in psychologically complicated circumstances. The crystallization of personality is another narrative strategy when "the favorable traits of character that resolve the discontinuity between their [the brothers] past and present behavior are not so much either created or unveiled as brought out by the pressure of events."[60] Joseph is the guide who reproduces the past and enables the reconciliation with his family. The story basically deals with life,

---

[56]   Exceptionally Gen 4:17–26 highlights the significance of women in fertility (yld, Qal); cf. Michaela Bauks, "Intratextual Exegesis in the Primeval History: The Literary Function of the Genealogies in View of the Formation of Gen 1–11," ZAW 131 (2019), 177–93; cf. Hieke, Genealogien, 278.

[57]   Concerning the formula to be fruitful and to multiply which is in opposition to the motive of the barren women, see Arnold, Genesis, 128.

[58]   Cf. Fokkelman, "Genesis," 42–43.

[59]   Cf. Alter, Art, 107.

[60]   See Meir Sternberg, The Poetics of Biblical Narrative: Ideological Literature and the Drama of Reading, Indiana Studies in Biblical Literature (Bloomington, IN: Indiana University Press, 1986), 285–308, esp. 296.

considering the circumstances of famine which force the brothers to move and shape the plot of the whole story.

With respect to life, the numerous genealogies present a very important rhetorical feature and shape the overarching structure of the book of Genesis. Nevertheless, the beginning of the book is surprising: Gen 1 has a different character in terms of its length, and at first glance also in terms of its topic. However, this text deals – as do the genealogies – with the topic of life in an upcoming movement of human history. Within the broader composition of Gen 1–11, Gen 1 forms an exposition in the form of the "genesis" of the physical preconditions which empower the human world. The text is reminiscent of the genre of theogonical texts of the Ancient Near East (cf. n. 15 above). The report is succeeded by a back-story in Gen 2–4, and both are harmonized by a secondarily introduced *tôlədôt* formula in 2:4a, which applies the genealogical scheme exceptionally to a cosmic topic. In this perspective Gen 1–4 form the "narrative prologue" to the "book or scroll of genealogies", which begins in Gen 5:1.[61] With regard to the ten *tôlədôt* formulas we have a symmetrical arrangement with 10 + 1 (Gen 1:1–2:4a) panels[62] which are equally devoted to (1) the origins of the world and first humanity and, starting from Gen 11:27, to (2) the prehistory of the Israelite nation. The *tôlədôt* clauses are used "in order to give the impression of a slow and gradual narrowing focus with fewer and fewer participants, accenting the particularizing effects of the blessing of God."[63]

While the primeval history as a primeval saga deals with distant time and distant land within a broken quality of mythical tradition,[64] the ancestral stories provide more concrete data by using genealogies combining the time-space factor with itineraries.

The embracing genealogical scheme shows a surprising feature within the narratives when the right of primogeniture (*bkwrh*),[65] which was widespread in the ancient Near East, is repeatedly transferred

---

[61] Carr, "Βίβλος γενέσεως Revisited 1," 164–69. Gertz characterizes the formula as "a carefully placed fermata in the narrative. Having done so, the following material appears to be an explication of the already reported creation in the sense of a later realization that seems to 'catch up' (*nachholende Vergegenwärtigung*)" (Gertz, "Formation," 114). Cf. for a critical evaluation of 2:4a as an old superscription placed before Gen 1:1, see Gertz, "Formation," 115.

[62] Gen 2:4a–4:26; 5:1–6:8; 6:9–9:29; 10:1–11:9; 11:10–26; 11:27–25:11; 25:12–18; 25:19–35:29; 36:1–37:1; 37:2–50:26.

[63] Arnold, *Genesis*, 6–7; and see chapter 14 in this volume by Joel S. Kaminsky.

[64] See Coats, *Genesis*, 35–38, esp. 38.

[65] The topic forms the background of the Hagar-Ishmael stories in Gen 16; 21; and it is spread out in Gen 27:1–28:5; see also the reversal from Reuben to Judah in Gen 49:3–4 (cf. 35:22).

to the second son (Ishmael – Isaac; Jacob – Esau; Perez – Zerah; Ephraim – Manasse) (see above). The paternal succession has been transferred from Abraham to Isaac (25:5; P absent), from Isaac to Jacob (27:27, 37; P 28:1–9; 35:11–12), and from Reuben to Judah (49:3, 9f.). The topic of the promise of land and offspring finds its most elaborated form in Gen 17:1–7, and in the probably most recent narrative in Gen 12. The latter narrative enlarges Abram's significance and includes theoretically all clans of the world in the blessing of this patriarch (12:3; see also 17:5–6). In this context the narrowed style of the ancestral narratives has been enlarged and universalized. In addition, Abram's itinerary becomes theologically important when he leaves Harran (12:4), arrives in Canaan at Shechem (v. 5), receives the land promised for his offspring (v. 7), pitches his tent between Bethel and Ai (v. 8; cf. 13:3), and journeys on in stages toward the Negev in the south (v. 9): "His subsequent journey 'by stages' means Abram has now traversed the 'promised land' itself."[66]

Despite the inclusion within the *tôlədôt* scheme (37:2), the Joseph Story falls out of the Genesis composition reported thus far for several reasons. Firstly, it "is arguably the finest narrative preserved in the Bible"[67] with unique storytelling skills which characterize in a most masterful way the main protagonists and create uniquely dramatic suspense such as the failed recognition by the brothers (42:29–45:1). The creation of tension in the tale is enlarged by several complications within the plot as a result of different initiatives by Joseph which lead to the two journeys of the brothers: the allegation that the brothers are spies causes Joseph to decide to send them or a part of them home to bring Benjamin to Egypt; then, in a second step, to send them back for inculpating Benjamin of having stolen a silver cup. The disparity of knowledge is only resolved when Joseph reveals himself to the brothers (45:3). Secondly, the novel is not composed as a series of segmented patriarchal traditions, but forms a continuous whole, a "novel", at least in chapters 37, 39–45 and small portions of 46–50. The coherence of the narrative process that characterizes the Joseph story is rarely encountered in the rest of the book. The few exceptions are, for example, the tale of Isaac's betrothal in Gen 24, where Rebekah is presented as the God-appointed bride (24:50)[68] among other descendants of Terah's lineage (22:20–24); or

---

[66]   Arnold, *Genesis*, 135.

[67]   Coats, *Genesis*, 351.

[68]   Sternberg, *Poetics*, 132–33, 151 about the multiple viewpoints in Gen 24; Adele Berlin, *Poetics and Interpretation of Biblical Narrative* (Winona Lake, IN: Eisenbrauns, 1994), 62 emphasizes that the new focus on Isaac in v. 63 is marked by *hinneh*. See Shimon Bar-Efrat, *Narrative Art in the Bible* (Sheffield: Scholars Press, 2008), 13–45,

the short narrative of the famous lentil stew in Gen 25. These two scenes involve descriptive detail that is composed of a more or less fixed sequence of motifs. Robert Alter interprets the chapters as "a perform-ance of a quotidian situation, and the Bible touches on the quotidian only as a sphere for the realization of portentous actions."[69] They focus on the patriarchal characters: the endogamous marriage of Isaac qualifies him as a rightful person in contrast to the fraudulent Jacob figure (see the triple presentation of his fraud in Gen 25:24–24; 29–34; 27:1–40).

A changing point of view marks the transition from the collective-ancestral perspective to an individually focused purpose in Gen 39. Although Joseph becomes the point of interest in Gen 37, his own point of view is not yet represented. That changes in 39:1, when the story begins to be told from his perspective.[70] In comparison to the patriarchs of Gen 11–36, the figure of Joseph has a minor impact on the history of Israel. Accordingly, the narrative does not manifest the same interests for eti-ology, time spans, and space. It forms a continuous storyline that explains finally how Israel came to Egypt and why the exodus became necessary. Important theological features of the patriarchal stories such as the-ophany, covenant, or ancestral promises are not touched upon.

This chapter has identified prominent literary features such as reports, etiologies, the role of space or geography and time, geography or history within the genealogies and their sociological impact on travel reports, cult notices, etymological notices, wordplays, short poems, and sayings. The first part of the book ("Primeval History") and the second ("Ancestral History") have more features in common than the Joseph narrative with its exceptional character. Due to several keywords around the topoi of life and divine benediction, an arrangement is provided which brings together the bouquet of different rhetorical features and narrative units of the book.

SELECT BIBLIOGRAPHY

Alter, Robert. *The Art of Biblical Narrative.* New York: Basic Books, 1981.
Bar-Efrat, Shimon. *Narrative Art in the Bible.* London: T & T Clark International, 2004.

concerning the different types of narrators in Hebrew Bible texts. He emphasizes the importance of the narrator's guidance in regard to the absorption of implicit values and attitudes of a particular text, so that the technique of the viewpoint fulfils a decisive role (16).

[69]   Alter, *Art*, 51, see also 96.
[70]   Berlin, *Poetics*, 76–77.

Bauks, Michaela. "Intratextual Exegesis in the Primeval History: The Literary Function of the Genealogies in View of the Formation of Gen 1–11." *ZAW* 131 (2019): 177–93.

Bauks, Michaela. *Die Welt am Anfang: Zum Verhältnis von Vorwelt und Weltentstehung in Gen 1 und in der altorientalischen Literatur.* WMANT 74. Neukirchen-Vluyn: Neukirchener Verlag, 1997.

Carr, David M. "Βίβλος γενέσεως Revisited: A Synchronic Analysis of Patterns in Genesis as Part of the Torah (Part One)." *ZAW* 110 (1998): 159–72.

Carr, David M. "Βίβλος γενέσεως Revisited: A Synchronic Analysis of Patterns in Genesis as Part of the Torah (Part Two)." *ZAW* 110 (1998): 327–47.

Carr, David M. *Reading the Fractures of Genesis: Historical and Literary Approaches.* Louisville, KY: Westminster John Knox Press, 1996.

Coats, George W. *Genesis, with an Introduction to Narrative Literature.* FOTL 1. Grand Rapids, MI: Eerdmans, 1983.

Finkelstein, Israel and Thomas Römer. "Comments on the Historical Background of the Jacob Narrative in Genesis." *ZAW* 126/3 (2014): 317–38.

Fokkelman, Jan P. "Genesis." Pages 36–55 in *The Literary Guide to the Bible.* Edited by Robert Alter and Frank Kermode. Cambridge, MA: Harvard University Press, 1987.

Gertz, Jan Christian. *Das erste Buch Mose (Genesis 1–11).* ATD 1/1. Göttingen: Vandenhoeck & Ruprecht, 2018.

Gertz, Jan Christian. "The Formation of the Primeval History." Pages 107–35 in *The Book of Genesis: Composition, Reception, and Interpretation.* Edited by Craig A. Evans, Joel N. Lohr, and David L. Petersen. VTSup 152. Leiden: Brill, 2012.

Gunkel, Hermann. *Genesis: Translated and Interpreted.* Translated by Mark E Biddle. Macon, GA: Mercer University Press, 1997. Translation of *Genesis übersetzt und erklärt.* HKAT 1.1. 3rd revised edition. Göttingen: Vandenhoeck & Ruprecht, 1910.

Hieke, Thomas. *Die Genealogien der Genesis.* HBS 39. Freiburg im Breisgau: Herder, 2003.

Sasson, Jack M. "A Genealogical 'Convention' in Biblical Chronography?" *ZAW* 90/2 (1978): 171–85.

Seeligmann, Isaac Leo. "Ätiologische Elemente in der biblischen Geschichtsschreibung." Pages 77–118 in *Gesammelte Studien zur Hebräischen Bibel.* Edited by Erhard Blum. FAT 41. Tübingen: Mohr Siebeck, 2004.

Sternberg, Meir. *The Poetics of Biblical Narrative: Ideological Literature and the Drama of Reading.* Indiana Studies in Biblical Literature. Bloomington: Indiana University Press, 1985.

Part II
Social World of Genesis

6 Genesis and Its Ancient Literary Analogues

ALICE MANDELL

IN THE BEGINNING: STORIES, SCRIBES, AND SCHOLARS

The book of Genesis stands apart from the rest of the Hebrew Bible in the diverse genres and topics that it covers, from creation accounts to shorter etiologies (e.g., the advent of clothing [Gen 3:7, 21], animal husbandry, agriculture, arts and crafts [Gen 4], dietary laws [Gen 9:3–4], the diversification of language [Gen 11:1–9]), and the early histories of specific linguistic and cultural groups descended from Noah's three sons, Shem, Ham, and Japhet. Genesis 12–50, which focuses on Shem's descendants, introduces key figures referred to here as the ancestors: Abraham/Sarah, Isaac/Rebecca, Jacob (renamed Israel)/Leah and Rachel (his two principal wives), and the twelve fathers of the tribes of Israel, Jacob's male offspring.

Genesis casts this clan as not only the ancestors of the people of Israel and Judah but also as the extended family, rivals, and (at times) allies of neighboring peoples. As a narrative block, the ancestor stories in Gen 12–50 foreshadow the emergence of the Iron Age kingdoms of Israel, Judah, Moab, Ammon, and Edom. Genesis also lays the groundwork for Israel's stint in Egypt, with its final piece, the Joseph story, serving as a bridge between the accounts of Jacob's children and the accounts of the generation of Israelites who follow Moses. In this way, the kinship networks and geography described in the ancestor stories in Genesis complement the story of the rise of the Israelite and Judean monarchies presented in the Deuteronomistic History; they harmonize disparate people under the banner of an ancestral god, YHWH, and the claim of a shared family lineage.

The history of Genesis scholarship elucidates key changes in how scholars approached the history of Israel's origins as they are presented in the Pentateuch. In the first phase of scholarship, the Genesis stories were treated as windows into Israel's early history – as "authentic" oral traditions that were written down by scribes during the monarchal period.

Scholars used key themes, narrative arcs, genres, and literary forms to connect Abraham, Isaac, Jacob, and the Exodus stories to specific historical periods, particularly those in the second millennium BCE. For example, scholars focusing on the Primeval History (Gen 1–11) have looked primarily to Mesopotamian analogues to explain the Priestly (P) and non-Priestly (traditionally J) creation stories, the flood matrix (both P and non-P), the Babel story, and the structure and significance of the genealogical lists that punctuate Gen 1–11 and form a bridge between the stories about Adam, Eve, and their descendants and the stories about the patriarchs and matriarchs in Gen 12–50. Those scholars interested in the descriptions of lifestyle and family customs in Gen 12–50, who (following Albright) identify Abraham as an Amorite and/or consider that Deut 26:5 and Abraham's time in Harran reflect a genuine Syrian origin for the ancestors in Genesis, seek ancient Near Eastern parallels for those social customs.

However, much of scholarship on Genesis today does not anchor these stories to the chronology given in the biblical text, and is increasingly skeptical of their historicity as presented in the biblical text (that is, scholars are skeptical that there was a discrete period of captivity or sojourn in Egypt, followed by a mass exodus; and that conquest events took place and enacted the birth of Israel as a territorially bounded people; there is also pushback against the view that David and Solomon's kingdoms represent the zenith of Israel's territories before a civil war). Such scholarship posits that the biblical stories in Genesis should first be evaluated as the product of Israel's social history, as defined by the Israelite and Judean experience of empire and exile into the first millennium BCE, and its scribal history, which places the composition of Genesis in a late- to post-monarchal context. This downdating of the composition of biblical literature correlates with the peak of Hebrew inscriptional findings (8th–6th centuries BCE).[1] Seen in the political context of the Neo-Assyrian, Neo-Babylonian, and Persian empires, Genesis is understood as an ideological composition that reflects the concerns of people living under the shadow of foreign empires in the second half of the first millennium BCE. Genesis, as a literary space, functions as an ark; it is designed as a curated representation of what was, while its language of covenant and promise speaks to future generations about what can be.

---

[1]   William M. Schniedewind, *How the Bible Became a Book* (Cambridge: Cambridge University Press, 2004), esp. 64–117.

THE PERILS OF PARALLELISM: METHODS
AND MOTIVATIONS

Genesis has also played an important role in the "genesis" of the comparative method in biblical and ancient Near Eastern studies. By comparing biblical writings to Iron Age Hebrew inscriptions and ancient Near Eastern analogues (or perceived analogues) dating to the first and second millennia BCE, scholars can clarify difficult or ill-understood terminology and/or practices, as well as elucidate the cultural backdrop of Israel and Judah's scribal institutions. The majority of studies of Genesis that adopt a comparative approach have focused upon the logo-syllabic cuneiform and alphabetic cuneiform texts of Israel's neighbors.

Beginning in the late nineteenth century, newly discovered cuneiform tablets recording stories with similarities to those in Genesis were seen by many as confirmation of the historicity of biblical literature. In 1872, George Smith identified a flood story on a fragment of Gilgamesh tablet XI with similar details to the Genesis flood composition. The growing corpus of cuneiform tablets was immediately seen as a way to supplement the biblical and classical writings, which had been the primary focus of historians and scholars of the ancient Near East.

Ancient Near Eastern written materials were particularly prized as potential correlates to the stories and events narrated in biblical writings. This interest in uncovering the cultures considered to be part of the biblical world fueled popular and institutional (both governmental and academic) interest in the archaeology of Mesopotamia.[2] This in turn yielded the financial backing needed to support renewed excavations in ancient Assyria and Babylonia. Both national museums and private individuals rapidly collected tablets from excavations and from the antiquities and black markets.

Cuneiform tablets recovered from Mesopotamia as well as third millennium BCE sites such as Ebla and second millennium BCE sites such as Alalakh, Emar, Hattusha, Mari, Nuzi, and Ugarit, have since transformed the study of the ancient Levant. These economic records, letters, legal materials, and ritual and literary texts predate biblical writings by over a millennium. In order to engage fully with the wealth of cuneiform materials, scholars specializing in the origins

---

[2]   George Smith died of dysentery in Aleppo on a subsequent trip to Nineveh to find more texts connected to the flood account. His description of the original findings is preserved in the archives of *Transactions of the Society of Biblical Archaeology*, vols. 1–5 (London: Longmans, Green, Reader, & Dyer, 1872–77).

and history of ancient Israel extended the scope of their research to include cuneiform corpora of the second and first millennia BCE. For example, in Hermann Gunkel's comparative study of the Enuma Elish, Gilgamesh, and the Genesis creation and flood stories, he proposed that Genesis 1–11 (in particular the sections attributed to P) both drew from and reacted to these Mesopotamian traditions.[3]

Since the late nineteenth century, ancient Near Eastern texts have been used in diverse ways to clarify the biblical text: both in microanalysis (e.g., to clarify individual words or formulae) and as points of comparison for the creation, transmission (spoken, enacted, and/or written), composition, and editing of biblical writings. Inherent to this enterprise is the search for the lived context of ancient texts as well as the search for those people creating and transmitting these "traditions" – an umbrella term in biblical studies, which includes narrative arcs (e.g., the sister-wife motif), theological claims (e.g., covenants regarding land/heirs/dynasty), as well as formulae (e.g., blessing and curse language).[4] In particular, a survey of cuneiform materials connected to Genesis in scholarship (especially during the twentieth century) reveals parallels of many different kinds (for example, general themes versus more specific plot points,[5] or such small details as the *hapax legomena* in the biblical flood narrative which find parallels in Akkadian flood accounts).[6]

The lack of consensus about what constitutes a parallel or analogous text-type has been a key issue in the comparative enterprise.[7] Moreover, once a tentative parallel has been drawn (even when scholars agree that the biblical and ancient Near

[3] Hermann Gunkel and Heinrich Zimmern, *Schöpfung und Chaos in Urzeit und Endzeit: Eine religionsgeschichtliche Untersuchung über Gen 1 und Ap Joh 12* (Göttingen: Vandenhoeck & Ruprecht, 1895).

[4] For an overview see Mark W. Chavalas, "The Comparative Use of Ancient Near Eastern Texts in the Study of the Hebrew Bible," *Religion Compass* 5.5 (2011): 150–65.

[5] In Atrahasis and Gilgamesh XI, a flood is devised as a means of population control, whereas in Genesis it is a punishment for human violence. In Gilgamesh XI, Utnapishtim sends a dove, a swallow, and a raven to look for dry land; in Gen 8:6–12, Noah sends a raven and then a dove to look for dry land.

[6] The term *kōper* in Gen 6:14, which describes the sealing agent that waterproofed the ark, is otherwise unattested in the Hebrew Bible; this is a cognate for Akkadian *kupru* "bitumen" used in the Gilgamesh Flood story and in Atrahasis (see *CAD* K, 553–55 for the list of parallels).

[7] For proposed criteria, see Brent A. Strawn, "Comparative Approaches: History, Theory, and the Image of God," in *Method Matters: Essays on the Interpretation of the Hebrew Bible in Honor of David L. Petersen*, ed. Joel M. LeMon and Kent Harold Richards (Atlanta, GA: SBL, 2009), 117–42.

Eastern texts share features), scholars differ about what the parallel means.[8] For example, it is debated whether or not the Genesis flood account was inspired by Mesopotamian flood stories (and if so, which one?), and whether or not the Akkadian and Hebrew flood accounts derive independently from well-known stories about a flood and the salvation of humans by a crafty god. Each view further raises the question of what was the mechanism for the transmission of these stories to Hebrew-writing scribes. A further complication is that ancient Near Eastern materials have their own complex composition histories. For example, before drawing parallels between the flood tablet of the Akkadian story of Gilgamesh and Genesis 6–9, we should consider the reception history of flood narratives as well as how Utnapishtim's story functions both as an independent tale and as an integrated part of Gilgamesh's quest for immortality.

Scholars of biblical literature and the history of ancient Israel have also looked to second-millennium BCE analogues to context-ualize the lifestyles and familial structures described in the Genesis ancestor stories and/or sought to identify a historic kernel under-lying the stories of Abraham and his family.[9] For example, Albright initially dated the stories of Abraham, Isaac, and Jacob to the early second millennium, viewing the story of Abraham's descent into Canaan as a description of the displacement of the Amorites that resulted in the foundation of the Middle Bronze Amorite king-doms in Syria and Mesopotamia (e.g., by figures like Hammurabi and Zimri-Lim).[10] In Albright's reconstruction, Abraham was a donkey-caravanner who lived in the early Middle Bronze Age. Albright further connected adoption practices at Nuzi (based on his understanding of the textual record's "sale adoptions") to Eliezer's status as an adopted heir (see Gen 15:1–6).[11]

[8] As Jack Sasson writes, "comparisons among words, stories, rituals, institutions, or artifacts can be homologous or analogous. They can be drawn analogously in the absence of a generic or genealogical linkage between two objects of comparison ... Most comparisons that refer to 'radiation,' 'dependence,' or 'archetypes,' are in fact analogic" (Jack Sasson, "About 'Mari and the Bible,'" RA 92 [1998]: 97–123, here 98).
[9] For an overview of attempts to connect these materials to the ancestor stories, see Martin J. Selman, "Comparative Customs and the Patriarchal Age," in Essays on the Patriarchal Narratives, ed. Alan R. Millard and Donald J. Wiseman (Winona Lake, IN: Eisenbrauns, 1980), 91–139.
[10] William F. Albright, "From the Patriarchs to Moses: From Abraham to Joseph," BA 36.1 (1973): 5–19.
[11] Cyrus H. Gordon, on the other hand, focused on family customs and argued for a mid-fourteenth-century BCE date for the ancestor stories in "Biblical Customs and the Nuzi Tablets," BA 3 (1940): 1–12.

Ephraim A. Speiser, similarly, connected social and legal customs at Nuzi to the ancestor stories of Gen 12–50.[12] He proposed that legal materials from Nuzi best explained the "sister-wife" triplet in Gen 12, 20, and 26, whereby Abraham (twice) and Isaac (once) pretend that their wives are their sisters.[13] However, Speiser viewed the received versions in the biblical text to be diluted, both through their oral transmission and through their arrangement by biblical writers.

In more recent scholarship, scholars seek to balance the study of such second millennium materials with textual analogues that are geographically and chronologically closer to ancient Israel and Judah (e.g., Iron Age alphabetic inscriptions, Egyptian texts and scribal practices, and historiographic works in Greek, as well as first-millennium BCE cuneiform comparanda).[14] This shift is in part due to two critical studies by Thomas Thompson and John Van Seters in the 1970s that contended that the Genesis ancestors were not historical figures.[15] Thompson and Van Seters pointed out anachronisms in the ancestor stories and argued that the familial customs and lifestyle described in Gen 12–50 fit better with the population movements and social concerns of the Levant in the

[12] See his discussion of "T," by which he means tradition, the pre-source material, which was "just as much an enigma to biblical writers themselves." See Ephraim A. Speiser, *Genesis: Introduction, Translation, and Notes*, Anchor Bible 1 (Garden City, NY: Doubleday, 1964), xl; see further xxxix–xliii.

[13] Ephraim A. Speiser, "The Wife-Sister Motif in the Patriarchal Narratives," in *Biblical and Other Studies*, ed. A. Altmann (Waltham, MA: Brandeis University Press, 1963), 15–28.

[14] See, for example, John Van Seters, *In Search of History: Historiography in the Ancient World and the Origins of Biblical History* (New Haven, CT: Yale University Press, 1983); David M. Carr, *Writing on the Tablet of the Heart: Origins of Scripture and Literature* (Oxford: Oxford University Press, 2005); Christopher A. Rollston, *Writing and Literacy in the World of Ancient Israel: Epigraphic Evidence from the Iron Age* (Atlanta, GA: SBL, 2010); Seth L. Sanders, *The Invention of Hebrew* (Urbana, Ill.: University of Illinois Press, 2009); Seth L. Sanders, *From Adapa to Enoch* (Tübingen: Mohr Siebeck, 2017); Karel van der Toorn, *Scribal Culture and the Making of the Hebrew Bible* (Cambridge, MA: Harvard University Press, 2007); William M. Schniedewind, *The Finger of the Scribe: How Scribes Learned to Write the Bible* (Oxford: Oxford University Press, 2019). See also Sara J. Milstein, *Tracking the Master Scribe: Revision Through Introduction in Biblical and Mesopotamian Literature* (New York: Oxford University Press, 2016).

[15] In the 1970s, both Thomas L. Thompson and John Van Seters wrote influential works that problematized Abraham and the Amorite hypothesis as well as the hunt for second-millennium BCE parallels. See Thomas L. Thompson, *The Historicity of the Patriarchal Narratives: The Quest for Historical Abraham* (Berlin: de Gruyter, 1974); John Van Seters, *Abraham in History and Tradition* (New Haven: Yale University Press, 1975); for a more recent treatment, see Thomas L. Thompson, *Biblical Narrative and Palestine's History: Changing Perspectives 2* (Bristol, CT: Equinox, 2013).

first millennium BCE.[16] Their critiques of past scholarship were also methodological; they noted that the so-called Albright School (primarily scholars in the United States) had theological aims and that the parallels that they proposed lacked substance.[17] Scholars of the ancient Near East should read these stories through the lens of first millennium BCE changes in the Levant, not in the light of Middle Bronze Age cuneiform comparanda.[18] This scholarship has also led to the down-dating of the composition and editing of the Pentateuch by certain scholars into the exilic and Second Temple periods.[19]

The overzealous application of the comparative method in biblical studies (perceived by some as "parallelomania"[20]) has faced criticism both in the broader study of the Levant and in other ancient Near Eastern fields.[21] A key critique is that ancient Near Eastern communities should be valued in their own right and not merely for their connection (or

[16]   For example, Van Seters sees the emphasis on Haran and references to nomadic elements as reflecting the movement of Arameans and nomadic groups (e.g., Arabian tribes), and most likely a Neo-Babylonian date (*Abraham in History and Tradition*, 29–38; 121; 310). He thinks that camel domestication fits best in an eighth–seventh centuries BCE context (17) and also argues that the references to the Philistines reflect a first millennium context (120–22). Other scholars, such as Richard Hess, have countered that the references to camels and Philistines could be later scribal additions or updates to older stories. See, for example, this recent exchange: Mark Elliott and Ed Wright, "Reply to the Richard Hess' review of Old Testament in Archaeology and History," February 2020, https://bibleinterp.arizona.edu/articles/re ply-richard-hess-review-old-testament-archaeology-and-history; Richard S. Hess, "Text and History: Reassessing the Relationship between the Bible and Archaeological Findings: A Review Essay of Jennie Ebeling, J. Edward Wright, Mark Elliott, and Paul V. M. Flesher, eds., *The Old Testament in Archaeology and History* (Waco: Baylor, 2017)," January 13, 2020, https://denverseminary.edu/article/text-and-history-reassessing-the-relationship-between-the-bible-and-archaeological-findings-a-review-essay-of -jennie-ebeling-j-edward-wright-mark-elliott-and-paul-v-m-flesher-eds-the-old-tes-tament-in-archaeology-and-history-waco-baylor-2017/.

[17]   Independently of Thompson and Van Seters, Samuel Greengus disproved the theory of a sister-wife at Nuzi, pulling out the moorings of such a theory as an explanation for the ancestor stories; see Samuel Greengus, " Sisterhood Adoption at Nuzi and the 'Wife-Sister' in Genesis," *HUCA* 46 (1975): 5–31.

[18]   As Thompson writes, "the quest for the historical Abraham is a basically fruitless occupation" (*Historicity*, 315).

[19]   For example, Van Seters dates the bulk of the composition of the ancestral narratives to the post-monarchal period. See *Abraham in History*, 310–11.

[20]   This expression was (to my knowledge) first introduced into the field of Biblical Studies in Samuel Sandmel's presidential address to the Society of Biblical Literature in 1961. In this speech, he critiqued the lack of controlled study of the New Testament texts and their relationships to the Dead Sea Scrolls and Rabbinic writings. See Samuel Sandmel, "Parallelomania," *JBL* 81.1 (1962): 1–18.

[21]   See, for example, Shemaryahu Talmon, "The 'Comparative Method' in Biblical Interpretation: Principles and Problems," in *Congress Volume Göttingen 1977*, ed. John Emerton, VTSup 29 (Leiden: Brill, 1978), 320–56; see also Helmer Ringgren, "The

perceived connection) to the world of the Bible.[22] In particular, the
search for parallels to biblical sources in cuneiform materials has
received a measure of resistance from Assyriologists.[23] Those
scholars who work on corpora so often compared to Genesis, such
as the cuneiform tablets from Mari, Nuzi, and Alalakh, have cau-
tioned biblical scholars that mining such cuneiform materials for
parallels to the biblical text is not a helpful enterprise if scholars
do not take the time to understand the contexts and composition
histories of these sources and to understand the points of
difference.[24] They also point out that there does not seem to be
a consensus on what constitutes a valid or meaningful parallel (do
shared word-pairs, formulae specific to a genre, common or shared
plot points, or similar names or cognate terminology suffice to argue
for textual dependence?).[25] And as they caution, it is important to be
aware of the motivations behind such comparative work. What is the
ultimate aim of the scholar – to anchor the biblical text in a specific
historical period in order to evaluate Israel's stories as part of
a broader royal and/or scribal endeavor to curate identity-driven

Impact of the Ancient Near East on Israelite Tradition," in *Tradition and Theology in the Old Testament*, ed. Douglas A. Knight (Philadelphia: Fortress, 1977), 31–46.

[22] In an extreme example, Friedrich Delitzsch proposed in an (in)famous set of lectures known as the "Babel und Bibel" series (1902–4) that the Hebrew Bible was both derivative of and inferior to Mesopotamian literature. He also argued that the Bible, an Israelite (that is, Jewish) text, had no place in modern Germany. This lecture series reflected the anti-Semitic climate of pre-World War II Germany, as well as efforts to create a German Christian identity stripped of the Hebrew Bible and its past. See Bill T. Arnold and David B. Weisberg, "A Centennial Review of Friedrich Delitzsch's 'Babel und Bibel' Lectures," *JBL* 121.3 (2002): 441–57.

[23] For a recent assessment and a call for more mindful use of Assyriological works, see Mark W. Chavalas, "Assyriology and Biblical Studies: A Century and a Half of Tension," in *Mesopotamia and the Bible*, ed. Mark W. Chavalas and K. Lawson Younger, Jr. (London: Sheffield Academic, 2002), 21–67. See also Benno Landsberger, *The Conceptual Autonomy of the Babylonian World* (Malibu, CA: Undena, 1976).

[24] William W. Hallo, "Compare and Contrast: The Contextual Approach to Biblical Literature," in *The Bible in Light of Cuneiform Literature: Scripture in Context III*, ed. William W. Hallo, Bruce William Jones, and Gerald L. Mattingly (Lewiston, NJ: Mellen, 1990), 1–30.

[25] See, for example, the critique of the use (and abuse) of cuneiform corpora by biblical scholars in Wilfred G. Lambert, "Review Article: The Mari Texts and the Old Testament," *PEQ* 126.2 (1994): 160–63. Jack Sasson's push back against the use of the Mari archives in Biblical Studies is equally acute; he cautions against "the drive to privilege historical research in authenticating biblical events" (Jack M. Sasson, "Mari and The Holy Grail," in *Orientalism, Assyriology and the Bible*, ed. Steven W. Holloway [Sheffield: Sheffield Phoenix, 2007], 186–98, here 188). See also Sasson, "About 'Mari and the Bible,'" 98.

literature, or to harmonize the biblical text with archaeology in a way that appeals to a contemporary faith community?[26]

READING GENESIS IN THE FIRST MILLENNIUM BCE

The paradigm shift in the downdating of the biblical text to the first millennium BCE coincided with a fundamental change in the study of the archaeology of the southern Levant.[27] Even the nomenclature used to describe the archaeology of this region was impacted. The "biblical archaeology" of the so-called Albright school (i.e., archaeology heavily influenced by the biblical text) has largely been replaced by "Syro-Palestinian" or "Levantine" archaeology. The later designations place emphasis on a geographic region bounded by similarities in material culture and political history, whereas the former label subordinates the complex social and political histories of diverse peoples to their relationship to a single textual corpus.[28] According to archaeologists, in particular those of the "Tel Aviv" school, biblical narratives such as the ancestor stories in Genesis should not be used as a starting point by archaeologists.[29] Such stories should,

[26] For example, one approach to reconcile the downdating of the composition of the biblical text into the Iron Age with a desire to situate the stories of Abraham and his family into a second millennium BCE setting is to argue for the passing down of small units of oral tradition, which, over time, were written down and became reframed by Hebrew scribes. See for example, the discussion of the story of Abraham and his family in the revision of John Bright's classic work, *A History of Israel*, 4th ed. (Louisville: Westminster John Knox, 2000), 67–103. The discussion of second millennium BCE comparanda concludes with the claim that "the Bible's picture of the patriarchs is deeply rooted in history" (ibid., 103).

[27] Much of this work was spearheaded by archaeologists such as William G. Dever who adopted the methods of processual archaeology, an approach that arose in the 1960s and emphasized scientific and statistical methods. For an overview of key shifts in the study of archaeology of the southern Levant, see Thomas E. Levy, "The New Pragmatism: Integrating Anthropological, Digital, and Historical Biblical Archaeologies," in *Historical Biblical Archaeology and the Future: The New Pragmatism*, ed. Thomas E. Levy (London: Equinox, 2010), 3–44.

[28] See, for example, J. Maxwell Miller and John Hayes's more cautious introduction to the Genesis ancestor stories in the second edition of their history of Israel and Judah. They write: "The parallels between biblical names and customs, on the one hand, and those known from Middle and Late Bronze Mesopotamian texts on the other, become less impressive when one considers that the sorts of names and customs involved were not confined to the second millennium BCE but were apparently characteristic of the first millennium as well. This renders the parallels relatively useless for pinpointing any particular period as 'the patriarchal age.'" See J. Maxwell Miller and John H. Hayes, *A History of Ancient Israel and Judah*, 2nd ed. (Louisville: Westminster John Knox, 2006), 53.

[29] See the exchanges between Israel Finkelstein and Amihai Mazar, which reflect different approaches to the presentation of history offered in the biblical text, in *The Quest*

however, be carefully sifted for what they might reveal about the attitudes of biblical writers, either toward a received history or toward concurrent political and social issues.[30]

Archaeologists and those textual scholars who work with material culture (that is, specialists who reconstruct Israel's history from datable remains) have also called for a more balanced use of biblical materials.[31] Accordingly, those scholars who adhere to a more traditional dating schema have had to respond to both text and material culture specialists who advocate for a much later context for these stories.[32] While there are scholars who seek to reclaim and redefine the intellectual territory lost by figures such as Albright, they offer a revised assessment of second millennium BCE comparanda, taking into account the increase in inscriptional and archaeological data in the past century.[33] The middle road in the field, which looks at all available evidence with a critical eye, is the most prudent in light of the extant evidence. Mark W. Chavalas offers the excellent advice that "we must not succumb either to 'parallelomania' or to 'parallelophobia.'"[34] This also means taking seriously any differences between suggested parallel sources as well as the literary and historical backdrops of the texts in question.[35]

for the Historical Israel: Debating Archaeology and the History of Early Israel, ed. Brian B. Schmidt (Atlanta, GA: SBL, 2007).

[30]   For example, anachronistic references to camels, Philistines, and sites that were either non-existent in the Middle Bronze Age or better-established in later periods suggest that the world of the ancestors, as described in Genesis, does not fit a Middle Bronze Age context. For a summary of the study of the ancestors in Gen 12–50 in archaeology, see the popular but influential work by Israel Finkelstein and Neil Asher Silberman, *The Bible Unearthed: Archaeology's New Vision of Ancient Israel and the Origin of Its Sacred Texts* (New York: Touchstone, 2002), 27–47, 319–25.

[31]   For example, William G. Dever has argued that historians should prioritize archaeology, not the biblical text; yet, he is equally critical of scholarship that denies the usefulness of biblical writings in fleshing out the details of ancient Israel's history (*Beyond the Texts: An Archaeological Portrait of Ancient Israel and Judah* [Atlanta: SBL, 2017]).

[32]   For example, the collection of essays in *Essays on the Patriarchal Narratives*. ed. Alan R. Millard and Donald J. Wiseman (Winona Lake, IN: Eisenbrauns, 1980) attempts to reevaluate the ancestor narratives in response to Thompson and Van Seters. For a less conciliatory position, see Kenneth A. Kitchen, *On the Reliability of the Old Testament* (Grand Rapids, MI: Eerdmans, 2003).

[33]   See the collection of essays in defense of "biblical archaeology" in *The Future of Biblical Archaeology: Reassessing Methodologies and Assumptions*, ed. James K. Hoffmeier and Alan Millard (Grand Rapids, MI: Eerdmans, 2004).

[34]   "Assyriology and Biblical Studies," 43.

[35]   For a defense of the integration of the "contextualist" (seeing the text within its cultural context) and "diffusionist" (i.e., comparative) approaches, see Howard Eilberg-Schwartz, "Beyond Parallel-anoia: Comparative Inquiry and Cultural Interpretation,"

More recent work, which balances the descriptions of family life in the biblical text with both archaeological and comparative Near Eastern evidence, also highlights how Genesis offers a window into broader Israelite ideologies about the family. This new emphasis has opened up the study of Genesis to research with an important comparative component, which includes targeted studies of kinship, gender, and the domestic economy and cult in ancient Israel.[36] The descriptions of the ancestors and their families in Genesis are critical to this vein of scholarship, as their stories touch upon birth and post-partum practices, naming customs, infant and child mortality, infertility, adoption, childhood, marriage and concubinage, and coming of age rites in ancient Israel.[37]

The study of ancient Near Eastern comparanda has ushered in a fundamental change in the study of the Hebrew Bible. Scholars can no longer treat the Bible as a bounded text unique to ancient Israel. Rather, scholars using the comparative method are expected to analyze the biblical text as a curated collection of diverse text types – an intricate tapestry that shares stylistic, thematic, linguistic, and ideological characteristics with the texts of neighboring peoples, and presumably with their non-written traditions and practices. In short, for those scholars who adopt a comparative linguistic or comparative literary method (including those scholars who adopt a tradition-historical or form-critical approach), the study of the Bible is inextricable from the study of the ancient Near East.

GENESIS AND HISTORY WRITING (OR SELF-REFLECTIVE STORYTELLING) IN THE ANCIENT NEAR EAST

So how did (or does) Genesis operate both as a collection of Israelite (and/ or Judean) origin stories and as an ancient Near Eastern text? This question is central to the comparative approach to ancient Near

---

in *The Savage in Judaism: An Anthropology of Israelite Religion and Ancient Judaism* (Bloomington, IN: Indiana University Press, 1990), 87–102.

[36] See for example, Cynthia Chapman's analysis of the portrayals of matrilineal kinship in Genesis; this work draws upon kinship terminology in Semitic comparanda to reconstruct the important role of the "house of the mother" in ancient Israel. See *The House of the Mother: The Social Role of Maternal Kin in Biblical Hebrew Narrative and Poetry* (New Haven, CT: Yale University Press). Kristine Henriksen Garroway incorporates diverse Near Eastern comparanda into a targeted study of children and the family in the Hebrew Bible, with a heavy emphasis on the descriptions of childbearing and rearing in Genesis. See *Growing Up in Ancient Israel: Children in Material Culture and Biblical Texts* (Atlanta: SBL, 2020).

[37] See further the chapters by Steinberg and Shectman in this volume.

Eastern texts and scribal practices more broadly. If we accept the premises that a comparative approach offers us (1) a better understanding of the world presented in the Bible, and (2) a glimpse into the worldview of the people creating and passing down Israel's literary traditions, there remains a methodological issue: how should we go about identifying parallels between the biblical and other Near Eastern texts, and when we find them, what do they mean?[38]

Detaching Genesis from a particular historical moment fundamentally changes how scholars use ancient Near Eastern texts that share structural and thematic similarities. Drawing on Johan Huizinga's description of history-making as a process, we might consider Genesis as a form of ancient historiography, a self-reflective intellectual and ideological enterprise.[39] This approach is not interested in proving (or disproving) the existence of the characters in Genesis 12–50, but is rather concerned with examining the process of textual creation and transmission in the Iron Age in order to better understand the complexity of Israel's cultural and political genesis, which includes the formative periods of exile and reconstruction into the Persian Period. While the building blocks of Genesis claim an ancient origin (in the world of the text) from before the days of Israel's temple, priests, or kings, the broader aim of Genesis is to forge a discrete social and religious community. The juxtaposition of the primeval narratives (Gen 1–11), which have clear Mesopotamian analogues, with the stories of YHWH's pact with Abraham, Isaac, and Jacob (Gen 12–50), which are identity-statement stories, suggest that the aims of Genesis lie not in presenting an accurate view of a received oral history but in creating a unifying origin myth, one that would appeal to contemporary and future generations. This understanding reframes the ancestor stories as a reshaping of history in order to make history. Genesis, as a curated work, was crafted as a response to the social and political crises arising from the Neo-Assyrian, Neo-Babylonian, and Persian periods.[40]

[38] My thanks to Theodore J. Lewis for introducing me to a satirical Onion article on the comparative method which gets to the heart of a key critique of this approach, entitled "Professor Sees Parallels Between Things, Other Things," *The Onion* 43.20, May 16, 2007, www.theonion.com/professor-sees-parallels-between-things-other-things-1819569111. The mock-professor states, "By drawing parallels between things and other, entirely different things, I not only further my own studies, but also encourage young minds to develop this comparative method ... It's not just the similarities that are important – the differences are also worth exploring at length."

[39] As Johan Huizinga writes, "History is the intellectual form in which a civilization renders account to itself of its past" (in "A Definition of the Concept of History," in *Philosophy and History: Essays Presented to Ernst Cassirer*, ed. Raymond Klibansky and H. J. Paton [Oxford: Clarendon, 1936], 1–10, here 9).

[40] In recent years, trauma theory has increasingly been valued as a lens through which to evaluate the interest in identity creation and preservation demonstrated in the biblical

The compositional complexity of Genesis also reflects the diverse aims of the people who selected, wrote, and revised its materials. Following this line of inquiry, we may also consider the structure of Genesis – both the macro arrangement of its materials and the micro-elements within individual pericopes (e.g., why the P and non-P creation accounts are juxtaposed, whereas the P and non-P flood accounts are integrated) – as a crafted, scribal work.[41] The very organization of its diverse components (lists, stories, etiologies, religious ideologies, descriptions of family customs, ritual practices, and conceptions of geography) reflect the scribes' ideologies about Israel's place in the world and its relationship with their god. Seen in this light, the differences between biblical and ancient Near Eastern analogues become as important as any parallels. Points of divergence are attributed to later monarchal and post-monarchal claims about Israel's unique status among the nations (perhaps reflecting a Deuteronomistic or exilic outlook) or to the creativity of scribes trained in Hebrew, who were knowledgeable about the literary traditions of their neighbors and perhaps harnessed (and/or subverted) them in order to transform ancient Near Eastern mythologies into pro-Yahwistic propaganda.[42]

Those scholars still interested in the origins of the stories in Genesis can now also approach these narratives through the conduit of a shared "cultural" or "collective" memory, which had earlier second millennium BCE precursors.[43] This vein of scholarship borrows concepts

text. See, for example, Daniel L. Smith-Christopher, *A Biblical Theology of Exile* (Minneapolis, MN: Fortress, 2003); see also the collection of essays in *Bible Through the Lens of Trauma*, ed. Elizabeth Boase and Christopher G. Frechette (Atlanta, GA: SBL, 2016).

[41] See, for example, the series of questions raised about the internal composition of Gen 1–11 in David M. Carr, "The Politics of Textual Subversion: A Diachronic Perspective on the Garden of Eden Story," *JBL* 112.4 (1993): 577–95; David M. Carr, *Reading the Fractures of Genesis: Historical and Literary Approaches* (Louisville: Westminster John Knox, 1996), 48–77; see also Seth L. Sanders, "What If There Aren't Any Empirical Models for Pentateuchal Criticism?," in *Literacy, Orality, and Literary Production in the Southern Levant: Contextualizing Sacred Writing in Ancient Israel and Judah*, ed. Brian B. Schmidt (Atlanta, GA: SBL, 2015), 298–302; see also Jack M. Sasson, "The 'Tower of Babel' as a Clue to the Redactional Structuring of the Primeval History [Gen. 1–11:9]," in *The Bible World: Essays in Honor of Cyrus H. Gordon*, ed. Gary A. Rendsburg, Ruth Adler, and Arfa M. Winter (New York: Ktav, 1980), 211–19.

[42] For a more cautious approach, however, see Carly L. Crouch, *Israel and the Assyrians: Deuteronomy, the Succession Treaty of Esarhaddon, and the Nature of Subversion*, Ancient Near East Monographs 8 (Atlanta, GA: SBL, 2014).

[43] For example, in his work on Abraham, Ronald Hendel argues that while Gen 12–50 reflects a shared "collective memory" about Israel's past, this work functions as a "countermemory," that is, as a "deliberate recasting of memories of the past ... to

from the fields of history, sociology, and psychology to consider the process by which groups of people stake a claim on a shared set of memories and their interpretation;[44] in particular, scholars interested in this set of questions make use of cultural memory studies to consider how the very choice of what is relevant, important and worth commemorating, or worth forgetting, shapes our understanding of the past.[45]

THE ORIGIN STORIES IN GENESIS AND THEIR ANE ANALOGUES

This section focuses on four main tradition-complexes in Genesis and addresses the ways in which they have been studied in relation to cuneiform analogues from Syria and Mesopotamia: (1) the creation, Gen 1–3; taken here together with (2) the flood, Gen 6–9; (3) the genealogical lists (Gen 5, 11:10–32); and (4) the ancestor stories (Gen 12–50).

CREATION AND FLOOD STORIES

Overwhelmingly, the stories of creation reflected in Gen 1–3 are treated in scholarship as a literary creation that presents an alternative to other ancient Near Eastern creation stories. The key differences, such as the lack of a moment of copulation or conflict with other gods (see, however, the combat theme in Exod 15; Pss 74, 89, 97, 104; and Job 9), reflect

---

refute, revise, and replace a previously compelling or accepted memory ..."
(*Remembering Abraham: Culture, Memory, and History in the Hebrew Bible*
[Oxford: Oxford University Press, 2005], 41). This approach draws from the study of collective or social memory-making; it is a mode of analysis that derives from the study of "the invention of tradition" of the nineteenth and twentieth centuries. During the wars and interwar periods, heightened European nationalisms (pl.) culminated in the creation of national narratives that were commemorated in history writing, state monuments, and civic ceremonies. See Maurice M. Halbwachs, *The Collective Memory* (New York: Harper & Row, 1980); and Peter Burke, "History as Social Memory," in *Varieties of Cultural History*, ed. Peter Burke (Ithaca, NY: Cornell University Press, 1997), 43–59.

44 This focus on collective memory (also called cultural memory in some contexts) draws from the works of scholars such as Hayden White, *Metahistory: The Historical Imagination in Nineteenth-Century Europe* (Baltimore: Johns Hopkins University Press, 1973); Paul Ricoeur, *Memory, History, Forgetting*, trans. Kathleen Blamey and David Pellauer (Chicago: University of Chicago Press, 2004); Halbwachs, *Collective Memory*; and Paul Connerton, *How Societies Remember* (Cambridge: Cambridge University Press, 2014).

45 As Burke writes: "What are the modes of transmission of public memories and how have these modes changed over time? What are the uses of these memories, the uses of the past, and how have these uses changed? Conversely, what are the uses of oblivion?" ("History as Social Memory," 46).

ideologies about Israel's god as a superior deity. YHWH is the supreme being, able to marshal space and matter; astral, organic, and liquid bodies; as well as language (particularly in P's creation account) to create a stage for human and divine interaction.

While Egyptian creation stories have been examined by biblical scholars,[46] traditionally cuneiform creation and cosmogonic stories have been the focus of comparative studies.[47] Hermann Gunkel's treatment of Genesis was an early attempt at the comparative method, which compared and contrasted the Babylonian Enuma Elish and biblical creation accounts.[48] According to Gunkel, P's creation story was an intentional departure from the *Chaoskampf* motif that he identified in Marduk's combat with Tiamat. He argued that the deep and the waters described in Gen 1 are substances controlled and sculpted by Israel's god, and not independent divinities; he concluded that creation in Genesis is demythologized, as God creates without rival or opposition. This work also demonstrated a strategy for identifying what Gunkel viewed to be original oral literary traditions that predated the writing down and editing of the Pentateuch. Gunkel (and later scholars who adopted a similar form-critical approach) have sought to understand these originally oral stories, poems, or sayings in their original socio-political and religious contexts, in part by drawing upon ancient Near Eastern texts of a similar genre and function.

Since Gunkel's early foray into the comparative method, studies comparing the primeval accounts in Genesis to cuneiform analogues have been common, although the claim that biblical writers were referencing a specific Mesopotamian text in the creation story has been backgrounded to some degree.[49] Today, more attention is paid to the

---

[46]   See James K. Hoffmeier, "Some Thoughts on Genesis 1 & 2 and Egyptian Cosmology," *JANES* 15 (1983): 39–49.

[47]   By way of example, both of the following studies use comparative approaches to the study of creation in Genesis, yet they draw upon quite different ancient corpora. See Hoffmeier, "Some Thoughts on Genesis 1 & 2 and Egyptian Cosmology" and David T. Tsumura, "Genesis and Ancient Near Eastern Stories of Creation and Flood: An Introduction," in *I Studied Inscriptions From Before the Flood: Ancient Near Eastern, Literary, and Linguistic Approaches to Genesis 1–11*, ed. Richard S. Hess and David T. Tsumura (Winona Lake, IN: Eisenbrauns, 1994), 27–57.

[48]   This interpretation relied heavily on cognates between Akkadian and Hebrew. A crucial argument has been the connection between the Hebrew term *tǝhôm* "the deep" and the name of the god Tiāmat (Gunkel and Zimmern, *Schöpfung und Chaos*, 115–16). For a key critique of this linguistic argument, see David T. Tsumura, *The Earth and the Waters in Genesis 1 and 2: A Linguistic Investigation* (Sheffield: Sheffield Academic, 1989), 45–50.

[49]   Key studies have dismissed many of the proposed parallels between the Genesis creation stories and the Enuma Elish; see, for example, Wilfred G. Lambert, "A New

differences between these stories.[50] For instance, in the case of the Enuma Elish, the creation of humans is merely a by-product in a story about divine conflict; the real purpose of this story is to announce Marduk's rise to the head of the pantheon and his sovereignty over Babylon.[51] In contrast, in Genesis 1–3, Israel's patron god acts alone, unfettered by any divine competition. And while in both stories humans are derived from both divinity and the materiality of the earth (dirt or clay), in Genesis humans are the most important creations, created as guardians rather than slaves.

The publication of literary tablets from the ancient kingdom of Ugarit, written in an alphabetic cuneiform script, has also impacted the study of biblical creation stories.[52] This corpus is written in a Northwest Semitic language and refers to deities known from the Hebrew Bible and Iron Age inscriptions (El, Baal, Yam [the Sea], Asherah, Anat, etc.); it opened the proverbial floodgates for a new range of comparative studies. The focus of this scholarship is on biblical and Ugaritic poetic texts involving a "struggle" against the waters or other divine beings, which many see as analogous cosmogonies, in particular between Israel's god as a creator and divine king and the descriptions of the god Baal in the so-called Baal Cycle. There is no Ugaritic creation story akin to the accounts in Gen 1–3 (or to the Enuma Elish), yet some scholars argue that key themes that tie together the Baal stories and the disparate creation accounts in the Hebrew Bible include the theme of a conflict between a principal god and a water god (Yam; Tiamat and the "deep" in Gen 1);

Look at the Babylonian Background of Genesis," *JTS*, n.s., 16.2 (1965): 287–300; Alan R. Millard, "A New Babylonian 'Genesis' Story," *TynBul* 18 (1967): 3–18.

[50] For an overview, see Tsumura, "Genesis and Ancient Near Eastern Stories." See also the collection of essays adopting a comparative approach to the creation and flood stories in Genesis and cuneiform comparanda, reprinted in Tikva Frymer-Kensky, *Studies in Bible and Feminist Criticism*, JPS Scholars of Distinction Series (Philadelphia: Jewish Publication Society, 2006).

[51] For a comparison from an Assyriologist's perspective, see Wilfred G. Lambert, "Mesopotamian Creation Stories," in *Imagining Creation*, ed. Markham J. Geller and Mineke Schipper (Leiden: Brill, 2008), 15–59. See also the classic treatments in Alexander Heidel, *The Babylonian Genesis: The Story of the Creation*, 2nd ed. (Chicago: University of Chicago Press, 1951), 82–140; and Wilfred G. Lambert and Alan R. Millard, *Atraḫasīs: The Babylonian Story of the Flood* (Oxford: Oxford University Press, 1969). For a more updated translation, see Benjamin R. Foster, *Before the Muses: An Anthology of Akkadian Literature*, 3rd ed. (Bethesda, MD: CDL, 2005).

[52] For a discussion of Ugarit's place among the Amorite kingdoms of the second millennium BCE, see Mary E. Buck, *The Amorite Dynasty of Ugarit: Historical Implications Linguistic and Archaeological Parallels*, Studies in the Archaeology and History of the Levant 8 (Leiden: Brill, 2020).

the world's order created as the by-product of a struggle for sovereignty; and temple building as the conclusion of an altercation between divine beings. All of these shared events are seen by scholars to connect Baal's rise to that of Marduk in the Enuma Elish, as well as to the varied descriptions of Israel's god in battle and victory.[53] While past scholars perhaps were too eager to connect the Baal materials to Israelite literature, more recent work evaluates the materials from Ugarit in their own historical and scribal contexts. For example, reading the rise and fall of Baal in the context of the political climate at Ugarit elucidates key differences between Baal and Marduk of the Enuma Elish account and the creation accounts in biblical writings. Baal's story reflects Ugarit's precarious political situation at the end of the Late Bronze Age, as a kingdom caught between political superpowers (the Egyptian and Hittite empires) and regional enemies.[54]

Comparisons between the flood narratives in Gen 6–9 and Mesopotamian flood accounts or references to the flood in genealogical materials also abound.[55] In Gen 6–9, Israel's god wipes out his creation through a cataclysmic flood and starts over through Noah, his family, and the animals they herd into an ark. The two most famous Mesopotamian analogues are Atrahasis and Gilgamesh Tablet XI, as they share both general plot points (e.g., a god sends a cataclysmic flood against humans; and a savior god ensures the survival of life [Israel's god plays both roles in Genesis]) and specific details (a hero, his community, and diverse animals are saved by a vessel sealed with bitumen; birds are used to discover dry land). There are numerous differences, however, that speak to the reformulation of this stock flood-deliverance story in Genesis as a way to champion Yhwh as both the punisher and deliverer of humankind.[56] For example, in the Mesopotamian flood stories overpopulation (which causes raucous noise) is the main motivation for the extermination of humans;[57] and a hero god (Enki/Ea) is pitted against

---

[53] See, for example, the classic treatment by Frank Moore Cross, *Canaanite Myth and Hebrew Epic* (Cambridge, MA: Harvard University Press, 1973).

[54] Aaron Tugendhaft, "Unsettling Sovereignty: Politics and Poetics in the Baal Cycle," *JAOS* 132.3 (2012): 367–84; Aaron Tugendhaft, *Baal and the Politics of Poetry* (New York: Routledge, 2017).

[55] Tikva Frymer-Kensky, "The Atrahasis Epic and Its Significance for Our Understanding of Genesis 1–9," *BA* 40.4 (1977): 147–55; Tikva Frymer-Kensky, "What the Babylonian Flood Stories Can and Cannot Teach Us About the Genesis Flood," *BAR* 4.4 (1978): 32–41.

[56] Frymer-Kensky, "The Atrahasis Epic," 148–50.

[57] Anne D. Kilmer, "The Mesopotamian Concept of Overpopulation and Its Solution as Reflected in Mythology," *Or* 41 (1972): 167–69, 172–75; see also William J. Moran, "The Babylonian Story of the Flood," *Bib* 40 (1971): 51–61, here 56, 58–59.

a destroyer god (Enlil). However, in the biblical flood story in Genesis, the mass killing that targets all humans outside of Noah's immediate family (not to mention all animals that are not able to accompany them in the ark), is framed as a positive act. It is framed as an act of divine punishment against evil-doers as well as an opportunity to restart humanity through Noah and his three sons, Shem, Ham, and Japhet, and their spouses. It has also been suggested that the Genesis story offers deliberate contrast to the concern with overpopulation in the Atrahasis story; it encourages fertility and human procreation (see in particular P's refrain "be fruitful and multiply" both in the creation and flood stories).[58] Moreover, the Genesis flood story is connected to ritual and law. In Gen 8:20–22, which forms the conclusion to the non-P flood account, Noah builds an altar and sacrifices to Yhwh; Yhwh then promises not to resort to mass destruction in the future. In P's conclusion to the flood story in Gen 9:1–7, Israel's god introduces the first set of prescriptions about human behaviors (humans are to procreate, not to eat blood or shed human blood); he also enacts a covenant with humans and promises not to send another flood to destroy them.

THE GENESIS GENEALOGIES AND CUNEIFORM KING LISTS

Genealogies play an important role in Genesis. They connect the Primeval History (Gen 1–11) to the ancestor stories that focus more narrowly upon Abraham and his descendants (Gen 12–50); within these two textual collections, the genealogies offer internal structure and connect disparate narrative units. These lists also serve a narrative function in Genesis. They contextualize figures who will be important in Israel's history down the road (e.g., Abraham, Isaac, Jacob, and their descendants, but also neighboring peoples who are ascribed a shared heritage). The genealogies are introduced with the heading אֵלֶּה תּוֹלְדֹת ("these are the descendants"), which expresses that the people named therein share a lineage based upon kinship; this heading also functions as a structural marker to signal the inclusion of a list into the broader structure of Genesis. In all, the total number of human genealogies introduced with the term (10) תּוֹלְדֹת (in Gen 5:1; 6:9; 10:1; 11:10; 11:27; 25:12; 25:19; 36:1; 36:9; 37:2), may intentionally mirror the generational division of the

---

[58] Kilmer, "The Mesopotamian Concept of Overpopulation," 174–75; see also Isaac M. Kikawada, "Literary Convention of the Primeval History," *AJBI* 1 (1975): 3–21, here 12–13 (see also p. 14).

numbers of ancestors before and after the flood story.[59] There are ten ancestors before the flood in Gen 5 and ten ancestors recorded after the flood in Gen 11.[60]

There are five genealogies in the Primeval History (Gen 4:17–26; 5:1–32; 10:1–32; 11:10–26); they punctuate pivotal narrative units, which include the creation story and that of Adam and Eve and their children; that of Noah and his children, and the flood story; the Tower of Babel story; and finally, the account of Terah and his descendants. The genealogical information in Gen 11 plays a critical role as it connects the Primeval generations to Terah, Abram's father (Gen 11:24–32). Abram (Abraham) is introduced in Gen 11:26 ("When Terah had lived seventy years, he became the father of Abram, Nahor, and Haran"). This verse is the conclusion to the Primeval History and serves as a bridge to the stories about Israel's ancestors.[61]

There are also five genealogical groupings in the ancestor narratives (Gen 11:27–11:32; 25:12–18, 19; 36:8, 9–43; 37:2).[62] Gen 11:27 transitions to a new list that focuses specifically on Terah and his children, paving the way for the ancestor stories in Gen 12–50. This second grouping of genealogies offers an origin story for Israel's twelve tribes, as they group Abraham, Isaac, and Jacob and their descendants into a cohesive family unit; these genealogies also serve to contextualize Israel's geographically and culturally proximate neighbors, the descendants of Ishmael (Gen 25:12) and Esau (Gen 36:1, 9). While the emphasis in the study of Genesis has been on the patrilineal ancestors (with a focus on these genealogical lists), it is important to note that the comparative approach is also critical to the work of reconstructing the matrilineal relationships, which are less represented both in the biblical text and in biblical scholarship.[63]

---

[59] It is important to note that Gen 2:4a, the conclusion of the P creation account, uses this same expression (translated in the NRSV as "these are the generations of the heavens and the earth ... ". Gen 5:1 introduces the story of Adam's descendants, but departs from the formula used in the other genealogy lists in Genesis ("This is the list of the descendants of Adam ... ").

[60] For an overview that considers their broader role in the Genesis narratives, see Ron Robinson, "Literary Functions of the Genealogies of Genesis," *CBQ* 48 (1986): 595–608.

[61] Naomi A. Steinberg, "The Genealogical Framework of the Family Stories in Genesis," *Semeia* 46 (1989): 41–50.

[62] Robert R. Wilson describes two main categories: linear (one person per generation; Gen 5:3–31) and segmented (those looking at multiple descendants, with more than one person per generation; Gen 10:1–32). See *Genealogy and History in the Biblical World* (New Haven, CT: Yale University Press, 1977), 19–20.

[63] For example, Cynthia Chapman's study of the matrilineal relationships in the ancestor stories relies upon targeted lexical parallels, particularly from Akkadian and

Turning to Mesopotamian comparanda for the genealogical lists in Genesis, scholars have looked to cuneiform king lists as either a textual source or model for the Genesis genealogies, or as a resource for understanding their function and recension history.[64] Two key lists are compared to cuneiform analogues: Gen 5 (Adam's immediate descendants down to the sons of Noah, the antediluvian list) and Gen 11:10–32 (a tailored list of ancestors beginning with Shem and ending with Abraham's family).[65] These lists are divided by the flood story and are therefore presented as two groups of ancestors: those living before the flood, with longer life spans, and those living after the flood, with shorter life spans (compare Noah's 950 years and Shem's 600 years to Terah's 205 years in Gen 11:32 at the end of the list).[66] The use of the flood as a means of demarcating historical time is an important feature, which some view as a direct parallel to the function of the references to the flood in the king lists in Mesopotamia.[67] The decrease in human life span that takes place after the flood story in the biblical account is also considered to be a shared parallel.

The Mesopotamian king lists span the second millennium BCE in their various recensions, and are seen to share some general structural similarities to the lists in Gen 5, 11:10–32:1. They include:

(1) the names of very prominent people with a number (length of life in Genesis and length of reign in the king lists).
(2) They include occasional comments about key events in the lifetimes of these important people.
(3) The numbers (reigns and lifespans) decrease as the lists progress.[68]

There are two key lists that are studied as potential parallels to Genesis 5 and 11:10–31. The first, the Sumerian King List (SKL) (2000–1700 BCE),

Ugaritic, which elucidate the complex kinship relationships and obligations described in the biblical text. See Chapman, *The House of the Mother.*
[64] See Lambert, "A New Look," 292–93.
[65] These two lists are separated by the flood account (Gen 6–9), the "Table of Nations" list (Gen 10), and the tower of Babel story (Gen 11:1–9). Both Gen 5 and 11:10–32 are attributed to the Priestly source, comprise ten individuals, and include comments about key figures (Enoch and Noah).
[66] The reference to limitations on human life spans in Gen 6:3 precedes the flood narrative; it comes between the antediluvian list in Gen 5 and the story of the flood in Gen 6:5–9:29.
[67] Y. S. Chen, "The Flood Motif as a Stylistic and Temporal Device in Sumerian Literary Traditions." *JANER* 12.2 (2012): 158–89.
[68] William W. Hallo, "Biblical History in Its Near Eastern Setting: The Contextual Approach," in *Scripture in Context: Essays on the Comparative Method,* ed. Carl D. Evans, William W. Hallo, and John B. White (Pittsburgh, PA: Pickwick, 1980), 1–26, here 9.

which exists in several different versions, is much more than a scribal list of the names of past kings. It is a political text that speaks to the political ideologies and concerns of the contemporary Isin Dynasty.[69] This work situates the Isin kings as the heirs of more ancient and (in some cases) mythical rulers. Some scholars have sought to identify exact parallels between the SKL and Gen 5 and 11:11–32 (e.g., to connect the names in Gen 5 to the names of specific kings in the SKL who lived "before the flood," or to draw parallels with the years of their lifespans/ reigns).[70] The second key king list compared to Genesis genealogies, the Lagash King List (also known as the Lagash Rulers), dates to a similar period to the SKL. It combines myth and etiology with a list of the names of the rulers of Lagash (e.g., an explanation for the life spans of humans and the beginning of agriculture).[71] However, it presents a different periodization from the SKL, which reflects an Isin-focused outlook; the royal genealogy in the Lagash list focuses on Lagash and includes rulers omitted from the SKL.[72]

For those of us less comfortable with positing that Mesopotamian king lists of the second millennium BCE served as a textual source for the Genesis genealogies (which raises the question of the mode of transmission and the impetus behind this borrowing), another line of inquiry into the relationship between Genesis and the king lists could be productive. For instance, we might ask what the function of the SKL as a form of Mesopotamian history-writing can elucidate about the form and function of the

---

[69] Thorkild Jacobsen, *The Sumerian King List*, Oriental Institute of the University of Chicago Assyriological Studies 11 (Chicago: Oriental Institute of the University of Chicago, 1939).

[70] See George A. Barton, "A Sumerian Source for the Fourth and Fifth Chapters of Genesis," *JBL* 34.1/4 (1915): 1–9. See also the argument for the number 10 in the grouping of ancestors in these lists in Abraham Malamat, "King Lists of the Old Babylonian Period and Biblical Genealogies," *JAOS* 88.1 (1968): 163–73; John Walton, "The Antediluvian Section of the Sumerian King List and Genesis 5," *BA* 44.4 (1981): 207–8; Speiser, *Genesis*. For the argument against this view, see Thomas C. Hartman, "Some Thoughts on the Sumerian King List and Genesis 5 and 11B," *JBL* 91.1 (1972): 25–32.

[71] See Jean-Jacques Glassner, *Mesopotamian Chronicles*, SBLWAW 19 (Atlanta: Society of Biblical Literature, 2004), 144–49; and Jeremy A. Black et al., "Rulers of Lagash: Translation," The Electronic Text Corpus of Sumerian Literature, www.etcsl.orinst .ox.ac.uk/section2/tr211.htm.

[72] For this reason, Sollberger has argued that the Lagash Rulers is a satirical scribal response to the SKL in which history begins with a description of the remaking of the world after the flood – that is, time (re)starts after the flood. See Edmond Sollberger, "The Rulers of Lagaš," *JCS* 21 (1967): 279–91.

lists in Genesis 1–11.[73] Or, how can the study of these texts in the field of Assyriology serve as a guide for how we can analyze the function of the Genesis lists as scribal and geo-political works?[74] The Mesopotamian king lists connect royal genealogies, mythic events, and mythic figures but also provide commentary about the past and about contemporary political issues.[75] In addition, they serve to order time – that is, they craft a royal narrative about the origins of historical time from which subsequent people and events are ordered.

The genealogies in Genesis are not overtly royal lists and they seem to do an altogether different work than their Mesopotamian counterparts.[76] What then do such texts achieve, both as independent lists and as participants in the larger textual spaces of Genesis and the Pentateuch? While we might initially think about the family tree that is crafted through these genealogies as being linear or, in a sense, telic (moving forwards in time to the last member of a family line), the Genesis genealogies are better conceptualized as overgrown thickets (to use another PLANT IS KINSHIP metaphor). The genealogies are complex and they intersect temporal, geographical, and political boundaries (including textual spaces). As Ron Robinson writes,

> It is a remarkable fact that, thanks to the genealogies, virtually every character in Genesis can be related to every other by specific degrees of kinship – grandson, cousin, nephew. Even characters lacking a full genealogy, such as the kings of the East who do battle with Abraham, can be located broadly within ancestral houses by the so-called Table of Nations in Genesis.[77]

[73] See for example, Richard E. Averbeck, "The Sumerian Historiographic Tradition and Its Implications for Genesis 1–11," in *Faith, Tradition, and History: Old Testament Historiography in Its Near Eastern Context*, ed. Alan R. Millard, James Karl Hoffmeier, and David W. Baker (Winona Lake, IN: Eisenbrauns, 1994), 79–102; see also Mark W. Chavalas, "Genealogical History as 'Charter': A Study of Old Babylonian Period Historiography and the Old Testament," in *Faith, Tradition, and History*, 103–28. Note that this collection of essays seeks to respond to Thompson's and Van Seters's attempts to date the Pentateuch to the second half of the 1st millennium BCE. The scholars represented offer a defense of reading the ancestor accounts in Genesis and Exodus in a second millennium context, albeit their view is more tempered by the evidence than those of earlier scholars.
[74] Averbeck, "The Sumerian Historiographic Tradition"; see also Chavalas, "Genealogical History."
[75] Piotr Michalowski, "History as Charter: Some Observations on the Sumerian King List," *JAOS* 103.1 (1983): 237–47.
[76] Richard S. Hess, "The Genealogies of Genesis 1–11 and Comparative Literature," in *I Studied Inscriptions from Before the Flood*, 65–71.
[77] Robinson, "Genealogies of Genesis," 601.

Seen in this light, the genealogies both create and comment upon human networks forged by kinship, by shared cultural traits, and by geographic proximity. Furthermore, if we think about their impact in the broader plot of Israel's history in the Pentateuch, it is clear that they function as identity-forming texts which play an integral role in the formation of Israel's history.[78] These avenues of inquiry shift the study of the Genesis lists from the search for a source or mode of transmission to an inquiry into the functions of these types of lists in the ancient Near East as a form of history-writing.[79]

SOCIAL AND RELIGIOUS PRACTICES IN GENESIS 12–50 AND ANCIENT ANALOGUES DATING TO THE SECOND MILLENNIUM BCE

The idea that the lifestyle of the ancestors in Genesis is best understood as a reflection of the Amorite culture of the second millennium BCE has been particularly resilient among biblical scholars. The fascination of sites like Mari, Alalakh, and Ugarit stems in part from their identification as part of an "Amorite" or West Semitic cultural horizon, comprising shared features of language, material culture, lifestyle, and religion.[80] Consequently, the cuneiform materials from these sites, as well as other relatively contemporaneous sites north of Canaan, have been seen by some as a treasure trove for ancient Near Eastern analogues to the ancestor accounts in Genesis.

The Mari corpus in particular has been crucial to attempts to date portions of Genesis to the second millennium BCE, and more recently to explain the lives of the ancestors as stories that reflect facets of Israel's northern origin.[81] Scholars have viewed the cuneiform tablets from Mari as windows into the names, kinship terminology, geographic designations, and ritual formulae and practices described in the biblical ancestor stories in Gen 12–40.[82] For example, those

---

[78] As Ronald Hendel writes, biblical genealogies "mark the boundary between the inside and outside, between Israel and the nations" (*Remembering Abraham*, 10).

[79] See, for example, the attempt to integrate anthropological models into the discussion of genealogies in Wilson, *Genealogy and History*.

[80] See the argument for an Amorite koine in Aaron A. Burke, *The Amorites and the Bronze Age Near East: The Making of a Regional Identity* (New York: Cambridge University, 2020); see also Aaron A. Burke, "Entanglement, the Amorite Koiné, and Amorite Cultures in the Levant," *Aram* 26.1–2 (2014): 357–73.

[81] For an overview of scholarship connecting Genesis ancestors to Mari, see André Lemaire, "Mari, the Bible, and the Northwest Semitic World," *BA* 47 (1984): 88–99.

[82] For an overview of proposed parallels, see Sasson, "About 'Mari and the Bible,'" 100–108.

scholars advocating a close cultural connection between Mari and Israel argue that the personal names in the ancestor stories (e.g., Jacob and Benjamin) have closer linguistic parallels in second millennium cuneiform texts at Mari than in later phases of Hebrew (or other West Semitic varieties of the first millennium BCE).[83] Related are potential parallels in kinship/tribal terminology. The personal and tribal name Benjamin in Genesis and references to the Binu Yamina (sons of the right [or south]), which is paired with the name Binu Sam'al (sons of the left [or north]) at Mari, are at the crux of these discussions. It is debated whether or not these are designations that refer to a specific tribe or are generic designations for "southerners" or "northerners," which can be used in any geographic context.[84] For example, Richard Hess maintains that the name Benjamin (tribe of the south) reflects Benjamin's territorial holdings to the south of the lands of his brothers.[85] Thomas Thompson, who represents the opposite camp in terms of dating, argues that "Benjamin" operated as a broader designation for people considered to be "southerners."[86] Alternatively, more recent scholarship by Daniel Fleming (see below) argues that the designation Binu Yamina at Mari was a tribal name connected to the area the tribe(s) used as grazing territories in the local geography around Mari; the term was reanalyzed in the Iron Age and connected to the tribe of Benjamin.[87]

---

[83]   Richard S. Hess, *Studies on the Personal Names of Genesis 1–11*, AOAT 234 (Kevelaer: Butzon & Bercker, 1993). See, however, John Huehnergard's contention that Amorite "is negatively defined, simply as non-Akkadian Semitic ... it is not subject to normal linguistic tests for meaning, structure, and development, since names may lack any firm connection to the language spoken by their bearer." See John Huehnergard, "Languages of the Ancient Near East: Introduction," *ABD* 4:159.

[84]   Again, this calls for analysis as to the geographic context of the Binu Yamina and Sam'al at Mari. Giorgio Buccellati, who specializes in the historical geography, texts, and archaeology of Mari argues that in the "perceptual geography" of its people, the steppe was further defined by its relation to the Euphrates river: "yamina, for the steppe to the right side of the Euphrates; and sam'al for the left side." He views these terms as reflecting social, geographic, and, implicitly, economic distinctions, rather than mere tribal designations that reflect identity ("'River Bank,' 'High Country,' and 'Pasture Land': The Growth of Nomadism on the Middle Euphrates and the Khabur," in *Tall al-Ḥamīdīya* 2, ed. Seyyare Eichler, Markus Wäfler, and David Warburton, OBO.SA 6 [Göttingen: Vandenhoeck & Ruprecht, 1990], 105–7).

[85]   Richard S. Hess, *Israelite Religions: An Archaeological and Biblical Survey* (Grand Rapids, MI: Baker, 2007), 63 (cf. 59); Richard S. Hess, "The Ancestral Period," in *Behind the Scenes of the Old Testament: Cultural, Social, and Historical Contexts*, ed. Jonathan S. Greer, John W. Hilber, and John H. Walton (Grand Rapids, MI: Baker Academic, 2018), 187–89.

[86]   Thompson, *Historicity*, 58–66.

[87]   Fleming writes, "When the Binu Yamina are recognized to be the primary tribal people from the Mari evidence who move through the back country of southwestern Syria in this period, and we can be fairly sure that a tribe named Benjamin played a leading role

Scholars have also argued that the integrated urban/pastoral economy reflected in the Mari tablets contextualizes the tribal and land allotments in the Genesis ancestor accounts. Key in these discussions is Michael B. Rowton's study of the "dimorphic" economy divided between agriculture and animal herding, dependent on both urban and steppe spaces. This model has been applied both to Mari (or the Amorites) and to early Iron Age polities.[88] One caveat in the comparisons between the Genesis and Mari corpora, however, is the geographical and chronological gulf between the kingdoms of Mari and Judah (as the crow flies, slightly over 600 km and 1,000 years). Another is the fact that many of these proposed parallels are not unique to Mari and to Iron Age Israel, but are widespread through the ancient Near East, whether these parallels consist of practices conditioned by climate (e.g., the complex inter-dependency of "built" spaces, cultivated lands, and "wild" grazing areas); aspects of treaty-making rituals (e.g., the use of animals in treaty making); or practices that reflect the complexity and uncertainty of family life (related to marriage, adoption, and inheritance).[89]

For these reasons, Fleming proposes a subtle shift in the use of Mari to understand the ancestor stories in Genesis. He examines how and why claims to an ancestry with origins outside of Canaan were integrated into a comprehensive history about national identity that was composed during the Iron Age.[90] Thus, while Fleming focuses upon the similarities in tribal terminology in the Mari tablets and in Genesis 12–50, he does not use these parallels to date the Genesis

in Israel at the end of the 2nd millennium, the insistence on treating these tribal names as totally unrelated becomes artificial." See "Genesis in History and Tradition: The Syrian Background of Israel's Ancestors, Reprise," in *The Future of Biblical Archaeology*, 193–232; quote on p. 218.

[88] See the classic work by Michael B. Rowton, "Dimorphic Structure and the Parasocial Element," *JNES* 36.3 (1977): 181–98. Thompson has critiqued the use of Rowton's work in describing the economy and landscape of the southern Levant in Thompson, *Biblical Narrative and Palestine's History*, 28–38, esp. 33.

[89] For example, scholars have compared the practice of animal dismemberment in a ritual for treaty-making in Genesis 15 and in several Mari tablets (ARM II 37; A. 1056; A. 2226). See Abraham Malamat, *Mari and the Bible* (Leiden: Brill, 1998); Abraham Malamat, *Mari and the Early Israelite Experience* (Oxford: Oxford University Press, 1989); Abraham Malamat, "A Note on the Ritual of Treaty Making in Mari and the Bible," *IEJ* 45.4 (1995): 226–29.

[90] For Daniel Fleming both the theological outlook (one god, YHWH) and the descriptions of the local geography and affiliated people (e.g., Esau=Edom; Lot's descendants Moab and Ammon) are those of the Iron Age southern Levant ("Genesis in History and Tradition," 209).

stories to the second millennium BCE.[91] Rather, the Genesis stories
are understood to reflect the ancestral origins of a particular group
within Iron Age Israel and Judah.[92] Ultimately, the ancestor stories of
Genesis transform inherited tribal terminology into a terminology of
kinship and descent that casts the peoples of Israel as a family from
a foreign territory.

CONCLUSION

This chapter has sought to contextualize the comparative approach to
the study of biblical literature within larger issues in the study of the
Hebrew Bible (e.g., dating, methodology, and the compositional history
and aims of biblical writers [and scholars]). Ultimately, the revised dating
of the composition of the bulk of biblical literature suggests that we
should accordingly contextualize Genesis in the first millennium BCE.
Furthermore, we should view it as a work meant to unify the disparate
people of Israel and Judah into a cohesive family unit (e.g., to forge
a shared history and identity) in the wake of Assyrian and Babylonian
military operations and deportations from the southern Levant and
onward into the exile and reconstruction periods (from the late sixth to
the mid-fourth century BCE). Yet, as William W. Hallo reminds us,

> We should neither exempt biblical literature from the standards
> applied to other ancient Near Eastern literatures, nor subject it to
> standards demanded nowhere else ... Israelite traditions about its
> own Bronze Age, though these traditions were written down in the
> Iron Age, have to be given as much credence as Middle and neo-
> Assyrian notions about the Old Assyrian past.[93]

When we analyze the origin stories in Genesis as ancient Near Eastern
texts, we must look at all extant (or potential) data. We must keep in
mind the periodization of Hebrew scribalism, social and political
changes, and keep in check our own inherent biases – that is, what we
ourselves bring to the text regarding what it communicated to ancient
audiences and what we wish to see (or not see) in it.

[91] He proposes the following parallels: references to the Binu Yamina at Mari and the
     tribe of Benjamin in Genesis; the importance of Harran as a tribal homeland; the
     connection between *ibrum* and the Binu Yamina, assuming that this term is con-
     nected to the adjective Hebrew as used in the Joseph Story; and the "division of pasture
     by right and left hands in Gen. 13:9" as a reference to tribal territory and its designa-
     tion. See Fleming, "Genesis in History and Tradition," 214.

[92] See ibid., 194–95.

[93] Hallo, "Biblical History," 5.

SELECT BIBLIOGRAPHY

Chavalas, Mark W. "The Comparative Use of Ancient Near Eastern Texts in the Study of the Hebrew Bible." *Religion Compass* 5.5 (2011): 150–65.

Chen, Y. S. "The Flood Motif as a Stylistic and Temporal Device in Sumerian Literary Traditions." *JANER* 12.2 (2012): 158–89.

Finkelstein, Israel and Amihai Mazar. *The Quest for the Historical Israel: Debating Archaeology and the History of Early Israel*. Edited by Brian B. Schmidt. Atlanta: SBL, 2007.

Fleming, Daniel E. "Genesis in History and Tradition: The Syrian Background of Israel's Ancestors, Reprise." Pages 193–232 in *The Future of Biblical Archaeology: Reassessing Methodologies and Assumptions*. Edited by James K. Hoffmeier and Alan Millard. Grand Rapids, MI: Eerdmans, 2004.

Hallo, William W. "Biblical History in Its Near Eastern Setting: The Contextual Approach." Pages 1–26 in *Scripture in Context: Essays on the Comparative Method*. Edited by Carl D. Evans, William W. Hallo, and John B. White. Eugene, OR: Pickwick, 1980.

Hendel, Ronald S. *Remembering Abraham: Culture, Memory, and History in the Hebrew Bible*. Oxford: Oxford University Press, 2005.

Hess, Richard S. "The Genealogies of Genesis 1–11 and Comparative Literature." Pages 65–71 in *I Studied Inscriptions from Before the Flood*. Edited by R. S. Hess and D. T. Tsumura. Winona Lake, IN: Eisenbrauns, 1994.

Lambert, Wilfried G. "Mesopotamian Creation Stories." Pages 15–59 in *Imagining Creation*. Edited by Markham J. Geller and Mineke Schipper. Leiden: Brill, 2008.

Levy, Thomas E. "The New Pragmatism: Integrating Anthropological, Digital, and Historical Biblical Archaeologies." Pages 3–44 in *Historical Biblical Archaeology and the Future: The New Pragmatism*. Edited by Thomas E. Levy. London: Equinox, 2010.

Sasson, Jack M. "Mari and the Holy Grail." Pages 186–98 in *Orientalism, Assyriology, and the Bible*. Edited by Steven W. Holloway. Sheffield: Sheffield Phoenix, 2007.

Steinberg, Naomi A. "The Genealogical Framework of the Family Stories in Genesis." *Semeia* 46 (1989): 41–50.

Thompson, Thomas L. *The Historicity of the Patriarchal Narratives: The Quest for Historical Abraham*. Berlin: de Gruyter, 1974.

Tsumura, David T. "Genesis and Ancient Near Eastern Stories of Creation and Flood: An Introduction." Pages 27–57 in *I Studied Inscriptions From Before the Flood: Ancient Near Eastern, Literary, and Linguistic Approaches to Genesis 1–11*. Edited by Richard S. Hess and David T. Tsumura. Winona Lake, IN: Eisenbrauns, 1994.

Van Seters, John. *Abraham in History and Tradition*. New Haven, CT: Yale, 1975.

7 Genesis and the Conceptual World of the Ancient Near East

JOHN H. WALTON

Genesis reflects a robust example of inter-cultural conversation. This chapter will summarize the major categories of commonality between Genesis and the ancient Near Eastern world in three major categories: (1) creation and humanity; (2) perceptions about the gods; (3) ancestor narratives. A truism of comparative studies is that similarities as well as differences require attention, and examples of both will be discussed.

All cultures have origin stories, and such literature reflects its native cognitive environment in numerous and often subtle ways. For cultures that share a cognitive environment and have historical points of contact, it would be no surprise that their origin stories reflect some commonalities. The implied authors and audiences of these stories are engaged in a conversation that takes place within a cultural context ("inner-cultural") and assumes familiarity with that context. Whether the ideas under consideration are mutually accepted ideas or are debated, the ideas themselves have a similar currency among the participants. At times conversations can encompass different cultural contexts ("inter-cultural"). One particularly dominant culture's tradition could potentially prompt how others around it construct or reconfigure their stories. Regardless, commonalities would be expected; some due to shared cultural perspectives, others to cross-pollination. Such commonalities are always worthy of consideration, but the differences are more telling. This is true whether those differences represent the independent traditions of each culture or, alternatively, reflect interactions that prompted differentiation, clarification, or perhaps pointed polemic.

CREATION AND HUMANITY

History has a beginning in the minds of those who trace the flow of events, but history is insufficient to portray *the* beginning.[1] Consequently, many cultures use "myth" to convey the deeper, and in most ways more important, realities that shape their understanding of themselves, the world, and the gods. The "beginning" was too remote to have yet become history. It could only be imagined on a grand scale; the finite abilities of humans prevent us from encompassing its scope and ordering it as Time. True beginnings transcend time rather than being rooted in it, for time itself is a creation.[2] From the exigencies of myth, history was eventually born, and a culture's understanding of its myth will determine its understanding of history. Cultures that hold parts of their histories in common with the cultures around them may view those histories very differently from one another depending on the shape of the larger reality posited in their myths, because their myths reflected their values, and their values shaped their perception of history and of events.

One of the highest values in the ancient world was Order. In Egyptian thinking, the value is represented by a major deity, Maat. In Mesopotamia, the sun god, Shamash, by virtue of his light, is associated with justice, itself one of the lynchpins of order. Throughout the ancient world, the value of order is articulated, for example, in legal literature focused on justice and in proverbial literature circumscribing the smooth operation of society. Order is sought in political relationships and informed by divinatory observations. Philosophy, economics, history, and ritual all seek to establish, maintain, and comprehend order in the cosmos as well as in society. It is reflected in nearly every sort of literature in the ancient world from the most mundane business documents to the lofty pinnacle of sophisticated literary texts. Its sway is attested across the cultures and the time periods of the ancient Near East and is as strong in Israelite values and literature as in that of her neighbors. Most obviously, the book of Proverbs seeks to address what order would look like in a variety of contexts. Less intuitively, we could consider how order is the priority in the covenant, which uses vassal treaty as the metaphor of Israel's relationship to the God, Yahweh. Treaties in the ancient Near East contained instructions concerning what manifested order would look like in the realm, in terms ranging from generic to

---

[1] In Mesopotamia, history, in one sense, begins when kingship descends from heaven, but more specifically, history begins after the flood. See Àngel Menargues Rajadell, "Mesopotamian Ideas of Time Through Modern Eyes," in *Time and History in the Ancient Near East*, ed. L. Feliu et al., RAI 56 (Winona Lake, IN: Eisenbrauns, 2013), 211–28.

[2] Gonzalo Rubio, "Time before Time: Primeval Narratives in Early Mesopotamian Literature," in *Time and History in the Ancient Near East*, ed. L. Feliu et al., RAI 56 (Winona Lake, IN: Eisenbrauns, 2013), 3–17.

specific, and exhorted the vassal to establish and maintain that order for the sake of the reputation of the suzerain and for their own survival. The documents of the Torah contain a similar picture of manifested order and exhortations to establish and maintain that order to retain the favor of their divine patron.[3]

It is no surprise, then, that texts that talk about the origins of the cosmos and the role of humanity within the cosmos are more likely to shape the conversation in terms of establishing and shaping order than in terms of material or physical objects. Rochberg observes, "Conceptions of order, norms, and schemata based upon such norms were central features of the scholarly corpus of texts dealing with the phenomena, and consequently of what was deemed in those texts to be knowable and significant."[4]

In contrast, our modern discussions of origins tend to focus primarily on how the material world came to be. Science provides the significant data and the framework for the modern models that we use. By contrast, the ancient world showed more interest in the origins of order in the cosmos. Documents of this type are conceptually more like a company's organizational chart, in contrast to modern scientific models, which may be compared more to the blueprints of a factory. Literature addressing the origin of order deals more with the functions and operations of the cosmos and humanity rather than scientific explanations of the origins of the material existence of the cosmos or humanity. To use another metaphor, the material "stage" and "set" for time and history is assumed and already in place as they focus attention on the unfolding drama of life and order.

This focus on functions and operations pertains not only to order, but to role, identity, and purpose. The result is that the treatments of cosmology provide the sort of insight that today we would include in a vision statement. It would be like identifying a college more by its curriculum than by its campus; like being more interested in the play than the set or the theater. Because of this, we find that the gods are the primary actors who operate by making decisions and issuing decrees more than engaging in production of objects. This conceptual framework is common to Israel and its neighbors even as it differs from modern categories of thinking.

Building on these observations, we may now delve into the literature to illustrate this proposed ancient ideology. Two documents from opposite

---

3   John H. Walton and J. Harvey Walton, *Lost World of the Torah* (Downers Grove, IL: InterVarsity, 2019).
4   Francesca Rochberg, *Before Nature* (Chicago, IL: University of Chicago Press, 2017), 85.

ends of the time, space, and genre spectrums of the ancient world can serve as an *inclusio* for our observation: *Enki and the World Order* (Sumerian Myth,[5] late third millennium), and *Papyrus Insinger* (Egyptian Demotic Instruction, Ptolemaic, late first millennium, 24th instruction[6]).

ENKI AND THE WORLD ORDER

When Enki brings order to the cosmos, he is doing so to establish justice and as he does so he decides the fates (ll. 74–76). He is engaged in administering ME – a Sumerian word with no English equivalent for the governing attributes of order in the world (both cosmic and societal), and often perceived as plural MES.[7] In the *Myth of Enki and Inanna*,[8] we are given a list of over 90 MES that circumscribe the category demonstrating its wide range. The list is far from comprehensive, but includes various crafts, abstractions such as wisdom, attentiveness, and respect, everyday trivialities such as the shepherd's hut and glowing coals, social interactions such as counseling, comforting, and decision-making, and others such as song, old age, kissing, grandiloquent speech, and heroism. It is logical that Enki is in charge of this ordering process because he is the god of wisdom, and wisdom is the path to order in the ancient world.

It is clear from the myth that establishing order and maintaining order together represent an unbroken and largely undifferentiated continuum. The scene that most suggests the material origin of something is when Enki apparently brings the Tigris and Euphrates into existence. But the fact that he does so by ejaculating his semen (ll. 253–60) warns us against thinking in strictly materialistic terms. His act insinuates what the rivers *are* (the fertility of Enki) rather than anything about their material properties or even how they came to be. Herman Vanstiphout interprets the text as referring to Enki conferring "extra *power* rather than *volume*" to the river systems.[9] The result is the grain that grows for people to eat. The text also immediately moves to talking about which

---

[5]   "Enki and the World Order," trans. Richard E. Averbeck (COS 4.91:340–51). Since the piece features extensive veneration of Enki, some have found it defensible to label it a Hymn rather than a Myth. Herman Vanstiphout proposes that it is didactic, in " Why Did Enki Organize the World?" in *Sumerian Gods and Their Representations*, ed. I. Finkel (Groningen: Styx, 1997), 117–35, here 131.

[6]   "The Instruction of Papyrus Insinger" (*AEL* 3:210–11).

[7]   John H. Walton, *Genesis 1 as Ancient Cosmology* (Winona Lake, IN: Eisenbrauns, 2011), 46–68; Yvonne Rosengarten, *Sumer et le sacré: le jeu des prescriptions (ME), des dieux, et des destins* (Paris: Boccard, 1977).

[8]   http://etcsl.orinst.ox.ac.uk/cgi-bin/etcsl.cgi?text=t.1.3.1#.

[9]   Vanstiphout, "Why Did Enki Organize," 121.

god is given control of the rivers. Vanstiphout concludes by indicating the nature of Enki's creative work: On the whole one sees that Enki is "creating", after a fashion, where *technique* of some sort is involved, such as is the case with irrigation, the readying of instruments, or building work. For the rest he is organizing, regulating, and managing already existing things.[10] Vanstiphout then observes that the myth turns its attention to what he refers to as the "infrastructure." This entails setting boundaries for the terrain (watercourses, marshlands, etc.), establishing rains, irrigation, and tending of crops (interestingly the same sorts of things that are addressed in Gen 2:5–6), and arranging for the management of animals and resources.[11]

Enki is creating an ideal set of conditions,[12] not an array of material objects. For example, consider his ordering of time: "Counting days and making months enter into their houses, in order to complete years; to present completed years to the assembly (for a) decision; making a decision to put days in good order: father Enki, you are king among its assembled people."[13]

INSTRUCTION OF PAPYRUS INSINGER

"Like all earlier Egyptian sages, the author of *Papyrus Insinger* believed in an all-embracing divine order which governed nature and human existence."[14] In the twenty-fourth instruction of this Ptolemaic era wisdom literature, the sage presents a list of what the god has created. The eighteen lines enumerate examples of order in the ancient world including light and darkness, life and death, time, seasons, food, constellations, fresh water, life in the egg, birth in the womb, sleep, remedies, dreams, wealth, work, and the succession of generations. The section concludes with the summary, "Great is the counsel of the god in putting one thing after another."[15] Like *Enki and the World Order*, we find that order frames the ancient interest in creation.

Since order is a core value in the ancient world, it is no surprise that it dominates the mythology as nothing else does. It is also unsurprising that it therefore pervades many of the other types of literature found in the ancient world (e.g., legal texts, historical texts, divination texts,

[10]   Ibid., 121–22.
[11]   Ibid., 124.
[12]   Ibid., 132.
[13]   "Enki and the World Order," lines 17–20.
[14]   "The Instruction of Papyrus Insinger", 185.
[15]   Ibid., 211.

wisdom texts). Consequently, understanding creation requires us to focus on order, and our understanding of order must be drawn from the wide spectrum of ancient literature.

To the extent that it is accurate to think of creation as primarily an ordering, function-granting, and identity-giving activity, it is also therefore essential to understand that creation is not just a one-time inaugurating event. That is, it is not an event as much as a continual, defining activity of the gods, and it is not just inaugurating, it is sustaining, because order, if not maintained, tends to degenerate. Jan Assmann thus observes, "[the world as conceived in the traditions of the ancient world] cannot be left alone. Its 'natural' tendency is toward chaos, entropy, dissolution, and cessation. It has to be constantly maintained by cultural efforts."[16] Order is not a natural equilibrium. Israel holds this perspective in common with the rest of the ancient world.

It is no challenge then to deduce why the gods create – everyone desires order. But order for whom? In the ancient world, it is the unanimous opinion that the gods are the center, source, and focus of order. They have ordered the cosmos for their own purposes and their own benefit.[17] Creation accounts are therefore, not unexpectedly, focused on the gods. The cosmos is ordered around them and functions for them. Creation therefore often eventuates in the construction of a temple from which the gods rule. In the *Enuma Elish*, though only rarely in other cosmological literature from the ancient Near East, this order is established through conflict. Genesis shows no sign of this aspect, and as such is more similar to Sumerian cosmologies.[18]

As is well recognized in the ancient world, however, a stable rule needs to be facilitated by those who serve. This is where people play their role. They are created so that the gods can enjoy the fruits of their ordering activities and rule at their ease. In their ordered world, the

---

[16] Jan Assmann, *Moses the Egyptian* (Cambridge, MA: Harvard University Press, 1997) 190.

[17] In the modern world, this could be considered the issue that drives economics, politics, and society. Who gets to establish order for their purposes and for their own benefits? This can be seen on a national level as some countries receive benefits at the expense of others, as well as in the private business world as wealthy and powerful individuals pursue their own agendas.

[18] The bibliography on this is massive see summary, discussion, and bibliography in John H. Walton, " Creation in Genesis 1:1–2:3 and the Ancient Near East: Order out of Disorder after Chaoskampf," *CTJ* 43 (2008): 48–63. See also Mark Smith, *The Origins of Biblical Monotheism* (Oxford: Oxford University Press, 2001), 167–72. Paul K.-K. Cho, *Myth, History, and Metaphor in the Hebrew Bible* (Cambridge: Cambridge University Press) has suggested that this conflict myth has had a more pervasive influence in various ways in the Hebrew Bible.

gods need food, housing, and clothing, and in general, desire to be pampered in every way. People are created to meet the needs of the gods. In that way, they play their role in the ordered cosmos. But since the gods have needs, they become dependent on people to meet those needs. Thus, a mutual dependence characterizes the system. The people need the gods to protect them and provide for them, which the gods must do because they are dependent on people to meet their needs. This co-dependence can be called the "great symbiosis" since it undergirds the people's understanding of all reality, sustained in both myth and history.

Here, finally, is where we see Israel taking a different perspective on creation and humanity. In contrast to the view in the rest of the ancient world, the view expounded by the implied authors of the Hebrew Bible is that Yahweh did not create for himself. He did not create out of need and did not expect the Israelites to meet his needs. Nevertheless, order remains the highest value. In the ancient Near East, the role of people was to maintain order in the human world so that they could continue to provide for the gods efficiently and effectively. In Israel, Yahweh establishes order in the human world with people delegated to work alongside him bringing order through the task of subduing and ruling (Gen 1) or tending and keeping (the garden) and naming the animals (Gen 2). In the ancient Near East the images of the gods serve as mediators for the gods' needs to be met; in Israel, humanity is the image of God, standing by his side as vicegerents and stewards. Admittedly, these are sweeping comparisons, but for all their limitations as generalizations, they capture an inherent difference even amidst the broad-spectrum similarities in how to think about creation in general.

A final observation that pertains to cosmology concerns the role of the flood. Israel and the Assyro-Babylonian world both recognize the centrality of this catastrophe near the dawn of history. They both consider the devastation to be massive and threatening to world order, engineered by the gods to wipe out humanity because of human noise (Mesopotamia) or human violence (Genesis). Nonetheless, humanity survives. The Mesopotamian gods do not preserve human order for its own sake since the humans survive only by treachery. Only *post facto* do they realize that the order of their own world was in jeopardy without the food that the humans provide, and therefore grudgingly allow the humans to continue to live. The same event in Israelite tradition, however, portrays accumulated human disorder being eliminated by the return of pre-cosmic non-order, as the waters once again cover the land and reset the cosmos to its "default settings." After this, the cosmic order is re-established, including the (deliberately preserved) human survivors, who are reinstated in their stewardship role in a recapitulation of the original cosmogony.[19] Both cultures interpret the catastrophe against their own views of the role of the gods in maintaining order in the cosmos, but they see those roles differently.

PERCEPTIONS ABOUT THE GODS

One of the great challenges of talking about the gods in the ancient world is that of cognitive categories. In our modern world, we often talk about deity using metaphysical terms and categories: sovereignty, omniscience, impassability, contingency, aseity, etc. These represent attempts to describe the nature of deity in abstract terms of being. In contrast, in the ancient world they do not use such metaphysical categories to describe gods. The result is, that when we try to compare how Israel thought about Yahweh to how Babylonians or Egyptians thought about their gods, we are inclined to use our metaphysical categories for the comparison, which, if they do not think in those categories, does not do justice to either Israel or the other civilizations of the ancient Near East. They are more inclined to talk about the gods *doing* than the gods *being*.

It is not difficult to compile a list of ways in which the Israelites perceived and portrayed Yahweh as distinct from the ways that gods were perceived and portrayed in the rest of the ancient Near East. Over the years, some of the initial distinctions have been mitigated by further analysis,[20] but the list remains substantial.[21] The comparative task is complicated by the many uncertainties that continue to exist concerning the dating of the perceptions reflected in the Hebrew Bible. The reality of long phases of oral transmission and untraceable stages and processes of composition that led to the texts we have today makes it difficult to discern which theological perspectives were resident in the traditions from the start as opposed to those that developed over time. Genesis is not immune to those questions. Acknowledging that difficulty, and having no other feasible choice, we will here bypass the composition questions to assess what the book of Genesis holds in its current form about the thought world pertaining to the gods, regardless of when those elements may have developed. We can compare the ideas without dating

[19] Tremper Longman III and John H. Walton, *The Lost World of the Flood* (Downers Grove, IL: InterVarsity, 2018).

[20] Marjo Korpel, *Rift in the Clouds: Ugaritic and Hebrew Descriptions of the Divine*, UBL 8 (Münster: Ugarit-Verlag, 1990).

[21] Theodore J. Lewis, *The Origin and Character of God* (Oxford: Oxford University Press, 2020).

them, though obviously the comparison will remain tenuous with dating and compositional process issues lurking unresolved.

DIVINE INTERRELATIONSHIPS

In the cosmology of the ancient world it is common to find a homological relationship between the gods and the elements of the cosmos (e.g., sun/ sun god). This inevitably indicates a level of interrelationship that extends beyond divine control of the elements.[22] Another level of interrelationship is found in the polytheistic system characterized by distinct delegated jurisdictions within the community of the gods. A third level of interrelationship, that between gods and humans, has already been mentioned in the great symbiosis. These three levels of interrelationship are defining aspects of the gods of the ancient Near East. Yet in Genesis and in the rest of the Hebrew Bible, every perspective on Yahweh resists these three levels of interrelationship. Level one: Yahweh is believed to be constantly and significantly active in the cosmos, but his identity is outside the cosmos with no homological relationships to its elements. Level two: He is not portrayed as operating within a divine community (regardless of the determination between monolatry, henotheism, and philosophical monotheism and when any of those had actually taken shape). Being autonomous, Yahweh yields no jurisdiction to other gods, even if he engages in delegation or on the occasions when their presence or existence may be tacitly allowed (in divine council). Yahweh is not part of a divine community with shared governance of the cosmos. Consequently, the Hebrew Bible is characterized by an intrinsic divine sufficiency located in Yahweh as the autonomous and singularly efficacious deity. This concept proved difficult for Israel to embrace because in human communities, people found their identity in their role and status in the various communities in which they were involved (civil, social, ethnic, clan). A person without a community was a person without an identity.

Level three: instead of the idea that people have been created to meet Yahweh's needs by feeding him, he plants the garden to provide food for them. Genesis neither explicates a contrast between Yahweh and ancient Near East gods at any of the three levels nor does it develop such a polemic. Instead, creation is discussed with no homology with the

---

[22]   Francesca Rochberg, "'The Stars and Their Likeness': Perspectives on the Relation Between Celestial Bodies and Gods in Ancient Mesopotamia," in *What Is a God?*, ed. B. N. Porter (Winona Lake: Eisenbrauns, 2009), 41–92.

cosmos and no divine community (the existence of a modified heavenly council notwithstanding).

ORDER BY DECREE AND THE ORDER MATRIX

In the ancient world the gods governed the cosmos by their decrees. The static components of the cosmos (ME) had been established time out of mind and were entrusted to the gods.[23] But the dynamic elements (NAM) were managed continually as the gods decreed the destinies.[24] Little if anything of this system is evident in Genesis, but it is notable that creation takes place in Gen 1 by decree. It has long been recognized that the Memphite Theology in Egyptian literature refers to *creation by the spoken word*, but the Mesopotamian element of *governing by divine decree* also offers interesting comparisons.[25] The decrees are the means by which the gods maintain order in the cosmos and in creation the gods have inaugurated that ordered system.

As in the rest of the cognitive environment, the Israelites view the world in three categories: non-order, order, and disorder (the Order Matrix).[26] In this way of thinking, non-order is the default situation. It is undesirable, but not evil, that is, not morally defined. The gods act to establish order in the midst of non-order, and regularly delegate humans (e.g., kings, priests) to work alongside or in place of them in that task. In Genesis, all humankind is so delegated by the blessing that calls on them to subdue and rule (Gen 1), by the commission to tend the garden (Gen 2), by the commission to work the ground (Gen 3), and by the commission to avenge bloodshed (Gen 9). The resulting order must be sustained by active agency (*creatio continua*) with regard to nature, family, interpersonal relationships, society, international relations, etc. Disorder is

---

[23] Extended discussion in Walton, *Genesis 1 as Ancient Cosmology*, 46–68.

[24] A. R. George, "Sennacherib and the Tablet of Destinies," *Iraq* 48 (1986): 133–46; Jack Lawson, *The Concept of Fate in Ancient Mesopotamia of the First Millennium* (Wiesbaden: Harrassowitz, 1994).

[25] "Prayer to the Divine Provider (K. 9902)" (Takayoshi Oshima, *Babylonian Prayers to Marduk* [Tübingen: Mohr Siebeck, 2011], 101), lines 4–5; "Epic of Creation," trans. Benjamin R. Foster (COS 1.111:390–402, esp. 393 [I:155–62] and 395 [II:159–63]. Also note that if Metcalf has rightly reconstructed the broken text of the Sumerian Hymn to Ninimma, she is identified as the "great word creating everything": Christopher Metcalf, *Sumerian Literary Texts in the Schøyen Collection*, CUSAS 38 (University Park, PA: Eisenbrauns, 2019), 48–49, line 4.

[26] This stands in contrast with the modern tendency to view the world according to the moralistic dichotomy of good/evil. The ideas in this paragraph were developed in conversation with J. Harvey Walton, who also contributed significantly to the ideas of the entire chapter.

likewise not inherently a moral category, but would include what the Israelites call "sin," as well as whatever behavior is considered offensive to the gods (in the ancient Near East, generally ritual offense or neglect). Disorder is what happens when someone disrupts the order that someone else is actively working to establish. Disorder in the human world usually occurs when humans undermine the order that is being sustained by either the gods or the social authorities, and can occur in the cultic, legal, moral, or political sphere. Warfare is undertaken in the ancient world on the premise that the king and his armies are responding to disorder promulgated by another city or country, and that the war will reestablish order even as the enemy is reduced to non-order.[27] The penalty for disorder is that the established order is undermined and collapses into non-order, as we also see in the flood narratives of both Babylon and Genesis.

In Genesis, the acquisition of the knowledge of good and evil (i.e., the capacity to perform the task of establishing order) returns humans to non-order (banishment into the liminal world), where they try to establish order by themselves and for themselves (Gen 4, comparable to the ancient Near East human prerogative), and partially succeed (cities and civilization), but are immediately undermined by disorder (Cain, Lamech, antediluvian population), and consequently return to the default of non-order (flood, scattering). All these elements in Genesis track well with the categories of the Order Matrix also observable in the ancient Near East.

In the ancient Near East, non-order is depicted in the descriptions of the world prior to the creative (ordering) acts of the gods. In Egyptian literature, this is reflected in the concept of "non-existence."[28] In Mesopotamian literature, the condition of non-order is everywhere evident as the pre-cosmic status before creation takes place. Examples include Sumerian NBC 11108, where the description includes darkness, waters not flowing, nothing produced, no rituals or high priest, unified heaven and earth, and inactive gods.[29] *Enuma Elish* begins similarly with

[27] Charlie Trimm, *Fighting for the King and the Gods* (Atlanta, GA: SBL, 2017), 43–51; Mattias Karlsson, *Relations of Power in Early Neo-Assyrian State Ideology* (Berlin: de Gruyter, 2016), 125–33.
[28] Egyptian terminology includes "non-existence" (iwtt/ iwti), "disorder" (isft), both of which are resolved by bringing "order" (m₃ʿt). Discussion in Erik Hornung, *Conceptions of God in Ancient Egypt* (Ithaca, NY: Cornell University, 1982), 174–76; Walton, *Genesis 1 as Ancient Cosmology*, 25–30.
[29] R. J. Clifford, *Creation Accounts in the Ancient Near East and in the Bible* (Washington, DC: Catholic Biblical Association, 1994), 28; similar descriptions in Gilgamesh, Enkidu, and the Netherworld (the Ḫuluppu Tree), The Electronic Text

a situation in which no names had yet been given, no gods brought forth, and no destinies ordained. The Sumerian *Enki and the World Order* does not begin with a description of the "before" picture, but by observing all the varied ways that Enki goes about ordering, it is easy to infer what the prior "non-order" would have been. In the Hebrew Bible, non-order is expressed through the term *tōhû* in Gen 1:2 and throughout its usage across the corpus.[30]

The contrasting state of order is achieved by the gods in creation in terms not unlike that found in Gen 1. Note for example the introduction to the disputation poem, *Series of the Spider*: "When the gods in their assembly created [*the universe*], brought into being the [S]ky, put tog [ether *the Netherworld*], they brought forth all living beings, all creatures, wild animals of the steppe, beasts of the steppe, and all creatures of civilization. *After t[hey had distribu]ted* all sanctuaries to the living beings, (and) to the wild animals and creatures of civilization had distributed the temples."[31] Another example among many is found in the acrostic *Nabu Hymn of Nebuchadnezzar II*. There Nabu holds the dome of the heavens in his hand and establishes the homes of the great gods. He forms humanity, which is further defined as assigning shepherds their animals. He controls life and health, and instructs humanity in the fear of the gods. The poem then proceeds to focus on how Nabu gave kingship to Nebuchadnezzar.[32] A final example from Egyptian literature, *The Hymn and Prayer to Ptah* (Papyrus Harris I), portrays Ptah as Creator in a variety of descriptive phrases. He shaped mankind and formed the gods, but also created events. He created the sky, raising it up like a feather, and encircled the world with the Ocean. He provided the netherworld for the dead and allows Re to sail across the heavens for their comfort. He provides both breath and sustaining food and has dominion over time, fate, and fortune. He created the concept of offerings for the gods and provided for kingship.[33]

Shifting attention to the historical frame of the human world, we find non-order is also evident in ancient categorizations. In the trope of

Corpus of Sumerian Literature, http://etcsl.orinst.ox.ac.uk/cgi-bin/etcsl.cgi?text=t .1.8.1.4#.

[30] See the extended discussion and consideration of all occurrences in Walton, *Genesis 1 as Ancient Cosmology*, 139–44.

[31] Enrique Jiménez, *The Babylonian Disputation Poems*, CHANE 87 (Leiden: Brill, 2017), 303.

[32] "Nabu Hymn of Nebuchadnezzar" (Oshima, *Babylonian Poems of Pious Sufferers*, 477).

[33] " Hymn and Prayer to Ptah" (John Foster, *Hymns, Prayers and Psalms: An Anthology of Ancient Egyptian Lyric Poetry*, SBLWAW [Atlanta, GA: SBL, 1995], 109).

the archetypal enemy hordes, the enemies ("Umman-Manda") are viewed as representatives of the non-ordered world who must be defeated to restore order.[34] Perhaps the epitome of non-order within the human world is the characterization of the barbarians in the Sumerian *Marriage of Martu*, where the subjects have monstrous features, show no reverence to the gods, roam about in primitive clothing, live in tents, and have no established burial practices.[35] In the Hebrew Bible the non-order of the terrestrial world is expressed in Gen 2:5–6 and resolved by acts of creation and garden-planting, by God's provision of clothing, and then by humans in Cain's line who develop musical instruments, domesticate animals, and engage in metal working.

One of the most distinctive ancient Near Eastern accounts of disorder in the human world is found in *Erra and Ishum*,[36] in which the god Erra responds to the human sin of neglect of him. Historically the piece is connected to the invasion of Babylon by the Sutu people.[37] The initial threat to order in the cosmos (Akk. *šiptu*, "governing order") is posed by Marduk's absence from the throne (1:170–89). Erra offers to maintain order in his place. As the piece progresses, however, Erra himself becomes a force of disorder. As in the flood story in Genesis (or the destruction of Jerusalem by Babylon), a god is destroying human order in response to human disorderly conduct. Erra brings the non-ordered world (Sutu) against the disordered world in order to reestablish order (an attempt to find rest), just as Yahweh brings non-order (the flood waters) against the disordered world (antediluvian violence) to re-establish order and bring rest (note the name of Noah). As Machinist notes concerning *Erra and Ishum*, "'Destructive fury,' in other words, does not simply oppose 'rest.' It can also bring it about, by the cleansing exhaustion it creates."[38]

---

[34] Selim Ferruh Adalı, *The Scourge of God: The Umman-Manda and Its Significance in the First Millennium BC*, SAAS 20 (Helsinki: The Neo-Assyrian Text Corpus Project, 2011). For the question about whether they should be considered non-order or disorder, see discussion in John H. Walton and J. Harvey Walton, *The Lost World of the Israelite Conquest* (Downers Grove, IL: InterVarsity Press, 2017), 138–47.

[35] Marriage of Martu, see lines 127–41. The Electronic Text Corpus of Sumerian Literature, http://etcsl.orinst.ox.ac.uk/section1/tr171.htm. See also Beate Pongratz-Leisten, "The Other and the Enemy in the Mesopotamian Conception of the World," in *Mythology and Mythologies: Methodological Approaches to Intercultural Influences*, ed. R. Whiting, Melammu II (Helsinki: The Neo-Assyrian Text Corpus Project, 2001), 195–231.

[36] "Erra and Ishum," trans. Stephanie Dalley (COS 1.113:404–16).

[37] Peter Machinist, "Rest and Violence in the Poem of Erra," *JAOS* 103 (1983), 221–26.

[38] Ibid., 224.

The vision of the Genesis flood story is again observable in the Mesopotamian flood accounts. The two share not only the basic narrative of the flood and the survival of a few, they also coincide on the sequence of disorder to non-order to renewed order. Despite that common trope, it is obvious that the biblical narrator(s) interpreted the account far differently from what we find in any of the Mesopotamian versions.[39] All versions construe the flood as representing a reset of order in response to encroaching and pervasive disorder. Despite the commonality they share in connection to the Order Matrix and the general similarities of plot, the biblical narrators reflect a variation in their interpretive path, however, as they offer no hint of divine interactions or humans fulfilling the needs of the gods.

In the Genesis account of the flood, cosmic order is restored first, then order between God and humans in the covenant made with Noah. The sign of the covenant, the rainbow, is assigned a significance of representing order when it might appear to be threatened. This is typical of phenomenological omens in Mesopotamia that offer a sense of order (achievable through divine communication) even as the sign itself is often considered an abnormality or lapse of cosmic order.

Another Mesopotamian example of disorder in the human realm can be found in the irreverent king motif.[40] Naram-Suen (2213–2176) in the dynasty of Akkad remains the most prominent example of this motif,[41] but Amar-Suen (2046–2038) from the Ur III is another outstanding example.[42] The motif features a king who desires to build or restore a temple and fails to gain divine permission to do so. When he attempts the project anyway, it not only fails but it brings destruction on the city or country. The account of the Tower of Babel in Gen 11 offers a possible example of the motif, though the king is unnamed. The project involves construction of sacred space (a ziggurat) and God is displeased with it, resulting in the failure to complete the work and, in Genesis, in the scattering of the people. In this way it can be seen that an attempt by

[39] For detailed analysis see Longman and Walton, *Lost World of the Flood*, 53–87.

[40] C. D. Evans, "Naram-Sin and Jeroboam: The Archetypal Unheilsherrscher in Mesopotamian and Biblical Historiography," in *Scripture in Context II: More Essays on the Comparative Method*, ed. W. W. Hallo, J. Moyer, and L. Perdue (Winona Lake, IN: Eisenbrauns, 1983), 97–125.

[41] Cf. "The Cuthean Legend of Naram Sin," translated and discussed in Joan Goodnick Westenholz, *Legends of the Kings of Akkade* (Winona Lake, IN: Eisenbrauns, 1997), 263–368.

[42] Piotr Michalowski, "Amar-Su'ena and the Historical Tradition," in *Essays on the Ancient Near East*, ed. M. J. Ellis (Hamden, CT: Archon, 1977), 155–57. Compare also Nabonidus as portrayed in early Achaemenid sources.

humans to establish order for themselves (making a name by bringing
a god down among them) ends in the disruption of that order (by means of
the confusion of tongues = non-order). It is interesting to note that Amar-
Suen desired to complete the temple and ziggurat of Enki at Eridu (considered the first city in history), but could not get approval from the god.
He eventually proceeds, doing so "to make his name everlasting."[43]
Already the dynasty of Ur began to collapse in the time of Amar-Suen,
but did not meet its final demise until the time of his successor, Shu-
Suen.[44]

ANCESTOR NARRATIVES

The thought world of the ancient Near East can also be explored through
the ancestral narratives that unfold in Gen 12–50. One issue of particular
interest concerns what we can discover about the developing worship of
Yahweh (though the book shows no interest in such analysis) and how he
was perceived as interacting with the family of Abram. In the initial
covenant offer in Gen 12:1–3, no introduction of the God is provided (e.g.,
I am Yahweh, or I am El Shaddai as we get in numerous other conversations). The narrator neither attempts a history of Yahweh, nor locates
him geographically or ethnically. He neither identifies Yahweh with
a pantheon nor distinguishes him as lacking one. No indication is
given that Yahweh expects to be understood as sole God or the exclusive
recipient of Abram's worship and ritual. In that sense, no information is
given in this initial conversation that would distinguish Abram's new
God as a different sort of god from what he would have been used to in his
world.

Scholars have noted that in the early second millennium, people
were inclined to interact with lower-level deities who became their
clan god; these acted as special caregivers who in turn then became the
primary focus of their rituals.[45] The interaction between Abram and his
God would easily fit that paradigm. Whether he knew the name Yahweh
is not our concern here. The narrator represents Abram, and later Jacob,

---

[43] Peeter Espak, *The God Enki in Sumerian Royal Ideology and Mythology* (Wiesbaden: Harrassowitz, 2015), 61. See also the text "Amar-Suena and Enki's Temple" (Amar-Suena A), http://etcsl.orinst.ox.ac.uk/cgi-bin/etcsl.cgi?text=t.2.4.3.1&charenc=j#.
[44] Further discussion in Longman and Walton, *Lost World of the Flood*, 134–35.
[45] Karel van der Toorn, *Family Religion in Babylonia, Syria and Israel: Continuity and Change in the Forms of Religious Life* (Leiden: Brill, 1996); T. Jacobsen, *Treasures of Darkness* (New Haven, CT: Yale University Press, 1976); Tzvi Abusch, "Witchcraft and the Anger of the Personal God," in *Mesopotamian Magic*, ed. Tzvi Abusch and Karel van der Toorn (Groningen: Styx, 1999), 81–122, especially 105–7.

interacting with Yahweh, though other names are attested. Our interest here is not in the history of the name but in how the God of Abram, by whatever name, was understood by him (as the narrator characterizes the relationship), and how that compares to the experience of general population in the second millennium BCE.

Abram is not given a new way to worship this presumably new God. He receives no instruction on that count at all, and nothing distinguishes his ritual activity, as little as we see of it, from anyone else in the ancient world. If Abram had lived in the urban centers of Ur and Haran (as opposed to being a pastoralist on the periphery of the urban centers) he would have been used to having a temple serve as the focus of his ritual attention. Now, instead, the narrator presents him as building altars to locate places of divine presence where rituals could be performed (although we note that the reports of the construction of altars are not generally accompanied by a comment about sacrifices being offered, except in the case of his son). Construction of such altars would not be an unusual practice for those outside the urban centers where the temples of the gods were less accessible.

The expectations that Abram and his clan had of this God do not vary from those that would have been current for any worshipper of this time: provision of food and family, protection, and a modicum of success. Yahweh's regular expectations of Abram and his descendants as faithful worshippers likewise show nothing out of the ordinary. In fact, Yahweh communicates little about his expectations, so all the defaults of the ancient Near East remain in place and govern how everyone acts. We might be surprised that more attention to ritual is not evident, but no new components of interaction appear.[46] Circumcision is not universally practiced but is not innovative as a ritual act (although the timing is so far unprecedented). Even the request for a human sacrifice is not something outside the range of possibility in that world. The idea that a god actively converses, directs activity, and is engaged in events is likewise not out of the ordinary, as remarkable as it may seem to modern readers.

We can mention in passing that in the issues of day-to-day life in a household, we also find little that distinguishes Abram's family from any family at this time. Marriage, adoption, inheritance, and clan inter-actions all follow common patterns that can be found throughout the archival materials of the second millennium and reflect human needs, wants, emotions, and problems. Occasional actions have yet to find

---

[46] The ritual of Gen 15 is largely unprecedented, but it is not given as a regular ritual practice – this is a special occasion.

parallels in the ancient world (e.g., wife masquerading as sister); this is more likely due to the inevitable incompleteness of our sources rather than reason to consider these narratives as reflecting a unique thought world.

A search for religious elements ill-fitted to the larger cognitive environment is largely unproductive, with only a few passing minor exceptions and one large feature that will demand more attention. Two of the minor ones can be briefly noted. The first is found in Abram's brief exchange with Melchizedek where he insists that his god, Yahweh, is El Elyon, and the creator of heaven and earth (Gen 14:22). This is an elevated claim for a family god. The second is when Jacob instructs his household to bury the foreign gods as they prepare to go to Bethel for him to fulfill his vow to Yahweh (Gen 33:2). Under normal circumstances in the ancient world, it is difficult to see why it would be a problem that they had images of other gods.[47] Each of these are often considered anachronistic supplementation, but regardless of the verdict on that count, they stand in Genesis as deviations. Many other narratives in Genesis could have been enhanced with anachronistic ideas yet were not.

These passing distinctions are all overshadowed by the issue that dominates these chapters and that distinguishes Israelite thinking from anything found thus far in the ancient world: the covenant. In the documents of the ancient world, the gods make bound and sworn agreements with kings.[48] Furthermore, treaties between suzerains and vassals from both the second and first millennia are informative for how relationships between human parties were formulated. Consequently, the idea of a covenant arrangement per se is not out of place in the ancient world. But a God making such an agreement with a clan is unattested.[49]

Beyond the idea of such a covenant, we are also struck by the terms and features that are stated. Though Yahweh does not demand exclusive worship, what he asks Abram to do will effectively cut at least some of his ties with whatever gods he has previously served. When Yahweh asks Abram to leave his family and his land, it is likely implied that as he does so his previous connections to the gods of his current land, and any

---

[47] It is unclear whether these would be the teraphim that Rachel had or perhaps images that had been plundered from Shechem in the previous chapter The teraphim have not played a major role to this point, and there was no reference to them plundering images from Shechem.

[48] Exploring Akkadian terms such as *adû* and *māmītu* can give the range of this practice. John H. Walton, *Ancient Near Eastern Thought and the Old Testament* (Grand Rapids, MI: Baker, 2018), 260; see *CAD*, A/1 *adû*, 134, and M/1 *māmītu*, 189–92.

[49] For a short discussion, see Walton, *Ancient Near Eastern Thought and the Old Testament*, 316 n. 2.

ancestral or clan deities worshipped in his family, will also be left behind (though perhaps Abram brought such figurines with him). Gods are tied to locations in the ancient world, not by spatial restrictions, but by the fact that sacrificial gifts are brought to the god at his sacred places (most importantly, temples). If one is no longer in proximity of a temple (or some other sort of shrine or altar), the sacrifices cannot be brought to that god. This is all interconnected with what we have called the great symbiosis. Gods only take care of people so that the people can meet their needs (through ritual performance). If no local shrine or temple exists, it is not practical to present gifts, in which case the god has no reason to act on one's behalf. As Abram travels further away from his homeland, he no longer has access to places where his former gods could be served. He therefore would have to construct sacred places for those gods (not something that can be done arbitrarily), or begin to worship gods whose sacred places are proximate to his new settlement, or focus on the worship of the family god who has brought him to a new place. It is the latter that characterizes Abram's worship.

The covenant as first discussed in Gen 12 has no stipulations.[50] It does not suggest ritual responses by Abram and it focuses on God's presence with Abram. We get no hint that the great symbiosis is in play, but admittedly, no denial of it either. At this point, therefore, the details of this covenant relationship evidence no expectations that differ from what would be found broadly in the ancient world, but the very idea of forming a covenant with a human family is striking, as is the overall nature of Yahweh's instruction. The idea of leaving one's community identity behind (homeland and family) is entirely counter-cultural. Furthermore, the lofty promise, "through you all the nations of the earth will be blessed," has no parallel. This is unprecedented in the extant sources from the ancient world and ill-suited to the cognitive environment which those sources reflect, though it is worth noting that narrative accounts of ancestors are largely absent from the textual material extant from the ancient Near East.

CONCLUSIONS

The history of cognitive environment criticism has often shown the tendency to become over-absorbed in the comparison of individual

---

[50] Though Gen 17:1 has some general stipulations such as, "Walk before me and be blameless", these would not be unusual expectations for a god to have of his worshipper in the ancient world.

passages from the Hebrew Bible with individual pieces of literature from the ancient world. Much greater gain is achievable when comparative analysis can focus on the similarities and differences in how these literatures interact with the cognitive environment they have in common. The result is that even when evidence is unable to demonstrate an indebtedness of the Hebrew Bible to a given piece of literature from the ancient Near East, our readings of both the Hebrew Bible and the ancient Near Eastern literature can be enriched by exploring the ways in which each is embedded in a world that is so different from ours today.

SELECT BIBLIOGRAPHY

Averbeck, Richard. "Ancient Near Eastern Mythography as It Relates to Historiography in the Hebrew Bible: Genesis 3 and the Cosmic Battle." Pages 328–56 in *The Future of Biblical Archaeology: Reassessing Methodologies and Assumptions*. Edited by J. K. Hoffmeier, and Alan Millard. Grand Rapids, MI, 2004.

Evans, C. D. "Naram-Sin and Jeroboam: The Archetypal *Unheilsherrscher* in Mesopotamian and Biblical Historiography." Pages 328–56 in *Scripture in Context II: More Essays on the Comparative Method*. Edited by W. W. Hallo, James Moyer, and Leo Perdue. Winona Lake, IN: Eisenbrauns, 1983.

Jiménez, Enrique. *The Babylonian Disputation Poems*, CHANE 87. Leiden, 2017.

Korpel, Marjo. *Rift in the Clouds: Ugaritic and Hebrew Descriptions of the Divine*, UBL 8. Münster: Ugarit-Verlag, 1990.

Longman, Tremper III and John H. Walton. *The Lost World of the Flood*. Downers Grove, IL: InterVarsity, 2018.

Oshima, Takayoshi. *Babylonian Poems of Pious Sufferers*. Tübingen: Mohr Siebeck, 2014.

Pongratz-Leisten, Beate. "The Other and the Enemy in the Mesopotamian Conception of the World." Pages 195–231 in *Mythology and Mythologies. Methodological Approaches to Intercultural Influences*. Edited by Robert Whiting, Melammu II. Helsinki: The Neo-Assyrian Text Corpus Project, 2001.

Rajadell, Àngel Menargues. "Mesopotamian Ideas of Time Through Modern Eyes." Pages 211–28 in *Time and History in the Ancient Near East*. Edited by Lluís Feliu et al. RAI 56. Winona Lake, IN: Eisenbrauns, 2013.

Rochberg, Francesca. *Before Nature*. Chicago, IL: University of Chicago Press, 2017.

Rochberg, Francesca. "'The Stars and Their Likeness': Perspectives on the Relation Between Celestial Bodies and Gods in Ancient Mesopotamia." Pages 41–92 in *What Is a God?* Edited by B. N. Porter. Winona Lake, IN: Eisenbrauns, 2009.

Rubio, Gonzalo. "Time before Time: Primeval Narratives in Early Mesopotamian Literature." Pages in 3–17 in *Time and History in the Ancient Near East.* Edited by Lluís Feliu et al., RAI 56. Winona Lake, IN: Eisenbrauns, 2013.

Toorn, Karel van der. *Family Religion in Babylonia, Syria and Israel: Continuity and Change in the Forms of Religious Life.* Leiden: Brill, 1996.

Vanstiphout, Herman. "Why Did Enki Organize the World?" Pages 117–35 in *Sumerian Gods and Their Representations.* Edited by Irving Finkel. Groningen: Styx, 1997.

Walton, John H. *Genesis 1 as Ancient Cosmology.* Winona Lake, IN: Eisenbrauns, 2011.

Walton, John H. and J. Harvey Walton. *The Lost World of the Israelite Conquest.* Downers Grove, IL: InterVarsity, 2017.

8 Family, Clan, and Tribe in the Book of Genesis

NAOMI A. STEINBERG

INTRODUCTION

Kinship studies are central for interpreting the ancestral narratives of Genesis. These studies are integral to understanding institutions such as marriage, as well as customary and traditional backgrounds to adoption, bartering, children, and many others, and provide a context for a close reading of this book in the texts of Genesis 12–50. In what follows, I rely on the Hebrew contextual application of the terms for family, clan, and tribe – the kinship units of ancient Israel – and define kinship as a culturally determined emphasis on blood and marriage as the preferred method for constructing the Israelite family, rather than solely on blood line.[1]

Systematic study of the levels and the functions of family structure in Genesis belies the assumption that the family – whether ancient[2] or modern – was ever a static entity with one definition fixed for all times. The biblical material is complicated because of the uncertain dates of biblical and related data and the diverse terms and the different modern translations of the contextual Hebrew terminology for social organization: family, clan, and tribe. The traditional meanings of these terms cannot be understood by imposing contemporary Western perspectives as though they are timeless universals. The data of any society must be studied in their original context and language in order to allow patterns reflective of that group to emerge. One of the problems to consider in discussing the world of the family in Genesis 12–50 is deciding the historical context for the practices reflected in the texts and when the texts were redacted and put into their final canonical form.[3] We will

---

[1] Naomi Steinberg, "Alliance or Descent? The Function of Marriage in Genesis," *JSOT* 51 (1991): 45–55.

[2] Leo G. Perdue, Joseph Blenkinsopp, John J. Collins, and Carol Meyers, eds., *Families in Ancient Israel* (Louisville, KY: Westminster John Knox, 1997).

[3] Stager and Schloen maintain that the texts reflect practices of pre-monarchical Israel. See Lawrence E. Stager, "The Archaeology of the Family in Ancient Israel," *BASOR*

mine the texts to retrieve kinship structure using a synchronic perspective but recognize that a diachronic approach might yield different analyses. Genesis may reflect the ideology of how family life should be rather than the reality of how it was lived.

Most studies that mention the relevance of kinship note that Genesis 12–50 are texts of the ancestral families of Genesis. Genesis 11:27 introduces the household of Terah, who has three sons: Nahor, Haran, and Abram/Abraham. Abraham is the father of Isaac who is the father of Jacob, who is the father of twelve sons who are later interpreted as the tribal unity called Israel. These terms and the dynamics of the narratives reveal that women are nevertheless important in these narratives.

In anthropological studies, as well as in past biblical research, the kinship terminology used viewed social structure from the vantage point of males. In what follows, I bring in gender and feminist studies which emphasize that a shift in perspective from the male point of view to the female point of view highlights the roles of women and provides a more inclusive model of the social world of the family than offered by a male perspective alone. Given this inclusivity, in what follows, women move from being on the fringes of kinship organization to being central to the social organization.

In Genesis there are many women in ancestral family life: Sarah, a primary wife, Hagar, a slave wife, and Keturah (Gen 25:1) a concubine, are all wives of Abraham. Esau had six wives; and two high-status women, Leah and Rachel, and two lower-status women, Zilpah and Bilhah, are all wives of Jacob. Finally, in studying the construction of kinship units, I address the presence and importance of children to family life.

ANTHROPOLOGICAL MODELS FOR BIBLICAL SOCIAL ORGANIZATION

The family as presented in Genesis has been reconstructed on three levels, described here from bottom to top. The basic foundational unit of the family is the *bêt 'āb*, the house of the father, the ancestral household, or a nuclear family. The *bêt 'āb* is both a descent group and a residential one and is the smallest unit of society. It is sometimes

260 (1985): 1–35; J. David Schloen, *The House of the Father as Fact and Symbol: Patrimonialism in Ugarit and the Ancient Near East*, Studies in Archaeology and History of the Levant 2 (Winona Lake, IN: Eisenbrauns, 2001), 108, 135.

referred to as a consanguineal family, or the joint family household. It consisted of "a conjugal couple and their unmarried children, together with their married sons and their wives and children, as well as other unmarried or dependent paternal kinfolk and slaves,"[4] who might bear children to the *bêt 'āb*. Not only does one note the presence of fathers and sons in the family but also wives, mothers, daughters, and concubines. Except for the latter, these women are marked typically as both maternally and paternally related individuals.

When more individuals are added to the nuclear family, the family is referred to as an extended family household. The term multiple-family household is used when a domestic unit is composed of more than one married couple who are tied to each other either by descent or marriage. In Genesis, if Laban's wife was alive at the time when Jacob and his wives Rachel and Leah lived with Laban (who was their father), then the *bêt 'āb* would be labelled a multiple-family household.

The kinship unit immediately above the family household was the *mišpāḥâ*, the clan (or maximal lineage), an enlargement of the *bêt 'āb* to include lineages related by marriage, intended as a "protective association of extended families."[5] The *mišpāḥâ*

> operated to preserve the minimal conditions for the integrity of each of its member families by extending mutual help as needed to supply male heirs, to keep or recover land, to rescue members from debt slavery, and to avenge murder. These functions were all restorative in that they were emergency means to restore the normal autonomous basis of a member family, and they were all actions that devolved upon the [*mišpāḥâ*] only when the [*bêt 'āb*] was unable to act on its own behalf.[6]

Sometimes the term *mišpāḥâ* is translated as "clan." Like the *bêt 'āb*, the *mišpāḥâ* can apply to more than one type of family organization. Both terms can refer to lineages; the Hebrew terminology is sometimes imprecise for the contemporary interpreter. In the ancestral narratives of Genesis, the level of the *mišpāḥâ* appears infrequently. One notable exception appears in Gen 24 when Abraham commissions his servant to return to Aram-naharim to seek a bride for Isaac from his kin. In Gen 24:38, 40–41, he specifies that a woman must be found from both his *bêt 'āb*, certainly intended to indicate the descent group of Terah through

---

[4]   Schloen, *The House of the Father*, 108.
[5]   Norman K. Gottwald, *The Tribes of Yahweh* (Maryknoll, NY: Orbis, 1979), 258.
[6]   Ibid., 267.

Abraham and his *mišpāḥâ*. The term *mišpāḥâ* also takes on significance in Gen 12:3 when God calls Abraham from his homeland and promises that the blessing to Abraham carries on to a social level hierarchically above Abraham.

In order to draw a clear picture of the hierarchical social structure of texts that serve as the foundation texts of an Israel assumed by family organization in Genesis we conclude with a discussion of the *šēbeṭ*, the tribe, a grouping which brings together clans related by descent from a common ancestor – whether related by blood or fictitious. Whether actual or ideal, Gen 49 lists twelve tribes, a band of the sons of Jacob. Dinah, daughter of Jacob borne to him by his wife Leah (Gen 34:1), is not counted among these tribes.

The tribes of Israel are presented as a kinship unit, although a larger group than the preceding kinship units. It is difficult to decide whether this tribal association refers to real individuals or are eponyms of these tribes, that is, symbolic of larger groups. From Genesis, and later biblical texts, it is also difficult to glean exactly how tribes were constituted or governed. It appears that the term *šēbeṭ* corresponds to a specific geographical area, although the biblical evidence in general is ambiguous about this level of social organization as a construct for understanding the family in ancient Israel.

These hierarchical concentric circles of kinship organization structured ancient Israel as depicted in Genesis, although an individual's life focused on the level of the *bêt 'āb*. The family story texts do not address the kinship connections that obligate the family household to the clan and the tribe; the focus is on fathers and sons, mothers and daughters, uncles and nephews, and cousins within the kinship unit descended from the apical ancestor Terah.

A more general perspective on those who reside in the *bêt 'āb* includes the resident alien, the *gēr* and the *tôšābîm* (workers and laborers). The text of circumcision appears to assume the presence of both groups living in the *bêt 'āb* when in Gen 17:27 Abraham is instructed to circumcise not only all the men of his *bêtô* (as a residence unit and a descent group, the reference is unclear) but those men he has purchased or are strangers (workers and craftsmen, presumably). Genesis does not explicitly refer to *gērîm* by name among the Israelite family, although Abraham himself is identified as a *gēr* in Kiriath-arba/Hebron (Gen 23:4) when he barters for land in the field of Ephron in Machpelah in order to bury Sarah.

Throughout these texts, family religion on the level of the *bêt 'āb* emerges. Abraham builds multiple altars (Gen 12:7–8; 13:8), which are sometimes linked to sacrificial offerings (including the case of the near sacrifice of Isaac, who is bound to an altar in Gen 22:9–14). On some occasions there is just a sacrifice, for example, Gen 15:9–21. Sometimes the ritual of altar-building is accompanied by a sacrifice and a meal is also eaten, as in the example of Gen 31:54, when Jacob and Laban separate. These practices together suggest evidence of family religion revolving around an ancestral cult and local deities in the religious world of the ancestral narratives of Genesis.[7]

Any study of life in the *bêt ʾāb* must address meal preparation as a feature characteristic of family structure. Jacob feeds Esau (Gen 25:29–34) and later Esau makes food for Jacob (Gen 27:31). Meals are sometimes for the purpose of hospitality (Gen 18:5–8). Here one notes that while women prepare meals, they do not eat with the recipients (Gen 18:6 regarding Sarah; Gen 27:7–9, 17 regarding Rebekah). Meals were also served at family celebrations, as at the time of the weaning of Isaac (Gen 21:8). Together, the building of altars, the offering of sacrifices, and the preparation of meals for different occasions (besides the assumed daily meals that are not discussed in the ancestral stories) provide a socioeconomic perspective on food in the texts.

Less familiar to the study of anthropological models of kinship and family organization is recent scholarship on the maternal subunits of the *bêt ʾēm*, literally, "the house of the mother." These subunits are not necessarily a distinct level of Israelite social structure.[8] However, they provide a gendered nuance to analysis of the level of the *bêt ʾāb*. The text of Gen 24:28 mentions "a *bêt ʾēm*, which represents a social and spatial subunit nested within the larger house of the father."[9] This terminology shows "how women and maternal kin marked social divisions within the house of the father and between houses."[10] Cynthia Chapman is surely correct that any study of the social structure of ancient Israel "must account for the mothers who served as its building blocks."[11]

[7] Karel van der Toorn, *Family Religion in Babylon, Ugarit, and Syria: Continuity and Change in the Forms of Religious Life*, Studies in the History and Culture of the Ancient Near East 7 (Leiden: Brill, 1996), 181–265.

[8] Cynthia R. Chapman, *The House of the Mother: The Social Roles of Maternal Kin in Biblical Hebrew Narrative and Poetry*, ABRL (New Haven, CT: Yale University Press, 2016).

[9] Ibid., 51. For a slightly different perspective, see Carol Meyers, "'To Her Mother's House': Considering a Counterpart to the Israelite *Bêt ʾāb*," in *The Bible and the Politics of Exegesis: Essays in Honor of Norman Gottwald on His Sixty-Fifth Birthday*, ed. David Jobling, Peggy L. Day, and Gerald T. Sheppard (Cleveland, OH: Pilgrim Press, 1991), 39–51, 304–7.

[10] Ibid., 200.

[11] Ibid., 228.

Chapman argues for the importance of "the house of the mother, *bêt 'ēm*, a phrase that occurs only once in Genesis.[12] A balanced theoretical discussion of family life will only occur when the kinship units of the *bêt 'āb* and the *bêt 'ēm* are fully integrated. Kinship studies will then be able to analyze both units as basic to family structure. Chapman argues that the presence of this term *bêt 'ēm* recognizes maternal kinship and its relevance for the construction of the social structure of kinship. She correctly states:

> When we include all of these maternally specific kinship terms in the analysis, it becomes clear that the biblical house of the father divides into maternally defined, unequal subunits. The house of Jacob divides into four subunits, two that trace their ancestry to wives and two that trace their ancestry to secondary, maidservant wives.[13]

As stated above, Gen 24:28 is the only text in Genesis that refers to the *bêt 'ēm*.[14] In the larger context of this chapter, Rebekah runs to her mother's house to tell her *bêt 'ēm* of her encounter with Abraham's servant, who has been sent by Abraham to find a wife for Isaac. The text traces Rebekah's kinship back to Abraham's brother Nahor, at the same time stating that she is tied to Nahor, and therefore back to Terah, through her mother Milcah. Milcah's lineage through Nahor identifies Rebekah as a preferred wife for Isaac because she is descended from both Nahor and Milcah (Gen 24:15, 24, 47 which link back to Gen 22:20–23). This genealogical kinship tie upholds the importance of the lineage of the wife Milcah, and the importance of her kinship credentials (as well as the choice of other ancestral wives traced back to Terah) in the choice of Rebekah as a wife for Isaac.

The economic brokering of marriage between Rebekah and Isaac, as well as the economic relationship between Rebekah and her brother Laban through their mother Milcah, comes to the forefront in Gen 24:22 where we find a list of the items given to Rebekah (as a demonstration of the wealth of Abraham) by their weight: "a gold nose ring weighing half a shekel and two bracelets for her arms weighing ten gold shekels." Presumably these items are what prompts Laban to quickly draw the servant into his house to "cash in" on the economic prosperity displayed by the servant (see also Gen 24:53b). The items

---

[12]   It appears also in Ruth 1:8; Song 3:4; 8:2.
[13]   Chapman, *The House of the Mother*, 19.
[14]   Chapman argues that each time this term appears, it is used from the perspective of a marriageable woman; ibid., 63.

given to Laban can later be used by Laban to barter for a wife. In her argument for the importance of the single reference to the *bêt 'ēm* in Genesis, Chapman remarks, "We are now focusing on Rebekah, her mother, and her brother."[15] The gifts from the servant not only go to Rebekah, and Laban, but to her mother. Although the mother is not named in Gen 24:53b, the narrative indicates her importance in Rebekah's life by identifying her from the perspective of Rebekah, as Rebekah's mother.

Chapman convincingly argues that tents are associated with women. Tents are maternal space in Genesis. Isaac goes into the tent of his mother when he marries Rebekah (Gen 24:67), Laban goes between the individual tents of his daughters and their maidservants (who share a tent) as he searches for his missing household gods. We have an indication that as physical spaces tents are typically divided up for individual women although this should not be conceptualized as the private/public sphere.

Also consistent with this perspective is the report of the encounter between Jacob and Esau when they meet again after years of separation caused by conflict between them over heirship to their father Isaac. Jacob fears for his life and the life of his family at Esau's hand. We are told, "So he [Jacob] divided the children among Leah and Rachel and the two maids with their children. He put the maids in front with their children in front, then Leah with her children, and Rachel and Joseph last of all" (Gen 33:2). Jacob's strategy is not only to separate multiple wives into subunits but to put the wives of lower status first in case Esau decides to attack. This arrangement is intended to make Jacob's primary, or higher-status, wives less vulnerable to attack than secondary wives and children.

Next we examine the theoretical significance of this kinship structure for reconstructing the social world of Genesis 12–50. This discussion recognizes the complexity of kinship structure when we include the perspectives of both men and women in the highly complex world of family relations.

ENDOGAMOUS MARRIAGE, PATRILINEAL DESCENT, AND PATRILOCAL RESIDENCE AND INHERITANCE

The purpose of marriage was economic, inasmuch as it was intended to guarantee production (growing food to guarantee the survival of the

---

[15] Ibid., 54.

group) and reproduction (offspring) of the family from one generation to the next. The pattern of marriage that emerges is certainly one that privileges men, but as noted above, it highlights the importance of women in kinship structure and explains recurring behavior from one generation to the next. Unless a male descended from the line of Terah marries a "preferred wife" he will not have a place in the vertical lineage of Abraham and Isaac (we discuss the horizontal lineage of Jacob below). The preferred wife is a woman who is descended from the men from the Terahite lineage. Husband and wife share patrilineal descent.[16] After marriage the new bride will live with her husband's family, which is also her family line through her father. Residence in the *bêt 'āb* of the groom is crucial so that the latter will inherit the property and land of his father and then produce (male) children to move the family into the next generation and address issues of inheritance.[17] The pattern described here makes clear that women and children are the glue that held together the *bêt 'āb* and helped maintain the values of production and reproduction in Genesis.

When a man marries a woman, who is a close blood relative, the type of marriage is labelled as endogamy. It is what might be called "in-group" marriage. In contrast, when a man marries outside of the boundaries established by an individual's kinship group, we have a form of marriage known as exogamy, or "marrying out."[18] The preference for endogamy, rather than exogamy, brings to the forefront the fact that marriage is based on economic considerations. A man and a woman from the same patrilineage bring their goods together and maintain them within the same kinship group. The property – whether brought to the marriage by either the bridge or the groom – does not pass to another patrilineage, as it does in cases of exogamy. The pattern of living on the land of the groom's father (patrilocal residence) guarantees that when the father dies his son will be on hand to inherit.[19] Despite the male perspective presented in this theoretical model,

[16] Naomi Steinberg, *Kinship and Marriage in Genesis: A Household Economics Perspective* (Minneapolis, MN: Fortress, 1993).

[17] Ibid., 137–38.

[18] For the argument that marriages in Genesis formed alliances, see Mara E. Donaldson, "Kinship Theory in the Patriarchal Narratives: The Case of the Barren Wife," *JAAR* 49 (1981): 77–87; Terry J. Prewitt, "Kinship Structures and the Genesis Genealogies," *JNES* 40 (1981): 87–98; Robert A. Oden, "Jacob as Father, Husband, and Nephew: Kinship Studies and the Patriarchal Narratives," *JBL* 102 (1983): 189–205; Robert A. Oden, *The Bible without Theology: The Theological Tradition and Alternatives to It* (San Francisco: Harper & Row, 1987), 106–30, 183–87.

[19] H. C. Brichto, "Kin, Cult, Land and Afterlife: A Biblical Complex," *HUCA* 44 (1973): 1–54.

women were not only present in the family household but their status determined the fate of their sons. One need only think of the example of the differing fates of the sons of Sarah, Hagar, and Keturah in the family household of Gen 11:27–25:11.

As the stories regarding Sarah's barrenness and the subsequent events because of her biological condition make clear, children were important to the family unit because they provided their mothers with sociocultural validation and their fathers with heirs to carry on the family line. As the story of the marriage of Sarah and Abraham makes clear, human biology may be a rather ineffective arrangement for perpetuation of the family. Various potential obstacles, the most obvious being barrenness, may interfere with reproduction, so it is no wonder that Genesis exhibits a variety of "solutions" to family continuity. When barrenness occurs in a generation to impede its continuity, barrenness is understood by the male authors of the biblical texts to be the "fault" of women, although the texts repeatedly demonstrate that wives are just as concerned with this problem as are their husbands (e.g., Sarah in Gen 16:2).

From the evidence of different cultures and Genesis itself, it is evident that there are multiple options by means of which a family could cope with the absence of progeny. Serial monogamy occurs when a man divorces a barren woman in the hopes of marrying a fertile one who will bear him a son. Even more effective than serial monogamy for producing heirs is polygyny (taking multiple, primary wives/ first-ranking wives; e.g., the marriages to Leah and Rachel by Jacob) or poly-coity, the attempt at reproduction by means of a woman of lower status than the primary wife/wives and who becomes a secondary wife as a result (e.g., Zilpah and Bilhah, the handmaids of Leah and Rachel). The desperation of a primary wife to maintain her socio-validation in the *bêt 'āb* is exemplified by the attempt by Sarah to provide Abraham with a child when she tells him to have sexual intercourse with her maid Hagar. Besides these examples, it is worth noting that the addition of women to the primary family unit can be not only for purposes of procreation but also for the sexual pleasure of the husband, but this was probably most likely done in cases of men of wealth.

An option other than adding women is for a couple to add a child or children, that is, they adopt. This would appear to be the strategy Abraham initially chooses when he leaves his father's homeland and takes his nephew Lot with him. Lot's father Haran is no longer alive, and Lot is descended from the patrilineage through Terah. Hence, to adopt Lot would be a natural choice for Abraham to consider in seeking an heir. Abraham's servant Eliezer, who is not from the descent line of Terah, is rejected as an adopted heir in Gen 15:2–5.

Although the evidence of the world of the child is meagre in the texts, we see that a son could be (nearly) sacrificed and he could be abandoned. A son could also be loved (e.g., Gen 21:11), but the texts do not reveal a child-friendly *bêt 'āb*.[20] Children live under the authority of their parents and are subject to their parents' wishes and for what they can contribute to the family. A family could not get along with them. Both daughters and sons are valued for their ability to contribute to the socioeconomic development of the *bêt 'āb*. To take two examples: first, in Gen 29:9, Rachel shepherds her father's sheep. Later in the *bêt 'āb* of Jacob, his sons tend to cattle in their father's field (34:5–7).

Childhood here appears to be a phase of life defined not only by chronological age, such as circumcision eight days after birth, but by developmental categories, such as weaning (probably at approximately three years of age).[21] The texts provide little other data on developmental stages of childhood. We can only speculate on the age of marriage, although as discussed below a groom was typically more than ten years older than his bride.

A final theoretical issue in the kinship patterns that emerge in the ancestral narratives is patrilocal residence, which requires that a man bring his bride back to live on the land he will inherit from his father (see Gen 24), another economic strategy intended to keep the property of the descent line within geographical boundaries of the patrilineage. This practice was predicated on the transmission of lineal heirship (although the texts describing the family of Jacob are distinct from those of the generations of Abraham and Isaac; the focus shifts from a lineal/vertical genealogy focused on the choice of only one son as heir to a segmented/horizontal genealogy, where all the sons of Jacob become his heirs; see the discussion above defining the term *šēbeṭ*).

In conclusion, we see that the paradigm described above upholds the family values of production and reproduction on the levels of the *bêt 'āb*, the *mišpāḥâ*, and the *šēbeṭ*. They maintain patrilineal, patrilocal endogamy as well as highlighting the importance of women and children for

---

[20] Naomi Steinberg, "Sociological Approaches: Toward a Sociology of Childhood in the Hebrew Bible." in *Method Matters: Essays on the Interpretation of the Hebrew Bible in Honor of David L. Petersen*, ed. Joel M. LeMon and Kent Harold Richards (Atlanta: Society of Biblical Literature, 2009), 251–69; Naomi Steinberg, *The World of the Child in the Hebrew Bible* (Sheffield: Sheffield Phoenix Press, 2013).

[21] Mayer I. Gruber, "Breast-Feeding Practices in Biblical Israel and in Old Babylonian Mesopotamia," *JANES* 19 (1989): 61–83, here 62–63, 66–68.

the kinship links in Genesis. I now apply these theoretical models to the kinship units in the book.

Abraham, Sarah, Hagar, and Keturah (Gen 11:27–25:11)

The introduction of Abraham as one of three sons to Terah appears to be in traditional genealogical format, linking a father to his sons in the descending generation. Abraham's household serves as one of the families of Israel that derives from the lineage of Terah. However, biology intervenes. Sarai/Sarah, the wife of Abram/Abraham, is barren. All societies that emphasize patrilineal descent must have strategies for overcoming this possibility.

The narratives of Gen 12–25 explore multiple options for establishing heirship for Abraham and socio-validation for Sarah as a mother. Initially the texts suggest that Abraham's *bêt 'āb* will continue through his nephew Lot, the son of his deceased brother Haran. Genesis 12:1 begins the with the *bêt 'āb* of Abraham's father and then makes mention of the *mišpāḥâ* of the earth (Gen 12:3), who although not from the household of Abraham, indicate the hierarchical nature of kinship social organization.

However, if Lot is to be designated the heir to his paternal uncle Abraham, he must reside on the land that will serve as his patrimony. But Lot moves outside the boundaries of the designated landed inheritance (Gen 13:2–18) due to conflict over this land. Later, family loyalty trumps family conflict when Abraham bargains for the preservation of Lot and his family in the destruction of Sodom and Gomorrah (Gen 19:29). With the departure of Lot, Abraham believes that his adopted heir will be his servant Eliezer of Damascus (an *'ebed*, servant, although the text does not specifically use this term; Gen 15:2–3).

Genesis 16 introduces the subject of an heir for Abraham, but this time from the perspective of his barren wife Sarah. Sarah is desperate for a child and her plan demonstrates the agency of a woman in the family unit. The plan for the pregnancy of Hagar, who must be understood as a surrogate mother who will turn her baby over to the married couple, introduces the perspective of a woman – a barren wife – whose social validation and future in the family are determined by her reproductive capabilities.

Genesis 16 brings Hagar, the Egyptian slave girl (*šipḥâ*), into the family household of Abraham and Sarah, a recognition of both the presence and the importance of slaves/servants/concubines in the *bêt 'āb*. The story assumes the existence of polycoity, a form of marriage,

mentioned earlier, in which a woman other than a primary wife functions as a secondary wife of lower status. Hagar remains a slave even
though she becomes pregnant.

Hagar is not consulted about Sarah's plan. She is forced to have
sexual intercourse with Abraham, just as Abraham is forced to procreate
because of the insistence of Sarah. Slaves do not have control of their
bodies. When Hagar becomes pregnant, Sarah is jealous; a pregnant slave
lords her biological condition over the barren primary wife Sarah. Sarah
retaliates and expels Hagar from the household. These dynamics indicate
both the competition of women over pregnancy as well as the perspective
of Hagar as a pregnant slave. The family household of Abraham is in
turmoil through the actions of the two women who cohabit with him.[22]

The household position of Sarah as primary wife is very different
from Hagar's position as a slave, because she is both a secondary wife and
a concubine. A primary wife is a woman bringing property into the
marriage (through either direct and/or indirect dowry) and who has
legal and economic rights not available to a woman who does not bring
in property. Her status is elevated if she is descended through the patrilineage of Terah, as is Sarah (Gen 20:12). By contrast, a slave, or servant,
or concubine has a lower status – economically and legally. She is
a secondary wife. Her marriage can easily be dissolved by the husband
whereas the primary wife has protection against divorce through the
property she brings to the marriage union. Hagar's status is separated
from the status of her child, who is considered a legitimate heir to his
biological father, Abraham, and to Sarah, Abraham's primary wife.
Hagar's role vis-à-vis "Sarah is to build up" and secure her place in the
bêt 'āb.[23]

The birth of Ishmael to his father Abram seemingly resolves the
problem of the continuance of the patrilineage of Terah through his son
Abraham in lieu of Eliezer (Gen 15:2–3), until the time that a son is borne
by Sarah to Abraham. Although it might seem that the birth of Isaac
would be interpreted to mean that Abraham is twice blessed, the pattern
in Genesis so far is that only one son is singled out to continue the
patrilineage, that is, the pattern is one of a lineal – as opposed to
a segmented – genealogy in order to preserve family land – that is, not
dividing it into smaller and smaller tracts. In Genesis 21, a choice is made
for Isaac over Ishmael as heir to the patrilineage of Terah. The choice

[22] Dolores S. Williams, *Sisters in the Wilderness: The Challenge of Womanist God-Talk*
      (Maryknoll, NY: Orbis Books, 1993), 15–34, *et passim*.
[23] Tammi J. Schneider, *Mothers of Promise: Women in the Book of Genesis* (Grand
      Rapids, MI: Baker Academic Press, 2008), 27.

appears to be an unexpected one because Ishmael is the first born son of Abraham. Here the first born does not inherit, as one might expect that he would.

Sarah is the agent who presses for the expulsion of Hagar and Ishmael in order that her son Isaac be designated heir to Abraham. Our analysis yields the following perspective on the life cycle of a woman in ancient Israel: "Being a woman is not enough; one has to become a wife. Being a wife is not enough; one has to become a mother." To this we might add: being a mother is not enough, one must be the mother of her husband's heir.

The kinship "rules" uphold Sarah's perspective that once Isaac is born, he is preferred over Ishmael as heir to Abraham, although both are biological sons of Abraham. The choice between the two sons brings us to the importance of the mothers, Hagar and Sarah, and to the kinship pattern that emerges: the preferred spouse for a son of the Terahite lineage is a woman descended from the same lineage as her husband and the preferred mother of this heir is a woman from the lineage. Sarah is from the lineage of Terah (20:12), whereas Hagar is of Egyptian origins and thus outside the boundaries of the line of Terah. Moreover, the course of events is determined by Sarah's insistence on the expulsion of Hagar and Ishmael. Abraham acts in both Gen 16 and 21 on the basis of Sarah's demands. As anthropologist Heather Montgomery states, "Whether children live in a polygamous or monogamous household, the relative status of their mother, whether they have kin around or whether they are legitimate all affect their status and the subsequent way that they are treated."[24] Thus, behind the dynamics of Gen 21 and the different childhoods of Ishmael and Isaac lay the antagonistic social status competition over fertility that came together in the polygamous household of Abraham going back to Gen 16.

Sarah's choice of her own son Isaac – over Ishmael – not only secures her son as heir to his father, but, using cross-cultural analogues, binds Isaac to her as a source of physical and economic security in her old age. Although the inflated ages of biblical characters in Genesis makes it difficult to be precise about their life spans, the age differential in extra-biblical marriage contracts between a groom and bride suggests that a wife would be expected to outlive her husband because the relative difference between the spouses' ages was typically over a decade.[25] The

---

[24] Heather Montgomery, *An Introduction to Childhood: Anthropological Perspectives on Children's Lives* (Oxford: Wiley-Blackwell, 2008), 54.

[25] Martha T. Roth, "Age at Marriage and the Household: A Study of Neo-Babylonian and Neo-Assyrian Forms," *Comparative Studies in Society and History* 28 (1987): 715–47.

age difference between Sarah and Abraham is in basic conformity with the data from ancient Near Eastern marriage contracts. According to Gen 17:17, Abraham is ten years old than Sarah.

Thus, Sarah's strategy in Gen 21 is to focus on building security for her old age through her son Isaac. Without a son, she could not have this security, and she almost does not when it appears that Abraham will sacrifice Isaac. We never hear from Sarah when Abraham leaves for this sacrifice. The near-sacrifice of Isaac brings in the child's perspective: he looks to his father for an interpretation of what is happening (Gen 22:7–8). Otherwise we hear little from Isaac and nothing from Ishmael when he is expelled with Hagar from the family household. Ishmael experiences a double abandonment. First Abraham abandoned Ishmael (Gen 21:14) and then Hagar abandoned Ishmael (Gen 21:15).

Genesis 24 illustrates that bartering was yet another aspect of the world of the ancestors. In Genesis, Jacob labors for Laban (Gen 29:15; 30:29; 31:6; using the verbal root 'bd) in exchange for marriage to Leah and Rachel. Abraham, who has reaped significant financial gains (Gen 12:16) in exchange for Sarah, uses his wealth as a bargaining chip with Rebekah's family in negotiations for her marriage to Isaac (Gen 24: 10, 22, 30, 35, 47, 53). As these events unfold, we are told in Gen 24:28 that Rebekah returns to her *bêt 'ēm* to tell them what has happened.

The gifts that are subsequently given to Rebekah serve the economic interests of her brother Laban. When Laban agrees to the marriage between Rebekah and Isaac, he is showered with gifts by Abraham's servant (Gen 24:53). Laban could later use these gifts as capital for acquiring a wife. Rebekah's marriage serves the economic interests of her brother and illustrates the dependence of a brother on his sister in order to gain a wife for himself. Women contribute to the socioeconomic development of the *bêt 'āb* and the *bêt 'ēm* in multiple ways.

Finally, Abraham takes another wife, Keturah (25:1–6), presumably a concubine, before dying. This marriage to a woman can be understood as one inferior to that between Sarah and Abraham. The marriage separates procreation from property. Keturah's sons receive gifts from Abraham but live far away from Isaac. As a result of our analysis from kinship studies, we understand that the matter of inheritance so carefully worked out with the birth of Isaac must not be tampered with.

This study of kinship in the lifetime of Abraham concludes with a brief discussion of the obscure text of Genesis 14 that highlights fighting between insiders and outsiders to the family. Abraham wages war (with the 318 trained men born in his *bêtô*) on behalf of his nephew Lot (14:14–16). The reference to these trained men (soldiers), suggests that military operations were a further aspect of the social structures in the world of Genesis.

We move now to study the family household of Rebekah and Isaac. Here again the importance and interdependence of the members of the *bêt 'āb* are brought to the forefront, but in this case the family dynamics focus on two sons borne by the same mother, Rebekah.

Isaac and Rebekah, Esau, Rachel, Leah, and Laban (Gen 25:12–36:43)

Isaac serves as the designated heir to Abraham because his mother Sarah is from the lineage of Terah and because his wife Rebekah is also descended from this lineage. Endogamous marriage occurs in the generation subsequent to Abraham. Rebekah goes with the servant back to the land of Abraham and the tent of Sarah, the maternal subunit of the *bêt 'āb*, maintaining the practice of patrilocal residence. Rebekah is an appropriate wife for Isaac not only due to endogamy and patrilocal inheritance, but because she is a virgin "whom no man had known" (Gen 24:16). The virginity of a bride signified that the first child she bore to her husband had been fathered by him and not by a previous lover of the new bride. The descent line from Terah must be a pure one.

No sooner than the marriage is arranged, Rebekah is living with Isaac. Initially Rebekah is said to be barren but cured of her condition quickly. Rebekah bears Isaac twin sons, Jacob and Esau. What ensues leads to friction in the *bêt 'āb*. Rebekah favors Jacob while Isaac favors Esau, another illustration of the power of women and the representation of their perspectives in the text.

Isaac, the patriarch of the family, is deceived by Rebekah and Jacob and manipulated into blessing Jacob instead of Esau (Gen 27). All the same, Isaac is clear regarding his role and his duty as head of the family: it is his responsibility to designate the son who will get the blessing needed to become heir to his *bêt 'āb*. Isaac does not know that Esau, the first-born son, has sold his birthright to Jacob in a moment of weakness occasioned by hunger (Gen 25:29–34). In addition, Esau violates the *sine qua non* for being reckoned his father's lineal heir through his exogamous marriages to Hittite women (Gen 26:34). Through these marriages Esau further distances himself from the possibility of being primary heir to his father Isaac. Esau loses his birthright, his father's blessing, and he makes the wrong marriage choices from the perspective of the Terahite lineage.

On the basis of Gen 27:5–17, Rebekah's love for her son Jacob and her favoritism toward him appear to be determined by her knowledge (Gen 25:23) that he will bring her personal security in the future as the lineal heir to his father Isaac. Subsequently she sends Jacob to her brother Laban, both to keep him safe from Esau's jealousy and to contract a marriage with a woman from her patrilineage. Through his labor for Laban, Jacob barters for his wives. Jacob's marriages to Rachel and Leah, daughters of Laban, descended from the lineage of Nahor (Gen 29:5), brother to Terah, secure his position as heir to Isaac. The marriage of a man to two sisters, who are women of equal social standing, is referred to as sororal polygyny. When Jacob marries his wives, each woman receives a maid, Bilhah for Leah and Zilpah for Rachel, who also bear sons to Jacob; the arrangement uniting Jacob to both his primary wives and to their maids is best characterized as polycoity.

From the perspective of the offspring Esau and Jacob, sons of Rebekah and Isaac, the emotions of both jealousy and fear surface. Rachel and Leah exhibit bitterness toward their father Laban (31:14–16). Particularly strong are the words of Rachel and Leah in v. 15, "Are we not regarded by him [Laban] as foreigners? For he has sold us, and he has been using up the money given for us." A *bêt 'āb* is divided against itself.

Jacob, Leah, Rachel, Zilpah, and Bilhah (Gen 37:1–50:26)

The pattern of kinship that governs the family of Jacob in Gen 37–50 is distinct from earlier kinship units. The generation of Jacob's children does not directly relate to marriage choices, inheritance, and heirship issues discussed above. Yet the emphasis on production and reproduction characteristic of the world of the Genesis family continues in the generation of Jacob's children.

In Gen 37–50, the focus shifts from a lineal/vertical genealogy, with only one son as heir to a segmented/horizontal genealogy, where all of Jacob's sons become his heirs. The lack of interest in exclusivity of heirship is clear when Jacob blesses his twelve sons in Gen 49. No one son is singled out as the sole heir to Jacob. Instead, the lineage clearly shifts from vertical to horizontal reckoning and all his sons are included in this blessing. Heirship has become decentralized.

The maternal subdivisions of Jacob's four wives (both those of higher status, Leah and Rachel, and those of lower status, Zilpah and Bilhah) give shape to family life as the generation of Jacob's sons moves from a family to the tribes and nation of Israel. Jacob's wives Leah and Rachel,

who are primary wives, and their maids Zilpah and Bilhah, *šipḥâ* and
'āmâ, literally maidservant and slave girl (although the terms probably
carry basically the same meaning), bear him twelve sons and one daughter. Dinah is the only named daughter; Leah is her mother (30:21). The
story of Dinah considers marriage, and the issue of marriage, from the
perspective of a daughter. This narrative (Gen 34) addresses issues of
endogamy and exogamy, but now from the perspective of an Israelite
woman. Despite her earlier tragic fate at the hands of Shechem the
Hivite, the later negotiations by her brothers with Shechem's father
Hamor for Dinah's hand in marriage highlight the economic aspects of
her marriage (Gen 34:10) with a primary emphasis on land as Shechem's
father, Hamor, presents the benefits this marriage would bring to Jacob
and his family. Other unnamed daughters of Jacob are referred to in Gen
46:15.

Just as earlier in the case of Ishmael and Isaac, the relative statuses of
the mothers of Jacob's children vis-à-vis his emotional reactions to his
wives determine how he views his offspring. Joseph is Jacob's favorite
because Rachel, Jacob's favorite wife, is Joseph's mother. The result is
that Joseph's brothers traffic (*mkr*, literally "sold") him into slavery due
to their jealousy (and to the dismay of their father Jacob, Gen 37:34–38;
45:4, who also favors Benjamin as a son of Rachel). Sibling rivalry
between the brothers for highest status in the house of their father
determines the course of events.

In Gen 49, none of the sons are excluded as tribes of Jacob/Israel; all
are his direct heirs. But the differences in the tribal blessings of the
twelve sons depends on the different statuses of their mothers, which
produces conflict between the women regarding fertility and mother-
hood, and between their sons.

Here kinship organization shifts from the *bêt 'āb* and a lineal heir to
horizontal kinship organization on the level of the *šēbeṭ*. The importance of the women in this generation once again provides evidence of
maternal subunits connecting wives, their children, and the husband of
these women and children. The statuses of Leah, Rachel, Zilpah, and
Bilhah give shape to the patterns of social organization in this kinship
unit.

Summary

In this chapter, we have linked family and kinship. The *bêt 'āb*, the house
of the father or ancestral home, included multiple individuals who, each
in their own way, determined the course of family life: a husband, a wife,

and an heir. The *bêt 'āb* was the most important level of family structure, the basic kinship unit, and refers to both lineage and residence.

The social structure of the family in Genesis depicts three levels of hierarchical family life. The level of social organization above the *bêt 'āb* was the *mišpāḥâ*, often translated as "clan" but our imprecise understanding of Hebrew terminology suggests that sometimes these two terms carry the same meaning. The term *mišpāḥâ* appears quite infrequently in Gen 12–50, which only adds to the problem of defining this word within these texts.

The highest level of social structure, the *šēbeṭ* (tribe), is particularly relevant for understanding the significance of the twelve sons of Jacob. It is not clear from references to the *šēbeṭ* exactly how tribes were organized or governed. Genesis 49 is the primary source for tribes in Genesis, but it is unclear whether the reference is to actual tribes whose eponymous names derive from the sons of Jacob or if it refers to the sons individually. The twelve tribes appear to represent specific geographical areas within ancient Israel. All three levels of social organization have socioeconomic functions.

Although past scholarship has focused on the ideal family as one characterized by patrilineal, patrilocal endogamy, all terms that take the perspective of the men of the household, our study has been able to demonstrate the importance of women in determining family life. It has been possible to see the pattern of preference for a wife who is descended from the lineage of Terah when an Israelite groom picks a wife. Isaac is the heir to Abraham because his mother Sarah was married through an endogamous marriage, but Ishmael was expelled from this household because Hagar, his mother, was an Egyptian. Here we experience the life of a child grounded in the endogamous versus the exogamous marriages of their mothers. This example and others establish that in Genesis the recipient of his father's blessings is different for different offspring based on the status of their mothers in the *bêt 'āb*. On the other hand, Deut 21:15–16 legislates for the rights of the primogeniture who is to receive a double portion of his father's inheritance regardless of whether his mother is liked or disliked by her husband, The discrepancy between these texts makes clear that childhood is a social construction and its meaning derives from a multiplicity of circumstances that extend beyond birth order.

Study of the passages concerning family organization confirm that any study of kinship and family organization must recognize the importance of gender for investigations of the family. The statuses of the women and their perspectives in the stories shape not only their individual futures but the future of both a woman's husband and her children. The importance of women and the presence of women's space, tents, indicate that in the study of the *bêt 'āb* we oversimplify social organization by strictly taking a male point of view, as both anthropologists and biblical scholars have done in the past. Examples of women's social roles in Gen 12–50 are too numerous to repeat here, but the mother-divisions seen through the wives Leah, Rachel, Zilpah, and Bilhah indicate the hierarchy that women's statuses have in forming the tribes of Israel, just as earlier the status differential between Sarah and Hagar shaped the formation of the lineage of Abraham.

Finally, neither men nor women nor children appear to have had peaceful ties with same-sex individuals within the family household. The world of the family is characterized by conflict over many issues.[26] Sibling rivalry is pervasive, and women compete over fertility. Failure to recognize these dynamics only serves to idealize the family, the clan, and the tribe in the social organization of Genesis.

SELECT BIBLIOGRAPHY

Chapman, Cynthia R. *The House of the Mother: The Social Roles of Maternal Kin in Biblical Hebrew Narrative and Poetry.* ABRL. New Haven, CT: Yale University Press, 2016.

Donaldson, Mara E. "Kinship Theory in the Patriarchal Narratives: The Case of the Barren Wife." *JAAR* 49 (1981): 77–87.

Meyers, Carol. "'To Her Mother's House': Considering a Counterpart to the Israelite *Bêt 'āb.*" Pages 39–51, 304–7 in *The Bible and the Politics of Exegesis: Essays in Honor of Norman Gottwald on His Sixty-Fifth Birthday.* Edited by David Jobling, Peggy L. Day, and Gerald T. Sheppard. Cleveland, OH: Pilgrim Press, 1991.

Oden, Robert A. "Jacob as Father, Husband, and Nephew: Kinship Studies and the Patriarchal Narratives." *JBL* 102 (1983): 189–205.

Perdue Leo G., Joseph Blenkinsopp, John J. Collins, and Carol Meyers, eds. *Families in Ancient Israel.* Louisville, KY: Westminster John Knox, 1997.

Petersen, David L. "Genesis and Family Values." *JBL* 124 (2005): 5–23.

Prewitt, Terry J. "Kinship Structures and Genesis Genealogies." *JNES* 40 (1981): 87–98.

Schloen, J. David. *The House of the Father as Fact and Symbol: Patrimonialism in Ugarit and the Ancient Near East.* Studies in Archaeology and History of the Levant 2. Winona Lake, IN: Eisenbrauns, 2001.

Schneider, Tammi J. *Mothers of Promise: Women in the Book of Genesis.* Grand Rapids, MI: Baker Academic Press, 2008.

---

[26] David L. Petersen, "Genesis and Family Values," *JBL* 124 (2005): 5–23.

Stager, Lawrence E. "The Archaeology of the Family in Ancient Israel." *BASOR* 260 (1985): 1–35.

Steinberg, Naomi. "The Genealogical Framework of the Family Stories in Genesis." *Semeia* 46 (1989): 41–50.

Steinberg, Naomi. *Kinship and Marriage in Genesis: A Household Economics Perspective*. Minneapolis, MN: Fortress, 1993.

Steinberg, Naomi. *The World of the Child in the Hebrew Bible*. Sheffield: Sheffield Phoenix Press, 2013.

Williams, Dolores S. *Sisters in the Wilderness: The Challenge of Womanist God-Talk*. Maryknoll, NY: Orbis Books, 1993.

Wright, C. J. H., "Family." Pages 761–68 in vol. 2 of *The Anchor Bible Dictionary*. Edited by D. N. Freedman. 6 vols. New York: Doubleday, 1992.

9 Women's Status and Feminist Readings of Genesis

SARAH SHECTMAN

There are very few books in the Hebrew Bible – Judges, Ruth, and Esther may be the only others – that contain such an abundance of women characters as does Genesis. This fact, coupled with the role of the creation narrative in women's status over the centuries, has resulted in a nearly endless body of feminist analysis of the book. This scholarship is diverse in its approaches and in its conclusions, reflecting multiple types of feminism. Indeed, the question of what constitutes feminist analysis is a sticky one: Is it any analysis that focuses on women? Is it analysis that seeks to make an argument about women's political empowerment? Must it proceed from a particular philosophical standpoint, incorporating works of feminist theory? Is a work feminist simply because it says it is – or can it be feminist even if it claims it is not?

Feminism on its own is not a method per se – it is, rather, a perspective on the text, one that chooses to take women as its focus. But that is only its starting point. Feminist analysis usually combines this focus with some other method, from historical and literary approaches to perspectival approaches, from African American (womanist) to Latinx (*mujerista*), to Asian, queer, postcolonial, and beyond.[1] Feminists also make use of archaeological, sociological, and economic theories and evidence in order to understand the biblical text and to reconstruct the history of the ancient Israelites who produced it.[2] Indeed, feminism can be used with any of the methods and approaches covered in other chapters of this book and is therefore complementary to rather than separate from them. Moreover, feminist interpretation is

---

[1]   L. Juliana Claassens and Carolyn J. Sharp, "Introduction: Celebrating Intersectionality, Interrogating Power, and Embracing Ambiguity as Feminist Critical Practices," in *Feminist Frameworks and the Bible: Power, Ambiguity, and Intersectionality*, ed. L. Juliana Claassens and Carolyn J. Sharp, LHBOTS 630 (London: T&T Clark, 2017), 1–9, here 1–2.

[2]   Katharine Doob Sakenfeld, "Feminist Biblical Interpretation: How Far Have We Come?," in Claassens and Sharp, *Feminist Frameworks and the Bible*, 11–18, here 12–13.

aware of the many intersections of power that individuals experience, along axes not only of gender but also of ethnicity and class, and it recognizes that power is relational.[3] As Carolyn Sharp notes, "Feminist biblical criticism seeks to make visible the countless ways in which authoritative sacred texts and their interpretations have lifted up some subjects while marginalizing or suppressing others, and have glorified certain ways of thinking about agency and power while dishonoring and harming subjects who inhabit agency and power in other ways."[4] For the purposes of this overview, I will treat feminist analysis as analysis that focuses specifically on texts or topics *because* they are related to women or gender in some way and because they focus on issues of power, status, and autonomy. Most of these works identify themselves as feminist, though not all do so explicitly.

Feminist interpretations of the Bible have generally tended to be more literary than historical, in part because feminism as a method has been more closely aligned with twentieth-century literary criticism than with historical-critical methods that were deemed overly positivistic.[5] Theological and reception-historical readings of the Bible have also played a major role, given the impact of theological readings of the Bible on women's status historically.[6] (Re)interpretations of the Bible have been critical to the feminist movement and to modern politics and theology.[7] But feminist interpretation has also been used as a tool for looking back on the history of the biblical text and of ancient Israel and as a means of reading the text literarily in a variety of contexts. Thus, feminism does not only look forward to the legacy of the Bible in its post-history, especially in the modern period. It is also a tool in the historical-critical toolbox, one that can illuminate the history of the biblical period and of the Bible's composition. However, as with all historical reconstruction, the Bible should be used cautiously in this regard – more so on

---

[3] Ibid., 14–15. See also Vanessa Lovelace, "'This Woman's Son Shall Not Inherit with My Son': Towards a Womanist Politics of Belonging in the Sarah-Hagar Narrative," *JITC* 41 (2015): 63–82, here 76–78; Lovelace argues that both Sarah and Hagar belong to an oppressed group, as women, but that Sarah also has the advantage of ethnicity and class in relation to Hagar, and she uses this power in order to enforce the boundaries between Israelites and Ishmaelites.

[4] Carolyn J. Sharp, "Character, Conflict, and Covenant in Israel's Origin Traditions," in *The Hebrew Bible: Feminist and Intersectional Perspectives*, ed. Gale A. Yee (Minneapolis, MN: Fortress Press, 2018), 41–72, here 43–44 (Kindle edition).

[5] See Sarah Shectman, *Women in the Pentateuch: A Feminist and Source-Critical Analysis*, HBM 23 (Sheffield: Sheffield Phoenix Press, 2009), 9.

[6] Ibid., 11–24.

[7] For a popular overview, see Cullen Murphy, *The Word According to Eve: Women and the Bible in Ancient Times and Our Own* (Boston: Houghton Mifflin, 1998).

the topic of women, who were likely not the authors of any of its texts –
and conclusions should focus especially on what the texts tell us about
the beliefs of the people writing the texts, rather than what they tell us
about broader ancient Israelite history.

Genesis can be divided roughly into three sections of unequal length:
the primeval history (Gen 1–11); the ancestral narratives (Gen 12–36);
and the Joseph story (Gen 37–50). This chapter will treat each of these
sections separately, exploring particular chapters and characters in some
detail. I will incorporate a diverse array of feminist voices, including
womanist, Asian American, African, and others, in recognition that
there is no single "feminist voice." This is not to suggest that minor-
itized and other perspectival views should be subsumed under the
umbrella of feminism generally, at the cost of their own unique voices.
Rather, it is a recognition that feminist interpretation is multivocal and
intersectional and that a discussion of feminist interpretation – and of
biblical interpretation generally – cannot be comprehensive without
including these viewpoints. The discussion herein will necessarily be
selective and is meant only as a glimpse into the many options that
feminist criticism gives us for reading the text.

THE PRIMEVAL HISTORY

It will come as no surprise that feminists have spent considerable time on
Gen 1–3, a short series of chapters that have had a disproportionate influence on the status of women across the centuries.[8] Feminist interpreters
began to revisit these chapters with the rise of the suffrage movement,
whose leaders saw the text's role in perpetuating women's second-class
political status.[9] Early Second Wave[10] feminists in the United States and
United Kingdom in the 1970s and 1980s also focused their attention on
these chapters. Two main elements of these texts were of particular
importance to feminists: the creation of woman in the two accounts in
Gen 1 and Gen 2 and the so-called punishment of the woman in Gen 3:16.

The first creation account (Gen 1:1–2:4a) reports the simultaneous
creation of man and woman together "in the image of God" (Gen 1:26–28).

---

[8]   See, e.g., Sharp, "Character," 48.
[9]   See Shectman, *Women*, 12–13; Sarah Shectman, "Feminist Biblical Interpretation:
      History and Goals," TheTorah.com, https://www.thetorah.com/article/feminist-
      biblical-interpretation-history-and-goals.
[10] On "waves" of feminism (and the problems with this model), see Nyasha Junior, *An
      Introduction to Womanist Biblical Interpretation* (Louisville, KY: Westminster John
      Knox Press, 2015), 7–9.

Feminist interpreters like Phyllis Trible used rhetorical criticism to emphasize this text's depiction of equality in the creation of men and women, arguing that "male and female" is synonymous with "the image of God."[11] Trible extends her positive reading of the creation of humans in Gen 1 to Gen 2, with its creation first of the man and then of the woman as "corresponding to" him, a depiction of equality and mutuality between the sexes.[12] According to Trible, the story takes a negative turn in Gen 3, with the transgression and the introduction of a sexual hierarchy: "Life has lost to Death, harmony to hostility, unity and fulfillment to fragmentation and dispersion."[13] Womanist scholar Wilda Gafney, however, focuses on the continued unity of the man and woman as the two parts constituting the entity "humanity." Created from the earth – and brown like it, as Gafney points out[14] – the humans continue together, both eating the fruit, both sewing clothes from leaves, and both expelled from the garden.[15] Cheryl Anderson also uses Trible's reading as a starting point for a womanist interpretation of the story, noting the damage that the "male dominance/female subordination gender paradigm" has caused Africans and African Americans by supporting a social structure that gives men sexual control over women.[16] These contrasting readings complicate our understanding of the text, demonstrating the ways in which the text constructs both positive and negative aspects of human relations.

Where Trible saw "male and female" in Gen 1:28 as synonymous with "the image of God," Phyllis Bird argued that "male and female" is a progression on God's image: humans are *not only* like God in some sense, but they are *also* male and female.[17] Bird argued that this mention of both man and woman was a practical detail, meant only to point out the sexual dimorphism of human beings, not to attribute any social significance (by means of similarity to the divine) to that fact. Carol Meyers follows Bird's interpretation of Gen 1,[18] but she goes further in

[11] Phyllis Trible, *God and the Rhetoric of Sexuality*, OBT 2 (Philadelphia: Fortress Press, 1978), 22.
[12] Ibid., 90.
[13] Ibid., 139.
[14] Wilda C. Gafney, *Womanist Midrash: A Reintroduction to the Women of the Torah and the Throne* (Louisville, KY: Westminster John Knox Press, 2017), 21.
[15] Ibid., 24–25.
[16] Cheryl B. Anderson, "The Song of Songs: Redeeming Gender Constructions in the Age of AIDS," in *Womanist Interpretations of the Bible: Expanding the Discourse*, ed. Gay L. Byron and Vanessa Lovelace, SemSt 85 (Atlanta: SBL Press, 2016), 73–92, here 77.
[17] Phyllis Bird, *Missing Persons and Mistaken Identities: Women and Gender in Ancient Israel*, OBT (Minneapolis, MN: Fortress Press, 1997), 133, 144.
[18] Carol L. Meyers, *Rediscovering Eve: Ancient Israelite Women in Context* (Oxford: Oxford University Press, 2013), 74.

her analysis of Gen 3:16, which reports the so-called punishment of the woman for her role in the humans' transgression of eating the fruit of the tree of knowledge of good and bad in Gen 3:6. Meyers uses sociological and archaeological evidence to argue that rather than simply being a punishment, the verse is meant to describe the life of a woman in a subsistence society like early Israel. She provides a new translation for the verse that makes this reading clear:

> I will make great your toil and many your pregnancies;
> with hardship shall you have children.
> Your turning is to your man/husband,
> and he shall rule/control you [sexually].[19]

According to Meyers, women's contributions to household labor and subsistence in early Israel were significant; thus the woman would have "great toil." The woman would also be under pressure to have multiple pregnancies, as children not only were extra hands in household and agrarian work but also were to care for elderly parents.[20] At the same time, pregnancy was risky both for the woman and for the child being born; the high infant-mortality rate also increased the number of pregnancies a woman needed to have in order to ensure offspring who would live into adulthood.

Gale Yee also offers a reading of Gen 3 focused on the social and economic reality that lies behind the composition of the text, though with different conclusions. Yee reads Gen 3 in light of the historical situation of political centralization – the creation and strengthening of the monarchy in Jerusalem in the early monarchic period (tenth–eighth c. BCE) – as the context for the composition of the Yahwist's creation narrative in Gen 2–3.[21] The monarchy worked to strengthen itself by weakening local power, vested in village and family power structures. One means of doing this was to regulate sexual activity, emphasizing the nuclear family and the marital bond at the expense of group loyalty to a larger kin group such as a clan or tribe, which posed a greater political threat.[22] Yee notes, "As the society itself becomes more stratified in the division of the ruling elite and the peasants, so relations between male and female become more hierarchically ranked. The increase in male

---

[19]   Ibid., 101.

[20]   Ibid., 97–98.

[21]   See chapters 2–3 of this volume on the sources that compose the book of Genesis; and see Shectman, *Women*, 123–29.

[22]   Gale A. Yee, *Poor Banished Children of Eve: Woman as Evil in the Hebrew Bible* (Minneapolis, MN: Fortress Press, 2003), 65–71.

status over the female ... becomes encoded in the literary production of Genesis 2."[23] The woman is also the intermediary between the serpent and the man, a literary device meant to position women as the greater threat to the stability of the state.[24] Feminist readings like Meyers's and Yee's move beyond the understanding of the creation story as simply encoding the subordination of one gender to the other. Rather, the narrative is revealed to reflect larger social realities, whether a description of an existing status quo or an attempt to justify an emerging political structure. At the same time, such feminist readings create possibilities for reading equality and mutuality between the sexes.

The story of creation leads into a series of genealogies interspersed with narrative episodes: Cain and Abel, the enigmatic Nephilim and the daughters of men, and the flood. The genealogies are combinations of material from two sources: the Priestly and the Yahwist/non-Priestly.[25] Women appear in the genealogies as wives and mothers, frequently at points where there is an interest in a particular family line, as at the end of Gen 11. As Cynthia Chapman notes, though the genealogies largely trace patrilines (lineages through men), the genealogies "frame narratives that feature maternally marked subgroups within the patriline."[26] Additions of mothers and wives into a man's story function to "add genealogical complexity" and to "present a certain line ... as legitimate, ascendant, and divinely chosen."[27]

THE ANCESTRAL NARRATIVES

The ancestral narratives (the stories about Abram/Abraham, Sarai/Sarah, and Hagar; Isaac and Rebekah; and Jacob, Leah, Rachel, Bilhah, and Zilpah) are a collection of family narratives that focus on marriage and children. In particular, they emphasize the choice of the "right" wife and the search for the "right" heir. Though these chapters are often called the *patriarchal* narratives, as the male characters in them are (mostly) the recipients of

---

[23]   Ibid., 70.

[24]   Ibid., 74.

[25]   See chapters 2–3 of this volume; and Shectman, *Women*, 123–29.

[26]   Cynthia Chapman, *The House of the Mother: The Social Roles of Maternal Kin in Biblical Hebrew Narrative and Poetry*, AYBRL (New Haven: Yale University Press, 2016), 4.

[27]   Ibid., 13; see also Shectman, *Women*, 79–83, 146–47, and Sarah Shectman, "Israel's Matriarchs: Political Pawns or Powerbrokers?," in *The Politics of the Ancestors: Exegetical and Historical Perspectives on Genesis 12–36*, ed. Mark G. Brett and Jakob Wöhrle, FAT 124 (Tübingen: Mohr Siebeck, 2018), 157–63.

God's promise of land and progeny, they are more accurately called the *ancestral* narratives, because women are so important to the events that transpire.[28]

The narrative begins with the introduction of women into the genealogy at the end of Gen 11 and with the notice that Abram's wife Sarai is barren. Sarai immediately becomes a key player in the story. Though the narrative is focused on the matriarchs attaining a male heir and thus serving what are ultimately patriarchal interests, feminist interpreters have mined these texts for details about Israelite social structures and where women fit into them – or were otherwise prohibited from fitting into them.[29] So, for example, the matriarchs all play some role in ensuring that their favored sons become the heirs to the blessing and promise (that is, the covenant with Yahweh).[30] Sarah drives out Hagar to ensure Isaac's inheritance; Rebekah subverts Isaac's will to ensure the blessing for Jacob; and Rachel and Leah jockey for position with Jacob in order to have multiple sons. Though all the sons, even those of the enslaved wives Bilhah and Zilpah, seem to inherit the blessing and promise equally in this last generation, becoming the eponymous tribes of Israel, Chapman points out that Rachel and Leah each have two sons from whom the entirety of the Israelite political and religious hierarchy derive.[31] As Chapman notes,

> Women and relationships forged through women play centrally strategic roles in the competition between houses to become the named, noble house of origin. Maternal kinship terms mark the dividing line between the central, named house of origin and the unnamed commoner houses that are cast to the side of the preserved memory that is the Bible.[32]

[28] See Irmtraud Fischer, *Die Erzeltern Israels: Feministische-theologische Studien zu Genesis 12–36*, BZAW 222 (Berlin: de Gruyter, 1994), esp. 375–78; Shectman, *Women*, 90. On the promise and the role of the matriarchs, see Shectman, *Women*, 55–90; and see Joel S. Baden, *The Promise to the Patriarchs* (Oxford: Oxford University Press, 2013). Note, though, that Hagar receives the promise of progeny that is elsewhere given only to the male characters; see Shectman, *Women*, 60–61; Nyasha Junior, *Reimagining Hagar: Blackness and Bible*, Biblical Refigurations (Oxford: Oxford University Press, 2019), 23, 25.

[29] See also "Family, Clan, and Tribe in the Book of Genesis," by Naomi A. Steinberg in this volume.

[30] Tammi J. Schneider, *Mothers of Promise: Women in the Book of Genesis* (Grand Rapids, MI: Baker Academic, 2008), 16.

[31] Chapman, *House of the Mother*, 216–19.

[32] Ibid., 36–37.

Mothers played a key role in establishing insider/outsider boundaries.[33]

Chapman uses anthropological methods to develop a detailed argument about the importance of the *bet 'em*, the house of the mother. The house of the mother is the counterpart to the house of the father (*bet 'av*), which appears frequently in the Hebrew Bible as a feature of the Israelites' social organization. The house of the mother appears less often, but the ancestral narratives in Genesis provide compelling evidence that it was also an important feature of the ancient Israelite social landscape. The house of the mother appears in the ancestral narratives when Isaac marries Rebekah, taking her into the tent of his mother to consummate the marriage. Rebekah also goes to her mother's household when she brings Abraham's messenger home, and her brother Laban, with whom she probably shares a mother, plays a significant role in her marriage, as is typical for uterine brothers.[34] Rachel, Leah, and Bilhah and Zilpah are said to each have their own tent, and their children at least at times seem to be clustered in or around those tents. Chapman argues that the mother's tent was the primary organizational element within the house of the father: a man's house (or household) might have one or more mothers' houses nested within it. One key role of the mother's house was in making marriage arrangements for its daughters, with uterine brothers taking a leading role alongside fathers.[35] The house of the mother remained important even after a son left the mother's household to establish his own household, as when Jacob flees to Laban's household to escape Esau.[36]

The biblical material emphasizes the roles of mothers and wives; far less visible are daughters, especially daughters who do not later become wives and mothers.[37] Kimberly Russaw's sociohistorical study of the roles and status of daughters in the Hebrew Bible argues that these often-overlooked biblical figures are "multidimensional characters that act strategically."[38] Russaw observes

> In the agrarian world of the Hebrew Bible, power is stratified along the axes of legal authority and control of economic surplus. Those

[33] Lovelace, "This Woman's Son," 76; Shectman, "Israel's Matriarchs."
[34] Chapman, *House of the Mother*, 54–55. Uterine siblings are those who share both a mother and a father. In a polygynous society like ancient Israel, all siblings are generally assumed to share a father, and distinctions are drawn based on shared maternity. See ibid., 15.
[35] Ibid., 74.
[36] Ibid., 175.
[37] Kimberly D. Russaw, *Daughters in the Hebrew Bible* (Lanham, MD: Lexington Books, 2018), 2–3.
[38] Ibid., 4.

with the greatest amount of legal authority and control of the largest amount of economic surplus have the most power. In this schema, daughters have little power.[39]

This situation left daughters vulnerable, but it also meant that a daughter could be "a mechanism for familial alliances via marriage," a position that might give daughters the ability to resist hierarchies of power despite the fact that they were generally required to follow the orders of their fathers, brothers, and/or husbands. This was another area in which the intersections of gender and class played a role, as a woman of higher social status might exert significant control over men of lower status and might even influence men of similar status.[40]

The daughters of Lot are the first daughters we encounter in a story of their own in Genesis. Feminist readings of this text (Gen 19) have focused on whether the daughters are being praised or criticized for their actions in the latter part of this narrative (vv. 31–38), where they commit incest and probably also rape with their father. The incestuous names of the nations they bear (Moab and Ammon) might suggest criticism of the daughters and their actions, but Russaw argues that in fact they are positive characters: they take bold action to perpetuate their father's lineage when they believe that it is endangered.[41] Johanna Stiebert also notes that sexually assertive women, like Lot's daughters here and like Tamar in Gen 38 (see below), are only acceptable if the sexual activity results in a legitimate male heir.[42]

Rebekah becomes a mother and a wife, but the extended narrative in Gen 24, which recounts her betrothal to Isaac, depicts her as a daughter. The narrative might seem focused on Abraham's servant and Isaac as potential groom, but it is filled with details about the social structure of Israelite families and the process of betrothal. Though the story is a piece of fiction, many biblical interpreters believe it is likely to reflect certain social realities. Russaw notes that "[t]he unique economic contribution of daughters to the household economy is income generating potential associated with the bride price,"[43] a phenomenon we see manifested in the servant's presentation of gifts to Rebekah when he meets her. This economic value is enhanced by the daughter's

---

[39]　Ibid., 106.
[40]　Ibid., 126–27.
[41]　Ibid., 73–74. See also Megan Warner, "Finding Lot's Daughters," in "Gendered Historiography: Theoretical Considerations and Case Studies," special issue, ed. Shawna Dolansky and Sarah Shectman, *JHS* 19.4 (2019): 49–58.
[42]　Stiebert, "Wife of Potiphar," 87; see also Warner, "Finding Lot's Daughters," 57–58.
[43]　Russaw, *Daughters*, 7.

virginity.[44] Tracy Lemos also writes about bridewealth – money or gifts given by the groom's family to the family of the bride. Bridewealth stands in contrast to dowry, which is given by the bride's family. The Hebrew Bible contains a number of mentions of bridewealth and none of dowry. As Lemos observes, this is typical of societies "in which pastoralism played an important economic and social role, ... in which lineages and corporate ownership of land were important organizing features on the local level, ... [and which were] lacking centralized governance."[45] This is the type of society that early Israel seems to have been, as Carol Meyers also argued.

Biblical authors use five different terms to describe daughters.[46] These terms may be used individually or in some combination for any given daughter, but strikingly, all five terms appear at one point or another in reference to Rebekah in Gen 24.[47] One such term, 'āḥôt, "sister," situates the daughter in the context of her brothers and is used in narratives where the brothers play a significant role, as in the Rebekah and Dinah stories in Gen 24 and 34, respectively.[48] This connects with Chapman's observations about the house of the mother and the importance of uterine brothers; in Gen 24, Rebekah's brother Laban is the most prominent male relative involved in negotiating Rebekah's betrothal.[49]

Gafney notes that Rebekah

> is one of the most dominant matriarchs in the Israelite story; she has agency and she uses her voice. A close reading of her story indicates that she is portrayed as one of the most active women in the canon. ...Rebekah's voice and agency are located in a matrilineal household, identified as her mother's household in Genesis 24:28. Her father identifies himself with a matronymic (maternal name) in Genesis 24:15 and 24.[50]

Rebekah is also less problematic than the other matriarchs, as she has no enslaved women to offer as surrogates (though she too experiences barrenness). The fact that she turns to underhanded means to help Jacob

---

[44]   Ibid., 13.
[45]   T. M. Lemos, *Marriage Gifts and Social Change in Ancient Palestine, 1200 BCE to 200 CE* (Cambridge: Cambridge University Press, 2010), 232.
[46]   See the summary in Russaw, *Daughters*, 93.
[47]   Ibid., 75.
[48]   Ibid., 58.
[49]   Chapman, *House of the Mother*, 54, observes that although the text does not specify that Laban and Rebekah share a mother, his role in the story and his appearance in the house of Rebekah's mother suggest that they are uterine siblings.
[50]   Gafney, *Womanist Midrash*, 45.

ensure Isaac's blessing is generally seen as a positive reflection on her resourcefulness and determination.[51] Likewise, when she experiences a difficult pregnancy and seeks an oracle, she receives a direct response from Yahweh (Gen 25:22–23).[52]

Having sons was important to ancient Israelite women for a number of reasons,[53] and each of the matriarchs experiences some problems in the endeavor, including infertility.[54] The sons Ishmael, Isaac, Jacob, and Esau are the result of Yahweh's promises that the women will conceive and give birth. Though the promise of a son has been incorporated into the larger theme of the promise (and covenant) to the patriarchs in Genesis, feminist interpretation has shown that the promises to the matriarchs were a separate and originally independent theme, focused on the birth of a specific son.[55] These motifs serve to emphasize the importance of the son, because the pregnancy and birth are hard-won. A son, especially a firstborn son,

> "builds up" his mother by raising her status in comparison to that of the other women in the household of her husband and by providing her with prestige among the community of women in her husband's village. ...[T]hrough him, she will secure economic maintenance for life and social prestige among women in her house and village.[56]

As a result, "In the narratives that cover the houses of Abraham and Isaac, insider mothers are credited with nation building and kingdom birthing, but in every case, the success of the mother in producing the heir is marked by her disappearance."[57]

In the case that a woman did not bear a child, she might turn to a surrogate wife; if the surrogate conceived, the child was considered the child of the primary wife, not the surrogate.[58] Sarah employs this tactic with Hagar, as do Leah and Rachel with their enslaved women, Bilhah and Zilpah. Feminists have explored the various ramifications of these episodes, from the expectations placed on and avenues available to

---

[51] See Shectman, *Women*, 85–86, and the literature cited there.
[52] As, e.g., Gafney, *Womanist Midrash*, 49, notes.
[53] Meyers, *Rediscovering Eve*, 97–98, and see above.
[54] Shectman, *Women*, 62–63; and see Candida Moss and Joel Baden, *Reconceiving Infertility: Biblical Perspectives on Procreation and Childlessness* (Princeton: Princeton University Press, 2015), esp. 21–69.
[55] See Shectman, *Women*, 71–74.
[56] Chapman, *House of the Mother*, 151; Lovelace, "This Woman's Son," 74.
[57] Chapman, *House of the Mother*, 201.
[58] See Gafney, *Womanist Midrash*, 34, on surrogate vs. concubine.

primary wives to the use and abuse of surrogates, who are primarily depicted as enslaved women.

Hagar, who is often included alongside the other matriarchs as a wife of the patriarch Abraham, is one such surrogate. Her story has raised a greater and more troubling set of concerns for feminist interpreters. Because Hagar is enslaved (as are Bilhah and Zilpah in the Jacob narrative), she occupies a unique position among the matriarchs. She embodies the intersections of gender, ethnicity, and class and is a rich source for feminist and womanist interpretation. As Gafney notes, Hagar "has one source of power: she is fertile; but she lacks autonomy over her own fertility."[59] When Sarai tells Abram to take her in order that Sarai might have a son through her, she is called a wife. But Nyasha Junior notes, "Hagar is only called a 'wife' when the text describes her sexual relationship with Abram in 16:3. . . . Even after she becomes a wife ('iššâ) of Abraham, the text emphasizes Hagar's enslaved status and her subordinate position."[60] Junior also observes that "Hagar's potential reproductive capacity, ethnicity, and enslaved status are key markers of difference within the text."[61] She is powerless against the whims of Sarai, who mistreats her when she becomes pregnant. She runs away, returns, and is ultimately expelled with her infant son, a harrowing story that resonates in a variety of ways. At every point, "the text stresses the hierarchical relationship between Hagar and Sarai."[62] Nor does Hagar ever indicate that she wishes to have children.[63] Hagar's wishes play no role in the story: "Hagar has no say over her body being given to Abram or her child being given to Sarai."[64]

Perhaps surprisingly, Hagar was only infrequently used as an example to argue against the enslavement of African people in the United States in the eighteenth and nineteenth centuries, nor was she seen as Black or African, despite her Egyptian origins.[65] However, womanist readers in the last decades of the twentieth century drew on a variety of Hagar traditions from across the centuries to read Hagar as

---

[59] Ibid., 41.
[60] Junior, *Reimagining Hagar*, 21–22. Junior also observes that in the genealogy in Gen 25, Hagar is "described as Sarah's slave woman and an Egyptian," rather than Abraham's wife (25). Note that Bilhah and Zilpah are also called wives once they are summoned to serve as surrogates.
[61] Ibid., 20.
[62] Ibid., 23. See also Lovelace, "This Woman's Son," 70, who notes that Sarah "uses her privilege to subjugate and exploit Hagar"; Gafney, *Womanist Midrash*, 34–35.
[63] Junior, *Reimagining Hagar*, 23.
[64] Gafney, *Womanist Midrash*, 41.
[65] Junior, *Reimagining Hagar*, 61–62.

a Black woman, both as a corrective to the "whitewashing" of biblical characters[66] and as a figure who resonates with the experiences of African American women.[67] Latina readers have noted the theme of migration in her story,[68] in addition to that of a domestic worker who is sexually abused and then thrown out when she has a child.[69] As Elsa Tamez notes, "Because Hagar is a woman she is a person oppressed three times over, owing to her slave status, her race, and her sex."[70]

Complicating our understanding of Sarah as Hagar's oppressor in Gen 16 and 21 are the so-called sister-wife narratives in Gen 12 and 20, in which Sarah is used for her sexuality, with little concern for her own safety.[71] As Gafney notes, "Sarah is a complex character who exercises privilege and experiences peril. ... Sarah's economic and social privilege and national origin separate her from Hagar, even though they share gender peril."[72] In the sister-wife episodes, Sarah seems to be complicit in her own subordination and potential rape, going along with Abraham's scheme. There are notable differences between the two stories, however, illustrating the ways in which a common tradition might develop and evolve in the imaginations of different authors.[73] Whereas the version in Gen 12:10–13:1 seems to celebrate the success of the ruse with little regard for Sarai, Gen 20:1–18 is sure to clarify that Sarah is never in any real danger of adultery or rape, and it absolves Abraham of lying by

---

[66]   Ibid., 122.

[67]   See the excellent overview of this interpretive process in Junior, *Reimagining Hagar*; on Black Hagar specifically, see esp. 101–25.

[68]   Nicole M. Simopoulos, "Who Was Hagar? Mistress, Divorcee, Exile, or Exploited Worker: An Analysis of Contemporary Grassroots Readings of Genesis 16 by Caucasian, Latina, and Black South African Women," in *Reading Other-wise: Socially Engaged Biblical Scholars Reading with Their Local Communities*, ed. Gerald O. West, SemSt (Leiden: Brill, 2007), 63–72, here 67.

[69]   Elsa Tamez, "The Woman Who Complicated the History of Salvation," *Cross Currents* 36.2 (1986): 129–39, here 134; and see Lovelace, "This Woman's Son," 73. For more on Hagar in an immigrant context, and on the connection between poverty and gender, see also Kari Latvus, "Reading Hagar in Contexts: From Exegesis to Inter-Contextual Analysis," in *Genesis*, ed. Athalya Brenner, Archie Chi Chung Lee, and Gale A. Yee, Texts@Contexts (Minneapolis, MN: Fortress Press, 2010), 247–74. On the idea that Hagar, as well as Bilhah and Zilpah, are raped, see, e.g., Rodney Sadler, "Genesis," in *The Africana Bible: Reading Israel's Scriptures from Africa and the African Diaspora*, ed. Hugh R. Page Jr. (Minneapolis, MN: Fortress Press, 2010), 70–79, here 75–77.

[70]   Tamez, "Woman," 132.

[71]   There is also a sister-wife episode involving Rebekah in Gen 26, but I will not discuss that one here.

[72]   Gafney, *Womanist Midrash*, 38.

[73]   On the issue of the sources of these two stories and their purpose in the narrative, see Shectman, *Women*, 74–79, and the literature cited there.

adding the new detail that Sarah is in fact his sister. Nevertheless, Gafney points out, "there is value in honoring Sarah as a survivor of sexual violence and domestic abuse and acknowledging her partner's complicity in that abuse."[74]

Dinah is another figure who has been a subject of intense focus by feminist interpreters. Chapman notes the prominence of the mother's household in this narrative, as also in Gen 24. As she observes, "It is unusual to identify a person through her mother, so the fact that this narrative [Gen 34] opens with a maternal genealogy suggests that we are dealing with an event where the house of Leah will prove central."[75] The focus quickly shifts to Dinah's brothers Simeon and Levi – her uterine brothers through Leah – who immediately eclipse her in the narrative. A primary role of male uterine siblings seems to have been to avenge affronts to their sisters, as Simeon and Levi do for Dinah.[76] Indeed, Dinah's father Jacob plays only a minor role in the story (as did Rebekah's in Gen 24).

Feminist analysis of the Dinah story, however, has focused heavily on the question of whether she is raped by Shechem – at stake is whether Dinah is a protagonist or a silent victim in her own story. The argument hinges on the meaning of the term *'nh* II (Piel; Gen 34:2), which scholars have argued means anything from "rape" to "oppress." Some degree of consensus appears to have emerged around the meaning of "debasement" for the verb, and it clearly points to some kind of mistreatment, though of what kind is still an open question. It is undeniably linked to sex and to sexual violence or coercion in some texts, even if that is not inherent in the verb itself.[77] Another danger in the Dinah story is the desire to blame the victim: "the detail that Dinah goes out to see the women of the land (that is, foreign women, 34:1) . . . is taken to mean that Dinah, essentially, has it coming."[78]

---

[74]   Gafney, *Womanist Midrash*, 33.
[75]   Chapman, *House of the Mother*, 64.
[76]   Ibid., 96.
[77]   On the question of whether Dinah is raped, see most recently Alison Joseph, "'Is Dinah Raped?' Isn't the Right Question: Genesis 34 and Feminist Historiography," in "Gendered Historiography: Theoretical Considerations and Case Studies," special issue, ed. Shawna Dolansky and Sarah Shectman, *JHS* 19.4 (2019): 27–37, and the literature cited there. See also the discussion in Russaw, *Daughters*, 78–82, 135–36; Johanna Stiebert, "The Wife of Potiphar, Sexual Harassment, and False Rape Allegation: Genesis 39 in Select Social Contexts of the Past and Present," in *The Bible and Gender Troubles in Africa*, ed. Joachim Kügler, Rosinah Gabaitse, and Johanna Stiebert, BIAS 22 (Bamberg: University of Bamberg Press, 2019), 73–114, here 83.
[78]   Stiebert, "Wife of Potiphar," 82.

Many feminist readers have noted the lack of overall agency that
Dinah demonstrates in the story, and the degree to which the action
quickly shifts from her (as subject only once and then as object) to the
various men involved.[79] Alison Joseph points out the difficulty in determining whether Dinah is raped as a question from a feminist-historical
perspective: rape as a modern category does not entirely fit with the
biblical material and biblical views about women's agency or lack
thereof. Yet sexual violence clearly happened in ancient Israel. The
great divide between (apparent) ancient and modern ideas of autonomy
and coercion make this text a minefield for feminist historians, Joseph
argues, forcing them to deny that Dinah is raped and thereby diminishing
the one thing that happens to her in the story. Many scholars argue that
despite the prominence of this sexual violence – and the circumcision
and murder of the Shechemite men, another act of sexual violence – the
story is not really about Dinah and what happened to her. Rather, it is
about honor and shame in a conflict between people and about the
dangers of intermarriage.[80] Joseph argues that "the Dinah story demonstrates that [intermarriage of Israelite women with foreign men] could be
a serious concern and poses a dangerous threat to Israelite identity." But
as she notes, "the historically contextualized perspectives on women's
sexuality in ancient Israel (as discussed above) eliminate rape from the
narrative." She concludes,

> "Is Dinah raped?" is not the right question because our modern
> definition of rape does not exist in ancient Israel, and the context-
> ual understandings of ענה ['nh II] do not support it, but furiously
> arguing that this narrative is not rape further demeans Dinah,
> while the focus of the narrative is not on her.[81]

Instead, Joseph suggests, "We can ask other historical questions, such as:
Why did the author use violence to establish Israelite identity? Why is
the prohibition against intermarriage told through the sexual violation of
Dinah? ... Why is consent not a concern for these ancient writers?"[82] It is
equally important for feminist historians to grapple with the ethical
implications of this material and what the removal of rape from the
picture means for readers in a modern context.

---

[79]   Joseph, "Is Dinah Raped?," 28; Russaw, *Daughters*, 81.
[80]   Joseph, "Is Dinah Raped?," 34.
[81]   Ibid., 36. On the issue of rape and consent in ancient Israel and in the Dinah story, see
       also Stiebert, "Wife of Potiphar," 81–83.
[82]   Joseph, "Is Dinah Raped?," 37.

THE JOSEPH NARRATIVE

The Joseph narrative contains considerably fewer women characters than the preceding chapters of Genesis. Notably, though, the narrative shifts to a story about a prominent woman after an initial chapter introducing Joseph as a key character. This chapter, Gen 38, moves to a story about Joseph's brother Judah and Judah's daughter-in-law, Tamar. Feminist interpreters have focused on Tamar's initiative and resourcefulness: seeing that the husband (and subsequent pregnancy and presumed birth of a son) promised her has been held back from her, she devises a clever ruse and traps Judah into making good on his obligations to her. She is rewarded with sons – twins! – and becomes an eventual ancestor of King David. The story also provides evidence for the biblical practice of Levirate marriage (see Deut 25:5–10), in which a widowed woman marries her deceased husband's brother in order to have a son who will function as the dead brother's offspring.[83]

A starting point for feminist readings of Gen 38 is the fact that Tamar, as a widow with surviving brothers-in-law, had the right to marriage and (ideally) a son – that is, feminists read the practice of the levirate not (just) as a means for patriarchal structures to perpetuate themselves but also as a way to ensure that a woman who might otherwise face social precarity would be taken care of. Mignon Jacobs's literary reading of the narrative in light of the themes of gender and power focuses on Tamar's initiative and use of disguise to achieve her desired ends: "upon perceiving that her rights are being violated, Tamar uses the advantages of her gender to secure what is being denied her."[84] That is, she uses sex and her subsequent pregnancy to force Judah to recognize her rights and fulfill his obligation to her. (Notably, the text does not say that she and Shelah married.) As Jacobs notes, "As subversive as it may be, Tamar's power is both in her restricted options [as a widow whose in-laws are not fulfilling their duty] and in the available avenues for securing her rights [namely, the

---

[83]   On the levirate, and specifically on connections between Gen 38 and Deut 25:5–10, see Dvora E. Weisberg, *Levirate Marriage and the Family in Ancient Judaism* (Lebanon, NH: Brandeis University Press, 2009), 28–30, and Ayelet Seidler, "The Law of Levirate and Forced Marriage – Widow vs. Levir in Deuteronomy 25:5–10," *JSOT* 42 (2018): 454–55. However, Mignon Jacobs argues that the levirate guaranteed only that the widow was "entitled to bear a child with her brother-in-law, but not entitled to be his wife"; *Gender, Power, and Persuasion: The Genesis Narratives and Contemporary Portraits* (Grand Rapids, MI: Baker Academic, 2007), 189.

[84]   Jacobs, *Gender*, 195.

ability to use sex].["85] Though Tamar "does not have the power to decide when to secure a levir,"[86] she formulates and executes a plan: "Tamar transforms herself from the passive woman who waits to the active woman who orchestrates her future."[87]

Though the story of Tamar has an early and prominent place in the Joseph story, the only other women to appear in the rest of the narrative are the wife of Potiphar (Joseph's Egyptian enslaver) and Joseph's eventual wife, Asenath (who seems to be the daughter of the same Potiphar).[88] Though the narrative tells us almost nothing about Asenath,[89] Gafney calls her "a treasure that has scarcely been mined in feminist and womanist scholarship, teaching, and preaching. ... Asenath is a woman of status in her native culture and in the Israelite narrative; she is among the treasures of Egypt with which Joseph is rewarded for his service and his loyalty."[90] Asenath, an Egyptian woman, is the mother of two of the most prominent tribes in Israelite lore: Ephraim and Manasseh.[91] However, the biblical text tells us little else about her.

Potiphar's wife has garnered more attention, predictably, given her role as a tempting *femme fatale* who turns on Joseph when he rejects her. For feminists, she raises questions about power, especially a story in which the usual balance of power is turned on its head. Alice Bach uses a literary approach to unpack the patriarchal values encoded in this text. She notes that "[g]etting at the suppressed story of the female in male-authored literature requires both filling the gaps in the narrative and reading the text for the patriarchal agenda that has shaped the telling of

---

[85]   Ibid., 189.

[86]   Ibid., 190.

[87]   Ibid., 196; and see Warner, "Finding Lot's Daughters," 55–56. In a more practical and immediate context, Tamar's story may speak powerfully to women in patriarchal societies who have restricted sexual and reproductive autonomy. See, e.g., Lilian Cheelo Siwila, "A Reading of Genesis 38 through Religio-Cultural Sexual and Reproductive Rights in the Ethiopian Context," *Journal of Theology for Southern Africa* 154 (2016): 141–55; Anderson Jeremiah, "Reclaiming 'Her' Right: Rereading the Story of Tamar (Genesis 38:1–27) from Dalit Women Perspective," *Bangalore Theological Forum* 38.1 (2006): 145–56.

[88]   See Stiebert, "Wife of Potiphar," 85.

[89]   Despite her opaque beginnings, Asenath became a figure of some importance in Second Temple Judaism; see Jill Hicks-Keeton, *Arguing with Aseneth: Gentile Access to Israel's Living God in Jewish Antiquity* (New York: Oxford University Press, 2018).

[90]   Gafney, *Womanist Midrash*, 71.

[91]   Ibid., 71–72. On the fact that the requirement of endogamous marriage seems to end with Jacob's sons, see Sarah Shectman, "Rachel, Leah, and the Composition of Genesis," in *The Pentateuch: International Perspectives on Current Research*, ed. Thomas B. Dozeman, Konrad Schmid, and Baruch J. Schwartz, FAT 78 (Tübingen: Mohr Siebeck, 2011), 207–22.

the story."[92] On a surface level, Joseph "embraces all the characteristics of the hero: loyal and pious, strong enough to resist the temptations of the female."[93] Potiphar's wife, whom Bach calls Mut-em-enet, following Thomas Mann,[94] "is the out-of-control female, slave to her passions,"[95] whose story "reflects the uncertainty of her position through the tepid response of her husband to her accusations, the silence of the servants, and Joseph's rejection of her immodest proposal."[96] Bach reclaims Mut-em-enet's agency and reads the story through her eyes, as a means to "prevent the seduction of the reader into the writer's world, where women are defined in relation to men, that is, by their sexual identity."[97]

Johanna Stiebert analyzes the story within the modern context of "rape culture – that is, a context where sexual violence occurs and sexual violence is widely normalized and sometimes ... even glamourized. Toxic attitudes that promote rape myths – including the suggestion that women very often lie about being raped – are part of rape culture."[98] But whereas rape today is a serious and punishable crime, the biblical stories suggest that it is adultery, rather than rape, that is the problem.[99] Though the usual roles are reversed in Gen 39 – the man is the victim and the woman the perpetrator – the power positions are not, and the story "demonstrates that sex and power are intimately entwined. ... In resisting [Potiphar's wife], Joseph, while socially inferior, is asserting his masculine autonomy."[100] At the same time, there is a widespread myth that women are likely to make false rape accusations. As Stiebert observes, "The effect of this is to downplay sexual assault, to downplay the often very powerful role of the men in these cases, and to ignore the much more self-evident fact that women in particular have been harassed and raped over a long expanse of time and with alarming frequency."[101]

---

[92]   Alice Bach, "Breaking Free of the Biblical Frame-Up: Uncovering the Woman in Genesis 39," in *A Feminist Companion to Genesis*, ed. Athalya Brenner, FCB 2 (Sheffield: Sheffield Academic Press, 1993), 318–42, here 318.

[93]   Bach, "Breaking Free," 322; and see Stiebert, "Wife of Potiphar," 74.

[94]   See Alice Bach, *Women, Seduction, and Betrayal in Biblical Narrative* (Cambridge: Cambridge University Press, 1997), 36–37, who adopts the name in recognition of Mann's "glorious" depiction of Potiphar's wife "that goes completely against biblical tradition" (ibid., 36).

[95]   Bach, "Breaking Free," 322; and see Stiebert, "Wife of Potiphar," 77–78.

[96]   Bach, "Breaking Free," 341.

[97]   Ibid., 342.

[98]   Stiebert, "Wife of Potiphar," 103.

[99]   Ibid., 104.

[100] Ibid., 105–6.

[101] Ibid., 108.

CONCLUSION

Feminist readings, not just of Genesis, focus not only on women but also on issues of power and the negotiation of relations between men and women in particular. Some such readings find positive aspects in what have traditionally been deemed negative texts for women (as, for example, with Meyers's reading of Gen 3:16), and some do the opposite (as with womanist readings of Sarah). Feminists may approach the text from a variety of angles – historical, literary, sociological, anthropological – but even readings that are not specifically historical run the risk of presenting the text as reflective of the real, lived experiences of women in ancient Israel. We must keep in mind that the biblical text is the product of men, even where it might incorporate earlier traditions created or circulated among women. Megan Warner cautions in this regard that "what we learn about power structures through [such] reading[s] doesn't relate to the historical situation of men and women per se, so much as to the way male writers employed women, or at least women characters, in their writing."[102] She continues,

> In the Genesis narratives the history of nations is played out as a domestic saga. The action therefore occurs in a realm in which women hold actual power and influence. Procreation and even family life are not possible without them. . . . [T]he Genesis narratives offered biblical authors a relatively safe place in which to negotiate religious, legal and ethical conundrums. I see women characters, too, offering a space of relative safety.

Genesis, then, by virtue of its content and genre, though it may appear to be an empowered and empowering source of traditions about women, should be approached with caution when we attempt to use it to make claims about women's status in ancient Israel. It is the product of men and necessarily reflects their perceptions and understandings of matters related to women.

Though feminist interpretations have complicated and even reversed traditional readings of the text, they also reveal the ways in which hierarchies of gender, race, and class are still deeply encoded in the text. The recognition of the constant relationality of men and women – their definition in relation to one another – and of women and other women and men and other men has led some feminist scholars to advocate for a more broadly gender-focused criticism rather

---

[102]   Warner, "Finding Lot's Daughters," 58.

than continuing to work within the parameters of feminist criticism.[103] Gender criticism recognizes that both men and women are affected by social gender constructions and norms and that the two are so closely connected to one another that it is impossible to understand the one without the other. It also recognizes that there is no single women's or men's experience but that gender coexists with and is impacted by factors such as ethnicity and class. This idea of intersectionality is only beginning to be explored in biblical studies, but it is a fundamental contribution of feminist criticism(s) to our understanding of the biblical text.

SELECT BIBLIOGRAPHY

Bird, Phyllis A. *Missing Persons and Mistaken Identities: Women and Gender in Ancient Israel*. Overtures to Biblical Theology. Minneapolis, MN: Fortress Press, 1997.

Brenner, Athalya, ed. *A Feminist Companion to Genesis*. FCB 2. Sheffield: Sheffield Academic Press, 1993.

Byron, Gay L., and Vanessa Lovelace, eds. *Womanist Interpretations of the Bible: Expanding the Discourse*. Semeia Studies 85. Atlanta: SBL Press, 2016.

Chapman, Cynthia R. *The House of the Mother: The Social Roles of Maternal Kin in Biblical Hebrew Narrative and Poetry*. AYBRL. New Haven: Yale University Press, 2016.

Claassens, L. Juliana and Carolyn J. Sharp, eds. *Feminist Frameworks and the Bible: Power, Ambiguity, and Intersectionality*. LHBOTS 630. London: T&T Clark, 2017.

Gafney, Wilda C. *Womanist Midrash: A Reintroduction to the Women of the Torah and the Throne*. Louisville, KY: Westminster John Knox Press, 2017.

Junior, Nyasha. *An Introduction to Womanist Biblical Interpretation*. Louisville, KY: Westminster John Knox Press, 2015.

Meyers, Carol L. *Rediscovering Eve: Ancient Israelite Women in Context*. New York: Oxford University Press, 2013.

Murphy, Cullen. *The Word According to Eve: Women and the Bible in Ancient Times and Our Own*. Boston: Houghton Mifflin, 1998.

Russaw, Kimberly D. *Daughters in the Hebrew Bible*. Lanham, MD: Lexington Books, 2018.

Schneider, Tammi J. *Mothers of Promise: Women in the Book of Genesis*. Grand Rapids, MI: Baker Academic, 2008.

Shectman, Sarah. *Women in the Pentateuch: A Feminist and Source-Critical Analysis*. HBM 23. Sheffield: Sheffield Phoenix Press, 2009.

[103] See Deryn Guest, *Beyond Feminist Biblical Studies*, Bible in the Modern World 47 (Sheffield: Sheffield Phoenix, 2012); Shawna Dolansky and Sarah Shectman, "Introduction: What Is Gendered Historiography and How Do You Do It?," in "Gendered Historiography: Theoretical Considerations and Case Studies," special issue, ed. Shawna Dolansky and Sarah Shectman, *JHS* 19.4 (2019): 3–18.

Trible, Phyllis. *God and The Rhetoric of Sexuality*. OBT 2. Philadelphia: Fortress Press, 1978.

Yee, Gale A., ed. *Poor Banished Children of Eve: Woman as Evil in the Hebrew Bible*. Minneapolis, MN: Fortress Press, 2003.

Yee, Gale A. *The Hebrew Bible: Feminist and Intersectional Perspectives*. Minneapolis, MN: Fortress Press, 2018.

Part III
Themes and Literary Motifs of Genesis

10 From *Imago* to *Imagines*: The Image(s) of God in Genesis

BRENT A. STRAWN

The image of God (Latin *imago Dei*) is a familiar, even fraught, biblical notion because it has served as something of an empty cipher that countless interpreters have sought to fill.[1] Despite a great deal of spilled ink, what, exactly, the *imago Dei* is remains no small mystery because the notion goes largely undeveloped and underdeveloped in the Bible.[2] References to the *imago Dei* appear

---

[1] For important studies, see J. Richard Middleton, *The Liberating Image: The* Imago Dei *in Genesis 1* (Grand Rapids: Brazos, 2005); W. Randall Garr, *In His Own Image and Likeness: Humanity, Divinity, and Monotheism*, CHANE 15 (Leiden: Brill, 2003); and Gunnlaugur A. Jónsson, *The Image of God: Genesis 1:26–28 in a Century of Old Testament Research*, ConBOT 26 (Stockholm: Alqvist & Wiksell, 1988), whose main conclusion is that factors other than scholarship alone "have played an important role in the history of imago Dei studies" (218). Other helpful overviews include Claus Westermann, *Genesis 1–11: A Continental Commentary*, trans. John J. Scullion (Minneapolis: Fortress, 1994), 147–55; David J. A. Clines, "Humanity as the Image of God," in *On the Way to the Postmodern: Old Testament Essays, 1967–1998*, 2 vols., JSOTSup 292–293 (Sheffield: Sheffield Academic Press, 1998), 2: 447–97 (originally published in TynBul 19 [1968]: 53–103); and Armand Puig I Tàrrech, ed., *Imatge de Déu*, Scripta Biblica 7 (Catalonia: Associació Bíblica de Catalunya, 2006). Most recently, see Ryan S. Petersen, *The* Imago Dei *as Human Identity: A Theological Interpretation*, JTISup 14 (Winona Lake: Eisenbrauns, 2016).

[2] Mark S. Smith, *The Genesis of Good and Evil: The Fall(out) and Original Sin in the Bible* (Louisville: Westminster John Knox, 2019), 52: a "somewhat abstract idea"; Andreas Schüle, *Theology from the Beginning: Essays on the Primeval History and Its Canonical Context*, FAT 113 (Tübingen: Mohr Siebeck, 2017), 13: "a thick but nonetheless vague *symbol* ... .provocatively fuzzy ... .highly suggestive and as such invit[ing] further interpretation" (his emphasis); Ellen F. Davis, *Opening Israel's Scriptures* (New York: Oxford University Press, 2019), 9: the "biblical phrasing is potent yet cryptic; in itself, it explains nothing, and perhaps for that very reason has proved to be endlessly intriguing." Andreas Wagner, *God's Body: The Anthropomorphic God in the Old Testament*, trans. Marion Salzmann (London: T & T Clark, 2019), 144 takes this lack of definition as proof that the concept is "not of central importance in the Old Testament." Cf. Westermann, *Genesis 1–11*, 148: "it has no ... significance in the rest of the Old Testament." James Barr famously said "there is no answer to be found" for the question of the meaning of the *imago Dei* because "[t]here is no reason to believe that this [biblical] writer had in his mind any definite idea about the content or the location of the image of God" ("The Image

almost exclusively in Genesis – "almost" because interpreters often find traces of the concept elsewhere, including in the New Testament.[3] Be that as it may, the clearest and most important loci for the idea – if only because they are the originary texts – are four passages in the so-called Primeval History of Gen 1–11:[4]

(1)   God said:
        Let us make humankind in our image (*bĕṣalmēnû*),
        according to our likeness (*kidmûtēnû*),
        that they might rule over the fish of the sea,
        and over the birds of the air,
        and over the animals, and over all the earth,
        and over all the things that creep upon the earth.
      So God created humankind in his image (*bĕṣalmô*):
        in the divine image (*bĕṣelem ʾĕlōhîm*), he created
        humankind –
      male and female, he created them.
                                                    (Gen 1:26–27)

(2)   This is the book of the genealogy of Adam:
        On the day God created humankind
          he made him in the divine likeness (*bidmût ʾĕlōhîm*)
          male and female he created them.
        He blessed them and named them "humanity" on the day he
          created them.
                                                    (Gen 5:1–2)

(3)   Now when Adam was 130 years old,
          he fathered a son in his likeness (*bidmûtô*),
          according to his image (*kĕṣalmô*).
      He named him Seth.
                                                    (Gen 5:3)

---

of God in the Book of Genesis – A Study of Terminology," *BJRL* 51 [1968]: 11–26). Surely Barr's is a counsel of despair.

3   Most especially 2 Cor 4:4 and Col 1:15 (of Christ; cf. Rom 8:29); see also 1 Cor 11:7; Jas 3:9; Wis 2:23; and Sir 17:3 (of humans; cf. Rom 8:29); and Wis 7:26 (of wisdom). I leave aside allusions to the notion (e.g., Psalm 8) since these are by nature debatable. For Gen 1:26–27 in later Second Temple Literature, see Armin Lange and Matthias Weigold, *Biblical Quotations and Allusions in Second Temple Jewish Literature*, JAJSup 5 (Göttingen: Vandenhoeck & Ruprecht, 2011), 54–55.

4   They are also all typically associated with the Priestly source.

(4) The one who spills human blood
a human will spill their blood,
because in the divine image (*bĕṣelem ʾĕlōhîm*)
God made humankind.

(Gen 9:6)[5]

The key Hebrew terms are *ṣelem* ("image") and *dĕmût* ("likeness"),[6] and even a cursory investigation of these four texts conveys a decent amount of information, including:

a. *ṣelem* occurs more than *dĕmût*: five times to three, respectively;
b. the literary form of texts (1) and (4) seems to be poetic, with texts (2) and (3) – or at least bits of them – also apparently on the high end of the poetry–prose spectrum;
c. it seems acceptable to speak of either "divine image" (*bĕṣelem ʾĕlōhîm*, twice) or "divine likeness" (*bidmût ʾĕlōhîm*, once), which may suggest some synonymity between these compound terms if not also between *ṣelem* and *dĕmût*;[7] and, finally,

---

[5] Translations are my own, adhere closely to the Masoretic Text (MT), and intentionally tend toward the dynamic. For text-critical issues, see the commentaries and Abraham Tal, *Genesis*, BHQ 1 (Stuttgart: Deutsche Bibelgesellschaft, 2015), ad loc.

[6] Translated in the Greek Septuagint and Latin Vulgate in intriguing ways that have often influenced subsequent interpretation: *ṣelem* by Greek εἰκών/*eikōn* ("image"; 1:26a, 27; 5:3b; 9:6) and Latin *imāgō* ("image"; 1:26a, 27; 5:3b; 9:6); *dĕmût* by Greek ὁμοίωσις/*homoiōsis* ("likeness") in 1:27b, εἰκών/*eikōn* in 5:1, and ἰδέα/*idea* ("appearance") in 5:3a; by Latin *similitūdō* ("likeness") in 1:26b; 5:1, 3a.

[7] So, e.g., Konrad Schmid, *A Historical Theology of the Hebrew Bible*, trans. Peter Altmann (Grand Rapids: Eerdmans, 2019), 431. Barr, "Image," 24 thinks *dĕmût* functions "to define and limit" the meaning of "the more novel and the more ambiguous" *ṣelem*. See Tal, *Genesis*, 79* for the tradition that treats the two terms as a unity; that perspective seems to be present in some early Versions (Symmachus, Theodotion, Syriac, Targum), with others (Samaritan Pentateuch, LXX, Aquila, Vulgate), however, consistently distinguishing the words. The Aramaic cognates *ṣlm*ʼ and *dmwt*ʼ appear together on an inscription from Tell Fekheriyeh, which many have taken as support that the two are somehow synonymous. See, e.g., Nahum M. Sarna, *Genesis*, JPS Torah Commentary (Philadelphia: Jewish Publication Society, 1989), 12. Cf., however, W. Randall Garr, "'Image' and 'Likeness' in the Inscription from Tell Fakhariyeh," *IEJ* 50 (2000): 227–34, who notes the distinct "rhetorical character" for these terms and the passages in which they appear, making them "pragmatically distinct," serving "different communicative functions" (233–34): "'Likeness' introduces the section that focuses on the ruler's petitionary role; 'image' introduces the section that illustrates his commanding presence and authoritative status … 'Likeness' is petitionary and directed at the deity; it is cultic and votive. 'Image' is majestic, absolute and commemorative; it is directed at the people" (231).

d. the reversal of the terms in text (3) compared to text (1) may function to *disassociate* Adam's likeness in his own offspring from the *imago Dei* in humanity.[8]

Indeed, text (3) seems quite different since it seems concerned with human (biological?) likeness. And yet, since it does employ the two key terms, many scholars think text (3) contributes something important to the proper interpretation of the *imago Dei* – namely, that it may have something to do with physical form.[9] Similarly, text (4) appears as part of a change in the diet of humanity after the Flood and has a somewhat different effect from texts (1) and (2), having the force of law.[10]

Given how few and how brief – even *opaque* – these four texts are, it is not surprising that many different possibilities for the meaning of the image of God have been offered in the history of interpretation.[11] The *imago* has been a particularly generative topic

---

[8] Cf. Barr, "Image," 25. This view is perhaps evident in Targum Onkelos, which does not render *kĕṣalmô* as it does in Gen 1:26, but uses an entirely different construction: "who resembled him" (*ddmy lyh*). Tal, *Genesis*, *91 deems this a theological change. Contrast Bill T. Arnold, *Genesis*, NCBC (Cambridge: Cambridge University Press, 2008), 85, who thinks text (3) "explain[s] how Adam actively continued God's creative work through fathering a child." For more on this text, see Jeffrey H. Tigay, "'He Begot a Son in His Likeness after His Image' (Genesis 5:3)," in *Tehillah le-Moshe: Biblical and Judaic Studies in Honor of Moshe Greenberg*, ed. Mordechai Cogan, Barry L. Eichler, and Jeffrey H. Tigay (Winona Lake: Eisenbrauns, 1997), 139–47.

[9] See the views discussed in Jónsson, *Image*, 54, 106, 112, etc. Texts like Exod 24:9–11 and Ezek 1:26–28 may also suggest some similarity between human and divine forms. On this matter, see already Maimonides in *Guide to the Perplexed* I.1; also Gerhard von Rad, *Genesis: A Commentary*, trans. John H. Marks, OTL (Philadelphia: Westminster, 1982), 58; and, more extensively, Wagner, *God's Body*; and Esther J. Hamori, *When Gods Were Men: The Embodied God in Biblical and Ancient Near Eastern Literature*, BZAW 384 (Berlin: Walter de Gruyter, 2008). Cf. also Tigay, "He Begot." Related here is the idea that the image notion suggests some sort of divine parentage of the human being – that God "fathers" humanity as did Adam Seth – but see further below.

[10] See Jónsson, *Image*, 59, 224–25 n. 40; Jeffrey H. Tigay, "The Image of God and the Flood: Some New Developments," in ללמד וללמד: *Studies in Jewish Education and Judaica in Honor of Louis Newman*, ed. Alexander M. Shapiro and Burton I. Cohen (New York: Ktav, 1984), 169–82 (174, 177); also James Barr, "Man and Nature: The Ecological Controversy and the Old Testament," *BJRL* 55 (1972): 9–32 (20): "Homicide was to be punished not because man [sic] had dominion over the animals, but because man [sic] was like God."

[11] The main ones are humanity's physical form, the ability to walk upright, intelligence and reason, various spiritual characteristics, authority over the animal kingdom, and capacity to relate to God (Jónsson, *Image*, 2). Problems with associating the *imago* with, say, cognition alone, are highlighted in works like George C. Hammond, *It Has Not Yet Appeared What We Shall Be: A Reconsideration of the* Imago Dei *in Light of*

in Christian theology.[12] In contrast, historical and comparative approaches to the subject have tended to set the notion in its literary and ancient Near Eastern contexts with more restricted results. While the constraints offered by the latter methodologies are instructive, it is clear that no study of the *imago* can be entirely confined to the four main texts if only because the *content* of these passages – limited as they are – nevertheless indicates that the "image of God" has two distinct referents: the divine (creator) and the human (creation), each of which is complex. The "image of God," that is, is *not* – not even in Genesis all by itself – a singular entity but, rather, a plural one. There is not just one *imago Dei* but *many images* of God. Indeed, if "image" is taken as a literary category, it is obvious that a large number of narrative and poetic representations of God are found in Genesis with the same holding true for images of human beings as well. These various *imagines* (plural of *imago*) – of both referents, human and divine, and in their interrelationship(s) – are taken up sequentially in what follows. First, however, the *imago Dei* should be put in its proper contexts.

THE IMAGE OF GOD: THREE CONTEXTUAL INSIGHTS

Once the ancient Near Eastern material was discovered and deciphered, then compared to Israelite literature, wide speculation about the meaning of the *imago Dei* "found certain reasonable controls."[13] These controls, found in "numerous parallels from both Egypt and Mesopotamia," clarified that, in its cultural context, the *imago* was "related to royal language, in which a king or pharaoh is

Those with Severe Cognitive Disabilities (Phillipsburg: P & R Publishing, 2017). As Jónsson's work demonstrates, "mental endowment" (*Image*, 33–43) is only one of many possible interpretations.

[12] See, e.g., Geoffrey Wainwright, *Doxology: A Systematic Theology* (New York: Oxford University Press, 1980), 15–44; Jason S. Sexton, "The Imago Dei Once Again: Stanley Grenz's Journey toward a Theological Interpretation of Genesis 1:26–27," *JTI* 4 (2010): 187–206; and, more recently Ian A. McFarland, *The Divine Image: Envisioning the Invisible God* (Minneapolis: Fortress, 2005). The *imago* is also important within Judaism: see, e.g., Michael Wyschogrod, "The Impact of Dialogue with Christianity on My Self-Understanding as a Jew," in *Die Hebräische Bibel und ihr zweifache Nachgeschichte: Festschrift für Rolf Rendtorff zum 65. Geburtstag*, ed. Erhard Blum, Christian Macholz, and Ekkehard W. Stegemann (Neukirchen-Vluyn: Neukirchener, 1990), 725–36 (736), who calls Gen 1:26 "the single most powerful in the Bible." See further Tikva Frymer-Kensky et al., eds., *Christianity in Jewish Terms* (Boulder: Westview, 2000), 321–56.

[13] Arnold, *Genesis*, 45.

the 'image of (a) god.'"[14] That the concept derives from the royal domain is now the consensus view among investigators who are historically and comparatively driven; it is also the first of three important contextual insights about the image of God.

In truth, however, the comparative material is not uniform.[15] It clusters around two loci: (i) the monarch as the image of a god and, in Mesopotamia, (ii) the monarch's use of his own image especially in statuary.[16] The first locus is manifest in the way the king could be described as, for example, "the image of (the god) Bel" (ṣalam Bēl) in Mesopotamia or, in Egypt, the way the pharaoh could be called "the likeness of (the god) Re" or even, via proper name: "the living image of (the god) Amun" (the meaning of Tutankhamun). The second locus is how kings set up images, particularly statues, of themselves as representations of the royal self in various places, including in devotional contexts or in conquered territories. In the case of occupied lands, the image of the king was to be carefully curated – alternatively, in instances of rebellion, the overlord's image was quickly defaced or destroyed. Wherever it was placed, however, the royal image served to "re-presence"[17] the monarch at a distance and/or in a particular role: sovereign, devotee, or both.

When applied to Genesis, this background suggests that humankind is the Divine Sovereign's stand-in within the created world, serving as God's

[14] Ibid. Note that the verbs in Gen 1:28 that describe the roles of humankind, "subdue" (k-b-š) and "have dominion" (r-d-h; also in 1:26), are used elsewhere of royal activity (e.g., 2 Sam 8:11; 1 Kgs 4:21, 24; Ps 72:8); however, von Rad deems these commissioning verbs to belong, not "to the definition of God's image," but rather "its consequence" (von Rad, Genesis, 59; cf. Jónsson, Image, 222).

[15] For the ancient Near Eastern material that follows, see extensively, Middleton, Liberating Image, passim; also Brent A. Strawn, "Comparative Approaches: History, Theory, and the Image of God," in Method Matters: Essays on the Interpretation of the Hebrew Bible in Honor of David L. Petersen, ed. Joel M. LeMon and Kent Harold Richards, SBLRBS 56 (Atlanta: Society of Biblical Literature, 2009), 117–42; Brent A. Strawn, "The Image of God: Comparing the Old Testament with Other Ancient Near Eastern Cultures," in Iconographic Exegesis of the Hebrew Bible/Old Testament: An Introduction to Its Method and Practice, ed. Izaak J. de Hulster, Brent A. Strawn, and Ryan P. Bonfiglio (Göttingen: Vandenhoeck & Ruprecht, 2015), 63–75; and Tigay, "Image," esp. 179 nn. 8 and 12.

[16] There are also abundant references to images of deities proper – i.e., artistic depictions of the gods.

[17] See Zainab Bahrani, The Graven Image: Representation in Babylonia and Assyria (Philadelphia: University of Pennsylvania Press, 2003), 121–48: "ṣalmu [the Akkadian cognate of Hebrew ṣelem] is better thought of as an ontological category rather than an aesthetic concept" (133); "[ṣ]almu is ... a mode of presencing" (137); "[t]he image repeats, rather than represents, the king" (144); "the image is no longer a representation but a being in its own right" (145). See also Irene J. Winter, On Art in the Ancient Near East, 2 vols., CHANE 34.1–2 (Leiden: Brill, 2010), 1:78–95.

viceroy, as it were, or, perhaps even more: as God's own "re-presence."[18] If correct, this line of interpretation indicates that in Genesis the *imago* is, on the one hand, *royal*, and, on the other hand, *thoroughly democratized*. It is no longer the monarch alone who participates in or somehow actually is the divine image.[19] Instead, according to text (1) above *all humans* – humanity as a whole – is (in) the image of God. This is theologically groundbreaking within the hierarchical polities of the ancient Near East (including ancient Israel),[20] since it dissolves any and all "classes" within the human species when it comes to God's image. There is no longer the singular king vs. all his subjects, the one monarch vs. the citizenry, royal vs. non-royal – so also there is no male vs. female (cf. Gal 3:28)[21] since humankind *en masse* and as such is (in) the image and likeness of God.[22]

A second contextual insight comes from those ancient Near Eastern texts that describe the creation of humans more generally. Unlike Genesis, the texts under consideration here do not employ the specific language of "image" and "likeness" but they occasionally suggest correspondence between the human and divine realms if not, in some instances, the divinity of humankind more generally, which is not unrelated.[23] The famous,

---

[18] Among other things, note, e.g., that in Gen 2:19, the human names the animals whereas in Gen 1, it is God who names things. See Victor Avigdor Hurowitz, "The Divinity of Humankind in the Bible and the Ancient Near East: A New Mesopotamian Parallel," in *Mishneh Todah: Studies in Deuteronomy and Its Cultural Environment in Honor of Jeffrey H. Tigay*, ed. Nili Sacher Fox, David A. Glatt-Gilad, and Michael J. Williams (Winona Lake: Eisenbrauns, 2009), 263–74 (273).

[19] Sarna, *Genesis*, 12 and 353 n. 22; Samuel Loewenstamm, *Comparative Studies in Biblical and Ancient Oriental Literatures*, AOAT 204 (Neukirchen-Vluyn: Neukirchener, 1980), 48–50.

[20] See Schmid, *Historical Theology*, 431–32; J. Gordon McConville, *Being Human in God's World: An Old Testament Theology of Humanity* (Grand Rapids: Baker Academic, 2016), 29.

[21] Brevard S. Childs, *Old Testament Theology in a Canonical Context* (Philadelphia: Fortress, 1985), 189: "Surely this is a witness of absolute [gender] equality." See further Maryanne Cline Horowitz, "The Image of God in Man – Is Woman Included?" *HTR* 72 (1979): 175–206; Wagner, *God's Body*, 151–52, 155; and Paul Niskanen, "The Poetics of Adam: The Creation of אדם in the Image of אלהים," *JBL* 128 (2009): 417–36; but cf. Phyllis Bird, "'Male and Female He Created Them': Gen 1:27b in the Context of the Priestly Account of Creation," *HTR* 74 (1981): 129–59.

[22] Note Benno Jacob, *The First Book of the Bible, Genesis: Augmented Edition*, trans. and ed. Ernest I. Jacob and Walter Jacob (Brooklyn: Ktav, 2007 [1974]), 10: the image in the first human couple together "is the opposite of racism and emphasizes the unity of [hu]mankind."

[23] See Hurowitz, "Divinity," 265. At least one Egyptian text, *Instruction for Merikare*, also speaks of all humankind as the image of god: "mankind – god's cattle . . . . They are his images, who came from his body" (*AEL* 1:106). For more on the Egyptian materials, see Middleton, *Liberating Image*, 99–111. An important study that drew attention to the Egyptian evidence is Siegfried Herrmann, "Die Naturlehre des Schöpfungsberichtes:

but also enigmatic, first line of the Babylonian flood story, *Atra-Ḥasis*, is a case in point: *i-nu-ma i-lu a-wi-lum*. This is often translated "when the gods *like* men ...," but there is no comparative particle in the text that would signal a simile.[24] Instead, the words for "gods" (*ilū*, plural) and "humans" (*awīlum*, here a collective singular) are "immediately juxtaposed as though they were one."[25] If so, "when the gods were human" is a possible translation, but so is "when humans were gods."[26]

An even more apt parallel for the *imago* in Genesis is found in an omen series called *šumma kataduggû*, which begins, "When the great gods put the soul in humankind for Enlilship and established *kataduggû*-omens to guide them ...."[27] The key term here is "Enlilship" (*illilūtu*), which is "specifically a divine characteristic and in all cases is possessed by gods and goddesses."[28] This text indicates, therefore, that humans' "soul" or "spirit" (*zaqīqu*)[29] is given to them so that they have "executive power, [the] highest rank (of gods and goddesses)."[30] In this view, humanity "is not just a supreme leader but is divine," indeed "of the highest divinity."[31]

The two insights mentioned thus far are mostly concerned with the historical and cultural background of the image concept. Unfortunately, studies in this vein have sometimes paid little attention to how they impact the interpretation of the biblical *imago Dei*; even when they do,

---

Erwägungen zur Vorgeschichte von Genesis 1," *TLZ* 86 (1961): 413–24. See further below on the question of divinization.

[24] W. G. Lambert and A. R. Millard, *Atra-Ḥasis: The Babylonian Story of the Flood* (Winona Lake: Eisenbrauns, 1999), 42–43 (emphasis added). Note that they argue that the word *awīlum* "has the locative *–um* with the meaning of the comparative *–iš*" (146). Cf. Benjamin R. Foster, *Before the Muses: An Anthology of Akkadian Literature* (Bethesda: CDL, 2005), 229 n. 1: "The line is a metaphor," though he adds that "this does not mean that the gods were actually human beings; rather, they had to work as humans do."

[25] Hurowitz, "Divinity," 266 n. 12.

[26] According to Hurowitz, "[a]t the beginning of the myth, the gods are manly, whereas at the time of its creation humanity is made godly" (ibid.). A very different interpretation is found in Thorkild Jacobsen, "Inuma Ilu awīlum," in *Essays on the Ancient Near East in Memory of Jacob Joel Finkelstein*, ed. Maria de Jong Ellis (Hamden, CT: Archon Books, 1977), 113–17, who renders the line: "When (the god) Ilu was the boss."

[27] *enūma ilāni rabiūtum ša amēluti zaqīqša ana illilūti iškunū u kataduggâša ana reteddîša ukinnū*, text and translation (slightly modified) from Hurowitz, "Divinity," 269–70.

[28] Ibid., 270.

[29] According to Hurowitz, *zaqīqu* "seems to mean some sort of intelligence distinguishing humanity from animals and permitting humans to utter comprehensible sounds rather than mere noises ... probably designates thoughts articulated verbally in the mind that are then expressed orally as speech" (ibid., 271).

[30] *CAD* I/J, 85.

[31] Hurowitz, "Divinity," 270, 272.

the discussion is often restricted to text (1). A third important contextual insight, therefore, comes from those studies that have been more concerned with the biblical image *in its present literary context*. Especially since the scriptural texts make no explicit mention of the cultural background (notwithstanding the importance of the same), these studies have suggested that the *imago* may best be understood as an open-ended, even processual conception. Put differently: if the image of God notion is somewhat unclear in Genesis (which it is), despite the helpful ancient Near Eastern background (which, while helpful, may not be determinative), perhaps the meaning of the *imago* is answered only in the unfolding of the book.[32] The image, that is, may not be an essential(ized) category but a functional one. *Imago* is what *imago* does. Human beings *will be* (in/as) the image of God – or show themselves to be (in/as) the image of God – if they *actually image* God. Image, according to this view, is a verb as much as it is a noun, an action more than a state of being, and is unfinished, not yet complete, with Genesis telling the story of if and how human beings do (and/or do not) turn out to image the Deity.[33] This line of interpretation is not only opened up by text (1) and its lack of specificity, it may even be present in the way text (1) is formulated: some interpreters argue that the preposition "in" (*bĕ-*) in "in our image (*bĕṣalmēnû*)" is perhaps better translated by "as": "Let us make humankind *as* our image . . . "[34] Be that as it may, Briggs nicely captures the gist of the third contextual insight: "Genesis uses the phrase 'image of God' to set us reading the canonical narrative with certain questions in mind,

---

[32] See Richard S. Briggs, "Humans in the Image of God and Other Things Genesis Does Not Make Clear," *JTI* 4 (2010): 111–26, esp. 123–24.

[33] Cf. Von Rad, *Genesis*, 59: "the text speaks less of the nature of God's image than of its purpose. There is less said about the gift itself than about the task." So also Schüle, *Theology*, 27–44; McConville, *Being Human*, esp. 29–45; Yochanan Muffs, *The Personhood of God: Biblical Theology, Human Faith and the Divine Image* (Woodstock, VT: Jewish Lights, 2005), 174–75: "as image, his is an unrealized potential. Only by becoming human under the guidance of the law does man [sic] actualize this potential"; and Leon R. Kass, *The Beginning of Wisdom: Reading Genesis* (Chicago: University of Chicago, 2003), 38–40. In Kass's opinion, the open-ended nature of the text indicates that the first chapter of Genesis "begins the moral education of the reader" (40). A similar sentiment may be present in the *šumma kataduggû* text: "To the extent that *zaqīqu* [the human "spirit"] is not a physical characteristic, humanity's divine quality is not physically embodied or expressed but is manifest by his spirit and behavior" (Hurowitz, "Divinity," 273–74). Similarly, Tigay, "Image," 172–73 notes that the king Tukulti-Ninurta's status as the image of the god Enlil appears to depend on his attentiveness to his subjects and his understanding.

[34] E.g., Davis, *Opening*, 9, 13 n. 1; similarly Gordon J. Wenham, *Genesis 1–15*, WBC 1 (Waco: Word, 1987), 29 who thinks "according to [with *kĕ-*] our likeness" is "an explanatory gloss indicating the precise sense of 'in [*bĕ-*] our image.'" For an analysis of such arguments, see Clines, "Humanity," 2:470–75.

or, as one might say, 'the image of God' serves as a hermeneutical lens through which to read the OT's subsequent narratives."[35] The *imago* is, therefore, an "anthropological question."[36]

It seems worthwhile to attempt to combine the three insights won by previous scholarship; even so, in their individuality, each evidences a range of potential meaning(s) for the image of God. And so, again, what the *imago* is, precisely, remains a live and lively question, as does another: how do (or perhaps better: will) humans manifest that image? The latter question depends on the former one in a primal way – the issue is not simply what the *image* of God means, but *how is God imaged* in the first place? What is God like, how is God understood? Only by answering these types of questions can one determine if (and how) human beings properly "image" God. But only so much can be gathered about God's own image from the four classic texts in Gen 1–11. Any investigation of the divine referent of the *imago* – the divine *self*-image, as it were – must look to the entirety of Genesis, if not also well beyond it. As Leon R. Kass puts it: "To see how man [sic] might be godlike, we look at the text to see what God is like."[37]

IMAGINES DEI, PART ONE: GOD'S OWN IMAGE(S) IN GENESIS

Taking his own advice, Kass notes that Genesis 1

> introduces us to God's *activities and powers:* (1) God speaks, commands, names, blesses, and hallows; (2) God makes, and makes freely; (3) God looks at and beholds the world; (4) God is concerned with the goodness or perfection of things; (5) God addresses solicitously other living creatures and provides for their sustenance. In short: God exercises speech and reason, freedom in doing and making, and the powers of contemplation, judgment, and care.[38]

All well and good – and quite correct, too. Two things seem missing, however. The first is the *nonviolent nature* of God's activities and powers and how those may come to be in the *imago Dei* in

---

[35] Briggs, "Humans," 123.
[36] Ibid., 124.
[37] Kass, *The Beginning of Wisdom*, 37. Similarly, von Rad, *Genesis*, 59: "If one wants to determine the content of this statement more closely, one must ask how ancient Israel thought in details of this Elohim," though he immediately goes beyond Genesis by mentioning the divine predicates "wise" (2 Sam 14:17, 20) and "good" (1 Sam 29:9).
[38] Kass, *The Beginning of Wisdom*, 37–38.

humanity.[39] In comparative perspective, the *imago* may well evoke a Divine Sovereign who has placed a "presence" of the royal self in subjugated territory,[40] but what is decidedly absent from Genesis 1 is any indication that the territory in question was subjugated in the first place.[41] Instead, the land in question is *created* – apparently generously and peacefully – and then *blessed*, even *sanctified* by God. The image the Deity sets in creation is, of course, nothing less than humankind, which is subsequently – and correlatively, it would seem – tasked with proper care of the earth in the next chapter (Gen 2:15);[42] but already in Gen 1, the human *imago* is given a diet that is altogether commensurate with the nonviolent ways of God: vegetables, not meat from slaughter, is what humans are to eat (1:29; see also 2:16). The same is true for all other animals as well: there is no such thing as a carnivore yet! The first (implied) mention of animal slaughter is Gen 4:4, outside of Eden, but it is for liturgical, not dietary reasons: when Abel brings a sacrifice of his flock to God.[43] There is no mention of animal consumption proper until Gen 9, in conjunction with text (4), the last of the image texts in Genesis. From Gen 9:3 forward, the non-violent *imago* is no longer replicated in humankind – at least in alimentary ways. Before that, however, human

---

[39] See Jerome F. D. Creach, *Violence in Scripture*, Interpretation (Louisville: Westminster John Knox, 2013), 26: "to bear God's image – means not to act imperialistically and coercively." More extensively, see Middleton, *Liberating Image*.

[40] So John T. Strong, "Shattering the Image of God: A Response to Theodore Hiebert's Interpretation of the Story of the Tower of Babel," *JBL* 127 (2008): 625–34, esp. 631.

[41] To be sure, scholars have argued that a divine combat myth lies behind Genesis 1, but for compelling critiques of such a perspective, see Middleton, *Liberating Image*, 235–69; Garr, *In His Own Image*, 191–211; and Jon D. Levenson, *Creation and the Persistence of Evil: The Jewish Drama of Divine Omnipotence*, rev. ed. (Princeton: Princeton University Press, 1994), esp. 122, 127. If a combat myth is present, it is at best only hinted at, as distant background, and would probably only have been activated for those with rather extensive extra-textual knowledge. For contrasting opinions, see recently C. L. Crouch, "Made in the Image of God: The Creation of אדם, the Commissioning of the King and the Chaoskampf of Yнwн," *JANER* 16 (2016): 1–21; and Jeffrey M. Leonard, *Creation Rediscovered: Finding New Meaning in an Ancient Story* (Peabody: Hendrickson, 2020).

[42] The second creation account in Gen 2:4(b)–3:24 is traditionally attributed to the J (non-P) source. Even so, for the resonance of Gen 2–3 with ancient Near Eastern image practices, see Schüle, *Theology*, 7–25, also 27–44; and, especially, Catherine L. McDowell, *The Image of God in the Garden of Eden: The Creation of Humankind in Genesis 2:5–3:24 in Light of the* mīs pî *and* wpt-r *Rituals of Mesopotamia and Ancient Egypt*, Siphrut 15 (Winona Lake: Eisenbrauns, 2015).

[43] Some interpreters think Gen 3:21 implies animal killing, but this is unnecessary. See Brent A. Strawn, "Must Animals Die? Genesis 3:21, Enūma Eliš IV, and the Power of Divine Utterance," *VT* 72 (2022), 122–150; (DOI: https://doi.org/10.1163/15685330-bja10020).

"dominion" over the animal kingdom does *not* include its death or destruction.[44]

Now, in truth, humanity proves itself incapable of imaging the nonviolent God long before its diet is changed in Gen 9. The most egregious transgression, given its sheer novelty, is Cain's murder of his brother Abel in Gen 4. Here, in the first human family according to Genesis, in the very first story outside the Garden of Eden, among the very first brothers, is a case of fratricide. Here is also the first mention of "sin" (*ḥaṭṭā 't*) in the Bible. Things go downhill quickly thereafter, which is not surprising since the murderous Cain is presented as the progenitor of urbanism and culture (4:17–22). One of Cain's descendants, Lamech, is remembered for his "doctrine of inordinate retaliation": murdering someone who merely wounded him (4:23–24). And so it is that, just a bit later, Genesis speaks of the great wickedness of humankind on the earth, how "every inclination of the thoughts of its heart was only evil always" (6:5), and how the planet "was full of violence" (6:11). Kass, evidently, is not the only one to have overlooked the nonviolent aspects of the divine image in Genesis! Humanity shows itself quick to fail in this aspect of divine imaging, and to be guilty of repeat offenses on the matter. Before all that, however, "in the beginning," the human image of God is *primordially nonviolent* toward animals (1:29; 2:16; 9:4) *and* also, ideally, toward humans (9:5–6; cf. 4:10).[45]

The second thing missing from Kass's list is actually plural: the *many ways God is imaged* beyond the first chapter of the Bible and beyond its first book. As Yochanan Muffs has noted:

> The image of God in the Bible is not a monolith; the divine persona is refracted through a wide range of personal prisms. [For example,] Isaiah sees God as a city sophisticate; Ezekiel as a country bumpkin ... .[E]ach prophet, in his own style, captures different aspects of the divine person.[46]

---

[44] Davis, *Opening*, 11, notes how the blessing of God comes before the verbs speaking of human rule and so "the human exercise of skilled mastery [how Davis translates 'to have dominion'] must be intended to reinforce that prior blessing, not to annul it." Care for the non-human world may be set in contrast to the royal image in comparative perspective since ancient Near Eastern monarchs were often presented in excessively violent ways vis-à-vis animals, especially in the royal hunt. See Strawn, "Comparative Approaches," esp. 132–35; Strawn, "Image," esp. 70–72: "The nonviolent *imago* reflects the non-violent *Deus*" (72).

[45] There are further exhibits of divine nonviolence: God does not execute capital punishment on the first human couple, despite their transgression (Gen 2:17), neither does God take Cain's life (4:15). In both of these cases, the Deity spares the offenders, proving both patient and merciful.

[46] Muffs, *The Personhood of God*, 97.

The same holds true for the different accounts found within Genesis itself and the various traditions that make up the book (however those are parsed out). Even if the Pentateuchal sources are reduced to three – "the Picasso called D ... the Rembrandt called J ... the Blake called P"[47] – the range of presentation, replete with distinct emphases, is remarkable and impossible to reduce, let alone capture, especially in a brief essay like the present one.

Painting in broad brushstrokes, therefore, one might say that the presentation of God in the Bible is tragic, with the Lord "constantly torn between His love for Israel and His profound exasperation with them."[48] More specifically with regard to Genesis, one could – following Muffs – see God as naïvely optimistic in Gen 1 (e.g., 1:31: "God looked at everything ... and it was very good") only to watch God turn deeply pessimistic in the Flood Narrative (e.g., 6:7: "I am sorry I made them").[49] What transpires after the Flood – in which God realizes that, despite that desperate measure, "the inclination of the human heart" was still "evil from youth" (8:21) – might be seen as a transformation of initial divine optimism and subsequent divine pessimism

> into what one may call divine realism. God now realizes that He cannot expect perfection from man [sic] and that human corruption is something He will have to make peace with. Man [sic] is not totally good, nor is he totally bad; he is simply human. God concludes that the appropriate reaction to man's sinfulness is not an outburst of punitive anger ... but rather forbearance and educational discipline in harmony with man's less-than-perfect nature.[50]

Perhaps so, although this interpretation is not airtight (none are). With reference to the matters at hand, if the *imago* is a moving target, something to be realized (or not) in the course of Genesis (and in human life/ lives), divine realism about humanity may be present from the very beginning, not simply or only a hard lesson God derives from the Flood. The *imago*, that is, may be an "anthropological question" or "hermeneutical lens" (see above). Regardless, Muffs seems more right than wrong when he asserts that

---

[47] Ibid., 98; Muffs leaves out mention of an E source.
[48] Ibid., 99.
[49] Ibid., 99–100.
[50] Ibid., 100.

[i]n the first chapters of Genesis, God emerges before us as a moral personality who grows and learns through tragedy and experimentation to become a model for man. The crucial message is that even God makes mistakes and actually learns from them.[51]

This summation is a far cry from the impassable God of the later philosophers but seems on point for the biblical portrayal of God writ large, not just in the opening chapters of Genesis. Indeed, a number of scholars have tracked how God is presented across the entire Old Testament, not just in Genesis, with the results bearing noteworthy similarity to Muffs's accounting.

W. Lee Humphreys, for instance, has concluded that God is very much a moving target in Genesis. This is to say once again that, in terms of literary presentation, there is no one singular *imago Dei* but, rather, many *imagines*. Humphreys identifies no less than twelve divine images, which he maps onto particular blocks of text:[52]

God as:	Chapters in Genesis:
Sovereign Designer	1, 12–14, 15, 16–17, 23–24
Struggling Parent	2–3, 4, 12–14, 15, 16–17
Disciplining Father	2–3, 4
Destroyer-Sustainer	5–9, 18–19, 22
Jealous	10–11
Patron	12–14, 16–17, 23–24, 25, 26, 27, 28–30, 31, 32–36, 37–41
Patron Challenged	15, 32–36
Judge	18–19, 31
Deliverer	20–21, 25, 28–30
Savage	22
Opponent	32–36
Providential Designer	42–50

It is easy enough to quibble with some of Humphreys' categories and/or the texts he has associated with each;[53] the point, regardless, is

[51]   Ibid., 100.
[52]   See the chart in W. Lee Humphreys, *The Character of God in the Book of Genesis: A Narrative Appraisal* (Louisville: Westminster John Knox, 2001), 234–35; further passim, esp. 237–56.
[53]   Cf., e.g., Jack Miles, *God: A Biography* (New York: Alfred A. Knopf, 1995), who catalogues 24 categories across the entire Hebrew Bible, but only four for Genesis: creator, destroyer, creator/destroyer, and friend of the family (25–84). The

that the depiction of God in Genesis is on the move, in no small
measure because – and this is crucial – the human images of God are
on the move.[54] As an example, in his treatment of God's character as
a parent "engaging a child with a mind of its own," Humphreys
writes:

> Yahweh's parental engagement with his human creations entails
> a continued becoming on his part as well as theirs ... God the
> parent is a God becoming.[55]

Or, again, more generally this time:

> [Various divine reactions in Genesis] suggest that God himself, espe-
> cially in relation to a creation that is not as fully under his control or
> as ordered a whole as first depicted, is more complex and in process of
> becoming than our first construction of him suggests.[56]

Hence:

> The movement [of God's character] is from type to full-fledged
> character to agent, as we move from God the sovereign designer
> in Genesis 1 to the complex, multi-faceted, and changing figure in
> the bulk of Genesis 2–36, to God as an agent silently shaping
> events in the stories other characters tell of him in the latter
> segments of Genesis.[57]

These citations show that Humphreys thinks that "the character God"
recedes in the course of Genesis – a recession or "removal" that might be

metaphorical nature of categories like Miles's and Humphreys's should not be missed;
these categories are not always explicitly flagged as such in the narratives proper.

54 Humphreys, *Character*, 252: "once God enters into real relationship with the humans
he creates in Genesis 2, he enters a dynamic story-world that is often marked by
tensions and conflicts with other characters who are dynamic as well. For God to
engage these other characters entails the real possibilities of dynamic change and
development in his own being."

55 Humphreys, *Character*, 61 (his emphasis); see also 244, which adds that the process of
becoming reveals that God is "at points ... torn by inner conflict"; and 252: "the
character God is on a learning curve." Contrary to Humphreys and others (e.g.,
C. L. Crouch, "Genesis 1:26–27 as a Statement of Humanity's Divine Parentage,"
JTS 61 [2010]: 1–15), it may be doubted that there is any divine parental metaphor prior
to Exod 4:22; still further, there is no explicit identification of God as a male parent
prior to Deut 1:31 (see 32:5, 18 for divine father and mother metaphors). See Brent
A. Strawn, "'Israel, My Child': The Ethics of a Biblical Metaphor," in *The Child in the
Bible*, ed. Marcia Bunge, Terence E. Fretheim, and Beverly R. Gaventa (Grand Rapids:
Eerdmans, 2008), 103–40.

56 Humphreys, *Character*, 239.

57 Ibid., 241 (his emphasis); further, 242–43 and passim.

seen as a disappearance, gradual or otherwise, from the human scene.[58] He is not alone, with Richard Elliott Friedman tracking the mystery of God's disappearance in Scripture, and Jack Miles asking, at the conclusion of his own literary reading, "does God lose interest?"[59] In Miles' own words:

> The Lord God's life in the Tanakh begins in activity and speech and ends in passivity and silence ... Why does this work take the form of a long decrescendo to silence? Why does it, so to speak, begin with its climax and decline from there?[60]

Humphreys's analysis of Genesis paints it as nothing less than a microcosm of what Friedman and Miles see across the whole Hebrew Bible:

> After Genesis 36, God rarely acts and speaks no more, with the single brief exception of his final meeting with Jacob at Beer-sheba where God joins him in the descent into Egypt [46:1–4]. It is now [after this point] largely in the words of other characters that we meet God. He becomes a God constituted through their words. And while they speak of him in ways that recall his sovereign mastery in Genesis 1, we must temper their constructions with our realization of their own partiality and with our own experience of God in Genesis 2–36.[61]

But what does this "becoming" or "decrescendo" of the divine *imago* (and *imagines*) mean and what might it have to do with the human *imago/imagines* of God?

IMAGINES DEI, PART TWO: GOD'S HUMAN (NON-) IMAGE(S) IN GENESIS

Perhaps it means that God has "no life unconnected to his human creature."[62] Or perhaps it is some sort of desperate bid for divine

---

[58] Ibid., 237, 240, 246, and 271 n. 1. Humphreys's identification of this literary movement is correct (e.g., 254), but his interpretation of why it is present (i.e., why God would self-remove) is unconvincing to my mind. I hold the same judgment for Miles. See further below.

[59] See Richard Elliott Friedman, *The Disappearance of God: A Divine Mystery* (Boston: Little, Brown & Company, 1995); Miles, *God*, 397–408. The idea precedes both Friedman and Miles; see, e.g., Erich Fromm, *You Shall Be as Gods: A Radical Interpretation of the Old Testament and Its Tradition* (New York: Henry Holt, 1991 [1966]).

[60] Miles, *God*, 402. Miles goes on to posit both Job (404: "God's most perfect image") and Nehemiah (406: "the perfect reflection, the comprehensive self-image, the quasi-incarnation") as images of God.

[61] Humphreys, *Character*, 248.

[62] Miles, *God*, 402.

omniscience, achieved at the cost of solitude, or an attempt to grasp divine sovereignty at the cost of silence.[63] Whatever the case, does it mean that humans, now, are to be gods or at least godlike after God's slow retreat? That is, after all, one way to understand the *imago*, especially in comparative perspective: that humans rule in God's stead (see above) – though in varying ways, alternatively beneficent or malevolent,[64] as humans understand and enact such rule in Genesis.

But there is another option. God's "subsiding," if that is in fact what it is, might be viewed more positively. Instead of God receding out of weakness or passivity, or whatever, the attenuation of God's direct communication, self-characterization, and activity in Genesis (and the Bible writ large) might be seen as nothing less than the continuation of the primal divine generosity evident in Gen 1 that made room for other subjects beyond the divine self.[65] J. Gerald Janzen has argued that "the word that initiates the creative process" in Gen 1 is *there*, as in "Let *there* be light," because that is the word that makes room for *everything* else.[66] The creation of humankind in the divine image is just one more, even if somehow climactic, instance of God creating space: *there-ness*. And if the *imago* is a matter of function and proper ethic, not a given of dignified essence, then the rest of Genesis and God's tempered direction makes room for humans to answer the anthropological question evoked by the *imago*: will they image God or not?

The answer humans give is decidedly mixed.[67] As already noted, Gen 4 is quick to showcase the presence of sin that eventuates in murder with things devolving quickly thereafter.[68] And yet, the relationship of real integrity – the dynamism within God summoned in part by the dynamism of the created world, especially the dynamic human *imagines* – means that both the divine image and the human *imago Dei* constantly interact and adjust.[69] When humans fail to image God

---

[63] See ibid., 402–3; and Humphreys, *Character*, 246, respectively.

[64] For the latter, see Donald E. Gowan, *When Man Becomes God: Humanism and Hybris in the Old Testament*, PTMS 6 (Eugene: Pickwick, 1975).

[65] Cf. Steven A. Rogers, "The Parent–Child Relationship as an Archetype for the Relationship Between God and Humanity in Genesis," *Pastoral Psychology* 50 (202): 377–85; see Strawn, "Israel, My Child," 137–38 for discussion.

[66] J. Gerald Janzen, *When Prayer Takes Place: Forays into a Biblical World*, ed. Brent A. Strawn and Patrick D. Miller (Eugene: Cascade, 2012), 51, see also 46, and further, 51–52.

[67] See Briggs, "Humans," 119–24.

[68] It is common to find such problems even earlier, particularly in Genesis 3. For a recent treatment of this material, see Smith, *Genesis*. See also below.

[69] More generally, see Terence E. Fretheim, *God and World in the Old Testament: A Relational Theology of Creation* (Nashville: Abingdon, 2005).

rightly, there is usually a calling to account, which is often accompanied by a new strategy, as it were, in the divine plan. This is the familiar cycle of disobedience–punishment–grace identified by many scholars in the Primeval History, but the pattern of divine–human interactivity continues on, and apace, in the ancestral stories, particularly around the problems of progeny and blessing. To be sure, this interactive story and vibrant process of (non-)imaging is not all dreary; there are real high points: the righteousness of Noah, for example, who walked with God (Gen 6:9), and God's remembrance of Noah and all the animals on the ark (Gen 8:1). Or, again, there is the obedience of Abraham, quite mixed at the start and at several points along the way, but decisive, though devastating, in the end (Gen 22:12). And then there is Joseph.

Genesis ends with an extended block of material devoted to Jacob's favorite son (chs. 37–50). What is significant for present purposes is how Joseph "in his commanding authority and effective control seems in many ways to assume God's place in the last segments of the Genesis story";[70] put differently, Joseph may be a final and remarkably successful instance of the *imago*. This is perhaps most clear in the two important theological statements Joseph makes with reference to his brothers' act of selling him into slavery:

> Now, don't worry, and don't be angry at yourselves that you sold me here because God sent me before you in order to save lives ... God sent me before you to establish a remnant for you on the earth and to save you in a great deliverance. So, *you* did not send me here: it was God! He has made me a father to Pharaoh, lord of all his house, and master of the entire land of Egypt ... God has made me lord of all Egypt.
>
> (Gen 45:5, 7–8, 9)

> Don't be afraid! Am I in God's place? You planned evil against me; God planned it for good in order to do as is the case right now: to save many people. So, don't be afraid! I will take care of you and your little ones.
>
> (Gen 50:19–21a)

Both statements are made *by Joseph*, not by the narrator and not by God, but they are striking nevertheless in what they say about God and how they paint Joseph as a privileged interpreter of God's acts, even God's intentions. With reference to the *imago*, does this index a closeness between Joseph and God, signaled already by the earlier

---

[70] Humphreys, *Character*, 256; see also 249.

notice that "the LORD was with Joseph" (Gen 39:1) – a fact that was evident even to others who were not native YHWH-worshippers (Gen 39:3; cf. 41:38–39) – and slightly later, where, even in prison, YHWH is again said to be "with Joseph" showing him steadfast love (*ḥesed*) and giving him favor in the sight of his jailor (Gen 39:21, 23)? It would seem so, and, from the other side of the equation, it should be observed how frequently Joseph is found mentioning God, depicted as concerned with God's ways, and fond of giving credit to the Lord (Gen 39:9; 40:8; 41:16, 25, 28, 32, 51–52; 42:18, 23; 43:29; 48:9; 50:24).

This is not to say that Joseph is perfect. Readers often wonder about Joseph, especially early on, when he is presented at odds with his brothers (Gen 37:2, 4–5, 8, 11) and worthy of rebuke by his father (Gen 35:10). But that is Joseph at the start, premature – failing, or so it would seem, to properly image God. Joseph at the end, mature, is a very different *imago* in at least two ways, beyond the closeness between him and God that has already been mentioned.

First and most importantly, Joseph not only understands what has happened to him to be God's doing, he explicitly states that it is for the purpose of *saving life*. The life that is saved, furthermore, is not limited only to his immediate family circle. Joseph includes his clan within the deliverance, to be sure (Gen 45:7; 50:21), but Joseph is equally clear that the preservation of life is larger still: somewhat nondescript, perhaps, in Gen 45:5 ("lives") but explicated clearly as "many people" (*'am-rāb*) in Gen 50:20, including, therefore, the Egyptians.[71] Indeed, according to the narrator, Joseph's agricultural strategy was highly effective, not only for Egypt but for "the whole world" (Gen 41:57).[72]

Second, Joseph's key theological assertions are made in the context of *forgiving his brothers*. Matthew Schlimm has observed that Joseph functions here as an "anti-Cain": he is "a brother who has all the power and all the reasons to harm his brothers but instead turns away from anger, and, despite the inherent difficulties, offers forgiveness."[73] Schlimm continues: "There is thus a chiastic interplay between Gen 4:7 and the book of Genesis as a whole, moving from fratricide to forgiveness."[74] In terms of the *imago*, Joseph

---

[71] See Jacob, *Genesis*, 342; and Claus Westermann, *Genesis 37–50: A Continental Commentary*, trans. John J. Scullion (Minneapolis: Fortress, 2002), 205.

[72] Westermann, *Genesis 37–50*, 251, who thinks the outlook of the Joseph story is "universal" and that it "served a critical function in a period of strong nationalistic aspirations," pointing "to the creator who is concerned for all his creatures."

[73] Matthew Richard Schlimm, *From Fratricide to Forgiveness: The Language and Ethics of Anger in Genesis*, Siphrut 7 (Winona Lake: Eisenbrauns, 2011), 178.

[74] Ibid., 179.

models the nonviolent primordial image in a way that Cain does not, and this is not to mention how Joseph also images God's habits of mercy vis-à-vis Cain (Gen 4:15) and others (e.g., Gen 3:21; 8:21). It is worth noting that, in the second forgiveness scene, the brothers speak to Joseph as if he were God by the strategic use of prayer language, especially the unusual rhetorical particle *'ānnā'* (Gen 50:17), which is otherwise used only in direct prayer to God (Exod 32:31; 2 Kgs 20:3; Isa 38:3; Jonah 1:14; 4:2; Pss 116:4, 16; 118:25; Dan 9:4; Neh 1:5, 11). Not surprisingly, Joseph – positive *imago Dei* that he is – recognizes what his brothers are doing, but also knows that, at best, he is only an *image* of God, not God. Hence his response: "Am I in God's place?" (Gen 50:19). While Joseph appropriately and humbly eschews identifying with God, he nevertheless replies to the brothers' "prayer" by offering them what God so often gives in response to the prayers of Israel: an oracle of salvation – "Don't be afraid!" – not once but twice (Gen 50:19, 21a), following that with a promise to provide for his brothers and their toddlers (*ṭappĕkem*). In this way, the narrator concludes, Joseph comforted his brothers and spoke tenderly to them (Gen 50:21b).

So, although Joseph is definitely *not* God, he certainly acts *like* God. Or, put differently, Joseph *images* God. It comes as no surprise, therefore, that later Christian interpreters often understood Joseph to be a type of Christ, another image of the invisible God (Col 1:15; cf. Heb 1:3).[75]

LIMITS TO THE *IMAGO*, THE *IMAGINES*, AND DIVINE–HUMAN IMAGING

That Joseph acts *like* God harkens back to text (1) at the beginning of Genesis, where humans are made not only "in [*bĕ-*] the divine image" but also "according to" or "like [*kĕ-*] the likeness" of God. Being or acting like God, whether for good, as in the case of Joseph (et al.), or ill, as in the case of Cain (et al.), are case studies in whether or not humanity can and will *image* God.[76] But one last aspect of being "like God"

[75]   Gary A. Anderson, "Joseph and the Passion of Our Lord," in *The Art of Reading Scripture*, ed. Ellen F. Davis and Richard B. Hays (Grand Rapids: Eerdmans, 2003), 198–215. This essay is useful in highlighting the many ways in which the ancestors' characters are "tied to the very identity of God" and how their individual roles are bequeathed "to a much larger sodality, the nation Israel" (198–99). See also, more extensively, Jon D. Levenson, *The Death and Resurrection of the Beloved Son: The Transformation of Child Sacrifice in Judaism and Christianity* (New Haven: Yale University Press, 1993).

[76]   See Briggs, "Humans," 123.

must be mentioned: the limits Genesis places on imaging and the divine–human relationship.

In the Eden narrative, the possibility to be "like God" (*kē'lōhîm*) is part of the first challenge posed to humankind (Gen 3:5).[77] This story is too profound to engage here properly; it is enough to observe that the desire to be "like God," at first just a possibility presented by the serpent, turns out to be an actual reality, recognized by none other than God. At the end of Gen 3, the Deity remarks: "Look! Humanity has become like one of us (*kē'aḥad mimmennû*) knowing good and evil" (3:22a).

Note: the humans have *already become* like us! The text makes immediately clear that this newfound divine-likeness on the part of humanity, which evidently surpasses the likeness in the *imago* – constitutes some kind of threat to the divine world. It is something that the Deity must properly contain, which is accomplished by denying humans access to the tree of life (Gen 3:22b). Human beings may have become divine, at least to some degree, by their actions in the Garden, but they are denied immortality. They are, at best, little godlings with limited lifespans (Gen 6:3) to do good or ill with their remarkable God-like capacities.

The notion of divinization (Greek *theōsis*) becomes an important part of mystical religious experience, especially Christianity, in later periods, but here in Gen 3 the idea is something that causes concern. Some sort of boundary has been transgressed, and the problem has precisely to do with being (too much) "like God." Said differently, the divine–human (inter)relationship has limits. Divinization, at least in this part of Genesis, is a real theological problem that the book seeks to redress. If not *sui generis*, the problem of divinization may have become known to ancient Israelites via the ways various kings and heroes from well-known ancient Near Eastern epics were thought to be divine.[78]

---

[77] For a classic interpretation of the temptation to be *sicut Deus* ("like God"), see Dietrich Bonhoeffer, *Creation and Fall: A Theological Exposition of Genesis 1–3*, trans. Douglas Stephen Bax, ed. John W. de Gruchy, DBW 3 (Minneapolis: Fortress, 1997), 111–14.

[78] Note, e.g., that in various versions of the Etana legend, the hero's name is differently written: in the Old Version, simply Etana, in the Middle Assyrian Version, ᵐEtana (with the masculine determinative), and, in the Late Version, ᵈEtana (with the divine determinative: "divine Etana"). See J. V. Kinnier Wilson, *The Legend of Etana: A New Edition* (Chicago: Bolchazy-Carducci, 1985). The divinity of Gilgamesh, whose name is often written with the divine determinative and who is said to receive cult, is attested already in the Early Dynastic god list from Šuruppak (mid-third millennium BCE) and continues on into Neo-Assyrian lists. See A. R. George, *The Babylonian Gilgamesh Epic: Introduction, Critical Edition and Cuneiform Texts*, 2 vols. (Oxford: Oxford University Press, 2003), 1:70–90, 119–35. The divinization of Mesopotamian

Patrick Miller has noted that all three of the passages in the Primeval History where God uses "we-language" (Gen 1:26; 3:22; and 11:7) are places where the human and divine worlds come into close contact.[79] Many reasons for the so-called divine plural ("Let us ... ") have been offered in the history of interpretation, but Miller thinks the plural is present because these texts deal "with the divine world as such and not simply the god Yahweh."[80] At the end of Gen 3, the relationship between the divine and human worlds is very close – uncomfortably so. And so, while it is apparently humanly "possible to overstep the bounds and seek to blend the two [realms] into one," Gen 3:22 and 11:7 resist that. A similar scenario, but without "we-language," is found in the highly enigmatic story in Gen 6:1–4, which David Clines has called "a satanic parody of the idea of the image of God in man."[81] In this instance, the "breakdown" between the divine and human arenas "is from the reverse direction."[82] At issue in each of these four stories is "the nature of humanity, its sphere of life and its powers, and to what extent human nature and human domain overlap with divine nature"; in each case, "limits upon the 'ĕlōhîm-like creature are ... enforced."[83] Still other passages depict human characters overstepping their creaturely bounds,

and Levantine kings is debated, though it seems likely especially in early periods. See, inter alia, Loewenstamm, *Comparative Studies*, 48; Jacob Klein, "Sumerian Kingship and the Gods," in *Text, Artifact, and Image: Revealing Ancient Israelite Religion*, ed. Gary Beckman and Theodore J. Lewis, BJS 346 (Providence: Brown Judaic Studies, 2006), 115–31; and Peter Machinist, "Kingship and Divinity in Imperial Assyria," in *Text, Artifact, and Image*, 152–88. Naram-Sin is apparently "the first attested ancient Mesopotamian ruler to have used the divine determinative before his name" (Winter, *On Art*, 1:87; citing Walter Farber, "Die Vergöttlichung Naram-Sins," *Or* 52 (1983): 67–72). Note also Michael C. Astour, "Rdmn/Rhadamanthys and the Motif of Selective Immortality," in *"Und Mose schrieb dieses Lied auf": Studien zum Alten Testament und zum Alten Orient: Festschrift für Oswald Loretz zur Vollendung seines 70. Lebensjahres mit Beiträgen von Freunden, Schülern und Kollegen*, ed. Manfried Dietrich and Ingo Kottseiper, AOAT 250 (Münster: Ugarit-Verlag, 1998), 55–89. For the Egyptian material, see Labib Habachi, *Features of the Deification of Ramesses II*, ADAIK 5 (Glückstadt: J. J. Augustin, 1969); and Racheli Shalomi-Hen, *The Writing of Gods: The Evolution of Divine Classifiers in the Old Kingdom*, Göttinger Orientforschungen IV, Reihe Ägypten 38 (Wiesbaden: Harrassowitz, 2006), 159–60.

79   Patrick D. Miller, *Genesis 1–11: Studies in Structure and Theme*, JSOTSup 8 (Sheffield: University of Sheffield, 1978), 25. See also Lyle Eslinger, "The Enigmatic Plurals Like 'One of Us' (Genesis I 26, III 22, and XI 7) in Hyperchronic Perspective," *VT* 56 (2006): 171–84.

80   Miller, *Genesis 1–11*, 25.

81   David J. A. Clines, "The Significance of the 'Sons of God' Episode (Genesis 6:1–4) in the Context of the 'Primeval History' (Genesis 1–11)," *JSOT* 4 (1979): 33–46 (37).

82   Miller, *Genesis 1–11*, 26.

83   Ibid.

misappropriating divine responsibilities. Cain is once again a paradigmatic example as he inappropriately plays the role of "brother's keeper" (though he actually disavows it); it is God alone who properly – and safely – keeps humanity (see Ps 121:4; cf. Ps 4:8).[84]

A FINAL IMAGE

In point of fact, limits for the human *imago* seem present already in text (1), which states that humans are *not* God but only (and at best) *in* God's *image* and *after* God's *likeness* – which is to say "*similar . . . but not identical.*"[85] The many different instantiations of the human *imago*, the many *imagines* in Genesis and beyond, reveal that there are countless ways in which humans properly image God and/or fail to do so in comparison with God's own *imagines*. The biblical material in Genesis and beyond contributes much by way of rounding out the latter, especially in God's relentless pursuit of humankind, despite its many schemes (cf. Eccl 7:29).

On this point, one last image is worth pondering. In Genesis, God is frequently portrayed as *Lord of the womb*. In Genesis 20, after Abraham has pawned off Sarah as his sister for a second time, we learn that "the LORD had shut up entirely every womb in the house of Abimelech on account of Sarah, Abraham's wife" (v. 18). Only after Abraham prays does God heal Abimelech, his wife, and his maidservants "so they could bear children again" (v. 17). In Gen 25:23, God knows the contents of Rebekah's womb: that she is carrying twins. In Gen 29:31a, when YHWH sees that Leah was unloved, he opens her womb, and later does the same for her sister, Rachel, who is said to be infertile (Gen 29:31b). Before that turn of events, however, Jacob, apparently exasperated by the two sisters' rivalry, blurts out to Rachel's request for children: "Am I in the place of God, who has kept from you the fruit of the womb?" (Gen 30:2). The first part is identical to Joseph's response to his brothers in Gen 50:19: "Am I in God's place?" No, just as was the case with Joseph, Jacob is most certainly *not* God. Therefore, only God can give Rachel what she wishes – something that God does very quickly thereafter by opening her womb (Gen 30:22). That divine action confirms, in retrospect, that Rachel's infertility, which

---

[84] See Paul A. Riemann, "Am I My Brother's Keeper?" *Int* 24 (1970): 482–91.

[85] Wagner, *God's Body*, 153 (his emphasis). Von Rad, *Genesis*, 58 thought the divine plurals functioned to prevent "one from referring God's image too directly to God the Lord. God . . . conceals himself in this multiplicity." For a fascinating fictional treatment of how pronounced divine–human similarity is inescapably still distinct, see C. S. Lewis, *Perelandra: A Novel* (New York: Scribner, 1944), 176–77.

is *divinely rectified*, may also have been *divinely caused* (see 1 Sam 1:5–6). A bit earlier, in the previous generation,

> Isaac prayed to the LORD for his wife because she was infertile. The LORD granted his prayer, and his wife Rebekah conceived.
>
> (Gen 25:21)

The Hebrew word for "infertile" is *ʿăqārāh*. Besides the mentions in Gen 25:21, of Rebekah, and Gen 29:31, of Rachel – both of whose inability to conceive is reversed by God – there is only one other instance of *ʿăqārāh* in Genesis, at the very end of the Primeval History:

> Now Sarai was infertile (*ʿăqārāh*). She had no children.
>
> (11:30)

In light of Genesis as a whole, one might wonder if Sarai's infertility is yet another instance of God's control of the womb, its closing and also its opening. Genesis goes on to report, after all, that "the LORD visited Sarah just as he said, and the LORD did for Sarah just as he promised: Sarah conceived and gave birth" (Gen 21:1–2a; cf. also Pss 113:9; 127:3). If so, what Gen 11:30 may signal – in a subtle and yet not-so-subtle way – is nothing short of *the calling of Sarai*, prior even to the more famous calling of her husband, a calling that, in Sarai's case, occurs within and precisely because of her infertility. If so, the mystery of divine election does not wait until Abram in Gen 12, but is present already in the mysterious workings of God amid humanity – in this specific case, amid one family, one elderly couple, one woman and her womb – and how God uses that to set the world aright with humanity as *imago Dei*. What an image!

SELECT BIBLIOGRAPHY

Briggs,Richard S. "Humans in the Image of God and Other Things Genesis Does Not Make Clear." *JTI* 4 (2010): 111–26.

Garr, W. Randall. *In His Own Image and Likeness: Humanity, Divinity, and Monotheism.* CHANE 15. Leiden: Brill, 2003.

Humphreys, W. Lee. *The Character of God in the Book of Genesis: A Narrative Appraisal.* Louisville: Westminster John Knox, 2001.

Jónsson, Gunnlaugur A. *The Image of God: Genesis 1: 26–28 in a Century of Old Testament Research.* ConBOT 26. Stockholm: Alqvist & Wiksell, 1988.

Kass, Leon R. *The Beginning of Wisdom: Reading Genesis.* Chicago: University of Chicago, 2003.

McDowell, Catherine L. *The Image of God in the Garden of Eden: The Creation of Humankind in Genesis 2: 5–3:24 in Light of the* mīs pî *and* wpt-r *Rituals of Mesopotamia and Ancient Egypt.* Siphrut 15. Winona Lake: Eisenbrauns, 2015.

Middleton, J. Richard. *The Liberating Image: The* Imago Dei *in Genesis 1.* Grand Rapids: Brazos, 2005.

Miles, Jack. *God: A Biography.* New York: Alfred A. Knopf, 1995.

Petersen, Ryan S. *The* Imago Dei *as Human Identity: A Theological Interpretation.* JTISup 14. Winona Lake: Eisenbrauns, 2016.

Strawn, Brent A. "Comparative Approaches: History, Theory, and the Image of God." Pages 117–42 in *Method Matters: Essays on the Interpretation of the Hebrew Bible in Honor of David L. Petersen.* Edited by Joel M. LeMon and Kent Harold Richards. SBLRBS 56. Atlanta: Society of Biblical Literature, 2009.

Strawn, Brent A. "The Image of God: Comparing the Old Testament with Other Ancient Near Eastern Cultures." Pages 63–75 in *Iconographic Exegesis of the Hebrew Bible/Old Testament: An Introduction to Its Method and Practice.* Edited by Izaak J. de Hulster, Brent A. Strawn, and Ryan P. Bonfiglio. Göttingen: Vandenhoeck & Ruprecht, 2015.

11 Genesis, Science, and Theories of Origins

JITSE M. VAN DER MEER

INTRODUCTION

Discussions of religious faith and science have proceeded along four tracks: science, philosophy, systematic theology, and scriptural interpretation. The dominant dialogue between theology and science is mediated by philosophical categories. While less prominent, the engagement of science and Scripture has been addressed in several intersecting classifications each with a specific focus. James P. Hurd sketches three scenarios seeking to harmonize the paleontological record of human origins with Scripture.[1] Nicolaas Rupke surveys five discourses about Scripture and science in their social context from 1750 to 2000.[2] Gijsbert van den Brink describes five types of interpretation of Genesis 2–3, addressing the historicity of Adam and the Fall.[3] Deborah Haarsma and Loren Haarsma as well as Denis Alexander distinguish attempts at creating consistency between science and Scripture (scenarios, models).[4] Mark Harris addresses the "neglect of the Bible by the science-religion field" more broadly.[5] All aim at conflict resolution.

In this chapter, I focus first on material realities as interpreted in the experimental and historical natural sciences that engage the interpretation of creation texts in the Bible. This focus excludes readings of the

[1] James P. Hurd, "Hominids in the Garden," in Perspectives on an Evolving Creation, ed. Keith B. Miller (Grand Rapids, MI: Eerdmans, 2003), 208–33.
[2] Nicolaas A. Rupke, "Five Discourses of Bible and Science 1750–2000," in A Master of Science History: Essays in Honor of Charles Coulston Gillispie, ed. J. Z. Buchwald (Dordrecht: Springer, 2011), 179–95.
[3] Gijsbert van den Brink, Reformed Theology and Evolutionary Theology (Grand Rapids, MI: Eerdmans, 2020), 160–203; Jerry D. Korsmeyer, Evolution and Eden: Balancing Original Sin and Contemporary Science (New York: Paulist Press, 1998).
[4] Denis Alexander, Creation or Evolution: Do We Have to Choose? (Oxford: Monarch Books, 2014), 285–94, and 316–19; Deborah B. Haarsma and Loren D. Haarsma, Origins: Christian Perspectives on Creation, Evolution, and Intelligent Design, rev. ed. (Grand Rapids: Faith Alive, 2011).
[5] Mark Harris, The Nature of Creation: Examining the Bible and Science (Durham, UK: Acumen, 2013).

text that do not refer to material reality because science cannot address them. I include readings that refer to material reality irrespective of how the text is characterized. Further, I do not cover other attempts at conflict resolution – dismissal or reconstruction of science and dismissal of Genesis – because they do not address the interpretations of the creation stories. Finally, I omit non-scientific challenges to Genesis such as those originating in philosophical naturalism.

Second, I describe how historical science prompts a reinterpretation of Genesis. Third, this chapter covers the two decades following the period 1750–2000 covered by Rupke.[6] I consider cosmic evolution and human evolution. Along the way I address the reliability of specific methods and explanations for the natural sciences as a whole as well as for some of the specific conditions for the interaction of Genesis and evolutionary biology. I end with a concluding section. Thus, this chapter is not comprehensive in either a historical or systematic sense but instead offers a representative selection of developments during the last two decades focusing on the reliability of science and methodological issues in its interaction with Scripture.

THE COSMOS: BEGINNING AND END

I begin with an example of the common tendency to read science into the text. In the early 1930s some physicists and philosophers noticed a loose consonance of the Big Bang theory with the opening verse of Gen 1:1.[7] Michael Heller explains why caution is necessary in discussions about cosmology's relation to biblical interpretation. He distinguishes the mathematical description of the origin of the universe from its physical interpretation as the Big Bang theory, and the latter from its metaphysical and religious interpretation. Physical interpretation has no access beyond the point of origin of our universe. Thus, the nothingness our universe emerged from "is only what the model says nothing about.

[6]   Rupke, "Five Discourses," 185–88.
[7]   Dominique Lambert, *The Atom of the Universe : The Life and Work of Georges Lemaitre* (Krakow: Copernicus Center Press, 2015), 210–14; Lemaitre, who introduced the Big Bang theory, carefully kept his physical theory separate from the Genesis text. For purely theological and philosophical discussion, see Pirooz Fatoorchi, "Four Conceptions of *Creatio ex Nihilo* and the Compatibility Questions," in *Creation and the God of Abraham*, ed. David B. Burrell, Carlo Cogliati, and Janet M. Soskice (Cambridge: Cambridge University Press, 2010), 91–106; William R. Stoeger, "The Big Bang, Quantum Cosmology and *Creatio ex Nihilo*," in *Creation and the God of Abraham*, ed. David B. Burrell, Carlo Cogliati, and Janet M. Soskice (Cambridge: Cambridge University Press, 2010), 152–75.

What is outside the model, the model itself does not specify." This theoretical nothingness "has nothing in common with the 'metaphysical nonbeing' of philosophers and theologians."[8] Equating the theoretical nothingness of the model with an *ex nihilo* interpretation of Gen 1:1 assumes without justification that the two refer to the same reality. This not only fails to understand the limitations of the model, but also distorts the text by reading the theoretical nothingness of the model into an *ex nihilo* interpretation of the text of Gen 1:1.[9]

The Big Bang theory can have different interpretations provided they do not contradict the mathematical structure of the theory. One can interpret it as creation out of nothing or as a result of the loss of all information about a previous cycle of the evolution of the universe. This uncouples the physical theory from metaphysical or theological interpretation. Thus, the physical theory neither affirms nor denies the interpretation of Gen 1:1.[10] In this case, physics has no role in justifying the *ex nihilo* interpretation of a text taken to address the beginning of the universe.

Dissonance between science and the Bible exists about the end of the physical universe. The laws of physics predict that the universe will end in death by freezing or heating, whereas the Bible describes symbolically the creation of a new heaven and earth. Robert Russell and Joshua Moritz view the body of the resurrected Christ – the first-born of the new creation – as indicating that the new creation will be a transformation of the old one, not a replacement for it.[11] For Moritz, this transformation is an interpretation of 1 Cor 15: 36–46 and John 12: 24. Moritz takes these texts as an occasion to reinterpret scientific knowledge and thereby widen its scope. Russell makes two assumptions. First, the laws of nature are descriptive rather than prescriptive. He characterizes this as a philosophical assumption but interprets the laws of nature theologically as describing divine action in nature. Second, the faithfulness of divine action means that the laws of nature are uniform. The freezing

---

8   Michael Heller, *Creative Tension: Essays on Science and Religion* (Philadelphia, PA: Templeton Press, 2003), 84–86.

9   The *ex nihilo* interpretation is controversial: Fatoorchi, "Four Conceptions"; Mark Harris, *The Nature of Creation: Examining the Bible and Science* (Durham, UK: Acumen, 2013), 111–30.

10   Heller, *Creative Tension*, 85.

11   Joshua M. Moritz, "Big Bang Cosmology and Christian Theology," in *Theology and Science: From Genesis to Astrobiology*, ed. Joseph Seckbach and Richard Gordon (Hackensack, NJ: World Scientific, 2018), 345–72; Robert John Russell, *Time in Eternity: Pannenberg, Physics, and Eschatology in Creative Mutual Interaction* (Notre Dame, IN: University of Notre Dame Press, 2012).

or frying of the universe is a prediction based on this uniformity. But uniformity of the laws of nature is bounded by the notion of a new creation. Therefore, the freezing or frying end will not happen.[12] To conclude, in both Russell and Moritz we witness an engagement of science with texts about the new creation. In both, this engagement is mediated philosophically. In Russell via a presupposition of science. In Moritz, by the presupposition that the Bible and science address the same reality, that is, the end of the universe. The latter allows for a direct engagement of science; justification is not at issue because no new textual interpretations are offered.

HUMAN EVOLUTION

Numerous attempts at removing the dissonance between Scripture and evolutionary biology have taken Adam and Eve as material realities. Some of these will assume Adam and Eve are specific individuals, whether referred to literally or symbolically, while others address the first human couple as humankind in general or "Everyman." Below, I assess the main scientific claims regarding human ancestry and describe how the assumption of direct interaction with Scripture leads to exegetical challenges.

Adam's Contemporaries and Ancestors

Interpreters who take Adam and Eve to be the first and sole ancestors of modern humanity envision their special creation either *de novo* or from hominins created by evolution under divine guidance after which they were placed in the Garden. This view faces several scientific challenges. I limit myself to the issues of genetic diversity, nucleotide sequence similarity, ancient DNA, and genealogical ancestry.

Genetic Diversity

The proposal that Adam and Eve are not the only genetic ancestors of all humans is prompted by the study of population genetics and ancient DNA (below). According to Dennis Venema, the amount of genetic diversity in the human population today excludes Adam and Eve as the only genetic ancestors of humankind.[13] One measure of genetic diversity is the number of alleles of a gene in a population. Simplified, current

---

[12] Russell, *Time in Eternity*, 77–78.
[13] Dennis R. Venema and Scot McKnight, *Adam and the Genome* (Grand Rapids, MI: Brazos Press, 2017).

allelic diversity is proportional to its diversity in the founding population, the rate at which diversity increases through the accumulation of
mutations, and the time available for this accumulation since the founding population. A single ancestral couple, Venema suggests, does not
have enough allelic diversity to produce the diversity in humans today
even if they lived several hundred thousand years ago when anatomically
modern humans first appeared in the fossil record.[14] Only a large enough
ancestral population can supply this much diversity since anatomically
modern humans appeared. Estimates using genomic diversity data from
eighteen studies indicate that all humans today originate from
a population of slightly above 10,000 breeding individuals on average.[15]
Venema's conclusions have been questioned by population geneticists.[16]
Revisions of effective population size are expected.[17] More importantly,
more research is required to decide whether the human lineage had
a bottleneck of two individuals in the distant past.[18]

Nucleotide Sequence Similarity

Nucleotide sequences can be compared between extant organisms.
Similarities are used to construct DNA genealogies. When two populations become different species, they stop exchanging genes and start
accumulating genetic differences (mutations). The longer they have
existed as different species, the more differences have accumulated in

[14]   Ibid., 45–55.
[15]   The estimates reviewed by Cameron Smith, "Estimation of a Genetically Viable
       Population for Multigenerational Interstellar Voyaging: Review and Data for Project
       Hyperion," *Acta Astronomica* 97 (2014): 16–29 agree with those made independently
       by John H. Relethford, *Genetics and the Search for Modern Human Origins*
       (New York: Wiley-Liss, 2001). For a helpful review of the evidence, see Dennis
       R. Venema, "A reply to Dr. Richard Buggs," *BioLogos*, November 8, 2017, https://bi
       ologos.org/articles/a-reply-to-dr-richard-buggs/ which also has a clear nontechnical
       explanation of how past numbers of reproducing individuals are estimated. For
       a critique of Venema, see Richard Buggs, "Adam and Eve: Lessons Learned" (2018), h
       ttp://richardbuggs.com/index.php/2018/04/18/adam-and-eve-lessons-learned/#;mor
       e-220.
[16]   Richard Buggs, "Adam and Eve: A Tested Hypothesis?" (2017), https://natureecoevo
       community.nature.com/users/24561-richard-buggs/posts/22075-adam-and-eve-a-tes
       ted-hypothesis. Further discussion: http://theskepticalzone.com/wp/adam-and-eve-
       still-a-possibility/comment-page-3/.
[17]   Jinliang Wang, E. Santiago, and Armando Cabbalero, "Prediction and Estimation of
       Effective Population Size," *Heredity* 117 (2016): 193–206.
[18]   Preliminary discussion by William Lane Craig, *In Quest of the Historical Adam:
       A Biblical and Scientific Exploration* (Grand Rapids: Eerdmans, 2021), 338–55.
       Many of his arguments remain unresolved for lack of research published in the
       professional literature. For exceptions, see Richard Buggs, https://natureecoevocom
       munity.nature.com/posts/32171-adam-and-eve-lessons-learned.

their DNA. For instance, in a comparison of humans with chimps, gorillas, and orangutans, the number of differences increases in that order. That is, humans and chimps have the most recent common ancestor. The next common ancestor is that of humans, chimps, and gorillas and finally that of humans, chimps, gorillas, and orangutans. This approach uses the observation that similarities between offspring are inherited from a parent. Apart from occasional revisions due to new discoveries, DNA genealogies are well established. They show that if Adam and Eve existed as specific individuals, they had ancestors in the genus Homo and more remotely animal ancestors. That is, since extant humans inherited DNA segments from Neanderthals, Denisovans, and the common ancestor of chimpanzees, they cannot have Adam and Eve as their first and sole genetic parents.

Ancient DNA

Ancient DNA (aDNA) is recovered from ancient sources including frozen or mummified tissue, fossilized and non-fossilized bones, teeth, hair, feces, and chewing gum.[19] Comparative paleogenomics is the study of similarity of DNA segments between ancient and extant DNA. It shows that traces of Neanderthal DNA exist in all modern humans.[20] So some of the children of *Homo sapiens* and *Homo neanderthalensis* couples remained within the human population, and had children of their own.[21] This allows for the possibility that offspring of Adam and Eve intermarried with other species of the genus *Homo*. Both discoveries challenge the interpretation that Adam and Eve are the first and sole genetic ancestors of all humans.

The reliability and limits of aDNA recovery methods depend on preservation and contamination. Low temperature slows chemical breakdown, which can change the code. So, better preserved aDNA comes from cooler places and yields the best time limits. At 10 degrees Celsius, the Sima de los Huesos cave (Spain) yielded the oldest aDNA

---

[19] Theis Z. T. Jensen et al., "A 5700 Year-Old Human Genome and Oral Microbiome from Chewed Birch Pitch," *Nature Communications* 10.5520 (2019), 1–10.

[20] Reviewed in: Belen Lorente-Galdos, Oscar Lao, Gerard Serra-Vidal et al., "Whole-genome sequence analysis of a Pan African set of samples reveals archaic gene flow from an extinct basal population of modern humans into sub-Saharan populations," *Genome Biology* 20: (2019): 77.

[21] Evidence suggests that *H. neanderthalensis* mated with *H. sapiens*, not with a different taxon of hominins: Julia Galway-Witham, James Cole, and Chris Stringer, "Aspects of Human Physical and Behavioral Evolution during the Last 1 Million Years," *Journal of Quaternary Science* 34 (2019): 355–78. doi:10.1002/jqs.3137.

from the genus Homo at 430,000 years.[22] Ancient DNA from *Homo sapiens* reaches back 45,000 years.[23] But most of human evolution occurred in warm regions where aDNA breaks down fast. Fortunately, this problem has been circumvented and samples from places such as the Middle East have yielded aDNA that is up to 12,000 years old.[24] In the future the time limit for aDNA from the genus Homo may be further extended into the past.[25] Contamination is by DNA from microbes and researchers and is methodically minimized.[26] Thus, notwithstanding revisions required by new discoveries, the conclusions based on aDNA are reliable.

Genealogical Ancestry

Whereas genetic ancestry is based on similarity between nucleotide sequences, genealogical ancestry is based on family relations. Genealogical science documents these relations using archives, written family histories and, more recently, mathematical modeling and DNA. Genetic and genealogical ancestry are related ontologically in that similarities in nucleotide sequences are due to family relations. Put otherwise, the individuals in the family tree are the carriers of the similar DNA segments.

Family trees present a different perspective on human history from DNA trees. Any extant human has two parents, four grandparents, eight

---

[22]   Matthias Meyer, Juan-Luis Arsuaga, Cesare de Filippo, Sarah Nagel, Ayinuer Aximu-Petri, Birgit Nickel, Ignacio Martinez, et al., "Nuclear DNA Sequences from the Middle Pleistocene Sima de los Huesos Hominins," *Nature* 531.7595 (2016): 504–07. doi:10.1038/nature17405; Ewen Callaway, "Oldest Ancient-Human DNA Details Dawn of Neanderthals," *Nature* 531.7594 (March 17, 2016): 286.

[23]   Qiaomei Fu, Heng Li, Priya Moorjani, *et al*, "Genome sequence of a 45,000-year-old modern human from western Siberia," *Nature* 514, 445–449 (2014), https://doi.org/10 .1038/nature13810; Mateja Hajdinjak, Fabrizio Mafessoni, Laurits Skov, et al., "Initial Upper Palaeolithic humans in Europe had recent Neanderthal ancestry," *Nature* 592, 253–57 (2021). https://doi.org/10.1038/s41586-021-03335-3; Kay Prüfer, Cosimo Posth, He Yu, et al., "A genome sequence from a modern human skull over 45,000 years old from Zlatý kůň in Czechia," *Nature Ecology and Evolution* 5, 820–25 (2021), https://doi.org/10.1038/s41559-021-01443-x.

[24]   Iosif Lazaridis et al., "Genomic Insights into the Origin of Farming in the Ancient Near East," *Nature* 536. 7617 (2016): 419–24.

[25]   Enrico Cappellini et al., "Early Pleistocene Enamel Proteome from Dmanisi Resolves Stephanorhinus Phylogeny," *Nature* 574.7776 (2019): 103–7,

[26]   Bastien Llamas et al., "From the Field to the Laboratory: Controlling DNA Contamination in Human Ancient DNA Research in the High-Throughput Sequencing Era," *STAR: Science & Technology of Archaeological Research* 3.1 (2017): 1–14; Cesare de Filippo, Matthias Meyer, and Kay Prüfer, "Quantifying and Reducing Spurious Alignments for the Analysis of Ultra-Short Ancient DNA Sequences," *BMC Biology* 16.1 (2018): 121, https://doi.org/10.1186/s12915-018-0581-9.

great-grandparents, sixteen great-great-grandparents, and so on. Thus this individual has many genealogical ancestors. Since this applies to each extant human, each has many genealogical ancestors. That is, each genealogical ancestor has other offspring among extant humans. Therefore, extant humans share ancestors and going back in time their family trees are interconnected. As a result, "All humans alive descend from each of these" genealogical ancestors.[27] They are universal genealogical ancestors (UGAs). This was borne out by using mathematical models to simulate the full genealogy of humankind. They show that any particular couple in a population about 4,000 years ago can be a genealogical common ancestor of all present-day individuals.[28] The length of this period does not depend on its location on the time scale. For example, all humans alive at 1 CE could have had any particular couple in a population living about 4,000 years earlier as their universal genealogical ancestors. One of these couples could be interpreted as Adam and Eve, but there would have been other universal genealogical ancestors.[29] The genetic basis of Swamidass's proposal is sound and modeling of genealogical ancestry has produced well-established results.[30]

If the offspring of Adam and Eve married those outside the Garden, the genealogies of these two groups would have completed their merger about 4,000 years later. Only at that time could all extant humans be counted as their genealogical offspring. Before that time there would be humans who would not have Adam and Eve as their genealogical ancestors.

Combining the evidence in this section, the conclusion is that Adam and Eve are neither the first nor the sole ancestors of extant humans in

---

[27] S. Joshua Swamidass, "The Overlooked Science of Genealogical Ancestry," *Perspectives on Science and Christian Faith* 70.1 (2018): 19–35, here 22.

[28] Joseph T. Chang, "Recent Common Ancestors of all Present-Day Individuals," *Advances in Applied Probability* 31 (1999), 1002–26; Joseph T. Chang, Peter Donnelly, Carsten Wiuf, et al., "Reply to Discussants: Recent Common Ancestors of all Present-Day Individuals," *Advances in Applied Probability* 31 (1999): 1036–38; Jotun Hein, "Human Evolution: Pedigrees for all Humanity," *Nature* 431 (2004), 518–19; Rohde, Douglas L. T., Steve Olson and Joseph T. Chang, "Modelling the Recent Common Ancestry of All Living Humans," *Nature* 431 (2004): 562–66.

[29] S. Joshua Swamidass, *Genealogical Adam and Eve: The Surprising Science of Universal Ancestry* (Downers Grove, IL: IVP Academic, 2019), 42–47.

[30] Ibid., 43–47; Chang, "Recent Common Ancestors; Chang et al., "Reply"; Peter Donnelly, Carsten Wiuf, Jotun Hein, et al., "Discussion: Recent Common Ancestors of all Present-Day Individuals," *Advances in Applied Probability* 31 (1999): 1027–35.

both the genetic and the genealogical sense. Many view this as a challenge to the interpretation of Gen 2 and Rom 5:12–19 which is that all humans are sinners because two particular individuals, Adam and Eve, were the first and only parents of all humans.

Original Disobedience

Ancient Disease, Biological Death, and the Order of Nature
Paleontological and biological evidence challenges the interpretation of Gen 3 as referring to a change in the order of nature. Direct fossil evidence for disease includes a blood-engorged tick attached to a dinosaur feather fossilized in 99-million-year-old amber from the Cretaceous era,[31] a worm-shaped Arthropod (tongue worm) attached to its crustacean host (a marine invertebrate found in 425-million-year-old rocks),[32] cancer in fossil fish, amphibians, reptiles, and hominins,[33] and arthritis in dinosaurs.[34] Fossils also show evidence of predation.[35] Moving from extinct to extant organisms, food pyramids around the world incorporate predation in their function. On an individual scale, longevity in animals and humans is under genetic control.[36]

[31]   Enrique Peñalver et al., "Ticks Parasitised Feathered Dinosaurs as Revealed by Cretaceous Amber Assemblages," *Nature Communications* 8. 1924 (2017), https://doi.org/10.1038/s41467-017-01550-z.

[32]   David J. Siveter et al., "A 425-Million-Year-Old Silurian Pentastomid Parasitic on Ostracods," *Current Biology* 25.12 (2015): 1632–37.

[33]   For example: Bruce M. Rothschild and Larry D. Martin, *Paleopathology: Disease in the Fossil Record* (Boca Raton, FL: CRC Press, 1993); Bruce M. Rothschild, Brian J. Witzke, and Israel Hershkovitz, "Metastatic Cancer in the Jurassic," *Lancet* 354. 9176 (1999): 398; Patrick S. Randolph-Quinney et al., "Osteogenic Tumour in Australopithecus sediba: Earliest Hominin Evidence for Neoplastic Disease," *South African Journal of Science* 112. 7–8 (2016): 1–7; Edward J. Odes et al., "Earliest Hominin Cancer: 1.7-Million-Year-Old Osteosarcoma from Swartkrans Cave, South Africa," *South African Journal of Science* 112. 7–8 (2016), https://doi.org/10.17159/sajs.2016/20150471; Megan R. Whitney, Larry Mose, and Christian A. Sidor, "Odontoma in a 255-Million-Year-Old Mammalian Forebear," *Journal of the American Medical Association Oncology* 3. 7 (2017): 998–1000; Yara Haridy et al., "Triassic Cancer: Osteosarcoma in a 240-Million-Year-Old Stem-Turtle," *Journal of the American Medical Association Oncology* 5. 3 (2019): 425–26.

[34]   Jennifer Anné, Brian P. Hedrick, and Jason S. Schein, "First Diagnosis of Septic Arthritis in a Dinosaur," *Royal Society Open Science* 3.8 (2016).

[35]   Patricia H. Kelley, Michal Kowalevski and Thor A. Hansen, eds., *Predator-Prey Interactions in the Fossil Record* (New York: Kluwer Academic, 2003).

[36]   Serena Dato, Mette Soerenden, and Giuseppina Rose, "Untangling the Genetics of Human Longevity: A Challenging Quest," *Genes* (Basel) 10.8 (2019): 585, https://doi.org/10.3390/genes10080585 ; Giusi Taormina et al., "Longevity: Lessons from Model Organisms," *Genes* (Basel) 10/7 (2019): 518, doi:10.3390/genes10070518.

Finally, there are genetic diseases that are inevitable when a mutant gene is present.[37] Thus, predation, disease and biological death are not consequences of the Fall because they preceded the Fall. Further, without predation, disease and biological death, planet earth could not accommodate the numbers of plants and animals. Put otherwise, predation, disease and biological death belong to the order of creation. This evidence has prompted a reinterpretation of the curses in Gen 3:14–19, 4:11, 5:29, Deut 28:16–20.[38]

Behavioral Dispositions

What if humans inherited behavioral dispositions from hominin ancestors that were to be designated sinful by God, but existed before the Fall? For instance, paleontologists have discovered that *Homo sapiens* practiced lethal violence against other humans some 200,000 years ago, long before Adam and Eve are traditionally believed to have existed.[39]

Like ancient disease and biological death, such dispositions could not be the result of the Fall. Moreover, behaviors do not become sinful until after they have been declared to be so. Further, behaviors are not inevitable because they are influenced by many genetic and environmental causes. It is possible, but very unlikely, that hundreds of causes converge on an inevitable behavior rendering a person insane or incompetent and thus not responsible for his or her acts.[40]

Take, for instance, the disposition to empathy. Genes specific for a lack of empathy (psychopathy) have been reported.[41] There also is evidence for unspecific genetic influences in psychopathy.[42] They are correlated with the

---

[37] Denis Alexander, *Genes, Determinism and God* (New York: Cambridge University Press, 2017), 169–73.

[38] C. John Collins, *Genesis 1–4: A Linguistic, Literary, and Theological Commentary* (Phillipsburg, NJ: P&R Publishing, 2006), 162–66.

[39] Christopher P. E. Zollikofer et al., "Evidence for Interpersonal Violence in the St. Césaire Neanderthal," *Proceedings of the National Academy of Sciences of the United States of America* 99.9 (2002): 6444–48.

[40] Alexander, *Genes, Determinism and God*, 233–53.

[41] Kris H. Naudts, Ruben T. Azevedo, Anthony S. David, Kees van Heeringen, and Ayana A. Gibbs, "Epistasis between 5-HTTLPR and ADRA2B Polymorphisms Influences Attentional Bias for Emotional Information in Healthy Volunteers," *International Journal of Neuropsychopharmacology* 15.8 (2012): 1027–36; Shimon Saphire-Bernstein, Baldwin M. Way, Heejung S. Kim, David K. Sherman, and Shelley E. Taylor, "Oxytocin Receptor Gene (OXTR) is Related to Psychological Resources," *Proceedings of the National Academy of Sciences of the United States of America* 108.37 (2011): 15118–22; Varun Warrier et al., "Genome-wide meta-analysis of cognitive empathy: heritability, and correlates with sex, neuropsychiatric conditions and cognition," *Molecular Psychiatry* 23.6 (2017): 1402–9.

[42] "The results from 24 studies with quantitative data suggest that the heritability for CU [callous-unemotional] traits is likely between 36–67%." A. A. Moore, R. J. Blair,

neuroendocrine physiology of oxytocin.[43] But the epistemic status of this evidence is weak. "A majority of [the] 16 molecular genetic studies focused on candidate genes in the serotonin and oxytocin systems ... have not been well replicated."[44] Moreover, "Although two genome-wide association studies have been conducted, no genome-wide significant loci have been discovered."[45] It is well established that empathy depends on the normal functioning of molecular signals, hormones, and the brain like any human behavior. Their functions are genetically regulated and can be disturbed by mutation. But that does not make psychopathy inevitable because there are also environmental contributions. More broadly, with very few exceptions there is no scientific support for genetic determinism.[46] Finally, empathy depends on a material substructure which can suffer indirectly from genetic disturbances. This dependence leaves room for environmental contributions and for the exercise of free will.

A possible exegetical challenge may lie somewhere else. DNA-based studies put the genetic continuity between *Homo sapiens* and its evolutionary ancestors beyond reasonable doubt. Assume for the sake of argument that solid empirical evidence supports the conclusion that all humans including historical Adam and Eve (if they existed) inherited behavioral dispositions from animal ancestors. According to the synthetic theory, these dispositions were subject to random variation and natural selection and thus evolved in different directions. On the one hand, some would become sinful only after God revealed his expectations and only after they were directed against these expectations. Other tendencies would agree with the divine will.[47] This implies moral and religious relativism.[48]

J. M. Hettema, and R. Roberson-Nav, "The Genetic Underpinnings of Callous-unemotional Traits: A Systematic Research Review," *Neuroscience & Biobehavioral Reviews* 100 (2019): 85–97.

[43] T. R. Rice and N. E. Derish, "Oxytocin and Callous-unemotional Traits: Towards a Social-cognitive Approach to Forensic Analysis," *International Journal of Adolescent Medicine and Health* 27.2 (2015): 195–201.

[44] A. A. Moore, R. J. Blair, J. M. Hettema, and R. Roberson-Nav, "The Genetic Underpinnings of Callous-unemotional Traits: A Systematic Research Review," *Neuroscience & Biobehavioral Reviews* 100 (2019): 85–97.

[45] Ibid.

[46] Alexander, *Genes, Determinism and God.*

[47] Patricia A. Williams, "Sociobiology and Original Sin," *Zygon* 35.4 (2000): 783–812; Michael Ruse, *Can a Darwinian Be a Christian?* (Cambridge: Cambridge University Press, 2001), 205–6, 209–10; Gijsbert van den Brink, "Questions, Challenges, and Concerns for Original Sin," in *Finding Ourselves After Darwin: Conversations on the Image of God, Original Sin, and the Problem of Evil*, ed. Stanley P. Rosenberg, Michael Burdett, Michael Lloyd and Benno van den Toren (Grand Rapids: Baker Academic, 2018), 117–29, here 125.

[48] Ruse, *Can a Darwinian Be a Christian?*, 203–4.

Does this implication challenge Gen 1: 26–27 according to which humans have been created in the image of God? Take the view that the image of God includes the original perfection of Adam and Eve irrespective of whether they were a real couple or not. If original perfection is taken to mean 'sinless perfection,' it can be dismissed because it originates in an ancient non-canonical exegetical speculation.[49] Moreover, God considers sinful and imperfect people to be created in the divine image.[50] Religious and moral relativism can also challenge the interpretation of the image of God in terms of original holiness and righteousness. But sinful people can be holy and righteous by the grace of God.[51] What about the goodness of God? Perhaps God created people with good and evil dispositions because without evil dispositions a free rejection of God would not be possible. I am referring to a free will defense of moral evil, which is outside the scope of this study.[52]

To review, the initial question was whether the evolutionary creation of humans prompts reconsideration of traditional interpretations of Genesis. Therefore, my discussion focused on whether there are material causes of evil behavioral dispositions that would prompt such reconsideration. First, evolutionary creation of humans with sinful dispositions is consistent with an image of God understood as a characterization of people who by divine grace are holy, despite being imperfect and sinful. Second, if the evolutionary creation of humans was necessary to make free choice possible, then it does not challenge the exegetical grounds for the goodness of God.

EVALUATING SCIENCE

So far, I have assessed particular explanations in specialized domains of evolutionary biology that have prompted a reinterpretation of creation

---

[49] Harrison, Peter, *The Fall of Man and the Foundations of Science* (Cambridge: Cambridge University Press, 2007), 19–28, 155–56, 162–64; see also Wolfhart Pannenberg, *Systematic Theology*, vol. 2, trans. Geoffrey W. Bromiley (Grand Rapids, MI: Eerdmans, 2001), 212.

[50] Gen 9:6; Jas 3:9.

[51] 1 John 3:7; Jas 3:9; Thomas A. Noble, *Holy Trinity, Holy People: The Historic Doctrine of Christian Perfecting* (Eugene, OR: Cascade, 2013), 21–25; McCall, *Against God and Nature*, 368–78.

[52] Alvin Plantinga, *God, Freedom, and Evil* (Grand Rapids, MI: Eerdmans, 1977); James R. Beebe, "Logical Problem of Evil," *Internet Encyclopedia of Philosophy*, www .iep.utm.edu/evil-log/#;H8; Peter van Inwagen, *The Problem of Evil: The Gifford Lectures Delivered in the University of St. Andrews in 2003* (Oxford: Clarendon Press, 2006), 113; Rik Peels, "Does Evolution Conflict with God's Character?" *Modern Theology* 34 (2018): 544–64, doi:10.1111/moth.12435; Bethany N. Sollereder, *God, Evolution, and Animal Suffering: Theodicy Without a Fall* (New York: Routledge, 2019), 44.

texts. The next two sections are about assessing degrees of reliability of science as a whole, in order to determine the need for a reinterpretation of a text.

Assessing the Natural Sciences

I begin with conflict avoidance strategies that must be eschewed in such assessments. The first conflict is between literalistic interpretation of Genesis and science. This strategy targets explanation in the natural sciences. It emphasizes that observation underdetermines theory. This exposes explanation to subjective cultural influences since theories are human constructions.[53] A decision between a literalistic reading of Genesis or a scientific interpretation of the history of humankind is turned into a decision between equally subjective worldviews. The aim is to level the playing field between them and, thereby, to weaken the force of scientific knowledge.

Two objections apply. First, while it is true that culture can shape theory in the natural sciences, this does not diminish the role of theory testing. In fact, a theory can be both shaped by cultural influences (context of discovery) and supported by successful empirical tests (context of justification). Consider Dobzhansky, whose religion demanded that organisms be free to evolve. This was why he chose the so-called balance theory over the selection theory of evolution. But the balance theory also had empirical support. Culture alone does not determine theory content. Put otherwise, a cultural perspective can be logically disconnected from the theory it may have inspired.[54] Second, if cultural influence has led science astray, science can correct itself, for instance, by relying on mutually independent lines of evidence. Further, when new scientific knowledge forces the replacement of theories that support a worldview, new auxiliary hypotheses can connect the new theory with the existing worldview or the worldview can be corrected.

The second conflict avoidance strategy to be eschewed also involves literal interpretation. But the target is observation in the natural sciences rather than explanation. It extends the first strategy by arguing that since worldview shapes theory and theory directs observation, therefore

---

[53] Michael Ruse, *Monad to Man: The Concept of Progress in Evolutionary Biology* (Cambridge: Harvard University Press, 1996); Michael Ruse, *Mystery of Mysteries: Is Evolution a Social Construction?* (Cambridge, MA: Harvard University Press, 1999).

[54] Ruse, *Monad to Man*, 408; Jitse M. van der Meer, "Theodosius Dobzhansky: Nothing in Evolution Makes Sense Except in the Light of Religion," in *Eminent Lives in Twentieth-Century Science and Religion*, ed. Nicolaas Rupke (New York: Peter Lang, 2007), 79–101.

worldview directs observation. Thus observation is subjective. True, world-view as well as theory can *direct* observation. Darwin's observations of diversity came after he became familiar with his grandfather's speculations about evolution, but before he had his theory.[55] In physics, observation has become theory dependent as physics progressed to an advanced state of theoretical development. On the other hand, the discovery of meiosis and meiotic crossing over as one of the sources of hereditary variation was made by observing cell division without theory guidance.[56] The correlation between meiotic crossing over and genetic recombination was a theoretical proposal inferred from these observations. The point is that while worldview and theory may *direct* observation they do not *determine* what is observed and how it is interpreted. For instance, the new experi-mentalism has corrected the excessive emphasis on theory-dominated science by restoring the relative independence of experimental knowledge from high-level theory.[57] Thus, theory dependence of observation is not an all-purpose safety valve for conflict resolution with Genesis.[58]

A third conflict-avoiding strategy ranges from distinguishing to sep-arating the divine author's intended meaning (the literal meaning) from its accommodation to ancient Near Eastern culture. Walton and Swamidass exemplify the distinguishing strategy. No evaluation of their science is needed because Walton interprets Scripture independ-ently of science and Swamidass's science is sound. Lamoureux repre-sents the separating strategy. He wants to show that Scripture does not contain scientific knowledge – a view known as a form of concordism.[59]

[55] Janet Browne, *Charles Darwin: Voyaging*, vol. 1 (New York: Alfred A. Knopf, 1995).

[56] Gabriel Hamoir, "The Discovery of Meiosis by E. Van Beneden, a Breakthrough in the Morphological Phase of Heredity," *International Journal of Developmental Biology* 36 (1992): 9–15.

[57] Alan F. Chalmers, *What Is This Thing Called Science?*, 4th ed. (Indianapolis: Hackett, 2013), 179–96.

[58] For more on evaluating science, see Delvin Ratzsch, *Science and Its Limits: The Natural Sciences in Christian Perspective* (Downers Grove, IL: InterVarsity Press, 2000); C. John Collins, *Science and Faith: Friends or Foes* (Wheaton, IL: Crossway, 2003), 29–55; Vern S. Poythress, *Science and Hermeneutics: Implications of Scientific Method for Biblical Interpretation* (Grand Rapids: Zondervan Academic, 1988); Vern S. Poythress, *Redeeming Science: A God-Centered Approach* (Wheaton: Crossway, 2006); Philip Kitcher, *Vaulting Ambition: Sociobiology and the Quest for Human Nature* (Cambridge, MA: MIT Press, 1987); Philip Kitcher, *Abusing Science: The Case Against Creationism* (Cambridge, MA: MIT Press, 1982); Gijsbert van den Brink, Jeroen de Ridder, and René van Woudenberg, "The Epistemic Status of Evolutionary Theory," *Theology and Science* 15.4 (2017), 454–72.

[59] For different forms of concordism, see Denis Alexander, "The Various Meanings of Concordism," March 23, 2017, https://biologos.org/articles/the-various-meanings-of-concordism.

He argues that the scientific knowledge concordists believe is in the Bible – "ancient science" – has been falsified by modern science. Therefore, he rejects the "ancient science." Ancient science is the incidental form of the text that needs to be separated from its eternal theological message. Thus, there was no Garden, Adam and Eve did not exist nor did a Fall happen. The image of God and sin emerged gradually as humans evolved.[60] Van den Brink counters that form and message cannot be easily separated.[61] The theological meaning of the text is embedded in its form. For instance, the theological meaning of the dust from which Adam is created is that he is mortal because mortality is one of the meanings of 'dust.' You cannot throw out the dust without losing the mortality. Likewise, one of the theological meanings of the criticisms of ancient Near Eastern creation stories in Genesis is that the God of the Hebrews is unlike other gods.[62] You cannot throw out the form in which the criticisms are embedded without losing the God of the Hebrews. Collins notes Lamoureux's insistence on a literalistic reading of creation texts while he seems unaware of defensible alternatives that maintain the historical reality of Adam and Eve.[63] Lamoureux observes that "the identification of ancient science in Scripture requires modern scientific information."[64] Hence "science has hermeneutical primacy over Scripture in passages dealing with the structure, operation, and origin of the physical world."[65] But this overestimates the permanence of modern scientific knowledge. Moreover, the primacy of scientific knowledge ignores the possibility that worldview can influence scientific knowledge, without entailing it. This justifies the hermeneutical independence of the Bible's interpretation.

Evaluating Historical Science
Responses to challenges of Scripture by historical science range from dismissal or reconstruction of science, dismissal of Scripture, and viewing Scripture and science as complementary. Here are some examples from historical science.

---

[60] Denis O. Lamoureux, *Evolutionary Creation: A Christian Approach to Evolution* (Eugene, OR: Wipf & Stock, 2008), 205, 287–91, 319.
[61] van den Brink, *Reformed Theology*, 91.
[62] J. Richard Middleton, *The Liberating Image: The Imago Dei in Genesis 1* (Grand Rapids: Brazos Press, 2005), 185–231.
[63] C. John Collins, *Did Adam and Eve Really Exist? Who They Were and Why You Should Care* (Wheaton, IL: Crossway, 2011), 34, 115 n. 21.
[64] Lamoureux, *Evolutionary Creation*, 161.
[65] Ibid.

Comparative DNA studies indicate that life has a history. Some theologians and scientists take the scientific study of history to contradict a "plain sense" or "traditional" reading of the history of the world described in Genesis. To avoid this conflict they dismiss historical science as subjective in favor of objective experimental science.[66] But the distinction between objective and subjective science is outdated.[67] So, can the history of life based on comparative studies be taken as reliable science?[68]

Past events cannot be observed. Nevertheless, speciation has been observed in plants and animals though rarely, as expected.[69] Moreover, predictions have been made and tested. An evolutionary thought experiment by Alexander aimed at understanding what conditions might be required for a mammal to be eusocial. Subsequently a mammal was identified from an environment that matched the conditions of the prediction and it was found to be eusocial (the naked mole-rat).[70] The existence of feathered theropods in the fossil record was predicted using evolutionary principles before they were discovered. Four-winged gliding dinosaurs were predicted by Beebe nearly

---

[66]   Theologians: Norman L. Geisler and J. Kerby Anderson, *Origin Science: A Proposal for the Creation–Evolution Controversy* (Grand Rapids, MI: Baker Book House, 1987). Scientists: Charles Thaxton, Roger L. Olsen, and Walter Bradley, *The Mystery of Life's Origin* (New York, NY: Philosophical Library, 1984), 204–5; Henry Gee, *In Search of Deep Time* (New York: The Free Press, 1999), 5–8.

[67]   For in depth discussion, see Elliott Sober, *Philosophy of Biology*, 2nd ed. (Boulder, CO: Westview Press, 2000), 14–15, 18; Carol E. Cleland, "Historical Science, Experimental Science, and the Scientific Method," *Geology* 29.11 (2001): 987–90; Carol E. Cleland, "Methodological and Epistemic Differences between Historical Science and Experimental Science," *Philosophy of Science* 69.3 (2002): 447–51; Carol E. Cleland, "Prediction and Explanation in Historical Natural Science," *The British Journal for the Philosophy of Science* 62.3 (2011): 551–82; Carol E. Cleland, "Philosophical Issues in Natural History and Its Historiography," in *A Companion to the Philosophy of History and Historiography*, ed. Aviezer Tucker (Chichester, UK: John Wiley, 2011), 44–62.

[68]   John H. Walton, *The Lost World of Adam and Eve: Genesis 2–3 and the Human Origins Debate* (Downers Grove, IL: IVP Academic, 2015), 182–83.

[69]   Examples: Douglas E. Soltis and Pamela S. Soltis, "Allopolyploid Speciation in Tragopogon: Insights from Chloroplast DNA," *American Journal of Botany* 76.8 (1989): 1119–24; Jesús Mavárez, Camilo A. Salazar, Eldredge Bermingham, et al., "Speciation by Hybridization in Heliconius Butterflies," *Nature* 441 (2006): 868–71; J. Albert C. Uy, Robert G. Moyle, Christopher E. Filardi, and Zachary A. Cheviron, "Difference in Plumage Color Used in Species Recognition between Incipient Species Is Linked to a Single Amino Acid Substitution in the Melanocortin 1 Receptor," *The American Naturalist* 174.2 (2009): 244–54.

[70]   R. D. Alexander, "The Evolution of Social Behavior," *Annual Review of Ecology and Systematics* 5 (1974): 325–83.

ninety years before *Microraptor gui* was found.[71] The theory of plate tectonics and the theory that marsupials migrated from South America to
Australia via the Antarctic continent led to the prediction of fossil marsupials on the Antarctic continent which was confirmed.[72] Thus, predictions
derived from evolutionary theories can be tested, but less frequently than in
experimental science and provided they are formulated in a testable way.

Testing predictions is not the only similarity in the methodology
used by experimental and historical scientists. They also test interpretations of evolutionary phenomena using independent lines of evidence
converging on the same explanation.[73] For example, radiometric dating,
plate tectonics, and the geographic distribution of fruit flies on the
Hawaiian Islands represent three causally independent lines of evidence
converging on an explanation for the evolution of Hawaiian fruit flies.[74]

Finally, there are methodological differences between experimental
and historical science. In the experimental sciences reasoning predominantly moves from cause to effect. Experimentation serves to manipulate
causes in order to establish their effects. In the historical sciences reasoning
reverses direction from effect to cause. One has the effect – say the extinc-
tion of dinosaurs – and a set of hypothetical explanations. The task is to find
evidence that discriminates between them. When there are mutually independent lines of evidence converging on one account, explanation in the
historical sciences can be as reliable as that in the experimental sciences.[75]

CONDITIONS FOR INTERACTION OF GENESIS
AND SCIENCE

The use of scenarios (models) nuances the discourse about Genesis and
science. A scenario incorporates scientific knowledge and thus may go

---

[71]   C. W. A. Beebe, "A Tetrapteryx Stage in the Ancestry of Birds," *Zoologica* 2 (1915): 38–52.
[72]   W. J. Zinsmeister, "Cretaceous Paleogeography of Antarctica," *Palaeogeography,
       Palaeoclimatology, Palaeoecology* 59 (1987): 197–206, for the popular version:
       New York Times, www.nytimes.com/1982/03/21/us/antarctica-yields-first-land-
       mammal-fossil.html.
[73]   Example: radiometric dating, plate tectonics, and the geographic distribution of fruit
       flies on the Hawaiian Islands represent three causally independent lines of evidence
       converging on an explanation for the evolution of the fruit flies; see Stephen Stearns
       and Rolf F. Hoekstra, *Evolution: An Introduction* (Oxford: Oxford University Press,
       2005), 337–39.
[74]   Stephen Stearns and Rolf F, Hoekstra, *Evolution: An Introduction* (Oxford: Oxford
       University Press, 2005), 337–39.
[75]   Cleland, "Methodological and Epistemic Differences." For a helpful comparison
       between the approaches of historical scientists and legal experts, see Alexander,
       Creation or Evolution, 160–63.

beyond what can be justified by the text. It also incorporates knowledge from the Bible and theology and thus may go beyond what can be justified scientifically. Thus a scenario proposes a hypothetical reality which mediates interaction between Genesis and science.[76]

Science and the Bible can interact either directly or indirectly. Direct interaction is presupposed in the notion of scenario because it proposes a hypothetical reality which combines knowledge from both science and Genesis. Put otherwise, scenarios presuppose that science and Genesis are about the same hypothetical reality. This assumption can be problematic.

First, as Mark Harris observes, "Much of the perceived conflict between science and religion arises over competing claims regarding what is said to constitute reality."[77] Take social relationships as an example of reality. Some consider human friendship and animal cooperation as the same kind of reality by claiming that the former can be reduced to the latter. Thus, interaction between science and the Bible on social relationships would be direct. The competing claim is that friendship and animal cooperation are different categories of reality. Hence, interaction between science and the Bible would be indirect. The competition can be resolved empirically. For instance, in pursuing a common goal friends display a joint intentionality that marks human behavior as more than animal cooperation.[78] Epistemological reduction is also on the table. Even if there were an evolutionary explanation of religiosity, this would not explain the content of a particular religion. In these cases, ontological and epistemological claims are unwarranted metaphysical extensions of evolutionary explanation of human cooperation and religious belief. Such claims must be assessed in order to determine whether they are a scientific or a philosophical challenge to exegesis and whether the interaction between the Bible and science is direct or indirect.

Second, assuming that they are about the same reality before an independent interpretation has been completed runs the risk of reading scientific knowledge into the text as when Big Bang cosmology is read into Gen 1:1. We would then be assuming what needs to be argued,

---

[76]   For more on scenarios (models), see Alexander, *Creation or Evolution*, 284–88.

[77]   Harris, *The Nature of Creation*, 3, 172. My comments are merely scratching the surface of extensive debates about methodology in Scripture interpretation and in the interpretation of nature; see Ratzsch, *Science and Its Limits*.

[78]   Schloss, "Our Shared Yearnings"; Victoria Wobber et al., "Differences in the Early Cognitive Development of Children and Great Apes," *Developmental Psychobiology* 56.3 (2014), 547–73; Michael Tomasello, *A Natural History of Human Morality* (Cambridge, MA: Harvard University Press, 2016), 50–53.

namely, that Genesis and science are about the same reality. That question ought to be decided after interpreting the text and doing so independently of scientific concerns. During this stage many details of reading a text well come into view each contributing to this decision. Since I have no expertise in these areas I am happy to defer to others who do.[79]

Once it turns out that science and Genesis are about the same reality, the standard practice has been to let scientific developments provide the occasion for the reinterpretation of the Bible, provided the interpretation of the text is justified by the Bible itself.[80]

Third, science and Genesis may appear to address the same reality when in fact they are addressing categorically different aspects of that reality. As noted, many view the possibility that Adam and Eve had ancestors and contemporaries as a challenge to the interpretation of Gen 2 and Rom 5:12–19. According to this interpretation all humans are sinners because two particular individuals, Adam and Eve, were the first and only parents of all humans. To see this as a challenge presupposes that evolutionary biology is about the same reality as the creation texts and thus that they can interact directly. This view would seem to receive support from Gen 1: 26–28 which can be read as a story not about Adam and Eve as particular individuals, but about the origin of humankind as is evolutionary biology. A conflict arises when Gen 3:20, as well as the New Testament interpretations of Adam and Eve in Acts 17:26, Romans 5:12–21, and 1 Cor 15: 21–22, 45–49 are interpreted as affirming that a particular couple are the first and sole parents of all humans.[81]

---

[79] C. John Collins, *Reading Genesis Well* (Grand Rapids: Zondervan, 2018); John W. Hilber, *Old Testament Cosmology and Divine Accommodation: A Relevance Theory Approach* (Eugene, OR: Cascade Books, 2020).

[80] G. C. Berkouwer, *Studies in Dogmatics: Holy Scripture* (Grand Rapids: Eerdmans, 1975), 133 and Gijsbert van den Brink, "All the More Reason to Exercise Caution while Discussing Genesis: G. C. Berkouwer on Scripture and Science," in *Rerum Novarum: Neo-Calvinism and Roman Catholicism*, ed. George Harinck and James P. Eglinton (London: Blackwell, forthcoming). Others who use Berkouwer's approach include Henri Blocher, *Original Sin: Illuminating the Riddle* (Grand Rapids: Eerdmans, 1997), 39; Walton, *Lost World of Adam and Eve*, 103; Lydia Jaeger, "Theology: Implications for the Knowledge of Human Origins," *Themelios* 41.3 (2016): 427–46; Vern S. Poythress, *Science and Hermeneutics* (Zondervan: Grand Rapids, 1988), 24; Vern S. Poythress, *Interpreting Eden* (Wheaton: Crossway, 2019), 57–58; Ted Cabal, Loren Haarsma, and Kenneth Richard Samples, "The Original Couple: What is the Range of Viable Positions Concerning Adam and Eve?" in *Old-Earth or Evolutionary Creation?*, ed. Kenneth Keathley, Jim B. Stump and Joe Aguirre (Downers Grove, IL: IVP Academic, 2017), 50–55.

[81] A similar distinction between categorically different aspects of reality, i.e., between biological and theological humans, is made for the same reasons by Kenneth W. Kemp,

This conflict arises for at least two related reasons. First, there is a methodological conflict between the general and the particular. Biology is about human origins *in general*. By contrast, the way the apostle Paul reads Gen 3: 20 in Acts 17: 26 has been interpreted as affirming that Adam and Eve are *particular* individuals.[82] Second, assuming direct interaction allowed biological evidence to challenge the view that there was a particular couple who were the first and only parents of all humans. That status was theologically essential because it could explain the introduction and continuation of disobedience.[83]

These problems do not arise when biology and Genesis are taken to address categorically different aspects of human reality. This difference has been characterized variously as between biological and theological humans, between the evolution of the body and the origin of sin, and between genetic and genealogical ancestry.[84] For instance, according to Walton, the wider context of Rom 8: 17–26 and 1 Cor. 15: 21–22 and 45–49 shows that Gen 1 and 2 as well as Gen 3:20 and Acts 17: 26 are about the origin of sin and the need for redemption.[85] In contrast, evolutionary biology is about bodily evolution of the species *Homo sapiens*, transmission of DNA, etc. Thus, evolutionary biology and the creation texts address different aspects of humankind. As Walton observes, "the transmission of sin cannot logically be an issue of DNA."[86] This is also the point of Kemp's distinction between biological and theological humans as well as of Swamidass's distinction between genetic and genealogical ancestry.

S. Joshua Swamidass argues that the biological challenge to an historical interpretation of Adam and Eve raised in previous sections is due to the mistaken assumption that biology and Genesis are addressing the same reality, namely the reality of Adam and Eve as specific individuals.[87] He differentiates between three accounts of human history. First, population genetics and DNA sequence similarity offer

---

"Science, Theology, and Monogenesis," *American Catholic Philosophical Quarterly* 85.2 (2011): 219–36.

[82] For instance, Collins, *Genesis 1–4*, 166–67.

[83] See Gen 2; 3: 20 (Collins, *Genesis 1–4*, 166–67) as well as the New Testament interpretations of Adam and Eve in Acts 17:26, Romans 5:12–21 (Collins, *Genesis 1–4*, 180–82) and 1 Cor 15: 21–22, 45–49 (Collins, *Genesis 1–4*, 180 n. 80, 146–47; Collins, *Adam and Eve*, 78–80).

[84] Respectively: Kenneth W. Kemp, "Science, Theology, and Monogenesis," *American Catholic Philosophical Quarterly* 85.2 (2011): 219–36; Walton, *Lost World of Adam and Eve*; Swamidass, *Genealogical Adam and Eve*.

[85] Walton, *Lost World of Adam and Eve*, 92–95, 100–3, 186–89, 206.

[86] Ibid., 157.

[87] Swamidass, *Genealogical Adam and Eve*, 10, 25–26.

a *genetic* account of human history based on the transmission of segments of DNA. Second, a *genealogical* account concerns the family
history of individuals. Third, genealogical accounts in Scripture differ
from other genealogical accounts by virtue of their spiritual meaning in
the history of Israel.[88] Next, he uses genealogical science to show that in
the recent past Adam and Eve could have been among multiple genealogical ancestors of all extant humans.[89] That is, Adam and Eve are
neither the first nor the sole parents of all humans in the general genealogical sense. But they could be in the spiritual sense of the genealogies in
Scripture.

In sum, the genealogical account in the Bible is not about DNA and
the genetic account is not about spiritual meaning. That is, Genesis and
science are describing categorically different aspects of the same reality.
Therefore, the genetic account cannot challenge the Genesis text directly. For instance, it cannot challenge the spiritual meaning of the text
of Genesis. Nor can it challenge the creation of some humans in the
image of God (Gen 1: 26–27). But indirectly the genetic account has
prompted a reconsideration of traditional interpretations of the text
with the aim of creating consonance between science and Scripture.[90]
Finally, if Genesis is read genealogically it could be taken to address
spiritual realities among others.

By way of contrast consider Russell and Moritz, who take the resurrection of the body of Jesus as a hint at what reality in the new creation
looks like. They assume that the Bible and science address the same
physical reality – the end of the universe – and this makes direct engagement possible. But Harris raises the prior question of the extent to which
"the Bible's eschatological texts predict the *literal* fate of the physical

---

[88] Robert R. Wilson, *Genealogy and History in the Biblical World*, Yale Near Eastern
      Researches 7 (New Haven and London: Yale University Press, 1977); Joseph
      A. Fitzmeyer, review of *The Purpose of the Biblical Genealogies: With Special
      Reference to the Setting of the Genealogies of Jesus*, vol. 8, by Marshall D. Johnson,
      Theological Studies 30.4 (1969): 700–704.
[89] Swamidass, *Genealogical Adam and Eve*, 42.
[90] Alexander, *Creation or Evolution*; Gijsbert van den Brink, "Questions, Challenges,
      and Concerns for Original Sin," in Stanley P. Rosenberg, Michael Burdett,
      Michael Lloyd and Benno van den Toren eds., *Finding Ourselves After Darwin:
      Conversations on the Image of God, Original Sin, and the Problem of Evil* (Grand
      Rapids: Baker Academic, 2018), 117–29; Benno van den Toren, "Original Sin and the
      Coevolution of Nature and Culture," in *Finding Ourselves After Darwin:
      Conversations on the Image of God, Original Sin, and the Problem of Evil*, ed.
      Stanley P. Rosenberg, Michael Burdett, Michael Lloyd, and Benno van den Toren
      (Grand Rapids: Baker Academic, 2018), 173–86; Swamidass, *Genealogical Adam and
      Eve*, 184–200.

world." If "its apocalyptic predictions instead be meant metaphorically for social, political or religious transformation in history," then the Bible and science are addressing different realities.[91] So, to determine whether science and Genesis can interact in a particular case it is imperative to assume provisional independence.

When science and the Bible do not refer to the same reality, interaction may be mediated by philosophical categories such as the notion of control beliefs.[92] Three examples come to mind. First, Russell avoids direct interaction between science and the Bible by moving it to the methodological level. On that level the eschatological transformation of the cosmos described in Scripture functions to limit the scope of the uniformity of the laws of physics which is a philosophical issue. Since these laws describe divine action and God is free to act, God can introduce the radically new kind of action that introduces a new creation.

Second, philosophical mediation requires scientific and biblical concepts to be 'translated' into philosophical ones so that interaction can take place between them.[93] Take the notion of freedom in the thought of the geneticist Theodosius Dobzhansky. He read the Genesis story symbolically as referring to God's desire to create people who would freely love him. He "translated" this notion of freedom metaphorically into the notion of free organisms, that is, animals free to evolve in any possible direction. The latter notion appears as adaptability in the so-called balance theory of population genetics which he supported.[94]

The third example concerns the discussion of the image of God. Evolutionary psychology studies human behavioral dispositions inherited from animal ancestors in which they evolved in random directions. This can be interpreted as God preparing the creation of humans who can freely choose to behave according to or against God's will. Some of the dispositions that humans inherited from animals would be judged sinful once God revealed his expectations. Further, in preparation for revealing himself, God used evolution to create humankind with the

[91]   Harris, *Nature of Creation*, 161.

[92]   Nicholas Wolterstorff, *Reason Within the Bounds of Religion* (Grand Rapids: Eerdmans, 1976); Nicholas Wolterstorff, "On Christian Learning," in *Stained Glass: Worldviews and Social Sciences*, ed. Paul A. Marshall, Sander Griffioen, and Richard J. Mouw (Lanham, MD: University Press of America, 1989): 56–80.

[93]   Jitse M. van der Meer, "Assessing Metaphor as Mediator Between Christianity and Science," *Philosophical Inquiries* 3.1 (2015): 157–82; Jitse M. van der Meer, "Interpreting Nature and Scripture: A New Proposal for their Interaction," in *Christianity and the Human Body: A Theology of the Human Body*, ed. Robert Brungs, SJ and Marianne Postiglione, RSM (St. Louis, MO: The ITEST Faith/ Science Press, 2001), 38–72.

[94]   van der Meer, "Theodosius Dobzhansky."

capacity for religiosity and thus for responding to his call. This new calling was for humans to live in a loving relationship with God, that is, to be an image of God.[95] The recipients of this call were not morally perfect. They displayed both good and bad behavior. But they would know that they were sinful because God had revealed his expectations for a holy and righteous life.

Such scenarios assume that evolutionary psychology and the Bible are addressing the same reality. But this implies that God would have created dispositions to morally corrupt behavior questioning the goodness of God.[96] For some the evolution of human freedom is the greater good that justifies God's manner of creation as in Plantinga's free will defense of moral evil.[97] But the consensus is that this defense has limited value as a solution for the human case.[98]

Consider instead that Genesis and evolutionary psychology are dealing with two different aspects of the same reality. Genesis 1 – interpreted symbolically – is about humankind being created in the image of God for a relation of love and trust. Evolutionary psychology is about behavioral dispositions humans inherited from animals. Bethany Sollereder connects the two with the notion of divine love. She interprets the freedom of animals to evolve in any direction as a manifestation of divine love "allowing radical freedom of the other," which precludes complete control but includes direction.[99] This mediating notion of divine love is an idea in philosophical theology. Thus the interaction between the two different realities is mediated philosophically.

CONCLUSIONS

The challenges from science for readers of Genesis originate in the historical natural sciences. This chapter covered challenges to diverse interpretations of Gen 1–3 prompted by cosmic and human evolution.

---

[95] Eph. 4:24 and Col. 3:10 look forward to the holiness and righteousness of humanity in the new creation. According to van den Brink (*Reformed Theology*, 139) they do not refer to the original creation of humankind in the image of God in Gen 1:26–27. Since the texts themselves make that comparison, I take them that way in this paragraph.

[96] Sollereder, *God, Evolution, and Animal Suffering*, 107: "God is culpable for setting up a system with such significant freedoms that grave harms may occur, but such a system with real and effective choice is essential to the nature of the love that creates."

[97] Alvin Plantinga, *God, Freedom, and Evil* (Grand Rapids, MI: Eerdmans, 1977).

[98] James R. Beebe, "Logical Problem of Evil," *Internet Encyclopedia of Philosophy*, https://www.iep.utm.edu/evil-log/#;H8.

[99] Sollereder, *God, Evolution, and Animal Suffering*, 94, 115, 135–37, 163, 165–73.

Circumstances under Which Challenges from Science Arise

Science can challenge readers of Genesis either directly or indirectly. Which one applies ought to be decided after interpreting the text and doing so independently of scientific concerns. This is to avoid assuming what requires proof, namely, that they are about the same reality.

When science and the Bible address the same material reality science can challenge the Bible directly as exemplified by how Russell and Moritz addressed the future of the cosmos. This applies independently of whether the scientific account is inspired by philosophical materialism or reductionism provided there is solid empirical support. It is, therefore, essential to distinguish natural phenomena from their explanation in the natural sciences and the latter from their philosophical interpretation. This also applies irrespective of whether the text is read literally or symbolically. Therefore, it also is crucial to distinguish the biblical text from its interpretation and the latter from wider philosophical frameworks.

Science can challenge the Bible indirectly when they address different realities or address the same reality in categorically different ways and the challenge is mediated philosophically (see Russell, Sollereder). Without philosophical mediation, the challenge of science to Genesis fails.

How Scholars of Genesis Have Responded to Challenges from Science

Biblical scholars have considered a larger range of interpretative options than could be covered here. For instance, an adequate treatment of the principle of accommodation was not possible within the available space.[100] Moreover, the focus on challenges to the interpretation of texts is just one of several responses to evolutionary biology and to failing conflict resolution strategies.

One strategy for dismissal of science appeals to the subjectivity of both the natural and the historical sciences as human enterprises. This fails because their subjectivity does not diminish their reliability. Another dismissal strategy appeals to the subjectivity of the historical sciences in particular, but opposes it to the objectivity of the natural

---

[100]   On accommodation applied to interpretation of texts about nature in relation to science: Amos Funkenstein, *Theology and the Scientific Imagination from the Middle Ages to the Seventeenth Century* (Princeton: Princeton University Press, 1986); Hilber, *Old Testament Cosmology and Divine Accommodation*; Denis O. Lamoureux, *The Bible and Ancient Science* (Tullahoma, TN: McGahan Publication House, 2020), 53–58, 137–45.

sciences. This fails because while the natural and the historical sciences are distinct in methodology, they can be similar in reliability and subjectivity.

Conflict between Genesis and science is an occasion for a mutually independent re-evaluation of science and textual interpretation. Evaluation of science must include its limitations and presuppositions. Evaluation of textual interpretation must be separate from science in order to respect their methodological independence.[101]

SELECT BIBLIOGRAPHY

Alexander, Denis. *Creation or Evolution: Do We Have to Choose?* Oxford: Monarch Books, 2014.

Blackwell, Richard J. *Galileo, Bellarmine, and the Bible.* Notre Dame, IN: University of Notre Dame Press, 1991.

Bono, James J. *The Word of God and the Languages of Man: Interpreting Nature in Early Modern Science and Medicine 1: Ficino to Descartes.* Madison, WI: University of Wisconsin Press, 1995.

Collins, C. John. *Science and Faith: Friends or Foes.* Wheaton, IL: Crossway, 2003.

Craig, William Lane. *In Quest of the Historical Adam: A Biblical and Scientific Exploration.* Grand Rapids: Eerdmans, 2021.

Haarsma, Loren. *When Did Sin Begin: Human Evolution and The Doctrine of Original Sin.* Grand Rapids: Baker Academic, 2021.

Harris, Mark. *The Nature of Creation: Examining the Bible and Science.* Durham, UK: Acumen, 2013.

Harrison, Peter. *The Bible, Protestantism, and the Rise of Modern Science.* Cambridge: Cambridge University Press, 1998.

Hilber, John W. *Old Testament Cosmology and Divine Accommodation: A Relevance Theory Approach.* Eugene, OR: Cascade Books, 2020.

Howell, Kenneth J. *God's Two Books: Copernican Cosmology and Biblical Interpretation in Early Modern Science.* Notre Dame, IN: University of Notre Dame Press, 2002.

Ratzsch, Delvin. *Science and Its Limits: The Natural Sciences in Christian Perspective.* Downers Grove, IL: InterVarsity Press, 2000.

Rupke, Nicolaas A. "Five Discourses of Bible and Science 1750–2000." Pages 179–95 in *A Master of Science History: Essays in Honor of Charles Coulston Gillispie.* Edited by J. Z. Buchwald. Dordrecht: Springer, 2011.

Swamidass, S. Joshua. *Genealogical Adam and Eve: The Surprising Science of Universal Ancestry.* Downers Grove, IL: IVP Academic, 2019.

[101] I am grateful for comments by Richard Averbeck, Koert van Bekkum, Clayton Carlson, Mark Harris, John Hilber, Lydia Jaeger, Hans Madueme, Joshua Swamidass, and David Wilcox.

van den Brink, Gijsbert. *Reformed Theology and Evolutionary Theology*. Grand Rapids, MI: Eerdmans, 2020, chapter 3.

van der Meer, Jitse M. and Scott Mandelbrote, eds. 2008. *Nature and Scripture in the Abrahamic Religions: Up to 1700*. 2 vols. Leiden: Brill.

van der Meer, Jitse M. and Scott Mandelbrote, eds. 2008. *Nature and Scripture in the Abrahamic Religions: 1700–Present*. 2 vols. Leiden: Brill.

Walton, John H. *The Lost World of Adam and Eve: Genesis 2–3 and the Human Origins Debate*. Downers Grove, IL: IVP Academic, 2015.

12 Genesis and Ethics

ECKART OTTO

A MORAL CHALLENGE: HERMENEUTICAL PROBLEMS OF AN ETHICS OF THE BOOK OF GENESIS

Biblical ethics reflects upon maxims of moral behavior from the perspective of normative good and examines its legitimations and justifications, as well as the consequences of what can be called a morally positive or negative behavior. If maxims of good behavior are to be derived from historical narrative traditions, such an undertaking is confronted with the problem that implicit maxims of moral behavior are entangled with a number of other motifs and can never be isolated purely. The narratives of the Bible are subject to this challenge for any reconstruction of a historical ethos and its ethics. Their moral maxims were also anchored in the cultural contexts and ideals of their time. Although biblical narratives, including some in the book of Genesis, were ethically self-reflecting, they participated in the historicity of the cultural ideal motifs of their time.[1] The solution for the resulting hermeneutical problem for any historical ethics due to the "nasty gap of history" (Gotthold Ephraim Lessing) – the tensions between modern ethical maxims and those of the Bible – is the main problem for any biblical ethics of the Torah or more specifically, the book of Genesis. The methodological consequence of this tension is that an ethics of the book of Genesis must first be descriptive in nature, before any questions of its applicability to the ethics of the twenty-first century can be discussed, which will be beyond the scope of this contribution.

If someone takes up the Bible today to find ethical guidance for his or her daily life and starts to read the book of Genesis as its entrance gate, the reader will become more and more puzzled. They will discover that

[1] For maxims of biblical ethos and their anthropological foundations in their East Mediterranean contexts, see Eckart Otto, "Encountering Ancient Religions: Law and Ethics," in *Religions of the Ancient World*, ed. Sarah Isles Johnston (Cambridge, MA: Harvard University Press, 2004), 84–97.

all the holy characters of the venerable patriarchs and their wives from Abraham up to Jacob and his sons acted again and again rather selfishly and immorally. Abraham delivered his wife Sarah to foreign rulers and did not protect her from the king in Egypt (Gen 12:10–20) nor from Abimelek, the king in Gerar (Gen 20:1–18), even claiming that she was his sister. Sarah, because she was barren, delivered her slave-girl Hagar to Abraham. But when Hagar became pregnant with Ishmael, Sarah treated her harshly (Gen 16:1–15) and expelled her from Abraham's house, so that Hagar had to flee to the desert ready to die (Gen 21:8–21).[2] Abraham's son Isaac copied his father, when he disowned his wife Rebekah delivering her to the king of Gerar, Abimelek, claiming that she was his sister. The patriarch Jacob did not act any better than his father or grandfather and was so immoral in many aspects of his behavior that the people gave him the name "the deceiver." His name, which was semantically derived from the Semitic root 'qb, meaning "God is near," was also interpreted via a folk etymology in Gen 27:36 (cf. also Hos 12:4), which was connected with the Hebrew root 'āqab "to deceive." This interpretation highlighted Jacob's role as a deceiver, recalling the time Jacob defrauded his brother Esau of his birthright in Gen 27:1–40 and then later cheated his uncle Laban out of his flock, while Rachel, Jacob's wife, stole Laban's deities (Gen 31:1–21). The pattern of immorality continued to the next generation as well – in Gen 34 Jacob's sons Simeon and Levi illegally killed all the male citizens of Shechem, although they had contracted a connubium with the Shechemites. In Gen 35:22 Reuben had intercourse with his father's concubine Bilhah. In Gen 37 Jacob's sons sold their brother Joseph into slavery because of their jealousy over Jacob's love for him. These misdeeds of the patriarchs and the apparent condoning of their numerous lapses in judgment are rather confusing for readers of the Bible, who do not expect moral ambiguity here but a clear and ideal moral profile of its acting heroes as moral paradigms.

The moral ambiguity in the narratives of the book of Genesis caused readers to look for apologetical strategies to create a morally unequivocal text by eliminating or downplaying especially those aspects in the narratives which contradicted modern moral standards and sentiments. One of the apologetic strategies was to find an answer in the anthropology of the primeval stories in Gen 1–11, especially in the narrative of the fall of

---

[2] For the Ishmael texts in Gen 16 and Gen 21, which had a tendency to parallelize Ishmael and Isaac, see Thomas Naumann, *Ismael: Israels Selbstwahrnehmung im Kreis der Völker aus der Nachkommenschaft Abrahams*, WMANT 151 (Göttingen: Vandenhoeck & Ruprecht, 2018).

humankind in Gen 3, so that the negative aspects in the ethos of the patriarchs was interpreted as expression of a sinful human nature, which should be the result of the fall of mankind in Gen 2–3. In this interpretation it was God's grace alone which elected Israel's patriarchs. But this apologetical solution was theologically thwarted by another problem. If Israel's patriarchs in their moral ambiguity cannot be models and examples of morals, then God himself should be this ethically unequivocal model without any kind of moral ambiguity. But examining God's actions in the primeval history narrated in the book of Genesis also raises theological problems. In the meta-mythical perspective of monotheism in the creation-narrative of Gen 1:1–2:3 God was thought to be both almighty and good as His creation of the world and human beings was portrayed as perfect and morally good. The main presupposition of the acting God in the following narratives was His omnipotence and goodness. Gen 1:31 told the reader "God saw all what he had made, and it was good" and this judgment included the creation of mankind in Gen 1:26–30. But looking at God's actions in Genesis with these criteria for God's divinity in mind, starting with the narrative of the fall of mankind in Gen 2–3, raises doubts in the mind of the reader. The consequence of the divine opacity in Gen 2–3 was the catastrophe of all the pre-diluvian generations of mankind, so that its annihilation with the exception of Noah's family was a further aspect of divine moral ambiguity in the book of Genesis. Even more problematic and not at all unequivocal seemed to be God's position in the narrative of "Isaac's binding" in Gen 22, where God demanded Abraham kill and sacrifice his son Isaac. This divine command was unethical, because what God demanded from Abraham contradicted any human ethos and any program for an ethics of *imitatio Dei*,[3] which sought to see in the divine actions a model for an ideal human ethos. Moral ambiguity on the human and the divine side in Genesis seems to shatter any ethics which tries to find ethical models and examples in the narratives of this book.

A second apologetic strategy beyond looking for any *imitatio hominis sive Dei* argues that the moral ambiguity of human actions in the narratives of Genesis owed to the fact that the divine legal and moral order of the Sinai-pericope was not yet revealed, so that the patriarchs and their families did not yet know of this divine legal and moral order.

---

[3] For an ethics of imitation of God in the Hebrew Bible, see John Barton, *Ethics in Ancient Israel* (Oxford: Oxford University Press, 2014), 263–72; see also Eckart Otto, *Theologische Ethik des Alten Testaments*, Theologische Wissenschaft 3/2 (Stuttgart: Kohlhammer, 1994), 85–86; Otto, " Ethics. III. Bible. 1. Old Testament," in *Religion Past and Present*, vol. 4, ed. Hans Dieter Betz et al. (Leiden: Brill, 2008), 580–82.

But this explanation does not solve the theological problem of moral ambiguity of the patriarchs and their wives, because after the revelation of the divine legal order at Mount Sinai the moral ambiguity in the actions of the people did not stop but continued as in Genesis (so in the narratives of murmuring of the Exodus generation in the desert in Num 14; 20 and 25). The Sinai revelation did not solve the problem of moral ambiguity in the narratives of biblical protagonist. On the contrary the divine revelation at Mount Sinai itself causes problems for any biblical ethics, for example by the death penalty for a son who was rebellious against his parents, or for adultery (Lev 20:10; Deut 21:18–21; 22:22), and by mutilation as penalty for an assault (Exod 21,23–24; Lev 24:19–20; Deut 19:21). The Sinai-revelation did not solve the problem of ethical ambiguity in the book of Genesis but represented a moral problem of its own because of the fundamental differences between its ancient moral standards and modern maxims of ethics. Once again, we see the hermeneutical "nasty gap," which could not and cannot be overcome by any hermeneutical or exegetical ploy.[4]

A third apologetical strategy to deal with the moral ambiguity in narratives of Genesis and their morally negative traits of behavior was offered by liberal Old Testament scholarship of the late nineteenth and early twentieth centuries. These scholars tried to overcome the "nasty gap" of historicity of biblical ethos by reconstructing the development of biblical ethics as a process of moral progress. By recognizing the increasing denaturing, internalization, individualization, and universalization of interiorized moral values in biblical texts, pre-Deuteronomistic and pre-priestly narratives in Genesis could be seen as mirrors of early moral standards in Israel's history, which were in part an inheritance of a pre-Canaanite nomadic life in the desert and in part a product of Canaanite agricultural culture. These early influences still impacted the ethics in Israel after the conquest of its Promised Land. J. M. Powis Smith wrote in 1925:

> The wonder is not that there is so much of the crude and primitive and sensuous in the morals of the early Israel, but that the soul of the people persisted in seeking after the higher things and gradually shook off all these lower materialistic habits and developed for itself a moral life that has held the admiration of mankind.[5]

---

[4] See also John Barton, *Ethics and the Old Testament*, 2nd ed. (London: SCM Press, 2002), 1–7.

[5] See J. M. Powis Smith, *The Moral Life of the Hebrews* (Chicago: University of Chicago Press, 1925), 5–6.

In his construction of Israel's moral evolution, God's moral development was seen as part of the improvement of moral standards in Israel's history of ethics. In the early pre-Deuteronomistic and pre-priestly history of biblical religion and ethics God was credited with sentiments, purposes, and actions, "that are very human, and indeed in some cases, quite inhuman."[6] In order to spotlight the higher moral values of the prophets, the pre-priestly patriarchal narratives of the book of Genesis were interpreted as witnesses of a primitive moral standard.[7] This kind of construction of the development of Israel's moral standards in liberal nineteenth-century scholarship was based on historico-critical decisions of what was early and what was late in the Hebrew Bible, which meant that the ethics were built on a kind of circular reasoning. It was unsatisfactory that these kinds of evolutionary constructions were based on what is now considered the rather problematic exegetical hypotheses of Wellhausian source criticism in the Pentateuch and on the application of ethical criteria taken from nineteenth-century models of the evolution of morals. As we have seen, the moral ambiguity in the narratives of Genesis can cause readers to call into question the biblical ethics of Genesis, but we can also expect that the narratives of this book can give an answer to such doubtful and critical attitudes.

NARRATIVE TRACTATES ON META-ETHICS IN THE BOOK OF GENESIS

In Gen 49:2–7 Jacob blamed Reuben, "for you went up onto your father's bed, onto my couch and defiled it," and Simeon and Levi were cursed, "for they have killed men in their anger and hamstrung oxen as they pleased."[8] Where did Jacob derive the values to blame his sons Reuben, Simeon and Levi? Jacob's son Joseph acted in an entirely different way from his brothers by striving for reconciliation. Again, one must ask, where did he get the maxims for his actions? If, in the narratives, the behavior of the patriarchs was implicitly valued positively or negatively, one must ask for the criteria and implicit values for such an evaluation and, ultimately, for the legitimation of these implicit values in the

---

[6] See ibid., 7.
[7] For a history of writing on Old Testament ethics in the last two centuries see Eckart Otto, *Theologische Ethik*, 12–17; Otto, "The Study of Law and Ethics in the Hebrew Bible/Old Testament," in *Hebrew Bible/Old Testament: The History of Its Interpretation III/2: The Twentieth Century*, ed. Magne Sæbø et al. (Göttingen: Vandenhoeck & Ruprecht, 2015), 594–621.
[8] For a post-exilic reception and interpretation of Gen 49:3–7 see Deut 33:6.8–11. For the omission of Simeon in Moses' blessings in Deut 33, see Eckart Otto, *Deuteronomium 23,16–34,12*, HThKAT (Freiburg: Herder, 2017), 2233–34.

narratives of Genesis, so that the readers of this book could agree to them and receive ethical guidance for their lives. The legitimation and justification of fundamental moral values and norms of behavior inherent in the narratives of Genesis was a topic of an inner-biblical meta-ethics. Genesis contains several narrative tractates on meta-ethics, so in Gen 2–3; 22 and 38, which differed categorically from didactic-sapiential narratives which aimed at the imitation of their moral "heroes" as representatives of an implicit moral behavior like Joseph in Gen 37 and 39–50.[9] The narrative in Gen 38 was written and incorporated into the Joseph story in order to argue for a Judean openness to foreign strangers[10] comparable to the book of Ruth,[11] but Gen 38 was not a didactic narrative in the sense that the acting subjects were representatives of different moral standards and values of biblical wisdom literature as was the case with the Joseph narrative. The acting persons were drawn as characters who had to decide in situations of moral conflicts and dilemmas: God chastised Er and Onan because of their selfishness and wickedness disregarding the levirate duty, so that both had to die. Judah, who had not realized that it had been God himself who killed his sons, was afraid of losing his last son and prevented him from fulfilling his levirate obligation. The readers of this chapter should realize that Judah was in a tragic conflict and aporia between following the obligation of continuing the family and genealogy of his eldest son on the one hand and risking the life of his youngest son on the other. For the readers it was evident that Judah's decision, to save the life of his youngest son, was an obviously terrible mistake, caused by the fact that Judah did not know the real reasons for the death of his sons. Therefore, the readers themselves should identify the criteria for Judah to decide in such a morally aporetic conflict. If they were of the opinion and came to the solution that in such

---

[9]   See Gerhard von Rad, "Josephsgeschichte und ältere Chokma," in *Gesammelte Studien zum Alten Testament*, 4th ed., ed. Gerhard von Rad, TB 8 (Munich: Kaiser, 1958), 272–80. For several perspectives on a biblical anthropology in the Joseph narrative, see Eckart Otto, "Die 'synthetische Lebensauffassung' in der frühköniglichen Novellistik Israels: Ein Beitrag zur alttestamentlichen Anthropologie," *ZTK* 74 (1977): 82–97.

[10]   This attitude was related to the integrative perspective of the Elohim-texts in Genesis; cf. Reinhard Achenbach, "The Post-Priestly Elohim: Theology in the Book of Genesis," in *Ein Freund des Wortes*, ed. Sebastian Graetz et al. (Göttingen: Vandenhoeck & Ruprecht, 2019), 1–21; cf. also n. 25.

[11]   For Genesis 38 as a narrative of biblical ethics, see Thomas Krüger, "Genesis 38 – ein 'Lehrstück' alttestamentlicher Ethik," in *Konsequente Traditionsgeschichte*, ed. Rüdiger Bartelmus et al., OBO 126 (Fribourg: Universitätsverlag; Göttingen: Vandenhoeck & Ruprecht, 1993), 205–26. For the legal background in the narrative in Gen 38, see Otto, *Theologische Ethik*, 57–61.

a conflict the decision required him to follow the legal obligations of the Torah – in this case the duty to fulfill the levirate according to Deut 25:5–10 – then the narrative explained to them that this solution would be far too simple. When Judah learned that his daughter, although widowed, became pregnant by prostituting herself, he decided to kill her according to the legal obligation of that time to protect the genealogy of his son by the death penalty for his daughter-in-law according to Deut 22:21 and Leviticus 21:9.[12] Once again Judah did not know the real facts and circumstances, so he was unaware that his decision to simply follow the legal obligations and commands of the Torah would be responsible for an act of plain injustice. The readers of the story again knew more than Judah, who was not aware of the fact that Tamar had decided to strive for the survival of the family and its genealogy of her deceased husband. The first lesson the readers of this narrative tractate on meta-ethics had to learn, was to accept that situations which called for moral decisions were often more complex and complicated than they seemed to be on the surface, because, and this is a second lesson the readers had to learn, God could be the acting subject hidden behind the scene and under the surface of human actions and this could imply that the real facts were hidden for a naïve observer of the scene, as Gen 38:7.10 demonstrated. The third lesson the readers had to learn was that they must know the criteria by which to decide what a moral action would be and what made an action unmoral. Simple reliance on Torah could sometimes lead to a hasty decision, since the application of the legal and moral rules of the Torah to a concrete situation might result in an injustice without a comprehensive and exact knowledge of all the real facts and circumstances as they are told in Gen 38:24–26. One may argue that the authors of Gen 38 intended to demonstrate that without the revelation of a divine moral and legal order at Mount Sinai ethical conflicts like those in Gen 38 could not be solved. But one has to admit that none of the rules and prescriptions of the revealed Sinaitic order could have helped Judah to solve these ethically aporetic conflicts. Furthermore, the literary history of Gen 38 speaks against such an apologetic theory – that the authors of Gen 38 intended to demonstrate the necessity of revelation of the Sinai-Torah for solving a moral aporia. Gen 38 represents a rather late, post-exilic, narrative, which was inserted into the Joseph story in order to argue against the prohibition of intermarriage of the Torah in Exod

---

[12] For the legal-historical context of the family law in Deut 22:21 and Lev 21:9, see Eckart Otto, *Deuteronomium 12,1–23,15*, HThKAT (Freiburg: Herder, 2016), 1705–26.

34:11–16 and Deut 7:1–7.[13] So the question of criteria for moral decisions needs another answer and the authors of Gen 38 did not hesitate to deliver it in Gen 38:24–26, when Judah commented on Tamar's effort to enforce her right for levirate by rather dubious means:

"She is more righteous than I am (ṣādəqāh mimmennî)" (Gen 38:26).

The root ṣdq does not mean "justice" here in the sense of an Aristotelian *iustitia distributiva* but rather in the sense of loyalty to a community where the acting subject was living, so that the noun could also be used in the plural form for several acts of solidarity.[14] Judah qualified Tamar's behavior as "just" in the sense of "loyal" to the welfare of the family by saving its genealogy and future with a son. In cases of moral conflicts of different ethical values and options, acting for the welfare of the societal community in which they were living had to be a decisive criterion for their moral decisions. This means that the narrative in Gen 38, read as a tractate of meta-ethics, was pleading for a type of ethos of responsibility. This kind of ethos corresponded to the biblical anthropology of the social nature of human beings as corporate persons. Commentaries of Genesis often qualify the narrative of Gen 38 as "profane" or "secular," because its core section in Gen 38:12–30 does not speak of any divine actions or revelations. But Gen 38:7–10 shows God as a secret actor in the background, so that the narrative is not at all profane. The portrayal of God as only acting in a secret manner in the background meant that the human actors had to make decisions based on their own conscience and orientated on the value of the concept implied by the verbal root ṣdq.[15] This solution of a meta-ethics in the narrative in Gen 38 begs the question: how is the freedom and competence of the individual human being to decide on his or her own how to realize ṣedeq (the noun) for his or her societal context, theologically and anthropologically founded and legitimized in the narratives of Genesis?

[13] For the legal historical context of the prohibitions of intermarriage in Exod 34 and Deut 7, see Eckart Otto, *Deuteronomium 4,44–11,32*, HThKAT (Freiburg: Herders, 2012), 847–49, 855–58, and 862–64.

[14] See Otto, "Synthetische Lebensauffassung," 371–74; Otto, "Law and Ethics," 84–87.

[15] One can qualify the ethos as one of the types of an ethics of responsibility ("Verantwortungsethik") and separate it with Max Weber from the ethos of an ethics of ultimate ends ("Gesinnungsethik"). For Max Weber's interpretation of "ethics in the time of the patriarchs" see his *Ancient Judaism*, trans. Hans H. Gerth and Don Martindale (Glencoe, IL: The Free Press, 1952), 49–57. For the interpretation of Max Weber's economical ethics of Ancient Israel in the context of his program of an "Economical Ethics of the World Religions" see Eckart Otto, "Max Weber's Sociology of Ancient Judaism as Part of His Project on the Ethic of the World Religions," in *Max Weber's "Economic Ethic of the World Religions": An Analysis*, ed. Thomas C. Ertman (Cambridge: Cambridge University Press, 2017), 307–45.

The narrative in Gen 2–3 answers these questions. This narrative was also to be read as a narrative tractate on meta-ethics as a key text not only for all of Genesis but for all the Torah in the Pentateuch. Like Gen 38, the narrative in Gen 2–3 too showed a certain distance from the divine order of the Torah, which was revealed at Mount Sinai. Gen 2:24 reads: "A man leaves his father and mother and is united to his wife, and they become one flesh." Gen 2:24 dissolved the rule of exogamy by subversively turning it round. This rule was constitutive for biblical family law in the revelation of Torah in the Sinai-pericope and in its interpretation by Moses in Deuteronomy.[16] Gen 2–3 should be read from the perspective of Gen 1 implementing in Gen 2:24 the idea of the equality of man and woman in Gen 1:27,31: "So God created mankind in his own image, in the image of God he created them ... God saw all that he had made, and it was very good. And there was evening, and there was morning – the sixth day."

But the life-experiences of all the readers of these priestly verses told them something entirely different – namely, male dominance over women and many other evils in the world. Neither world nor human beings were perfect and good – on the contrary, there was much human suffering from many evils in the world, which had been, as Gen 1 told, so well created. The authors of the narrative tractate in Gen 2–3 intended to give a solution of this contradiction between the priestly theological theory of a perfect divine creation of the world and humankind in Gen 1 and the realm of human experiences in the real world. They tried to answer the question how and why evil came into a perfectly created world.[17] A long tradition of exegetical scholarly interpretation of the narrative in Gen 2–3 as a story of the

---

[16]   See Otto, *Theologische Ethik*, 39–54; Otto, " Die Rechtsgeschichte von Familie und Ehe im antiken Judentum der Hebräischen Bibel: Die Dialektik genealogischer und religiöser Normenbegründung im Familienrecht," in *Ehe – Familie – Verwandtschaft: Vergesellschaftung in Religion und sozialer Lebenswelt*, ed. Andreas Holzem and Ines Weber (Paderborn: Schöningh, 2008), 65–88.

[17]   See Eckart Otto, "Der Urmensch im Paradies: Vom Ursprung des Bösen und der Freiheit des Menschen," in *Die Tora: Studien zum Pentateuch. Gesammelte Schriften*, ed. Eckart Otto, BZABR 9 (Wiesbaden: Harrassowitz, 2009), 679–89. For the literary historical context of Gen 2:4–3:24 which was incorporated into Genesis, after the priestly creation account in Gen 1:1–2:3 was written and followed this priestly creation narrative also in a literary historical perspective, see Eckart Otto, "Die Paradieserzählung in Genesis 2–3: Eine nachpriesterschriftliche Lehrerzählung in ihrem religionshistorischen Kontext," in *"Jedes Ding hat seine Zeit". Studien zur israelitischen und altorientalischen Weisheit*, ed. Anja Diesel et al., BZAW 241 (Berlin: de Gruyter, 1996), 167–92; cf. also Joseph Blenkinsopp, *The Pentateuch: An Introduction to the First Five Books of the Bible*, ABRL (New York: Doubleday, 1992), 60–67, and Jean-Louis Ska, *Introduction to Reading the Pentateuch*, trans. Pascale Dominique (Winona Lake, IN: Eisenbrauns, 2006), 191.

"fall" understood its theological intention in that way – that the authors of Gen 2–3 wanted to say that the first human couple was responsible for the evil which came into human lives after the good and perfect creation because they had disregarded a divine command.[18] Thereby the authors of the narrative in Gen 2–3 intended to warn their readers of the dangers of eating from the fruits of the "tree of knowledge" and aspiring after "being like God." This meant that these authors of Gen 2–3 intended to exhort their readers to follow the divine prohibitions and orders.[19] But this interpretation misses the intention of the authors of Gen 2–3, the theological kerygma of this narrative, and its meta-ethical theory. The story does not promote or forbid specific human behavior but says simply that the first couple did, in fact, eat forbidden fruit. This is a decisive difference.[20] The authors of Gen 2–3 took part in a post-exilic biblical debate about human abilities to distinguish between good and evil and, in this context, to recognize the divine moral order which was thought to determine what was good and what was evil, and which was responsible for the success and disaster of those who were obedient to this order or neglected it.[21]

These questions were already controversially debated in Job and its supplements with Job 32–37 on the one side and Job 28 on the other.[22] The author of Job 28 asks,

> Where can wisdom be found? Where is understanding dwelling? No mortal comprehends its worth, it cannot be found in the land of the living ... God understands the way to it and he alone knows where it dwells, for he views the ends of the earth and sees everything under the heavens.
>
> (Job 28:13–14, 23–24)

---

[18] See *Paradise Interpreted: Representations of Biblical Paradise in Judaism and Christianity*, ed. Gerald P. Luttikhuizen, Themes in Biblical Narrative 2 (Leiden/Boston: Brill, 1999); Philip C. Almond, *Adam and Eve in Seventeenth-Century Thought* (Cambridge: Cambridge University Press, 1999); Martin Metzger, *Die Paradieserzählung: Die Geschichte ihrer Auslegung von J. Clericus bis W.M.L. de Wette*, Abhandlungen zur Philosophie, Psychologie und Pädagogik 16 (Bonn: Bouvier, 1959).

[19] Cf., e.g., Odil Hannes Steck, *Die Paradieserzählung: Eine Auslegung von Genesis 2,4b–3,24*, BibS(N) 60 (Neukirchen-Vluyn: Neukirchener, 1970).

[20] Cf. Konrad Schmid, *Theologie des Alten Testaments* (Tübingen: Mohr Siebeck, 2019), 110.

[21] See Eckart Otto, "Woher weiß der Mensch um Gut und Böse? Philosophische Annäherungen der ägyptischen und biblischen Weisheit an ein Grundproblem der Ethik," in *Recht und Ethos im Alten Testament: Gestalt und Wirkung*, ed. Stefan Beyerle et al. (Neukirchen-Vluyn: Neukirchener, 1999), 207–31.

[22] See also Barton, *Ethics in Ancient Israel*, 169.

Qohelet resumes Job 28's acknowledgment of the human incapacity to recognize the divine order and what was good or bad *sub specie Dei*, in God's eyes, so that we mortals had to discover on our own what was good and what was evil. Qohelet 8:16–17 refers to Job 28, saying,

> When I applied my mind to know wisdom and to observe what is done on earth ... no one can comprehend what goes on under the sun. Despite all their efforts to search it out, no one can discover its meaning. Even if the wise claim they know, they cannot really comprehend it.

Ben Sirach voted for the opposite position[23] on the basis of a priestly theology of creation and the covenant theology, writing,

> Counsel, and a tongue, and eyes, ears, and a heart He gave them to understand. Withal He filled them with knowledge of understanding, and showed them good and evil. He set His eyes upon their hearts, that He might show them the greatness of His works. He gave them the glory in His marvelous acts forever, that they might declare His works with understanding. And the elect shall praise his holy name. Besides this He gave the knowledge and His law of life for a heritage. He made an everlasting covenant with them, and showed them His judgment.
>
> (Sirach 17:6–12)

The authors of the narrative tractate in Gen 2–3 took part in this debate between the authors of the books of Job, Qohelet, and Ben Sirach and advocated for a position of their own – criticizing the positions of Qohelet on the one side and Ben Sirach on the other[24] by arguing that mortals did not possess any knowledge of what was good and what was evil *sub specie Dei* nor did mortals make use of this knowledge as a divine gift. For the authors of the narrative in Gen 2–3 the knowledge

---

[23]   For the probability of a direct literary connection between the authors of the books of Qohelet and Ben Sirach see Johannes Marböck, "Kohelet und Sirach," in *Das Buch Kohelet: Studien zur Struktur, Geschichte, Rezeption und Theologie*, ed. Ludger Schwienhorst-Schönberger, BZAW 254 (Berlin: de Gruyter, 1997), 275–301.

[24]   This dialogue was possible because the narrative of Gen 2–3 in its final form was a post-exilic and post-priestly text; cf. the literature above in n. 17 and also Andreas Schüle, *Der Prolog der hebräischen Bibel: Der literar- und theologiegeschichtliche Diskurs der Urgeschichte (Genesis 1–11)*, ATANT 86 (Zurich: Theologischer Verlag Zürich, 2006), 150–77; Martin Arneth, *Durch Adams Fall ist ganz verderbt ... Studien zur Entstehung der alttestamentlichen Urgeschichte*, FRLANT 217 (Göttingen: Vandenhoeck & Ruprecht, 2007), 97–147; cf. also Jan Christian Gertz, *Das erste Buch Mose (Genesis): Die Urgeschichte Gen 1–11*, ATD 1 (Göttingen: Vandenhoeck & Ruprecht, 2018), 8–149.

of good and evil was the result of a human rebellion against the divine command not to eat from the tree of knowledge of good and evil. Background for this theological solution was the motive found in Job 15:8 that a mortal human being had been listening to the divine council and had stolen divine wisdom from this realm.[25] As in Gen 38 the readers of Gen 2–3 had to learn some lessons from this narrative tractate and one lesson was to learn to read this narrative as a tractate about human freedom in deciding moral matters.[26] The first and theologically decisive aspect of Gen 2–3 was the freedom God granted to humanity either to follow his order or to neglect it, knowing well the consequence of mortality for disregarding God's command. Granting humanity freedom to decide to follow His order or to disregard it implies a divine withdrawal by limiting His divine omnipotence and renouncing His sovereignty in relation to humankind. The kabbalah described the divine withdrawal as God's concentration and contraction. But for the authors of Gen 2–3, this withdrawal was different from its kabbalistic interpretation and not a matter of rendering possible all the divine acts of creation of the world. The authors of the narrative in Gen 2–3 connected the implicit motive of divine withdrawal only with God's relationship to the human beings by granting them the freedom to decide to follow His divine command or to disregard it. These authors knew that there was no freedom without the possibility to fail and that a freedom without this possibility was no freedom at all. Gen 2–3 told the reader that the two mortals failed on account of the freedom God had granted to them. The freedom God conceded to humans had its price, a *pretium libertatis*, in the form of fundamental reductions of human life spelled out in the divine curses in Gen 3:17–20. This was the next lesson the readers of Gen 2–3 had to learn. The integration of mortals into their natural environment was and is disturbed by enmity. In a similar way, the relation of love between men and women was and is disturbed by male domination over women. From now on the mortals had to live with their moral ambiguity, which would be responsible for the increasing violence with each generation in the primeval history. The story of Cain and Abel in Gen 4 directly follows the narrative in Gen 2–3 and forms a unit of

[25] As the authors of the dialogues in Job knew that human beings did not possess the divine knowledge to correlate God's almightiness with all the evil in the world and to mediate these aspects, they made use of a mythological language for presenting their solution in the divine answer in Job 38–42, as Plato also did in his dialogues; cf. also the oracle against the king of Tyre in Ezek 28:2–5.

[26] See Otto, "Urmensch im Paradies," 688–89; Rainer Kessler follows this interpretation in *Der Weg zum Leben: Ethik des Alten Testaments* (Gütersloh: Gütersloher, 2017), 108–9.

meta-ethical narratives in Gen 2–4. Gen 4 demonstrates the dangerous dimensions of moral freedom for the mortals, a freedom that God had granted as a divine gift to mankind but one that also required its limitation. To establish the necessity of this limitation was the ethical topic and function of the narrative in Gen 4 in relation to Gen 2–3. Human life had to be protected, so that, if Gen 2–3 claimed that human freedom had its price, it must not be another human life. Killing means that the murderer also destroys his own life, or so is the moral message of Gen 4:

> Then God said: What have you done? Listen! Your brother's blood cries out to me from the ground. Now you are under a curse and driven from the ground, which opened its mouth to receive your brother's blood from your hand. When you work the ground it will no longer yield its crops for you. You will be a restless wanderer on the earth.
>
> (Gen 4:10–13)

The motif of a harsh divine intervention in this narrative established the prohibition of homicide as a definite and fundamental norm at the beginning of human history, long before this norm became part of the revelation of the divine order of the Torah at Mount Sinai. The narratives in Gen 2–3 and Gen 4 were together part of one theological discourse on meta-ethics. The moral freedom God had granted to humanity meant that there would be conflicts between them, even between brothers, because true moral freedom came with the possibility of failure. The lesson the readers of Gen 4 had to learn was that any freedom God had granted to the mortals received limitations in the prohibition of solving conflicts by homicide. The story of the deluge in Gen 6–8 demonstrated the fatal consequences of neglecting this fundamental prohibition. The world is described as filled with violence due to the moral failures of humanity in exercising their freedom and all the mortals except from one family were annihilated by God. In this, Gen 6–8 reads as a kind of counter-narrative to Gen 1.[27] But within Gen 2–4, Gen 4 was the necessary counter narrative to Gen 2–3.

---

[27] Gen 6:1–4 delivers another interpretation of the reasons for the deluge in Gen 6–8. Human guilt was not responsible for it, but a fatal disregard of the borderlines between the celestial and human realm by the sons of God. The redactors, who were responsible for the integration of the narrative of Gen 2–3 into the priestly primeval stories were also those who integrated Gen 6:1–4 into Gen 6–8 in order to relieve the first couple from the burden of responsibility for the annihilation of a whole generation as a consequence of their failure with the freedom God had granted them.

Gen 2–4 as narratives of meta-ethics had another counter-narrative in the story of Abraham's binding of his son Isaac at God's command to sacrifice Isaac in Gen 22.[28] This narrative of a meta-ethics could be read as a story of a Torah conflict:[29] the divine command to Abraham in Gen 22 to kill and sacrifice Isaac contradicted the divine prohibition of killing a human being found in Gen 4 and Gen 9. The narrative in Gen 22 was construed as a prolepsis to the Sinai-pericope so that the revelation at Mount Sinai was not a complete novelty[30] but was anticipated by Abraham's experience of the presence of God demanding obedience to His commandments and the ritual offering of a whole burnt sacrifice.[31] This narrative dealt with many theological aspects of the relationship between God and humankind and did not hide the "dark sides of God."[32] It was also to be read as a tractate of meta-ethics in Genesis in its relation to the narratives of the primeval history; not only in the way that Gen 22 transcended any dimension of a human ethics and opened the realm of an intimate personal relationship of trust between God and a single human being beyond any hope for his or her own life in the future, but

[28] The narrative in Gen 22 in its context in Gen 20–22 is neither part of a sources of a "Jahwist" nor "Elohist." The change of the divine epithet from YHWH and Elohim in Gen 20–22 had a hermeneutical function and was a literary tool comparable to the "Numeruswechsel" in Deuteronomy, but was not a sign of different sources in Genesis, see Eckart Otto, "Die narrative Logik des Wechsels der Gottesnamen zur Differenzierung zwischen Erzählzeit und erzählter Zeit in der Genesis," in *Die Tora. Studien zum Pentateuch. Gesammelte Aufsätze*, ed. Eckart Otto, BZABR 9 (Wiesbaden: Harrassowitz, 2009), 587–600. Reinhard Achenbach also renounces a source-hypothesis and understands the "Elohistic" parts of Genesis which use the epithet Elohim as an interpretation of a post-priestly redaction of the Hexateuch, which was characterized by an integrative view on the narratives in Gen 12–50; see Achenbach, "The Post-Priestly Elohim."

[29] See Matthias Millard, *Die Genesis als Eröffnung der Tora: Kompositions- und auslegungsgeschichtliche Annäherungen an das erste Buch Mose*, WMANT 90 (Neukirchen-Vluyn: Neukirchener, 2001), 144–50.

[30] See Georg Steins, *Die "Bindung Isaaks" im Kanon (Gen 22): Grundlagen und Programm einer kanonisch-intertextuellen Lektüre*, HBS 20 (Freiburg: Herder, 1999), 163–202.

[31] See Walter Moberly, "Christ as the Key to Scripture: Genesis 22 Reconsidered," in *He Swore an Oath. Biblical Themes from Genesis 12–50*, 2nd ed., ed. Richard S. Hess et al. (Eugene, OR: Wipf & Stock, 2007), 143–73, here 155–56.

[32] On Gen 22 as a story about the "dark sides" of God, see Kessler, *Wege zum Leben*, 147, who builds his approach on Walter Dietrich and Christian Link, *Die dunklen Seiten Gottes* (Neukirchen-Vluyn: Neukirchener, 2000). For the problem of the "moral character of God," see Barton, *Ethics in Ancient Israel*, 245–72. Barton critically discusses *inter alios* Frederik Lindström, *God and the Origin of Evil: Contextual Analysis of Alleged Monistic Evidence in the Old Testament*, ConBOT 21 (Lund: Gleerup, 1983).

in the sense of a limitation of God's dark sides as God had promised already after the deluge in Gen 8:21–22:

> Never again will I curse the ground because of humans, even though every inclination of the human heart is evil from childhood. And never again will I destroy all living creatures, as I have done. As long as the earth endures, seedtime and harvest, cold and heat, summer and winter, day and night will never cease.

As the human hearts did not and would not change for the better, it was God himself who changed after the deluge. Henceforth his dark sides would be limited by the knowledge that He would always keep His promises like those in Gen 9:7 and 12:1–3 and keep to His own rule in Gen 4, which prohibited any killing of a single human life, a norm which was reiterated after the deluge in Gen 9:6. At the end of the narrative in Gen 22 God confirmed that He himself would keep to His own ethical rules and the legal commands that He had given to all the mortals, so that He would be morally reliable for them. In this sense Gen 22 was laying the theological and meta-ethical basis for the divine revelation of His legal and moral order in the Sinai-pericope.

POLITICAL AND MORAL THEORIES
OF CONFLICT-SOLUTION IN THE BOOK OF GENESIS

In Genesis the creation narratives of Gen 1–3 were followed by a narrative on a fatal conflict between two brothers in Gen 4 constituting the divine prohibition of homicide. The narratives of the patriarchs in Gen 12–50 took up the topic of conflict and developed some strategies for conflict resolution. One suggestion for resolving such conflicts, even between brothers, was a spatial separation of the opponents and rivals. The first narrative of this type of conflict resolution was the story of Lot's separation from Abraham in Gen 13:7–13. Their close family ties were emphasized by calling them "brothers," but this close proximity also made rivals out of them, because the land could not support both of them as long as they were living together. So Abraham suggested they should separate and yielded the privilege to Lot to choose that part of the land where he wanted to live. Abraham did this even at the cost of his own disadvantage: "If you take the left hand, then I will go to the right, or if you take the right hand, then I will go to the left" (Gen 13:9). Lot chose the fertile Jordan valley leaving the arid hills to Abraham.[33] This model of conflict resolution was related to the principle of separation of families and peoples in the primeval narrative in Gen 10:5,32 (*prd*), which had its foundation in the divine separations in the creation narrative in Gen 1:4.6–7, 14, 18.[34] The application of this cosmic principle, which functioned as a kind of natural law,[35] to the narratives of the patriarchs as a method for resolving conflicts was repeated several times in subsequent chapters: in the narration of an upcoming rivalry between Isaac and Ishmael[36] by sending Ishmael off from Abraham's family in Gen 21:8–20, in a conflict between Abraham and Abimelek in Gen 21:22–34, in a dispute between Isaac and the Philistines in Gen 26:1–32, and in the rivalry between Jacob and Esau in Gen 28–33.[37] At the end of the conflict the two brothers embraced each other after more than twenty years of spatial separation.[38] Jacob bowed to his brother and offered Esau a part of his possessions as a reconciliatory present (Gen 32:13–21; 33:1–11). Peace between Jacob and Esau became possible, because of their mutual forgiveness. Esau forgave Jacob, because Jacob did not insist on the prophecy that "the elder shall serve the younger" and did not implement his privilege by birth, which he had tricked out of Esau.[39] In this case brotherly restraint preserved peace between Jacob and Esau and their families, and by extension between the nations they were representing. After they reconciled, they stabilized

---

[33] For Waldemar Janzen (*Old Testament Ethics: A Paradigmatic Approach* [Louisville: Westminster/John Knox, 1994], 10–11, 32–33) the essence of the ethical message of this story is not only Abraham's peaceful and nonassertive disposition but also Abraham's "model behavior" of his self-abandoning trust in God.

[34] See Eckart Otto, *Das Gesetz des Mose* (Darmstadt: Wissenschaftliche Buchgesellschaft, 2007), 14–38.

[35] For aspects of natural theology in the Hebrew Bible, see James Barr, *The Concept of Biblical Theology: An Old Testament Perspective* (London: SCM Press, 1999), 468–96.

[36] Cf. Benedikt Hensel, *Die Vertauschung des Erstgeburtsegens in der Genesis: Eine Analyse der narrativ-theologischen Grundstruktur des ersten Buches der Tora*, BZAW 423 (Berlin: de Gruyter, 2011), 113–35; cf. above n. 2.

[37] For the ancient literary history of the Jacob narratives see Konrad Schmid, "Von Jakob zu Israel: Das antike Israel auf dem Weg zum Judentum im Spiegel der Fortschreibungsgeschichte der Jakobsüberlieferungen der Genesis," in *Identität und Schrift: Fortschreibungsprozesse als Mittel religiöser Identitätsbildung*, ed. Marianne Grohmann, BibS(N) 169 (Neukirchen Vluyn: Neukirchener, 2017), 33–67.

[38] Cf. Hensel, *Vertauschung*, 135–79.

[39] For this motif as a model for political ethics, see Frank Crüsemann, "Dominion, Guilt, and Reconciliation: The Contribution of the Jacob Narrative in Genesis to Political Ethics", in *Ethics and Politics in the Hebrew Bible*, ed. Douglas A. Knight and Carol Meyers, Semeia 66 (Atlanta: Scholars Press, 1995), 67–77; Barton, *Ethics in Israel*, 30–31, 210.

their relationship and the peace between their nations[40] by separating again, this time once for all (Gen 33:12–16). The Joseph narrative in Gen 37, 39–50[41] also deals with separations and reconciliations beginning with the forced separation of Jacob's sons from their brother Joseph by selling him into slavery in Gen 37. Years later, Jacob's sons meet their brother again in Egypt and the story ends with their reconciliation. For the authors of the Joseph story, reconciliation as a theological topic explicitly meant both Joseph's forgiveness and his restraint in exacting vengeance for all the selfish misdeeds and wrongdoings his brothers had committed against him. In Joseph's renouncement of revenge, the narrative repeated what had been already implicitly foreshadowed in the story of the reconciliation of Jacob with his brother Esau in Gen 33. But Joseph forgives his brothers only after first playing a sardonic game with them to bring their wrongdoing home to them.[42] As John Barton notes,

> His forgiveness clears all the way to the reunion of the family and its safe preservation in Egypt until the time appointed for the exodus. Joseph does not insist on his right to vengeance, and this abstention from revenge enables his family to blossom again after the danger of complete collapse. Forgiveness is thus a theme in the Old Testament, even though nothing is said about it in law or wisdom.[43]

But divine forgiveness and reconciliation are an important theological topic of the prophetic literature in the Hebrew Bible as especially Hosea 11:1–9 shows.[44] So Genesis ends up with a prophetic perspective on

---

[40] For the historical context of the Jacob-Esau-cycle, see Eckart Otto, *Jakob in Sichem: Überlieferungsgeschichtliche, archäologische und territorialgeschichtliche Studien zur Entstehungsgeschichte Israels*, BWANT 110 (Stuttgart: Kohlhammer, 1979), 24–158; Otto, "Jacob I. Old Testament," in *Religion Past & Present*, vol 6, ed. Hans Dieter Betz et al. (Leiden: Brill; 2009), 634–36; Israel Finkelstein and Thomas Römer, "Comments on the Historical Background of the Jacob Narrative in Genesis," *ZAW* 126 (2014): 317–38.

[41] For a pre-exilic origin of the Joseph narrative, see Erhard Blum and Kristin Weingart, "The Joseph Story: Diaspora Novella or North-Israelite Narrative?," *ZAW* 129 (2017): 501–21.

[42] See Otto, "Synthetische Lebensauffassung", 387–400.

[43] So John Barton, *Understanding Old Testament Ethics: Approaches and Explorations* (Louisville, KY: Westminster John Knox Press, 2003), 7.

[44] See Otto, *Theologische Ethik*, 109–11, and 265–66. For reception in the New Testament as a topic of a biblical theology see Eckart Otto, "Hermeneutics of Biblical Theology, History of Religion and the Theological Substance of Two Testaments," in *The Reception of Psalms in Hebrews*, ed. Dirk J. Human and Gert Steyns, LHBOTS 527 (New York: T&T Clark, 2010), 3–26. For a theology of divine mercy in the Torah, i.e., in the book of Deuteronomy, see Deut 4:31; 30:3–4; cf. Otto, *Deuteronomium 23,16–34,12*, 2068–69.

forgiveness as all the Pentateuch has its prophetic finale in Deut 29–34.[45] The theological paradox found in the verses at the end of Genesis hint at the prophetic finale of the Torah in Deuteronomy: "You intended evil against me, but God intended it for good to accomplish what is this day, to save many lives" (Gen 50:20). Even the evil which is a consequence of human freedom that according to Gen 2–3 God has granted to humankind will be subordinated to God's fulfillment of his promises of grace.

SELECT BIBLIOGRAPHY

Barr, James. *The Garden of Eden and the Hope of Immortality*. London: SCM Press, 1992.

Barton, John. *Ethics in Ancient Israel*. Oxford: Oxford University Press, 2014.

Crüsemann, Frank. "Dominion, Guilt, and Reconciliation: The Contribution of the Jacob Narrative in Genesis to Political Ethics." Pages 67–77 in *Ethics and Politics in the Hebrew Bible*. Edited by Douglas A. Knight and Carol Meyers. Semeia 66. Atlanta: Scholars Press, 1995.

Fischer, Georg. "Die Josefsgeschichte als Modell für Versöhnung." Pages 243–71. in *Studies in the Book of Genesis: Literature, Redaction and History*. Edited by André Wenin. BETL 155. Leuven: Peeters, 2001.

Krüger, Thomas. "Genesis 38 – ein 'Lehrstück' alttestamentlicher Ethik." Pages 205–26 in *Konsequente Traditionsgeschichte*. Edited by Rüdiger Bartelmus et al. OBO 126. Fribourg: Universitätsverlag; Göttingen: Vandenhoeck & Ruprecht, 1993.

Millard, Matthias. *Die Genesis als Eröffnung der Tora: Kompositions- und auslegungsgeschichtliche Annäherungen an das erste Buch Mose*. WMANT 90. Neukirchen-Vluyn: Neukirchener, 2001.

Otto, Eckart. "Encountering Ancient Religions: Law and Ethics." Pages 84–97 in *Religions of the Ancient World*. Edited by Sarah Isles Johnston. Cambridge, MA: Harvard University Press, 2004.

"The Study of Law and Ethics in the Hebrew Bible/Old Testament." Pages 594–621 in *Hebrew Bible/ Old Testament: The History of Its Interpretation III/2: The Twentieth Century*. Edited by Magne Sæbø. Göttingen: Vandenhoeck & Ruprecht, 2015.

Theologische Ethik des Alten Testaments. Theologische Wissenschaft 3/2. Stuttgart: Kohlhammer, 1994.

"Der Urmensch im Paradies: Vom Ursprung des Bösen und der Freiheit des Menschen." Pages 679–89 in *Die Tora: Studien zum Pentateuch. Gesammelte Schriften*. BZABR 9. Wiesbaden: Harrassowitz, 2009.

---

[45]   See Eckart Otto, "Deuteronomy as the Legal Completion and Prophetic Finale of the Pentateuch," in *Paradigm Change in Pentateuchal Research*, ed. Matthias Armgardt et al., BZABR 22 (Wiesbaden: Harrassowitz, 2019), 179–88.

"Woher weiß der Mensch um Gut und Böse? Philosophische Annäherungen der ägyptischen und biblischen Weisheit an ein Grundproblem der Ethik." Pages 207–31 in *Recht und Ethos im Alten Testament: Gestalt und Wirkung.* Edited by Stefan Beyerle et al. Neukirchen-Vluyn: Neukirchener, 1999.

Schlimm, Matthew R. *From Fratricide to Forgiveness: The Language and Ethics of Anger in Genesis.* Winona Lake, IN: Eisenbrauns, 2011.

Schmid, Konrad. *Theologie des Alten Testaments.* Tübingen: Mohr Siebeck, 2019.

Steck, Odil Hannes. *Die Paradieserzählung: Eine Auslegung von Genesis 2,4b–3,24.* BibS(N) 60. Neukirchen-Vluyn: Neukirchener, 1970.

Steins, Georg. *Die "Bindung Isaaks" im Kanon (Gen 22): Grundlagen und Programme einer kanonisch-intertextuellen Lektüre.* HBS 20. Freiburg: Herder, 1999.

13 Genesis and the Problem of Evil: Philosophical Musings on the Bible's First Book

PAUL M. GOULD

In the book of Genesis, we find stories about beginnings. We read of God's creation of the universe, the origin of man, the fall into sin, the first murder, the father of faith, the birth of Israel, and more. It is a world strangely unfamiliar to modern readers, yet familiarly strange. When it comes to the origin, nature, and explanation of evil, discussions among analytic philosophers usually focus on the relationship between propositions, found within arguments, that aim to show God's existence is either compatible or incompatible with the reality of evil, or probable or improbable given the reality of evil. God, in the analytic mode, is understood as a personal being worthy of worship. This conception of God is common to the great monotheistic traditions found in Judaism, Christianity, and Islam. Much progress can be – and has been – made on the problem of evil at the level of "mere theism."[1] Yet, as we shall see, there is much more that can – and should – be incorporated into a full-blown account of God and evil. Importantly, what is missing are more fine-grained explorations of God and evil that enfold individual narratives and second-person experiences of dreadful suffering *and* joyful resolution within the larger framework of the world as described in the Bible, and in particular the Bible's first book. In this chapter, my aim is to rectify this lacuna in much, though not all, philosophical theorizing related to the problem of God and evil, by incorporating the insights we learn from the stories found in the book of Genesis. In the first portion of this chapter, I shall specify, building on the work of Eleonore Stump, how biblical narratives can aid philosophical investigations of the problem of evil. The second portion will turn to the narrative of Genesis to explore from the inside a world created by God yet full of suffering. In the final

---

[1] The term "mere theism" denotes the minimal set of propositions held in common by the three great monotheistic traditions. This set includes the propositions that "God is a personal being worthy of worship," "God is the creator and sustainer of the physical universe," and "God is omniscient, omnipotent, and omnibenevolent," among others.

section, I apply the insights gained from our analysis of Genesis to the topic of theodicy.

NARRATIVE AND THE PHILOSOPHICAL PROBLEM OF EVIL

After examining the four biblical narratives of Job, Samson, Abraham, and Mary of Bethany, the philosopher Eleonore Stump asks how these stories should be brought into philosophic discussions about evil.[2] Perhaps, Stump suggests, biblical stories can function as *illustrations* for philosophical claims.[3] Abraham suffers the loss, for many years, of the deep desire of his heart to be a patriarch. In God's test over Isaac, this deep desire is in danger of being blotted out. Yet Abraham trusts God, receiving, in the end, this deep desire of his heart, now enfolded within his deepest desire for God. Abraham became not only the father of a great nation but the father of faith. Biblical stories illustrate, among other things, how suffering produces character. To use biblical stories as mere illustrations for some philosophical point, however, is according to Stump to "wreck them as stories" by treating them as "gratuitous helps for those who like their philosophy with entertainment along the way."[4] I think Stump is being a bit harsh. Stories engage our imagination and, in doing so, help us *understand* the meaning of concepts and propositions.[5] Still, while I do not think using stories to illustrate concepts is completely gratuitous, I follow Stump in thinking this is not their chief value.

Likewise, Stump continues, to use biblical narratives as *support* for a premise in a philosophical argument is also to misuse, or at least to overlook, the chief value of stories for the problem of evil.[6] Using the biblical narratives as support for philosophical premises is to look at the stories from the outside, as it were, as "external descriptions of a case of

---

[2]   Eleonore Stump, *Wandering in Darkness: Narrative and the Problem of Suffering* (Oxford: Oxford University Press, 2010), 371–75. See Part III of Stump's book for the detailed examination of these biblical narratives.

[3]   Ibid., 372.

[4]   Ibid.

[5]   Alasdair MacIntyre, *After Virtue*, 3rd ed. (South Bend, IN: University of Notre Dame Press, 2007), 208–11 argues that basic actions (human or divine) cannot even be rendered intelligible if shorn from their narratival context. For more on the role of the imagination in shaping our view of the world and aiding our understanding of concepts and propositions, see James K. A. Smith, *Imagining the Kingdom* (Grand Rapids, MI: Baker, 2013) and Holly Ordway, *Apologetics and the Christian Imagination* (Steubenville, OH: Emmaus Road, 2017).

[6]   Stump, *Wandering in Darkness*, 372–73.

suffering, without insight into the inner life of the sufferer."[7] Rather, stories should enter into philosophical discussions on their own terms, in all their messiness, richness, and texture, providing for us "something of what we would have had if we ourselves had been participants, even just as bystanders, in the second-person experiences that the story describes."[8] Stories help us to enter into a worldview, in this case, the world as viewed from the perspective of the Bible, and to experience it from the inside.

The chief philosophical value then of biblical narratives, according to Stump, is to "inform in subtle ways our intuitions and judgments"[9] regarding possible theodicies by providing us with insights into the inner experiences of the sufferer (in the case of fully functioning adult human persons) as well as an enriched perception of God's goodness and power (in all cases of suffering human and non-human). In summary, the chief value of the biblical narratives vis-à-vis the problem of evil is to give us something like a *lived experience*, a second-person experience, of the biblical worldview from which we can interpret and judge attempted theodicies as intelligible or unintelligible.[10]

Following Stump's lead, I shall treat the biblical narratives as stories, understood as second-person accounts that function for the reader like a lived experience, an experience that conveys knowledge of other persons that is not reducible without remainder to the propositional knowledge prized by analytic philosophers. In understanding the biblical narrative as a story, I shall not concern myself, when possible, with matters of history or revelation. In doing so, I side-step issues related to historical biblical scholarship, on the one hand, and the nature of divine revelation, on the other.[11] This narratival approach seems especially helpful when addressing the problem of evil, since the problem is largely, though not entirely, about how a wholly good and powerful personal being – God – can allow or bring about evil and suffering in the lives of other (human and angelic) persons. It is time to turn to the salient biblical narratives that speak to the problem of evil in the Bible's first book.

---

[7] Ibid., 373.
[8] Ibid.
[9] Ibid.
[10] A first-person experience is a direct and immediate awareness of a person as a person, and that person is me. In a third-person experience, the person has knowledge of a state of affairs that is "outside" the person. In a second-person experience one person has direct and immediate awareness of a person as a person, and that other person is a distinct person. See ibid., 75–77.
[11] For more on this approach to biblical narratives, see ibid. 23–38.

NARRATIVES IN GENESIS ON GOODNESS AND EVIL

We begin with the origin story of the universe (Gen 1–2) and move on from there to examine the fall of man and sin's ever-widening scope (Gen 3–11), and finally, the stories of Abraham, Isaac, Jacob, and Joseph (Gen 12–50). Setting aside the Genesis 1–2 narrative where God's goodness and power are on full display, we find in the narratives examined in this section God either allowing or causing the suffering found in the story.

Genesis 1–2

Genesis 1–2 portrays God as alive and active: "In the beginning God created the heavens and the earth" (Gen 1:1; NIV). The *living* God, in contrast to the dead and false idols of other ancient traditions, is good and powerful, preparing a place suitable for creatures, especially humans.[12] As divine image bearers, humans are created by God to represent God and rule over creation as vice-regents (Gen 1:26–28). Seven times in Genesis 1, we read of God declaring that which he has made as good – or very good (Gen 1:4, 10, 12, 18, 21, 25, and 31). The created order is good because it fits together and functions as God intended, providing a place for animals and humans to flourish and God's goodness to be on full display. While God's reason for creating is not revealed in the text, the narrative encourages us to understand the objective scale of value within the created order relationally: non-human creation functions for the benefit of mankind and, in turn, the highest good for humans, and the primary good of the Garden of Eden (Gen 2), is union with and the presence of God. Man – finite, created, material, and spiritual (Gen 2:7) – finds his fulfillment in relationship with God, and in harmony with others (Gen 2:18) and the created world (2:19–20) as he lives out his God-given purposes. Everything fits together and points to the divine. As Calvin famously states, the universe is "a dazzling theatre" in which God's glory is on full display.[13]

Genesis 3–11

Something goes wrong, however. God's perception of original goodness in Genesis 1–2 and man's state of innocence (2:24) is replaced with the observation, in Genesis 6, that "the earth was corrupt" and "full of

---

[12] On those other ancient traditions, see the chapters in this volume by Mandell and Walton.

[13] John Calvin, *Institutes of the Christian Religion*, ed. John T. McNeill and trans. Ford Lewis Battles (Louisville: Westminster John Knox Press, 1960), 1.5.8, p. 61.

violence" (6:11). Genesis 3 explains this drastic reversal. The serpent is introduced without fanfare in 3:1 as a being "more crafty than any of the wild animals the Lord God had made." The serpent, identified canonic- ally as Satan, here represents a "chaos creature" and "the mouthpiece of a Dark Power."[14] The existence of the chaos creature signifies that an alien (and finite) force has already entered and disrupted the cosmic order established by God in Genesis 1–2. Genesis 3 records how sin and evil enter the human realm, locating the brokenness of the world in the disobedience of humanity's representative couple. The serpent slanders God's character, encouraging doubt in Adam and Eve. "You will not surely die" (3:4) if you eat from the tree of wisdom. Moreover, "you will be like God, knowing good and evil" (3:5). The serpent's temptation was too alluring: "the woman saw that the fruit of the tree was good for food and pleasing to the eye, and also desirable for gaining wisdom" (3:6). And so she ate. Then he ate. Then everything changed: disorder, strife, sin, curse, guilt, shame, death, and alienation entered the human realm (3:14–24). Yet, importantly, even as God delineates the devastating con- sequences to Adam and Eve's disobedience (3:14–19), we find evidence of divine love in the promise that a future offspring of Eve's will "crush" the head of the serpent (3:15) and in God's provision of clothing as Adam and Eve are banished from the Garden (3:21–24).

From the moment of their banishment, the trajectory of human life in Genesis 4–11 is toward ever-increasing wickedness, beginning with the first murder in Genesis 4. This does not mean all was as bad as it could be, of course. Order and disorder, blessing and curse, unfold side by side. For example, even as the murderous Cain was driven "out from the Lord's presence" (4:16) to wander east of Eden, we find through him or his descendants the development of civilization (4:17), the invention of musical instruments (4:21), primitive technologies (4:22), and the domestication of animals (4:20).

By the time of Genesis 6, however, as we have noted, the earth was "corrupt" and "full of violence" (6:11). God was not pleased. The text reads, "The Lord saw how great man's wickedness on the earth had become, and that every inclination of the thoughts of his heart was only evil all the time" (6:5). This state of affairs grieved God and so he determined to "wipe out mankind ... from the face of the earth" (6:7), with the exception of Noah, his sons, and their wives. Given human

[14]   For more on the serpent as a "chaos creature," see John H. Walton, *The Lost World of Adam and Eve* (Downers Grove, IL: InterVarsity, 2015), 128–39; for more on the serpent as "the mouthpiece of a Dark Power," see C. John Collins, *Genesis 1–4* (Phillipsburg, NJ: P&R, 2006), 171–72.

wickedness, God is morally justified in rendering his act of judgment. Yet, we find something quite startling as the flood waters recede in Genesis 8. God knows that humans are *still* wicked and that "every inclination of his heart is evil from childhood" (8:21), but, with language reminiscent of the creation narrative, God makes a covenant to never again "destroy all living creatures," including humans (8:21–22). In this divine concession, we find *mercy*.

The Noahic covenant signifies a dramatic turn in the Genesis narrative, a turn that has far-reaching implications for the problem of evil: from at least the time of Noah, God decides to work with *suboptimal conditions* and fallen creatures to achieve his purposes. The living God has extended *mercy* to fallen humans, determining to work with and through them to display his goodness and glory. God has not, and will not, destroy humankind. Rather, God will work to bless and restore. In Genesis 11:10–26, we find the genealogy of Shem, Noah's blessed son (9:26). The genealogy ends with Abram (11:26) and his barren wife Sarai (11:30). God's unfolding story is about to get personal.

Genesis 12–50

Tradition tells us that Moses wrote Genesis to prepare the Israelites, as they stood at the foot of Mount Sinai, to enter the promised land.[15] The God of Abraham, Isaac, and Jacob had promised they would become a great nation. God also promised them land, a place to flourish and live and serve God and man for the blessings of all. The Israelites' story begins with Abram and his wife Sarai. God calls Abram to leave his country, his people, and his father's household and go to a new land (12:1). God will make Abram the father of a new nation with many descendants, and through this nation, "all peoples of the earth will be blessed" (12:3).

The central Abrahamic promise – to bless through Abram the entire world – is absolute and unconditional. The fulfillment is assured. The means of its fulfillment, however, involves fallen humans and a causal nexus of God and man, sin and obedience, faith and doubt, blessing and curse. Through deception (e.g., lying about Sarai to the Egyptian king in 12:10–20 and the Philistine king in chapter 20), doubt (e.g., turning to Hagar for a solution to Sarai's infertility in chapter 16), and trial (e.g., God's testing of Abraham to fulfill the deep desire of his heart to be

---

[15] John H. Walton, *Genesis: The NIV Application Commentary* (Grand Rapids, MI: Zondervan, 2001), 399–400. But see William P. Brown, *Sacred Sense* (Grand Rapids, MI: Eerdmans, 2015), 16–17, for a different possible historical context to Genesis.

a great patriarch in chapter 22) Abraham (renamed in 17:5) forges
a relationship with God, becoming the father of faith. While Abraham's
story is given 13 chapters in Genesis (12–25), these chapters reveal more
about God than Abraham. In the climactic scene with Isaac on Mount
Moriah, God provides a sacrificial lamb (22:13). So too, in Genesis 24,
God provides a fitting spouse for Isaac. God is a God who provides
(22:8,14). Abraham dies at 175 years of age (25:7) at rest. Just as God has
provided for him, so too God will provide for his descendants.

God's redemptive plan for humankind unfolds in chapters 25–36
through Isaac's son Jacob, who emerges from Rebekah's womb clutching
his brother Esau's heel (25:26). The young Jacob is a self-centered oppor-
tunist, stealing Esau's birthright through manipulation and deceit (25:
27–34). God first speaks to Jacob at Bethel as he flees Esau (28:10–22),
offering friendship, forgiveness, and purpose. Somewhat surprisingly,
given Jacob's moral depravity, we learn that it is through Jacob's line
that all the people of the world will be blessed (28:14). Transformation is
needed, however, if Jacob is to be a fitting conduit of the divine promise.
After twenty years in service to the deceitful Laban, the Lord instructs
Jacob to return home (31:3). As he prepares to meet Esau, Jacob first
meets God. Appearing in the form of a man, God wrestles with Jacob
for a night. Through this divine–human struggle, Jacob is mysteriously
transformed (32:22–31). While wounded from the struggle, Jacob is given
a new name and character. He is now "Israel," one who "struggles with
God" yet prevails (32:28). Reconciled with God and Esau (chapter 33),
Jacob returns to the promised land. In the climactic scene of this section,
Jacob builds an altar to Yahweh at Bethel (chapter 35). Abraham's God is
now Jacob's God. The covenant – 200 years later – still stands.

In chapters 37–50, the focus narrows once again, to Joseph, Jacob's
eleventh and favorite son, "born to him [i.e., Jacob] in his old age" (37:3).
As a young man, Joseph has two dreams. These dreams are from God and
reveal Joseph's destiny. One day Joseph will lead, in some way, his
brothers. Joseph's report of this future reality is met with anger and
envy by his brothers, who sell him into slavery in Egypt (37:12–36).
Even in slavery, life initially goes well for Joseph as he is put in charge
of Potiphar's household. Potiphar's wife attempts without success to
seduce Joseph. When she realizes that Joseph will not comply, she lies
about him and as a result he is imprisoned (chapter 39). While in prison,
Joseph correctly interprets the dreams of Pharaoh's cupbearer and baker
(chapter 40). Two years later, Pharaoh has a series of troubling dreams
and Joseph is called upon to interpret them (41:1–36). God has revealed to
Pharaoh, according to Joseph, that there will be seven years of abundance

followed by seven years of famine. Thus interpreted, Joseph advises Pharaoh to appoint someone to lead the effort of preparing for the future famine. Pharaoh picks Joseph. Joseph is now the virtual leader – second only to Pharaoh – of Egypt (41:37–57). The remaining chapters of Genesis, 42–50, climax with Joseph's self-disclosure to his brothers of his true identity and their subsequent reconciliation. "You intended to harm me, but God intended it for good to accomplish what is now being done, the saving of many lives" (50:20). After Jacob dies, Joseph and his brothers settle in Egypt (50:14). Jacob's family is preserved. While there will always be threats to the divine promise, the promise still stands. As Genesis closes, the stage is set for Israel's impending enslavement in Egypt. But Joseph's story does not end with foreboding and despair. Refined through suffering, Joseph's faith in God is secure: "God will surely come to your aid and take you up out of this land to the land he promised on oath to Abraham, Isaac, and Jacob" (50:24).

Summary of the Genesis Narrative

How might the Genesis narrative inform theorizing about the problem of evil? Genesis encourages us to develop theodicies that move beyond "mere theism" and a generic conception of God and the cosmos. Yahweh – the living God – interacts with humans and intervenes in human history. Full of raw power *and* tender mercy, God is good but not safe. While the cosmos is orderly and lawlike, it is not fully explainable in terms of mechanical laws acting upon inert matter. The world is full of divinity, spiritual forces, agencies, intentionality, unpredictability, hierarchies of beings, telos, and mystery. Humans come into the world as part of an ongoing story and must take up their place within that story in order to find meaning and purpose. Each individual drama is constrained by the dramas of others and all are enfolded into the divine drama. While human life is fragile and vulnerable, we find reasons to think, given the narrative of Genesis 12–50, that God cares for individuals. While Abraham, Isaac, Jacob, and Joseph – the central characters in the story that begins in Genesis 12 – suffer, in the end, each finds rest, fulfillment, and divine provision. While evil *is* permitted, it is confounded. There is a reason to hope, given the stories' trajectory, that it will one day be eradicated.

Finally, it is important to note the evocative nature of the Genesis narrative. The story evokes an encounter with the living God, a God of wonder and awe. Any theodicy, I suspect, faithful to the world of Genesis (or the biblical world in general), will sound odd, even implausible, to

those in the grips of the mechanized world-picture, along with its preference for a conception of God as a distant and aloof architect of a universe
governed by immutable laws. This fact should not long detain us, however, for theodicies that settle for "mere theism" and the modern world-
picture are ultimately implausible and unfaithful to the narrative and
world as presented to us by Genesis. The question explored in this
chapter is this: how does the *Genesis narrative* inform our theorizing
about evil? It is to that question that we now turn.

GENESIS AND THE PROBLEM OF EVIL

It is customary to speak in terms of giving a defense or theodicy to the
ethical challenge from evil. A defense provides God's *possible* reason for
evil, a theodicy God's *actual* reason for evil. In this section, I assume
the truthfulness of the Genesis narrative and assess some, but not all,
of the most prominent and promising theodicies from the perspective
of the Bible's first book. The criteria I adopt in selecting candidate
theodicies are (1) *inclusion* of beliefs grounded in the Genesis narrative and (2) *consistency* with the lived experience and trajectory of the
Genesis narrative. We begin with a theodicy developed by Augustine
and more recently, as a defense of the logical problem of evil, by Alvin
Plantinga.

The Free Will Theodicy

Given the goodness of creation, it is reasonable to think that God is good.
Moreover, a natural reading of Genesis 1–2 suggests humans are significantly free. As image bearers of a creating and cultivating God, humans
are invested with certain powers of the will to create and cultivate in
a derivative mode. The command to work and care for the Garden of
Eden (Gen 2:15) suggests humans have an ethical responsibility, and the
command to refrain from eating the fruit from the tree of the knowledge
of good and evil (Gen 2:16–17) suggests that man has the ability to do
wrong. The question the text presses upon us as the narrative moves into
Genesis 3 is this: If God is good, why evil? In his treatise, *De libero
arbitrio voluntatis* (*On Free Choice of the Will*), Augustine famously
locates the source of evil in the misuse of creaturely (angelic and human)
free will.[16] God does not cause evil, rather he permits, but does not
desire, the creaturely misuse of freedom as a means to his good purposes.

[16]   Augustine, *On Free Choice of the Will*, trans. Thomas Williams (Indianapolis, IN:
Hackett, 1993).

In the 1970s, it was widely thought that Alvin Plantinga solved the logical problem of evil. His free will defense is essentially an updated version of Augustine's central insights found in *De libero arbitrio*. While Plantinga developed his free will reply to evil as a defense, his project can be recast as a theodicy. The Plantingian free will theodicy, developed in terms of God's actualization of a possible world (understood as mega states of affairs) that is on balance very good, is as follows.[17] A world containing incompatibilist free creatures is more valuable than a world containing none at all. In creating, God actualizes a world containing incompatibilist free creatures. While omnipotent, God cannot *cause* free creatures to only do what is right. Thus, in actualizing a world full of creatures capable of moral good, God must bring into being creatures who are also capable of moral evil. Some incompatibilist free creatures – humans – possess "transworld depravity": in every possible world where they exist, they go wrong at least once.[18] Human misuse of creaturely freedom explains much, if not all, moral evil. Other finite creatures – Satan and the demonic horde – who misuse their freedom are responsible for much, if not all, of the natural evil (hurricanes, tsunamis, disease, and the like) in this world. Thus, all sin, evil, and suffering trace back to the misuse of (human and angelic) creaturely incompatibilist freedom. Still, God created this world because it contains the most favorable balance of moral good over evil that God can bring about, taking into account the great good of incompatibilist freedom.

A strength of the free will theodicy is that it explains evil in terms of God's permission. God does not desire evil, sin, and suffering, yet he permits them as a means to his good purposes. As Augustine argued, since God is good, he cannot be the cause of evil. The free will theodicy helps us understand how God's creation can be functionally good, yet there is evil. Creaturely freedom is good but corruptible. When angelic or human beings turn away from the good that is God, sin, evil, and suffering result.

From the perspective of the Genesis narrative, however, there are three problems with the (Plantingian) free will theodicy.[19] First, while it

---

[17] This paragraph loosely follows Plantinga's summary of his free will defense in *The Nature of Necessity*, Clarendon Library of Logic and Philosophy (Oxford: Oxford University Press, 1974), 166–67.

[18] For more on transworld depravity, see ibid., 184–89.

[19] There are also two philosophical worries that I shall note in passing only to set aside. The first has to do with the charge made by some that incompatibilistic freedom is incoherent. If incompatibilistic freedom is incoherent, then the free will theodicy is an obvious non-starter. While the debate over the nature of freedom is ongoing, I set it aside for three reasons. First, I am convinced that there is no logical incoherence to the

is *possible*, for all we know, that every incompatibilist free creature suffers from transworld depravity, there is nothing provided from within the Genesis narrative to render it *plausible*. Neither the fall of humanity's first couple nor the existence of the "chaos creature" in Genesis 3 provides support for transworld depravity. From the fact that angelic and human creatures misused their freedom in the actual world, it does not follow that any possible free creatures God could create would misuse that freedom. Second, in endorsing a spiritual world, the Genesis narrative does raise the plausibility of Plantinga's suggestion that natural evil is produced by fallen angels. The problem is not the existence of angelic beings, however. The problem is that the free will theodicy *by itself* provides no evidence that angelic beings produce much, if not all, natural evil in the world. Finally, the free will theodicy leaves much of the evil in the actual world mysterious.[20] As noted, in Genesis 1–2, we find a God concerned with what we might call *cosmic excellence*.[21] This cosmic

notion of incompatibilistic freedom. Second, some, but not all, compatibilists agree, even if they reject incompatibilism on other grounds, e.g., John S. Feinberg, *The Many Faces of Evil: Theological Systems and the Problems of Evil*, rev. ed. (Wheaton, IL: Crossway Books, 2004). Finally, I submit that a natural reading of Genesis, indeed of all of Scripture, suggests some version of incompatibilistic human freedom. For more on the debate over free will in general, see Robert Kane, *A Contemporary Introduction to Free Will*, Fundamentals of Philosophy Series (Oxford: Oxford University Press, 2005). For more on the debate over free will, Scripture, and the problem of evil, see, e.g., Jerry L. Walls, "Why No Classical Theist, Let Alone Orthodox Christian, Should Ever Be a Compatibilist," *Philosophia Christi* 13.1 (2011): 75–104; Steven B. Cowen and Greg A. Welty, "Pharaoh's Magicians Redivivus: A Response to Jerry Walls on Christian Compatibilism," *Philosophia Christi* 17.1 (2015): 151–73; and Jerry L. Walls, "Pharaoh's Magicians Foiled Again: Reply to Cowan and Welty," *Philosophia Christi* 17.2 (2015): 411–26. The second philosophical worry I will mention only to set aside is the problem of reconciling incompatibilism with divine foreknowledge. Again, while admitting that the issue is still debated, I think the Molinist and Ockhamist approaches to resolving the apparent contradiction between future contingent acts and divine foreknowledge are both viable options. Even if they are not, however, compatibilism does not follow. For the incompatibilist could simply deny, as the Open Theist does, that God knows the future. For a robust theodicy from the perspective of Open Theism, see William Hasker, *The Triumph of Evil: Theodicy for a World of Suffering* (Downers Grove, IL: InterVarsity Press, 2008). For more on Molinism, see Thomas P. Flint, *Divine Providence: The Molinist Account*, Cornell Studies in the Philosophy of Religion (Ithaca, NY: Cornell University Press, 1998). For more on Ockhamism see Alvin Plantinga, "On Ockham's Way Out," *Faith and Philosophy* 3.3 (1986): 235–69.

20   Eleonore Stump, "The Problem of Evil," *Faith and Philosophy* 2.4 (1985): 392–423, here 394.

21   Marilyn McCord Adams points to Genesis 1 as evidence of God's "global" goodness and desire for "cosmic excellence" and to the overall biblical portrayal of God as loving and merciful to individuals as evidence for God's "person-oriented" goodness. See Marilyn McCord Adams, "Plantinga on 'Felix Culpa': Analysis and Critique,"

excellence, no doubt, includes the significant (incompatibilist) freedom of created persons. The main thrust of Genesis 12–50, however, with its focus on the narratives of Abraham, Isaac, Jacob, and Joseph, suggests that God is also concerned with *particular excellence* (i.e., the flourishing of individuals, especially humans). If so, then it is reasonable to think that for any particular person who suffers, that suffering must produce an outweighing good *for that person*. The free will theodicy helps us see how significant freedom contributes to the cosmic excellence of a world created by God, but it does not help us understand the intensity, duration, and amount of suffering experienced by individuals; surely a good God could prevent or lessen particular instances of suffering in one way or another without curtailing, or significantly curtailing, human freedom.

I conclude that a more promising theodicy will incorporate incompatibilist freedom into a broader range of beliefs and good-making properties as a solution to the problem of evil, suffering, and sin. We turn now to theodicies that incorporate such freedom within more fine-grained accounts of the relations of God and evil in the world.

The *Felix Culpa* Theodicy

Felix Culpa theodicies share the following feature in common: sin, evil, and suffering are God's necessary means to accomplish his good purposes. *Felix Culpa* theodicies have a long and rich history and include the soul-making theodicy of John Hick (who finds inspiration from Irenaeus), the best-world theodicy of Gottfried Leibniz, as well as various iterations of the greater-good theodicy.[22] The story of Joseph is often cited as biblical evidence of God using, even ordaining, evil for some greater good. Joseph's being sold into slavery, like Christ's death on the cross in the Christian tradition, were both ordained by God "for the saving of many lives" (Gen. 50:20).[23] While there are many viable kinds

---

Faith and Philosophy 25.2 (2008): 123–45, here 129. See also Stump, "The Problem of Evil," 411.

[22] On the soul-making theodicy, see John Hick, *Evil and the God of Love* (New York: Harper & Row, 1966); for a concise summary of Hick's theodicy see his " Soul-Making Theodicy," in *God and the Problem of Evil*, ed. William L. Rowe (Malden, MA: Blackwell, 2001), 265–81. For a helpful summary of Leibniz's treatment of evil, see Feinberg, *The Many Faces of Evil*, 45–66. For a decent exposition of greater-good theodicies in general, see Bruce A. Little, *A Creation-Order Theodicy: God and Gratuitous Evil* (Lanham, MD: University Press of America, 2005).

[23] James Spiegel, "The Irenean Soul-Making Theodicy," in *God and Evil*, ed. Chad Meister and James K. Dew Jr. (Downers Grove, IL: InterVarsity, 2013), 80–93, here 90.

of *Felix Culpa* theodicies, in this section, I will explore one of the most sophisticated versions of the theodicy as developed by Alvin Plantinga.[24]

The theodicy runs as follows. Prior to the divine decree to create, God aims to bring into being a really good world. Plantinga asks: what are good-making properties among worlds? Some good-making properties are of finite value. Creaturely happiness, beauty, pleasure, justice, and the like, are examples of finite good-making qualities. A world where the aggregate of good-making qualities outweighs the bad-making qualities (sin, evil, suffering) is a good world, and the more the overall good, the better the world. The picture is a bit more complicated, however, since there are also good-making qualities that are infinitely valuable. Plantinga has two infinitely valuable states of affairs in mind: God's existence and "the unthinkably great good of divine incarnation and atonement."[25] God exists in every possible world, given his necessary existence. So, every possible world, including worlds where God refrains from creating, are already very good – infinitely valuable – worlds. Still, some very good worlds, worlds of infinite value, are better than others. Plantinga thinks that worlds containing incarnation and atonement are better than worlds without these towering goods. In fact, worlds with incarnation and atonement are the best possible *kinds* of worlds; they cannot be matched by any aggregate of creaturely goods nor could any aggregate of creaturely badness outweigh the goodness of incarnation and atonement.

With these assumptions about valuable states of affairs in place, we can now discern God's reason for creating a world that includes evil and suffering. God actualizes this world because it is the best *kind* of world, a world containing the incommensurable and infinitely valuable goods of incarnation and atonement. Man's fall into evil is a "happy sin," a necessary part of the best possible kind of world.

An obvious strength of Plantinga's *Felix Culpa* theodicy is its incorporation of Adam and Eve's fall into sin as part of the solution to the problem of evil. While suggestive, I think Plantinga's *Felix Culpa* ultimately fails as a successful theodicy, as do all *Felix Culpa* theodicies. Regarding Plantinga's version, the theodicy is most plausible when

---

[24] For years Plantinga refrained from offering a theodicy (although we recast his defense as a theodicy in the previous section). In the early 2000s, however, Plantinga applied his considerable philosophical acumen to the question of theodicy. As a result, see his "Supralapsarianism, or 'O Felix Culpa'," in *Christian Faith and the Problem of Evil*, ed. Peter van Inwagen (Grand Rapids, MI: Eerdmans, 2004), 1–25.

[25] Ibid., 7.

considering the issue of cosmic excellence, but it does not provide an explanation, or much of an explanation, for individuals who suffer.[26] For the redeemed, it is not hard to see how incarnation and atonement are great goods, but what of the unredeemed? How is God's cosmic end valuable for them? Plantinga proffers no answer to this question. One solution is to adopt universalism and the idea that in the end all sinners are saved.[27] Genesis does not rule out universalism, but arguably, the rest of Scripture does, and for that reason, it is not clear that *Felix Culpa* theodicies can accommodate agent-centered concerns regarding evil. A second problem, however, is more devastating.[28] Recall that Genesis 1–2 encourages us to understand man's highest good relationally. Humanity is created *for* relationship with God. *That* is the towering good suggested by Genesis. On Plantinga's version of the *Felix Culpa* theodicy, however, the towering good in view is God's display of unmatched love brought about by incarnation and atonement, not the redemption that is accomplished by these acts.[29] Thus, Plantinga's *Felix Culpa* theodicy confuses the means (incarnation and atonement) to a great good (union with God) with the great good itself. Finally, according to Kevin Diller, there is a problem that infects all versions of the *Felix Culpa* theodicy: *evil itself* – something essentially irrational – is rendered reasonable and part of God's functionally good creation.[30] What the lived experience of the Genesis narrative teaches us, however, is that evil is an alien invader, something *permitted* but not originally willed, required, or desired by God. A perfectly loving God can and will use evil for his good purposes, including our moral and spiritual growth, but for an answer to the problem of evil, we must look elsewhere.

---

[26]   This objection is discussed in Adams, "Plantinga on 'Felix Culpa': Analysis and Critique," 128–31 and in Kevin Diller, "Are Sin and Evil Necessary for a Really Good World? Questions for Alvin Plantinga's Felix Culpa Theodicy," *Faith and Philosophy* 25.1 (2008): 93–95.

[27]   As do John Hick and Marilyn Adams. For Hick, see sources cited in n. 22; for Marilyn Adams see " Redemptive Suffering: A Christian Approach to the Problem of Evil," in *Rationality, Religious Belief, and Moral Commitment*, ed. Robert Audi and William J. Wainwright (Ithaca, NY: Cornell University Press, 1986), 248–67.

[28]   This objection is discussed by Diller, "Are Sin and Evil Necessary for a Really Good World?," 92–93.

[29]   See Plantinga, "Supralapsarianism, or 'O Felix Culpa'," 7. As Diller expounds Plantinga, "The fall now becomes the means to the ultimate end of the display of God's love in the suffering of the atonement" (Diller, "Are Sin and Evil Necessary for a Really Good World?", 92–93).

[30]   Diller, "Are Sin and Evil Necessary for a Really Good World?," 95–96.

The Eschatological Theodicy

Every theodicy, according to Eleonore Stump, is embedded within a larger vision of the world.[31] This grand vision includes an account of God's character and purposes, the nature of the world created by God, and man's place within the divine drama. Humans, as we have noted, were created for relationship with God, others, and perhaps other sentient creatures as they live out their calling to rule and steward God's good creation. The reality of a created order in which all things find their place points to an objective side to suffering for humans: humans suffer evils when their flourishing is undermined. The reality of embodied individuals – particular humans – points to a subjective side to suffering as well: humans suffer evils when deprived of the deep desires of the heart such as the loss of a loved one or a project about which one cares. Stump seeks a theodicy that defeats both kinds of evils for humans and thinks that any successful theodicy must include some notion of the afterlife.[32] I begin with Stump's 1990 article "The Problem of Evil" and then fill in some details of an eschatological theodicy by drawing from her discussion of Aquinas's theodicy in her magisterial book *Wandering in Darkness*.

In addition to the beliefs that God is maximally perfect, evil exists, and humans have incompatibilist freedom, Stump incorporates three beliefs into her theodicy that flow from her distinctively Christian approach: Adam fell, natural evil entered the world as a result of Adam's fall, and after death, human beings either go to heaven or hell.[33] The big idea, according to Stump, is that all post-fall humans have a defective will such that they have a powerful inclination to will what they ought not to will. In this condition, humans cannot attain their highest good – shared union with God – and hell – understood as the

---

[31] Stump, *Wandering in Darkness*, 17.

[32] Ibid., 419.

[33] Stump, "The Problem of Evil," 398. There is considerable debate among Christian philosophers and theologians regarding the doctrine of original sin. For insightful discussions on the coherence of original sin see Paul Copan, "Original Sin and Christian Philosophy," *Philosophia Christi* 5.2 (2003): 519–41; Michael C. Rea, "The Metaphysics of Original Sin," in *Persons: Human and Divine*, ed. Peter van Inwagen and Dean Zimmerman (Oxford: Clarendon Press, 2007), 319–56; and W. Paul Franks, "Original Sin and Broad Free-Will Defense," *Philosophia Christi* 14.2 (2012): 353–77. For a provocative discussion that attempts to show the compatibility of original sin with evolution, see Hud Hudson, *The Fall and Hypertime* (New York: Oxford University Press, 2014). For a novel attempt to reconcile scientific consensus regarding evolution with belief in a literal Adam and Eve, see S. Joshua Swamidass, "The Overlooked Science of Genealogical Ancestry," *Perspectives on Science and Christian Faith* 70.1 (2018): 19–35.

permanent absence of God – is the best alternative to annihilation. A wholly good God *wants* to fix defective humans, but since the defect is a defect of a *free* will, even an omnipotent God cannot remove the defect without removing the person's freedom. Neither is self-repair an option. The will, after all, is defective; it is bent toward evil. The only remaining option, according to Stump, is for a person to will that God fix her defective will. On this account, human freedom is maintained since God's alteration of the will is freely chosen, yet it is God who alters the will. The experience of moral and natural evil can produce, and "[may be] the only effective means"[34] of producing, the appropriate psychological state in humans such that they freely seek divine assistance. There is no *guarantee*, given free will, that evil and suffering will make people better. The chief good that free will produces and which outweighs subsequent evil and suffering is not the ability to exercise significant freedom, but the "willing in accordance with the divine will and thus making possible union with God."[35]

In *Wandering in Darkness*, Stump further unpacks and extends this line of thinking by locating God's justification for evils within the objective and subjective scale of value for humans. The best thing *simpliciter* for human persons is to enter, upon death, into "unending shared union of loving personal relationship with God" and the worst is to enter, upon death, into "the unending absence" of God.[36] With this objective scale of value in view, God's morally sufficient reason for permitting evils in a person's life are (i) to provide the chance of warding off the greater harm of permanent absence from God (for the yet unredeemed) or (ii) the chance to provide the greater good of an increased degree of everlasting shared union with God (for the redeemed). A perfectly loving God cares about what humans care about too. This means that God cares about suffering due to the loss of a heart desire. This subjective scale of value, however, raises two problems for Stump's (and Aquinas's) theodicy. First, the grief stemming from the loss of a heart desire results in internal fragmentation. But then, heartbreak stemming from the loss of something one cares about works against a key condition for closeness and union with God, internal psychological integration. Second, a person may not care more about flourishing than about the loss of her heart's desire, and so it difficult to see how God could justifiably defeat the suffering stemming from such heartbreak. Stump's theodicy addresses

---

[34]   Stump, "The Problem of Evil," 409.
[35]   Ibid., 416. See also Stump's discussion in *Wandering in Darkness*, 151–73.
[36]   Stump, *Wandering in Darkness*, 388.

these difficulties by noting that in the case of human persons, the two scales of value ultimately converge: the deepest (subjective) desire of the heart is one and the same as man's (objective) highest good. Since a person's deepest heart desire is for God, it is possible to weave together all the things she cares about into her flourishing. If that happens, then all the other things a person cares about become gifts, "gifts had or hoped for, or even gifts lost or not given."[37] When we learn to receive, and even enjoy, all things as a gift in creaturely response, we enter into the divine drama and open ourselves to the happiness there is, not the happiness there is not.[38] Importantly, we need not cease caring about the things we care about, rather, when we locate them within our deepest heart desire for God, they are enfolded and reconfigured – without losing their identity – in such a way that evil can be defeated and God can be trusted as perfectly good and loving.

From the perspective of the Genesis narrative, Stump's eschatological theodicy is attractive for at least three reasons. First, the future-directed nature of the benefit that accrues to the sufferer is consistent with the lived-experience of the Genesis narrative. Man is created with great dignity for a purpose. Even as the effect of sin expands, we see blessing and divine provision too. If humans were only created for a this-worldly existence, it is difficult to see how many of the evils that impede human flourishing or the deep desires of the heart could be defeated. The spirit-infused world of Genesis, as well as its trajectory, give us reason to hope. In the Garden, on the Ark, through one nation of people, the seed of divine blessing is sustained and carried forth. God has not – and will not – give up on his creation. One day, *El Roi*, the God who sees (Gen 16:13), will restore.

Second, Stump's eschatological theodicy accommodates the book's emphasis on cosmic and personal excellence. It is appropriate to speak of an objective scale of value for humans because God created humans to flourish in light of their nature. It is also appropriate to speak of a subjective scale of value for humans because God created individual persons with unique loves, longings, and projects. The suffering in need of justification, and ultimately defeat, occur when something goes significantly contrary to the nature or will (or both) of the sufferer.

Third, by incorporating the doctrine of original sin, Stump's eschatological theodicy correctly locates the human propensity for moral evil in

---

[37]   Ibid., 445.
[38]   As C. S. Lewis colorfully describes the second-person nature of gift in *The Problem of Pain* (New York: HarperCollins, 2001 [1940]), 47.

humans and not God. God does not *desire* evil; his *antecedent* will is for
a world without sin, suffering, and evil. Given the outweighing good of
free creatures capable of uncoerced relationships of self-surrendering
love with God and self-giving love with others, God permits evil as part
of his consequent will. While we might not be able to discern God's
reason for the particular suffering of a particular sufferer at a particular
time and place, there is *no* pointless suffering. On Stump's theodicy,
every instance of suffering can benefit the sufferer in such a way that it
outweighs the suffering and could not have been obtained as well without the suffering.[39] Finding closeness to and thus union with God
requires surrender. For those who enter into relationship with God
through the surrender of justification and sanctification, there is con-
solation for suffering in this life and final defeat of evil in the next.

There are three shortcomings to the eschatological theodicy as presented. These shortcomings, acknowledged by Stump, would need to be
addressed in order to provide a fully generalized theodicy explaining
God's reasons for evil. First, recall that evil is already on the scene, as
evidenced by the serpent, *before* Adam and Eve fall into sin. Stump's
theodicy locates natural evil's origin in the fall of man, but the origin of
evil itself is left unexplained. There are also two other kinds of evils left
unexplained in Stump's eschatological theodicy, those associated with
the suffering of animals and non-fully functioning humans (e.g., infants,
mentally impaired adults, etc.). In the final section, I consider a possible
extension to Stump's eschatological theodicy that takes these shortcomings into account. If successful, there is at least one plausible theodicy
consonant with the lived-experience of Genesis that explains God's
reasons for evil.

Cosmic Conflict and Rules of Engagement

Given the reality of celestial beings, we can locate the origin of evil in the
misuse of angelic freedom. Satan and his cohorts rebelled against God
and as a result, evil – understood as that which opposes God's antecedent
will – entered the created order. Satan, as we have seen in Genesis 3, is
the arch-slanderer, calling into question the goodness of God. Since the
charge against God is moral, and since genuine union with God entails
epistemic freedom to trust or distrust God, it follows that God could not
immediately bring about a state of affairs (via omnipotence) such that
fallen humans *freely* recognize the goodness of God. "Demonic allegations," according to John Peckham, "call for rules of engagement that

---

[39]   Stump, *Wandering in Darkness*, 455.

provide the parameters in which the allegations could be proven true or false via demonstration."[40] God grants Satan and his cohorts limited jurisdiction over the world in order to demonstrate his goodness. Given God's agreement to abide by "rules of engagement," he is morally bound to do so, introducing the concepts of self-limitation and cosmic conflict as additional resources from which to explain God's reasons for permitting evil. Given God's commitment to promise-keeping and his desire to demonstrate his goodness in the cosmic court, we now have the resources to understand why God would permit the suffering of non-fully functioning humans and nonhuman animals: such evils are the result of the angelic fall (ultimately) and permitted by God to demonstrate his goodness in the face of slander via negotiated covenantal "rules of engagement."[41] As Peckham states, summarizing what he calls a theodicy of love,

> [God] may wish to mitigate or eliminate the vast amount of animal [and non-fully functioning human] suffering in this world. However, it might be against the rules of engagement for God to do so – that is, doing so might affect the jurisdiction of the temporary ruler of this world. If so, it is not that God desires this state of affairs but that, as Jesus states, "an enemy has done this" (Matt. 13:28).[42]

God does not always get what he wants, given his commitment to love, freedom, and promise-keeping. Yet, in the end, his goodness is vindicated, and evil is defeated. By enfolding the concepts of cosmic conflict, divine self-limitation, and covenantal rules of engagement into Stump's eschatological theodicy, we find a plausible way to understand the

---

[40] John C. Peckham, *Theodicy of Love: Cosmic Conflict and the Problem of Evil* (Grand Rapids, MI: Baker Academic, 2018), 104.

[41] Due to space limitations, I sidestep the question of how immaterial angels causally influence the world. For helpful discussions on the topic, see Garry Deweese, "Natural Evil: A 'Free Process' Defense," in Meister and Dew, *God and Evil*, 53–64; and Kent Dunnington, "The Problem with the Satan Hypothesis: Natural Evil and Fallen Angel Theodicies," *Sophia* 57.2 (2017): 1–10.

[42] Peckham, *Theodicy of Love*, 117. Alternatively, it could be argued, regarding nonhuman animals, that they do not genuinely suffer and thus there is no problem of animal suffering. See, e.g., B. Kyle Keltz, "Neo-Thomism and the Problem of Animal Suffering," *Nova et Vetera*, (English Edition), 17.1 (2019): 93–125. Keltz surveys the scientific literature regarding animal cognition and concludes that there are good reasons to think that while animals are conscious of pain, they are not self-aware of pain and thus do not truly suffer. See also Michael J. Murray, *Nature Red in Tooth and Claw: Theism and the Problem of Animal Suffering* (New York: Oxford University Press, 2008).

suffering of all creatures great and small consonant with the goodness of God and the lived experience of Genesis.

SELECT BIBLIOGRAPHY

Adams, Marilyn. "Redemptive Suffering: A Christian Approach to the Problem of Evil." Pages 248–67 in *Rationality, Religious Belief, and Moral Commitment: New Essays in the Philosophy of Religion*. Edited by Robert Audi and William J. Wainwright. Ithaca: Cornell University Press, 1986.

Augustine. *On Free Choice of the Will*. Translated by Thomas Williams. Indianapolis: Hackett, 1993.

Feinberg, John S. *The Many Faces of Evil: Theological Systems and the Problems of Evil*. Revised and expanded edition. Wheaton, IL: Crossway Books, 2004.

Flint, Thomas P. *Divine Providence: The Molinist Account*. Cornell Studies in the Philosophy of Religion. Ithaca, NY: Cornell University Press, 1998.

Hasker, William. *The Triumph of God Over Evil: Theodicy for a World of Suffering*. Downers Grove, IL: InterVarsity Press, 2008.

Hick, John. *Evil and the God of Love*. New York: Harper & Row, 1966.

Hudson, Hud. *The Fall and Hypertime*. Oxford: Oxford University Press, 2014.

Kane, Robert. *A Contemporary Introduction to Free Will*. Fundamentals of Philosophy Series. Oxford: Oxford University Press, 2005.

Lewis, C. S. *The Problem of Pain*. San Francisco: HarperCollins, 2001 [1940].

Little, Bruce A. *A Creation-Order Theodicy: God and Gratuitous Evil*. Lanham, MD: University Press of America, 2005.

Peckham, John. *Theodicy of Love: Cosmic Conflict and the Problem of Evil*. Grand Rapids, MI: Baker Academic, 2018.

Plantinga, Alvin. *The Nature of Necessity*. Clarendon Library of Logic and Philosophy. Oxford: Clarendon Press, 1974.

Stump, Eleonore. "The Problem of Evil." *Faith and Philosophy* 2.4 (1985): 392–423.

Wandering in Darkness: Narrative and the Problem of Suffering. Oxford: Oxford University Press, 2010.

Swamidass, S. Joshua. "The Overlooked Science of Genealogical Ancestry." *Perspectives on Science and Christian Faith* 70.1 (2018): 19–35.

Walls, Jerry L. "Why No Classical Theist, Let Alone Orthodox Christian, Should Ever Be a Compatibilist." *Philosophia Christi* 13.1 (2011): 75–104.

Part IV
Reception History of Genesis

14 Modern Philosophical Receptions of Genesis

FREDERICK D. AQUINO

The book of Genesis is replete with philosophical issues. Some include the nature of the human condition (e.g., the propensity for evil and goodness), freedom, contingency and necessity, ecological responsibility, and the contours of human interaction and flourishing.[1] However, a perennial philosophical issue focuses on the relationship between divine commands and ethical evaluation. An important and related question is whether what God says and does is fitting if judged by a more developed concept of the divine nature. What, for example, is befitting of the divine? What is involved in determining whether the actions of the divine are befitting?

The story of the binding of Isaac in Genesis has been a central text along these lines. Crucial moral and epistemological issues have been raised in the modern philosophical receptions of this story. One issue involves clarifying the relationship between the Bible, as well as this story, and philosophy (e.g., the nature, function, and purpose of Scripture, especially as it pertains to the task of engaging in philosophical reflection). Another (and related to the previous inquiry) seeks to identify, clarify, and address the relevant philosophical issues in this story (e.g., the relationship between divine commands and ethical evaluation; determining *what* counts as a divine revelation and *how* to adjudicate among competing claims to divine revelation).

Accordingly, I will restrict the focus of this chapter to these two areas of philosophical inquiry. First, I will highlight three recent scholarly accounts of the relationship between the Bible (and in one case

---

[1] See, for example, Paul W. Kahn, *Out of Eden: Adam and Eve and the Problem of Evil* (Princeton: Princeton University Press, 2007), Hud Hudson, *The Fall and Hypertime* (Oxford: Oxford University Press, 2014), Thomas L. Pangle, *Political Philosophy and the God of Abraham* (Baltimore, MD: The Johns Hopkins University Press, 2003), Kenneth Seeskin, *Thinking about the Torah: A Philosopher Reads the Bible* (Philadelphia: The Jewish Publication Society, 2016), and Shira Weiss, *Ethical Ambiguity in the Hebrew Bible: Philosophical Analysis of Scriptural Narrative* (Cambridge: Cambridge University Press, 2018).

Genesis) and philosophy. A discussion of this sort raises and tackles questions about the nature, scope, and function of Scripture. Should one, for example, approach the Bible as a philosophical text? Is it alien to such philosophical schemes? Or, can it be appropriated via philosophical analysis? Second (by extension and related to the discussion in the first section of this chapter), I will focus on the story of the binding of Isaac (Gen. 22:1–19), underscoring the various modern philosophical readings of the story while unpacking some of the relevant philosophical issues. This story and the philosophical receptions of it open fruitful avenues of philosophical inquiry. What, for example, are we to make philosophically of the story of the binding of Isaac? Does it support and call for a blind kind of faith? Does divine command suspend the ethical? Or does the story offer a safeguard against or condemnation of the violation of human well-being? Third, I will conclude with some brief and constructive suggestions concerning the relationship between the disciplines of philosophy and biblical studies.

SCRIPTURE AND PHILOSOPHY

There has been a growing interest in thinking critically and constructively about the intersection of Scripture and philosophy.[2] Some of the scholarly discussion has sought to clarify the nature, function, and scope of Scripture and the extent to which it can be appropriated philosophically. It has also explored philosophical issues that are identified in Scripture while seeking to offer constructive possibilities. With this discussion in mind, I will focus briefly on the works of Leon Kass, Yoram Hazony, and Eleonore Stump.

In his book, *The Beginning of Wisdom*, Leon Kass seeks to offer a philosophical reading of Genesis. However, it is not immediately clear, as he acknowledges, what is involved in reading this text philosophically. What Kass seems to have in mind is something comparable to (or what he takes as) the ancient conception of philosophy, namely, the

---

[2] See, for example, William J. Abraham, *Canon and Criterion in Christian Theology: From the Fathers to Feminism* (Oxford: Clarendon Press, 1998); William J. Abraham, *Crossing the Threshold of Divine Revelation* (Grand Rapids: Eerdmans, 2006); Sandra Menssen and Thomas D. Sullivan, "Revelation and Scripture," in *The Oxford Handbook of the Epistemology of Theology*, ed. William J. Abraham and Frederick D. Aquino (Oxford: Oxford University Press, 2017), 30–45; Paul Moser, ed., *Jesus and Philosophy: New Essays* (Cambridge: Cambridge University Press, 2009), Samuel Fleischacker, *The Good and the Good Book* (Oxford: Oxford University Press, 2015), and Jaco Gericke, *The Hebrew Bible and Philosophy of Religion* (Atlanta, GA: Society of Biblical Literature, 2012).

love and pursuit of wisdom. More exactly, the aim is to decipher how this ancient text can help us acquire relevant wisdom for living an enlightened life in the twenty-first century. Kass's approach is concerned with nothing less than the art of living in our contemporary context.[3] It seeks to explore critically and thoughtfully the "truth about the world and our place within it and to find thereby guidance for how we are to live."[4] In essence, Kass is reading Genesis for wisdom, but not as a text in which the authors are engaged in a specialized discipline of philosophical inquiry. Consequently, he approaches it in the same spirit in which he reads "Plato's *Republic* or Aristotle's *Nicomachean Ethics* – indeed, any great book – seeking wisdom regarding human life lived well in relation to the whole."[5] The overall project, then, is to provide a more holistic and humane reading of Genesis while exploring its constructive promise.

Consequently, Kass does not think that Genesis should be read as a textbook, for example, in epistemology, metaphysics, philosophy of mind, philosophy of language, and philosophy of religion, or that it operates with "some method of reasoning and questioning practiced by card-carrying professional philosophers."[6] The Bible, in a narrower and more technical sense, is not a work of philosophy. Neither its manner, Kass adds, "nor its manifest purposes are philosophical. Indeed, there is even good reason for saying that they are *anti*philosophical, and deliberately so."[7] In other words, Kass thinks that religion and philosophy are fundamentally different habits of mind. The former offers "wisdom based on divine revelation" and relies on "prophecy," whereas the latter seeks "wisdom looking to nature and relying on unaided human reason."[8] This stems primarily from the fact that the beginning of wisdom "comes not from wonder but from awe and reverence, and the goal is not understanding for its own sake but rather a righteous and holy life." As a result, the "wisdom of Jerusalem is not the wisdom of Athens."[9] Thus, "biblical wisdom" is motivated by "fear (awe-reverence) for the Lord, not open

---

[3] For further reflection on the conception of philosophy as a way of life in antiquity, see Pierre Hadot, *Philosophy as a Way of Life: Spiritual Exercises from Socrates to Foucault* (Malden: Blackwell, 1995).

[4] Leon R. Kass, *The Beginning of Wisdom: Reading Genesis* (New York, NY: Free Press, 2003), 1.

[5] Ibid.

[6] Ibid.; Gericke, *The Hebrew Bible and Philosophy of Religion*, 9, says, "contrary to popular belief, therefore, we actually need more – not fewer – philosophical inquires, precisely because the Hebrew Bible is not a textbook in the philosophy of religion." Instead, he is interested in providing a philosophical account of ancient Israelite religion.

[7] Kass, *The Beginning of Wisdom*, 3.

[8] Ibid.

[9] Ibid., 2–3.

inquiry spurred by wonder." The aim here is the cultivation of a "righteous and holy life," not the pursuit of "understanding for its own sake."[10]

The Jerusalem and Athens dichotomy accordingly shapes Kass's understanding of the nature, function, and scope of Scripture (and in particular Genesis). His wisdom-seeking approach also seems to differ from the standard historical critical approach and a kind of fideism that affirms the Bible as the revealed word of God but exempts it from critical investigation. Alternatively, he reads Genesis in a "spirit and manner that is simultaneously naïve, philosophic, and reverent."[11] That is, he comes to the text with the "attitude of thoughtful engagement of suspended disbelief, eager to learn."[12] Underlying this approach is an attempt to "understand the text on its own terms" while exploring how it illumines "some of the most important and enduring questions of human existence."[13]

By contrast, Yoram Hazony claims that the Hebrew Bible is primarily a work of reason. He parts ways with (and challenges) those who maintain and employ the dichotomy of reason and revelation in their approach to the Hebrew Bible. This traditional distinction, he contends, is neither helpful, nor is it an apt way to approach the Hebrew Bible. Such a dichotomy becomes "a kind of distorting lens."[14] It rests on a fundamental mistake, namely, a false understanding of the purpose of the Hebrew Bible. It presumes there are two ways of addressing "ultimate issues – those that are the product of *reason*; and those that are known by way of *revelation*."[15] The former, as illustrated in the works of Plato, Aristotle, Kant, and so on sought to "to assist individuals and nations looking to discover the true and the good as best as they are able in accordance with [their] natural abilities."[16] By contrast, the Hebrew Bible, as the traditional dichotomy stipulates, is "a text that reports" God's thoughts about things. It "bypasses [our] natural faculties" and thus gives us "knowledge of the true and the good by means of a series of miracles."[17] So, what the Hebrew Bible "offers is miraculous knowledge, to be accepted in gratitude and believed on faith."[18] With this distinction

[10]   Ibid., 3, 15.
[11]   Ibid., 15.
[12]   Ibid., 16.
[13]   Ibid., 15–16.
[14]   Yoram Hazony, *The Philosophy of Hebrew Scripture* (Cambridge: Cambridge University Press, 2012), 3.
[15]   Ibid., 1.
[16]   Ibid.
[17]   Ibid.
[18]   Ibid.

in mind, divine revelation and reason are radically different ways of addressing ultimate issues. An appeal to divine revelation "requires the suspension of the normal operation of our mental faculties, calling on us to believe things that don't make sense to us – because they are supposed to make sense to God."[19]

Alternatively, Hazony argues that the Hebrew Bible is more readily understood if it is read and approached primarily as a work of reason rather than as a work of revelation. In particular, he sets out to offer a "methodological framework" that can move in the direction of offering a "well-articulated understanding of the philosophical content of the Hebrew scriptures."[20] The more modest or weaker claim is to say that the Hebrew Bible can be appropriated philosophically (e.g., Kass). However, Hazony advances a stronger claim. That is, the Hebrew Bible can be read as a work of philosophy, with an "eye" to exploring and "discovering" what it says about the "nature of the world" and the conditions under which humans ought to pursue and embody a "just" way of being in the world.[21] The "integrated" and "instructional narrative" that extends from the creation of the world in Genesis to the collapse of the kingdom in the book of Kings investigates and advances arguments regarding fundamental questions in ethics, political philosophy, and metaphysics.[22]

Hazony therefore sets out to clarify "the biblical mode of argument as it finds expression in the narratives."[23] Underlying his proposal is an epistemological assumption, namely, that the Hebrew Bible invites the reader to engage in a long search for truth in the "epistemic jungle – a confused and frightening reality in which such knowledge is chronically distant."[24] The characters in Scripture as well as the writers of it "believe that such wisdom can be found in the world, because they believe that God has spoken it. To find it is the difficulty, and the subject of a lifelong quest."[25] As we have seen, Hazony does not think that the Hebrew Bible fits the Athens and Jerusalem model, nor does it impose a rule of faith or catechism on its hearers or readers. Instead, Hazony contends that a biblical religion, shaped by the Hebrew Bible, "must be skeptical with respect to attempts at imposing a rule of faith or

---

[19] Ibid.
[20] Ibid., 259.
[21] Ibid., 4.
[22] Ibid., 23, 79.
[23] Ibid., 66.
[24] Ibid., 256.
[25] Ibid.

catechism due to the Bible's oft-repeated observation that ultimate knowledge of God's thought is beyond" our "fallible and frail" powers.[26]

The Hebrew Bible, according to Hazony, is "an artful compendium, whose purpose is not – and never was – to present a single viewpoint."[27] The claim here is not a denial of a core teaching in the Hebrew Bible. Hazony is simply reiterating the point that such a core must be sought or pursued in the midst of "a family or a school of viewpoints."[28] Moreover, the purpose of the Hebrew Bible, like any work of philosophy (at least in its classical mode), "was to assist individuals and nations looking to discover the true and the good in accordance with [their] natural abilities."[29] It employs the literary form of narrative to make arguments concerning the social and political structures that support and promote human flourishing. Grace, then, is not a precondition to the process of making and deciphering these lines of argumentation. The God of the Hebrew Bible "is not particularly impressed with piety, with sacrifices, with doing what you are told to do and what your fathers did before you. He is not even that impressed with doing what you believe has been decreed by God."[30] Instead, God is intent on increasing human freedom and human wisdom. "The final author of the History," he argues,

> wished to persuade his readers that there exists a law whose force is of a universal nature, because it derives from the way the world itself was *made* ... [and] that the law of Moses was the very first systematic expression of this natural law, written down for the benefit of Israel and of all [humanity].[31]

Eleonore Stump likewise thinks that narrative plays an indispensable role in the discussion of certain philosophical issues.[32] Though an advocate of the analytic approach to philosophy, she thinks this approach tends to side-step "complex cases drawn from real life or from the world's great literature,"[33] especially when it comes to the task of providing a complex and robust analysis of human interactions. Instead,

---

[26]   Ibid., 227.
[27]   Ibid., 41.
[28]   Ibid.
[29]   Ibid., 31.
[30]   Ibid., 109.
[31]   Ibid., 249.
[32]   On the relationship between Stump's approach and divine revelation, see Stump, *Wandering in Darkness: Narrative and the Problem of Suffering* (Oxford: Clarendon Press, 2010), 35–37. Stump would probably fall in the category of appropriating the Bible philosophically rather than taking it as a work of philosophy. For more on Stump's approach, see chapter 12 in this volume.
[33]   Stump, *Wandering in Darkness*, 25.

it employs "thin stories" that involve "the philosophical crash-dummies Smith and Jones."[34] Yet, Stump contends that personal relations "are at the heart of certain philosophical problems" (e.g., the problem of human suffering).[35] The analytic approach's response to the problem of suffering has been predominantly the result of left-brain thinking (e.g., the formulation of precise principles that aim to justify God permitting the suffering we experience and observe). However, Stump claims that inasmuch as "analytic philosophy is one of the pattern-processing arts, it will be incomplete at best when it comes to describing the parts of reality including persons."[36]

Stump does not intend to denigrate the analytic approach's focus on precision, clarity, and rigor, but she does argue that it is unnecessarily limiting in terms of the scope of its inquiry. Rather, she thinks a constructive way forward (especially with respect to the problem of evil) involves marrying analytic philosophy to the "study of narrative" (including biblical narratives) while "preserving" the virtues of the analytic method.[37] Undergirding Stump's project is the basic assumption that not all knowledge is reducible to propositional knowledge. We can acquire knowledge of things that are "philosophically significant but that are difficult or impossible to know or express apart from stories" (e.g., knowledge of persons conveyed to us through our own second-person experiences and narratives; the complex give-and-take of interpersonal interactions).[38]

Accordingly, Stump makes a distinction between "Dominican" and "Franciscan" epistemologies. The former categorizes "on the basis of sets of abstract properties and abstract designations,"[39] and such a focus is in keeping with the analytic approach to philosophy. This kind of knowledge comes by way of rigorous argumentation. However, this is not the only way to categorize things. The Franciscan approach is "based not so much on abstract properties as on stories, and the labels used for classification are the proper names of the stories' figures." This way of categorization can be thought of as "a kind of typology."[40] This kind of non-propositional knowledge is derived from personal experiences and human interaction. In essence, Stump thinks that narratives (including

---

34   Ibid.
35   Ibid., 23.
36   Ibid., 38.
37   Ibid., 25.
38   Ibid., 40, 62.
39   Ibid., 41.
40   Ibid.

biblical narratives) can convey important knowledge of persons and personal relations, and thus help us see how suffering contributes to the ultimate flourishing of various biblical characters (e.g., Abraham, Job, Mary of Bethany) and to the process of achieving the desires of their hearts.

As we have seen, the recent scholarly discussion about the relationship between Genesis and philosophy is complex. A crucial issue involves determining whether Genesis should be read as a work of philosophy or appropriated philosophically. Hazony says the Bible is a work of philosophy while Kass thinks that it can be read for philosophical profit but it is not, strictly speaking, a work of philosophy. Stump seems to think that the Bible is not a work of philosophy in the strict sense but "it is legitimate to examine biblical narratives philosophically."[41] In fact, the Bible offers, in its narrative mode, Franciscan knowledge with respect to knowledge of persons.

MODERN PHILOSOPHICAL RECEPTIONS
OF THE BINDING OF ISAAC

Many philosophical issues emerge while reading the story of the binding of Isaac on its own terms and in light of the canons of philosophical reflection.[42] What, for example, are we to make of God's command to Abraham, "Take your son, your only son Isaac, whom you love, and go to the land of Moriah, and offer him there as a burnt offering"? (Gen 22:2). Why, in the first place, would God ask Abraham to sacrifice his son? Moreover, what are we to make of Abraham's willingness to kill his own child? Is there an underlying purpose or justification? If so, what is it? Why would God desire such a sacrifice or see it as desirable? Does the story actually call for blind obedience to divine commands? Or, are we left with the choice between the rightness of obedience to divine commands or the rightness of moral duty?

---

[41]   Ibid., xix; see also chapters 2–4.
[42]   For example, Ze'ev Levy, "On the Aqedah in Modern Philosophy," *Journal of Jewish Thought and Philosophy* 15.1 (2007): 85–108, here 89, says that the philosophical interest of the story "might be recapitulated as follows: The ethical (or, more exactly, unethical) connotation of the story – Abraham's willingness to kill his son – cannot be justified under any circumstances; and the religious connotation of the story – Abraham's willingness to sacrifice Isaac – is, to say the least, controversial." Kass, *The Beginning of Wisdom*, 333, adds: "No story in Genesis is as terrible, as powerful, as mysterious, as elusive as this one. It defies easy and confident interpretations, and despite all that I shall have to say about it, it continues to baffle me."

It is not surprising, then, that this story has given birth to different philosophical inquiries and readings. The plural in the title of this section is deliberate. The different receptions of the text wonderfully illustrate the complexity of the story itself and the various issues that materialize in light of philosophical reflection. However, the aim of this section is not to be comprehensive in terms of coverage, nor is it to determine which philosophical reading is correct. Instead, the primary focus will be on how philosophers have read, interpreted, and evaluated this story. I will highlight the different philosophical issues that emerge in the receptions of the story and the ways in which they have been taken up and addressed by different philosophers. The thinkers covered in this section will serve as a springboard for broader scholarly discussion of the text and the relevant philosophical issues that emerge in light of it.

A fitting place to begin is with the philosophical receptions of Immanuel Kant and Søren Kierkegaard. They come from radically different philosophical points of view and thus offer profoundly different ways of reading the story of the binding of Isaac. More importantly, they have deeply shaped the modern philosophical discussion of this story.[43] In fact, most of the modern philosophical receptions can be traced back in some ways to one or both of these points of view. The philosophical receptions are generally framed in moral and epistemological terms. For example, what are the morally and epistemologically relevant issues in the text? What are the moral and epistemic criteria by which we evaluate the story? How do we determine what counts as a divine revelation or a manifestation of the divine?

Kant clearly frames his reading of the story in moral terms. He thinks that the moral law is the criterion by which we ought to evaluate any moral action and or requirement, even in the case of the binding of Isaac. He "reasons that the moral law is certain, at least insofar as not killing one's innocent son is concerned, whereas divine commands are

---

[43] As Seeskin, *Thinking about the Torah*, 61, points out, the question of whether God could command the sacrifice of Isaac "takes us into the realm of philosophical interpretation. Again, we have a Scylla and Charybdis, only this time the opposing positions are represented by Kant and Kierkegaard." Robert Merrihew Adams, *Finite and Infinite Goods* (Oxford: Oxford University Press, 1999), 277, says that the salience of the story of the binding of Isaac "owes much to one of the classics of modern religious thought, Søren Kierkegaard's *Fear and Trembling*, in which ethical issues about the story are raised with exceptional sharpness and made the focus of a profound examination of the relation between religion and ethics." See also Levy, "On the Aquedah in Modern Philosophy," and Seizo Sekine, "Philosophical Interpretations of the Old Testament," in *Congress Volume Ljubljana 2007*, ed. André Lemaire (Leiden: Brill, 2010), 339–66.

profoundly uncertain."[44] What stands against the moral law must be rejected. So, what Abraham believes God is calling him to do, from the perspective of the moral law, must be rejected.

Kant also frames his reading of the story in epistemological terms, especially with respect to divine revelation. For example, are all claims to divine revelation equally valid? Did God actually command Abraham to kill his own son? If so, how do we weigh such appeals to divine revelation? Kant in fact claims that we are not in a position to *know* if God truly is speaking to us. "For if God should really speak [to us, we] could still never *know* that it was God speaking. It is quite impossible" for us to "apprehend the infinite by [our] senses, distinguish it from sensible beings, and *recognize* it as such."[45]

Though distinctive areas of inquiry, the moral and the epistemic seem to intersect in Kant's reading of the story. For example, he says that there are some cases in which we "can be sure that the voice [one] hears is *not* God's; for if the voice commands [one] to do something contrary to the moral law, then no matter how majestic the apparition may be, and no matter how it may seem to surpass the whole of nature," one "must consider it an illusion."[46] So, in the case of Abraham, even if he thought that he heard God command him to sacrifice his only son, he "should have replied to this supposedly divine voice" as follows: "That I ought not to kill my good son is quite certain. But that you, this apparition, are God – of that I am not certain, and never can be, not even if this voice rings down to me from (visible) heaven."[47] The claim here seems to be that Abraham, epistemically speaking, did not really hear God. If he thought that he did, he simply got it wrong and, morally speaking, he should reject it in light of the moral law.

An important issue, for Kant, is whether divine revelation can be reliably transmitted and interpreted. Are we, in other words, in a position

---

44   Matthew Levering, "God and Natural Law: Genesis 22 and Natural Law," *Modern Theology* 24.2 (2008): 151–77, here 152.

45   Immanuel Kant, *The Conflict of the Faculties*, trans. Mary J. Gregor (Lincoln, NE: University of Nebraska Press, 1979), 115. Adams, *Finite and Infinite Goods*, 284, thinks that Kant's main point is essentially correct. "Whatever one's source of information may be, if it indicates that God has commanded something truly terrible, one of the possibilities that should be considered is that we have been misinformed about the commands of the true God." Adams likewise thinks the dilemma most likely stems from an epistemological problem, namely, the inability to decipher God's will. "The problem, as he recognizes, has an epistemological dimension. Among purported revelations, which of them are authentic and really come from God? Hardly any religion supposes that all of them do."

46   Kant, *The Conflict of the Faculties*, 115.

47   Ibid.

to acquire (reliably) knowledge of divine revelation? As Filip Čapek points out, it is evident, for Kant, that "revelation as a medium conveying the divine will is not a reliable source. This revelation, being transmitted *via* historical documents, is never certain. This, expressed by Kant, refers to all historical and visionary faith. Such a form of experience always embraces the possibility of error."[48] Again, there seems to be a connection between the epistemic and the moral. The uncertainty of the former is tied to determining whether it would be fitting for God to command such a thing. Kant observes that in all likelihood persons who think that they receive commands from God suffer from a God delusion. As a result, Kant seems to think that the sacrifice of Isaac on the face of it is irrational, incoherent, and unintelligible.

Kierkegaard seems to operate with radically different theological and philosophical assumptions. When God asks Abraham to perform an act that, from an ethical point of view, is wrong, Abraham's decision can be justified by only one assumption – namely that God has the power to suspend the ethical. In other words, the ethical prohibition against killing an innocent person is overridden by God's command. Accordingly, faith is not merely about believing in God; it requires an "absolute relation" to God and an "absolute duty" towards God.[49] Kierkegaard seems to concede that the teleological suspension of the ethical is a violation of a moral principle, and it is certainly not to be universalized. As he says, the ethical "applies to everyone."[50] However, Abraham opts for the particular over the universal, especially when he comes to the call to renounce the finite for the infinite.

Why, then, did Abraham agree to offer up Isaac? Kierkegaard says, "For God's sake, and (in complete identity with this) for his own sake. He did it for God's sake because God required this proof of his faith; for his own sake he did it in order that he might furnish the proof."[51] That Abraham understands and accepts this feature of his existential situation is part of what makes him a "knight of faith." The problem, then, is not a matter of mishearing or an interpretive dilemma.[52] Instead,

---

48 Felip Capek, "A Philosophical Discourse on Genesis 22-Akedah Reflected by Kant, Fichte, and Schelling," *CV* 52.3 (2010): 217–27, here 220. See also Kant, *The Conflict of the Faculties*, 115–18.

49 Søren Kierkegaard, *Fear and Trembling: A Dialectical Lyric*, trans. Walter Lowrie (Princeton, NJ: Princeton University Press, 1941), 105, 106, 123.

50 Ibid., 79.

51 Ibid., 89.

52 Martin Buber, *Eclipse of God: Studies in the Relation Between Religion and Philosophy* (New York: Harper & Brothers, 1957), 117–18, argues that Kierkegaard's reading of the story does not sufficiently take into consideration "the fact that the

Kierkegaard draws attention to what the contours of faith entail in this story. The command is clear, and it is from God. As a "knight of faith," Abraham relinquishes the "finite" for the "infinite." In his particularity, Abraham acts "by virtue of the absurd, for it is precisely absurd that he as the particular is higher than the universal."[53]

The teleological suspension of the ethical, for Kierkegaard, is from the standpoint of a higher religious objective. In other words, obedience to God takes precedence over moral principles. As a "knight of faith," Abraham "follows the narrow way of faith," and so "no one can give counsel," nor can they understand him. In this sense, faith is a "miracle."[54] Abraham "knows that it is refreshing to become intelligible to oneself in the universal."[55] However, he "knows also that higher than this [the universal as his home] there winds a solitary path, narrow and steep; he knows that it is terrible to be born outside the universal, to walk without meeting a single traveler."[56] In his solitary existence and decision, Abraham remains silent before his son whom he has agreed to offer up as a burnt offering.

Eleonore Stump believes that Kierkegaard's way of reading the story is problematic and "mistaken."[57] Kierkegaard's account of the story of the binding of Isaac, according to Stump, lacks textual and philosophical coherence. His reading eclipses an important part of the story. That is, the binding of Isaac needs to be read within the context of the whole narrative of Abraham's life. Failing to do so misses the nuances of the story.

---

problematics of the decision of faith is preceded by the problematics of the hearing itself." See also Sekine, "Philosophical Interpretations of the Sacrifice of Isaac," 345.
[53] Kierkegaard, *Fear and Trembling*, 90, 83.
[54] Ibid., 100, 122. For a contemporary philosophical reception of Kierkegaard's isolation and silence, see Emmanuel Levinas, *Proper Names*, trans. Michael B. Smith (Stanford, CA: Stanford University Press, 1996) and Jacques Derrida, *The Gift of Death*, trans. David Wills (Chicago: University of Chicago Press, 1995).
[55] Kierkegaard, *Fear and Trembling*, 115.
[56] Ibid.
[57] Stump, *Wandering in Darkness*, 261. Fleischacker, *The Good and the Good Book*, 138, says that "Abraham is often cited as an example of someone who suspends all ordinary moral and pragmatic concerns when he offers up his beloved son" to God. However, he also seems to challenge God to "live up to an independent standard of justice" (Gen. 18:25). More exactly, Fleischacker draws attention to the complex relationship between human autonomy and obedience in the Hebrew Bible. Thus, Abraham's willingness to sacrifice Isaac "has always been a terrifying mystery to believers. It remains that; we are and should be disturbed by it, not hold it up as a model of faith, as Kierkegaard does" (Fleischacker, *The Good and the Good Book*, 138; see also 110).

A central theme in the story centers on the desires of Abraham's heart – the promise of a great nation and posterity. The core of Stump's argument is that the faith of Abraham consists not in detachment from the desires of the heart but rather the question of what it means to trust in the goodness of God to fulfill those desires.[58] In addition, the themes of promise, reliability, and faith are interwoven into the larger narrative of Abraham's life. Stump also draws attention to the "pattern" of Abraham's double-mindedness, especially with respect to "God's promises to give him his heart's desire."[59] More exactly, the pattern of Abraham's double-mindedness is "interspersed with episodes in which Abraham's trust in God's goodness is wholehearted, most notably in the binding of Isaac. But the overall pattern is only highlighted by the few notable exceptions to it."[60] Thus, the dilemma is not between God's command and morality. Instead, "it constitutes a test of Abraham's character that he passes precisely by committing himself to the belief that morality and obedience to God are on the same side."[61]

In terms of the story of the binding of Isaac, Stump thinks it is crucial to note that when God speaks to Abraham, it is clear that Abraham immediately recognizes that the speaker is in fact God (Gen. 22:1). "This initial step, in which God says Abraham's name and Abraham responds with immediate recognition and shared attention, makes subsequent doubt on Abraham's part much harder and less plausible."[62] In other words, Abraham does not seem to be suffering from a God delusion. Stump seems implicitly, if not explicitly, to be rejecting the claim that Abraham is incapable of recognizing the voice of God. The content of God's command is certainly different, but the voice of the one commanding Abraham to sacrifice Isaac is the same. In the previous divine speeches, the content "has been or at least included great promises about Abraham's offspring and their descendants," but in the story of the binding of Isaac, "without explanation, God abruptly demands that Abraham sacrifice his son to him."[63]

Stump sees the story as a test that challenges Abraham's double-mindedness about God's promises while seeking to refine his faith. An important backdrop in this respect is the expulsion of Ishmael (Gen. 21:9–21). In particular, Abraham has to face honestly "the fact that he

---

[58] Stump, *Wandering in Darkness*, 259.
[59] Ibid., 282.
[60] Ibid., 282.
[61] Ibid., 261.
[62] Ibid., 294.
[63] Ibid.

was willing to expel his first-born son into the desert on the strength of God's promise to make of him a great nation."[64] Abraham, Stump adds, will fail the test presented to him in the story of the binding of Isaac "if he does not treat Isaac in the same way in which he treated Ishmael."[65] To deal with both cases in "the same way, then, requires believing that, even if he sacrifices Isaac, Isaac will live and flourish."[66] In essence, Abraham "must now place his hopes on God's goodness, or he must make clear that in the expulsion of Ishmael he was just using God as a means to a seriously wrong act, without supposing that God cared much or took much notice of that wrongness."[67] Abraham, Stump concludes, "passes the test only if he believes that in obeying God he is *not* giving up Isaac."[68]

Yoram Hazony agrees that it is a fundamental mistake to read the story of the binding of Isaac in isolation from the larger narrative of Abraham's life. Like Stump, Hazony couches the story within the context of the whole narrative. A broader reading recognizes the complex character of Abraham, a person who embodies some extraordinary virtues (e.g., generosity; justice) while exhibiting normal patterns of self-interest. A neglected virtue, according to Hazony, is Abraham's "horror over the shedding of innocent blood."[69] This virtue can be seen in various places, but it is perhaps most evident in Abraham's dialogue with God concerning the fate of the righteous in Sodom. Abraham "believes that the dangers to the lives of the innocent of Sodom merits such a risk [of courting God's wrath] on his part."[70] In this situation, "Abraham's sense of the need to protect innocent human life, even if this involves a risk to oneself, stands out as a virtue that God is concerned to see handed down to future generations."[71] Abraham's concern over the well-being of others (especially the righteous or innocent) should factor into the reading of the binding of Isaac story. Instead, most think that Abraham's actions in Genesis 22 are horrific, "morally repugnant," unintelligible, and "absurd."[72]

---

[64] Ibid., 297.
[65] Ibid.
[66] Ibid., 300.
[67] Ibid., 298.
[68] Ibid., 300. On this point, Stump thinks Hebrews 11:17–19 offers a similar interpretation.
[69] Hazony, *The Philosophy of Hebrew Scripture*, 115.
[70] Ibid.
[71] Ibid.
[72] Ibid.

The different responses of Abraham in Genesis 18 and 22, however, seem to suggest that Abraham is not exhibiting blind obedience, but is trusting the character of God, which has already been established. In Genesis 18, Abraham boldly wonders whether God will act justly towards the righteous or "sweep away the righteous with the wicked" (see Gen. 18:23). He seems to be unsure about God's justice. This especially explains Abraham's line of questioning. The point in the story seems to be the question of whether God would behave justly with respect to the presence of select righteous people. The answer from God is obviously yes.[73] In the binding of Isaac, however, Abraham's disposition is different. Abraham does not question God's command, nor does he inquire about God's justice.

As a result, Hazony claims that the basic point of the story of the binding of Isaac is to show that God does not approve of human sacrifices. The story is meant to emphasize the radical difference between the gods of other nations, who seemingly take pleasure in child sacrifice, and the God of Abraham, who not only values innocent human life but deplores the shedding of innocent blood vis-à-vis child sacrifice. "Given the choice between the sacrifice of Abraham's most prized possession – his only son – and the sacrifice of a ram that Abraham did not even own, the God of Israel prefers the ram."[74] Thus, Hazony does not think, contra Kierkegaard, that the text is sanctioning blind obedience to God's commands. Rather, the text rejects human sacrifice. The main point of the story is the condemnation of human sacrifices, not the dilemma between blind faith and the suspension of the ethical. The universe accordingly "is ruled by a God who has no interest in seeing human beings make the ultimate sacrifice for his sake, because innocent life is more precious to him than such honor as can be bestowed by misguided" people or sacrifices.[75] Given God's commitment to the well-being of the innocent and hatred for the sacrifice of innocent humans, the intent on God's part was never for "Abraham to sacrifice his son."[76]

Hazony also does not think the text supports the claim that Abraham obeyed God because he believed that God would ultimately

---

[73] However, Stump, *Wandering in Darkness*, 284, says that though "Abraham is usually praised for his concern with justice and for his courage in confronting God in this exchange, the first thing to see here is in fact Abraham's double-mindedness about God's goodness." Abraham affirms that the God is the "judge of all the earth" but he also sees the need to talk the same judge into doing "what is just" (Gen. 18:25). Cf. Fleischacker, *The Good and the Good Book*, 136.

[74] Hazony, *The Philosophy of Hebrew Scripture*, 116.

[75] Ibid.

[76] Ibid., 116–17.

bring his son back from the dead.[77] Such a claim presumes that the
sacrifice of Abraham's only son foreshadows "the New Testament
God's sacrifice of Jesus, understood as his only son, on the cross."[78]
However, Hazony argues that this kind of interpretation of the story
cannot or should not "be accepted."[79] One reaches such a conclusion
by "reading the story out of the context of the larger narrative in which
the biblical author has placed it; and by ignoring those verses that indicate that Abraham was never 'willing' to sacrifice Isaac."[80] Again, the
point of the story is to show or draw a distinction between the God of
Abraham and the gods of the surrounding nations.[81] While "other
nations may expect a contempt for innocent human life from their
gods" (e.g., the Canaanite custom of child sacrifice), the God depicted
in Genesis 22 "values innocent human life above the piety of giving
honor and thanksgiving to the gods." In reality, "it is the *sacrifice of
a ram* that is the symbol of the God of Abraham, who is a god of
shepherds; and it pleases this God to accept such a sacrifice "in place
of his son," which is to say, in place of human sacrifice.[82]

[77] Ibid., 311 fn. 80, says, "This consideration of Isaac's possible resurrection comes from
the implicit parallel drawn here between Isaac and Jesus: Just as God was willing to
sacrifice 'his only son,' so too was Abraham. And because Jesus was then resurrected
from the dead, it becomes plausible to think that Isaac might have been. This was
defended, among others, by Stump" (see Stump, *Wandering in Darkness*, 300).
However, Hazony argues that such a reading risks "missing the entire point of the
story, which is that the God of Israel, unlike other gods of Canaan, would never will
the murder of an innocent person." Stump does include an appeal to Hebrews 11:17–
19 in a footnote. However, she also grounds her reading of Abraham's obedience in the
antecedent promises of God concerning the well-being of Ishmael.
[78] Hazony, *The Philosophy of Hebrew Scripture*, 115.
[79] Ibid.
[80] Ibid., 115–16.
[81] Ibid., 116.
[82] Ibid. John Levenson, *The Death and Resurrection of the Beloved Son: The
Transformation of Child Sacrifice in Judaism and Christianity* (New Haven, CT:
Yale University Press, 1993), 113, says that it is "strange" that the story would begin
with "that same God's demanding that from which he recoils." In other words, why
would the God who "finally opposes child sacrifice initially" command it? Also,
Levenson (113f.) says, "The cumulative evidence against the ubiquitous idea that
the aqedah opposes child sacrifice and substitutes an animal cult is overwhelming."
See also Samuel Lebens, "Hebrew Philosophy or Jewish Theology? A False
Dichotomy," *Journal of Analytic Theology* 2 (2014), 250–60, here 257. Weiss,
Ethical Ambiguity in the Hebrew Bible, 29, agrees that God's command is clearly at
odds with "autonomous moral standards." However, perhaps in commanding such an
offering God is seeking to "foster Abraham's religious fervor in a manner familiar to
him from his pagan background. Once Abraham actualized such passion as he prepared to offer his beloved son as a sacrifice, he could then be taught to sublimate such
a fervor in a more ethical way." As a result, "the divine command not to slaughter
Isaac is the climax of the narrative and takes an independent ethic into consideration."

Notwithstanding the nuanced examinations of the larger narrative of Abraham's life, the story of the binding of Isaac, and the focus on the desires of Abraham's heart, some philosophical questions remain. What, for example, does it mean for a good God to command the sort of sacrifice envisioned in the story of the binding of Isaac? Suppose it is the case that God really demanded such a sacrifice. How, as Robert Adams wonders, "should we respond if God confronted us with such a sign? Should we obey, trusting that God will see to it that obedience works out for the best, even if we do not see how? Or should we change deities?"[83] The concern here is whether a commandment of this sort would be befitting of a God who is omnibenevolent. In this case, much would depend on whether we could imagine and/or see the author of such a command as "the supreme Good. If we could, then perhaps trusting obedience might seem the right course."[84] Adams nevertheless thinks a situation in which he "would find it reasonable to believe that a good God had given such an abhorrent command seems," to him, "unimaginable."[85]

CONCLUDING REMARKS

Given the diverse landscape of the modern philosophical receptions of the story of the binding of Isaac, what, then, does it mean for biblical studies to maintain the integrity of its own methodological commitments while taking seriously and charting a constructive philosophical path? It certainly does not mean forgetting its own commitments (e.g., historical and linguistic rigor), nor does it mean exempting those commitments from engagement with the broader streams of philosophical thought and recent work in epistemology (e.g., normative questions about the philosophical issues that arise in the relevant biblical texts). There are clearly encouraging signs of scholarly interest in connecting the disciplines of biblical studies and philosophy. The key, in my estimation, is to foster instructive dialogue and interdisciplinary work in fruitful ways.

A nice place to begin is with reflection on the epistemological issues that are identified in Genesis. For example, one of the epistemological issues in the reception of the binding of Isaac focuses on the conditions under which one can hear or perceive the divine voice. Such an issue is

Abraham learned, by heeding the second divine call, that it would no longer "be an appropriate mode of sacrifice and offered a ram in Isaac's stead."
[83]   Adams, *Finite and Infinite Goods*, 290.
[84]   Ibid.
[85]   Ibid.

ripe for epistemological analysis. It would be helpful to get a greater clarification of what divine revelation entails and how it functions as an epistemic concept for individuals and for religious communities.[86]

Epistemological questions concerning the normative status of particular biblical texts are natural and inevitable. A project of this sort would seek to do historical, theological, and philosophical justice to various themes in Scripture while seeking to explore constructive epistemological possibilities. The interdisciplinary nature and scope of this project, however, is a vivid reminder of the importance and challenge of bringing together insights from various domains of inquiry.[87]

SELECT BIBLIOGRAPHY

Adams, Robert Merrihew. *Finite and Infinite Goods*. Oxford: Oxford University Press, 1999.

Capek, Felip. "A Philosophical Discourse on Genesis 22-Akedah Reflected by Kant, Fichte, and Schelling." *CV* 52.3 (2010): 217–27.

Fleischacker, Samuel. *The Good and the Good Book*. Oxford: Oxford University Press, 2015.

Gericke, Jaco. *The Hebrew Bible and Philosophy of Religion*. Atlanta, GA: Society of Biblical Literature, 2012.

Hazony, Yoram. *The Philosophy of Hebrew Scripture*. Cambridge: Cambridge University Press, 2012.

Immanuel Kant, *The Conflict of the Faculties*. Translated by Mary J. Gregor. Lincoln, NE: University of Nebraska Press, 1979.

Kass, Leon R. *The Beginning of Wisdom: Reading Genesis*. New York, NY: Free Press, 2003.

Kierkegaard, Søren. *Fear and Trembling: A Dialectical Lyric*. Translated by Walter Lowrie. Princeton, NJ: Princeton University Press, 1941.

Levenson, John. *The Death and Resurrection of the Beloved Son: The Transformation of Child Sacrifice in Judaism and Christianity*. New Haven, CT: Yale University Press, 1993.

---

[86] For recent philosophical and theological accounts of divine revelation, see Richard Swinburne, *Revelation: From Metaphor to Analogy* (Oxford: Clarendon Press, 1992); Keith Ward, *Religion and Revelation: A Theology of Revelation in the World's Religions* (Oxford: Clarendon Press, 1994); George Mavrodes, *Revelation in Religious Belief* (Philadelphia: Temple University Press, 1988); Abraham, *Crossing the Threshold of Divine Revelation*; William J. Abraham, *Divine Revelation and the Limits of Historical Criticism* (Oxford: Clarendon Press, 1982); Sandra L. Menssen and Thomas D. Sullivan, *The Agnostic Inquirer: Revelation from a Philosophical Point of View* (Grand Rapids: Eerdmans, 2007); and Menssen and Sullivan, "Revelation and Scripture."

[87] Thanks to Bill T. Arnold, Brian Shockey, and Taylor Bonner for helpful comments on earlier versions of this chapter.

Levy, Ze'ev. "On the Aquedah in Modern Philosophy." *Journal of Jewish Thought and Philosophy* 15.1 (2007): 85–108.

Stump, Eleonore. *Wandering in Darkness: Narrative and the Problem of Suffering.* Oxford: Clarendon Press, 2010.

Weiss, Shira. *Ethical Ambiguity in the Hebrew Bible: Philosophical Analysis of Scriptural Narrative.* Cambridge: Cambridge University Press, 2018.

15 Jewish Reflections on Universalism and Particularism in Genesis

JOEL S. KAMINSKY

Already in antiquity Jewish interpreters commented upon the oddity that the Torah, a book centered upon and preoccupied with the laws given at Sinai, contains such an extended prologue. Thus, the following reflection from the *Mekhilta of Rabbi Ishmael*, an anthology of legal midrashim from second/third-century CE Palestine, comments on why the Ten Commandments are not given in Genesis:

> *I am the Lord your God:* Why were the ten commandments not stated at the beginning of the Torah? An analogy: A man enters a province and says (to the inhabitants): I will rule over you. They respond: Did you do anything for us that you would rule over us? Whereupon he builds the (city) wall for them, provides water for them, wages war for them, and then says: I will rule over you, whereupon they respond: Yes! Yes! Thus, the Lord took Israel out of Egypt, split the sea for them, brought down manna for them, raised the well for them, brought in quail for them, waged war with Amalek for them, and then said to them: I will rule over you, whereupon they responded: Yes! Yes![1]

As one can see, the *Mekhilta* answers its own rhetorical question with a wonderful parable about how a king who wishes to rule over people must first do things to earn the respect of his subjects. Likewise, God first redeemed Israel from Egypt and also provided the Israelites with manna and quails before asking for their fealty. Similarly, Rashi, the great medieval Jewish exegete, initiates his running commentary on Genesis by asking why the Torah does not begin with the first commandment given to the whole people of Israel, a command that occurs in Exodus 12. Rashi sees the preceding materials in Genesis as necessary so that other nations cannot claim that Israel illicitly stole the Holy Land. Here God's

---

[1] *Mekhilta de-Rabbi Ishmael, Bahodesh,* 5, translation from Safaria: https://www .sefaria.org/Mekhilta_d'Rabbi_Yishmael.20.2.1?lang=bi.

ownership over creation is stressed as a way to explain God's right to take land from the Canaanites and give it to the Israelites (see Rashi on Gen 1:1).

While the *Mekhilta* and Rashi generate slightly different answers, each is an attempt to explain why we have an extended, mainly narrative, prologue placed before the bulk of the Torah's legal material. One could say that they both reply: to show you that the God of Israel is indeed the God who created and controls all the world. Yet, they do this in inverse ways, probably because each is commenting on a different passage in the Torah. The *Mekhilta* relates the vast bulk of the Torah and the larger Hebrew Bible, which focus on Israel more particularly, back to a more universal viewpoint by stressing God's control over creation as demonstrated by the miracles surrounding the Exodus and Israel's journey to Sinai. Ultimately, both the demonstration of God's control over nature and God's claim on Israel's fealty are grounded in the Genesis creation stories, a point underlined by the pervasive use of creation and flood related imagery within the Exodus story. On the other hand, Rashi shows that the wider viewpoint found early on in Genesis undergirds God's later election of Israel and God's right to deed Israel the land of Canaan. Both these interpretive moves are in substantial agreement that the early materials in Genesis, most especially those stressing God's creation of the natural world and of humanity, have a much more universalistic emphasis than other parts of the Torah, a reading that is in tune with the way many contemporary biblical scholars understand Genesis 1–11.

I concur with the notion that there is a productive tension between the universal framework found in Genesis 1–11 and the rest of the Torah's and larger Hebrew Bible's more particularistic stories and laws that follow. Yet, I would like to suggest that even within Genesis 1–11's rather universal thrust one finds substantial elements of particularism, albeit often in muted form. And, as will be noted later in this chapter, the more particularistic narratives concerning Israel's ancestors found in Genesis 12–50 may be more universalistic than often recognized. To focus this discussion, the chapter will begin by attending to Genesis 1–4 in some depth and then proceed by surveying a selection of passages from elsewhere in Genesis.

UNIVERSALISM AND PARTICULARISM IN GENESIS 1–4

Let us begin with the opening creation account in Genesis, a text often viewed as quite universalistic in its outlook. Thus Jon Levenson, in his seminal essay, "The Universal Horizon of Biblical Particularism," makes the following observations about the first creation account:

> [Gen 1–2:3] mentions no landmarks, no countries, no rivers, not even a Garden of Eden. Instead, men and women, created together, exist on undifferentiated dry land .... In the biblical story, the only *particular* vestige of the act of creation is a cultic rite, the Sabbath, through which man replicates the rhythm of the protological events (2:1–3) .... Like Esagila, the Sabbath recollects the divine repose after the work of creation, but in a nonspatial and therefore universalizable way. Unlike the *Enuma Elish*, Gen. 1:1–2:3 does not serve to buttress any particular political or cultic order. It is also highly significant that in both creation accounts at the beginning of Genesis (1:1–2:3 and 2:4–24), it is humanity in general and not any people in particular that is created. Israel is not primordial.[2]

Yet, even here, one need not look far to find notes of particularism beyond the Sabbath, which Levenson touches upon and perhaps too quickly suggests is spoken of here in a universalizable manner. Thus Dick Clifford, in an essay written in honor of Levenson, argues that:

> Genesis 1 contains covert references to several defining features of Israel, viz., the Sabbath, the Temple, the dietary laws, and the conquest. Despite its care for proper chronology, P evidently shared the ancient conviction that important elements of the world "were there from the beginning" and acquired their significance at their origin. If one may borrow computer language, P's references to Israel are "locked" in the disk of Genesis 1 and are accessible only to those possessing the code.[3]

To be sure, we should not overstate the difference between these two thoughtful scholars. Clifford acknowledges that each element of Israelite particularism he finds in Genesis 1 is in a subtle and nascent form. For example, Clifford does not assert that the Levitical dietary laws are mentioned in Genesis 1, but rather that these laws only make sense in relation to the separations and distinctions found in Genesis 1. Similarly, he does not think Israel's conquest of Canaan is overtly invoked, but

2   Jon D. Levenson, "The Universal Horizon of Biblical Particularism," in *Ethnicity and the Bible*, ed. Mark Brett (Leiden: Brill, 1996), 143–69, here 146–47 (emphasis his).
3   Richard J. Clifford, "Election in Genesis 1," in *The Call of Abraham: Essays on the Election of Israel in Honor of Jon D. Levenson*, ed. Gary A. Anderson and Joel S. Kaminsky (Notre Dame, IN: University of Notre Dame, 2013), 7–22, here 7–8.

rather subtly alluded to in that in Clifford's view the most likely referent of the word *kibšuhā* in Gen 1:28, often rendered to "subdue it," is to Israel's later conquest of Canaan.

Now one should not be shocked that Israel's portraits of universalism are colored by her own particularistic viewpoint. One finds a similar situation today among Western thinkers whose own universalist musings are equally tinged by a particularistic Western outlook. The truth is that even if certain universal ideals broaden the scope of a particular culture's worldview, they do so in ways that inevitably reflect the deepest particularistic ideals of that culture. In short, universal ideals grow in the soil of and thus remain rooted in a specific cultural context.

Even if one endorsed Clifford's view over Levenson's, Clifford himself points out that there is more than one way to understand these covert references to various Israelite cultural touchstones embedded within Genesis 1:

> According to the first, Genesis 1 is communicating to insiders that God's real interest in creating the world was Israel; other nations are mentioned, but they are present only as backdrop and audience for God's business with Israel. According to the second, the foreshadowing means that from the beginning there existed a complementarity between the elect nation and the other nations. The tasks and hopes of Israel and the nations, respectively, might be differently expressed and differently timed, but they are closely related. Israel is an example of a nation doing important things in its own way while sharing the experience and aspirations of other nations.[4]

In fact, both the view that God created the world for Israel and the notion that God's interactions with Israel are part of God's wider purposes for the nations and the larger world have been advanced in various biblical and postbiblical texts. One need only think of 4 Ezra 6:55–59, which derogates the place of all other nations and describes the world as created for Israel.

> All this I have spoken before you, O Lord, because you have said that it was for us that you created this world. As for the other nations that have descended from Adam, you have said that they are nothing, and that they are like spittle, and you have compared their abundance to a drop from a bucket. And now, O Lord, these nations, which are reputed to be as nothing, domineer over us and

4 Ibid., 8.

devour us. But we your people, whom you have called your first-born, only begotten, zealous for you, and most dear, have been given into their hands. If the world has indeed been created for us, why do we not possess our world as an inheritance? How long will this be so?

(NRSV, translation from the NOAB)

This passage contrasts with the tenor of parts of Second and Third Isaiah, which at times depict Israel as playing an important role in reconciling God and the other nations of the world in a renewed creation. What needs to be highlighted here is that 4 Ezra 6:55–59 likely builds upon Isa 40:15–17, and Isaiah 40 may well be in dialogue with Genesis 1. As both Levenson and Clifford affirm, the rather subtle way that Genesis 1–2 adumbrates certain Israelite cultural touchstones results in texts that feel much more universalistic in their orientation than comparable Mesopotamian texts, as highlighted by Levenson in the quotation from his essay "The Universal Horizon of Biblical Particularism" cited above. And yet we need to be careful not to overlook the notes of particularism found in even the most universalistic biblical texts. Otherwise, not only will we have great difficulty understanding how 4 Ezra arrived at his position, but we will have equal difficulty grasping how texts like Genesis 1–11 relate to the larger Jewish Bible, or for that matter the Christian Bible.

Moving further into Genesis 1–11, one finds the Garden of Eden story. I have no intention of arguing that this story is filled with cryptic particularistic references. I would contend, however, that this universalistic story about humanity has an uncanny resemblance to ancient Israel's more specific story that occupies much of the Hebrew Bible. The ancient rabbis, in a brilliant midrash from Genesis Rabbah, demonstrate that Genesis 2–3 mirrors Israel's later attainment of and expulsion from the land. I have included this rather lengthy excerpt, but following it I summarize its thrust and explain its exegetical arguments.

> R. Abbahu said in the name of R. Jose b. R. Hanina: It is written, *But they are like a man (Adam), they have transgressed the covenant* (Hos 6:7). "They are like a man (Adam)" means like Adam: just as I led Adam into the garden of Eden and commanded him, and he transgressed My commandment, whereupon I punished him by dismissal and expulsion, and bewailed him with אֵיכָה (how)! I led him into the garden of Eden, as it is written, *And the Lord God took the man, and put him into the garden of Eden* (Gen 2:15); and I commanded him: *And the Lord God commanded the*

man (2:16-17); and he transgressed My commandment: *Have you eaten of the tree, that I commanded you that you should not eat of it* (3:11)? and I punished him by dismissal: *Therefore the Lord God sent him forth from the garden of Eden* (v. 23); and I punished him by expulsion: *So he drove out the man* (v. 24); I bewailed him with אֵיכָה (how)! And said to him: איכה (אַיֶּכָּה is written [in the ancient consonantal only text]). So also did I bring his descendants into Eretz Israel and command them, and they transgressed My commandment, and I punished them by sending them away and expelling them, and I bewailed them with אֵיכָה! I brought them into Eretz Israel, as it is written, *And I brought you into a land of fruitful fields* (Jer 2:7); I commanded them: *And you will command the children of Israel* (Exod 27:20), also, *Command the children of Israel* (Lev 24:2); they transgressed My command: *All Israel have transgressed your law* (Dan 9:11); I punished them by sending them away: *Send them out of my sight, and let them go* (Jer 15:1); by expulsion: *I will drive them out of My house* (Hos 9:15); and I bewailed them with אֵיכָה: אֵיכָה *(how) the city sits solitary* (Lam 1:1).[5]

In this midrash, the rabbis find two primary verbal links to connect Israel's history to the events that take place in Genesis 2–3. One is that Hos 6:7 contains the enigmatic phrase, *wəhēmmâ kə'ādām 'ābərū bərît*, often understood to refer to some sinful event that took place at a specifically named locale. Thus, the NRSV renders, "At Adam, they transgressed the covenant." The rabbis, however, read the text more straightforwardly, and rendered it more literally as follows: "like Adam they transgressed the covenant." With this reading in mind, it is not difficult to see why they think the text is drawing an analogy between Adam's universal human story found in Genesis 2–3 and Israel's rise and fall. God places Adam in a lush garden, issues a command, only to have Adam break the command resulting in Adam and Eve's expulsion from Eden. Similarly, God brought Israel to the Holy Land and issued commandments for living in the land, which Israel disobeyed, eventuating in her exile. This set of thematic connections is substantially deepened by the rabbinic observation that God's question to Adam, *'ayyekkah*, "where are you," is consonantally identical (*'ykh*) to the first word in Lamentations 1:1, *'êkâ*, "How" as in "How the city sits solitary." In

---

5 Gen. Rab. 19:9. This and all later citations from Midrash Rabbah are based on the Soncino translation, as found in Davka Software's Soncino Classics Library, but have been modified to update the archaic language particularly in the verse citations.

sum, the rabbis see God's gift of the land and Israel's disobedience and eventual exile as hinted at, or perhaps even pre-enacted, in Genesis 3. The ease with which the rabbis can draw thematic, structural, and verbal parallels between the seemingly universal story of Genesis 2–3, which tells of the earliest fracture in the divine/human relationship, and the bulk of the Torah and Prophets, which narrates an analogous story about God's dealings with the people of Israel, suggests that the seemingly universal materials early in Genesis may reflect more particularistic concerns than sometimes recognized.[6]

Proceeding to Genesis 4, one finds what appears to be a universal story that probes the origins of the widespread human tendency toward violence and murder. Yet, the focus of this story adumbrates perhaps the deepest particularistic theme in Israelite culture and has obvious connections to several key biblical narratives. As I have argued elsewhere, this is the first of a host of passages that probe the meaning of God's special divine favor toward certain chosen people and its implications for the non-chosen.[7] This theme of chosen-ness and the relational tensions it often brings in its wake sits at the center of Israel's own theological identity. Later in Genesis and the rest of the Hebrew Bible, God repeatedly favors certain individuals, families, and tribes who turn out to play major roles in Israel's history. Furthermore, Israel understands herself to be God's specially beloved people. At the same time, the narrative also indicates that the non-chosen are not excluded from God's gracious plan for the world. In this account, God speaks at length only with Cain and grants him a measure of mercy even after jealousy drives him to kill Abel, his brother.

While the favor of the chosen and the resultant envy of the non-chosen is due to the particularity of God's own affections, this whole pattern is in some sense a universal story. Cain is an archetype for any human who in a fit of jealousy might lash out and kill his brother. This is what enables modern authors like Melville in *Billy Budd* and Steinbeck in *East of Eden* to use this text so productively. These modern authors build upon ancient precedents. The following midrash, for example, articulates why someone might even kill his own brother; and why in a perfectly egalitarian world it is still likely that people will continue to do so.

---

6   While seemingly unaware of this rabbinic antecedent, David Noel Freedman, in his book *The Nine Commandments: Uncovering a Hidden Pattern of Crime and Punishment in the Hebrew Bible* (New York: Doubleday, 2000), 2–6, also notes that the pattern of command, violation, and exile found in Genesis 3 and again in Genesis 4 is strikingly similar to Israel's larger story.

7   Joel S. Kaminsky, *Yet I Loved Jacob: Reclaiming the Biblical Concept of Election* (Nashville: Abingdon, 2007).

R. Joshua of Siknin said in R. Levi's name: Both took land and both took movables, but about what did they quarrel? One said, "The Temple must be built in my area," while the other claimed, "It must be built in mine." For thus it is written, *and when they were in the field*: Now *field* refers to the Temple, as you read, *Zion [i.e. the Temple] shall be plowed as a field* (Micah 3:12). Out of this argument, *Cain rose up against his brother.*[8]

This midrash imagines that Cain and Abel each stood to inherit half of all the land and half of all the movable property in the world. One might think that with such vast wealth and property holdings each brother would have no reason to feel cheated or deprived. But even in a completely egalitarian situation with ample resources for all parties, human jealousy quickly arises over the exact dividing point. In this instance, the rabbis speculate that each brother knows that in the center of the world stands the future Jerusalem, and in its center the future temple will be erected. In a profound observation on the way in which religious piety itself can lead to violence against others, Cain and Abel's quarrel over whose property will house the future temple results in the first murder. The ancient rabbis imagine a different scenario than Genesis 4 presents. In this midrash, Cain and Abel are both actively involved in a heated dispute that culminates in Cain's murder of Abel. Furthermore, it is a dispute about property rights. In an interesting twist, the rabbis' attempt to link Cain and Abel to Israel's later temple cult has the effect of making the moral of the story more, rather than less, universal. This is because they use this particularistic detail to help us recognize the universal truth that human jealousies are not just driven by actual inequities (as one might think on the basis of Genesis 4), but that jealousy can flare up even in totally egalitarian circumstances.

Now, one might suggest that the rabbinic attempt to link Genesis 4 to later, more particularistic Israelite concerns, while understandable, still cuts against the grain of the biblical story. But is this really true? After all, there is already a host of thematic links between Genesis 4 and the other sibling rivalry stories in Genesis. Furthermore, the Wise Woman of Tekoa in 2 Samuel 14 evokes Cain and Abel when hinting at Absalom's banishment after he murdered Amnon.[9] In fact, 2 Samuel

---

[8] Gen. Rab. 22:7.

[9] The story of the Wise Woman of Tekoa actually contains a host of allusions to a number of the sibling stories in Genesis, as discussed at length in Larry Lyke, *King David with the Wise Woman of Tekoa: The Resonance of Tradition in Parabolic Narrative*, JSOTSup 255 (Sheffield: Sheffield Academic Press, 1997).

may well have supplied much of the exegetical basis of this midrashic comment inasmuch as it implies that the father character had died and that his two sons fought each other in the field. It is not a great distance to assuming that the fight in the wake of their father's death was caused by an argument over inheritance rights. The fact that God promised David that his successor would build the temple and that he had two sons who came to mortal blows might have given rise to the notion that Cain and Abel also fought over who would have the temple built on his property.[10] My point here is simply that what appear to be generic and somewhat universal stories like this one in Genesis 4 already have quite substantial links to Israel's deeply particularistic stories about her identity and later history. Even when Israel tells a seemingly universal story, she is conveying her own story and when she narrates her own very particular story it is a story with universal human import.

UNIVERSALISM AND PARTICULARISM IN GENESIS 6–9 AND 12:1–3

Later within Genesis 1–11, one finds additional and at times more explicit evocations of particularism. Here the pure and impure animals mentioned in J's version of the flood story and the cursing of Ham's son Canaan in Genesis 9 quickly come to mind. The mention of clean and unclean animals is itself instructive (Gen 7:1–3). Traditional source critics see this trope as reflecting J's rather broad-minded conception that any human might legitimately offer sacrifice to God (Gen 8:20), while P is depicted as more parochial. Thus, Gerhard von Rad tells us that in J, "the chief importance of God's activity suddenly lies outside the sacred

---

[10] Further proof that the stories surrounding David's family troubles may have provided the fodder for this rabbinic attempt to explain the cause of Cain and Abel's fight can be found in two midrashic comments also found in *Gen. Rab.* 22:7, which follow the one by R. Joshua of Siknin cited above. Thus, immediately after this midrash about the fight being over whose property would house the future temple, one finds two alternate explanations suggesting the brothers fought over a woman. The first of these midrashic comments imagines that when Adam had died, each brother claimed Eve, leading to the mortal fight in the field. The second midrashic comment suggests that a single twin girl had been born with Abel. Here Cain as the older brother claims he has rights to this woman, while Abel asserts that as his twin, she rightfully belongs to him. Interestingly enough, one finds an example resembling each of these cases in the stories surrounding David's sons. Thus, the older brother Amnon's rape of his half-sister Tamar eventuates in the younger brother Absalom, Tamar's full brother, avenging Tamar by murdering Amnon. Then in 1 Kings 2 Solomon has Adonijah executed when Adonijah makes a claim on Abishag, the last potential consort of King David.

institutions"[11] and Richard Friedman explains that "the author of P, it seems, did not want to promote the idea that there was a precedent for anyone besides an Aaronid priest to offer a sacrifice."[12] But if J is democ-ratizing and universalizing sacrifice, he is expressing it in a way that is shot through with Israel's own views about what animals are permissible to sacrifice.[13]

A P analogue to this might be found in Gen 9:3–5, which now allows the consumption of animal meat with one qualification. Here one finds a prohibition on the consumption of animal blood in language that suggests P thought of this as a type of natural law recognized by all, as noted by von Rad: "Here, therefore, it is not an isolated 'dietary law' at all (what would be the meaning of a rite without an existing cult?) but an ordinance for all mankind."[14] Yet, what P assumes is universal reflects specific Israelite or perhaps wider ancient Near Eastern mores. We know today that not every culture frowns upon the consumption of animal blood. Similarly, one could ask whether the adjacent P command requir-ing capital punishment for murder would be acknowledged by all to be a universal human value.

It seems that even many of what at first glance appear to be the Bible's most universalist declarations turn out to be much more particu-laristic upon closer inspection. This will trouble those seeking to mute the Bible's particularism in hopes of arriving at a less offensive univer-salism. But it might suggest that we cannot isolate some universal core of biblical truth from the very particularistic theological claims that per-vade the larger biblical corpus. I am not saying that it is wrong to draw out the universal implications of Israel's theology, but rather that we should acknowledge that any such universalism is not generic. It remains a specifically Israelite universalism that is inseparable from ancient Israel's highly particularistic theology. So too later Jewish and Christian uses of Israel's theology remain equally particularistic.

The difficulty of striking the proper balance between the Bible's more universalistic and particularistic tendencies can be seen quite clearly in the scholarly debates surrounding Gen 12:1–3. A number of

[11] Gerhard von Rad, Genesis: A Commentary, OTL (Philadelphia: Westminster, 1973) 30.
[12] Richard Elliott Friedman, Who Wrote the Bible (New York: HarperCollins, 1987), 191.
[13] This is far from the only instance of J expressing a deeply Israelite viewpoint within the early materials in Genesis. Thus, source critics like Speiser see J as the author of Gen 9:18–27, a story that portrays the Canaanites whom Israel would later displace very negatively. See Ephraim Speiser, Genesis, AB (New York: Doubleday, 1962), 60–63.
[14] von Rad, Genesis, 132.

Christian critics have, in my opinion, placed a disproportionate emphasis on what I call the "instrumental" aspects of Israel's election. They do so because they wish to argue that God's special relationship to Abraham, and thus to the people of Israel as a whole, is primarily for the sake of the eventual universal salvation of all the Gentiles. For example, in his influential essay "The Kerygma of the Yahwist," Hans Walter Wolff, puts tremendous weight on Gen 12:1–3, particularly on the final phrase in 3b translated by the NRSV as "in you all the families of the earth shall be blessed."[15] The attempt to read this text in missional and instrumental terms recurs regularly among Protestant exegetes, as demonstrated by the following statement from Terence Fretheim's book on Abraham: "God's choice of Abraham is an initially exclusive move for the sake of a maximally inclusive end. Election is for mission (in the broadest sense of the term)."[16] Frequently, Christian readings that stress instrumental and missional aspects of election at the expense of the intrinsic elements of God's bond with the people of Israel tend toward supersessionism.

Interestingly enough, it was Walter Moberly, a Christian scholar, whose work has convincingly argued that Gen 12:1–3 is primarily directed to Abraham as a message of assurance rather than being addressed to those others with whom Abraham and his children will interact. Note Moberly's words concerning Abraham in Gen 12:1–3:

> He is a solitary figure, who in response to God is leaving behind the usual securities of territory and family. As such, he may fear rapid extinction and oblivion.... Because of God's blessing the solitary and vulnerable Abraham will become a nation to be reckoned with, and the object of extensive respect and prayer for emulation.[17]

While Moberly's reading of the *Niphal* of the root *brk* in Gen 12:3b as implying emulation remains hotly contested, his point that this passage is aimed primarily at assuring Abraham seems on the mark.[18] This is not

[15] Hans Walter Wolff, "The Kerygma of the Yahwist," in *The Vitality of Old Testament Tradition*, ed. Walter Brueggemann and Hans W. Wolff (Atlanta: John Knox, 1975), 41–66.
[16] Terence Fretheim, *Abraham: Trials of Family and Faith* (Columbia, SC: University of South Carolina, 2007), 34.
[17] R. W. L. Moberly, *The Bible, Theology, and Faith: A Study of Abraham and Jesus* (Cambridge: Cambridge University Press, 2000), 123–24.
[18] For a fuller discussion of the possible options for translating Gen 12:3b, see Paul R. Williamson, *Abraham, Israel and the Nations: The Patriarchal Promise and its Covenantal Development in Genesis*, JSOTSup 315 (Sheffield: Sheffield Academic Press, 2000), 220–34, or Keith Nigel Grüneberg, *Abraham, Blessing and the*

to deny the theological importance of the idea that all the families of the earth will somehow obtain blessing through their relationship to Abraham and his descendants. However, the blessing that the other nations of the world experience is better viewed as a consequence that flows from God's special election of Abraham and his descendants through Isaac and Jacob rather than as something that explains the primary purpose of Israel's election. In fact, this is exactly how Rashi understands the plain sense meaning of 3b, citing Gen 48:20 as a supporting analogue. Here again it turns out that what many view as one of the most universalistic texts in Genesis or perhaps even within the larger Tanakh, upon close inspection may be much more particularistic than commonly recognized.

This is not to say that Jewish tradition always read the text in an equally particularistic fashion. One could argue that God's call of Abraham in Gen 12:1–3 contains no explanation for God's choice of Abraham. Thus God's choice remains stubbornly particularistic regardless of whether or not Gen 12:3b is understood as a particularistic statement of assurance to Abraham or as support for the universal implications of God's election of Abraham. While early Christian sources like Paul's letters remain fully comfortable with such divine arbitrariness (e.g., Rom 9:10–15), there is a stream of ancient rabbinic midrashic tradition that posits that Abraham merited God's attention because he reasoned his way to monotheism. In effect, the midrash cited just below turns Abraham into a universal figure, the founder of monotheism, thereby making God's selection of Abraham much less arbitrary and hence making aspects of Abraham's story much less particularistic.

> Terah was a manufacturer of idols. He once went away somewhere and left Abraham to sell them in his place.... [Once] a woman came with a plateful of flour and requested of him, "Take this and offer it to them." So he took a stick, broke them, and put the stick in the hand of the largest. When his father returned he demanded, "What have you done to them?" "I cannot conceal it from you," he replied. "A woman came with a plateful of fine meal and requested me to offer it to them. One claimed, 'I must eat first,' while another claimed, 'I must eat first.' Thereupon the largest arose, took the stick, and broke them." "Why do you make sport of me," he [Terah] cried out; "have they then any knowledge!" "Should not

Nations : A Philological and Exegetical Study of Genesis 12:3 in its Narrative Context, BZAW 332 (New York; Berlin: Walter de Gruyter, 2003).

your ears listen to what your mouth is saying," he [Abraham]
retorted.[19]

A BRIEF SURVEY OF GENESIS 12–50

Apart from Gen 12:1–3, which as we have noted is often read as being
quite universalistic, the vast bulk of Genesis 12–50 is usually thought of
as being much more particularistic than the materials found in Genesis
1–11. While it is not possible within the confines of this brief essay even
to survey all of Genesis 12–50, let alone to discuss these materials and
classical Jewish interpretations of them in any depth, we will examine
a few key examples. Close attention to the nuances in these narratives
suggests a deeper interest in non-Israelites than is sometimes recognized.
Thus, just as Genesis 1–11 may be more particularistic than often recognized, perhaps the materials in Genesis 12–50 may not be quite as
particularistic as some have imagined. Here we begin by noting that
many of the stories between Genesis 12–36 narrate the narrowing of
the covenant to one family line at the expense of other possible choices
and explore the family dynamics that occur in the wake of this fact. Over
the course of Genesis 13, Lot, Abram's nephew and a potential contender
to inherit the land of Canaan, finds himself separating from his uncle and
moving his family to Sodom near what would later become the Dead Sea.
Yet, even after Lot is marked as non-chosen, the chosen Abraham twice
intervenes to help save Lot and his family from peril and possible death.
First, in the enigmatic story found in Genesis 14, Abraham successfully
fights an alliance of kings who had taken Lot and his family and property
as booty and frees his nephew, also recovering Lot's household and lost
property.

Then, in Gen 18:16–33, Abraham bargains with God to attempt to
save all of Sodom if at least ten righteous men can be found in it. While
Sodom is ultimately destroyed, Lot and his family are again rescued, this
time by God's angels. Abraham's election results in the exclusion of Lot
from God's covenantal promises, but at the same time Genesis highlights
a special concern on the part of the elect Abraham to intercede on behalf of
the now non-chosen Lot. This is one of several instances in which
a storyline that at first blush suggests a narrowing of God's concern to
an ever smaller group of the elect at the expense of everyone else is, upon
deeper examination, seen to contain a strong interest in the non-elect. In
Gen 18:17–19, immediately preceding Abraham's extended plea to save all

[19]   Gen. Rab. 38:13.

of Sodom if enough righteous people can be found in it, God indicates that he feels he must inform Abraham of what he is about to do to Sodom precisely because Abraham's chosen status entails that the chosen are expected to act with justice and righteousness. The placement of this passage in such close proximity to Abraham's plea for mercy for Sodom appears to indicate that part of the job of the elect is to intercede with God on behalf of non-chosen others, even non-chosen others who are residents in a city as wicked as Sodom.

On this point, it is worth citing a well-known rabbinic midrash that further fills in the discussion that took place between God and Abraham in Genesis 18.

> R. Levi commented: *Shall not the judge of all the world act justly?* (Gen 18:25). If you desire the world to endure, there can be no strict justice, while if you desire absolute justice, the world cannot endure. Yet, You hold the cord by both ends, desiring both the world and strict justice! Unless You forego a little, the world cannot endure. The Holy One, blessed be He, said to Abraham: *you loved righteousness* (Ps 45:8a): you loved to justify My creatures; *and hated wickedness* (Ps 45:8a): you hated to condemn them. *Therefore God, your God, anointed you with the oil of gladness above your fellows* (Psalm 45:8b). From Noah to you there were ten generations, and out of all of them I remembered but you alone.[20]

Here the ancient rabbis utilize a single verse from Psalm 45 (verse 7 in the English), which describes the ways the king should ideally act, and they apply it to Abraham. They do so by creatively interpreting the first half of this verse against its plain sense meaning; reading it as if it said, "you loved to justify my creatures and you hated to find them guilty." This midrashic excerpt demonstrates that the ancient rabbis understand Abraham not only as someone who interceded on behalf of Sodom to attempt to save it from destruction, but as a person who regularly sought to intercede on behalf of all the world inasmuch as humans will always fall short when justice is strictly reckoned (Ps 130:3). And while one could argue that Abraham failed in his bid to save all of Sodom, the rabbis see him as ultimately triumphing by convincing God that the world could only endure if God's mercy trumped God's justice.

Interestingly enough, there is a stream of Jewish tradition that sees Abraham, who in Judaism is imagined as the first Jew, as superior to

---

[20] *Gen. Rab. 49:9.* A very similar midrash can be found in *Gen. Rab. 39:6.*

Noah, who in some sense represents a generic righteous universal human being. This claim is grounded in the fact that Abraham interceded to save even the wicked inhabitants of Sodom, while Noah raises no objections whatsoever to God's announcement that he should build an ark because God was about to destroy the entire world.[21] Such a reading suggests that the Torah's shift in focus from narratives dealing with all of humanity to those concerning Israel's oldest ancestors need not be seen as signaling a diminishing concern for humanity at large.

One finds similar complexity in the Isaac/Ishmael and Jacob/Esau sibling rivalry stories inasmuch as the non-favored brother in each narrative is neither hated by God nor excluded from God's blessing. In fact, within Genesis both Ishmael and Esau are presented with great pathos and sympathy. When one carefully examines the language in Genesis 17 and 21 describing Ishmael's status, it becomes clear that even though he is outside of the covenant (17:19, 21), he is barely outside of it. Not only is he circumcised, thereby receiving the bodily mark of the very covenant from which he is explicitly excluded, but furthermore he receives a special divine blessing (Gen 17:18–26; 21:12–13). More telling yet is the fact that the very same P text of Genesis 17, which in verses 19 and 21 twice declares that God's covenantal promises to Abraham will be passed on to the soon to be born Isaac rather than to Abraham's only currently living son Ishmael, takes special interest in Ishmael and depicts his future quite positively in verse 20.[22] While Isaac is mentioned twice by name in Genesis 17 (three times if one counts the pun when Abraham laughs at God's announcement that he at 100 and Sarah at 90 years old will soon produce Isaac), Ishmael is mentioned five times by name in this short section of Genesis 17. Furthermore, the text emphasizes that Ishmael was indeed circumcised as *Abraham's son* (vv. 23, 25, and 26 all refer to Ishmael as "his son") as God commanded. While the narrowing of the covenant to Isaac's descendants signals a deepening theological particularism, it is accompanied by an awareness that some non-Israelites are blessed by God and that certain non-Israelites are even part of Abraham's family and as such they too are circumcised. It seems that the plea that the chosen Abraham makes on behalf of Ishmael in

---

[21] See Nehama Leibowitz, *Studies in Bereshit (Genesis) in the Context of Ancient and Modern Jewish Bible Commentary* (Jerusalem: World Zionist Organization, 1972), 61, citing the *Zohar* commenting on Genesis 18 (*Zohar* A 106a, Davka software).

[22] John T. Noble, *A Place for Hagar's Son: Ishmael as a Case Study in the Priestly Tradition* (Minneapolis: Fortress, 2016) makes a case that P's portrayal of Ishmael is more positive than the earlier J and E materials from which P drew and thus that P's theology is in fact more universalistic than many previous scholars have recognized.

Gen 17:18 influences God: "As for Ishmael, I have heard you" (Gen 17:20a). Now Ishmael is explicitly included in God's promise of blessing even if he is excluded from God's covenant with Abraham: "I will bless him [Ishmael] and make him fruitful and exceedingly numerous; he shall be the father of twelve princes, and I will make him a great nation" (Gen 17:20b).[23]

Much the same can be said of Esau, who at times is depicted with great pathos (e.g., Gen 27:30–38) and who prospers in life, eventually fathering a host of progeny (Genesis 36). Even when we arrive at the Joseph story, which focuses much attention on the complex family dynamics between Jacob, Joseph, and Jacob's other sons, this very particularistic story is set on a wider world stage in which the resolution to the story not only entails the healing of the rift in Jacob's family but also results in mitigating the effects of a famine ravaging the larger population inhabiting the Near East (Gen 41:55–57).

CONCLUDING REFLECTIONS

The nuances and complexities that I have highlighted throughout this essay may help provide a more balanced way to approach the question of how the universal relates to the particular not only within Genesis but also within the Torah as a whole as well as within the larger Hebrew Bible. Some recent interpreters such as Regina Schwartz in her book *The Curse of Cain* tend to see the Hebrew Bible's more universalistic and more particularistic ideas as two streams of biblical thinking that are at war with each other.[24] Such thinkers too often end up endorsing the rather tired Enlightenment position that embracing the universal requires a rejection of all things particular. Other contemporary interpreters rightly recognize the inseparability of the Bible's deep particularism from the various universal ideals it projects. Yet at times, even these interpreters favor the universal over the particular inasmuch as they see God's particular story with Israel as a long detour between the universalistic passages mostly concentrated in the early chapters of Genesis (1:1–12:3) and the eschatological universalism proclaimed by various

---

[23] For an account of the representation of Ishmael in rabbinic tradition, see Carol Bakhos, *Ishmael on the Border: Rabbinic Portrayals of the First Arab*, SUNY series in Judaica: Hermeneutics, Mysticism, and Religion (Albany: SUNY Press, 2006).

[24] Regina Schwartz, *The Curse of Cain: The Violent Legacy of Monotheism* (Chicago: University of Chicago Press, 1997). For a larger critique of Schwartz's approach, see R. W. L. Moberly, "Is Monotheism Bad for You? Some Reflections on God, the Bible, and Life in the Light of Regina Schwartz's *The Curse of Cain*," in *The God of Israel*, ed. R. P. Gordon (Cambridge: Cambridge University Press, 2007), 94–112.

prophets, an eschatological universalism that many Christians believe is echoed in Jesus' message.[25] Such an understanding elides the fact that even the most universalistic images in the Hebrew Bible are heavily tinged by Israel's particularistic worldview, and more importantly, it fails to acknowledge that these universal ideals grow out of and only make sense in relation to the very specific theological claims that lie at the heart of Israel's scriptures. It also fails to see that many of the biblical passages that articulate Israel's particularistic identity, such as the narratives in Genesis 12–50 that highlight Israel's ancestral stories and revolve around the election of one sibling and the non-chosen status of another child or group of siblings, contain both a wider interest in and often a more positive view of non-Israelites than many scholars have recognized.

Here it worth recalling that what is arguably the single most universalistic statement in the whole biblical tradition found early in Genesis, that all humans were created in the image of God, comes from P, a source that is far from shy in asserting Israel's special status and the additional obligations Israel's sacral status entails. The following short rabbinic excerpt attributed to Rabbi Akiva demonstrates how within both the Hebrew Bible and classical rabbinic sources universalistic and particularistic ideas are not seen as belonging to two contradictory streams of tradition, but rather, they are seen as differing aspects of one unified tradition and in effect they actually reinforce one another.

> He used to say: Beloved is man in that he was created in the image [of God]. [It is a mark of] superabundant love [that] it was made known to him that he had been created in the image [of God], as it is said: *For in the image of God made he man.* Beloved are Israel in that they were called children of the All-Present. [It was a mark of] superabundant love [that] it was made known to them that they were called children of the All-Present, as it is said: *You are children of the Lord your God.*[26]

In this passage, Rabbi Akiva first declares that God loves human beings in general and has in fact even told them so, using Genesis 9:6b as a proof

[25] For numerous examples and a fuller critique of the way in which a host of Christian thinkers more generally seek to soften God's choice of Israel by seeing it as a temporary step on the way toward a greater universalism, see Joel N. Lohr, *Chosen and Unchosen: Conception of Election in the Pentateuch and Jewish-Christian Interpretation*, Siphrut 2 (Winona Lake, IN: Eisenbrauns, 2009), 3–31 and Kaminsky, *Yet I Loved Jacob*, 1–9 and 137–58. Or more recently, see Joel Kaminsky, "Election Theology and the Problem of Universalism." *HBT*, 33 (2011): 34–44.
[26] *Pirkei Avot* 3:14. Soncino translation from Davka software with slight modifications.

text. He immediately goes on to assert that God has special love for his people Israel and has told this to Israel, citing Deuteronomy 14:1 as support. While today many assume that universalism and particularism are inversely related so that where one increases the other must in turn decrease, the biblical and rabbinic evidence suggests that Israel's deepening understanding of her unique identity as God's chosen people went hand in hand with Israel's growing awareness that Israel's God is indeed a universal God who created and continues to relate to all human beings in the world.

SELECT BIBLIOGRAPHY

Bakhos, Carol. *Ishmael on the Border: Rabbinic Portrayals of the First Arab.* SUNY series in Judaica: Hermeneutics, Mysticism, and Religion. Albany: SUNY Press, 2006.

Clifford, Richard J. "Election in Genesis 1." Pages 7–22 in *The Call of Abraham: Essays on the Election of Israel in Honor of Jon D. Levenson.* Edited by Gary A. Anderson and Joel Kaminsky. Notre Dame, IN: University of Notre Dame, 2013.

Freedman, David Noel. *The Nine Commandments: Uncovering a Hidden Pattern of Crime and Punishment in the Hebrew Bible.* New York: Doubleday, 2000.

Fretheim, Terence. *Abraham: Trials of Family and Faith.* Columbia, SC: University of South Carolina, 2007.

Grüneberg, Keith Nigel. *Abraham, Blessing and the Nations: A Philological and Exegetical Study of Genesis 12:3 in its Narrative Context.* BZAW 332. New York; Berlin: Walter de Gruyter, 2003.

Kaminsky, Joel S. *Yet I Loved Jacob: Reclaiming the Biblical Concept of Election.* Nashville: Abingdon, 2007.

Leibowitz, Nehama. *Studies in Bereshit (Genesis) in the Context of Ancient and Modern Jewish Bible Commentary.* Jerusalem: World Zionist Organization, 1972.

Levenson, Jon D. "The Universal Horizon of Biblical Particularism." Pages 143–69 in *Ethnicity and the Bible.* Edited by Mark Brett. Leiden: Brill, 1996.

Lohr, Joel N. *Chosen and Unchosen: Conceptions of Election in the Pentateuch and Jewish-Christian Interpretation.* Siphrut 2. Winona Lake, IN: Eisenbrauns, 2009.

Lyke, Larry. *King David with the Wise Woman of Tekoa: The Resonance of Tradition in Parabolic Narrative.* JSOTSup 255. Sheffield: Sheffield Academic Press, 1997.

Moberly, R. W. L. *The Bible, Theology, and Faith: A Study of Abraham and Jesus.* Cambridge: Cambridge University Press, 2000.

Moberly, R. W. L. "Is Monotheism Bad for You? Some Reflections on God, the Bible, and Life in the Light of Regina Schwartz's *The Curse of Cain.*"

Pages 94–112 in *The God of Israel*. Edited by R. P. Gordon. Cambridge: Cambridge University Press, 2007.

Noble, John T. *A Place for Hagar's Son: Ishmael as a Case Study in the Priestly Tradition*. Minneapolis: Fortress, 2016.

Schwartz, Regina. *The Curse of Cain: The Violent Legacy of Monotheism*. Chicago: University of Chicago Press, 1997.

Williamson, Paul R. *Abraham, Israel and the Nations: The Patriarchal Promise and its Covenantal Development in Genesis*. JSOTSup 315. Sheffield: Sheffield Academic Press, 2000.

Wolff, Hans Walter. "The Kerygma of the Yahwist." Pages 41–66 in *The Vitality of Old Testament Tradition*. Edited by Walter Brueggemann and Hans W. Wolff. Atlanta: John Knox, 1975.

16 Before Moses: Genesis among the Christians

IAIN PROVAN

Christians have been reading the book of Genesis for a very long time now, because from the beginning of the Christian movement they have believed that "all Scripture is God-breathed and ... useful" in one way or another (2 Tim 3:16, NIV) – and they have held this to be true, first and foremost, of what they have regarded as the Old Testament (OT). They have read Genesis, then, in pursuit of what they should believe and how they should live.

MODES OF READING

In this pursuit they have approached Scripture in various ways.[1] Many of them have been interested in what we might call nowadays the text's "literal" or "historical" meaning – the meaning we might reasonably conclude that the original (human) author intended to communicate. Among the Church Fathers, Augustine (for example) places a high value on grasping this meaning; concerning the interpretation of Genesis 2–3, he writes that "if anyone wanted to take everything that was said according to the letter ... and could avoid blasphemies and explain everything in harmony with the Catholic faith, we should ... regard him as a leading and highly praiseworthy interpreter."[2] Jerome devotes an entire treatise to *Hebrew Questions on Genesis*, addressing textual and exegetical difficulties in the book with reference to both Hebrew language and Jewish interpretation.[3]

---

[1] For a fuller account of Christian modes of reading Genesis, see Iain Provan, *Discovering Genesis: Content, Interpretation, Reception* (Grand Rapids: Eerdmans, 2016), 12–48; for an extensive discussion of Christian hermeneutics more generally, see Iain Provan, *The Reformation and the Right Reading of Scripture* (Waco, TX: Baylor University Press, 2017).

[2] Augustine, *Two Books on Genesis against the Manichees*, 2.2.6, in *On Genesis: Two Books on Genesis against the Manichees, and on the Literal Interpretation of Genesis, an Unfinished Book*, trans. R. J. Teske, FC 84 (Washington, D.C.: Catholic University of America Press, 1991), 45–143 (95).

[3] C. T. R. Hayward, *Saint Jerome's Hebrew Questions on Genesis*, Oxford Early Christian Studies (Oxford: Clarendon, 1995).

Such literal reading remains important throughout all the succeeding Christian centuries. We encounter it in pre-Renaissance times in the writings of Peter Abelard and Nicholas of Lyra, for instance. In the succeeding period Renaissance Humanism, with its clarion call *ad fontes* ("back to the sources"), further encouraged close attention to the literal sense of the biblical text in its original languages, and thereby prepared the way for the Protestant Reformation. At the very heart of this movement lay a profound emphasis on the plain meaning of the biblical text, as articulated by its original, ancient authors; it was here, Martin Luther proclaimed, that the theological value of the Bible was to be found. In due course this emphasis on an understanding of the past as crucial to the interpretation of a book like Genesis produced the beginnings of what some call the historical-critical and others the grammatical-historical project, as Christian readers (along with all sorts of others) began to ask questions about the authorship of this or that biblical text, or its date, or the sources out of which it was constructed, or its genre.

At the same time, the literal sense has not been the only one of interest to Christians – not least because they have understood Scripture as comprising a unified, self-consistent, and divinely communicated text that revealed truth and exhorted virtue. Especially where coherence has been under threat, either within Scripture or between Scripture and other recognized guides concerning what should be believed and practiced, Christian readers have been apt to move beyond the literal sense to other levels of meaning. Immediately after having lauded the interpretation of the literal sense in the passage cited above, then, Augustine goes on to propose that "if there is no way in which we can understand what has been written in a manner that is pious and worthy of God without believing that these things have been set before us in figures and in enigmas," then there is apostolic warrant for doing so "according to the Catholic faith."[4] This was the view of many others in the early post-apostolic church as well, and Origen is perhaps the best example. The primacy of this way of reading a book like Genesis in the Middle Ages is suggested by this comment of Peter Abelard: "Although many men put together many allegorical or moral interpretations of Genesis, among us [Latin Christians] the insightful intellect of most blessed Augustine alone undertook to explicate

---

[4] Augustine, *Against the Manichees*, 2.2.7–8.

the literal-historical in this matter."[5] As one modern author has put it: "The concentration of allegory in the air in the Middle Ages was heavy."[6]

As we begin to move from the Middle Ages toward the modern period, we still find many Christian readers of Genesis interested in spiritual readings that extend beyond the plain sense of the text. As we transition from the middle of the seventeenth century into modernity proper, however, we increasingly find an emphasis on the literal sense dominating discussion of the Bible at least among educated Christians operating in the field of public discourse. The subsequent postmodern environment, interestingly, has once again loosened the grip of the literal sense of the biblical text upon the scholarly imagination. In structuralist and poststructuralist reading of Genesis, for example, the long-standing modern preoccupation with authorial intent is abandoned, and the focus of interest falls instead either upon the deep structures of thought in the text that transcend individual authors and determine their writing, or upon the ways in which readers themselves determine the meaning of the text.

Deploying these various approaches, then, how have Christians read Genesis in pursuit of what they should believe and how they should live? What follows is naturally illustrative rather than exhaustive.[7]

Creation: Genesis 1:1–2:25

An important idea derived from the opening chapters of Genesis is that we inhabit a world *created* by a *Person*, and not something else: "In the beginning God created the heavens and the earth" (Gen 1:1). He does so first by transforming a desolate, brooding landscape such that the waters become useful as the rains and the oceans, and the darkness becomes useful as night (1:3–10). He then proceeds to create everything else. The orderly creation that thus begins to emerge is described on many occasions as "good" (e.g., 1:4) and ultimately as "very good" (1:31). This "good" has sometimes been interpreted in the Christian tradition as implying "perfect," that is, as lacking in everything that we might think of as "evil," including suffering; John Calvin holds, for example, that "[t]he inclemency of the air, frost, thunders, unseasonable rains,

---

[5] " Dedication Letter to the Commentary on the Six Days of Creation," in *Letters of Peter Abelard: Beyond the Personal*, ed. J. M. Ziolkowski (Washington, D.C.: Catholic University of America Press, 2008), 52–63, here 62.

[6] P. E. Beichner, "The Allegorical Interpretation of Medieval Literature," *Publications of the Modern Language Association of America* 82 (1967): 33–38 (33).

[7] For a fuller account, see Provan, *Discovering Genesis*, 59–189.

drought, hail, and whatever is disorderly in the world, are the fruits of sin."[8] Yet Genesis 1 itself speaks of human beings ruling and subduing creation, which implies that there are already forces in the good world that *require* such actions. So "goodness" clearly does not imply that there is no work to be done in the world, and no progress to be made in it. Creation is good – but it is also, from the beginning, on a journey whereby what is "good" will one day become "better." In the meantime other biblical texts like Psalms 8 and 104 already celebrate God's beautiful and functional creation as we find it right now, and this theme of celebration has remained an important one in the Christian interpretive tradition down through the ages. It was indeed such deeply held Christian convictions about the divinely ordained order of the cosmos that created the conditions in which modern science arose and flourished.[9] The scientific developments of the succeeding centuries have, of course, caused significant reflection among Christian Bible-readers as to how far Genesis 1 and 2 should themselves be read as science, with the great majority concluding along with John Calvin that they should not – that they speak to philosophical questions such as the nature of God, the world, and the human person, rather than to the questions of physics, chemistry, and biology that so interest modern scientists.

Related to this point, the sequence of God's creative acts in Genesis 1 has generally been considered in the Christian tradition to be instructive, but not always in plausible ways. Some have believed that the intention of the author is to communicate thereby the sequence of space-time events that resulted in our present reality – a chronology of the cosmos. Yet long before the modern period Origen already noted the difficulty of reading the chapter in such strictly chronological terms: "Who that has understanding," he asked, "will suppose that the first, and second, and third day, and the evening and the morning, existed without a sun, and moon, and stars? And that the first day was, as it were, also without a sky?"[10] The problems that Origen hints at here have not become any less severe with the passing of time. More astute are those readings of Genesis 1 that understand the primary purpose of the ordering as relating to the importance of humanity in biblical thinking: a sequence of

---

[8] John Calvin, *Commentaries on the First Book of Moses Called Genesis*, ed. and trans. John King, Geneva Series Commentary (London: Calvin Translation Society, 1847), 177.

[9] M. B. Foster, "The Christian Doctrine of Creation and the Rise of Modern Natural Science," *Mind* 43 (1934): 446–68.

[10] Origen, *Princ.* 4.1.16 (*ANF* 10:325).

creative steps that rise to an apex in the creation of human beings. Genesis 2:4–25 communicates the same truth using a different "order." Here creation is described as something that cannot function properly without human beings. This is probably why shrubs and plants "precede" humanity in Genesis 1:11–12 (cf. 1:29–30), whereas in Genesis 2:4–7 there must be a gardener before there can be shrubs and plants. This is also why the animals in Genesis 2:19 are created after humanity, whereas in Genesis 1:24–25 they appear beforehand.

Whatever one makes of this particular point, certainly Christian reading of Genesis 1–2 has greatly *emphasized* the idea of the importance of humanity in the cosmos – those created according to Genesis 1:26 in the ṣelem ("image") and dəmût ("likeness") of God. Ancient Christian exegesis from Irenaeus onwards tended to interpret these two terms as relating to two distinct aspects of humanness (natural qualities like reason, over against supernatural graces).[11] However, "according to our likeness" is in reality merely an explanatory gloss on "in our image"; both are ways of saying the same thing. Regarding specifically *what* they are saying, there has been much Christian discussion concerning the human qualities to which image and likeness together might refer, with "reason" being the most popular. In this respect and others, humans are "like God" in a manner that other creatures are not.

The human vocation that arises from this endowment has also been a key matter of interest. Genesis 1:26 and 28 talk about humanity "ruling" (rādâ) and "subduing" (kābaš) creation. This is the language of kingship, and it has sometimes been interpreted within the Christian tradition as justifying an aggressive, instrumentalist human approach to the rest of creation. Yet it is not as autonomous beings, but as God's representatives, that humans are made in God's image. "The earth is the LORD's, and everything in it" (Ps. 24:1), and we govern it only on God's behalf. Then again, the vocation of kings in the ancient world involved not only ruling and subduing, but also looking after the welfare of their subjects and ensuring justice for all. The royal commission, then, is not a mandate to exploit and ravage the earth in one's own self-interest. Genesis 2 makes it especially clear, in fact, what "dominion" looks like in relation to non-human creation, as it explains it in terms of earth-keeping. Here human beings are placed in God's garden in order to "serve it and keep/guard it" ('ābad and šāmar). This is religious language, which underlines the importance and the sacred nature of the task: it is worship and conservation. It is precisely the language that is used in Num 3:7–8

---

[11] Note, e.g., Origen, *Princ.* 3.6.1 (*ANF* 10:262–63).

when the work of the priests in the Tabernacle is described. The world is a sacred place, like a temple, and human beings are its priests. The dominion given to human beings in Genesis 1, then, is evidently not a *lording it over* the rest of creation, but rather a sacrificial *looking after* creation. Every human being – as John Calvin puts it – should "regard himself as the steward of God in all things which he possesses. Then he will neither conduct himself dissolutely, nor corrupt by abuse those things which God requires to be preserved."[12]

That God does retain the kind of interest in the whole of his creation that makes sense of this ongoing moral imperative for the Christian is particularly clear in the New Testament (NT). Here it turns out that "in the beginning ... the Word" (Jesus) was not only "with God," but *was* God, and that "[t]hrough him all things were made" (John 1:1–3). "From him and through him and to him are all things," writes Paul – "the earth ... and everything in it" (Rom 11:36; 1 Cor 10:26; cf. Rev 4:11). Christ then enters into this world that he created along with the Father, and he does so as the one in whom human image-bearing reaches its highest point – "the image of the invisible God," of whom Paul says that "all things were created by him and for him ... in him all things hold together" (Col 1:15–20). It is he who "fulfills God's design for all creation and displays what had always been intended for all humankind."[13] The redemption that Christ thus initiates is naturally cosmic in its scope – as broad as the original creation: "God was pleased ... through him to reconcile to himself *all things* [my emphasis], whether things on earth or things in heaven" (Col 1:19). For this cosmic redemption the entirety of non-human Creation – currently "subjected to frustration" – has in fact long been waiting "in eager expectation for the children of God to be revealed" (Rom 8:19–20). How it became "subjected" in such a manner leads us on to our next set of reflections.

The Entrance of Evil: Genesis 3:1–24

The setting for the story told in Genesis 3 is the "garden in Eden" in which the human gardeners have already been placed in Genesis 2:8–14. Many Christian readers have speculated about its location, and some have set out in search of it. Basil of Caesarea used it to account for the fact that ancient Christians prayed facing toward the east.[14] But in all probability

---

[12]   Calvin, *Genesis*, 125.
[13]   W. L. Lane, *Hebrews 1–8*, WBC 47A (Dallas: Word, 1991), 48.
[14]   Basil, *On the Holy Spirit* 27.66, trans. David Anderson (Crestwood, NY: St. Vladimir's Seminary Press, 1980), 100.

the "garden" is intended, not as a specific *place* in the world, but as a picture of a *state of being* in the world. This is the kind of interpretation offered in the seventeenth century, for example by Oliver Cromwell's chaplain, Peter Sterry, who "believed that Paradise had been in the midst of man and had not so much been lost or ruined as hid beneath the besmirched image of God."[15] Many of the motifs of Eden in the book of Genesis are in fact those of the divine dwelling place described in Mesopotamian and Canaanite myth, redeployed in Genesis in distinctive ways.[16] This itself supports the idea that Eden is "the world," since the dwelling of God in biblical thinking is not a single country or temple, but the entire world.[17]

The beauty of this "garden" as it is portrayed throughout Genesis 1–3 – and in particular the beauty of its first human beings – is a matter of great significance in the Christian interpretive tradition, especially as it is expressed in art: Dürer's *Adam and Eve* (1504), for example, in which the primal couple appear in nearly symmetrical, idealized poses. More generally, Eden has inspired all kinds of music, art, and literature that wistfully notes its loss and (or) pines for its retrieval. Its loss is alluded to in Shakespeare's *Hamlet*, for example, where it is choked by weeds and governed by the serpent Claudius, who has taken his father's crown.[18] Its retrieval is anticipated in the early modern notion that the development of modern science would "restore that which had been damaged in the Fall, and ... return the earth to its primevally perfect state."[19]

Among the many beautiful things in the garden are the trees – two of which are especially important. One is the tree of life, from which (apparently) the human pair never get to eat (3:22), and therefore never achieve immortality. The other is the tree of the knowledge of good and evil, and the question has often been asked: which kind of knowledge is in view? Some Christian interpreters have considered it to be sexual in nature. For John Milton in *Paradise Lost*, for example, Adam's rationality is overcome by his love for Eve; he follows her willingly to his doom,

[15]   P. C. Almond, *Adam and Eve in Seventeenth-Century Thought* (Cambridge: Cambridge University Press, 1999), 66.

[16]   For access to these various ancient Near Eastern texts, see "The Epic of Gilgamesh," trans. E. A. Speiser (*ANET*, 72–98), "Enki and Ninhursag: A Paradise Myth," trans. S. N. Kramer (*ANET*, 37–41), and "The Balu Myth," trans. Dennis Pardee (*COS* 1.86:242–83). See further the chapters by Alice Mandell and John H. Walton in this volume.

[17]   This idea already shows up in earlier Christian authors like Clement of Alexandria and Hugh of St. Victor, as well as in Luther's *Table Talk* (Almond, *Adam and Eve*, 74–75).

[18]   William Shakespeare, *Hamlet*, 1.2.133–37.

[19]   Almond, *Adam and Eve*, 35.

more desirous of possessing her than of obeying God.[20] Others have thought that the forbidden knowledge is the cultural kind described in Genesis 4, and still others that it is moral insight. The most satisfactory Christian reading, however, focuses not on the nature of the knowledge but on the nature and timing of its acquisition. In the same way that a child grows up to become an adult, "knowing good and evil" and having wisdom or insight, so God intended human beings one day to "know good and evil" as "adult" creatures. Instead, they prematurely *grasped after* knowledge in independence of God.

The woman happens to be the one who replies to the serpent in the exchanges that lead up to the eating of the fruit (cf. 2 Cor 11:3; 1 Tim 2:14), but the text does not imply that the man is elsewhere and uninvolved; his presence is explicitly indicated in Gen 3:6 (he was "with her"). This narrative fact has not been given sufficient weight in many Christian readings through the ages, with the consequence that the woman has tended to attract much more blame than the man for the human rebellion against God.[21] Eve easily becomes in these readings, not just the occasion of Adam's sin, but the cause of it.[22] All sorts of reasons have then been developed for why the serpent chose to approach the woman and *not* the man. In the Middle Ages the theme of Eve's *credulity* was often "repeated in the temptation scenes of the mystery plays."[23]

The consequences of eating the fruit are serious. Here begins the long-term, biblical battle between humans and the forces of chaos and darkness (represented by the serpent) that in the Christian tradition will not come to an end until Jesus Christ – having entered history once already as "the last Adam" who saves his people from their sins (Rom 5:12–20; 1 Cor 15:12–58) – returns to lead his armies to victory over all the dark powers. It is this twofold victory of Christ over evil that is read into Gen 3:15 itself by various of the early Church Fathers and then by many other interpreters.[24] In the meantime, human beings encounter in their

[20]   John Milton, *Paradise Lost*, 9.990–99.
[21]   Note, e.g., Tertullian, *Cult. Fem.*, 1.1.1–2, in *Tertullian: Disciplinary, Moral and Ascetical Works*, trans. Rudolph Arbesmann, E. J. Daly, E. A. Quain, FC 10 (Washington, D.C.: Catholic University of America Press, 1959), 117–18.
[22]   E.g., in Ambrose, *Paradise* 6.33, in *Saint Ambrose: Hexameron, Paradise, and Cain and Abel*, trans. J. J. Savage, FC 42 (Washington, D.C.: Catholic University of American Press, 1961), 311.
[23]   D. Danielson, "Eve," in *A Dictionary of Biblical Tradition in English Literature*, ed. David L. Jeffrey (Grand Rapids: Eerdmans, 1992), 251–54 (253).
[24]   So. e.g., Irenaeus, *Haer.* 5.21.1 (ACCS OT 1:90–91).

fallen state many troubles. John Chrysostom captures some aspects of the consequences of the Fall for the woman in this respect when he paraphrases Gen 3:16 in the following way:

> In the beginning I created you equal in esteem to your husband, and my intention was that in everything you would share with him as an equal, and as I entrusted control of everything to your husband, so did I to you; but you abused your equality of status. Hence I subject you to your husband.[25]

The remainder of the "curse" on the woman has often been understood in Christian tradition as pertaining to female biology (labor pains). For various reasons it is much more likely, however, that the "pain" envisaged is bound up with the difficult *circumstances* into which the woman now brings children.[26] She suffers pain (*'iṣṣābôn*, 3:16) in the home just as the man – in conflict with the earth – eats the produce of the earth in "pain" (*'iṣṣābôn*, 3:17). Beyond pain, there is now only death for both of them – if they persist in walking the path upon which they have now set out. This is an important qualification, given the strong fatalism that has marked some Christian understandings of "the Fall," as the event in Genesis 3 is sometimes called. Yet Christian Scripture itself, both OT and NT, does not justify such fatalism, as if there were nothing that human beings could do about their condition. To the contrary, creation remains a place in which the goodness of God is everywhere experienced (e.g., Ps 104); ongoing relational problems between God and human beings are not inevitable (e.g., Gen 5:24; 6:9); and the predominant note struck when mothers and children are described is joy, and not pain (e.g., Ps 113:4–9; 127:3). The righteous Noah overcomes the curse on the ground in Gen 9:20, and Deuteronomy promises agricultural blessings more generally to others who obey God. Christian Scripture does not regard it as inevitable, then, that humanity must live in the world of Genesis 3. In fact, it urges its readers *not* to do so, but instead to know a different world by turning back to God.

[25] John Chrysostom, *Hom. Gen.*, 17.36, in *Saint John Chrysostom: Homilies on Genesis 1–17*, ed. T. P. Halton, trans. R. C. Hill, FC 74 (Washington, D.C.: Catholic University of America Press, 1986), 240.

[26] See further my " Pain in Childbirth? Further Thoughts on 'An Attractive Fragment' (1 Chronicles 4:9–10)," in *Let Us Go Up to Zion: Essays In Honour of H. G. M. Williamson on the Occasion of his Sixty-Fifth Birthday*, ed. Iain Provan and Mark Boda (Leiden: Brill, 2012), 285–96.

From Cain to the Tower of Babel: Genesis 4:1–11:26

As Genesis 4 opens, and despite the sin of chapter 3, we find a world still
operating under God's blessing: two brothers are born. However,
a problem arises between them, apparently because Abel is careful to
bring his very best to God while Cain fails do to so – a view already taken
by Ephrem the Syrian: "Abel selected and offered the choicest of his
firstborn and of his fat ones, while Cain either offered young grains or
certain fruits that are found at the same time as the young grains."[27]
Cain's resulting anger brings him to a crossroads in his relationship with
God; two ways open up before him, and he opts for the murderous one.
He becomes in the process, in later books of the Bible, a prototype of the
wicked, just as the victim Abel becomes a prototype of the righteous (e.g.,
Heb 11:4; 1 John 3:12). In the early post-apostolic Christian tradition,
Augustine's *City of God* likewise invites its readers to consider that "the
conflict between Cain and Abel displayed the hostility between ... two
cities ..., the city of God and the city of men" – an ongoing conflict,
spanning the entirety of time, between the redeemed and the unredeemed "who love this world as their home and find their happiness in
the worldly felicity of the earthly city."[28] As such this story has inspired
a considerable amount of Christian art and music – it is the subject of
famous paintings by Titian, Tintoretto, and Rubens, for example – as
well as literature and drama. Abel's innocent blood is alluded to in three
of Shakespeare's plays (*Hamlet*, *Richard II*, and *Henry VI*), for instance,
and in Milton's *Paradise Lost*.[29]

Genesis next follows the line of Cain down through several generations, noting its contributions to human culture (4:20–22) but also its
violent tendencies, before returning to the primal couple Adam and Eve
in order to describe the different line of descent that begins with Seth.
A long time then passes, chronologically, before we get to the Great
Flood (beginning in 6:9). The central character in this part of the story
is the righteous Noah, whose family is chosen along with the remainder
of creation "in-miniature" to survive the watery chaos that all too
quickly descends upon the earth (6:14–22) – an image alluded to in the
NT when Jesus refers to the sudden coming of the judgment of God at the
end of time (Matt 24:36–41; Luke 17:26–27). The boat involved in this
salvation is unsurprisingly read in later Christian tradition as analogous

---

[27] Ephrem, *Commentary on Genesis*, 3.2.1 (ACCS OT 1:104).
[28] Augustine, *Civ.* 15.5, 15, trans. G. G. Walsh and Grace Monahan, FC 14 (Washington, DC: Catholic University of America Press, 1952).
[29] Shakespeare, *Hamlet*, 3.3.36–38; *Richard II*, 1.1.104–106; *Henry VI*, 1.3.38–40; Milton, *Paradise Lost*, 11.429–47.

to the church, by way of a passage like 1 Pet 3:20–21, "God waited patiently in the days of Noah while the ark was being built. In it only a few people, eight in all, were saved through water, and this water symbolizes baptism that now saves you also." In such Christian reading, Noah is seen as prefiguring Christ himself, as well as exemplifying the Christian believer (Heb 11:7). These links having been made between Noah and Christ, ark and church, we find the Noah story being evoked in the art of the early Christian catacombs in Rome, in the medieval mystery plays, in the carvings of Gothic cathedrals like Wells and Salisbury, and, perhaps most famously, by Michelangelo in the Sistine Chapel in the Vatican.

The immediate aftermath of the flood story has sometimes been read in the Christian tradition as giving divine permission to abandon an originally vegetarian state (Gen. 1:29) and embrace instead a carnivorous one. Thomas Aquinas alludes to this interpretive tradition as follows: "In the opinion of some, those animals which now are fierce and kill others, would, in that [original] state, have been tame, not only in regard to man, but also in regard to other animals."[30] Some Christian translations of Gen 9:2–3 do imply as much:

> The fear and dread of you will fall on all the beasts of the earth, and on all the birds in the sky, on every creature that moves along the ground, and on all the fish in the sea; they are given into your hands. Everything that lives and moves about will be food for you. Just as I gave you the green plants, I now give you everything. (NIV)

Since other parts of the OT tradition that describe creation do not however reflect any belief that the existence of carnivorous animals in the world results from anything other than God's good creation purposes (e.g., Ps 104:21; 147:9), other Christian interpreters have sought a better-grounded interpretation. The clue to it lies in the observation that one class of animals, "livestock" (bəhēmâ), is not mentioned in the Hebrew text of Gen 9:2; this verse only concerns animal life in the *non-domestic sphere*. It is the wild creatures, and not animals in general, that in the aftermath of the Flood now live their lives in fear and dread of human beings. This is not a passage about the beginning of meat-eating but rather concerns a change in the human relationship with the world whereby wild animals become first and foremost targets of human

---

[30] Thomas Aquinas, *Summa Theologica*, 1.96.1, trans. Fathers of the English Dominican Province, 2 vols. (New York: Benziger, 1947), 1: 486.

aggression rather than subjects of human governance and care. The force of Gen 9:3 in this context is not "just as I gave you plants, now I give you animals," but "just as I gave you the plants of the earth that you had not cultivated, now I give you the wild animals of the earth that you have not domesticated."[31]

As this part of the Genesis story comes to an end, we find Noah in a less than impressive state as a consequence of his over-indulgence in the fruit of his vines (9:18–29). As he lies insensible in his tent, we also encounter the great (but obscure) sin of Ham in "seeing his father's nakedness." It is a curious episode that has attracted much attention. It has inspired medieval art, for example, that portrays Noah "unconscious and exposed ... perhaps soiled by excessive wine" as a type of Christ, "faint, bloodied, and naked" at his scourging.[32] It has also wrongfully led some Christians, by way of a highly dubious interpretation of the curse on Canaan in this context, to justify enslavement based on racial/ethnic identity.[33]

The subsequent Tower of Babel incident in Gen 11:1–9, where humanity attempts to construct a city possessing a tower that reaches "to the heavens" in the hope of making "a name" for itself and avoiding being scattered over the face of the whole earth" (11:4), has also been given considerable attention. It appears in Dante's *Inferno*, for example, as the starting point of his journey,[34] and in Milton's *Paradise Lost*, where it is built at the very mouth of hell itself.[35] In Bruegel's famous 1563 painting, *The Tower of Babel*, an impressive-looking Colosseum-like building is revealed upon closer inspection to be in the process of falling down – an inconsequential structure in the end, just like the biblical tower.

Abraham, Sarah, and Isaac: Genesis 11:27–25:18

The Table of Nations and the "Babel incident" in Genesis 10–11 provide the immediate backdrop for the story that follows. The peoples of the ancient world having been assigned their proper places in the world, we

[31] For a more extensive discussion, see Iain Provan, *Seriously Dangerous Religion: What the Old Testament Really Says and Why It Matters* (Waco, TX: Baylor University Press, 2014), and .

[32] A. C. Labriola, "The Bible and Iconography," in *The Oxford Handbook of Reception History of the Bible*, ed. Michael Lieb, Emma Mason, Jonathan Roberts, and Christopher Rowland (Oxford: Oxford University Press, 2011), 175–99 (188).

[33] S. R. Haynes, *Noah's Curse: The Biblical Justification of American Slavery* (Oxford: Oxford University, 2002).

[34] Dante, *Inferno*, 3.25–30.

[35] Milton, *Paradise Lost*, 12.24–62, esp. 40–45.

now meet one extended family whose story will occupy the remainder of
the book. Gen 11:27–25:18 focuses mainly on Abraham and his wife
Sarah, and secondarily on their son Isaac, but there is also a supporting
cast that includes Abraham's concubine Hagar, his nephew Lot, and
others. The story is primarily about trusting in God. Its key verse is
Gen 15:6, "Abram believed the LORD, and he credited it to him as
righteousness," which is picked up in the NT, in different ways, by
both Paul and James (Rom 4; Gal 3; Jas 2). The key passage that relates
to this verse is Genesis 22, where Abraham's trust is pushed to the very
edge of reason.

The promise to Abraham that lies at the heart of the story first
appears in Gen 12:2–3. Here we learn that this one family now stands
at the center of God's intention to bless his creation, and we hear about
the particular land in which this family will live. A subsequent "covenant" (bərît) between God and Abraham undergirds the promise (15:8–19),
which builds on the earlier covenant with the whole created order in Gen
9:1–17. The Abrahamic promise and covenant take on a particular kind
of significance in the NT. Here Jesus, "son of Abraham" (Matt 1:1),
accepts that his fellow Jews who oppose him are also Abraham's descendants, but points out that they do not do the things that Abraham did,
and are in another sense the children of the devil (John 8:31–47). In due
course it becomes clear that it is actually all those who accept Jesus as
Lord, both Jew and Gentile, who are the true heirs of the promise to
Abraham (e.g., Rom 4:1–25; 9:1–9; Gal 3:1–14). It is to the new global
people of God, the church, that the promise of Genesis 12 ultimately
points – including the promise of a "land" (Heb. 4:1–11).

Among the minor characters in the Abraham story, the mysterious
priest-king of Salem, Melchizedek, is certainly one who has attracted
significant Christian interest (Gen 14). Psalm 110 already claims that the
Davidic king in Jerusalem is "a priest forever, in the order of Melchizedek"
(Ps 110:4) and that it is in him that God's plans for the world are focused.
The Epistle to the Hebrews picks up this thread in the course of its argument that, despite his non-Levitical ancestry, Jesus is a priest. The author
deploys as a precedent here precisely the figure of Melchizedek: "without
father or mother, without genealogy, without beginning of days or end of
life, like the Son of God he remains a priest forever" (7:2–3). This notion of
Melchizedek later gave rise to various heterodox opinions in the Christian
church, and there even arose for a while a sect that regarded Melchizedek as
equal or superior to Christ. The NT connection between Christ and
Melchizedek also greatly influenced the Christian art of the succeeding
centuries, and resulted in many representations of Abraham's encounter

with him. Two parallels have been emphasized in this work: the first, between Abraham offering tithes to Melchizedek and the wise men offering gifts to the infant Jesus (Matt 2:1–12); and the second, between Melchizedek offering bread and wine to Abraham, and the Eucharist. Among many examples are some fifth-century CE mosaics in the church of Santa Maria Maggiore in Rome and some sixth-century ones in Ravenna, as well as Rubens's *The Meeting of Abraham and Melchizedek* (c. 1625).[36]

Sarah's slave-girl Hagar has been another person of interest. In the NT she becomes a picture of the slavery to the Jewish law that the apostle Paul wants to see abolished in the church of Galatia (Gal 4:21–31). By the middle of the third century she has already come to stand for Judaism as such, and this theme is clearly articulated in the fifth century by Augustine, who argues that all Jews have descended from Hagar rather than from Sarah: "Christians, not Jews, are the seed of Abraham, the inheritors of the promise through Isaac."[37] In the seventeenth century Hagar's exile in the desert then becomes a popular theme among Dutch artists such as Rubens (*Hagar Leaves the House of Abraham*, c. 1615) and Rembrandt (*Abraham Dismissing Hagar and Ishmael*, 1640).

Another popular subject of Christian art has been Abraham's encounter in Genesis 18 with three mysterious strangers. In the eastern Christian world these have often been represented artistically as a prefiguration of the Trinity. The most famous example is probably the fifteenth century icon of the Russian artist Andrei Rublev (c. 1360–1430), which pictures them seated around an altar, with a chalice representing the Eucharist standing at the center. The same idea is found in the West in Rembrandt's etching *Abraham Entertaining the Angels* (1656). This reading of the story stands in continuity with an earlier tradition represented by Ambrose of Milan:

> Abraham, who was glad to receive strangers, faithful to God and tireless in his service and prompt in fulfilling his duty, saw the Trinity typified. He added religious devotion to hospitality, for although he beheld three, he adored one, and, while keeping a distinction of the persons, yet he called one Lord.[38]

Of all the well-known stories about Abraham's immediate family in the book of Genesis, it is the one told in Gen 22:1–14 that has attracted

---

[36]   N. M. Sarna et al., "Abraham," *EncJud* 1:280–88 (287–88).
[37]   E. A. Clark, "Interpretive Fate amid the Church Fathers," in *Hagar, Sarah, and their Children: Jewish, Christian, and Muslim Perspectives*, ed. Phyllis Trible and L. M. Russell (Louisville, KY: Westminster John Knox, 2006), 127–47 (136).
[38]   Ambrose, *On His Brother, Satyrus*, 2.96, cited from Genesis 12–50 (ACCS OT 2:61).

the most attention. The NT itself already connects Isaac with Jesus in the Gospels, when it is announced in Mark 1:11 (and parallels) that Jesus is "the beloved son" of God, evoking the Septuagint of Gen 22:2, 12, and 16. We also hear echoes here of Isa 42:1 ("in whom I am well pleased") and its surrounding context, which speaks of a suffering servant, persecuted unto death yet bringing redemption to others. Jesus is in this way associated with notions of both binding and sacrifice. Elsewhere he is connected directly with the lamb of the Passover feast who takes away the sins of the world (John 1:29). It is in this context that the NT representation of Jesus as "beloved son" becomes especially meaningful. Here is the Son of God given up by the Father for the sake of the redemption of many, carrying the instrument of his death with him to the place of execution (as Isaac also did, Gen 22:6). Thus, for the writers of NT the Genesis story prophesies a higher truth: the divine mystery proclaimed in Christ. We see this reflected in the Gospel of John, where "God so loved the world that He gave his one and only son" (John 3:16). We see it also in Paul: "He who did not spare his own son, but gave him up for us all" (Rom 8:32). Jesus is the supreme example of parental sacrifice and of willing martyrdom, as the averted death of the son in Genesis becomes the literal death – and resurrection – of the Son. It is Jesus, then, who is ultimately "the offspring" mentioned in Gen 13:15 and 17:8 (cf. Gal 3:13–16). This is how the story is read, for example, by Tertullian.[39] This Christian interpretation of Genesis 22 inevitably plays out among Christian writers, musicians, and artists of the succeeding centuries. The story figures in all the important English miracle play cycles, and numerous later dramas, and it is reflected in the artistic works of Donatello (*The Sacrifice of Isaac*, c. 1418), Caravaggio (*The Sacrifice of Isaac*, 1601–2), and Rembrandt (*The Sacrifice of Isaac*, 1635), among others.

The Jacob Story: Genesis 25:19–37:1

The story of Isaac's son Jacob, bound up with that of his brother Esau, occupies another substantial section of the book of Genesis. It is a story about manipulation and cheating. Esau claims that Jacob has cheated him twice, taking first his birthright and then his blessing (Gen. 27:36), and when Jacob flees north to escape his brother's anger at the behest of the scheming Rebekah, *he* is then cheated by his uncle and her brother Laban. It is also a story, though, not only about Jacob's *character* (as a cheat), but about his *vocation* as the chosen one of God. Interestingly, the second of

---

[39] Tertullian, *Marc.* 3.18 (*ANF* 3.336).

these themes tends to predominate over the first in many Christian appropriations of the Jacob story in the succeeding centuries, to the extent that Jacob's character flaws often all but disappear from view as his chosenness is emphasized. That is to say, Christian reading (just like Jewish reading) tends to try to "clean up" the portrait of Jacob in the biblical text and make him into a mere saint – and as such, a prefigurement of Christ. Esau, for his part, becomes merely a sinner. Augustine, for example, held that Jacob did not lie to Isaac, but spoke figuratively to him, and in fact Isaac "knew what was happening since he had the spirit of prophecy, and he himself was acting symbolically."[40] Pelagius agrees with Augustine as to Jacob's virtue (and Esau's contrasting vice), and makes use of these realities to argue (against Augustine) that "God's foreknowledge of merits was the cause of his subordinating Ishmael to Isaac and Jacob to Esau."[41] Ambrose urges his readers to imitate Jacob in precisely his virtue.[42] It is only with the Enlightenment that we see a general shift away from regarding Jacob in particular in such a favorable light.

Two moments in the Jacob story have proved to be of particular interest to Christian interpreters. The first relates to Jacob's journey north to Laban, and his overnight stay in a lonely place near the city of Luz (Gen 28). Here he has a dream involving a stairway linking earth and heaven, in the course of which he encounters God and receives a divine promise. Although he is fleeing, he will one day return – God will preserve him and bring him back to the land (28:15). Jacob responds by transforming his pillow into a sacred pillar, thereby creating a shrine (28:18), since this will be God's house for him when he eventually returns to the land (28:22). In early Christian literature the main emphasis in reading this story is Christological. Augustine, for example, tells us that "Christ is the ladder reaching from earth to heaven, and from the carnal to the spiritual."[43] The Protestant Reformers tend to follow him in this view, as do later hymn writers like Charles Wesley. In the Middle Ages, however, the ladder typically comes to represent spiritual progress in the Christian *believer*, as in the Rule of St. Benedict and in the

[40] Augustine, *Serm.* 4.21 (ACCS OT 2:174).
[41] Mark Edwards, "Augustine and Pelagius on Romans," in Lieb et al., *Reception History*, 609–20 (618).
[42] Ambrose, *On the Death of His Brother Satyrus*, 2.100, in *Funeral Orations by Saint Gregory Nazianzen and Saint Ambrose*, ed. R. J. Deferrari, trans. J. J. Sullivan and M. R. P. McGuire, FC 22 (Washington, D.C.: Catholic University Press of America, 1968), 161–259 (242).
[43] Augustine, *Reply to Faustus the Manichean*, 12.26 (NPNF¹ 4:192).

teaching of Bonaventure, who uses the ladder to represent six stages of the ascent of the soul to God.

The second "moment" is Jacob's encounter with God on the way back *into* the Promised Land in Genesis 32, as he awaits with some trepidation at the Jabbok river his inevitable reunion with his brother Esau (32:22–32). Here "a man wrestled with him till daybreak" (32:24), but he was not able to overpower Jacob (32:25). Jacob does pick up an injury in the fight, but he holds on, looking for a blessing, and he receives one. In return he is compelled to give up his name, which evokes all the cheating in his life up to this point; he is no longer to be called Jacob, but Israel (32:28). The crossing of the river symbolizes a new beginning, marked by this new name. In the midst of it all Jacob realizes that he has seen God face to face – as the name given to the site indicates (Peniel, "face of God," 32:30). This wrestling match became a popular subject for Christian artists in the Middle Ages – for example, for the composer of the eighth-century fresco in Santa Maria Antica in Rome and for later artists like Rembrandt (*Jacob Wrestling with the Angel*, c. 1659). Musically, the fight forms the basis for Johann Sebastian Bach's cantata, *Ich lasse dich nicht, du segnest mich den* (1727), and for a motet written by Johann Christoph Bach (1642–1703) that was published in English in the nineteenth century as *I Wrestle and Pray*.[44]

The Joseph Story: Genesis 37:2–50:26

The final section of the book of Genesis tells us about "the descendants of Jacob" (Gen 37:2–50:26). It is typically referred to as the "Joseph story," because the spotlight in the narrative mainly falls on this *one* of Jacob's descendants; it is however to a significant extent also a "Judah story."[45] It is a narrative about how the promise to Abraham continues to work its way out through his early descendants in spite of significant obstacles – in this case human wickedness and natural famine. By its end the promise is still alive, and Joseph himself foresees a time when "God will surely come to your aid and take you up out of this land to the land he promised on oath to Abraham, Isaac, and Jacob" (50:24). Joseph thus occupies a pivotal place in the biblical story, and comes to be regarded in the interpretive tradition as one of the great men of biblical history (e.g., in Acts 7:9–16; Heb 11:22).

The story opens with a portrait of a brash young man possessing little tact, who provokes his brothers into violent behavior. It is important to

---

44   N. M. Sarna et al., "Jacob," *EncJud* 11:17–25 (22–24).
45   See Provan, *Discovering Genesis*, 185–87.

say this, given that some interpreters have wished to portray Joseph in rather glowing terms; his righteousness, in fact, is frequently stressed in the early Christian tradition. Athanasius and Cyprian, for example, consider him to be "a model of constancy to God in the face of enemies, temptations and trials."[46] This reading has a lot to do with the associated reading of Joseph as a "type" of Christ, most extensively developed in Ambrose's *On Joseph the Patriarch*, where the author notes many correspondences between Joseph and Jesus, including their suffering at the hands of others and their betrayal by Judah/Judas.[47] As late as the nineteenth century, Franz Delitzsch's commentary on Genesis (1852) still represents this stream of the interpretive tradition.[48] Joseph's remarkable robe has correspondingly been associated with Christ's assumption of humanity in the Incarnation; as Cyril of Alexandria puts it, "The multicolored garment is the symbol of the multiform glory with which God the Father clothed the Son made similar to us through his human nature."[49]

Having been taken down to Egypt against his will, Joseph next becomes a slave in the household of a powerful man named Potiphar. He soon gets into an awkward position with Potiphar's wife, who finds him to be very handsome (Gen 39:13–17; cf. 39:6–7) – a physical attractiveness that is often commented upon in the early interpretive literature. Ambrose, for example, tells us that:

> although he was good-looking . . . he did not direct the charm of his countenance toward another's wrongdoing but kept it to win grace for himself . . . That is the true beauty that does not seduce the eyes of others or wound their fragile hearts but gains the approval of all.[50]

John Chrysostom declares that "it was remarkable and unprecedented that this remarkable young man had his clothes torn from him by this frenzied and intemperate woman without yielding to her."[51] The story could also be read typologically in the pre-modern period. For example, in Bede's *Commentary on the Pentateuch* (eighth century) Joseph is Christ, who did not commit adultery by accepting the teaching

---

[46]   A. Jacobs, "Joseph the Patriarch," in Jeffrey, *Biblical Tradition*, 414–16.

[47]   Ambrose, *Jos.*, 3.13–14, 18 (ACCS OT 2:237, 241).

[48]   Franz Delitzsch, *A New Commentary on Genesis*, trans. Sophia Taylor; 2 vols. (Minneapolis: Klock & Klock, 1978), 2: 252–53.

[49]   Cyril of Alexandria, *Glaphyra on Genesis*, 6.4 (ACCS OT 2:231–32).

[50]   Ambrose, *Jos.* 5.22 (ACCS OT 2:251).

[51]   John Chrysostom, *Hom. Gen.* 62.19 (ACCS OT 2:252–53).

of the scribes and the Pharisees, but left his life in their hands (as Joseph left his garment in the hand of the temptress).[52] As we move toward the modern period, we find John Bunyan in the seventeenth century picking up the theme of chastity in *The Pilgrim's Progress* (1678–84), in which Potiphar's wife appears as the character Wanton, who attempts to seduce Christian's companion Faithful. At the same time Christiana's son, also named Joseph, is exhorted to be like his biblical counterpart, "Chaste, and one that flees from Temptation."[53]

Ultimately Joseph rises to a high position in Egypt as a result of his ability to interpret dreams, and in the course of a famine in the land he once again encounters his brothers (Gen 42:6–8). Eventually he breaks down and reveals himself to them, delivering in the midst of his tears a theological reflection on the entire preceding story (45:5–8). The whole family ends up in Egypt as a result, and as Jacob approaches his death there he blesses Joseph's sons Manasseh and Ephraim (48:1–22) and then all of his own sons (49:1–28). One of the key elements here is Jacob's oracle about Judah (49:8–12), who is celebrated as the premier tribe: "your father's sons will bow down to you" (49:8). Judah, it seems, is the one who ultimately inherits Joseph's dream in Genesis 37. In Gen 49:10, indeed, Judah is pictured as seated with his royal scepter held upright in front of him, ruling "until he comes to whom it belongs," at which point the nations will give their obedience to that person. The NT picks up this idea from Gen 49:9–10 and relates it to Jesus (Heb 7:14; Rev 5:5).

Joseph appears in most of the medieval European mystery cycles, and by 1560 there were in Christian Europe a dozen "English plays on the subject [of the Joseph story] and dozens more in French, Spanish, Italian, Dutch, and German."[54] He is an important figure in the Renaissance, represented for example on Ghiberti's bronze doors for the Baptistery in Florence and in Raphael's frescoes in the Vatican. The attempted seduction by Potiphar's wife was a very popular story among sixteenth- and seventeenth-century artists, among them Tintoretto (1555) and Rembrandt (1634). The latter also shows Joseph relating his dreams to his family (1638) and standing over the dying Jacob while the latter lays his hands on Manasseh and Ephraim (1656). So although in Genesis itself – and in Christian Scripture as a whole – it is Judah who inherits Joseph's dream, being the one to whom all the other brothers bow down

52 Bede, *Commentary on the Pentateuch*, referred to by M. Siebald, "Potiphar's Wife," in Jeffrey, *Biblical Tradition*, 625–26 (625).
53 John Bunyan, *The Pilgrim's Progress*, ed. Roger Pooley (London: Penguin Classics, 2008), 250.
54 N. M. Sarna et al., "Joseph," *EncJud* 11:406–13 (411).

(Gen. 37:5–7), in the Christian reception history of Genesis 37–50 there is no question about who it is that eventually comes out "on top" among the sons of Jacob. Before Moses, among the Christians, it is clearly Joseph.

SELECT BIBLIOGRAPHY

Danielson, Dennis. "Eve." Pages 251–54 in *A Dictionary of Biblical Tradition in English Literature*. Edited by David L. Jeffrey. Grand Rapids: Eerdmans, 1992.

Jacobs, Alan. "Joseph the Patriarch," Pages 414–16 in *A Dictionary of Biblical Tradition in English Literature*. Edited by David L. Jeffrey. Grand Rapids: Eerdmans, 1992.

Labriola, A. C. "The Bible and Iconography." Pages 175–99 in *The Oxford Handbook of Reception History of the Bible*. Edited by Michael Lieb, Emma Mason, Jonathan Roberts, and Christopher Rowland. Oxford: Oxford University Press, 2011.

Oden, Thomas C., ed. *Ancient Christian Commentary on Scripture*. 29 vols. Downers Grove, IL: InterVarsity Press, 2001–10.

Provan, Iain. *Discovering Genesis: Content, Interpretation, Reception*. Grand Rapids: Eerdmans, 2016.

Provan, Iain. *Seriously Dangerous Religion: What the Old Testament Really Says and Why It Matters*. Waco, TX: Baylor University Press, 2014.

Sarna, N. M. et al. "Abraham." Pages 280–88 in *Encyclopaedia Judaica*. Edited by Michael Berenbaum and Fred Skolnik. Vol. 1. 2nd ed. Detroit, MI: Macmillan Reference USA, 2007.

Sarna, N. M. "Jacob." Pages 17–25 in *Encyclopaedia Judaica*. Edited by Michael Berenbaum and Fred Skolnik. Vol. 11. 2nd ed. Detroit, MI: Macmillan Reference USA, 2007.

Sarna, N. M. "Joseph." Pages 406–13 in *Encyclopaedia Judaica*. Edited by Michael Berenbaum and Fred Skolnik. Vol. 11. 2nd ed. Detroit, MI: Macmillan Reference USA, 2007.

Siebald, Manfred. "Potiphar's Wife." Pages 625–26 in *A Dictionary of Biblical Tradition in English Literature*. Edited by David L. Jeffrey. Grand Rapids: Eerdmans, 1992.

Scripture Index

Genesis
  1, 32, 39, 42, 44, 54, 67, 83, 102, 104,
      105, 114, 135, 154, 157, 220,
      223, 225, 227, 258, 270, 274,
      284, 325, 344, 346
  1, 238, 284, 323, 343
  1–2
    3, 66, 108, 264
    4, 101, 114, 190, 324
  1–4, 101
    16, 101
  1–11
    32, 100
  1–12
    3, 337
  2, 13, 159
  3, 13
  3–10, 343
  4, 277, 284
  5–2
    3, 94
  6–7, 277
  10, 284
  11–12, 345
  12, 284
  14, 277
  16, 13
  18, 277, 284
  21, 284
  24–25, 345
  25, 284
  26, 232, 345
  26–27, 212, 247, 256
  26–28, 190, 254, 284
  26–30, 264
  27, 110

27–31, 270
28, 112, 191, 325
29, 221, 351
29–30, 345
31, 264, 284, 343
1–2, 255, 284, 291, 326, 344,
    345
1–3, 5, 13, 31, 35, 134, 136, 190, 258,
    276, 347
1–4, 114
1–11, 6, 43, 48, 55, 62, 65, 69, 71, 90,
    100, 101, 114, 122, 124, 132,
    138, 142, 190, 212, 220, 263,
    323, 326, 334
2, 32, 84, 154, 157, 193, 244, 254,
    284, 345
2, 13
4, 36, 101, 103, 104
4–25, 345
4–3
  19, 34
4–4
  16, 102
4–7, 345
4a, 66
4b, 31
5–6, 152, 160
7, 108, 284
8, 106
8–14, 346
9, 95
15, 221, 289, 326
16, 221
16–17, 289
17, 327
18, 284

Genesis (cont.)
    19, 345
    19–20, 284
    23, 108, 111
    24, 101, 108, 270, 284
    25, 108
  2–3, 5, 13, 44, 95, 236, 264, 267, 270,
      272, 279, 326, 327, 341
  2–4, 105, 114, 274
  2–36, 225
  3, 17, 18, 32, 157, 191, 192, 231, 244,
      264, 285, 289, 291, 298,
      346, 349
    1, 108, 285
    5, 231
    6, 192, 348
    7, 108, 121
    8, 18
    11, 327
    14–19, 111, 245
    15, 348
    16, 190, 192, 206, 349
    17, 103, 111
    17–20, 273
    19, 95, 108
    20, 101, 113, 254, 255
    21, 121, 230
    21–29, 101
    22, 95, 231, 232
    23, 327
    24, 95, 106, 327
  3–11, 284
  4, 13, 84, 105, 158, 222, 227, 275, 276,
      328, 330, 348
    1, 101, 105
    2, 84
    4, 221
    6–7, 111
    7, 229
    10–13, 274
    11, 245
    14, 13
    15, 230
    16, 106, 285
    16–25, 104
    17, 84, 285
    17–24, 111, 139
    17–26, 101, 105, 113

    19–24, 103
    20, 107, 285
    20–22, 84, 101, 111, 350
    21, 285
    22, 285
    25–26, 101, 139
  4–11, 285
  5, 102, 103, 104, 105, 134, 140
    1, 36, 66, 104, 105, 114, 138
    1–2, 101, 212
    1–32, 101, 139
    2–3, 103
    3, 110, 212
    5–31, 103
    21–24, 103
    22, 111
    22–24, 103
    24, 103, 349
    29, 111, 245
  6, 284, 285
    1–4, 232
    1–9
      17, 101
    3, 95, 231
    5, 96, 285
    7, 223, 285
    9, 36, 66, 101, 103, 104, 105, 138,
      228, 349, 350
    10, 101
    11, 285
    14–22, 350
  6–8, 274
  6–9, 33, 34, 65, 85, 125, 134, 137
  7
    6, 101
    10–8
      7, 85
  8
    1, 228
    20–22, 138
    21, 223, 230, 286
    21–22, 276, 286
    22, 101, 112
  9, 66, 157, 275, 330
    1, 94
    1–7, 138
    1–17, 353
    2–3, 351

3, 221
3–4, 121
3–5, 331
4–6, 66
6, 110, 213, 276, 338
7, 276
11, 94
17–29, 101
18, 101
18–29, 352
20, 349
25, 101
26, 286
28, 101
10, 67, 104, 106
  1, 36, 66, 101, 103, 105, 138
  1–32, 101, 139
  2–5, 104
  2–7, 84
  3–18, 101
  5, 277
  5–32, 104
  6–20, 104
  8–10, 104
  9, 112
  20, 84
  21–25, 106, 109
  21–31, 104
  22–23, 84
  24–30, 104
  32, 101, 103, 277
  31, 84
10–11, 352
11, 104, 139, 161, 194
  1–9, 95, 101, 121, 352
  7, 232
  10, 36, 66, 101, 105, 138
  10–23, 101
  10–26, 139, 286
  10–31, 140
  10–32, 140
    1, 140
  11, 103
  14–16, 106
  26, 106, 286
  27, 36, 66, 101, 105, 114, 138,
    139, 169
  27–25

11, 176
18, 353
27–32, 139
28, 45
30, 113, 234, 286
31, 45, 106, 107
32, 140
11–36, 116
12, 64, 71, 90, 101, 115, 126, 165, 200,
    234, 353
  1, 106, 178
  1–3, 61, 162, 276, 331, 333, 334
  2, 61
  3, 171, 178
  4–11, 107
  6–7, 108
  7, 19
  7–8, 68, 171
  10–13
    1, 200
  10–20, 54, 63, 106, 263
  16, 181
12–25, 45, 48, 68, 287
12–36, 65, 100, 190, 334
12–40, 143
12–50, 6, 48, 62, 65, 72, 121, 122, 126,
    132, 134, 138, 139, 145, 162,
    168, 169, 174, 185, 276, 284,
    288, 292, 323, 334, 338
13, 334
  1, 107
  1–13, 72
  2–18, 178
  7–13, 276
  8, 68, 171
  9, 276
  18, 72
  15, 355
14, 34, 82, 181, 334, 353
  19–22, 112
  22, 164
15, 33, 44, 67, 96
  1–6, 125
  2–3, 178, 179
  2–5, 177
  7, 45
  8–19, 353
  9–21, 172

Genesis (cont.)
  19–21, 106
 16, 86, 178, 200
  1, 113
  1–15, 263
  2, 176
  6, 107
  13, 297
  21, 107
 17, 33, 44, 66, 67, 103, 336
  1–7, 115
  4–8, 94
  5, 108
  5–6, 115
  6, 81
  8, 355
  9, 66
  10, 95
  10–14, 94
  13–14, 66
  17, 181
  18–26, 336
  23–27, 94
  27, 171
 18, 72, 317, 354
  1–15, 44
  5–8, 172
  6, 172
  12–15, 109
  16–33, 334
  17–19, 334
  22, 96
  23, 317
  25, 335
  33, 96
 18–19, 72
 19, 88, 96
  22, 109
  29, 178
 20, 72, 97, 126, 200, 233
  1, 107
  1–18, 33, 54, 63, 64, 200, 263
  12, 179
 20–22, 44, 62
 21, 72, 179, 200
  1–2, 234
  1–7, 72
  2–3, 86

  4, 94
  6, 109
  8, 86, 172
  8–20, 277
  8–21; 263
  9–21, 315
  11, 107, 177
  12–13, 336
  14, 181
  15, 181
  20, 107
  22–34, 277
  31, 109
 22, 5, 72, 100, 264, 267, 275, 276, 316,
    353, 355
  1, 315
  1–14, 354
  1–19, 6, 44, 96, 304
  2, 310, 355
  6, 355
  7–8, 181
  8, 287
  9–14, 172
  12, 228, 355
  14, 19, 108, 109, 287
  16, 355
  19, 107
  20–23, 173
  20–24, 115
 23, 107
  4, 171
  15, 197
  16, 182
  22, 173
  24, 72, 86, 115, 177, 181, 196,
    201, 287
 27, 86
  28, 172, 197
  38–41, 170
  40, 103
  67, 174
 25, 116
  1, 169
  1–6, 181
  7, 287
  9, 107
  11, 107
  12, 36, 66, 103, 105, 138, 139

12–18, 139
19, 36, 66, 105, 138
21, 113, 234
22–23, 198
23, 112, 183, 233
24–26, 94
26, 287
29–34, 172, 182
25–27, 88
25–33, 71
25–36, 48
26, 64, 71, 72, 82, 88, 126
1–11, 54, 63, 97
1–23, 107
1–32, 277
2–5, 44
6–11, 33
25, 108
34, 182
27, 86, 182
1, 87
1–40, 116, 263
5–17, 183
7–9, 172
28–29, 112
30–38, 337
31, 172
36, 109, 263, 355
39–40, 112
27–34, 287
28, 71, 82, 108, 356
2–29
13, 107
10–22, 62
10, 86
10–20, 107
10–22, 33, 63, 287
11–19, 88
17–19, 110
28–33, 277
29
5, 183
9, 177
15, 181
31, 113, 233
29–30, 86
30
1, 113

2, 233
22, 233
29, 181
31
1–21, 263
3, 287
6, 181
14–16, 183
17–33
18, 107
33, 108
48, 88, 109
54, 172
31–33, 86
32, 108, 357
2–3, 88, 110
13–21, 277
22–31, 287
22–32, 100, 357
23–33, 88
28, 109, 357
30, 110, 357
34, 357
35, 357
33, 278, 287
1–11, 277
2, 164, 174
12–16, 278
17, 110
18–20, 108
18–34
31, 34
34, 184, 201, 263
1, 171
5–7, 177
35, 287
1–7, 108
8, 88
9–15, 33
10, 229
10–12, 94
11, 81
20, 88
22, 263
22–26, 105
22–29, 104
22a, 93
22b–26, 93

Genesis (cont.)
36, 112, 337
  1, 36, 66, 105, 138, 139
  1–43, 34
  4, 113
  6–8, 107
  8–43, 139
  9, 36, 66, 105, 138, 139
  31–39, 17
36, 112, 337
37, 20, 33, 72, 89, 97, 116, 263, 278
  1, 107
  2, 36, 66, 103, 105, 115, 138, 139,
    229
  2–50
    26, 357
  3, 287
  3–11, 62
  4–5, 229
  5–7, 360
  8, 229
  11, 229
  12–36, 287
  21–22, 93
  26–27, 93
  29–30, 93
  34–38, 184
  39–50, 267
37–50, 48, 58, 65, 100, 183, 190, 228,
  287, 360
38, 5, 20, 94, 95, 196, 203, 267, 273
  7–10, 268, 269
  12–30, 269
  24–26, 268
  28, 109
39, 36, 89, 97, 116, 205, 287
  1, 116, 228
  2–3, 113
  3, 229
  6–20, 89
  6–7, 358
  9, 95, 229
  13–17, 358
  21, 229
  23, 113
39–50, 72, 278
40, 89, 287
  8, 95, 229

41, 89
  16, 95, 229
  25, 95, 229
  28, 229
  32, 229
  37–57, 288
  38–9, 229
  39, 95
  50–52, 93
  51–52, 229
  55–57, 337
  57, 229
42
  6–8, 359
  18, 229
  22, 93
  23, 229
  29–45
    1, 115
  37, 93
42–50, 288
43
  3–5, 93
  8–10, 93
  29, 229
44
  14–34, 93
45
  4, 184
  5, 229
  5–8, 359
  5–9, 228
  7, 229
46, 20
  8–27, 93
  12, 20
  18–25, 113
  25, 184
47
  1–6, 24
48
  1–22, 359
  5, 93
  9, 229
  20, 112, 333
49, 105, 171, 183, 184, 185
  1, 112
  1–27, 34

1–28, 359
2–7, 266
2–27, 112
3–4, 93
8, 110
8–12, 359
28, 112
29–30, 107
50
  12, 229
  13, 107
  14, 288
  17, 230
  19, 230, 233
  19–21, 113, 228
  20, 97, 229, 279, 288, 292
  21, 230
  24, 229, 288

Exodus
  1–14, 65
  1–15, 62
  2, 32, 54
  3
    14, 32, 44, 57
  12, 6, 322
    14–20, 66
  14
    3, 18
  15, 134
  16–18, 62
  19–24, 62
  21
    23–24, 265
  24
    4, 12
  24–31, 42
  25
    1–2, 94
    8, 94
  27
    20, 327
  29
    43, 94
    45, 94
  31
    12–17, 66

32
  31, 230
32–34, 62
34
  11–16, 268
35–40, 42

Leviticus
  11
    41–45, 66
  17, 66
    3–7, 66
  17–26, 66
  20
    10, 265
  21
    9, 268
  24
    19–20, 265
    2, 327

Numbers
  3, 102
  7–8, 345
  11–20, 62
  14, 265
  20, 265
  24, 17
  25, 265

Deuteronomy
  12, 68
  14
    1, 339
    16–20, 245
  19
    21, 265
  21
    18–21, 265
  22
    21, 268
    22, 97, 265
  25
    5–10, 95, 203, 268
  26
    5, 122
    5–9, 60, 78

Deuteronomy (cont.)
28
29–34, 279
31, 60, 61
9, 12
34
1–7, 269
1–12, 12
3, 95
5
14–15, 108
6
20–24, 78
7
10–12, 12

Joshua
24, 60, 61
2–13, 78
3–4, 60, 61
Judges
3
1, 111

Ruth
4
18–22, 109

1 Samuel
1
5–6, 233
27
2, 87
2 Samuel
2
9, 79
7
9, 61
13
37, 87
14, 329
21, 111

1 Kings
1
1, 87
11

14, 17
19, 17
40, 87
12, 108
3
4–15, 88
2 Kings
20
3, 230
22–23, 37

1 Chronicles
1, 106
8
2, 111

4 Ezra
6
55–59, 325

Nehemiah
1
11, 230
5, 230
8
1, 26
9
7, 45

Job
15
8, 273
28, 271
13–14, 271
23–24, 271
32–37, 271
9, 134

Psalm 110, 353
Psalms
45
8, 335
74, 134
89, 134
97, 134
104, 134, 344, 349
21, 351

110
4, 353
113
4–9, 349
9, 234
116
16, 230
118
25, 230
121
4, 233
127
3, 234, 349
130
3, 335
147
4
8, 233
97, 351

Ecclesiastes
8
16–17, 272

Isaiah
38
3, 230
41
8–9, 68
42
1, 355
51
2, 68

Jeremiah
2
7, 327
15
1, 327

Lamentations
1
1, 327

Ezekiel
33
23–29, 68

Daniel
9
4, 230
11, 327

Hosea
6
7, 326, 327
9
15, 327
11
1–9, 278
12
4, 263

Jonah
1
14, 230
4
2, 230

Micah
3
12, 329

Sirach
17
6–12, 272

Matthew
1
1, 353
2
1–12, 354
24
36–41, 350
Mark
1
11, 355

Luke
17
26–27, 350

John
1
1–3, 346

John (cont.)
  29, 355
  12
    24, 238

Acts
  9–16, 357
  17
    26, 254, 255

Romans
  4, 353
    1–25, 353
  5
    12–19, 244, 254
    12–20, 348
  9
    1–9, 353
  11
    36, 346

1 Corinthians
  10
    26, 346
  15
    12–58, 348
    21–22, 254
    36–46, 238
    45–49, 254
2 Corinthians
  11
    3, 348

Galatians
  3, 353
    1–14, 353
    13–16, 355
    28, 217
  4
    21–31, 354

Colossians
  1

15, 230
15–20, 346
19, 346

1 Timothy
  2
    14, 348

116
  4, 230

2 Timothy
  3
    16, 341

Hebrews
  1
    3, 230
  4
    1–11, 353
  7
    14, 359
  11
    4, 350
    7, 351
    22, 357

James
  2, 353

1 Peter
  3
    20–21, 351

1 John
  3
    12, 350

Revelation
  4
    11, 346
  5
    5, 359

Subject Index

Abraham ibn Ezra, 19–21
Albright, William Foxwell, 122, 125–27, 129, 130
Alt, Albrecht, 68, 76
amphictyony, 61, 79
ancient DNA (aDNA), 241–42
Aqiba, Rabbi, 11, 338
Astruc, Jean, 32–33, 53–55
Augustine, 14, 341, 342, 354
   City of God, 350
   De doctrina christiana, 21
   De libero arbitrio, 289
authorship, Mosaic, 12, 19, 28, 34, 53–54

balance theory, 248, 257
Big Bang theory, 237–38, 253

clan, 49, 121, 162–64, 170–71
collective memory, 51, 133–34
cult, Israelite, 40, 107–8

de Wette, Wilhelm Martin Leberecht, 37–39
diaskeuastes. *See* Homer
Documentary Hypothesis, 33, 36, 39, 40, 42, 43, 55, 57–59, 60–62, 70
   D (source), 42, 44
   E (source), 36, 40, 44, 61, 64
   J (source), 43, 48, 60–61, 62–64, 67–70, 90, 330
   P (source), 35, 39, 42–43, 47, 57, 64–67, 82, 85, 90–91, 324, 330–31, 336, 338

Eichhorn, Johann Gottfried, 33–35
Elohist. *See* Documentary Hypothesis

Enki (Sumerian deity), 151–53, 159
Enuma elish, 81, 84, 102, 124, 134–36, 153, 158, 324
epic. *See* myth
etiology, 76, 88, 102–5
evolution, theory of, 239, 247, 252, 257
evolutionary biology, 247, 254–55, 259
ex nihilo, 238

Fragmentary Hypothesis, 33, 39, 55

genealogical ancestry, 242–44, 255
genealogy, function of, 28, 34, 42, 51, 81, 93, 100–5, 114, 138–43
genetic diversity, 239–40
Gilgamesh, epic of, 81, 85, 88, 123–25
Great Symbiosis, 156, 165
Gunkel, Hermann, 28, 30, 45–47, 74–79, 99–100, 124

Hazony, Yoram, 306–7, 316–18
Homer, 12, 17, 31, 36, 42
hypothesis, mosaic, 55

Ilgen, Karl David, 35–37
Image of God, 190, 191, 211–34, 247, 250, 256, 258, 284, 289, 338, 345
Instruction of Papyrus Insinger, 152–55
Ishmael, Rabbi, 11

Jahwist. *See* Documentary Hypothesis
Jerome, 13, 341
justice, 92, 95–97, 149, 269

Kant, Immanuel, 311–13
Kass, Leon R., 220–23, 304–6, 310

Kierkegaard, Søren, 313–14
kinship, 121, 138, 142–46, 168–86

legend. *See* Gunkel, Hermann

Midrash, 18, 19, 92–93, 326–30
myth, 35, 38, 41, 43, 83–85, 100, 106,
    148–53, 154

neo-documentarians, 49, 56, 70
New Criticism, 49, 50
Nicholas of Lyra, 22, 342
Noth, Martin, 47, 59, 61, 78–79
nucleotide sequence, 240–41

omnisignificance, 11, 19
oral tradition, 28, 45, 60, 75, 79–80,
    90, 121, 126, 129
Origen, 13–14, 38, 344

philology, study of, 29, 30
Priestly Source. *See* Documentary
    Hypothesis

Rashi de Troyes, 18–19, 323
Rendtorff, Rolf, 44, 47–48, 61

saga. *See* Gunkel, Hermann
Spinoza, Baruch, 25–26, 38
Stump, Eleonore, 282–83, 295–98,
    308–9, 314–15
Supplementary Hypothesis, 39, 55,
    63, 64

theodicy, 289–300
Thompson, Thomas L., 48–49, 126,
    144
toledot, 36, 66, 102–5, 114
tribe. *See* clan

Van Seters, John, 48, 65, 68–69,
    126, 127
von Rad, Gerhard, 47, 57–59, 60, 68,
    78, 102

Wellhausen, Julius, 41–44,
    55–56
wisdom, 95, 151, 267, 271–73,
    285, 304–5
wordplay, 108–10

Yahwist. *See* Documentary
    Hypothesis

CAMBRIDGE COMPANIONS TO RELIGION *(continued from page iii)*

FEMINIST THEOLOGY Edited by Susan Frank Parsons

FRANCIS OF ASSISI Edited by Michael J. P. Robson

GENESIS Edited by Bill T. Arnold

THE GOSPELS Edited by Stephen C. Barton

THE GOSPELS, SECOND EDITION Edited by Stephen C. Barton and Todd Brewer

THE HEBREW BIBLE/OLD TESTAMENT Edited by Stephen B. Chapman and Marvin A. Sweeney

HEBREW BIBLE AND ETHICS Edited by C. L. Crouch

THE JESUITS Edited by Thomas Worcester

JESUS Edited by Markus Bockmuehl

JUDAISM AND LAW Edited by Christine Hayes

C. S. LEWIS Edited by Robert MacSwain and Michael Ward

LIBERATION THEOLOGY Edited by Chris Rowland

MARTIN LUTHER Edited by Donald K. McKim

MEDIEVAL JEWISH PHILOSOPHY Edited by Daniel H. Frank and Oliver Leaman

MODERN JEWISH PHILOSOPHY Edited by Michael L. Morgan and Peter Eli Gordon

MOHAMMED Edited by Jonathan E. Brockup

THE NEW CAMBRIDGE COMPANION TO ST. PAUL Edited by Bruce W. Longenecker

NEW RELIGIOUS MOVEMENTS Edited by Olav Hammer and Mikael Rothstein

NEW TESTAMENT Edited by Patrick Gray

PENTECOSTALISM Edited by Cecil M. Robeck, Jr and Amos Yong

POSTMODERN THEOLOGY Edited by Kevin J. Vanhoozer

THE PROBLEM OF EVIL Edited by Chad Meister and Paul K. Moser

PURITANISM Edited by John Coffey and Paul C. H. Lim

QUAKERISM Edited by Stephen W. Angell and Pink Dandelion

THE QUR'AN Edited by Jane Dammen McAuliffe

KARL RAHNER Edited by Declan Marmion and Mary E. Hines

REFORMATION THEOLOGY Edited by David Bagchi and David C. Steinmetz

REFORMED THEOLOGY Edited by Paul T. Nimmo and David A. S. Fergusson

RELIGION AND TERRORISM Edited by James R. Lewis

RELIGIOUS EXPERIENCE Edited by Paul K. Moser and Chad Meister

RELIGIOUS STUDIES Edited by Robert A. Orsi

FREIDRICK SCHLEIERMACHER Edited by Jacqueline Mariña

SCIENCE AND RELIGION Edited by Peter Harrison

ST. PAUL Edited by James D. G. Dunn

SUFISM Edited by Lloyd Ridgeon

THE SUMMA THEOLOGIAE Edited by Philip McCosker and Denys Turner

THE TALMUD AND RABBINIC LITERATURE Edited by Charlotte E. Fonrobert and Martin S. Jaffee

THE TRINITY Edited by Peter C. Phan

HANS URS VON BALTHASAR Edited by Edward T. Oakes and David Moss

VATICAN II Edited by Richard R. Gaillardetz

JOHN WESLEY Edited by Randy L. Maddox and Jason E. Vickers

CPSIA information can be obtained
at www.ICGtesting.com
Printed in the USA
LVHW050943250522
719703LV00009B/437

9 781108 438322